D0893710

IMF

CONDITIONALITY

IMF

CONDITIONALITY

Edited by
John Williamson

Institute for International Economics

Washington, DC
1983
Distributed by
MIT Press/Cambridge, London, Tokyo

JEROME LIBRARY-BOWLING GREEN STATE UNIVERSITY

Dr. John Williamson is a Senior Fellow at the Institute for International Economics. He was formerly Professor of Economics at leading universities in Brazil, England, and the United States, Consultant to H.M. Treasury, and Advisor to the International Monetary Fund.

INSTITUTE FOR INTERNATIONAL ECONOMICS
C. Fred Bergsten, Director
Kathleen A. Lynch, Director of Publications
Rosanne Gleason, Publications Assistant

Copyright © 1983 Institute for International Economics
All rights reserved.

First Printing, May 1983; Second Printing, June 1984;
Third Printing, March 1985.

With the exception of short quotations in news articles or reviews, this publication may not be used or reproduced in any form without written permission from the Institute for International Economics.

The Institute for International Economics was created, and is principally funded, by The German Marshall Fund of the United States.

The views expressed in this publication are those of the authors. The publication is part of the research program of the Institute, as endorsed by its Board of Directors, but does not necessarily reflect the views of individual members of the Board or Advisory Committee.

Library of Congress Cataloging in Publication Data
Main entry under title:

IMF Conditionality.
Based on a conference which was held at Airlie House, Virginia, Mar. 24–26, 1982, sponsored by the Institute.

Includes bibliographies and index.
1. International Monetary Fund Congress. 2. Loans, Foreign Congresses. I. Williamson, John 1937–. II. Institute for International Economics (U.S.) III. Title: IMF Conditionality. IV. Title: Conditionality.
HG3881.5.I58I4 1983 332.1′52 82 21352

ISBN 0–88132–006–4

Distributed by MIT Press/Cambridge, Massachusetts, and London, England
ISBN 0–262–23116–6

Contents

Figures

INSTITUTE FOR INTERNATIONAL ECONOMICS
11 Dupont Circle, NW, Washington, DC 20036
(202) 328-0583 Telex: 248329 CEIP

C. Fred Bergsten, *Director*

BOARD OF DIRECTORS

Peter G. Peterson, *Chairman*
Raymond Barre
W. Michael Blumenthal
Alan Greenspan
Abdlatif Y. al-Hamad
Reginald H. Jones
Frank E. Loy
Donald F. McHenry
Saburo Okita
Karl Otto Pöhl
Donna E. Shalala
Mario Henrique Simonsen
Anthony M. Solomon
John N. Turner
Dennis Weatherstone

Ex officio
C. Fred Bergsten
Richard N. Cooper

ADVISORY COMMITTEE

Richard N. Cooper, *Chairman*
Robert Baldwin
Lester Brown
Rimmer de Vries
Carlos Diaz-Alejandro
Rudiger Dornbusch
Isaiah Frank
Herbert Giersch
Gottfried Haberler
Mahbub ul Haq
Arnold C. Harberger
Dale E. Hathaway
Peter B. Kenen
Ryutaro Komiya
Lawrence B. Krause
Stephen Marris
Richard R. Nelson
Joseph S. Nye
Rudolph A. Oswald
John C. Sawhill
Ernest Stern
Henry Wallich
Marina Whitman
Alan W. Wolff

Preface

This first book to be published by the Institute for International Economics addresses a topic which is both of great policy importance at present and promises to remain so for the indefinite future: the terms on which the International Monetary Fund provides financial resources to its member countries. The volume includes twenty-one papers on that topic presented to a conference sponsored by the Institute in March 1982, along with an analysis of conclusions and policy recommendations published separately as *The Lending Policies of the International Monetary Fund* in August 1982.

Interest in the issue of Fund conditionality has grown even further since the conference was held and we released our initial publication on the topic last August, due to the critical role of Fund programs in responding to the debt crisis in major developing countries including Argentina, Brazil, Mexico, and Yugoslavia. It is our hope that the volume will provide useful background material for understanding the nature and implications of Fund programs, both for the individual countries involved and for the functioning of the international economy and financial system as a whole.

The Institute for International Economics is a private nonprofit research institution for the study and discussion of international economic policy. Its purpose is to analyze important issues in that area, and to develop and communicate practical new approaches for dealing with them.

The Institute was created in November 1981 through a generous commitment of funds from the German Marshall Fund of the United States. Financial support has been received from other private foundations and corporations, including a grant from the Ford Foundation in support of the conference on which this volume is based. The Institute is completely nonpartisan.

The Board of Directors bears overall responsibility for the Institute and gives general guidance and approval to its research program—including identification of topics that are likely to become important to international economic policymakers over the medium run (generally, one to three years) and which thus should be addressed by the Institute. The Director of the Institute, working closely with the staff and outside Advisory Committee, is responsible for the development of particular projects and makes the final decision to publish an individual study.

The Institute hopes that its studies and other activities will contribute to building a stronger foundation for international economic policy around the world. Comments as to how it can best do so are invited from readers of these publications.

C. Fred Bergsten
Director

Introduction

John Williamson

The International Monetary Fund's conditionality policies, the terms on which it lends, have been a perennial source of controversy. The traditional criticisms, which initially stemmed primarily from left wing elements in borrowing countries, were that the Fund adopts a doctrinaire monetarist approach, that it is insensitive to the individual situations of borrowing countries, that it imposes onerous conditions, that it is ideologically biased in favor of free markets and against socialism, and that it overrides national sovereignty and perpetuates dependency.

Until recent years the Fund did not respond to such criticisms. Its aloofness seems to have aggravated the critics, until hostility came to dominate the posture of the Group of 24 and the Group of 77 and misgivings spread even to the US Congress. There was little systematic evidence with which to evaluate these criticisms. In part this was because of the Fund's own reticence: such studies as it made public were uninformative on the vital questions, which involve making value judgments. Most accounts provided by the critics were not just presented in polemical terms but were analytically flawed by the absence of any convincing description of feasible alternatives to the Fund policies under attack. In this situation it seemed that a conference might be unusually illuminating. Such a conference was convened by the Institute for International Economics in March 1982 and held at Airlie House, Virginia.[1] This volume reports the proceedings of that conference.

When the idea of holding a conference on IMF conditionality was conceived, the main purpose was therefore to provide a body of case studies that would provide an adequate base for informed judgments on the Fund's role and performance in promoting adjustment in coun-

[1] See Appendix A for details.

tries borrowing from its high-conditionality facilities. The prime need seemed to be for a series of case studies asking the right questions about the feasible alternatives to what actually happened. It seemed natural to precede that review by some consideration of criteria for judging the success of stabilization cum adjustment programs and current professional views on the way such policies should be conducted. The conference sessions intended to fill that function appear as Part II in this volume; the case studies comprise Part III.

By the time plans for the conference were set in train in 1981, the situation had changed in several respects. In the first place, much more material on the Fund's role in promoting adjustment was becoming available.[2] An important reason for this was the Fund's own more forthcoming attitude both reflected in and promoted by its External Relations Department. Thus the Fund cooperated with the substantial research project undertaken by the Overseas Development Institute (London), two of whose studies (on Jamaica and Kenya) are included in this volume. The Fund has also published an occasional paper describing the program in Portugal and a volume based on the IMF Institute course on Kenya. And, of course, the Fund agreed to take an active part in our own conference.

In a second major change, the Fund had come under attack from a new direction. The criticisms of the Reagan administration were the obverse of those traditionally heard: that in its attempt to expand its role in the recycling process after the second oil shock, the Fund had "gone soft," approving programs that offered no hope of lasting adjustment, thereby devaluing the Fund's "seal of approval"; that the Fund had overextended itself into areas like structural adjustment; and that it had been lending to countries that could perfectly well borrow from the commercial banks instead.

To address those criticisms, the Fund's overall role in the intermediation process had to be considered, including its relationship to the World Bank and the commercial banks. That suggested that proposals for extending and systematizing the Fund's low-conditionality facilities should also be covered. This range of issues is treated in Part I of the volume, introduced by a wide-ranging paper by the Fund's Deputy Managing Director William B. Dale.

Part IV attempts to draw conclusions and policy implications. The first of its three chapters is a record of the panel discussion that introduced the concluding session of the conference. The second is a post-conference expansion of Dragoslav Avramovíc's comments during the conference. The last chapter consists of the monograph that I wrote after the conference, which draws on it to evaluate the Fund's recent performance and discusses the five main policy issues confronting the Fund in its lending operations.[2] These are: its role in the intermediation process; the division of labor between Fund and World Bank; the policy advice dispensed by the Fund regarding the design of adjustment programs; the monitoring of adjustment programs; and the desirability of the Fund's varying its lending policies with the state of the world economy.

My analysis is intended neither as a distillation of views presented at Airlie House nor as a conference report. Indeed, the last of the five topics listed above was scarcely discussed at Airlie House. It arose from a passing remark by Richard Cooper (Chapter 22, this volume) to the effect that the Fund should be more lenient during world recessions than world booms, on the grounds that a need to resort to the Fund when world conditions make it easy to run a surplus is more suggestive of inadequate policies than is a deficit at a time like 1981–82. But, as documented in Chapter 24, the Fund moved in the opposite direction in 1981, tightening its policies despite the deepening of the recession. This incongruity demanded analysis although it was not on the original agenda.

The final section of Chapter 24 offers an evaluation of the criticisms that have been directed at the Fund. It generally supports the Fund's performance, arguing that, at least in the cases studied (which were not chosen with the object of making it easy for the Fund to defend itself), there seems to be little basis for the traditional complaints. It is not clear that the Fund would have deserved equally warm endorsement had a somewhat earlier period been studied nor whether a similar exercise in the future, looking back at the present period, will be as supportive. In other words, even if readers find themselves in sympathy with my conclusions from the case studies in this volume, "monitoring the Fund" cannot be accomplished by a single conference or a single volume; it needs to be pursued continuously. The Fund's ability to modify its policies without open debate, as happened in 1981, makes the monitoring process both more difficult and more necessary.

The study concluded with an attempt to calculate the size of the quota increase that would be needed to provide the Fund with financial resources adequate to sustain the role advocated for it. This calculation implied that an increase of about two-thirds would be called for. But, even as the study was published, eruption of the Mexican crisis suggested that this estimate was too conservative, for

[2] John Williamson, *The Lending Policies of the International Monetary Fund,* POLICY ANALYSES IN INTERNATIONAL ECONOMICS 1 (Washington: Institute for International Economics, 1982).

Mexico drew not the 100 percent of quota assumed necessary to provide the confidence-restoring "seal of approval," but rather 450 percent of its quota. To enable the Fund to meet calls of that size on its resources, quotas would have needed to be at least doubled.

The official world also concluded that a quota increase was much more urgent than had previously been assumed, and an agreement was actually reached at the meeting of the Interim Committee in February 1983, as this book was going to press. The agreed increase was 47.4 percent. However, taken in conjunction with the enlargement of the General Arrangements to Borrow and the decision to make these potentially available to any Fund member, the increase in the resources available to the Fund is roughly equivalent to a doubling of quotas.

PART I

Role of the Fund

CHAPTER **1**

Financing and Adjustment of Payments Imbalances

William B. Dale

I shall first recapitulate the main problems that members of the International Monetary Fund have currently been facing. I shall then discuss how these problems have made it necessary for the Fund to reorient its policies so that it can play an active role in problem resolution and describe the support that the Fund is currently giving to members' adjustment efforts. I shall next take up some specific issues that have been raised concerning the Fund's financing role. My concluding remarks will look toward the evolution of the Fund's role in the years to come.

The International Economic Scene

The world economic situation in recent years has remained difficult and complex; problems of stagflation and large payments imbalances continue to cast gloom over the entire economic scene.

There have been some positive developments—in particular, inflation has eased in most countries in 1981 following the unprecedented levels of 1979 and 1980. However, the wide dispersion in the rates of inflation among the major industrial countries is likely to persist, and the average rate of inflation itself in the near term is expected to be about as high as in the latter part of the 1970s, or about twice as high in the decade ending in 1972. The situation of the non-oil developing countries, where consumer prices had risen

Note: This paper is reproduced by permission of the International Monetary Fund, Washington.

by about 30 percent in 1980–81, is still more disturbing. The fight against inflation must continue to concentrate heavily on demand management. Although the increase in oil prices was earlier an important contributing factor, oil prices have recently softened, and the major impulse behind inflation in both industrial and developing countries has come from expansionary financial policies mainly associated with large budgetary deficits and/or from a complex of cost-push factors and expectations.

The sharp setback to economic growth that the industrial countries have suffered is not likely to be quickly reversed. Total output, which grew at an annual average rate of 4 percent in 1976–79, rose by only 1.5 percent in 1980, and the growth rate has been still lower in 1981. While some improvement may be expected in 1982, the growth rate will still remain low if only because the control of inflation is likely to exercise a depressing influence. The setback in growth in the industrial countries is reflected in the high overall level of unemployment in these countries, which is projected to rise to perhaps 7.5 percent in 1982, and in the sharp decline in the growth of the volume of world trade, which reached no more than 1.5 percent in the last two years compared with 7 percent in the period 1976–79.

In the aggregate, the non-oil developing countries have managed to maintain their growth rates at about 5 percent. This aggregate growth rate may appear reasonably satisfactory, but against a background of low absolute income levels and continuing population growth it implies no more than a negligible growth of per capita income in many countries. The rapid rise of the import prices of non-oil developing countries and the weak demand for their exports have combined to bring about a sharp deterioration in their trade position, and, despite a sizable reduction in the volume of import growth, there has been a dramatic increase in the aggregate current account deficit of the non-oil developing countries.

This enlarged deficit is perhaps best seen in the context of the overall shift in the global distribution of current account imbalances. The current account surplus of oil-exporting countries, which almost disappeared by 1978, rose to $115 billion in 1980. Correspondingly, the combined current account position of industrial countries (excluding official transfers) moved from a surplus of $30 billion in 1978 to a deficit of $45 billion in 1980, whereas the combined current account deficit of non-oil developing countries more than doubled to $86 billion. For 1981, our projections now indicate a fall in the current account surplus of oil-exporting countries to about $70 billion. In the softer oil market of 1982, it will again decline sharply to perhaps $25 billion. For the oil-importing countries, an uneven picture emerges.

The deficit of the largest industrial countries is expected to improve from 1980 to 1982 and to move sharply into surplus, whereas that of the smaller industrial countries would remain very high. In as many as half of the industrialized and non-oil developing countries, the ratio of the current deficit to GDP is projected to exceed 7 percent in 1980–81, with much higher ratios in the case of certain countries, compared with an average of 3 percent at the beginning of the 1970s. The projections, however, are particularly difficult. We have not yet been in a position to distribute among countries and groups of countries the projected 1982 fall in the OPEC (Organization of Petroleum Exporting Countries) surplus apart from the evident proposition that the large industrial countries, the biggest oil importers, will benefit most.

Imbalances of this magnitude cannot be sustained: the burden of debt resulting from their financing is already weighing heavily on countries and is becoming, in some instances, unmanageable. If the international financial system is to remain viable, the adoption of policies to bring about a marked reduction in these deficits, by industrial and developing countries alike, is essential.

Prospects for the medium term, which the Fund has sketched, reinforce this conclusion. Our analysis shows that if the industrialized countries were to decide to relax their demand policies, the consequences could be seriously adverse. Growth rates might well improve in the near term, but inflation would flare up again, and the results would be damaging both domestically and internationally. The process of overcoming stagflation requires not only a sustained and integrated approach with continued accent on demand restraint, but also specific attention to supply policies. A premature resort to fiscal and monetary expansion would call for a still more costly process of adjustment in the future. Our analysis also shows that, even with reasonably favorable assumptions such as moderate growth rates in the industrial countries and effective adjustment policies in deficit countries, the combined current account deficits of the non-oil developing countries may well continue to increase in nominal terms through the middle of the 1980s. Although these deficits will decline somewhat in relation to exports of goods and services, from 21 percent in 1981 to about 18 percent in 1985, they will nevertheless remain large in comparison with historical norms. The prospects are particularly worrisome for some 38 poorest countries in this group and also for some 50 middle-income countries whose exports consist mainly of primary commodities. In this scenario, the ratio of debt-service payments to exports of goods and services for the poorest countries would remain, on average, at the historically high level of 20 percent between 1981 and 1985, while the ratio for the middle-income countries would increase from 17 percent to 24 percent of exports.

Need for a Strong Role of the Fund

With the emergence of the deeply rooted internal and external imbalances in member countries, it was evident that there was need for increased international cooperation among individual countries and groups of countries and that the Fund should play an active role in helping its member countries to deal with the complex policy issues. For the Fund this has meant redefining its role and policies both as a regulatory body and a forum for international collaboration, and as an agency to provide balance of payments financing to promote adjustment. The Fund has strengthened its procedures to carry out its general responsibility for surveillance over member countries' exchange rate policies. The regular consultations with individual members, a principal vehicle for such surveillance, have provided opportunities to assist members in the diagnosis of economic problems and in the prescription of requisite policies. These consultations are supplemented by more informal policy discussions with member authorities. Another means of surveillance, the periodic reviews of economic developments and policies in the context of the *World Economic Outlook*, has become an increasingly important forum for dialogue and cooperation. In the area of adjustment and financing of payments imbalances—the subject of this paper and this conference—the Fund recognized that it had to play a greatly increased role.

Two sets of considerations that are closely interrelated gave, and continue to give, urgency to this need. The first stems from the characteristics of bank lending. Private financial institutions have been and will continue to be the major providers of financing. However, for many deficit countries the existing position is not altogether satisfactory. The banks have to be concerned with the commercial viability of their operations; their criteria for allocation of resources do not necessarily meet the requirements of all countries. Some countries have found it difficult, at one time or another, to maintain conditions that can assure the banks of the soundness of additional or even existing loans. In such circumstances bank lending has at times been abruptly reduced, with very harsh consequences for the countries concerned. Resolution of the problems that have arisen has been particularly difficult because the commercial banks are not generally well placed to negotiate with the authorities of the affected countries on the policies that might enable lending to be resumed.

Furthermore, the banks tend to consider that it is not their role to assume the risks involved in maintaining flows in difficult and uncertain situations. These situations have become more frequent in the last two years and are likely to increase in the future because of the sharp rise in the external debt of many developing countries and because of the difficulty that these countries will face in adjusting to the deterioration in their terms of trade. Although prudential concerns have not proved to be a significant constraint on the expansion of bank lending to countries where banks are already relatively heavily exposed, market resistance has stiffened for individual countries whose adjustment policies are viewed as inadequate, and it probably will continue to do so in the future.

The second set of considerations arise from the problems the developing countries have been facing, problems that cannot be solved by mere financing. Alone, financing is useful only to gain time. Far from dealing with fundamental problems, borrowing by itself would result in levels of indebtedness that in the course of time would become insupportable. Financing and the adjustment of imbalances must therefore go hand in hand, and the Fund can play a critical role in helping to bring about a proper mix of these two elements. The nature of current imbalances requires in many cases considerable changes in the pattern of demand and supply in members' economies, and the Fund is, I believe, well placed to encourage members to make these changes and to help design programs serving that end. It is also important that Fund members adopt such programs in good time, that the availability of financing does not postpone adjustment, and that situations are avoided in which corrective policies are introduced only at an advanced stage of economic deterioration.

The situation today is quite different from the one prevailing in 1974–75, when the Fund established its oil facilities. Lending under these facilities—particularly under the one applied in 1974—had very mild conditionality. Under the 1974 facility, access was made conditional mainly on a representation by the member that it would avoid measures destructive to international prosperity including, in particular, restrictions on trade and payments. Although the use of the 1975 facility called for a statement of policies from the member to achieve a medium-term solution to its balance of payments problems, a solution the Fund would consider adequate, there was no requirement of a comprehensive quantified program. The concern at that time was that countries should not attempt to adjust too quickly, on the grounds that such an attempt, if collectively pursued, could lead to an undesirable deepening of global recession. Subsequently, as inflation became the principal threat and as domestic imbalances in the members' economies became pervasive, the emphasis shifted to a fundmental adjustment of the imbalances that includes attention to structural elements.

Decline in the Fund's Lending Capacity

A strong role for the Fund in promoting adjustment requires that the Fund have sufficient resources to place in support of members' efforts, and that Fund policies permit members to obtain assistance on a scale commensurate with the members' financing needs while strong adjustment programs are under way. The growth in the size of the Fund's available conditional resources (including those involving low conditionality, such as resources provided under the oil facility and under the Trust Fund), however, lagged well behind the increase in payments imbalances faced by members during the 1970s. The Fund's basic resources are derived from currency subscriptions by its members. At any time, only part of these resources is in fact available to be used by members because the currencies of members that are in need of balance of payments assistance are not ordinarily used. On the basis of historical data, a plausible assumption would be that members accounting for slightly over one-half of aggregate quotas might be expected to be in a sufficiently strong position so that their currencies could be used to assist members in deficit. The maximum possible drawings on this assumption would be, say, 55 percent of total quotas. Although most borrowing arrangements, under ordinary circumstances, can be used in their entirety, we have assumed that only about half of the agreed total amount for the General Arrangements to Borrow can actually be used in any one time because that arrangement envisages financing of the deficits of some members by borrowings from other members within a closed group.

Measured in this way the size of the Fund's conditional resources, compared to the sum of the current account imbalances of some 111 countries for which data are available, fell from 50 percent on average during 1966–70 to about 20 percent in 1977–78. When compared with the sums of overall payments imbalances, it fell from 81 percent to about 27 percent between the same periods. Both the size of the Fund and the sum of Fund quotas have declined relative to world imports since the 1960s; the erosion in the real value of quotas has been particularly sharp. In 1960, total quotas were 12 percent of world imports; in 1970, they were 10 percent; and at present they are below 3 percent. Until recently, a member's access to the Fund's conditional resources was ordinarily limited to 100 percent of quota; the limit was raised to 165 percent under the extended Fund facility (EFF), which was established in 1974. During the 1970s, when imbalances rose dramatically, the full use of the Fund thus gave a member resources that were often quite inadequate to meet the member's need for financing.

The lagging growth in the size of the Fund has had significant consequences for the international monetary system. This development has meant that countries' financing needs arising from payments imbalances have been met increasingly through international bank lending rather than through the use of Fund resources, and it in part explains the reluctance, until 1979, of many member countries to have recourse to the Fund's conditional resources. This lag in the capacity of the Fund is not likely to have raised the cost of finance to members, but it may also have been a severe constraint on the capacity of the Fund to promote adjustment through the provision of financial support for economic stabilization programs. In other words, the inability of the Fund to keep pace with the rise in payments imbalances may have contributed to a slowing in the pace of balance of payments adjustment by countries with large external deficits.

Recent Changes in the Fund's Lending Policies

Major initiatives were clearly necessary to increase the Fund's lending capacity. In 1979 the supplementary financing facility (SFF) became operative, with resources borrowed from oil-exporting and major industrial countries for a total amount of SDR 7.8 billion. In 1980 the Seventh General Review of Quotas became effective and led to a 50 percent increase in quotas, which by historical standards was relatively large. With the full commitment of resources available under the SFF, the Fund engaged in new borrowings to maintain an enlarged lending capacity. An agreement was concluded last year with the Saudi Arabian Monetary Agency that enables the Fund to borrow up to SDR 4 billion a year for two years, with the possibility of additional amounts in the third year. An agreement has also been reached under which the monetary institutions of 13 industrial countries have undertaken to lend SDR 1.3 billion to the Fund either bilaterally or through the Bank for International Settlements. Other bilateral arrangements, as well as a possible approach to the private markets, if required, are under study.

As a result of these initiatives, the Fund's capacity to provide finance to support adjustment programs has increased dramatically since the end of 1978 by nearly 90 percent. While the initiatives have reversed the downward trend in the relation between the size of the Fund and the relevant measures of its financing tasks, they have restored the relative capacity of the Fund only to its level of about 1975, far below that of any earlier period in the Fund's history.

Along with an increase in available resources, the Fund has progressively revised its lending limits in the last few years. Such a revision was required not only by the need to encourage members to undertake adjustment programs but also by the very nature of the programs that are appropriate in current circumstances. Because the imbalances faced by members arose in many cases from structural factors, adjustment programs need to emphasize measures to achieve a major reallocation of resources to improve supply capacity, as well as policies of aggregate demand restraint. Such an adjustment is likely to take time, and the programs therefore have to be set in a medium-term time frame, their objective being to bring about a sustainable current account by the end of this period. The essential ingredients of the supply side of the program are to increase domestic savings, to encourage net capital inflows, and to reorder incentives and priorities to ensure that investment is directed particularly to projects and uses that will benefit the balance of payments. These measures on the supply side are, of course, to be closely supported by measures to maintain aggregate demand within the constraints set by available financing. Because the programs often involve a reexamination of private and public investment policy and of the operations of the public enterprises, the Fund has relied heavily and increasingly on collaboration with the World Bank in helping members assess these programs.

The Fund has recognized that, to provide adequate support to such programs, it would have to make available much larger resources relative to quota than were permitted previously, and for a period of several years when necessary. Following the most recent revision of Fund policy, in January 1981, countries making strong efforts to correct their payments imbalances may draw up to a maximum of 150 percent of their newly enlarged quotas, or a total of up to 450 percent over a three-year period, not counting any drawings under the special facilities for compensatory and buffer stock financing. This policy—which in essence restored a member's total access to the Fund to the level of the mid-1960s—has yielded very rapid and encouraging results since 1979. In 1980 new Fund loan commitments and other drawings totaled SDR 9.5 billion, which is more than double the average during the preceding five years. In 1981 total new commitments and other drawings have jumped further to some SDR 16 billion.

There has been in the past 18 months an impressive growth in medium-term arrangements extending over two or three years. More recently, Fund analysts have noted that members find it difficult to make specific policy decisions beyond one year and, if such decisions are made in advance, to implement them when the time comes. Some of the longer term arrangements have, therefore, been cancelled or have been allowed to lapse, and they have been replaced by one-year arrangements. Nevertheless, programs continue to be set in the medium term, even when specified for a shorter period, because of the nature of the adjustment problems I have mentioned.

Because policies to redress structural imbalances are not likely to yield quick results, the repayment period for Fund drawings has been extended from the range of three to five years for drawings under ordinary tranche policies, to four to ten years for drawings under the EFF, and to three-and-one-half years to seven years for drawings under the SFF or its successor, the policy on enlarged access.

Broader Use of the Fund

One or two issues that have been prominently featured in recent discussions on the financing policies of the Fund need further elaboration.

Is the Fund to be regarded as a lender of last resort, or is it to be a routine provider of financing to meet balance of payments deficits? At the time the Fund was being set up, there was a strong body of opinion, most forcefully led by Lord Keynes, that the Fund should be a regular intermediary between surplus and deficit countries, that the resources of the Fund should constitute for members, after their own reserves, the next line of defense for the balance of payments. The original Articles of Agreement set a limit of 25 percent of quota on members' drawings each year, and in the early discussions on the Fund's lending policies several executive directors argued that a member should have an automatic right to drawings up to this amount in any year—subject, of course, to the limit specified in the Articles on the aggregate use of the Fund. Although this never became the Fund's policy, the Fund in 1947 did assure members that, until a member had been informed to the contrary by the Fund, it could count on obtaining prompt assistance in more moderate amounts. In fact, for a period the Fund applied a rule that, if the requested drawing did not exceed 5 percent of a member's quota within a 30-day period, the request could be dealt with by the managing director without prior reference to the Executive Board. Indeed, several transactions were made under this procedure, including successive drawings by the same country. There was growing dissatisfaction among the Board members as a whole, however, with the simplicity of the operation contemplated by this rule, since it was felt that the policy provided little assurance that a temporary use of Fund resources was being made. In early 1948 the Board decided that the Fund had the power to postpone, reject, or approve a request for a drawing subject to conditions designed to safeguard the Fund's purposes.

In subsequent years, as a systematic framework of the Fund's policies on the use of its resources began to evolve, the main consideration was to strike a balance between assurance to members that they would be able, in times of need, to draw on the Fund and assurance to the Fund that the revolving character of its resources would be protected. The introduction of the concept of stand-by arrangements attempted to provide such a balance. The intention of the arrangement, as first announced in 1952, was to give members an advance assurance, after the Fund had discussions with a member on its general position, that the member would be able to draw on the Fund if, within a period of six months to a year, a need for drawing presented itself. In later years, annual stand-by arrangements became the principal vehicle of Fund assistance in cases where a member had both an immediate and a prospective need to draw. However, the initial conception of the stand-by arrangement as a sort of precautionary device to assure the availability of financing in times of need also survived. Particularly in the 1960s, there were several countries that came to the Fund for this assurance, often for successive years. Their balance of payments position at the time they concluded the arrangements was not necessarily troublesome; in fact, their actual drawings on the Fund were generally well below the amounts that were committed by the Fund. The existence of a stand-by arrangement helped to maintain the confidence of foreign creditors in the economic policies of the member, and frequently the dominant reason for seeking an arrangement with the Fund was not so much the availability of the Fund's resources, although this was not unimportant, as it was the sustaining of capital inflows from abroad. Even apart from such uses of the Fund, in the 1950s and 1960s the Fund was involved in the financing of various balance of payments situations that were not necessarily critical ones.

During most of the later period, however, a different situation has prevailed. By and large, members have approached the Fund when their financial positions have already suffered extreme deterioration and when the possibilities of borrowing from other sources have either sharply diminished or have even temporarily disappeared. In this period the Fund has been largely a lender of last resort. I have already given one reason for this turn of events—the greatly reduced size of the financing that could be obtained from the Fund relative to the need for such financing, and the relative ease with which financing could be obtained from the international markets. Other reasons are also advanced: that the conditions the Fund may require for its assistance are difficult; that the Fund resources are cut off if a performance criterion is breached, even if marginally, perhaps causing a seriously adverse effect on the ability of the country to maintain its borrowing from other sources. And there is, of course, an understandable reluctance for governments to submit to the scrutiny of their economic situation and policies by an outside agency as long as this can be avoided. Whatever the reason, the publicity that is given to negotiations with the Fund and the widespread impression that is created that an approach to the Fund signals a desperate situation have clearly been a deterrent to many countries that might decide to negotiate with the Fund.

We in the Fund have regarded this development as unfortunate. In recent discussions of Fund policies by our Board, much attention has been given to the need to attract to the Fund countries other than those in extreme distress. The guidelines on conditionality that were established in March 1979 put this matter at the top of the Fund's concerns. The first guideline says that "members should be encouraged to adopt corrective measures, which could be supported by use of the Fund's general resources in accordance with the Fund's policies, at an early stage of their balance of payments difficulties." It notes that the Fund's regular consultations with members are among the occasions at which the Fund would be able to discuss with members the adjustment policies that may be needed to overcome any existing or potential problems and the circumstances under which the Fund would be able to provide financial support. At these and other occasions, the Fund is making it clear to members that adjustment measures, if taken in time, need not be too rigorous and that if the authorities set such measures in motion, may well satisfy the criteria for Fund lending when the member approaches the Fund. The increase in the resources of the Fund and the liberal limitations for members' access to these resources that I have mentioned are also intended to encourage a broader use of the Fund.

I believe that these initiatives are beginning to bear fruit. In recent years the Fund has concluded stand-by or extended arrangements with some countries—I might cite India, Pakistan, and Yugoslavia among others—when the approach to the Fund has not been prompted by a critical situation. We in the Fund have been reviewing our procedures and policies in order to promote further the diversification of the use of the Fund, and I shall have something to add on this matter in my concluding remarks.

Nature of Imbalances and the Pace of Adjustment

A second issue that I will briefly touch on concerns the relation between the origin of the payments imbalances and the nature of adjustment that is appropriate. The imbalances currently faced by Fund members in part stem from external factors, in particular the increase in import prices and, in many cases, downturns in export prices. There is no dispute, I believe, that imbalances, whatever their origin, must eventually be adjusted as long as the developments giving rise to them are not themselves transitory or self-reversing. If there is a lasting change in the situation, whether it is due to domestic inflation or to an adverse turn in the terms of trade, an adjustment of the supply-demand balance must take place. The question then is whether adjustment of imbalances of external origin should take a different form or time path from that of internally caused imbalances. The practical significance of this question is a limited one because in most cases it is difficult to separate the relative contributions of domestic and external factors to payments imbalance. But the question has some relevance for imbalances induced by the higher costs of imported energy.

In this sense, the issue has been fully recognized by the Fund. Recent programs supported by the Fund have paid particular attention to structural changes in the economy that are designed to bring about savings in the use of imported energy. Such changes have involved adjustment of energy prices, other measures to economize on energy consumption, and an active policy to expand and develop energy production; in all these the Fund has closely collaborated with the World Bank. Adjustment to higher international energy prices is bound to take time, and the Fund does not expect that such adjustment will necessarily be completed by the end of the period of a Fund arrangement. But it does expect that policies pursued during this period will enable the member to achieve a viable balance of payments in the sense that sustainable means of financing will be available to meet any continuing deficit in the current account. The Fund's role is to encourage the member to manage its domestic policies in a manner that will enhance its ability to attract capital inflows, and thus to maintain a viable balance of payments position for the entire period needed to bring about a full adjustment.

Concluding Remarks

I briefly referred to the medium-term projections the Fund recently made that indicate serious problems of adjustment and financing for a large number of countries in the years to come. The financial environment in these years is not easy to predict. There is no question that the intermediation process by the private market has so far been remarkably smooth and efficient. Whether it will be as smooth in the 1980s is less clear. There are several indications that some strains on the system could develop: external indebtedness in many countries has grown rapidly in the 1970s; some countries have reached or have exceeded the limits of their creditworthiness; and some banks are showing signs of making their lending policies more restrictive and more selective. Even when intermediation is adequate, as was the case in past years, it may not always work to meet adjustment needs. The easy availability of financing in the past has not served the fundamental interests of some countries, particularly when such financing has bolstered consumption rather than supporting investment and the growth of productive capacity. Reliance upon such financing has enabled some members to delay, sometimes for excessively long periods, the needed domestic and external adjustment. The criteria on which banks have judged the creditworthiness of some of the borrowing countries have often not been clear, and in some cases the abrupt decline in credit flows, as the true nature of the risks became manifest, has caused serious problems. This is not to cast doubt on the efficiency with which intermediation has generally taken place, but the fact remains that in a number of cases intermediation—by the private banks and, in some cases, by governments—has worked at cross purposes with the adjustment process. One cannot rule out that such problems may reemerge in the future.

In addition to the particular need for financing for some countries, the more general need for adjustment of payments imbalances continues to require, I believe, a strong role for the Fund in the 1980s. This role is not to be seen as taking up a specific share of the intermediation business or as competing with other financing channels. The unique function of the Fund is to promote the adjustment process; it cannot in today's circumstances engage in intermediation without ensuring that adjustment is also taking place. It is true that the oil facility, especially for 1974, came close to pure intermediation, but the uncertainties that justified it—in particular uncertainties concerning the adequate availability of financing and the nature of the policy response that was called for—do not currently prevail.

There will be countries facing, or continuing to face, crisis and near-crisis situations, and the Fund will have to collaborate with them, helping them to make steady progress toward a viable position. However, as I have said, restricting the financial activities of the Fund only to helping members when all other sources of finance have failed would cast too narrow a role for the Fund. We in the Fund hope that international cooperation would be able to limit the frequency of these situations. In particular, we would like to see the commercial banks, regardless of competitive pressures, weigh carefully the merits of financing deficits in cases where such financing allows the countries concerned to defer adjustment policies. We also see in other cases the need for the banks to stand fast and maintain, or even increase, exposure levels when a country in acute difficulty has finally brought itself to set a new course toward payments viability.

From the point of view of effective international adjustment, the use of the Fund should clearly be broadened to include use by countries that now rely primarily on commercial banks but that do face adjustment problems. Early access to the Fund, with parallel borrowing from commercial sources, would give assurance to such members, and to the international community, of continued flows of funds in the context of well-designed programs of economic adjustment. To induce members to design such programs, the Fund's capacity to provide finance relative to the total of imbalances should be strengthened. This would be all the more necessary if smaller industrial countries, and large developing countries, should find it necessary to approach the Fund.

As to the means of strengthening the Fund's resources, there is a widespread consensus in our Board that this should take the form of quota increases. A quota increase is, in effect, a set of arrangements with all members, and it can, in principle, give the Fund a larger access to resources than can a set of borrowing arrangements with only a few members. Moreover, securing the access to resources through an overall quota increase accords well with the cooperative nature of an institution such as the Fund. This does not necessarily mean that borrowing can be dispensed with in the future—that depends on the size and nature of the coming quota increase. Borrowing arrangements provide a useful supplement to quota resources whenever there is a significant difference, as is the case at present, between the distribution of quotas and of payments surpluses, or when quota increases turn out to be insufficient relative to the desired capacity of the Fund. Borrowing arrangements may be necessary to maintain the Fund's lending capacity during the interval between reviews for general quota increases.

CHAPTER **2**

Stabilization: The Political Economy of Overkill

Sidney Dell

In his remarkable essay on stabilization plans in the Southern Cone of Latin America, Carlos Diaz-Alejandro (1981) suggests that these plans have been a case of "overkill" in that the economic retrenchment the plans have brought about has gone much further than is strictly necessary for what could have been regarded as reasonable objectives.

The term overkill used by Diaz-Alejandro could well be used much more generally to describe the national and international programs of adjustment adopted in the 1970s and early 1980s. The following discussion deals first with international aspects of this process of overkill, and later with some of the national aspects.

International Aspects

The "purposes" of the International Monetary Fund (IMF) are set out in the first of its Articles of Agreement. Six such purposes are defined, including international monetary cooperation, the expansion and balanced growth of international trade, the promotion of exchange stability and of a multilateral system of payments, the mitigation of disequilibria in balances of payments, and the provision of resources to facilitate the correction of such disequilibria.

The "primary objectives" underlying these purposes are described in Article I(ii) as being "the promotion and maintenance of high

Note: The views expressed in this paper are those of the author and not necessarily those of the United Nations Secretariat.

levels of employment and real income and. . . the development of the productive resources of all members as primary objectives of economic policy." Further reference to these primary objectives is made in Article I(v), which specifies that the correction of maladjustments in the balance of payments should be undertaken "without resorting to measures destructive of national or international prosperity."

The Distortion of Priorities

The international community seems to have strayed quite far from these "primary objectives of economic policy." In a situation of increasingly inadequate effective demand, growing underutilization of productive capacity, and soaring unemployment, the pressure continues for even greater reductions of demand, which are likely to increase the volume of idle capacity and unemployment still further. The singlemindedness of the attack on inflation[1] seems to have gone beyond the point at which trade-offs with other objectives are even considered, so that monetary restriction has almost become an end in itself. This is a distortion of IMF priorities, of the priorities of Article 55 of the United Nations Charter, and of the International Development Strategy drawn up under that Charter.[2]

It is ironic that the first industrial country to express alarm at the current situation is precisely the one that, throughout the postwar period, had maintained the strongest orthodoxy in fiscal and monetary matters, and that on past occasions had invariably resisted proposals for economic expansion that might carry with them the smallest risk of inflation. On the insistence of Chancellor Helmut Schmidt of Germany, the Washington communiqué of January 6, 1982, contained the following warning: "The Chancellor referred to the danger of a worldwide depression."

In the present circumstances, it might be expected that world leadership would be concerned with charting a program of economic recovery and with seeking international cooperation in such a program. In fact, however, IMF management takes the position that:

[1] The purposes of the IMF as stated in its Article I did not, even after the amendments adopted in 1969 and 1978, include the elimination or reduction of inflation. Inflation is relevant to the IMF purposes to the extent that it contributes to balance of payments disequilibrium.

[2] Article 55 of the United Nations Charter calls for the promotion of "higher standards of living, full employment, and conditions of economic and social progress and development."

> The fight against inflation must continue to concentrate heavily on demand management. Although the increase in oil prices was earlier an important contributing factor, oil prices have recently softened, and the major impulse behind inflation in both industrial and developing countries has come from expansionary financial policies mainly associated with large budgetary deficits and/or from a complex of cost-push factors and expectations. (Dale, Chapter 1, this volume.)

This statement exemplifies the fundamental error of much current thinking about both the world economy and the problems faced by individual countries, whether industrial or developing.

It is interesting to examine this statement in reference to the United States, whose economy is still so large in relative terms that it plays the leading role in determining the level of economic activity of the industrial countries as a whole and, hence, to a considerable extent, of the developing countries as well.

At present (April 1982), unemployment in the United States is at a level of approximately 9 percent and is rising. There is idle productive capacity in every sector of the economy, and the rate of capacity utilization has fallen to a level of 70 percent or lower in manufacturing industries. If it is true that current financial policy in the United States is expansionary as a result of the large budget deficit, why is it that output is not rising? Why, on the contrary, has real GNP been falling at an annual rate of no less that 4.5 percent for the past six months? And if real income—hence, real demand—is falling, what sense does it make to say that the fight against inflation is essentially a problem of demand management?

The mistake here is twofold. First, a budget deficit per se tells nothing about whether aggregate demand is excessive. It is only when the budget deficit is considered in conjunction with other demands on private saving—gross investment and net exports—that one can judge excessive aggregate demand. This, of course, is just as true for developing countries as it is for industrial countries.

Second, under conditions of substantial unemployment and excess capacity, one must distinguish between the part of a budget deficit that is an automatic response to the low level of business activity, leading to reduced government revenues and higher government transfers, and the rest of the deficit, which would add to demand even at a high level of employment. Despite the ascendancy of monetarism, the US Department of Commerce continues to estimate the high-employment budget deficit at regular intervals, and not long ago it issued a revised series going all the way back to 1955. Unfortunately, the department has over the years progressively raised the percentage of unemployment used as a basis for defining the concept of high employment, so that this percentage now stands at 5.1, a level that seems much too high. Nevertheless, even at this level the high employment budget was in surplus in the United States in 1979, 1980, and the first three quarters of 1981, whereas the deficit in the fourth quarter of 1981 was equivalent to considerably less that 1 percent of GNP—well within the order of error of the estimates. Now, if the high employment budget was balanced or in surplus throughout the period 1979–81, it can hardly be said that inflation in the United States during that period was due to "expansionary financial policies mainly associated with large budgetary deficits," as Mr. Dale contends. The source of inflation must clearly be sought elsewhere. Even for 1982, available projections indicate that the expansionary thrust of the deficit, adjusted for the level of employment, is likely to be small or negligible.

Although the notion of a high employment budget deficit cannot be applied mechanically to developing countries because of conceptual problems with the definitions of unemployment and excess capacity, it is just as true in these countries as in the industrial countries that, at reduced levels of economic activity, budget deficits increase because of the associated declines in government revenue. Consequently, the expansionary thrust of a budget deficit in a developing country, as in an industrial country, cannot be assessed without allowing for the level of economic activity.

It has been necessary to dwell upon this matter because it is typical of the errors of diagnosis that so often lead to the disorientation of stabilization programs and, hence, to the process of overkill. Deflationary policies, however essential they may be in cases where balance of payments disequilibrium is due primarily to excess demand, should not be regarded as a panacea for all problems. Nor should the explicit injunction of Article I(v) of the IMF be forgotten—that measures to restore external equilibrium should not be "destructive of national or international prosperity." In many cases, measures that carry the obvious risk of being destructive of national prosperity are nevertheless considered indispensable in overcoming inflation, or in restoring external balance, or in both. Moreover, such measures are commonplace not only in countries where balance of payments support is being sought, but in many other countries also.

Some comfort is derived from the recent slowing down of cost inflation, as if this single measure of economic health could be given priority over all others. No one ever doubted that, with sufficient determination it would be possible to cut back the level of business activity to the point at which demand inflation would be eliminated and cost inflation at least slowed down. The question was rather that of determining whether it was really necessary to burn down the house to discover roast pig, whether there was some better way of doing things that would give higher priority to "national and international prosperity" and somewhat less importance to the rate of increase in prices.

This is not to say that inflation is a matter that can be neglected. On the contrary, it is clear that inflation can seriously distort the development process by encouraging the use of resources in socially undesirable ways and by intensifying inequity in the distribution of income. But if the real problem is cost-induced inflation, and the remedy applied is demand deflation, the cure is likely to prove worse than the disease. Instead of reducing social tension, demand deflation is likely to aggravate it; even if the cost inflation is slowed down temporarily, the benefits are likely to last only as long as demand is maintained at subnormal levels.

A permanent solution to the problem of cost inflation cannot be obtained by seeking to play on the fear of rising unemployment among those who try to protect themselves against increases in the cost of living by demanding higher wages. Where a cut in living standards is unavoidable, price stability in a democratic society requires general agreement on the way in which the burden should be shared. Intimidation through unemployment is likely to make any long-lasting agreement on burden sharing more difficult to achieve, not less.

The ultimate futility of the deflationary approach becomes particularly clear in the prospects for the world economy foreseen by the adherents of this approach. After a decade of stagnation, their program of action calls for little but further stagnation for some time to come, so as to ensure that inflationary psychology is broken. Such stagnation seriously prejudices the adjustment process, because adjustment is always easier in an expanding economy. But the real danger is more fundamental. Sooner or later persistent deflation—whether monetary, fiscal, or both—is bound to cause a crisis of confidence, and it is this crisis that Chancellor Schmidt no doubt had in mind in speaking of the danger of depression. If such a depression were to come, it would be the first to be brought about deliberately, on the misguided view that this is the only way of dealing with inflation.

The Problem of Symmetry

The IMF continues to insist that the origin of a balance of payments deficit, whether internal or external, has no bearing on the adjustment measures required. On this view, the only valid question is whether a deficit is temporary or persistent; if it is persistent, there is only one way of dealing with it.

In taking this position, the Fund appears to shrug off its responsibility for ensuring that the burden of adjustment is distributed equitably and efficiently among countries. Because the underlying principle seems to have been forgotten, it is perhaps worth restating it—in fact, worth putting it in the terms in which it has been advanced in the past by some of the industrial countries that are now most insistent in pressing for unilateral adjustment by deficit developing countries.

The need for equity and efficiency in the distribution of the burden of adjustment was advanced with particular emphasis by Paul Volcker, current chairman of the US Federal Reserve Board, representing the US Government in the Committee of Twenty at deputy level. The *Economic Report of the President* for January 1973 sets out the essential elements of the case argued before the Committee by Volcker as well as the text of a memorandum on this matter submitted to the Committee in November 1972.

The point was made that there had been nothing in the Bretton Woods system to assure compatibility of the balance of payments objectives of various countries, and that the breakdown of the system could be attributed to the failure to induce the adjustments required to achieve equilibrium. In the light of this experience, the US proposals for a new system were designed "to apply equivalent incentives for adjustment evenhandedly to all countries" (*Economic Report of the President 1973*, pp. 161–62).

Symmetry in the adjustment process was seen as partially a question of equity in sharing the political and economic costs of adjustment. But it was also necessary for efficiency:

> If countries on both the deficit and the surplus side of a payments imbalance follow active policies for the restoration of equilibrium, the process is likely to be easier than if the deficit countries try to bring about adjustment by themselves. Deficit countries would in any case be unable to restore equilibrium unless surplus countries at least followed policies consistent with a reduction of the net surplus in their payments positions. (*Economic Report of the President* 1973, pp. 124–25.)

The US view of the main shortcoming in the adjustment process was not, of course, shared by the European countries, which regarded the asymmetry between the reserve center and the rest of the world as the crucial problem, and asset settlement as the solution to that problem. But as John Williamson (1977) has pointed out, there was no necessary contradiction between these two approaches, and it would have been possible to construct a system that incorporated both. Unfortunately, the system (if system it can be called) that actually emerged incorporates neither approach.

Parallels Between the 1980s and the 1970s

The combined current account deficit of net oil-importing developing countries rose from $30 billion in 1978 to $80 billion in 1981. Against this increase of $50 billion, their bill for oil and interest payments alone increased by close to $70 billion. In fact, despite the world recession, the net oil-importing developing countries achieved a remarkable improvement in their exports and actually moved into surplus on non-oil trade account (de Larosière 1981). This refutes the assertion often made that the developing countries did not adjust after the first oil crisis. They certainly did adjust, and on an impressive scale. The deterioration in their current account that occurred in 1979–81 despite these significant efforts of adjustment was due entirely to factors beyond their control—the further rise in oil prices and the new upsurge in interest rates.

In January 1974, at a time when many countries were facing large deficits in their balances of payments as a result of a deterioration in their terms of trade, the managing director of the IMF presented a note to the Committee of Twenty in which he indicated that oil-importing countries would, in the short run, have to accept the deterioration of the current account of the balance of payments because:

> Attempts to eliminate the additional current deficit caused by higher oil prices through deflationary demand policies, import restrictions, and general resort to exchange rate depreciation would serve only to shift the payments problem from one oil-importing country to another and to damage world trade and economic activity. (Committee of Twenty 1974, pp. 25–26.)

Subsequently, in its communiqué of June 13, 1974, the Committee of Twenty noted (emphasis supplied):

> As a result of inflation, the energy situation, and other unsettled conditions, many countries are experiencing large current account deficits that need to be financed. . . . Sustained cooperation would be needed to ensure appropriate financing without endangering the smooth functioning of private financial markets and *to avert the danger of adjustment action that merely shifts the problem to other countries*. (Committee of Twenty 1974, p. 221.)

These were the considerations underlying the decision to establish an oil facility to provide balance of payments support at low conditionality in 1974–75. Any IMF member drawing on the oil facility was required to cooperate with the Fund in finding appropriate solutions for the member's balance of payments problem. This requirement of cooperation with the Fund was the same as that for the compensatory financing facility (CFF), but the character of the conditionality involved was quite different. Under the relevant decisions of the Executive Board on this matter,[3] member countries drawing on the oil facility were required to avoid "competitive depreciation and the escalation of restrictions on trade and payments" and to pursue "policies that would sustain appropriate levels of economic activity and employment, while minimizing inflation."

One would have thought that similar considerations and objectives would have been applied to the situation in 1981–82. Here again, the upsurge in oil prices of 1979–80, coupled with general inflation, had a major effect on the balances of payments of a large number of countries. And once more, as in 1974–75, it was important that deficit countries not adopt policies that would merely exacerbate the problems of other countries. But whereas in 1974–75 the emphasis of the IMF was on avoiding restrictive policies and on sustaining "appropriate levels of economic activity and employment," in 1981–82 the resources provided by the Fund bring with them all the rigors of upper credit tranche conditionality and generally involve severe economic retrenchment. The deflation brought about by the adjustment process is thereby superimposed on, and reinforces, the primary deflation that is the result of business recession in the industrial countries.

It is apparent that, in the view of responsible IMF authorities, the situation in the 1980s is quite different from that prevailing in the 1970s and is therefore not susceptible to the same treatment. The reasons for this view are, however, not altogether clear. At times it is suggested that the surpluses of the oil-exporting countries are likely to be more persistent in the 1980s than in the 1970s.[4] On the grounds

[3] Executive Board decision 4134 (74/4), January 23, and 4241 (74/67), June 13; (IMF 1974, p. 108, 122–23). I am indebted to Mr. Alexandre Kafka, Executive Director of the IMF, for this point.

[4] Alternative scenarios through the mid-1980s, explored in the IMF's *World Economic Outlook* (IMF 1981*b*) assumed that the real price of oil would either remain steady or continue to increase, so that the current account surplus of oil-exporting countries would either decline from $96 billion in 1981 to some $50 billion by 1985 or remain approximately unchanged; no consideration was given to the possibility that the real price of oil might decline.

that persistent imbalance calls for adjustment regardless of its character and origin, therefore, it is argued that a much greater effort of adjustment is required in the 1980s than in the 1970s.

The expectation that the oil surpluses will be more persistent in the 1980s is, however, open to question. Although the recent decline in the real price of oil is no doubt attributable in large part to the slackening of business activity, there also appears to be evidence of increased capacity for the supply of oil as well as, in the words of the Interim Committee, "a break in the previous close link between economic growth and oil consumption" (IMF 1981*a*, p. 200). In addition, the import demand of Organization of Petroleum Exporting Countries (OPEC) associated with development and defense has shown a tendency to increase faster than expected. A continuation of recent downward trends in oil prices and in the relationship between oil consumption and GNP in the industrial countries, together with further expansion in the import demand of OPEC countries, would eliminate the OPEC current account surplus in the near future. It is also relevant that the long-term component of financing the OPEC current account surpluses has been increasing significantly. For all these reasons there are grounds for doubting whether the evolution of OPEC balance of payments positions in the early 1980s calls for a greater degree of adjustment by deficit countries than that which occurred in the 1970s, which as shown above, was itself quite impressive.

The Burden of Unilateral Adjustment

The downward pressure of the adjustment process on non-oil developing countries in 1980–81 was much heavier than necessary in the circumstances in which these countries found themselves. In analyzing the situation of these countries in October 1979, the Interim Committee stated that:

> It was especially important, in the Committee's view, that the industrial countries, in the design of their economic policies, pay particular attention to the economic needs of developing countries. In this connection, a wide range of policies was seen to be relevant, including the reduction of protectionist measures; the opening of import markets to exports of manufactures and commodities from developing countries and of capital markets to outflows of funds to such countries; and measures to give new impetus to the flow of official development assistance, which had stagnated in recent years. (IMF 1980*b*, p. 153.)

That protectionist measures were actually intensified, that the flow of official development assistance continued to stagnate, and that private capital flows leveled off added greatly to the burdens imposed on the developing countries. Moreover, the particular mix of fiscal and monetary policies applied by the industrial countries in dealing with inflation, without regard to international consequences, worsened the imbalance still further by steeply raising the interest cost of foreign borrowing from both private and public institutions, including the IMF, the World Bank, and the regional development banks.

Here again the policy stance of the IMF is inconsistent. On the one hand, it seeks to encourage export supply in the developing countries through adjustment of exchange rates and other "outward looking" policies. On the other hand, it advocates further reductions in aggregate demand—hence, in the demand for imports—in the industrial countries that provide the principal markets for the additional export supplies thus generated. The Fund has been outspoken on the subject of protectionism, but its admonitions in this respect are nullified by its insistence that the industrial countries balance their budgets at low levels of employment and maintain or strengthen their policies of monetary restriction. After all, it is precisely the low level of employment that encourages protectionism.

Further inconsistency can be seen in the emphasis placed by the IMF on the need for governments to create market and other incentives for structural change while at the same time recommending deflationary policies that destroy any inducement to incur the risks of the investment in new capacity that would be required.

The Doctrine of Persistence

The logic of the IMF's position is, of course, that if the protectionism and other policy developments in the industrial countries mentioned above appear to be of a persistent character, there is no choice for the deficit countries but to adjust accordingly. The doctrine of persistence would appear to imply that—even if the policies pursued by one group of member countries were of a deliberately "beggar my neighbor" character and looked as if they would continue indefinitely, and if other countries encountering consequential deficits were to seek balance of payments support—the IMF would be compelled to insist on whatever degree of adjustment was called for in the circumstances as a condition of providing its support. But does this not raise the question that the IMF thereby becomes, albeit unwillingly, an accomplice in the beggar my neighbor policies in question?

Under current conditions of long-lasting business stagnation, the line to be drawn between persistent and temporary imbalance becomes indeterminate. In the past, deficits caused by a slackening of import demand owing to a business recession in major markets would have been regarded as coming unequivocally within the category of "temporary" and therefore as eligible for financing without adjustment. This was because recessions had hitherto been of relatively brief duration, and self-reversing. At the present time, however, recessions are not necessarily "temporary." As far as is known, it has not yet been suggested that a country should be declared ineligible for compensatory financing if its export shortfall is due to a decline in import demand in other countries resulting from a downturn in business activity that is expected to persist. Yet this is the logic of the IMF position, and it would also be required if the working of the decision establishing the CFF, which is intended only for cases of temporary shortfalls, were to be taken literally.[5] For the time being, efforts to neutralize the intent and effectiveness of the facility are taking the form of proposals to tighten the regime of conditionality that is applied.

Thus, a new situation may be approaching in which all deficits are considered to be of a character that calls for adjustment, and in which even the CFF becomes otiose.

The Basis of Conditionality

But what is it that requires the IMF to insist on stringent upper credit tranche conditionality regardless of whether a borrowing country is responsible for the deficit confronting it and regardless of whether the factors contributing to the deficit (such as protectionism) are compatible with the Fund's own "purposes" and "primary objectives"?

Originally the imposition of conditions on a potential borrower was considered to be justified largely in terms of the need to ensure prompt repayment of drawing so as to safeguard the revolving character of the Fund's resources. Thus Article I(v) provides for "making the general resources of the Fund temporarily available to [members] under adequate safeguards."

But, as Tony Killick (1981, p. 3; see also his study of Kenya, Chapter 16, this volume) has pointed out that "the stringency of conditionality has sometimes seemed disproportionate to the need to

[5] IMF Executive Board decision 6224 (79/135) provides in part that requests for drawings on the CFF will be met when the Fund is satisfied that "the shortfall is of a short-term character and is largely attributable to circumstances beyond the control of the member" (IMF 1979).

safeguard the repayment of Fund credits—credits which in the past have often been small relative to a country's total foreign exchange obligations." There is, moreover, no method of correlating the conditions imposed with the capacity to repay, if only because circumstances can change drastically over the period of the loan. For example, no matter how severe the conditions imposed on a primary producing country may be, the capacity to repay will inevitably deteriorate if the price of its principal export falls significantly, as happens not infrequently.

The World Bank and regional development banks have not hitherto made demands on borrowing countries of the type characteristic of IMF programs, yet no one imagines that repayment of their loans is less assured than that of loans made by the Fund. It is true that the projects for which financial support is obtained from the multilateral banks are appraised so as to determine that they will yield a return adequate to service the loans. But this does not provide any guarantee that foreign exchange will in fact be available in the amounts and at the times required. In practice, repayment to the multilateral banks is ensured not by project appraisal but by the fact that no country would willingly risk the drastic consequences for its access to all forms of credit that would result from a default to any one of these banks. And the same consideration applies to repayments to the Fund, whether or not the loans involved carry upper credit tranche conditionality.

In justifying its policies on conditionality, the IMF now relies relatively less on the idea that this will safeguard the revolving character of its resources and relatively more on its responsibility, under Article V.3(a), for assisting members "to solve their balance of payments problems in a manner consistent with the provisions of this Agreement." Moreover, Article IV.3(a) requires the Fund to "oversee the international monetary system in order to ensure its effective operation." Although this provision is included in the article concerning exchange arrangements, its significance may be regarded as being of a general character.

The Fund's Mandate

Thus, the IMF may be said to have a general mandate for watching over the international monetary system and for seeking viable and consistent balance of payments policies among its members. In carrying out this mandate, the Fund has at its disposal resources calling for various levels of conditionality. However, as shown elsewhere (Dell 1981, pp. 29–30), the low conditionality resources happen, at the present time, to constitute an abnormally low proportion of the total, because of the particular method that members have adopted for enlarging access to the Fund's resources—that is, by increasing access as a percentage of quota rather than by increasing quotas themselves. The effect is that, of the cumulative 600 percent of quota available to members for drawings, only 25 percent is provided at low (first credit tranche) conditionality; whereas, if quotas had been increased sixfold, which would have been the normal way of proceeding, first credit tranche conditionality would have applied to the equivalent of 150 percent of current quotas.

All this does not, however, mean that the IMF lacks discretion in determining the stringency of conditions to be applied, even if it is established that a source of imbalance is "persistent." As we have seen, the compulsion for a member to repay its drawings on the Fund is not derived from the provisions of the stand-by arrangement but is based on the profound interest of sovereign governments in maintaining their creditworthiness not only with the Fund but with all other potential creditors.

Nor do the more general responsibilities of the Fund in relation to the international monetary system require it to impose conditions on a deficit country that ignore the degree to which that country is responsible for the imbalance. On the contrary, the Fund has an implied responsibility *not* to act in a manner that appears to condone behavior on the part of other countries that is incompatible with the Fund's "purposes" and with "primary objectives of economic policy." In particular, the fund has an obligation to do all it can to assist a member that is suffering the effects of events beyond its control or of injurious policies pursued by other members.

The Fund has itself pointed out that the effort of non-oil developing countries to adjust to increased oil prices "is hampered by the slowing in the pace of industrial activity in the rest of the world, as well as by protectionist barriers to certain types of their exports to the industrial countries" (IMF 1980*b*, p.51). An additional obstacle mentioned by the Fund is the effect of unusually high rates of interest on external debt. As noted earlier, this is the result of the particular constellation of domestic fiscal and monetary policies employed by the industrial countries in attempting to deal with inflation, without regard to international repercussions.

In the light of these findings, the idea that the Fund's options are limited to a determination whether a deficit is temporary or persistent is far-fetched. The Fund cannot, of course, supply more resources than are available to it. But, subject to that constraint, there is much that the Fund can do to lighten the burden of adjustment and to avoid the application of severe and peremptory measures, especially of a deflationary character.

Developing countries must, of course, adjust to irreversible changes—this issue is not in dispute. But in determining the appropriate policy mix (including the amount of balance of payments support to be provided), the conditions required for the provision of that support, and the period over which adjustment should be programmed, it is important to distinguish between those elements of a balance of payments deficit for which a developing country is itself responsible and those elements that are due to factors beyond the country's control.

A Possible Solution: Liberalization of the CFF?

This is not a revolutionary idea. At one time, levels of activity had to be cut back even where external imbalance was due to a temporary decline in foreign demand for exports. The introduction by the IMF of the CFF and later of the oil facilities indicated clear recognition of the principle that it is improper to force standard adjustment policies on developing countries in circumstances for which they are not responsible. What is now proposed is an extension of that principle to all external sources of disturbance in the balance of payments.

Indeed, the Fund is itself well aware of the shortcomings of the CFF and has taken several steps to improve its coverage and relevance. The facility was established in 1963, but only 57 drawings, totaling SDR 1.2 billion, were made under the restrictive provisions that applied during its first 13 years. A turning point was the liberalization of the facility in December 1975. From January 1976 through December 1981, there were drawings totaling SDR 5.9 billion under the facility; these accounted for 32 percent of total drawings by non-oil-exporting developing countries during that period. (Goreux 1980, pp. 2–3, updated by the IMF).

Important as the liberalization of December 1975 was, the CFF was still subject to major shortcomings. Although CFF drawing rights were increased progressively from 50 percent to 75 percent and later to 100 percent of quota in any one year, even the last amount was in many cases insufficient to finance the full amount of export shortfalls, especially if these shortfalls persisted over periods longer than a year. Moreover, the reasoning that had been applied to export shortfalls was still not applied to import overages resulting from factors beyond the control of particular countries. In May 1981 a first and very limited step toward the latter objective was taken by the Fund when it agreed to extend financial assistance at low conditionality "to members that encounter a balance of payments difficulty produced by an excess in the cost of their cereal imports." As in the case of export shortfalls, the Fund must be satisfied that the source of difficulty is short term in character and is "largely attributable to circumstances beyond the control of the member" (IMF 1981*c*).[6]

It thus took no less than 18 years for the IMF to reach the conclusion that the logic it had introduced with respect to export shortfalls in 1963 was applicable also to import overages. Even then, in 1981, the step forward that was taken was extremely limited and inadequate in scope. There is, nevertheless, still the hope that the next stages of the process of liberalization can be accelerated and that the low-conditionality facility of the Fund will be enlarged to apply to all imports and to provide drawing rights that are much larger in relation to potential shortfalls and overages than drawing rights are today. If this were done, the Fund would have at its disposal, at last, an array of facilities that would allow it to adjust the volume and conditions of the balance of payments support that it provides to the circumstances of each case, including particularly the degree of responsibility of the country concerned for the difficulty encountered.

It has been suggested by William Dale (Chapter 1, this volume) that what he calls "pure intermediation" by the Fund is unnecessary because there is no longer any uncertainty about the adequacy of finance for that purpose. The implication here, presumably, is that pure intermediation is a function of the commercial banks only. In that case, however, the only countries entitled to have access to pure intermediation would be those that the commercial banks deem to be creditworthy in their terms—the industrial countries together with a minority of developing countries, as matters now stand.

As noted above, if the Fund had enlarged access to its resources by raising quotas instead of by increasing drawing rights as a percentage of existing quotas, the volume of resources available to members on first credit tranche terms would have been six times as large as they are under the method actually employed. The Interim Committee and the IMF management have stated repeatedly that the correct method of enlarging Fund resources is by increasing quotas. The Fund authorities must therefore see a role for a much increased

[6] *IMF Survey*, June 18, 1981. The use of the word "short term" appears unnecessarily restrictive. It is implicit in the wording of Article I(v) cited earlier, that the balance of payments difficulties for which Fund financing is appropriate may be characterized as "temporary" (that is, likely to be reversed in due course) rather than as merely "short term."

volume of first credit tranche resources, whether one calls it "pure intermediation" or something else.

National Aspects

The IMF approach to the balance of payments problems of developing countries starts out from three basic assumptions. The first of these is that there is sufficient flexibility in the economies of these countries to permit them to respond to standard adjustment formulas without undue cost. The second is that, by and large, the problems are of a short-term character that can and should be handled within a relatively short time frame. The third is that, within the framework of appropriate government policies, it is generally best to rely on market forces to bring about the requisite adjustment.

Evenhandedness or Discrimination?

These basic assumptions are considered equally valid for all members of the Fund, and evenhanded treatment of Fund members therefore requires that stabilization programs should be of roughly similar design regardless of the countries involved. This does not, of course, mean that the content of programs has to be the same from country to country. Obviously the degree of devaluation, if any, required in a particular case will depend on the circumstances of that case, and similar considerations apply to all other stabilization measures involved. Yet, given the degree of balance of payments pressure and the factors responsible for that pressure in any particular country, the stabilization measures required would be approximately the same whether the country were developed or developing.

This may imply evenhanded treatment of Fund members, but such treatment is not necessarily the practice. Indeed, evenhanded treatment as seen from the standpoint of the lender can, and frequently does, involve inequality of burden-sharing among borrowers. This can be illustrated by a hypothetical case involving two countries suspected of having overvalued exchange rates, one of which is completely dependent on primary commodities for its export revenues, whereas the other obtains most of such revenues from sales of diversified manufactures. Standard purchasing power parity calculations may show the degree of devaluation required to be the same in both cases. But the burden of such devaluation will be much greater for the exporter of primary commodities than for the exporter of manufactures because of the much smaller responsiveness of exports to be expected in the former case. In fact, the impact on primary exports may be perverse. On the one hand, the entire burden of correcting the disequilibrium falls on imports and, hence, on the curtailment of domestic consumption, investment, or both. The country exporting manufactures, on the other hand, may find itself in a position to correct its external balance entirely through an increase in exports and, hence, in the level of business activity. If used labor and capital are available, such a country may actually be able to improve its situation even from the standpoint of domestic consumption and investment.

In general, any approach to stabilization policies that overlooks the much lower mobility of resources in developing than in developed countries is bound to discriminate against the former if standard formulas are applied to purely monetary measures of internal and external disequilibrium. Moreover, correction of present imbalances calls for structural adjustment over periods longer than traditional Fund programs. Although the need for medium-term structural adjustment has been accepted in principle in statements by the Interim Committee and the IMF management, it is unclear how far the requirements of such adjustment are recognized in practice. The very fact that adjustment is programmed over a longer period would appear to imply a less rigorous and less demanding program of stabilization than if the same degree of adjustment had to be achieved within a shorter period. If has nevertheless been stated by the Fund that, on average, resources are now being provided at a much more exacting level of conditionality than they were in the mid 1970s, and that, whereas in the mid-1970s approximately three-quarters of the resources provided by the Fund to its members were at low conditionality, three-quarters of current new lending commitments involve upper credit tranche programs (IMF 1981*d*, p.35).

Finally, the effort to induce developing countries to rely on market forces in the adjustment process contrasts oddly with the steady increase in the number of products exported by developing countries that have been removed from the influence of market forces by the industrial countries.

If free market conditions were the key to development, there would be no dichotomy between developed and underdeveloped economies, since government intervention in the latter economies is a relatively recent phenomenon, following accession to economic independence. There is not a single industrial country that did not employ vigorous protection at some stage in its history. Among the much applauded newly industrializing countries, the most important have highly regulated economies. Even such a highly industrialized country as Japan, the miracle economy of the century, continues to this day to protect its industrial development in a variety of ways. Although Japan is under great pressure to dismantle this protection, the important lesson of Japan for the developing countries and for the Fund is that properly managed protection, far from being an obstacle to growth, is an indispensable instrument in promoting growth.

Where there is a case against regulation, it depends not on any inherent superiority of market forces but on the much simpler consideration that many developing countries do not have the administrative resources required for extensive or detailed regulation and control. Even where such resources do exist, it is often difficult to ensure that regulation and control are exercised in the interests of the public at large and not merely in the interests of the regulators and controllers. But this does not mean that developing countries should do away with all controls—only that they should limit themselves to the key controls they are able to operate efficiently.

The Capacity for Adjustment

Mention was made earlier of intercountry differences in the elasticity of supply of exports as a factor in explaining differences in the effectiveness of adjustment. This is one example—perhaps the most important—of a more general differentiation between countries in their capacity for adjustment. For example, countries differ considerably in the extent to which they can compress imports without suffering adverse effects. On the one hand, some countries are better equipped than others in the availability of skills and resources for developing import substitutes. On the other hand, whereas in some countries imports may include a substantial share of nonessentials that can be readily restricted without serious economic injury, in others they may consist entirely of essential foodstuffs, raw materials, and equipment, the curtailment of which would have damaging effects on basic consumption, investment, or production.

In the United Nations Development Programme/United Nations Conference on Trade and Development (UNDP/UNCTAD) study (Dell and Lawrence, 1980), it was found that much of the intercountry variation in performance during the 1970s could be attributed to differences in the capacity for adjustment. It was also suggested that adjustment programs and policies should be adapted to the particular capabilities for adjustment of each country. Mention has already been made of the potentially very different effects of devaluation in various countries, depending on the responsiveness of actual or potential exports to such a step in the short and medium term. Similarly, a cost benefit analysis of general measures to improve the trade balance by cutting consumption would yield one set of results in a country where exported goods were not consumed domestically and imported consumer goods consisted mainly of basic foodstuffs, and a different set of results in a country where a substantial proportion of exportables was consumed domestically and there was a wide range of imported consumer goods.

Exchange Rate Policies

Perhaps the greatest difficulties in relation to stabilization programs have arisen in the area of exchange rate adjustment. It is here that the effect of government intervention in the economy is particularly visible. Moreover, the effect of that intervention is usually to bring about a decline in domestic consumption and a shift in the distribution of income.[7] In many cases, in fact, it is precisely the fall in real income and the shift in income distribution that are the main goals of exchange rate adjustments, especially where supply and demand elasticities in foreign trade are relatively low.

It is not uncommon for exchange rate adjustments exceeding 50 percent to be proposed, often on the basis of the crudest calculations of purchasing power parity. It is not merely that the data themselves have serious shortcomings. There is also the problem of determining the composition and weighting of the two price or cost series to be compared, for which there is no unique solution. Doubtless in extreme cases the need for exchange rate adjustment is clear enough on the basis of any reasonable grouping of the available data. But establishing the required direction of change is not the same thing as determining the precise degree of adjustment needed.

More serious, however, is that, as Lord Kaldor has pointed out, it cannot be taken for granted that the internal distribution of income, which is the outcome of complex political forces, can be effectively changed by devaluation. A large scale devaluation may well be followed by a price upheaval that ends up by reproducing, at a much higher level of prices, the same price and cost relationships as had prevailed before the devaluation (Kaldor 1982).

A study of Tanzanian experience in the 1970s for the UNDP/UNCTAD project showed that Tanzania had resisted devaluation on the grounds that any attempt by Tanzania to raise its share of export

[7] Even if the fall in domestic consumption is unavoidable, the perception of the general public may be that a government that devalues is responsible for the decline in living standards.

markets for primary commodities would have provoked retaliation, and that there was a preference for using import controls and selective indirect taxation for limiting imports because those were the instruments of choice in the overall planning process. On the other hand devaluation was regarded as far too unselective a means of demand management that would tend to shift income from the relatively poor producers of food to the relatively richer exporters of cash crops, which is inconsistent with Tanzania's social objectives and the goal of raising food production. Tanzania nevertheless devalued in 1971 and 1975 when absolute cuts in domestic prices of export products or major export subsidies would otherwise have been needed.

Devaluations in Zambia in 1976 and 1978 were designed to maintain the profitability of the mining companies in the face of rising external costs (equivalent to 60–70 percent of total costs) and falling copper prices. The difficulty seen in the devaluation strategy, however, was that, to the extent that it succeeded, it tended to increase excess supplies and, hence, depress prices still further, thereby making it necessary to undertake recurrent devaluations.

Doubts about the effectiveness of the exchange rate weapon, however, are not limited to low-income primary producing countries. Brailovsky (1981) has studied the impact of exchange rate changes during the 1960s and 1970s in a group of 13 countries, of which 7 are among the leading industrial country exporters of manufactures—Canada, France, Federal Republic of Germany, Italy, Japan, Netherlands, and the United Kingdom; the remaining six are the more successful exporters of manufactures among the developing countries—Argentina, Brazil, Hong Kong, Republic of Korea, Mexico, and Singapore.

The data presented by Brailovsky suggest that changes in nominal exchange rates caused relatively small changes in real exchange rates during the period examined, and it is therefore not surprising that changes in nominal exchange rates account for only a small proportion of the shifts in market shares. The main impact of these changes was on rates of domestic inflation, not on real exchange rates.[8]

[8] Brailovsky defines the real exchange rate as the weighted average of the ratio between domestic and foreign prices, both converted to a common currency, the weights corresponding to the area composition of trade.

The Role of Monetarism

Despite a certain eclecticism to be found in the published IMF literature, most Fund programs are established within a common framework. According to members of the Fund staff, "in this framework there is a fairly well defined relationship between money, the balance of payments, and domestic prices, in which the supply of and demand for money play a central linking role" (Khan and Knight 1981, p.3).

A distinction is often drawn between what is called the new monetarism and the old monetarism, and between their respective prescriptions for stabilization. The important point, however, is not the differences but the similarities—particularly the incorrect diagnosis of problems—and the consequent shortcomings of would-be remedial programs.

The Case Against Monetarism

This is not the place to elaborate on the case against monetarism—there is an abundant and growing literature (see particularly Hicks 1975 and 1976 and Kaldor 1964, 1978, and 1981) in support of the following propositions.

- Correlations between the supply of money and levels of expenditure do not indicate the direction of causality, even if there is a time lag between the former series and the latter.
- Although narrow definitions of the money supply are not very useful for most purposes, broad definitions are arbitrary, and money supply broadly defined is surrounded by a halo of liquid assets that are not included but nevertheless are close substitutes for assets that *are* included.
- It is not the money supply, however defined, that is relevant to spending decisions but liquidity in the widest sense, including not only money but money substitutes. And liquidity in this widest sense is not under the control of the monetary authorities.
- In a credit economy, the fact that a substantial proportion of bank money is idle breaks the link between the total quantity of money and that part of it which is circulating. If monetary controls are effective at all, it is the rate of interest that is important and not the total quantity of money, however defined.
- If output is below capacity levels, it is likely that an increase in money supply will be noninflationary and that the effect will be a rise in output.

• Goodhart's law: any measure of the money supply that is used as a basis for an attempt at official control quickly loses its meaning.
• It is incorrect to group all forms of inflation together as being induced by a single factor—an increase in the money supply. In deciding on the remedy for inflation, it is essential, as noted earlier, to distinguish between demand inflation and cost inflation and to adapt the remedies accordingly.

Perhaps the most important single economic reason that the management of national economies is now in disarray throughout both the developed and the developing world is that problems of cost inflation are being attacked by measures to deflate demand even when economies are operating at 20 percent or more below capacity. As Tony Killick (1981, p. 28) concludes on the basis of replies to questionnaires addressed to IMF staff, "it appears on this evidence that the Fund is no less likely to require demand restraint even in countries in which its own staff does not believe excess demand to be a principal cause of the payments problems." Demand deflation, if taken far enough, will ultimately have an impact on cost inflation. There is no dispute about this. What is in question is the need for the heavy social and economic costs that are involved.

The Policy of Sackcloth and Ashes

As Diaz-Alejandro (1981, p. 125) has pointed out in examining the stabilization plans of the Southern Cone countries of Latin America:

> Even in cases where excess demand was a plausible explanation for the high rates of inflation during the preplan period, its explanatory power declines as the months go by and excess capacity and foreign exchange reserves pile up. Remaining fiscal deficits and/or high rates of increase in the money supply provide weak explanations under conditions of declining output and of shrinking real credit and cash balances. Excessive trade union power can hardly be blamed when real wages collapse and union leaders are jailed, or worse.

Despite continuing retrenchment, inflation rates were not brought down below the 15–20 percent level. The situation became one of overkill, in that reductions in aggregate demand went beyond what was required to make room for an expansion in the production of exportables and of those importables and nontraded goods benefiting from the new constellation of relative prices. The curtailment of demand brought with it severe weakness in capital formation as reductions in public investment were accompanied by lack of confidence on the part of the private sector. Diaz-Alejandro suggests that the process of overkill cannot be fully explained without reference to the authorities' wish to discipline the labor force by creating a soft labor market.

The situation thus described is characteristic of many countries in other parts of the developing—and, indeed, of the developed world. In some developing countries, stabilization programs in the 1970s induced declines in real wages of the order of 20–40 percent over relatively short periods (Dell and Lawrence 1980, p. 64). Programs of this kind were by no means limited to countries entering into stand by arrangements with the IMF. The wave of exaggerated economic retrenchment was and is an almost worldwide phenomenon; in many cases where adjustment policies of great severity were applied under stand-by arrangements, the government itself was at least as keen to cut back as the IMF mission involved. Moreover, as is well known, in a not inconsiderable number of cases ministries of finance and central banks welcomed the support given by IMF missions to retrenchment policies that these financial authorities were having difficulty in persuading other sectors of the government to accept.

Is evidence of the kind cited above relevant? John Williamson (1981, pp. 4–5) points out, quite correctly, that a comparison of "what is" with "what was" is "conceptually inappropriate" if one is trying to assess policy results and economic performance. What is implied here, however, is that alternative methods of adjustment were available that would not have involved so large a reduction in real income, in some cases perhaps no reduction at all. Such methods would have required correct identification of the sources of cost inflation and the mobilization of the social consensus required to slow down and ultimately halt the struggle between social groups to safeguard their respective shares of real income. Given such social consensus, the need for demand deflation would have been correspondingly reduced; devaluations, where they occurred, could have been much less drastic, and the fall in real wages would have been correspondingly smaller. In cases where idle resources could be shifted to exportables facing open markets abroad, the adjustment process could even have been carried out without loss of output and income—as occurred in countries such as Brazil and the Republic of Korea, where access to the international capital market made if possible for the two countries to escape the standard deflationary remedies, at least for a time. More recently, in the face of mounting debt and soaring interest rates in the international market, even Brazil has felt compelled to deflate.

As to why the sackcloth-and-ashes approach to adjustment was preferred, the reasons lie more in the realm of politics than of economics. Many governments, developing as well as developed, were seeking radical solutions to what they regarded as long-standing problems of income distribution and trade union militancy, and they came to the conclusion that their goals were too far from existing realities to be realized through the normal processes of negotiation and compromise required for the attainment of social consensus.

At the international level, the radical solution envisaged by developed countries takes the form of reducing, as far as possible, the transfer of concessional resources to developing countries and of relying on market incentives to generate the flows of private capital required to supplement the domestic efforts of these countries and to provide them with balance of payments support when it is needed. Under this concept, the role of the Bretton Woods institutions is to support the basic thrust of the above strategy by cooperating more closely with the private sector, and by negotiating the kind of stabilization programs that would help deficit countries to attract balance of payments support from the only source capable as matters stand of providing it in the volume required—namely the commercial banking system.

This strategy, of course, leaves out all those countries that are unable to attract large-scale commercial bank loans *under any conditions*. For them, the IMF is the lender of both first and last resort. Thus, the concept of the Fund as primarily a stimulus to and guarantor of the creditworthiness of developing countries, and only a residual provider of balance of payments support in its own right, is completely unacceptable to the low-income countries that have no other source of such support available to them. The strategy is also unwelcome to other developing countries, if only because the country limits for lending set by commercial banks for prudential reasons do not, in the aggregate, reflect an appropriate measure of the borrowing capacity of the countries concerned, especially under conditions of artificially high interest rates.

Pinpoint Targetry

One advantage of monetarist theories is that they make it possible to devise straightforward performance criteria in the form of precise monetary targets that can be readily monitored by the IMF. This creates an objective basis for determining whether member countries that have entered into stand-by arrangements with the Fund are performing sufficiently well to establish an entitlement to successive phased drawings on the lines of credit established by the Fund under these arrangements.

Tony Killick (1981, p. 25) finds that "in economic terms, by far the strongest evidence of a stereotyped approach is the almost universal inclusion of ceilings on bank credit, which in many cases are the chief test the government must pass," although he notes also that "there is a considerable diversity as to the forms which these take" to suit local conditions. Almost all stand-by arrangements include limits on the amount of new bank credit that could be extended to both the public and private sectors.

The fact is, however, that neither the developed nor the developing countries have had much success in achieving quantitative monetary targets, even when they have set the targets for themselves. The governor of the Bank of England (1978, pp. 36–38) has reported that from 1974 to the beginning of 1978 the mean error of forecasts of the public sector borrowing requirement (PSBR) made at the beginning of each financial year in the United Kingdom was of the order of £ 3 billion: the average annual level of the PSBR from 1974/75 to 1977/78 was £ 8.2 billion. For this and other reasons, the governor was sharply critical of procedures requiring a particular numerical target to be reached by a particular date: "Firm deadlines can force one either to adjust too fast to an unforeseen trend developing late in the period, or to appear to accept a failure to reach one's target."

Similar problems have arisen in the United States. As reported by Governor Henry Wallich (1980, pp. 12–13) of the Board of Governors of the Federal Reserve System:

> Since mid-1974, a whole collection of standard money demand functions used routinely in econometric models has misperformed on a large scale by overpredicting the amount of money that would be demanded at given levels of income and interest rates. By late 1979 this overprediction amounted to anywhere from 9–17 percent of M1A or M1B, or something like $35–70 billion. This overprediction of the amount of money required made the Federal Reserve's targets, which seemed quite restrictive, turn out relatively unrestrictive. . . . The uncertainties inherent in this approach underline the advisability of stating money supply targets in terms of a range rather than of a single number.

Governor Wallich suggests further that "it may be risky to become irrevocably committed to a numerical set of targets." And he points out that the most successful countries in conducting noninflationary monetary policies have been the Federal Republic of Germany and Switzerland and that both these countries have been "quite relaxed about their adherence to [money supply] targets."

Incidentally, the Federal Reserve study prompted Governor Wallich to conclude further that "monetary restraint, however steady, cannot quickly bring down inflation nor interest rates. The most plausible view is that the main impact of monetary restraint on prices occurs with a two-year lag." This is not a very promising time horizon even for stabilization programs based on IMF extended arrangements, let alone for standard one-year programs.

The Breakdown of Stand-by Arrangements

The IMF is, of course, not "irrevocably committed" (to use Governor Wallich's phrase) to precise monetary targets. Tony Killick reports that, on the average, as many as one-third of the Fund's stand-by arrangements are amended as a result of minor deviations from targets that are regarded as temporary or reversible or that result from unexpected changes in circumstances.

More serious, however, are the many cases in which credit ceilings are exceeded, or other targets breached, by margins that cannot be dealt with by waivers. Here the member government automatically loses its right to draw outstanding installments of its line of credit without, as Sir Joseph Gold (IMF 1969, p. 533) has pointed out, the need for a decision by, or even notice to, the Fund's Executive Board.

The government always has the option, in such cases, of negotiating a new understanding with the Fund, but there is no guarantee that such negotiations will succeed or that the new targets will be more easily achieved than the previous ones. Moreover, in many cases some of the damage done by the breakdown of the agreement may be irreversible, especially if it leads to a general loss of confidence and the government is forced into costly alternative courses of action.

The frequency of breakdowns indicates in itself that there is something wrong with the system of pinpoint targetry. Can so many governments all be guilty of incompetence or mismanagement? In some cases, the time lags involved in the preparation of the necessary statistics are such that the negotiators on both sides are unaware that the targets under discussion are already out of date and are impossible to achieve. Even when this is not the case, the above-mentioned experiences of the United Kingdom and the United States indicate that reliance on precise quantitative targets is full of pitfalls and that the errors of estimation may be of very large orders of magnitude.

These shortcomings would be serious even if it were clear that monetary targets were the right targets on which to concentrate. But this is not necessarily the case even if the primary objective is demand management. When demand is excessive, it may be much more important and effective to raise taxes than to restrict credit. In the many instances in which improvements in the balance of payments depend primarily on structural change, monetary targets may at best be of limited importance and may at worst be entirely irrelevant.

A good example of destabilizing error as a result of uncertainties in forecasting can be found in the experience of Peru in 1978–79. Peru was compelled to negotiate for an IMF stand-by in the third quarter of 1978 and had to accept stringent obligations to deflate the economy—less severely than the unrealistic agreement of December 1977 had provided, but still harsh enough.

Yet if one examines the balance of payments projections agreed upon as a basis for the stand-by negotiations, it is immediately apparent that, had the negotiators known that the price of copper would recover from $0.58 a pound in July 1978 to $0.90 a pound in March 1979, they would have realized that that fact alone would come close to restoring external balance without any cutting down of the economy at all. By April 1979, the Peruvian balance of payments was so strong and the inflow of capital so massive that the international financial press was reporting the country's inflation-inducing surplus of dollars.

Mistakes of forecasting are of course unavoidable, and a case of this kind underlines the dangers of pinpoint targetry. A more important source of concern is that here was a case in which the projected external imbalance was largely due to a temporary and reversible factor—the low price of copper. The cost to Peru in lost output and investment was out of all proportion to the magnitude of the external problem that had been encountered. It is disquieting that the economy of a country such as Peru—which among developing countries has relatively diversified exports—can still be at the mercy of the volatility of a single commodity. And it is alarming that such a country can find itself compelled to endure lasting damage to its economy because of circumstances that are reversible and because of inability to mobilize balance of payments support on a scale sufficient to avoid such damage.

Conclusions

Several forward-looking steps have been taken. The IMF (1980*a*, p. 42) has stated that:

> In view of the size of the current deficits and of the difficulties that may arise in private intermediation, the Fund must be prepared, when necessary, to lend in larger amounts than in the past. Also, the structural problems faced by many countries may require that adjustment take place over a longer period than has been typical in the framework of

> Fund programs in the past. Further, lending by the Fund must reflect the sort of flexibility, with an awareness of the circumstances of members, that is called for in the Executive Board's current guidelines on conditionality.

More recent developments, notably the severe tightening of conditionality, raise some doubts whether the promise of the above statement is being or will be realized. The concept of unilateral adjustment—with one group of countries at best neutral toward, and at worst frustrating, the adjustment process of the other group—is not an acceptable basis for IMF supervision of the international monetary system. There is a pressing need for the Fund to reconsider its position on this basic issue.

Furthermore, care should be taken to avoid overkill in determining the degree and character of adjustment needed in stabilization programs. This will require setting aside monetarist doctrines that lead to mistakes in the diagnosis of problems and in the specification of solutions, especially where problems of structural adjustment over the medium term are involved.

One useful device for dealing with some aspects of both these problems would be to liberalize and enlarge the CFF with the objective of applying the same kind of regime to both imports and exports. This would have the effect of providing the Fund with an array of facilities at low and high conditionality that would make it possible to design stabilization programs in a manner that would be more responsive to the particular situations of individual countries.

References

Bank of England. 1978. *Quarterly Bulletin,* vol. 18, no. 1 (March).

Brailovsky, Vladimiro, with the assistance of Juan Carlos Moreno. 1981. *Exchange Rate Policies, Manufactured Exports and the Rate of Inflation.* Mexico: Institute for Industrial Planning. Processed.

Committee of Twenty. 1974. *International Monetary Reform: Documents of the Committee of Twenty.* Washington: IMF.

De Larosière, Jacques. 1981. "Address to the 1981 Annual Meetings of the Fund and Bank." *IMF Survey* (October 12).

Dell, Sidney. 1981. *On Being Grandmotherly: The Evolution of IMF Conditionality.* Essays in International Finance, no. 144. Princeton, NJ: International Finance Section, Princeton University.

Dell, Sidney, and Roger Lawrence. 1980. *The Balance of Payments Adjustment Process in Developing Countries.* New York: Pergamon Press.

Diaz-Alejandro, Carlos F. 1981. "Southern Cone Stabilization Plans," in *Economic Stabilization in Developing Countries,* ed. William R. Cline and Sidney Weintraub. Washington: The Brookings Institution.

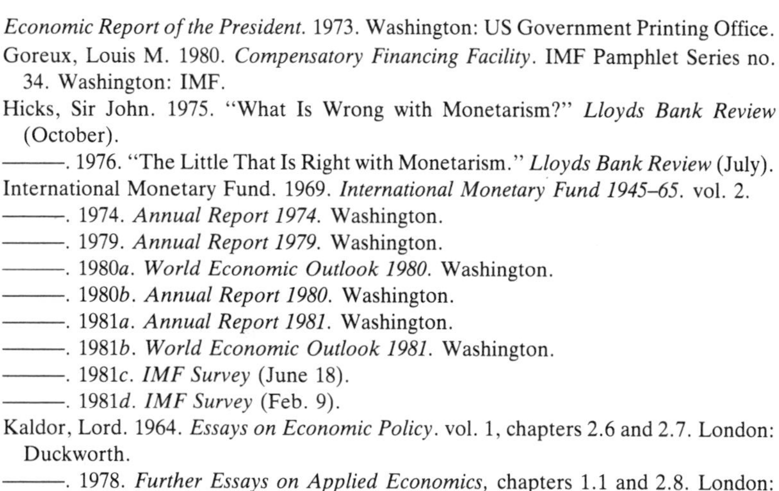

Economic Report of the President. 1973. Washington: US Government Printing Office.

Goreux, Louis M. 1980. *Compensatory Financing Facility*. IMF Pamphlet Series no. 34. Washington: IMF.

Hicks, Sir John. 1975. "What Is Wrong with Monetarism?" *Lloyds Bank Review* (October).

———. 1976. "The Little That Is Right with Monetarism." *Lloyds Bank Review* (July).

International Monetary Fund. 1969. *International Monetary Fund 1945–65*. vol. 2.

———. 1974. *Annual Report 1974*. Washington.

———. 1979. *Annual Report 1979*. Washington.

———. 1980*a*. *World Economic Outlook 1980*. Washington.

———. 1980*b*. *Annual Report 1980*. Washington.

———. 1981*a*. *Annual Report 1981*. Washington.

———. 1981*b*. *World Economic Outlook 1981*. Washington.

———. 1981*c*. *IMF Survey* (June 18).

———. 1981*d*. *IMF Survey* (Feb. 9).

Kaldor, Lord. 1964. *Essays on Economic Policy*. vol. 1, chapters 2.6 and 2.7. London: Duckworth.

———. 1978. *Further Essays on Applied Economics,* chapters 1.1 and 2.8. London: Duckworth.

———. 1981. *Memorandum of Evidence of Monetary Policy to the Selected Committee on the Treasury and Civil Service*. London: H.M. Stationery Office.

———. 1982. "The Role of Devaluation in the Adjustment of Balance of Payments Deficits." Report to the Group of 24. Forthcoming. Processed.

Khan, Mohsin, and Malcom D. Knight. 1981. "Stabilization Programs in Developing Countries: A Formal Framework." *IMF Staff Papers,* vol. 28, no. 1 (March).

Killick, Tony. 1981. *IMF Stabilization Programmes*. London: Overseas Development Institute. Processed.

Wallich, Henry. 1980. "Federal Reserve Policy and the Economic Outlook." Address to the Chesapeake Chapter of Robert Morris Associates, December 3. Processed.

Williamson, John. 1977. *The Failure of World Monetary Reform 1971–74*. Sunbury-on-Thames: Nelson.

CHAPTER 3

Appraising IMF Conditionality: Too Loose, Too Tight, Or Just Right?

Raymond F. Mikesell

Most of the debate on IMF conditionality found in the literature is concerned with whether conditionality has been too strict or has involved demands on member countries negotiating stand-by or extended Fund facility (EFF) agreements that are inappropriate or harmful to the member's welfare. There is also the position—associated with the US Department of the Treasury and with certain private individuals or groups—that IMF conditionality has not been sufficiently rigorous or comprehensive to achieve the objectives of IMF assistance and to assure the revolving character of IMF resources. The latter position, however, has not been well developed or articulated. It is the purpose of this paper to discuss the rationale for this argument.

Relative rigor or looseness of IMF conditionality may be judged from one or more of the following standpoints: (1) the specific elements and comprehensiveness of the policy reforms set forth in the agreement and the specific performance targets employed in the conditionality package; (2) the monitoring of performance by the Fund during the term of the agreement and the degree to which the Fund conditions its releases of resources on the achievement of performance targets, including both quantitative and qualitative targets; and (3) the adequacy of the policy reforms and performance targets for achieving the objectives of the conditionality program. Judging the degree of rigor or looseness of IMF conditionality is not necessarily the same as judging the success of the IMF conditionality programs in achieving their objectives, although the two are related. Thus IMF conditionality could be quite rigorous and yet fail in terms of certain measures of success, such as the improvement of a country's performance in relation to the best potentially feasible outcome or other measures of success suggested by John Williamson (Chapter 7, this volume). For example, a member country government might be unable or unwilling to undertake the policy measures set forth in the conditionality program, or external events during the period of the program may have altered the conditions necessary for achieving the best potentially feasible outcome.

An important consideration in judging the degree of rigor of IMF conditionality is the objectives of the program. If movement toward current account balance were the only objective, rigorous demand management for reducing absorption would suffice. But the Fund has other important objectives for its conditionality programs, such as maintaining the GNP growth rate and avoiding or minimizing the use of quantitative restrictions on imports. The existence of objectives other than current account balance requires the inclusion of policy instruments in addition to those concerned with demand management in the conditionality package.

Article I (ii) of the Fund Articles of Agreement states that a purpose of the Fund is "to facilitate the expansion and balanced growth of international trade, and to contribute thereby to the promotion and maintenance of high levels of employment and real income and to the development of the productive resources of all members." (IMF 1979) It is further stated that a purpose of the Fund is "to give confidence to members by making the general resources of the Fund temporarily available to them under adequate safeguards, thus providing them with opportunity to correct maladjustments in balance of payments without resorting to measures disruptive of national or international prosperity" [Article I(v)]. Clearly the Fund's purposes include not only progress toward balance of payments equilibrium (which I define for a developing country as a current account deficit that is not in excess of sustainable long-term capital inflows from private or nonconcessionary sources), but also the promotion of employment and growth of all the members of the Fund and the expansion of international trade. In the context of the Fund's purposes, IMF conditionality programs should not be directed *solely* to the welfare of the individual member receiving assistance from the Fund.

Types of Disequilibrium

Over the nearly 40 years since the Bretton Woods conference, there have been important changes in the Fund's concepts of balance of payments disequilibrium and the adjustment process. Before the 1970s three kinds of situations were recognized. First, temporary disequilibrium may be caused by a *reversible* loss of markets or reduction in the terms of trade. This situation might call for little or no change in policies. IMF resources would constitute a supplement to the country's own reserves and the country's reserve position would be restored when markets and/or terms of trade improved. The second type of disequilibrium is a consequence of expansionary monetary and fiscal policies; in this case demand management is clearly called for and required by the Fund for drawings in the higher credit tranches. The third condition, which was called "fundamental disequilibrium," was not defined in the Articles of Agreement, but it means that internal and external prices are so far out of line that an adjustment of the country's par value or exchange rate is required, usually combined with the exercise of demand management. In the latter two types of disequilibrium, IMF conditions embodied in the stand-by agreements have generally been limited to macroeconomic monetary, credit, and fiscal policies, with exchange rate adjustment in the case of fundamental disequilibrium.

In recent years other kinds of disequilibrium have been identified by the IMF that call for both financial assistance over a longer term and the inclusion of additional policy instruments in the IMF policy and assistance package. Thus the EFF, established in 1974, was designed to deal with two main categories of problems: "(1) Serious imbalance relating to structural maladjustments in production and trade and where cost and price distortions have been widespread, and (2) an economy characterized by slow growth and an inherently weak balance of payments position which prevents pursuit of an active development policy" (IMF 1976, p. 88).

Under the first category, IMF assistance is often designed to deal with disequilibrium caused by "external shocks," which are best represented by the sudden rise in petroleum prices in 1973–74 and again in 1979–80. The second category of payments imbalance for which the EFF was designed describes the typical slow-growing and poor developing country. We might question why this situation calls for IMF assistance rather than straightforward development assistance, and why it is called a "structural adjustment" problem rather than a development problem, but a discussion of this issue is outside the terms of reference of this paper. It should be noted, however, that many countries in this condition are receiving so-called structural adjustment assistance from both the IMF and the World Bank. There is little to distinguish between the assistance programs for structural adjustment provided by the two institutions from the standpoint of either the conditions they are designed to correct or the underlying perception of requirements for adjustment (Stern, Chapter 5, this volume). For reasons to be discussed later on, there are differences in the content of the conditionality packages of the two institutions. What is new in the approach of the IMF to disequilibrium embodied in the EFF is the emphasis on policies designed to deal with *supply* as contrasted with those relating to demand management.

Frequently associated with one or the other of the two categories of structural payments imbalance described above is the inability of a country to meet the debt service on its external obligations. In such cases the IMF stand-by may become the basis for a Paris Club negotiation with the creditors. It may be noted that in many cases large-scale external borrowing from the private international financial markets has enabled countries to postpone resolution of their payments imbalances for a number of years, and the country approaches the IMF only after it is faced with default.

The Nature of Supply-side Adjustment Policies

Any serious approach to balance of payments adjustment must begin with limiting the growth of real demand, or absorption, within available supply, or the capacity of the country to produce real goods domestically plus what external capital can be attracted on a sustainable basis. Although policy actions should promote both output expansion and the switching of output in favor of tradable goods, demand management is required to assure that higher output is not preempted by consumers and government expenditures not related to productive investment. Restricting demand while expanding domestic output calls for a set of policy and administrative actions that are appropriate for the conditions peculiar to the individual country. Supply-side actions involve microeconomic policies such as the elimination of internal price distortions as well as distortions between internal and external prices; the liberalization of trade; the removal of financial repression in the form of controls on interest rates and capital markets; and the elimination of constraints on domestic and foreign investment. Supply-side measures influence the volume and pattern of production, while fiscal and monetary restraints reduce demand. Exchange rate adjustments also serve to dampen real demand and to promote the production of tradable goods as contrasted with nontradable goods. If growth is to be maintained during the adjustment process, savings and investment must be encouraged and price distortions that impair incentives to production removed. In order to maintain investment, imports of investment goods may need to be financed for a time by IMF or other forms of financial assistance. What is required is a well-devised package of policy reforms rather than a conditionality package limited to monetary, fiscal, and exchange rate policies and performance targets that characterized the traditional IMF stand-by agreements.

The Content of IMF Conditionality

The importance of supply-side policies and programs designed to achieve structural adjustment has been emphasized in several publications by IMF officials, but there is a certain amount of obfuscation regarding the role of supply-side policies in recent IMF conditionality packages designed to achieve structural adjustment. For example, an article by Manuel Guitián, a member of the Fund's staff, states as follows:

> It is also common to have a number of important policy understandings in the formulation of an adjustment program, which provide the basis on which the feasibility of the domestic financial policies is predicated. These understandings are rarely made performance criteria in programs supported by the Fund, but they can be critical for the attainment of financial balance and sustainable growth rates. They normally include: public sector policies on prices, taxes and subsidies, which can contribute to eliminate financial imbalances and to promote efficiency and public sector activities; interest rate policies, which foster the generation of domestic savings and improve resource allocation; exchange rate policy, which helps to control absorption in the external accounts but is also a powerful tool for development; and incomes policies, which keep claims on resources from outstepping their availability.
>
> Actions in these policy areas are of direct interest to the Fund because they foster savings and investment—the basis for expanding supply and for the sound development of an economy. Measures of this type elicit supply responses on two different levels: by insuring appropriate pricing in the broadest sense, the flow of output out of a given stock of resources is maximized, the medium-term to long-term growth rate of output is enhanced (Guitián 1981, p. 16).

Guitián's article goes on to discuss the collaboration between the World Bank and the Fund and the jurisdiction of each with respect to different types of policy advice. Guitián states that "In providing policy advice, the Fund continues to focus on the macroeconomic and balance of payments adjustment policies, while the Bank concentrates on the quality and effectiveness of development plans and investment priorities" (Guitián 1981, p. 16). This statement reflects an understanding between the two institutions that the Fund has primary responsibility for exchange rates and restrictive systems, for adjustment of temporary balance of payments disequilibrium, and for evaluating and assisting members to work out stabilization programs. The Bank has primary responsibility for the composition of development programs and project evaluations, including development priorities. Further, IMF conditionality is primarily concerned with macroeconomic variables relating to monetary, fiscal, foreign borrowing and exchange policy; the Bank's structural adjustment agreements emphasize microeconomic factors such as price distortions, the composition of development programs, development priorities, and institution building for transferring seeds, fertilizer, and credits to agriculture.[1]

Although the texts of stand-by and extended facility agreements are not made public by the Fund, public statements issued by the Fund indicate that a wide variety of supply-side policies are included in the "Letters of Intent" of the members receiving IMF assistance. For example, in a statement contained in the *IMF Survey* (supplement on the Fund, May 1981, p. 3), it is stated that "The adjustment programs call attention to supply-related measures, such as export promotion policies or measures to increase the efficiency of government spending, because these contribute to the elimination of imbalances without jeopardizing the economy's growth prospects."

These and other supply-side factors mentioned in Guitián's article are not included in the performance criteria set forth in the Fund's conditionality agreements for determining releases of funds. Instead, they are considered in the course of periodic reviews or consultation during the term of the program. In IMF press releases, these policy reforms are usually stated in rather vague and imprecise terms indicating the intentions of the member government, and while there may be stand-by agreements that are very specific with respect to these policy reforms, it is my impression that conditions with respect to them are not precise, lack a timetable, and are generally not monitored in a rigorous way. This impression is strengthened by the US executive director's criticism of the $5.8 billion IMF loan to India approved on November 9, 1981, in which the conditionality package

[1] According to Ernest Stern, this division of responsibilities is not based on differences in objectives or of concerns of the two institutions with respect to macroeconomic and microeconomic issues, or with respect to financial aspects as contrasted with real resources. "On the contrary, the difference lies primarily in the orientation of each institution's staff and the experience and expertise it is capable of mustering" (Chapter 5, this volume).

was characterized as lacking "a detailed statement of concrete structural adjustment measures to be implemented during the three years and consistent with its objective of removing structural rigidities in the economy which are a significant source of its balance of payments problem. Such structural rigidities include administered prices, export restraints, import restrictions, and government regulations" (Erb 1981).

Judging IMF Conditionality Packages Without Seeing Them

Since IMF stand-by agreements are secret and the statements regarding their content are limited to generalities, how is it possible for an outsider to evaluate them in terms of the degree of rigor with respect to the nature and comprehensiveness of the policy conditions set forth, the monitoring of performance, or the degree to which conditionality has been enforced? Ex post examination of monetary and fiscal performance is important, but the achievement of macroeconomic performance targets is often frustrated by a variety of internal and external conditions despite the best efforts and intentions of the country in controlling credit and the budget. What may be the most important factors for achieving the Fund's objectives are the policies required for adjustment with minimum impairment of growth. Therefore, a feasible approach to evaluating the Fund's conditionality programs may be to look at the current policies of the developing countries that have been receiving IMF assistance under stand-by and extended facility arrangements in relation to the policies that have proved to be most effective in achieving balance of payments adjustment with successful growth. This approach implies that the degree of rigor in IMF conditionality programs in the past is reflected in the current policies pursued by the developing countries that have negotiated IMF conditionality agreements. Of course, some countries may have adopted policies appropriate for successful adjustment in the absence of Fund conditionality programs. But if a high proportion of countries that have received IMF assistance under conditionality agreements are not currently following appropriate policies, there is evidence of a lack of rigor in the content or enforcement of the conditionality programs.

In February 1982 there were some 40 IMF stand-by and extended facility arrangements in effect with the less developed countries (LDCs), and during the past four or five years a high proportion of the IMF's LDC members have received assistance under these arrangements. The countries include many of the larger non-oil-exporting LDCs, for example, India, Korea, Pakistan, the Philippines, Thailand, Turkey, Yugoslavia, Zambia, and Zaire. Some of the countries that have negotiated extended facility arrangements with the Fund are in the upper per capita GNP range of the middle-income LDCs, for example, Mexico and the Philippines, while others have per capita GNPs of under $300 per year, for example, Sri Lanka and Sierra Leone. Some of the countries that have negotiated conditionality agreements had relatively good performance records during the 1970s, including Korea, the Philippines, Thailand, Uruguay, and Yugoslavia, while others had poor performance records, including Bolivia, Ghana, Tanzania, Zaire, and Zambia. Since IMF assistance has been made available to a large number of countries representing a wide range of adjustment success in dealing with their imbalances, no attempt will be made in this paper to relate conditionality programs to policies on an individual country basis, except for citing a few examples. Rather I shall consider the current policies of the developing countries as a whole in relation to those policies that have been shown to be the most effective in promoting adjustment without seriously impairing growth.

In pursuing the above approach I propose to examine two questions: (1) What policies have proved most effective in promoting balance of payments adjustment while maintaining growth or avoiding serious impairment of growth? and (2) To what degree have developing countries been pursuing policies associated with successful development?

Policies Associated with Successful Adjustment and Growth

Over the past decade a number of country studies have examined the relationship between growth experience and balance of payments adjustment on the one hand, and the policies pursued by individual

[2] The extensive studies authored or co-authored by Bela Balassa are referenced in Bela Balassa, Chapter 8, this volume. In addition, the NBER sponsored a comprehensive project on foreign trade regimes and economic development under the joint direction of Professors Jagdish Bhagwati and Anne Krueger. The project included case studies of the following 10 countries, each of which resulted in a volume written by different authors: Brazil, Chile, Colombia, Egypt, Ghana, India, Israel, Philippines, South Korea, and Turkey. In addition to the 10 country volumes that appeared during the mid-1970s, two volumes were published analyzing the results and implications of the case studies: Anne O. Krueger (1978) and Jagdish Bhagwati (1978).

countries on the other. These studies have been prepared by an impressive group of authors whose work has been sponsored by prestigious institutions such as the National Bureau of Economic Research (NBER), the World Bank, the Organization for Economic Cooperation and Development (OECD) Development Centre, and the Agency for International Development[2] (Krueger 1978; Bhagwati 1978; Jaspersen 1981).

Although there are substantial differences in the economic and political histories of the countries studied—so that many factors have affected their export and development experience—two broad conclusions are almost universally supported by the evidence derived from these case studies covering a substantial proportion of the developing countries. First, the movement from heavy import restrictions and overvalued exchange rates toward more open economies and equilibrium exchange rates was accompanied by a rise in the rate of growth of both exports and GNP and the rapid adjustment of payments imbalances associated with the rise in oil prices in 1973–74 and with other external shocks. Second, countries that failed to liberalize their trade and foreign exchange regimes and continued import substitution policies and overvalued exchange rates experienced slow economic growth or stagnation and poor export performance. Moreover, these same countries experienced the most difficulty in achieving balance of payments adjustments and tended to rely heavily on borrowing as contrasted with improving their current account balance through increased exports. The poor performance accompanying inward-oriented as contrasted with outward-oriented policies arose from price distortions that discourage exports in favor of high-cost import substitution, increased costs due to delays and inefficiencies of the bureaucracy imposing controls, stifled competition within the country, and reduced rates of saving and domestic investment traceable to government-imposed negative real rates of interest and government intervention in the capital markets.

It is sometimes asserted that the policies associated with successful adjustment in the middle-income LDCs have less relevance for the very poor and primitive agricultural economies such as the countries of sub-Saharan Africa. Nevertheless, a recent World Bank (1981*a*) study, *Accelerated Development in Sub-Saharan Africa*, finds that "exchange rate and trade policies are especially critical for African economies," and that "overvalued exchange rates discouraged local production," and "direct controls over trade (for example, import bans and quotas) which are widely imposed to deal with balance of payments problems, have proved extremely costly to apply . . . and have frequently been ineffective." Moreover, the study emphasizes "reform of incentive structures to ensure better prices, more open and competitive marketing systems and greater availability of consumer goods" as essential conditions for growth (World Bank 1981, *a* pp. 5–6). In short, nearly all the policy reforms that have proved effective for successful adjustment and growth in the middle-income countries are also recommended for the countries of sub-Saharan Africa.

The *World Development Report 1981* (World Bank 1981b) identifies three ways in which countries have responded to external shocks during the 1970s: (1) structural adjustment, which includes switching resources to the production of exports and import substitutes, including domestic substitutes for imported energy; (2) external financing; and (3) slower growth, which narrows current account deficits by restricting imports. Of those countries relying heavily on structural adjustment, the most successful were the countries following an outward-oriented approach leading to an expansion of exports (for example, South Korea). Those countries following an inward-oriented approach relied more heavily on external borrowing (for example, Turkey). By and large the countries with an outward orientation, including both semi-industrial countries and primary producing countries, maintained their growth rates, while those following inward orientation had reduced growth rates. The outward-oriented economies used external financing to cover increases in the cost of oil imports until they were able to pay for them with increased exports. In these countries "most of the extra investment needed to effect adjustment was financed by increased domestic saving, and their strong export performance meant that debt-service ratios rose only slightly. By contrast, reliance on external borrowing was significantly greater in the inward-looking group which did not undertake structural adjustment" (World Bank 1981b), p. 75).

The Record of Oil-Importing LDCs

The growth record of the middle-income oil-importing LDCs during the period 1970–80 has been remarkably good in the face of the sharp rise in oil prices and the periods of worldwide recession. For these countries the average annual rate of growth in per capita GNP was 3.1 percent for the period in contrast with 2.5 percent for the industrialized countries. The average annual rate of growth in per capita GNP for the low-income oil-importing LDCs was only 0.8 percent during the period. For many LDCs growth rates have been maintained by large external borrowings rather than by means of adjustment. With certain notable exceptions, the record of policy reform of the oil-importing LDCs has not been favorable, despite the fact that a substantial number of them have negotiated one or more stand-by agreements with the IMF.

Progress toward policy reform is difficult to quantify, but certain indicators may be noted. For example, more than two-thirds of the non-OPEC (Organization of Petroleum Exporting Countries) LDCs maintained quantitative payments restrictions on current transactions in 1981, and more than half the 32 countries that did not have quantitative restrictions impose some form of cost-related import restrictions, such as import surcharges. (Nearly all the OECD countries have abolished quantitative payments restrictions on current transactions.) Countries that do not impose quantitative payments restrictions on current transactions include Chile, Hong Kong, Ivory Coast, Korea, Liberia, Malaysia, Mexico, Singapore, Thailand, and Uruguay (IMF 1981*a*), pp. 470–77). It may be noted that this list includes some of the outstanding examples of countries that achieved successful adjustment to payments imbalances caused by external events during the 1970s, for example, Chile, Ivory Coast, Korea, Malaysia, Singapore, Thailand, and Uruguay.

High rates of inflation have existed in the non-oil developing countries reaching a (weighted) average of 32.5 percent in 1980 as contrasted with an average of 12 percent in the industrial countries (IMF 1981b, p. 16). In addition, a substantial proportion of the developing countries' economies are characterized by internal price disparities created by administered prices and negative real rates of interest for domestic savers. A number of developing countries have maintained overvalued exchange rates for long periods of time. According to a recent article in *World Financial Markets*, overvalued exchange rates in Latin American countries have "retarded the expansion and diversification of export-oriented and import-competing sectors; they have stimulated destabilizing flows of speculative capital; and by eventually requiring sharp cutbacks in real economic growth, they have raised needlessly the cost of adjustment to higher oil imports, falling commodity prices, and other adverse external developments" (*World Financial Markets* 1982, pp. 4–10). The fact that most non-oil-exporting LDCs peg their currencies to the dollar or other major currencies, while their domestic rates of inflation tend to be two or more times the rates of inflation in the United States and other industrial countries, inevitably makes for overvalued exchange rates.

In the absence of an adequate empirical investigation, I shall support my contention that most oil-importing LDCs are not pursuing policies associated with successful adjustment and growth by reasoning that Charlie Kindleberger would call "casual empiricism." On the basis of dozens of recent reports on individual LDCs and of global reports by international agencies such as the IMF, World Bank, and OECD, I conclude that currently most of the following conditions exist in over half the oil-importing LDCs: (1) exchange rates are overvalued by 20–50 percent or more; (2) quantitative import restrictions are heavy and extensive; (3) real rates of interest on savings in financial institutions are negative; (4) there are administered prices for a number of important domestically produced goods that create price distortions that reduce incentives for productive investment; (5) prices charged by government enterprises supplying goods or services for the domestic market do not cover full economic costs; (6) the rate of inflation is in excess of 20 percent per annum.

The continued existence of these conditions in a substantial proportion of the LDCs suggests that not enough attention is being given to policy reform in the negotiation and implementation of the IMF conditionality programs. Moreover, in the case of a number of countries that have received IMF assistance under stand-by and extended facility agreements, the funds were largely disbursed during the first year of the agreement on the basis of promises for policy reform that the governments have been slow to undertake and which often have never been implemented at all. This suggests that releases under the IMF's conditionality practices should be made only after the agreed policy reforms have been undertaken since the IMF has little leverage once the funds are released.

An Approach to More Effective Conditionality

With the abandonment of the par value system and the huge accumulation of official reserves, 80 percent of which are held by the industrial and oil-exporting countries, the Fund's resources are being used primarily for assistance to developing countries. Moreover, the availability of the enormous pool of private international capital to the more industrialized, higher-income LDCs has tended to concentrate the assistance activities of the Fund on middle- and low-income developing countries. The problems of these latter countries are largely development problems and not the short-term, reversible balance of payments deficits for which the Fund's resources were originally intended. The IMF has justified its role in development financing by calling it assistance for structural balance of payments adjustment. Several years after the Fund began making structural balance of payments loans, the World Bank also entered the field of structural adjustment loans; the objectives and rationale for these loans are virtually identical for the two institutions. Nevertheless, as has been noted, the conditionality packages of the two institutions have tended to differ, even though the policy reforms and financial performance requirements necessary to achieve adjustment with growth are identical. This has been recognized by collaboration between the two institutions when they are both making structural adjustment loans to the same country. In most cases, however, countries have not negotiated conditionality programs with both institutions at the same time, with the result that the full complement of conditionality instruments is not being utilized or implemented in a rigorous manner.

Since both institutions make loans to the same countries, even though in some cases the World Bank is making project loans while the Fund is making loans under stand-by or extended facility arrangements, I would recommend a common conditionality program, including quantitative financial performance targets and specific policy adjustments, together with a timetable and strict monitoring of performance. The joint conditionality package should then be jointly enforced by means of withholding funds by both institutions in the event of nonperformance.

Under the approach I am suggesting, it would not be necessary for both institutions to make general balance of payments loans (or what the World Bank calls structural adjustment loans). This function might well be left to the IMF while the Bank might make sectoral and multiproject loans in support of high-priority development programs.[3] The joint conditionality package, which should include all elements currently contained in both the IMF and World Bank structural adjustment loan agreements, would greatly strengthen the development assistance programs of both institutions for achieving their common objectives.

One further recommendation would be to replace the IMF extended facility with a series of one-year stand-by agreements, which would be renewable, provided performance under the conditionality agreements was achieved. Repayment terms could be adjusted in accordance with the estimated time required for balance of payments adjustment or the availability of external private capital, which is likely to increase with progress toward balance of payments adjustment, especially with an increase in exports.

[3] In another paper I have questioned the desirability of structural balance of payments loans by the World Bank (Mikesell 1982).

Arguments for Loose Conditionality

Those who criticize the Fund's conditionality on the grounds that it is "too tight" may be divided into three categories: (1) those who want no conditions on the use of the Fund's resources drawn under the higher credit tranches and the extended facility; (2) those who argue that the Fund's policy prescriptions place "adjustment" above employment and growth; and (3) those who argue that the burden of adjustment should be more equitably divided between the deficit and the surplus countries. The argument of the first group, which represents a position held by some government representatives at the time of the Bretton Woods conference in 1944, is untenable for an institution with limited resources. There must be rules for the allocation of the Fund's resources; otherwise the resources would become a political grab bag or would be allocated in accordance with some formula based on population or GNP of its members, but which would bear no relation to the purposes for which the Fund was organized and financed. The second group of critics of Fund conditionality bases its argument on the existence of an incompatibility between progress toward adjustment and growth. There is substantial evidence that the very policies that promote adjustment will also promote growth, and this is the kind of conditionality package that the Fund ought to be striving for. Some members of this group also take the position that where the cause of payments imbalance can be traced to external factors beyond a member's control, rather than to the member's own internal policies, different standards of conditionality relating to policy adjustments should be imposed.[4] But the alternative to adjustment is a continuous flow of resources from the Fund (whose resources are limited) or from the private international capital markets, from which loans will not be available beyond a certain level of indebtedness. In fact, many countries come to the Fund only after they have exhausted their ability to obtain or service additional external debt from private lenders. In the absence of assistance from the Fund, adjustment would inevitably take place, but possibly at a far greater cost in unemployment and impairment of growth. There is nothing in the cause of a country's payments imbalance that relieves it of the necessity for adjustment, given the limitations on the availability of external resources.

[4] This argument has been forwarded by Sidney Dell (1981, pp. 17–19) and Alexandre Kafka (1976).

The latter argument is related to that of the third group of critics of conditionality, namely, that fairness demands that the surplus countries share the obligation to adjust with the deficit countries. It is true, of course, that the Fund has an obligation to bring pressure on surplus countries where the surplus is being generated by undervalued exchange rates or the maintenance of import restrictions and/or export subsidies. The Fund has also played an important role in recycling the surplus funds of the OPEC countries, but the Fund lacks the ability to induce OPEC countries to reduce their surpluses by lowering the price of oil or by increasing imports from the non-oil producing LDCs. Whatever the moral arguments in favor of fairness, the facts of life are that deficit countries cannot go on delaying adjustment, and the purpose of the Fund's conditionality program is to make the adjustment process as painless as possible given the existence of limited IMF resources and the necessity of revolving these resources.

References

Bhagwati, Jagdish. 1978. *Anatomy and Consequences of Exchange Control Regimes*. New York: National Bureau of Economic Research.

Dell, Sidney. 1981. *On Being Grandmotherly: The Evolution of IMF Conditionality*. Essays in International Finance, no. 144. Princeton, NJ: International Finance Section, Princeton University.

Erb, Richard D. 1981. Statement before House Subcommittee on International Trade, Investment and Monetary Policy, December 10, 1981. Washington: US Department of the Treasury. Processed.

Guitián, Manuel. 1981. "Fund Conditionality and the International Adjustment Process." *Finance and Development* (June).

International Monetary Fund. 1976. *Annual Report 1975*, Washington.

———. 1979. *Articles of Agreement*. Washington.

———. 1981. *IMF Survey* (May). Washington.

———. 1981a. *Annual Report on Exchange Arrangements and Exchange Restrictions, 1981* (June). Washington.

———. 1981b. *Annual Report 1981*. Washington.

Jaspersen, Frederick Z. 1981. *Adjustment Experience and Growth Prospects of the Semi-Industrial Economies*. Staff Working Paper no. 477 (August). Washington: World Bank.

Kafka, Alexandre. 1976. *The International Monetary Fund: Reform Without Reconstruction?* Essays in International Finance, no. 118 (October). Princeton, NJ: International Finance Section, Princeton University.

Krueger, Anne O. 1978. *Liberalization Attempts and Consequences*. Cambridge, Mass.: Ballinger.

Mikesell, Raymond F. 1982. "The Economics of Foreign Aid and Self-Sustaining Development." Washington: Departments of Treasury and State and the Agency for International Development. Forthcoming.

Morgan Guaranty Trust Company. 1982. *World Financial Markets* (February). New York.

World Bank. 1981a. *Accelerated Development in Sub-Saharan Africa.* Washington.

———. 1981b. *World Development Report 1981*. New York: Oxford University Press.

COMMENTS, CHAPTERS 1–3

Rimmer de Vries and Arturo C. Porzecanski

It was a little over two years ago, amidst growing concern about the scale of the Organization of Petroleum Exporting Countries (OPEC) current account surpluses and the large recycling burden these imposed on private markets, that calls were heard for a greater role to be played by the International Monetary Fund (IMF). Partly in response to those calls, the Fund expanded its lending authority substantially and encouraged countries with major payments deficits to make use of its credit facilities as an aid to their adjustment process. Now that some time has passed and that energy conservation and substitution and austere demand management policies in the main industrial countries have resulted in a whittling down of the OPEC surplus, an assessment of the IMF's enhanced role is warranted. The objective is to take a factual look at what, in the aggregate, the Fund's lending has amounted to in the recent past, and at what its realistic role can be expected to be in the foreseeable future.

An examination of IMF lending must recognize from the start that, despite the successful completion of the Seventh General Review of Quotas and the borrowings arranged with Saudi Arabia and certain industrial countries, the Fund's resources remain limited both in absolute terms and in relation to the world's recycling needs. The amount available to the IMF for lending to deficit countries is derived from its pool of usable currencies. As of the first quarter of 1982, the pool is made up of the quotas of 7 industrial, 8 oil-exporting, and 15 developing countries, and its totals some $36 billion. In addition, the IMF has access to its Special Drawing Rights (SDR) holdings in the General Account, to resources under the supplementary financing Facility, and to lines of credit from Saudi Arabia and the Bank for International Settlements (BIS) under the enlarged access policy. Currently, these could yield an extra $21 billion, for an estimated total of $57 billion. This is not a fixed, absolute ceiling but represents a reasonable approximation of resources at the Fund's disposal. In actual practice, the IMF would not feel comfortable about disbursing all of these funds because the external position of some of the countries deemed to have usable currencies could deteriorate unexpectedly.

With regard to the utilization of IMF financial resources, its loans outstanding under all conditional and unconditional facilities are presently in the neighborhood of $16 billion, and undrawn commitments under existing stand-by and extended Fund facility (EFF) arrangements are almost $15 billion, for a total of $31 billion. Beyond this, the Fund must keep resources readily available for disbursement under facilities to which countries have relatively immediate and automatic access. The compensatory financing facility, for example, under which countries obtained about $1 billion in the past 12 months, probably will be tapped heavily in the near future given the recent widespread decline of basic commodity prices. For repayments of earlier IMF loans as a source of new funding, the available data reveal that the volume of amortizations reached a peak in 1978 and has declined steadily since then, and that many loans made in 1980–81 for the most part do not come up for repayment until the mid-to-late 1980s.

The implications are clear. The Fund, like other official institutions, faces certain practical financial limitations. For precautionary reasons, the IMF surely would not wish to disburse more than half of the $26 billion that is available to it. In view of its *masse de manoeuvre*, the Fund cannot sustain the pace of new loan commitments witnessed last year, when approvals of new stand-by and extended arrangements (net of cancellations of earlier commitments) totaled a record $15 billion. Even in the absence of further expansion and liberalization of its facilities, or a weakening of conditionality, its remaining resources could be consumed by the approach of just a few major deficit countries, or by the extension of assistance to a portion of the more than 70 developing countries that have yet to sign up for a stand-by or a three-year program.

To envision a still greater role for the IMF in the near future, therefore, implies the acceptance of two heroic assumptions. On the supply side, it assumes that there is a willingness to endow the IMF with additional resources. This is highly unlikely. First, it will take at least three years to raise member quotas once again. Second, during the course of this year the OPEC surplus is projected to disappear and Saudi Arabia's international reserves to stop growing, which may mean that the Fund will have to tap additional countries that generally prefer to maintain their reserve position liquid and that do not favor making long-term investments. Third, there is reluctance on the part of several key member governments to allow IMF recourse to the private capital markets, largely out of concern that the institution's character would be altered in unforeseeable ways. On the demand side, proponents of a greater role assume that countries somehow will flock to the IMF, despite the fact that conditionality must and will be maintained, and that this will deter all but the financially weakest countries from seeking Fund assistance.

A pragmatic assessment, therefore, leads to the conclusion that the IMF is playing, and probably will continue to play, a qualitatively important but nevertheless quantitatively limited role in the international financial arena. This becomes quite clear when the Fund's lending is compared with that of the commercial banks. During 1980 and 1981, use of IMF credit by non-oil developing countries net of repayments amounted to $6.6 billion. Given a $1 billion increase in these countries' reserve position with the Fund, however, the IMF resources they obtained to finance their current account deficits accordingly was $5.6 billion. In contrast, the amount of credit the non-oil less developed countries (LDCs) received from the commercial banks in the industrial countries amounted to approximately $90 billion—also net of repayments—of which $4.5 billion was returned to the banks in the form of higher private and official deposits. Thus, a net amount of about $85 billion was received by the non-oil LDCs from the banks—15 times the amount the IMF was able to provide in this two-year period of heightened Fund involvement. This is not to say, of course, that IMF resources were not of critical importance to some individual deficit countries.

The second issue to be considered involves the qualitative aspects of the IMF's lending program and how changes in it have altered in a major way the relation between the Fund and the commercial banks. The IMF traditionally served the financial needs of both industrial and developing countries. For example, during the late 1960s, two-thirds of its outstanding loans were to industrial countries and the remaining third to non-oil LDCs. By the mid–1970s, outstandings in industrial countries were down to roughly half of the total. At present, use of Fund credit by industrial countries accounts for less than 5 percent of the total, while credit to non-oil LDCs has risen correspondingly to over 95 percent of outstandings (Table 1).

A breakdown of IMF lending to various subgroups of non-oil LDCs also reveals substantial changes. Fund outstandings in Western Hemisphere countries are down sharply (from 24 percent of the non-oil LDC subtotal as of end–1977 to 10 percent as of end–1981), as are outstandings in the non-oil exporting nations of the Middle East (from 9 percent to 1 percent). On the one hand, the IMF's exposure in the lesser developed countries of Europe (including Turkey) has declined somewhat from 12 percent to 9.5 percent of the non-oil LDC subtotal.

TABLE 1 IMF CREDITS OUTSTANDING, END-1977 TO END-1981

Item	December 31, 1977		December 31, 1979		December 31, 1981	
	Billion dollars	*Percentage of total*	*Billion dollars*	*Percentage of total*	*Billion dollars*	*Percentage of total*
Industrial countries	7.84	49.3	2.19	20.8	0.64	4.1
Oil-exporting countries	0.00	0.0	0.00	0.0	0.00	0.0
Non-oil developing countries	8.05	50.7	8.32	79.2	14.92	95.9
Western Hemisphere	1.90	12.0	1.53	14.6	1.56	10.0
Middle East[a]	0.70	4.4	0.65	6.2	0.20	1.3
Africa	1.65	10.4	2.03	19.3	3.88	24.9
Excluding South Africa	(1.18)	(7.4)	(1.93)	(18.4)	(3.88)	(24.9)
Asia[b]	2.16	13.6	2.13	20.3	5.41	34.8
Europe[c]	0.97	6.1	1.10	10.5	1.42	9.1
Communist countries	0.65	4.1	0.88	8.4	2.46	15.8
Total	15.89	100.0	10.50	100.0	15.56	100.0

Source: International Financial Statistics, various issues.
a. Egypt, Israel, Jordan, Syria, and Yemen.
b. Excluding China, Kampuchea, Laos, and Viet Nam.
c. Cyprus, Greece, Portugal, and Turkey.

On the other hand, it has increased noticeably in African countries (excluding South Africa), whose share is up from 15 percent to 26 percent; in Asian countries (up from 27 percent to 36 percent); and in the six Communist countries that are members of the Fund (China, Kampuchea, Laos, Romania, Viet Nam, and Yugoslavia), which currently account for 16.5 percent of credit to non-oil LDCs versus 8 percent as of end–1977.

Another breakdown of the IMF's loan portfolio portraying significant change is by the per capita income of the borrowers (Table 2). Five groups have been identified: countries with a 1978 GNP per capita of less than $300 per annum, which are the poorest; those with average incomes between $300 and $699; middle-income countries with a GNP per capita ranging from $700 to $2,999; upper income countries where the corresponding range is $3,000 to $6,999; and countries with income per capita exceeding $7,000. A comparison of the IMF's portfolio as it stood on December 31, 1981, versus its composition as of end–1979, shows that outstandings in the poorest countries have tripled (to account for one-fourth of the Fund's total portfolio), while outstandings in upper and highest income countries have fallen by 58 percent and 82 percent, respectively (to account for a combined total of 5 percent of the portfolio). IMF exposure in middle-income countries (the single most important group of borrowers) has risen by 170 percent, to represent a 39 percent share, and net lending has doubled to countries with a GNP per capita of between $300 and $699, to 30 percent of the total.

These trends are likely to be accentuated in the near future, as suggested by the available data on loan commitments under the credit tranches and the extended and enlarged access facilities (Table 3). For instance, IMF commitments to the poorest countries have jumped to $9.8 billion and now comprise nearly half of the $20.8 billion in total commitments. The two low-income country categories together represent two-thirds of total commitments.

In sum, in recent years Fund and commercial bank lending have evolved in different directions. In the past, the IMF and the banks frequently found themselves involved in lending to the same countries at the same time, and their activities complemented each other. A successful IMF agreement could unlock significant amounts of additional bank lending and contribute to the early resolution of external payments difficulties through a mixture of adjustment and financing. In contrast, at the present time the IMF increasingly finds itself in countries where the banks have a relatively small stake that, for the most part, they are not eager to increase. To illustrate, the two groups of low-income countries to which the Fund has pledged $13.9 billion,

TABLE 2 IMF CREDITS OUTSTANDING TO COUNTRIES GROUPED BY 1978 GNP PER CAPITA
(million dollars, December 31, 1981)

Country/GNP	*Credit outstanding*
Less than $300	
Bangladesh	322
Burma	57
Burundi	12
Central African Rep.	23
Chad	8
China	524
Equatorial Guinea	17
Ethiopia	114
The Gambia	17
Guinea-Bissau	3
Haiti	37
India	659
Kampuchea	15
Laos	15
Madagascar	87
Malawi	87
Mali	8
Mauritania	35
Nepal	22
Pakistan	757
Sierra Leone	56
Somalia	34
Sri Lanka	404
Tanzania	99
Uganda	186
Viet Nam	59
W. Samoa	5
Zaire	346
Subtotal	4,008
Percentage of total	25.8
$300–$699	
Bolivia	71
Cameroon	3
Dominica	7
Egypt	99
El Salvador	44
Ghana	28
Grenada	6
Guyana	86
Honduras	37
Kenya	204
Liberia	101
Morocco	450
Papua N.G.	52
Peru	388
Philippines	958
St. Vincent	2
Senegal	149
Sudan	482
Thailand	705
Togo	21
Yemen	5
Zambia	731
Zimbabwe	44
Subtotal	4,673
Percentage of total	30.0
$700–$2,999	
Barbados	1
Chile	49
Costa Rica	102
Cyprus	26
Dominican Rep.	23
Guatemala	112
Ivory Coast	371
Jamaica	470
Korea	1,247
Malaysia	221
Mauritius	149
Nicaragua	24
Panama	93
Portugal	55
Romania	590
St. Lucia	5
Turkey	1,322
Yugoslavia	1,252
Subtotal	6,112
Percentage of total	39.3
$3,000–$6,999	
Gabon	13
Greece	16
Israel	102
New Zealand	40
Spain	165
United Kingdom	364
Subtotal	700
Percentage of total	4.5
$7,000 and over	
Finland	61
Iceland	7
Subtotal	68
Percentage of total	0.4

TABLE 3 IMF COMMITMENTS UNDER CONDITIONAL PROGRAMS TO COUNTRIES GROUPED BY 1978 GNP PER CAPITA
(million dollars, December 31, 1981)

Country	*Commitment*
Less than $300	
Bangladesh	931
Burma	31
Ethiopia	79
India	5,820
Madagascar	127
Malawi	58
Mauritania	30
Pakistan	1,070
Sierra Leone	216
Somalia	50
Tanzania	209
Uganda	131
Zaire	1,062
Subtotal	9,814
Percentage of total	47.1
$300–$699	
Dominica	10
Grenada	4
Guyana	175
Honduras	55
Kenya	281
Liberia	64
Morocco	951
Senegal	73
Sudan	497
Thailand	948
Togo	55
Zambia	931
Zimbabwe	44
Subtotal	4,088
Percentage of total	19.6
$700–$2,999	
Costa Rica	322
Guatemala	22
Ivory Coast	564
Jamaica	556
Korea	670
Mauritius	35
Romania	1,283
Turkey	1,455
Uruguay	37
Yugoslavia	1,935
Subtotal	6,879
Percentage of total	33.0
$3,000–$6,999	
Gabon	40
Subtotal	40
Percentage of total	0.2
$7,000 and over	
None	0

Source: International Monetary Fund.

or two-thirds of its total commitments, account for a mere 7 percent of the commercial banks' exposure in non-oil LDCs. One major implication is that the IMF cannot afford to weaken its conditionality because, given the paucity of official concessional aid and the lack of commercial bank involvement, failure to insist on these countries' external and domestic adjustment could easily turn the Fund into a foreign aid agency dispensing monies it knows cannot be repaid. This would imply a radical departure from the Fund's original objective—in fact, its *raison d'être*—to provide temporary balance of payments support to a changing group of countries.

Looked at from another perspective, the IMF's expanded lending program has, with few exceptions, failed to attract countries that are major borrowers from the commercial banks and that have large external financial requirements. Industrial countries such as Belgium, Denmark, Ireland, and Spain do not have programs with the Fund, and neither do developing countries such as Argentina, Brazil, Chile, Greece, Israel, Portugal, and Mexico. All this illustrates that the IMF and the commercial banks increasingly have operated, and are likely to continue to operate, in different markets. As in the recent past, the bulk of the Fund's resources can be expected to be channeled to countries that, by and large, are excluded from ready access to private capital markets. Countries enjoying such access probably will remain reluctant to sign up for conditional Fund assistance. Only in a few instances—such as in Korea, the Philippines, and Turkey—will there be a commonality of interests and informal collaboration among the IMF, the commercial banks, and other interested parties.

The commercial banks, therefore, must come to the realization that they are on their own when it comes to international lending because the Fund is no longer a catalyst for prompt external adjustment in the major deficit countries. In smaller and poorer countries, IMF involvement all too frequently takes place at a very advanced stage of balance of payments deterioration and, as evidenced by a growing number of failed stand-by and EFF arrangements, often does not result in prompt or sustained payments improvement. Thus, the Fund must now be viewed as a protective umbrella under which the international banking community can find shelter in times of trouble.

This means that the banks must stand ready to make judgments on economic policy performance in individual countries and on their degree of internal and external adjustment to adverse circumstances. This evaluation of the direction and speed of adjustment policies is essential, for experience strongly suggests that excessive reliance on external finance to the detriment of economic adjustment is what usually leads deficit countries down the path to debt servicing crises. Whenever the commercial banks conclude that the cause of adjustment is not being served, they—much as the IMF does when a program is not being observed—must be ready to modify lending postures accordingly, slowing down the extension of international credit to signal the need for improved policies.

What does all this imply for the Fund and its relationship with the banking community? Clearly, one avenue that ought to be explored is the supportive role the IMF could play in international finance by providing market participants, both borrowers and lenders, with more timely economic information and more relevant policy analyses of the main borrowing countries. Until now, most of the member governments have taken the narrow view that the Fund's original work is virtually always of a confidential nature. A far more enlightened approach would recognize that, although the IMF staff's policy recommendations are proprietary, there is a great deal of analytical research on adjustment indicators that could be developed and should be placed in the public domain. It is good to remember that several years ago other international institutions, such as the BIS and the Organization for Economic Cooperation and Development, took the initiative and began to compile data and to issue reports of relevance to the private capital markets. The BIS, for example, undertook to publish statistics on the international claims of banks in the industrial countries, and this filled a major information gap. As a service to the international financial community, the Fund could regularly produce and release timely estimates of monetary, fiscal, and external payments performance developed by its country analysts to supplement the historical data published already by its Bureau of Statistics. A start in this direction would be the publication, for the principal borrowing countries, of the kind of adjustment indicators that the IMF staff would monitor under a Fund-supported adjustment program and that normally would serve to establish performance criteria. In this way the IMF could appreciably improve the efficiency of private capital markets and thereby minimize, on the part of both borrowers and lenders, the miscalculations and misperceptions that often have paved the way for payment crises.

PART II

Issues Relating to Conditionality

CHAPTER 4

Adjustment Policies and Conditionality

C. David Finch

In Chapter 1, Mr. Dale provides a broad description of the setting of the problems of adjustment and financing. This paper addresses some specific issues relating to the design of adjustment programs. It first discusses certain matters on which, as explained below, debate is complicated by underlying assumptions and perceptions and is frequently not enlightening. It then proceeds to elaborate other issues that would benefit from active debate and on which well-reasoned conclusions drawn by this seminar will be particularly helpful to the Fund staff and to the authorities in Fund member countries who struggle with the complex task of improving economic performance in a world environment of growing difficulty.

The first group of issues generally concerns the Fund's basic approach to adjustment. The debate on this question in large part reflects basic economic—and political—philosophies. Frequently the positions adopted largely exclude differing viewpoints. Attitudes taken on these issues have varied, but some are strong and uncompromising. For instance, on the one side, there are those who believe that market forces behave most efficiently when they are left alone and therefore do not support any guiding or monitoring role for an international agency. On the other side, there are those who believe that any institution whose voting and decision-making structure is dominated by the economically powerful countries is by definition imperialistic in the broadest sense and designed to perpetuate an economic system that keeps most countries dependent. Both groups have certain ob-

Note: This paper is reproduced by permission of the International Monetary Fund, Washington.

jections to the goals and activities of the Fund, although for different reasons. Arguments of this nature involve essentially political judgments, and they have to be consciously and deliberately set to one side if progress is to be made in the discussion of the important issues that form the basis of this conference.

The general proposition regarding the Fund's role in adjustment is relatively simple: it is that the task of the Fund is to oversee a distribution of capital in support of policies that will ease the adjustment problems of member countries over time. It is expected that adjustment will enable the member to make repayment at a later stage, and that the process as a whole will be of net benefit to the member. There are, of course, many other tasks that are undertaken by the Fund in the financing area. The Fund provides direct liquidity through SDR allocations and it provides financing for temporary shortfalls of export receipts and for buffer stocks. While in a broad sense there is some degree of conditionality attached to all of the financial facilities of the Fund, conditionality in a stricter sense is related only to those cases where Fund assistance is requested because there is an adjustment problem—that is, cases in which an existing balance of payments deficit needs to be converted into a future surplus of a size adequate to allow repayment of the resources drawn.

In the light of this, it should be clear that it is the nature of the problem facing the member that dictates many of the policy responses that are attributed to arbitrariness or shortsightedness on the part of the Fund staff, management, and Board. The existence of a balance of payments problem means that policies have to be directed toward redressing the imbalance. First, the absorption of resources in relation to production must be reduced; second, resource allocation will be directed efficiently to ease the balance of payments constraint. In this context, it seems a rather futile exercise to debate whether the Fund supports policies that unduly emphasize deflation or devaluation, because, generally speaking, what the Fund is doing is addressing the nature of the problem. In all cases of continued payments difficulties, the authorities' attention will have to be focused on ways of reducing the level or the rate of growth of demand—which broadly means deflation—and on redirecting resources—which broadly calls for devaluation.

Such policies, of course, have certain implications. It is evident, and therefore to be expected, that reducing the domestic absorption of resources is generally painful and politically unpopular. Particularly if the government that was responsible for the unsustainable expansion of demand is still in office, there is likely to be adverse reaction to the measures designed to respond to the realities of the situation, and the reaction may take the form of political upheaval or social unrest. But this point must not be overstated. People are not as naive as analysts often seem to imply. We have found a remarkable readiness to support realistic, although difficult, action in many instances. There is frequently a basic understanding of the constraints that tends to give rise to support for political leaders who are perceived as facing up to the needs of the situation. It is notable that those who have led an austere adjustment program have frequently gone on to positions of greater leadership.

The reality of painful adjustment that may engender a political crisis also gives rise to concern about the growth performance that can be expected under an adjustment program. It almost seems paradoxical to suggest that an effort to reduce absorption can also be expected to lead to economic growth. Yet experience indicates that the road to recovery and economic growth need not be as long delayed as is often feared. The actual path is, of course, dependent on initial conditions. A country still in the flush of overexpansion inevitably tends to experience a reduction in growth in the immediate period of adjustment. But all too often delay in taking adjustment action has already brought about a slowdown in growth or, even more frequently, absolute declines in production. In these cases, well-designed economic programs, by encouraging and facilitating remedial policy action, can provide the best course toward early recovery. In all cases the eventual solution of the balance of payments constraint is a key to the achievement of economic growth on a more sustained and larger scale than before. Consequently, there is no conflict between balance of payments recovery and economic growth when a time horizon appropriate to both objectives (that is, the medium term) is specified.

This leads to another set of issues on which discussion would seem to be of limited usefulness. They relate not so much to ignoring the circumstances in which adjustment action is undertaken, but to the responsibility of the Fund to press objectives other than balance of payments recovery in the policy programs supported by Fund resources. The variety of objectives that are considered appropriate for the Fund to promote includes, among others, the meeting of basic human needs and the improvement of income distribution. It is refreshing to see such faith in the power of an international agency, but the arguments are essentially misguided. The Fund has not been given power to act in these fields. It has not been established to give guidance on social and political priorities, nor has its voting system been designed to give it the moral authority to oversee priorities of a noneconomic nature. Its functions have to be kept narrowly technical if it is to be effective in the exercise of its role as a promoter of the adjustment process. For this purpose, the Fund has to accept that the authorities of a country are the sole judges of its social and political priorities. And, of course, that has been, and is, the practice. When a president or a prime minister is confronted with what may turn out to be the most difficult decisions of his career, it is not an occasion for the Fund to press its view of political priorities. All that the Fund is called to do is to form a judgment on the assurance given by the authorities that the resources it may provide will be appropriately used to support a program of balance of payments recovery. It is to be expected that the basis for such assurance can exist only if the priorities are reasonable. In fact, it can be argued that even in critical areas, such as those related to income distribution, the policies that are generally desirable from the point of view of economic efficiency tend to be the ones that provide the most likely assurance of improving income distribution. Many balance of payments recovery programs involve an improvement in the terms of trade for the rural sector, which is universally the poorest sector of the country's population.

This principle of political neutrality, if it may be so described, has an important bearing on another aspect of the Fund's approach, the use of aggregate monetary variables as one of the instruments of control in programs of adjustment. This approach evolved in large part from the desire to place as much distance as possible between the sphere of influence of the Fund and the specific decisions relating to policy implementation. In the formulation of any adjustment program there is, of course, a necessity to undertake specific actions. Measures are often needed to cut specific subsidies, reduce protection, or increase specific prices and taxes. The choice among actions of this character is essentially political, and the Fund has no right to prefer one action over another, provided that the final result is the required recovery of the balance of payments. Consequently, it was accepted as a general practice that access to Fund resources should be regulated in accordance with developments in the broadest of macroeconomic indicators, that is, global monetary aggregates, which give the needed assurance of continued adherence to the adjustment effort, and not in accordance with the implementation of the specific measures that lie behind the global developments.

Turning now to the issues that may profit more from debate, it may be useful to start by briefly outlining the approaches that have been followed by the Fund staff in discussions of adjustment policy. These involve, first, a general assessment of the balance of payments situation and prospects in order to arrive at a common understanding with the member both on the payments profile that is to be sought in the medium term and on the payments outcome that seems feasible for the immediate future. The discussion of medium-term prospects tends to be in terms of the current account of the balance of payments, while that of the immediate prospect tends to be in terms of the overall balance, the limits of which are frequently bound by resource constraints. Policy discussions then focus on the immediate actions that are necessary to achieve results in the first year that are compatible with the recovery path that has been designed for the medium term. The annual program normally contains a specification of the maximum amount of resources available to the authorities (consistent with a return to a medium-term viability of the balance of payments) and, given this amount, a determination of the measures deemed necessary to improve the balance between demand for and supply of resources. Once the amount of foreign borrowing and the amount of Fund resources that is likely to be used are agreed, the problem is to determine the amount of domestic resources that will be available from the banking system, given the conditions that are expected to prevail with respect to prices and output. That amount of domestic resources is then divided among those necessary for various purposes, as well as between the private and the public sectors. The tasks that the authorities have then to address are, broadly: which categories of expenditures are to be reduced, which categories of revenues are to be raised, and what other measures should be taken to increase savings and allocate the available resources to the most productive activities.

The decisions that have to be made to frame a policy program are by no means simple. The relative role that is to be accorded to the use of improved price incentives as against the use of quantitative controls, the degree to which inflation is to be reduced, the speed and sequence of the implementation of agreed policies (to put it in its sharpest form, the adoption of a shock versus a gradual strategy of reform), and the combination of tax measures, expenditure cuts, and credit restraint, as well as the role to be played by incomes policy and public investment are all issues that will have to be faced. In the making of these decisions, there is an unavoidable and complex interplay of politics and economics. It would serve no purpose to insist that the purely economic considerations must dominate, simply because an ideal solution is of no interest if political power to implement and achieve it does not exist. On the other hand, the prevalence of political weakness cannot be accepted as a justification for failure to take the necessary economic actions.

It is in these areas that discussions such as those to be undertaken in this seminar can be most productive. First, the perception of the authorities with respect to the political feasibility of economic measures is affected by the climate of expert opinion. Too great a difference in the direction and tone of expert advice and too large a margin for doubt can weaken the willingness of governments to undertake economically appropriate action. Second, there is a need to have the issues explained in terms that are widely understood by the authorities and their constituencies, and this is a process that can only be aided by the widest discussion and exchange of views. Third, there is a need for improved analysis of the sources and resolution of economic imbalances in the light of experience and for that experience to be constantly tested in the light of changing conditions.

Before a discussion of these broad topics, it would be desirable to narrow somewhat the focus of the circumstances to be analyzed. There is a potentially very wide range of conditions underlying payments problems that can lead to the adoption of a program qualifying for support by the Fund. It seems most productive at this point to concentrate on the circumstances prevailing in the relatively large group of countries that face the more acute imbalances at this time. A distinguishing feature of such cases is that the balance of payments constraint has become the overriding consideration. These countries typically have already had serious problems in meeting current payments to the point that arrears in payments have developed. As a result, it is not unusual to find that the countries have suffered a consequent worsening of the terms and conditions under which they trade, e.g., import prices are raised because of the application of risk premiums to cover the uncertainty of payments; the supply of credit is reduced, if not totally curtailed; normal short-term credits to cover imports in transit are not made available; and, to compound the difficulties, domestic capital tends to flee in search of safer and better returns. In response to these pressures, imports and other exchange transactions are controlled, with inevitable adverse side effects on the efficiency of resource allocation. The tightening foreign exchange constraint all too frequently leads to lower production levels together with increasing unavailability of consumer goods.

When a member country is confronting conditions such as those just described, what is the advice that should be given to the authorities? In attempting to answer this question, it would be appropriate to set out some of the more important considerations affecting the range of possible policy actions and outcomes. This is indeed a difficult path to tread. There is a need to explain the rationale behind a rather eclectic range of policy actions that have been accepted by the Fund as the basis for the extension of its financial assistance. At the same time, there is also need to offer a clear guidance for the thrust of the broad policies that our experience would suggest to be the most appropriate. If some of the conclusions that are drawn appear venturesome, the purpose is indeed to stimulate a useful interchange of views. There is, however, one qualification that should be made at the outset. Whatever conclusions are reached, they cannot be timeless or absolute. A clear example is the attitude on inflation. When the system of exchange arrangements in the world was based on fixed parities, it was critical to feature the objective of inflation control as an essential part of the process of regaining overall financial balance so that the system could continue to prevail. With the general acceptance of flexibility of exchange rates, the emphasis given to the control of inflation has become less urgent.

The first issue that may be raised relates to the relative role to be allowed for controls and restrictions in members' foreign exchange systems. In principle, the Fund in its policy advice stands for their elimination as a critical element contributing to the growth and welfare of the world economy. But in practice we have found that exchange and trade controls, including particularly import controls imposed for balance of payments reasons, soon acquire and generally play such an important role in the political sphere that less than clearcut commitments and actions in this area have to be temporarily accepted. It is evident that insistence on the strict and rapid elimination of all controls would simply result in sharply limiting the scope of the financial assistance of the Fund. It seems that on the basis of the weight of economic logic, Fund policy advice must lean heavily in the direction of an elimination of controls and restrictions as rapidly as possible. The growth of the smaller economies will inevitably remain well below their potential unless there is an effective attempt to integrate them into the world economy.

It is also clear, however, that for the essential purposes of conditionality, an absolute standard in this area is not necessary at this time. It is possible to argue that the Fund's assistance can play a useful role by encouraging a steady reduction over time in the degree of restrictiveness, thereby lessening the cost of adjustment. This compromise standard, however, cannot be stretched to permit the indefinite accumulation of external payments arrears. If a program of balance of payments recovery does not at least envisage the elimination of arrears on current payments, it can hardly be considered to involve a serious adjustment effort, nor can the repayment of resources to the Fund be assured under such a program. In this context, one aspect of the compromise standard just outlined needs a further comment. If the rate of inflation in the country exceeds that of its trading partners, there virtually always has to be provision for exchange rate flexibility. Otherwise, there would be an implicit acceptance of the possibility that repayment of resources to the Fund would be made by intensifying restrictions on foreign payments. Such a situation, by discouraging capital flows into the country, would make the task of balance of payments adjustment even more difficult.

On the question of inflation, there is also a measure of conflict between the requirements of economic efficiency and those dictated by political expediency. There can hardly be any doubt that the performance of an economic system suffers when decisions have to be made against a background of uncertainty with respect to the size and variability of the general price increases that may occur in the future. There is a diversion of resources away from productive activities and a general loosening of the association between economic reward and economic efficiency. There are growing conflicts as attempts are made to redress the transfers that occur between debtors and creditors and between groups of workers pressing to maintain their advantage or reduce any disadvantage through wage bargaining. On the other hand, to halt an ongoing price-wage spiral requires political action sustained with very considerable strength, often over an extended period. It is evident that, in the circumstances prevailing in the world economy, it would not be realistic to expect the political strength that would be required to reestablish stable price and wage relationships in the majority of cases that face this type of problem. But, unfortunately, even in such cases the problem still has to be addressed. Quite often the willingness to accept a continuation of existing rates of inflation will quickly lead to an accelerating escape from monetary assets. Consequently, it must be recognized that an important effort to slow inflation should normally be a critical objective in a program of adjustment. The extent of the improvement of price performance will, of course, depend on the circumstances—in particular, on the speed with which the earlier price increases had taken place. It is quite evident too that some economies have demonstrated a remarkable tolerance for inflation, as shown by the readiness to accept its consequences for exchange rate arrangements and the structure of domestic interest rates; in these rare cases, the urgency for inflation control is clearly less marked.

There is one other point to note. In a number of member countries inflation has been repressed through controls, particularly on prices of state enterprises and imports. Such situations make it likely that an adjustment program will include a period in which corrective price adjustments will have to be undertaken with the result that recorded price increases may exceed the levels of the past. Such an adjustment strategy is quite compatible with the general aim of a later slower price advance and is a relatively frequent feature in programs supported by Fund resources.

On the related issue of the pace of adjustment, an important issue is the individual circumstances of the country in question. If the conditions indicate that the imbalances have been allowed to prevail for a protracted period of time, there is much to be said in favor of the adoption of decisive early action if only because, in order to be effective in influencing behavior, such action needs time. Moreover, in many cases the political tolerance for resolute policy measures cannot be maintained beyond a limited time, and it is important to use it to the greatest advantage while it exists. Our experience predisposes us generally to stress the importance and appropriateness of decisive early action. There are necessarily many instances, however, in which the strategies are less clearcut. If resources are available to avoid abrupt curtailments in domestic absorption, and if real wage levels do not have to be reduced in the process of adjustment, there is, of course, a good basis for adopting a firm but gradual approach to adjustment. It may be noted here, however, that these are not by any means the characteristics most common to the situations in which Fund assistance is requested.

In designing a policy program, the most time-consuming process is undoubtedly the determination of the mix of specific actions that will be undertaken to manage aggregate demand and to stimulate the recovery of production. The variety of factors—political and economic—to be taken into account for this purpose necessitates the most careful examination of alternative courses of action and, naturally, makes the choices highly dependent on the particular circumstances of the case. Nevertheless, our experience does suggest that a number of generalizations can be made.

In virtually all cases, the whole spectrum of policy action has to be reviewed. It is rare indeed that corrective action can be limited to only one area without need for reinforcing action in other areas. In the more serious situations of imbalance, there is need for restraining aggregate demand; for changing the structure of incentives by adjusting exchange rate, interest rate, and price policies; and for reexamining the investment priorities in order to redirect scarce investment resources along more efficient lines. This last aspect is being given increased emphasis in recent programs because of the structural factors in payments imbalance and the fact that in many developing countries the bulk of investment is carried out in the public sector. While adjustment of relative costs and prices provides a better guide to decisions on resource allocation, direct action is frequently needed in the near term to remove supply bottlenecks by tapping existing productive potential and by speeding up the completion of the more productive projects. In a number of countries this involves a substantial modification of existing development programs that frequently are well beyond the limits of foreseeable resources. In these areas the Fund is acting in close collaboration with the World Bank, so that the adjustment programs supported by the Fund are consistent with the investment needs of the economy.

Turning now to specific policies, we feel that major contributions to the adjustment effort frequently have to be made by means of a reduction in subsidies of various types. This is not to say that subsidies always have to be eliminated. Their complete elimination is very rare and it is often likely that some subsidies will increase to keep some of the more undesirable aspects of the impact of the adjustment within acceptable bounds. But there is little question that in many economies in difficulty, existing subsidies—usually in the form of losses on the operation of state enterprises—are a critical element contributing to the weakness of the economic performance in general, and of the public sector finances in particular. Thus, for budgetary reasons, quite apart from the issue of the establishment of adequate incentives, the whole gamut of subsidies has to be examined in detail. In many instances, the growth of subsidies over time can be explained as part of an attempt to mask the deterioration of economic conditions. Whether that deterioration results from exogenous causes, such as a rise in energy prices, is not the relevant factor in this context; rather the permanent or transitory nature of the imbalance will determine the need for and the extent of adjustment. It is virtually impossible to improve the external payments position without directly facing these issues and seeing that the cost borne by the economy is passed to the consumer.

In the course of reviewing the cost of subsidies, the efficiency of operations of the state enterprises frequently arises as an issue. It often becomes apparent that charging a cost that would provide for financial balance would be an imposition on the consumer because the operating efficiency of the state enterprises has deteriorated over time for reasons that generally can be described as pressures of a political nature. Closer Fund-Bank collaboration has already been noted; this is an area where problems that we face call for assistance of other agencies, notably the World Bank. The appropriate degree of coordination, however, often takes a considerable amount of time and effort on the part of the institutions and members' authorities.

For this reason it is not easy to ensure such coordination where immediate action is needed.

Tax decisions are another relatively frequent element in programs supported by the Fund. The scope for tax increases is often available when progress is made in the exchange rate and import control areas. An exchange rate adjustment frequently is of a magnitude that allows for the possibility of taxation of unexpected increases in income of export agencies; the higher valuation base in local currency also enlarges receipts from import duties. Relaxation of import controls can also open tax revenue possibilities. Notably, if limited volumes of luxury goods become available, they can frequently be taxed at high rates. Unfortunately, for essentially political reasons, the possibility of such action is quite limited.

At this point it might be useful to digress briefly on the attitude that the Fund has taken with respect to multiple exchange rates and export subsidies. While the Fund, by its charter, does not welcome such devices, they will be found to exist in a number of programs. In particular, there are a number of occasions on which a dual market has been accepted as an interim arrangement toward the initiation of exchange rate flexibility. If a part of exports can be transferred to an efficient market, many of the appropriate incentive effects begin to operate, and the proceeds can then be used to permit imports that were kept out because of foreign exchange shortage. Equally, export subsidies can on occasion be used to start the movement to greater emphasis on investment in the export sector. The transitory nature of these expedients, however, must be stressed. Investment in export industries on the desired scale requires the assurance that comes from an adequate return at a realistic exchange rate—not that conveyed by a possible temporary political privilege. Finally, order in world trading is dependent on working within a well-defined system of generally accepted rules, which normally cannot be expected to be based on individually decided subsidies.

Returning now to the problems of budgeting, we have found that a critical element in all plans has turned out to be the wages for the public sector employees. It is impossible to act on subsidies and the exchange rate without also facing the issue of the implication that these have for wage policy. In this area the issue of proper timing of action is particularly important. It is essential that public opinion be prepared for the wage adjustment to be made, and this necessarily involves time. The authorities must be the sole judges of this particular aspect of the program, but, of course, the Fund has a responsibility to formulate a judgment and determine when adequate adjustment action has been taken. The need for a judgment of this nature can, of course, lead to increasing pressure on the authorities to act. Sometimes the difficulty can be overcome by the provision of outside assistance by friendly governments. But the tensions involved in some negotiations are real and undoubtedly can give rise to some resentment at the apparent unwillingness of the Fund to support a member's strategy.

This argument leads into the issue of whether the Fund should be involved in providing financing in all cases, even when the resources given would simply be used in an unsuccessful attempt to ensure the political survival of a government, leaving an incoming administration with a debt to the Fund that had been incurred for no lasting purpose. There will certainly be a number of cases where it would be inappropriate for the Fund to enter into an agreement leading to use of its resources. There has to be a readiness on both sides to help establish conditions in which the resources can be most constructively used.

Having said all of this, it needs to be stressed that even in the most difficult of circumstances there is potential for recovery. In fact, it may well be that it is when the most disorderly conditions prevail that the recovery can be most rapid. The issue at stake in deciding on Fund intervention is solely one of timing, of waiting until the political conditions have reached the stage to permit the authorities to implement action that gives reasonable assurance that the Fund resources will be used in support of appropriate policies, and that they can be repaid within the prescribed period.

In concluding, this paper has touched on some of the major issues likely to be raised in the course of this conference. This introduction of our attitudes and experience, based as they are on the generality of cases, has to be unavoidably brief, but the concrete examples that are to be discussed will provide the opportunity to supplement the points made above. It is to be hoped that some conclusions emerging from this conference will be useful to us and to the authorities of our member countries in these difficult times. There are few more challenging tasks than to improve the ability of those in charge of economic policy decisions to cope with the desperate problems their countries face.

CHAPTER 5

World Bank Financing Of Structural Adjustment

Ernest Stern

Since the early 1970s the developing countries have faced a difficult and volatile international economic environment in which major developments seem to be neither transitory nor cyclical. Countries have adjusted to the resulting marked deterioration in their balance of payments through increased borrowing, expansion of exports, increased import substitution, and lower growth rates. As the 1981 *World Development Report*[1] points out, oil-importing countries were quite successful in adjusting without reducing their rates of growth, with the exception of low-income countries in sub-Saharan Africa. But the process of adjustment is becoming increasingly difficult. The previous rapid expansion of debt has limited the net incremental borrowing capacity of a number of countries. Trade growth has slowed while, simultaneously, more countries emphasize export development. The opportunities for easy import substitution have been increasingly exploited, and further progress may involve relatively heavy investment. Having exhausted these externally oriented adjustment factors, a great many more developing countries will likely be forced to accept lower growth, or no growth, in the next several years as the primary means of adjusting to the international economic environment.

Slow growth and high interest rates have created a much less favorable investment climate, making it more difficult for a country to achieve a rapid adjustment in its production structure. The adverse external trends have been compounded in many instances by inap-

[1] World Bank, *World Development Report, 1981* (New York: Oxford University Press, August 1981), ch. 6.

propriate domestic policies and weak institutions that are incapable of adapting promptly to changing circumstances. For example, external inflationary pressures from the rapid increase in the cost of imported manufactures have often been intensified by an expansionary domestic monetary policy. Export growth has been handicapped by overvalued exchange rates, inadequate price incentives for producers, and the mismanagement of agencies handling credit, marketing, and export promotion. Mobilization of domestic resources has been undermined by negative real interest rates.

Some developing countries postponed domestic policy reforms, or introduced them only slowly, and relied instead on increased external borrowing. In others, government sought to offset constraints imposed by external factors or uncertainty on the part of private investors through increased deficit financing to expand public sector investment programs. But as economic activity slowed down and external capital flows, both commercial and concessional, became less buoyant, the costs of such partial adjustments became increasingly severe. This was reflected in growing expenditures on subsidies and in unsustainable budget deficits. To limit inflation and control the balance of payments deficit, some of the countries then resorted to price controls and import restrictions, which led to a misallocation of resources and to an incentive system biased against exporters.

Remedial actions at this stage are often politically difficult because the degree of change needed is large. Moreover, the economic effects can be seriously perverse. Efforts to reduce credit expansion can, unless accompanied by other policies, squeeze out the private sector at the expense of the public. Reductions in overall investment may leave a disproportionate share of large, public sector projects of long gestation while reducing investments in quick-yielding activities. Reductions in public expenditures may easily result in cutting back on such essential investments as education and health while safeguarding steel mills, or in reducing expenditures on maintenance of plant and infrastructure rather than reducing subsidies. Even where reductions in public investment are undertaken, both scarcity of relevant data and political commitments make it extraordinarily difficult to prune selectively, rather than to cut across the board, thereby delaying the productive benefits from a wide range of investments.

The objective for the developing countries must be to introduce policy changes to permit a reduction in the current account deficit over the next several years while minimizing the penalties to growth in the long run, hence allowing continued progress toward the achievement of their development objectives. Because some of the mitigating mechanisms, such as external borrowing, have been used extensively, and because delays in action have exacerbated problems of pricing and subsidies, a complex set of changes in policies and incentives are now required. It is to support such changes that the World Bank developed its program of structural adjustment lending.

There is, without doubt, considerable scope for strengthening economic management. Structural adjustment lending is intended to assist governments to adopt necessary, though often politically difficult, policy and institutional reforms designed to improve the efficiency of resource use. By focusing on the policy and institutional reforms required to correct distortions in the pattern of incentives and to adapt each economy to the changed international price structure and trading opportunities, structural adjustment lending also helps create a more appropriate environment for the Bank's project lending. In this way, the two forms of assistance are complementary, not alternatives.

Rationale for Structural Adjustment Lending

In response to the increasing severity of the balance of payments problems faced by its members and the related need for assistance—both in financing and in policy analysis and formulation—the Bank proposed to initiate a program of structural adjustment loans (SAL) at its Annual Meeting in September 1979. This new form of lending would:

- support a program of specific policy changes and institutional reforms designed to reduce the current account deficit to sustainable levels
- assist a country in meeting the transitional costs of structural changes in industry and agriculture by augmenting the supply of freely usable foreign exchange
- act as a catalyst for the inflow of other external capital to help ease the balance of payments situation.

It was clear from the outset that the issues faced by individual countries would vary greatly, as would the institutional and management capacity to deal with them. Consequently, the specifics of the structural adjustment programs would vary among countries. Many countries would have to undertake programs of financial discipline to moderate or reduce the level of aggregate demand for goods and services in order to bring their current account deficit to levels that could be supported more realistically by external capital flows. Such programs could be supported by the International Monetary Fund

(IMF), particularly through the use of its extended Fund facility (EFF). But merely reducing aggregate demand was not enough. Unless stabilization measures were accompanied by specific actions, at both the operating and policy levels, that were designed to make more effective use of productive capacity and to reduce aggregate demand in ways consistent with development objectives, the cost in growth forgone was likely to be excessive, and the imbalances were likely to recur when growth resumed. Thus, from the outset Bank lending for structural adjustment assumed the existence of a stabilization program, normally supported by a Fund stand-by or EFF arrangement, which would provide the foundation for more detailed measures to improve incentives, eliminate distortions, promote production, and increase the efficiency of resource use.

The structural adjustment programs might involve a variety of sectors and policy issues. Although in many developing countries it is possible to work out limits for budgetary expenditures and credit controls, there are few countries that have the data and the analytic capacity to trace the specific impact of such changes on the economy. Countries as advanced as Turkey and Brazil lack consolidated accounts of public investment programs; others may even lack financial statements accurately reflecting performance in the most recent years. Financial requirements for public investment projects may only be known in the most general terms for a budget year. Yet, if the external payments problem is not merely temporary, limiting public investment without understanding the longer term impact on production and incentives may lower demand, but it will result in limited structural change.

Similarly, in limiting noninvestment expenditures, it is important to follow a set of priorities that reflect explicit development objectives rather than to reduce expenditures across the board. For instance, despite overall stringency it may well be that expenditures for agricultural extension and research should be expanded, rather than curtailed, if there are prospects for a rapid increase in production. And often there is scope for providing services such as education and health at lower unit cost, thereby avoiding a reduction in service levels despite reduced funding.

The same requirement for detailed analysis, leading to the design of soundly based action programs, exists in the areas of exports. It is, of course, essential that the exchange rate be realistic and that interest rates reflect the scarcity of capital, matters that are typically a central concern of the Fund. But beyond these issues lies a range of concerns: the relative roles of the public and private sector; the responsibility and capacity of governments to organize and control markets; the process and criteria by which the structure and level of agricultural prices are set; the tariff, licensing, and incentive schemes that determine the composition and location of industrial investment; the appropriate structure of energy prices to bring about desired levels of conservation; and the infrastructure—both physical and institutional—that is required, in addition to incentives, to expand exports and support investors in new, less capital-intensive areas.

Distortions in the policy and allocation framework that were undesirable in the 1960s have become unsustainable in the much more difficult international economic environment of the 1980s. The flexibility to cushion the impact of change, to move gradually on politically contested reforms in the context of fragile political structures, and at the same time to avoid further reducing the incomes of already very poor people was gradually exhausted. Today policymakers have little room for maneuver. It can be argued that governments should have acted sooner; indeed, some countries have exhibited a remarkable unwillingness to come to grips with these issues, an unwillingness often combined with an inadequate understanding of the scope of the problem. But the risk of political failure in implementing the more urgently required actions is now much greater. It is the acceptance of the more urgent requirement for change—not the need for changes nor, often, the specifics of change—that is the new element. That present policies are proving unsustainable has given rise in some countries to a willingness to reexamine basic premises and development strategies that was absent before and makes feasible a public call for increased sacrifices in the face of political opposition.

Structural adjustment lending enables the Bank to address basic issues of economic management and development strategy more directly and more urgently than before. The advantage of SALs over alternative lending instruments derives from three features of SAL operations: the comprehensiveness of their coverage in terms of both macro and sector issues of policy reform; the exclusive focus on policy and institutional reform; and the detailed articulation of the precise modifications in policy necessary to adjust the economy to a changed economic environment.

Design of Structural Adjustment Lending Operations

In brief, the objective is to support—by means of a series of (possibly three or four) discrete lending operations over a period of approximately five years—measures specifically designed to strengthen countries' balances of payments over the medium term (i.e., within a five-year to seven-year time frame).

SALs normally address both macro and sector issues of policy and institutional reform. For macro policy, SAL operations typically cover agreement on the size and composition of the public investment program and often specify important components of recurrent expenditure. Precise changes in the institutional arrangements, procedures, and criteria by which public development expenditure programs are determined and implemented are also typically part of the agreement. In addition, SAL agreements would also cover policies required to mobilize resources for development purposes. As regards sector coverage, SALs cover the directly productive sectors of agriculture and industry as well as the energy sector. Within each of these sectors the approach is generally sector-wide, although the SAL agreement might include understandings on subsectoral policies as part of the sector-wide approach.

Because the level of development, current situation, prospects, and policital framework vary from country to country, the Bank has stressed that there can be no single model to guide adjustment. Although the objective is the same in all countries in which structural adjustment lending is considered, the content of programs would vary. The main features of structural adjustment programs have evolved on a case-by-case basis. To date, 12 countries have received such assistance. Although the Bank's experience with the implementation of the structural adjustment programs is as yet limited, it is already possible to discern some of the strengths and weaknesses of this form of assistance. The scope and variety of the structural adjustment programs so far supported by the Bank is summarized in Table 5.1.

The structural adjustment programs comprise three distinct elements. First, the SAL programs set out a statement of specific structural objectives to be achieved over an approximate period of five-to-seven years; for example, increasing nontraditional exports, reducing levels of protection, removing export bias in incentive systems, expanding incentives for private investment, reducing the rate of growth of total energy use and of imported energy by given amounts, and increasing agricultural output.

Second, the SAL programs present a statement of the measures that will be taken over an approximate five-year period to achieve the adjustment objectives. These might include reforming the pattern and level of industrial protection to erase its anti-export bias and to make industry more efficient by stimulating those subsectors in which the country has a comparative advantage and by subjecting manufacturers to greater external competition; increasing the real price of energy and also the pattern of energy pricing to conserve energy and to increase domestic supplies in an efficient manner; modifying the internal terms of trade of the agricultural sector of the economy; undertaking major changes in the organization of agricultural marketing, including the respective roles of the public and private sectors, and so on.

The third component of a SAL program is a set of specific actions, to be taken by a government and monitored by the Bank, either before approval of the SAL operation by the Bank's Board or during the following 12 to 18 months. Each loan typically is provided in two tranches in order to establish a formal opportunity for reviewing implementation of the adjustment program in general and to consider progress in carrying out specific key measures identified in advance. The monitorable program of actions might include the first (or subsequent) actions to modify tariffs, to strengthen export incentive schemes, to remove quantitative restrictions on imports and exports, and to introduce industrial investment incentive schemes. Similarly, in energy and agriculture there may be agreement on a precise set of monitorable actions relating to prices and institutional agreements. These monitorable programs embody detailed actions for both policy changes and institutional reforms that a government obligates itself to implement according to an agreed timetable. To the extent that some of the precise actions can only be defined after further study, the terms of reference and timetable for such studies are incorporated in the monitorable program. Actions based on the findings of these studies would form part of subsequent SALs.

Because the strengthening of the balance of payments over the medium- to long-term is the fundamental aim of structural adjustment lending, programs to date have covered a broad range of policies related to the more efficient use of resources in the key sectors (see Table 5.1). The measures mainly fall within four areas: (1) *the restructuring of incentives,* which covers pricing policies, tariff reforms, taxation, budget subsidies, and interest rate policy; (2) the revision of *public investment* priorities in light of the changed international price structure and resource availabilities; (3) improvement in *budget and debt management;* and (4) the *strengthening of institutions,* particularly public enterprises. Each program is a combination of complementary and mutually reinforcing measures.

Structure of Incentives

A frequent concern—especially for middle-income countries—has been to reduce the bias that has crept into the industrial incentive

TABLE 5.1 SCOPE AND VARIETY OF STRUCTURAL ADJUSTMENT PROGRAMS SUPPORTED BY THE WORLD BANK

Item	*Senegal*	*Turkey*[a]	*Guyana*	*Kenya*	*Bolivia*	*Philippines*	*Mauritius*	*Malawi*	*Ivory Coast*	*Korea*	*Thailand*
Trade policy											
Exchange rate policy		X			X						
Tariff reform and import liberalization	X	X		X		X					
Export incentives and improved institutional support	X	X	X	X		X	X	X	X	X	X
Sector policies											
Energy											
Pricing policy		X	X		X		X	X		X	X
Conservation measures		X	X							X	X
Development of indigenous sources		X	X				X			X	
Agriculture											
Pricing policy	X	X	X		X		X	X	X	X	X
Improved institutional support (marketing, etc.)	X	X					X	X	X		X
Industry											
Incentive system	X	X		X		X	X			X	X
Institutional improvements and subsector programs		X	X			X	X	X		X	

Public investment program										
Revision and review of structural priorities	X	X	X	X	X	X	X	X	X	
Strengthening of institutional capacity to formulate and implement public investment program	X		X				X	X		X
Public sector enterprises										
Financial performance	X	X	X		X		X		X	X
Institutional efficiency	X	X			X		X		X	
Resource mobilization										
Budget policy	X	X	X	X			X		X	X
Interest rate policy		X	X	X			X		X	
Debt management										
Strengthening of institutional capacity to manage external borrowing	X	X	X	X	X	X	X	X		

Source: World Bank.

a. Includes two structural adjustment loans to Turkey.

systems. High tariffs and import controls have often encouraged high-cost production for import substitution and have, therefore, been biased against exporting. SALs have incorporated agreement to phase out quantitative import restrictions and to modify the level and structure of tariffs, export subsidies, and excise and sales taxes in order to equalize the incentives for production for both the export and domestic markets. For example, the Philippine structural adjustment program aims to even out the effective rates of protection and to liberalize trade with the objective of stimulating a radical improvement in industrial efficiency. Reforms are also being introduced to reduce or to simplify administrative procedures that have obstructed exports. These measures will encourage Philippine industry to become increasingly competitive in both domestic and foreign markets; they not only will benefit local consumers but also will serve as a precondition for achieving sustained growth of output and employment in this sector. However, given the existence of an industrial structure built up behind protectionist barriers, transitional measures are also required to assist in the rehabilitation or phasing out of uncompetitive plants.

For most structural adjustment programs, revised prices are crucial to foster production in the agricultural sector. Substantial empirical evidence exists that farmers respond well to price incentives, yet in many countries producer prices have been allowed to fall well below export or import parity prices. Under SAL operations, the Bank has frequently sought agreement on price changes in both output and input prices and the related tax and subsidy arrangements. In addition, criteria have been established for determining the level and structure of agricultural prices. For example, improved price incentives to stimulate food production, both for the domestic market and for export, were a key feature of the SAL programs in Bolivia, Guyana, and Senegal.

Although most structural adjustment programs give priority to reforms relating to agriculture and industry, problems in other productive sectors have been addressed. In Bolivia, for example, mining taxation was modified to provide greater incentives for investment in new mines and to encourage existing mines to exploit marginal ore bodies. Incentives to stimulate both energy conservation and import substitution are also, at least in part, a pricing issue—to ensure that domestic fuel prices adequately reflect international prices. In Bolivia, the price of oil produced locally was raised to encourage fuel conservation and, hence, to raise export earnings. Higher fuel prices also provide an added incentive for oil and coal exploration.

Public Investment

A critical review of public investment programs is an integral part of most structural adjustment programs, with priority being given to projects that will ease the foreign exchange constraint. The most obvious examples are investments in hydroelectric power, oil exploration, and the expansion of export crops. Often, too, the level of public investment has to be cut back to match reduced resource availabilities. Considerable attention was given to the structure and size of public investment, for example, in the Turkey SAL. In this case the shortage of investment funds had led to cuts across the board in many of the ongoing projects, whereas what was needed was selectivity and careful attention to priorities determined in the context of the objectives of the structural adjustment program.

The public sector too often makes investment decisions without adequate attention to the likely economic rate of return. Moreover, with a binding constraint on the balance of payments, project analysis needs to assume a realistic shadow price for foreign exchange that is determined within a long-term planning frame. This consideration will normally lead to preference being given to the more quickly gestating projects, which are more capital saving and more employment creating. Unfortunately, many countries lack well-staffed and authoritative units within their government to undertake the required rigorous project evaluation. Thus, strengthening the planning capacity has also been a feature of several programs.

Budget and Debt Management

Although it has been important to reduce budget deficits to achieve greater financial stability, the expenditure items to be reduced must be carefully chosen to ensure that the cuts have the minimum adverse effect on productive activities. It must be remembered that inadequate maintenance of infrastructure has often created production bottlenecks, and reducing operating expenses may be more expensive in the short term than reducing capital outlays. Moreover, it may be found that expanded agricultural production will depend on improved agricultural services, as was the case in the Kenya SAL. Achieving the objective of expanded production to save or earn foreign exchange while containing or reducing the budget deficit requires selective cutbacks to shift expenditure away from nondevelopmental activities. One approach is to target welfare programs and consumer subsidies more sharply on the needy, as well as to seek ways of reducing unit costs of social programs; another is to take a hard look at nondevelopmental expenditure (e.g., military and administrative services).

With the high levels of debt prevalent in so many countries, careful attention must be paid to the character of the foreign debt. Debt restructuring has been a precondition for several SALs, and in one case (Mauritius) a clear understanding on debt policy was incorporated in the SAL program. In these matters the Bank has worked particularly closely with the Fund; the Bank, through its debt-recording system and related technical assistance, has played an important institution-building role.

Institutional Reform

Recognizing that many of the management problems in developing countries stem from weak institutions, structural adjustment lending has given special emphasis to institutional reform. For example, agricultural pricing incentives are not likely to be effective unless measures have also been introduced to improve marketing, access to credit, and the supply of tools, seed, fertilizer, and pesticides. In Senegal the SAL program provided for major reform of the agricultural parastatal enterprises, including exposing state marketing organizations to competition from the private sector to encourage efficiency.

Since parastatal organizations often enjoy a monopoly, their mismanagement can constitute a major bottleneck to production. An important component of Turkey's program involves the progressive reform of state economic enterprises by introducing tighter financial discipline, more economic staffing, and greater managerial autonomy. Other examples of institutional reforms include measures to improve agricultural extension services in Turkey and to provide better credit and insurance facilities for exporters in Kenya and the Philippines. In the case of the Ivory Coast SAL, agreement was reached on a whole series of measures to improve public investment planning. Finally, establishing better systems for maintaining external debt records—for example, in Kenya and Turkey—was also seen to be essential for sound financial management.

The Phasing of Structural Adjustment

It is recognized that structural change can only take place over a period of several years. Modifications to the productive structure depend to a large extent on new investment. This process is inevitably slowed down when the rate of investment is reduced as a consequence of short-term balance of payments constraints. Furthermore, in periods of economic difficulty there is likely to be political resistance to reforms that entail short-term costs, as may be the case with reforms of the system of industrial protection. In this context, structural adjustment lending serves both to initiate reforms and to maintain their momentum—hence the need for a series of SAL operations spaced over several years.

The precise scheduling of reforms is clearly a matter of judgment for each country, with the political preference normally being to postpone painful decisions. While this is understandable, the Bank, as an international financial institution, has a responsibility to assess whether the scope and timing of the program of reform that it is asked to support will be adequate to achieve the government's goals of adjustment.

Nature of SAL Conditionality

It follows from the earlier discussion that the Bank must reach a firm understanding with each government on the monitorable action programs, specifying both the steps to be taken and the studies required as a basis for further progress. The practice is for this understanding to be spelled out in detail in a Letter of Development Policies that is explicitly referred to in the loan agreement. The tranching of disbursement involves the identification of a few key actions that are specified as preconditions for the release of the second tranche. However, satisfactory progress on the implementation of the overall program is also a requirement.

While this procedure may be called "conditionality," it is in principle no different from the relationship involved in Bank sector or project lending. The action programs for structural adjustment are of course different in scope from the issues dealt with in most projects, and they often involve policy matters in sectors in which there is no project lending. There will be many countries for which structural change is necessary, but for which there will be no basis for structural adjustment lending because of political constraints faced by the government or because of institutional weaknesses that would make the implementation of broad policy changes unduly uncertain. In many of these cases, there nonetheless would remain a sound and valid basis for project financing.

Key Issues

The introduction of structural adjustment lending has led to protracted discussions among member countries. Three key issues frequently raised are: (1) the roles of the Bank and Fund, (2) project versus nonproject lending, and (3) additionality in the flow of external capital assistance. These are briefly addressed below.

Roles of the Bank and Fund

The Bank's structural adjustment lending clearly interfaces with the Fund's stabilization programs and extended facility arrangements. Both institutions now provide funds that are available to finance a broad range of imports, and both impose conditionality that requires the development of action programs focused on policy and management issues. The Fund is increasingly taking into account considerations of supply as well as demand management, and its programs now have a medium-term perspective. The Bank, for its part, is acutely aware that effective long-term development programs cannot be undertaken by a country that is disrupted by an immediate financial crisis. In such cases priority must be given to stabilization measures. Experience over the past two years has shown that the Bank's SALs and the IMF programs are in practice both complementary and mutually reinforcing.

Though both institutions share the same ultimate aim—to foster broadly based growth in incomes and employment in their member countries—they nonetheless have distinct roles and pursue distinct operational objectives. The immediate focus of the Fund's attention is primarily the country's overall financial situation, while the Bank's central preoccupation is primarily the efficiency of resource use in the productive sectors. In practice both institutions, each from its respective vantage point, will have views about the appropriateness of the key elements of a country's economic policy. For example, both will be concerned that the exchange rate should not become overvalued, since this will have an impact not only immediately on the balance of payments, but also in the medium term on the structure of production that will be determined by the price structure, which in turn reflects the exchange rate. Another example is subsidies. The Fund often advocates reducing subsidies to state enterprises to limit the budget deficit. The Bank's complementary objective is to encourage the enterprise to operate more efficiently.

The nature of the structural changes required provides in large measure the answer to the question of the respective roles of the Bank and the Fund and of the connection between Fund conditionality and the policy actions agreed to by the Bank. It is not, as is sometimes simplistically suggested, that one institution is concerned with macroeconomic issues while the other is concerned with microeconomic issues. The case of Ghana demonstrates, if any demonstration of the obvious is needed, that development cannot proceed when exchange rates are seriously out of line for prolonged periods. Equally, a stabilization program is not likely to succeed if domestic energy prices differ markedly from border prices or if agricultural prices result in insufficient incentive to produce. It is similarly obvious that many policy measures will have an impact on both demand and the volume and pattern of supply. Changes in interest rates affect aggregate demand and individual investment decisions; increasing prices of food may reduce subsidies and increase incentives to producers. There are a multitude of similar examples.

There has been, and to some extent still is, a difference in the time horizons of the Bank and the Fund. However, this difference is becoming less as account is taken of the medium-term nature of the balance of payments problem of the developing countries. Providing EFF resources with eight- to ten-year maturities focuses the Fund's attention not only on the actions agreed for the first three years, but also on the repayment capacity of the country for the next five.

The complementarity between Fund arrangements and action programs supported by the Bank's structural adjustment lending derives from two factors. The first has already been alluded to—structural adjustment can only take place effectively in the context of actions to limit aggregate demand and, where necessary, external borrowing. Thus, conditions adequate to permit access to Fund resources are usually a prerequisite to a detailed program of structural change. Second, as a consequence of the distinct mandates of the institutions, their respective staffs have different specializations.

The Fund, when it deals with prices—for example, of oil, foodgrains, or parastatal products—is concerned with the effect on aggregate public expenditure and on the distributional aspects of such expenditures. But such changes are not only often highly controversial politically, they also require specialized technical and economic knowledge to be implemented effectively. Changing the price of a principal crop when it is markedly out of line is relatively easy in the direction and initial order of magnitude required, but account must also be taken of the impact on the overall cropping pattern, on the balance of land use between domestic and export crops, on the capacity of the market system to assure the producer the price agreed on, and on the supporting services and supplies that will help to translate better incentives into higher production. It is in these areas, including the associated institutional issues, that the Bank can help to define programs that will not only support the stabilization objective, but that will also enable the country to expand output.

Similar considerations apply to such goals as eliminating parastatal deficits and further improving their performance to the point where the parastatal enterprises contribute to national savings by generating financial surpluses. Obviously, one important aspect of such a reform is its impact on the budget and government savings. But agreement on the objective, even when accompanied by agreement on greater price freedom and a more commercially oriented operation, will not ensure long-term institutional change. Managers who have grown up in a framework of controlled prices and access to budget funds or deficit financing are likely to have neither the capacity nor the tools nor the data to align prices with marginal costs, to reduce unit costs in a sensible manner, or to define their investment priorities in terms of market demand and competition. In the absence of programs to deal with these deficiencies, they will reduce investments, and possibly operating deficits, but these will recur as soon as conditions improve sufficiently to permit relaxation of the financial restraints. To translate the general objectives into permanent changes requires programs at the plant level to assist managers in developing analytical and monitoring systems, administrative and managerial policies, financial and accounting systems, and appraisal and marketing capacity quite different from the present ones. At times it may also require different managers. The Bank's staff is equipped to assist countries in these areas precisely because they involve the same expertise that the Bank has furnished and continues to furnish in its project operations.

In summary, the fundamental distinction to be made between the roles of the Bank and the Fund is not that of objectives, nor that one institution is concerned with the short term and the other with the long term, one with macroeconomic issues and the other with microeconomic issues, or one with monetary and financial aspects and the other with real resources. On the contrary, the difference lies primarily in the orientation of each institution's staff and the experience and expertise it is capable of mustering.

An important difference also arises in the procedures of the Bank and Fund. These reflect the difference in the nature and scope of each institution's operations. The Fund's involvement is restricted to a single type of operation—balance of payments support—with relatively infrequent and limited staff visits to a country, whereas the Bank has many missions relating to a wide range of operations. Fund support is generally, though not always, seen as a rescue operation in response to a crisis. In these circumstances, failure of a Fund arrangement is likely to have grave consequences for a country's international creditworthiness. The Bank's individual SAL operations have a much lower profile and are negotiated at a less intense pace. The consequences of failure to reach agreement are therefore much less serious. In these circumstances, negotiations tend to be less confrontational, and it may be possible for the Bank to achieve a more fundamental government commitment to reform.

Given the commonality of their interest but their different mandates, it is vitally important for the Bank and Fund to work together to harmonize policy advice. For this reason increased efforts have been made to ensure that Bank and Fund staff collaborate closely in the analysis of policy issues. In the process, a clear division of labor has arisen whereby each institution contributes in the areas where it has special expertise and is recognized as having the lead role. Over the past three years, the number of missions with staff participation from both institutions has more than doubled. In documents submitted to the Bank's Board, the position of the Fund is always clearly set out, and the Fund has adopted a similar practice.

Another issue often raised in defining the Bank's and Fund's distinct roles is whether balance of payments support should not be left to the Fund, implying that Bank financial assistance should exclusively take the form of project and sector lending. The argument against this has been set out above in the discussion on the rationale for structural adjustment lending. Nonetheless, it must be reemphasized that the primary purpose of a SAL is not to fill a current account deficit but to support a medium-term program of changes necessary to reorient the economy and to bring its current account deficit to a more sustainable level over a number of years. Of course, as do the disbursements under project loans, the disbursements under structural adjustment loans add to the country's external capital flows.

Project vs Nonproject Lending

Related to the concern about the respective roles of the Fund and the Bank is the proposition that the Bank should rely exclusively on project lending. The question is often asked why it has not been possible for the Bank to address key policy issues in the project context—or why it could not do so in the future. Of course, the issues that require attention today are not new, nor have they remained unidentified in most countries. Bank reports are replete with problems of subsidies, distorted incentives, unrealistic interest rates, excessive public deficits, and inefficient parastatal operations. Nor was the Bank merely crying in the wilderness, as some would suggest who view the depth of change required today. Producer prices were raised in many countries, agricultural services strengthened, operating subsidies reduced or abolished, tariffs raised to make public utilities viable—and there is a long list of countries where, at Bank insistence, interest rates have been raised repeatedly to ensure that they are at positive levels. But all such changes involved difficult political decisions, and the pace of change was modest.

Yet it has not been possible to achieve the same degree of comprehensive coverage of structural adjustment policies through project lending. A project operation is typically related to one subsector (e.g., a power project in the energy sector or a palm oil project in the agricultural sector), which inevitably limits the scope for taking a broad sectoral view. For understandable reasons, the less directly the policy issues are related to the project being financed and to the subsector of which it is a part, the greater the difficulty in both reaching agreement initially on these policy issues and subsequently ensuring that they are implemented. Sector lending—defined as an operation in which the Bank finances a slice of the sector investment program—provides greater opportunity to address broad sectoral policy issues. But in many countries the Bank is involved in only a limited number of sectors. Even in those countries where this is not the case, loans in each sector are typically spaced over three or more years. Given the low probability that the Bank would have a concurrent series of project or sector operations in all sectors in which the policy issues are important for structural adjustment, structural adjustment lending provides a unique opportunity to achieve a comprehensive and timely approach to policy reform.

Although Bank project operations have contained important covenants spanning the whole spectrum (from detailed technical, administrative, and financial issues relating to the project, through subsectoral policy and institutional issues, and on occasion sectoral policy), for obvious operational reasons priority is given to the immediate project objectives. In contrast, SAL conditionality is related entirely to issues of macroeconomic and sectoral policies. It raises the level of dialogue to the highest ranks of government and provides a single focus that helps ensure that adequate attention is given to the program's prompt implementation. Whereas in project lending, the Bank will typically be dealing with agencies or sectoral ministries, SALs are always the concern of the key government decisionmakers. The commitment to a series of operations spaced at 12–18 month intervals, and with tranching of each loan or credit, makes the monitoring of policy implementation a continuous process. The availability of SAL funds is made entirely dependent on progress in implementing policy reform.

Additionality for Structural Adjustment Lending

Although the SALs are intended to support much needed programs of structural change, it is sometimes suggested that such lending must be additional to the Bank's regular lending. It is argued that, if structural adjustment lending were to result in a noticeable reduction in project lending (i.e., if it is not additive), governments would be discouraged from negotiating SALs. There is no doubt that, despite the need to restrict investment levels in many countries, the investment requirements for increased energy self-sufficiency, for reorienting the industrial structure, and for making more effective use of existing capacity are considerable. There is justification, therefore, for increased Bank lending to countries prepared to undertake major structural change. However, in determining the global planning figure for Bank Group lending, current constraints have made it difficult to add a specific allowance for structural adjustment lending. Thus, although for Bank borrowers as a whole there is no explicit additionality because weight is given to country performance in allocating Bank resources, it is possible to increase lending to a country undertaking structural change for a few years. But even when the additionality is modest, countries recognize the importance of involving the Bank in the design and support of their programs of structural change.

The size of individual SALs is determined in relation to the size of the country's borrowing program, and a judgment is made on the optimum balance between project and nonproject lending in that country (Table 5.2). Although individual SALs usually are small com-

TABLE 5.2 WORLD BANK STRUCTURAL ADJUSTMENT LENDING OPERATIONS
(million dollars)

Country	*Amount*
Kenya	55
Turkey[a]	575
Bolivia	50
Philippines	200
Senegal	60
Guyana	22
Mauritius	15
Malawi	45
Ivory Coast	150
Korea	250
Thailand	150
Jamaica	75

Source: World Bank.
a. Includes two lending operations.

pared with a country's foreign exchange gap, the total program implicit in the intent to provide a series of such loans over a five-year period usually is of the same order of magnitude as resources available under an extended Fund loan over a three-year period.

Conclusion

The Bank's project lending provides many opportunities to address specific sectoral issues. These opportunities are increasingly being exploited to assist countries to improve the policy framework for development, but there are broad policy issues that cannot be appropriately addressed in a project context. Yet, although the Fund is effectively overseeing the management of the principal macroeconomic aggregates, it lacks the functional and sectoral specialists able to analyze in depth the long-term development implications of alternative macroeconomic strategies. Nor does the Fund have the frequent staff-government contacts afforded the Bank through its economic and sector missions and its extensive project work. Structural adjustment lending provides a framework for the Bank's intensive economic dialogue. It enables the Bank to provide support for an agreed program of action to change both policies and institutions to make more effective use of resources and to increase foreign exchange availability. Through SALs and associated project lending, the Bank helps to institutionalize changes at the operating level—in both plants and agencies. Without change at that level, countries are unlikely to establish a permanent basis for accelerated growth. Thus, the Bank's structural adjustment lending complements both Fund operations and the more traditional forms of its own lending.

Structural adjustment lending is one in a whole spectrum of lending instruments. Only a minority of countries are expected to be prepared to commit themselves to the explicit set of reforms required. Many countries lack the political and technical capacity to formulate credible programs. In these cases, existing forms of project and sector lending are available to support more limited, but more manageable, progress.

The Bank's structural adjustment lending is still in a pilot stage and has given rise to some misunderstandings. There is no intention to displace project or sector lending by structural adjustment lending. But the developing countries are facing difficult problems of adjustment in the face of a drastically changed, and considerably more hostile, economic environment. The Bank, as the largest development finance institution, cannot stand aside and fail to support these adjustment efforts. Structural adjustment is the central problem of development at present, and experience has shown that SALs are an important means of assisting a country—intellectually and financially—in reorienting its development strategies.

CHAPTER **6**

Private Bank Conditionality: Comparison with the IMF And the World Bank

Irving S. Friedman

The issues revolving around "conditionality" have gained much importance and sharpness because of the very large increase in commercial bank lending to developing countries (summarized in Tables 6.1, 6.2, and 6.3). I will focus on what might be called conditionality of private banks and draw some comparison with the International Monetary Fund (IMF) and the World Bank. My main thesis is that commercial banks that do significant (for them) external lending to developing countries are evolving what is the equivalent of conditionality practiced by official national and multilateral agencies, that for many borrowing countries this conditionality of private banks is decisively important, and that official lenders and borrowers are increasingly influenced in their own actions by the conditionality of private lenders. Finally, the conditionality of official national and multilateral lenders can play a major role in the lending practices of commercial banks, but the actions and practices of official lenders cannot substitute for the conditionality of private banks and for the full responsibility and accountability of private banks for their conditionality and implementation, unless the actions of official entities include full and unqualified guarantees of the loans made by private lenders. Measures short of guarantees will influence judgments on credit and country risk, but only as important inputs into the lending decision process among other important inputs.

Banks that cannot make adequate credit and country risk judgments are compelled to rely on the judgments of other banks or to act on other criteria, like portfolio diversification or minimal mag-

TABLE 6.1 TOTAL DISBURSED EXTERNAL TERM DEBT OUTSTANDING OF DEVELOPING COUNTRIES, 1970–81
(billion dollars at year-end)

Source of lending	*1970*	*1971*	*1972*	*1973*	*1974*	*1975*	*1976*	*1977*	*1978*	*1979*	*Prel. 1980*	*Est. 1981*
Total disbursed external term debt[a]	74.7	86.6	98.2	118.9	144.6	179.1	216.9	264.6	336.6	397.3	456.2	524.0
DAC/ODA	23.1	24.7	26.0	28.6	31.0	34.3	36.5	41.4	49.0	53.1	57.0	61.0
Multilateral agencies	8.8	10.0	12.0	14.3	17.5	21.8	26.7	33.5	40.2	47.9	56.0	65.0
Capital markets[b]	12.6	16.6	22.1	33.7	44.6	57.9	76.0	95.2	127.5	154.9	180.0	209.0
Bank loans	7.6	9.4	14.1	24.0	34.4	46.9	60.6	78.7	105.7	129.9	149.9	172.0
Export credits	23.8	27.5	29.0	31.4	35.5	45.4	54.2	65.8	85.3	100.7	114.0	128.0
Other[c]	6.4	7.8	9.1	10.9	16.0	19.7	23.5	28.7	34.6	40.7	49.2	61.0
Source of lending as a percentage of total debt												
DAC/ODA	30.9	28.5	26.5	24.1	21.4	19.1	16.8	15.6	14.6	13.4	12.5	11.6
Multilateral agencies	11.8	11.5	12.2	12.0	12.1	12.1	12.3	12.7	11.9	12.1	12.3	12.4
Capital markets	16.9	19.2	22.5	28.3	30.8	32.3	35.0	36.0	37.9	39.0	39.5	39.9
Bank loans	10.2	10.8	14.4	20.2	23.8	26.1	27.9	29.7	31.4	32.3	32.7	32.8
Export credits	31.9	31.8	29.5	26.4	24.6	25.3	25.0	24.8	25.3	25.3	25.0	24.4
Other	8.6	9.0	9.3	9.2	11.1	11.0	10.8	10.8	10.3	10.2	10.8	11.6
Percentage annual increase in total debt		16	13	21	22	24	21	22	27	18	15	15

DAC Development Assistance Committee of the Organization for Economic Cooperation and Development (OECD); ODA official development assistance.
Note: Figures are for approximately 150 developing countries, including capital-surplus oil exporters.
Source: OECD, *Development Cooperation, 1981 Review* (Paris, November 1981), and OECD, *External Debt of Developing Countries* (Paris, October 1981).
a. Includes external term debt whether public, publicly guaranteed, or nonguaranteed in the borrowing country.
b. Bank loans (other than export credits), including loans through offshore centers, bonds, and other private lending.
c. Includes lending by Organization of Petroleum Exporting Countries and centrally planned economies.

TABLE 6.2 NET FLOW OF FINANCIAL RESOURCES FROM DAC COUNTRIES TO DEVELOPING COUNTRIES AND MULTILATERAL INSTITUTIONS, 1967–69 TO 1980
(net disbursements, billion dollars, current prices)

Source of flow	*Average 1967–69*	*Average 1969–71*	*1970*	*1974*	*1975*	*1976*	*1977*	*1978*	*1979*	*1980*
Total net flows	12.7	15.7	15.9	22.4	44.8	46.7	51.9	71.0	75.7	75.1
Official flows	7.0	8.1	8.1	13.8	17.7	18.1	19.1	25.3	25.1	32.1
ODA	6.4	7.1	6.9	11.6	13.8	13.9	15.7	20.0	22.4	26.8
Other	0.6	1.0	1.1	2.2	3.9	4.1	3.4	5.3	2.7	5.3
Private flows (market terms)	5.7	7.0	7.0	7.3	25.7	27.2	31.2	44.0	48.5	40.6
Direct investment	2.6	3.3	3.7	1.1	10.5	7.9	9.5	11.0	12.9	8.9
Capital markets[a]	1.5	1.4	1.2	3.7	11.0	12.6	13.4	23.0	25.5	19.2
Export credits[b]	1.5	2.3	2.2	2.5	4.2	6.8	8.3	10.0	10.0	12.6
Capital markets and export credits as a percentage of the total net flow	23.6	23.6	20.9	27.7	33.9	41.5	41.8	46.5	46.9	42.3
Grants by private voluntary agencies	—	0.6	0.9	1.3	1.3	1.4	1.5	1.7	2.0	2.4

—Not available.
Note: Figures are for approximately 150 developing countries.
Source: OECD, *Development Cooperation, 1981 Review* (Paris, November 1981).
a. Mostly bank lending from banks resident in DAC countries, but excluding lending by offshore subsidiaries of these banks.
b. The bulk of which, however, is officially guaranteed in capital-exporting countries.

TABLE 6.3 TOTAL ANNUAL DEBT SERVICE OF DEVELOPING COUNTRIES, BY SOURCE OF LENDING, 1970–81
(billion dollars)

Source of lending	*1970*	*1971*	*1972*	*1973*	*1974*	*1975*	*1976*	*1977*	*1978*	*1979*	*Prel. 1980*	*Est. 1981*
DAC countries and capital markets	8.0	9.3	11.6	15.1	19.0	22.5	27.5	35.3	49.8	64.6	79.9	98.3
DAC/ODA	1.3	1.4	1.6	1.7	1.7	1.8	1.9	2.0	2.3	2.6	2.9	3.3
Capital markets[a]	2.0	2.7	3.6	5.6	8.0	9.6	12.4	16.5	26.5	36.5	46.0	57.0
Private banks	n.a.	n.a.	n.a.	n.a.	n.a.	7.8	10.5	14.2	23.3	32.3	41.0	51.0
Total export credits	4.7	5.2	6.4	7.8	9.3	11.1	13.2	16.8	21.0	25.5	31.0	38.0
Multilateral agencies	0.8	0.9	1.1	1.2	1.4	1.7	2.1	2.6	3.2	3.8	4.9	6.0
Other	0.6	0.7	0.8	0.9	1.7	2.0	2.6	3.1	3.9	5.2	6.4	7.4
Centrally planned economies	0.5	0.6	0.6	0.7	0.8	0.8	1.0	1.2	1.4	1.7	2.1	2.5
OPEC countries	—	—	—	—	0.1	0.2	0.3	0.6	0.9	1.4	1.8	2.0
Other developing countries	0.1	0.1	0.2	0.2	0.3	0.4	0.5	0.5	0.7	0.8	1.1	1.4
Unspecified and adjustments	—	—	—	—	0.5	0.6	0.8	0.8	0.9	1.3	1.4	1.5
Total debt service	9.4	10.9	13.5	17.2	22.1	26.2	32.2	41.0	56.9	73.6	91.2	111.7
Interest	2.8	3.3	4.0	5.3	7.3	9.5	11.8	14.3	19.8	26.0	34.9	46.5
Amortization	6.6	7.6	9.5	11.9	14.8	16.7	20.4	26.7	37.1	47.6	56.3	65.2
Annual nominal percentage increase	—	16	24	27	28	19	24	27	38	30	24	22

n.a. Not available; — Not applicable.
Source: OECD, *External Debt of Developing Countries*, Paris, October 1981.
a. Bank loans (other than export credits), including loans through offshore centers, bonds and other private lending.

nitudes. Such private lenders cannot, however, escape full responsibility and accountability for their own decisions. In time, these private lenders find that self-responsibility and self-accountability lead to self-reliance in making credit and country risk judgments and lending decisions based on such judgments.

IMF conditionality arises from the decision that access to the Fund's resources by member countries should not be automatic (in magnitudes, charges, and repurchase provisions), i.e., guided only by the Articles of Agreement or by procedures closely derived from such Articles, without substantial additional requirements. Conditionality arises when the Fund adds requirements for access to its resources that are legally compatible with the Articles of Agreement, but are not called for by the Articles. This results in a wide range of options, and even wider range in the application of options to individual country situations. The choice of such options becomes a key management decision involving executive directors, staff, and, at times, governors of the Fund.

The question of whether access to the financial resources of the IMF should be automatic or managed has been with us since the deliberations that preceded the Bretton Woods conference. My responsibilities within the Fund, and then in the World Bank, gave me the opportunity to play a leading role in this area of management in these institutions for nearly 25 years. A few remarks on these institutions may be helpful in understanding my views on private bank conditionality.

In the early years of the Fund, the issue was the broad question of an automatic versus a managed Fund. It was resolved in the early 1950s, but only after about five years of experience that nearly paralyzed the Fund as a financing institution. Automaticity was put aside in favor of management, but the ghost of the controversy lived on in the form of a debate concerning whether the Fund should have different conditions on accessing its financial resources for different magnitudes, usages, or needs of members. From the beginning, I had advocated conditionality, but believed that the content of conditionality had to be different for differing countries and changed over time as countries and the world economy changed. When I went to the World Bank in 1964 to create a general economic staff and a program of country economic work, I brought with me a bias in favor of conditionality, but conditionality applied realistically to achieve the purposes of the World Bank.

I did not worry in the Fund or Bank whether our approaches belonged to any particular school of thought. Outsiders had neither our responsibilities nor our sources of information. Our member countries defined our parameters, but the staff had to have independent views based on the best possible professional work. This insistence on the need for intellectual independence and the ability to base our decisions on our information, our analyses, our staff capabilities, and our judgments helped create the institutions as they are today. I have regarded myself as fortunate to have had the opportunity to contribute to this evolution. It did not happen by accident. These lessons I brought in 1974 and since to private international lending and private bank conditionality.

Countries within the Fund have changed their positions repeatedly on the issue of automaticity versus conditionality. Compromises have been found over the years with the help of the Fund management and staff. Much of the complexity of the Fund as it exists today is explained by the need to find workable compromises and the frequency with which countries have dramatically altered their general policy positions.

Successive changes in policies on access to the Fund resources were not arbitrary nor made without much deliberation. The international environment in which the Fund operated was undergoing major changes in the 1950s, 1960s, and 1970s; the perceived and agreed role of the Fund changed not only in response to those changes in the international environment, but also to changes in countries' views of the appropriate role of the Fund as the central international monetary institution.

Fund policies gave content to its purposes and procedures. Much of what the Fund did was not provided for in the Articles. Our program of periodic country visits, reports, recommendations, and Board deliberations on countries, which I had the opportunity to initiate and manage, were not provided for in the Articles, although they could be readily justified as one way of fulfilling the intentions of the Articles of Agreement. Fund policies on exchange rates were adapted to conflicting views on what was good for the international monetary system and for particular member countries, given their conditions and outlooks. Fund policies on use of its resources reflected the outcome of conflicting views on whether the Fund could better achieve its purposes by giving members easy and quick (and, if feasible, large) assistance in financing balance of payments deficits, or better help if based on prior deliberations and investigations of a member's conditions and policies and agreements on the future course of trends and policies. Since my responsibilities in the Fund were focused on achieving monetary behavior by member countries in conformity with their international obligations under the Articles, I had ample opportunity to experience what it meant in practice to apply the Fund's general views and policies to individual member country situations.

When I went to the World Bank, I found myself again in the midst of issues we can label as "conditionality." It is from this experience I learned that the Fund's assessments of countries can be useful for the World Bank and private banks and vice-versa, but such assessments could not substitute for each other. Close cooperation can avoid duplication and materially improve the quality of work. Much room exists for more cooperation and collaboration. Each institution, however, has unique areas of professional knowledge and skills that the others will not have. Each institution has to assume full and unambiguous responsibility for its own decisions, including its financial decisions. Their activities may be complementary, but they are distinctly separate.

The notion of "risk" is very different among these financing institutions. The primary risk for the IMF is that the members will not fulfill their international monetary behavioral obligations under the Articles of Agreement. The Fund's policies and procedures are designed to achieve certain specific international behavior. Financial obligations, particularly repurchase obligations, exist, but are secondary to the behavioral obligations. The Fund has to defend its financial liquidity. As we all know, it is a pool of national currencies. The Fund must protect both the total value of the pool and its currency composition. But the pool exists to help achieve the Fund's purposes—a particular internationally agreed code of behavior. To defend its liquidity at the expense of achieving or defending the international code of behavior would be topsy-turvy. In a private commercial bank, defending liquidity is a primary goal and obligation of its management.

In the World Bank, ability to access private capital markets to fund its loan portfolio creates incentives to behave more like the commercial banks than the Fund. The developmental purposes of the Bank, however, give it a mandate to take risks that commercial banks regard as unacceptable. Risk aversion cannot dominate the World Bank's lending policies. Therefore, unlike a commercial bank, usage of the loans rather than their *financial* quality becomes crucial. A commercial bank, first and foremost, must protect the *financial* quality of its portfolio.

Moreover, it became apparent in my Fund experience that the ability to fulfill the Fund's requirements on exchange rates and exchange restrictions involved a host of member country policies, and hence flows of information, exchange of views on a wide range of domestic conditions and policies, and, in one form or another, expressions by the Fund of views on domestic policies. The evolution and acceptance of this domestic role of the IMF was influenced by its financial responsibilities; but more important, I believe, have been its responsibilities for international monetary behavior. Long before Fund financing became of some importance, the Fund delved into domestic conditions and policies because it could not fulfill its obligations to achieve the withdrawal of restrictions on current payments by member countries without dealing with the causes of balance of payments difficulties and perceived needs for restrictions. With the help of the European Payments Union, its successors, and the Bank for International Settlements, the Fund led the world to convertibility in the 1950s. In so doing, we found ourselves deeply concerned with domestic policies outside the narrowly defined exchange rate and exchange restriction fields. Some member countries objected, but in time came to recognize the need for this broadening of IMF involvement with countries. As a staff, we tried to conduct ourselves to gain acceptance for this expanded role of the IMF. Our conditionality in the use of the Fund's resources reflected these aims and activities.

The Fund could not help being politicized in this sense; it came to live at the center of domestic policy making, policies that could change at any time. A continuous flow of country knowledge became essential to do the Fund's job. If access to the Fund's resources were to be related to a member country's policy performance, it had to be done in such way as to recognize these continuing concerns. The conditionality of the Fund had to be related to these continuing needs, whether they are confined to exchange rate and exchange restriction practices and policies, or more broadly related to domestic policies that affect exchange rates and the use of restrictive practices. (Indeed, through its relations with the General Agreement on Tariffs and Trade this is extended to trade practices as well.)

The World Bank, by comparison, does not have the international responsibility to enunciate or administer an international code of behavior. More like a commercial bank, its lending and funding policies are dictated by its own purposes, procedures, and policies. Its entry into more general conditionality is more like that of a private bank. It has to be a borrower in order to be a lender. It has to allocate scarce lending capability and limited International Development Association resources. It cannot meet all of the demands of its members. It has to choose among countries and among projects to finance.

In so doing, over the years, the World Bank became concerned with the quality of its portfolio, but repayment evaluations were secondary and became even more so when other lenders and borrowers accepted the Bank's position of being a "preferred creditor."

Repayment remained important to protect the ability of the Bank to borrow from private as well as public investors at acceptable market terms. Usage of the Bank's loans did, however, create the need to be concerned about country conditions and performance. We began to put these country concerns on a systematic basis in 1964–65 at the initiative of George Woods and this work was carried forward by Robert McNamara. It was the main reason that I was asked to come from the Fund to the Bank in 1964. We created a staff for this purpose. Our agenda of country concerns overlapped with the IMF, but much was distinctly different. Both Fund and Bank cared about existing domestic conditions and short-term outlooks, but the Bank gave much more weight to long-run trends, changes, and adjustments, social as well as economic. We entered such fields as education, population, agriculture, employment, and rural poverty—central issues in developing countries—as well as industrialization and infrastructure. Related to our projects were concerns like utility pricing and import policies. We entered into these fields because we could better fulfill our obligations under the Bank Articles of Agreement, not because the Articles told us to deal with these matters.

I emphasize this because it helps to understand what private banks do. They have no responsibilities for the public policies of countries unless they specifically and directly affect their borrowers or the banks' funding. They have no mandate to interfere in domestic policies, but they cannot avoid being deeply interested, concerned, and affected in their business decisions by such policies. They cannot make decisions that are abstracted from the social and political, as well as the economic, conditions of countries, whether domestic and external.

The World Bank does not dictate economic policies to borrowing countries, but it can make policy actions a precondition for lending. Private banks can, but mostly choose not to do so. They can because they, as lenders, can set conditions they wish to have met as part of their lending. The borrower can refuse to borrow. The borrower cannot object, in principle, to conditionality or, in principle, to specific conditions. The borrower can simply refuse to borrow and look for another lender if the conditions are not acceptable.

In practice, however, private banks *separate* conditionality from the act of lending. They express and implement conditionality very differently than do the Fund and the Bank, but it is a very important part of private international lending.

The marketplace severely constrains the behavior of any single lending bank in deciding on the financial terms of any loan—domestically or internationally. Interest rates, spreads above (or below) prime London interbank offered rate (Libor), collateral, maturities, grace periods, default clauses, jurisdiction, immunities, penalties in case of nonperformance, conditions for renewals, and the like are driven by market forces. Considerations such as whether to lend in the first place; the institutional standard like return on assets, and spreads between costs of money and lending rates; to increase or decrease exposure; to change maturity profiles; to change geographic distribution of assets; to alter customer and borrower composition; to enter or expand specific financial services, and so forth are *not* part of the loan decision. They *precede* the loan decision. They are not market driven in the sense that a bank's management has little choice. In these aspects, which are not market driven, the bank can decide any way it sees fit. It may mean that it will not even enter the market for a particular loan. It can decide not to subject itself to the market competition. Market conditions can, of course, influence such decisions. Inadequate returns on assets because of spreads available to the borrower in the market may affect the lending decision, but more basic are the factors that lead the lending bank to decide to compete for particular assets or to avoid such competition.

Lending banks are, however, in the lending business. Given acceptable risks (credit and country) and acceptable spreads or differentials, they want to lend and enter the market competition. They may be handicapped by a lack of knowledge or concern about capital, but these problems can usually be handled. A bank that cannot acquire more attractive, profitable assets because of capital inadequacy is still rare, as I see it. The major profitable activity of a bank is to lend at a profitable spread. Loan losses destroy profitability, so they must be avoided and financially guarded against, if they happen. Losses cannot be so large or frequent as to significantly weaken confidence in the bank as a borrower or erode the confidence of investors in the bank's shares. Again, banks can take measures to safeguard against creditor loan risk and country risk. The lure of profitability causes banks to improve their ability to assess credit and country risks and to manage such risks effectively. This process is now going on in international lending.

Given these incentives, a bank is led to have views about a country's conditions, outlook, and policies. It needs those views in the stage *before* lending. A loan is a contract—20/20 hindsight is nearly useless—it is better not to have made a loan than to be sorry you made it. The bank's evaluation is a precondition for many aspects of lending: magnitudes; acceptable financial terms, particularly interest rates, maturities and grace periods; geographic distribution (country limits and sublimits); services; type of borrowers; purposes; and relations with other lenders (like cofinancing).

During this stage, the bank is at the threshold of conditionality. By its decision to lend or not to lend, it exercises influence on a country's domestic and international behavior and policies. Borrowing countries realize this and act accordingly. A major consideration is to impress their bankers favorably. They will often not mention these considerations publicly; at other times, they will do so, even sending emissaries to the banks to explain and defend their policies, even though countries' policies will not be part of the terms of a loan contract. On the other hand, banks will visit potential clients and their governments. Bankers will express their views on country risks and policies. If reluctant to lend, they will often explain why. If changes are desired by lenders, these changes will be inferred or stated explicitly. The banker wants a country environment that makes the country an acceptable, profitable area for private lending. We are now in the middle of private bank conditionality.

If the lender sees the country as too risky, or becoming too risky, he is pleased to find others engaged in trying to change policies in accordance with his standards. The IMF is, at times, the most visible outside influence with standards deemed acceptable to lending banks. Fund policies concentrate on improving the balance of payments, keeping currencies free from restrictions on payments, including payments on external debt, and achieving the preconditions for more stable exchange rates. Like the banker, the Fund does not like inflation, budgetary deficits, and monetary excesses; it dislikes inefficient public sector activities, subsidies, artificial public utility pricing, domestic price controls, discrimination against foreign investment, and so forth.

The banker eagerly applauds a country in difficulty that goes to the Fund to agree on some kind of stand-by arrangement embodying a set of policies endorsed by the Fund. However, whether he is dealing with a country already in difficulty serious enough to require debt renegotiation, in lesser difficulty, or in danger of experiencing difficulties, the Fund arrangement is not sufficient by itself to assuage anxieties regarding country risk.

Bankers have different reasons, in any case, for continued anxieties. Perhaps most important is the fear that the Fund will agree to a program that is inadequate because of its own management views on how to deal with a country under a specific set of circumstances. The banks do not often feel they have better analytical skills, but still their judgments can and, at times, do differ from the content of a Fund-agreed program.

Perhaps especially important is the fear—gained from experience—that a country may not be able to live up to the intent of the stand-by with the Fund. A bank cannot withdraw from a loan contract unless it specifically provides—as some do—a continued ability to access the Fund. In some cases, the anxiety is that a country is not fulfilling a program, but the fact is not made public or cannot be inferred until a specified date when a country is able to access the Fund in accordance with a schedule of drawings reflecting the agreed phased use of the Fund. Bank loans made in the interim cannot be withdrawn.

In addition, the bank may have fears about the long term and what may happen if a country is faced with difficulties. Will the IMF help a country financially? If so, how much? Will it encourage a country to give the highest priority to external debt servicing to private lenders? Will it try to influence the banks to lend more when the banks are still reluctant? The private lender sees that the Fund can be confronted by a dilemma: a choice between a program that is "tough" enough to satisfy anxious private lenders, but is less likely to be implemented, or a "softer" program that is more likely to be implemented, but is not seen as overcoming the fundamental causes of the bank's anxieties. Thus, even aside from the commercial bank's financial considerations like portfolio composition, earnings, capital, loan loss experience, and so forth, the bank finds that the Fund cannot substitute for its management responsibilities in decisions on country risk and credits.

Then, the commercial bank's views of a country's conditions, outlook, and policies remain separate from the Fund and the World Bank, although often the actions of these two institutions are seen as most helpful. (The World Bank, perhaps because of its preferred creditor position, acts as an umbrella or life-line, particularly when acting in the same country for the same purposes, or with the kinds of relations built into cofinancing arrangements.) The World Bank seems to be moving toward conditionality more akin to that of the IMF. It nearly did so in the 1960s as part of a so-called supplementary financing facility (SFF) proposed to countries by the Bank staff, but not sufficiently supported by certain countries. Presumably, its new structural adjustment loans will also strengthen the Bank's role in conditionality. In the Peruvian situation in the late 1970s, the private banks tried to support a more active role for the World Bank, but the Bank did not move actively in this direction at that time. In any case, even an expanded role in conditionality by the World Bank, regional development banks, and the IMF would not eliminate the need or incentives for the private banks to have their own conditionality and implement it in a manner suitable to a private lender.

I will try to illustrate the role of conditionality in private bank lending under different conditions.

Mexico is a very large borrower from external private banks—perhaps larger than Brazil. For many years Mexico has enjoyed a strong position with foreign banks and institutional lenders, surely among the best of the developing countries. Its external debt has been relatively large for decades, and debt servicing has been a major element in balance of payments financing. Yet Mexico had no difficulties in accessing private loans in many billions, even before the recent spectacular increase in oil exports and earnings from oil. It could borrow for all purposes: budgetary support; balance of payments deficits; government entities like its government owned oil company, PEMEX, one of the largest multinational enterprises in North America; project financing and private sector borrowing for all purposes for which entities borrow and banks lend. The loan loss record has been very good for decades. Skillful negotiations kept spreads narrow. Declines in export prices for oil, minerals, and other primary products in 1981 could be offset, and were offset, by incremental borrowing in the billions. Mexican credit remained strong. In the late 1970s Mexico had entered into an arrangement with the Fund after a steep devaluation of its currency, the Mexican peso, but this was exceptional.

During the last year, the Mexican situation has deteriorated. The symptoms are manifold: high rates of inflation (40 percent per annum); an increasing balance of payments deficit reflecting high growth rates and requiring rising payments for imports; tourism falling off because of the overvalued exchange rate, which also encouraged more imports; declining oil and other export prices; limited capability in exporting manufactures; world inflation; higher interest rates pushing up debt-servicing magnitudes in a world of floating interest rates; wage increases; large real increases in public investments; bottlenecks in labor, transportation, communication, and the like; continued huge budgetary deficits; excessive monetary expansion, and so forth. Results were inevitable and clear despite a policy of minidevaluations: a huge depreciation of the currency combined with the need for stricter budgetary and monetary policies, reduced growth rates, changes in wage policies and cutbacks in investment programs, and so forth. The Mexican government must, however, continue to borrow almost $1 billion per month *net*! The private banks will be the largest single source of this required financing. How do the private banks react?

The answer is not yet clear because these events are so recent. Banks cannot postpone decisions—a decision *not* to lend is a decision. Every bank is on its own. No bank—I repeat, no bank—can defend itself by lending more. It can help rescue an individual credit, but it cannot rescue a country, nor its own exposure in a country. Banks do not act as a system or a group. They cannot act on the principle of doing good or being helpful. Their primary principle is to be profitable and to avoid relatively large losses. Mexico, despite its current difficulties, is a strong country with many ingredients for success. It is likely to remain a huge external borrower for many years, even if oil prices strengthen or exports of oil and other products rise. How to reconcile short-term anxieties with longer-term confidence?

The response is the special type of conditionality practiced by private banks. First, reexamine the bank's loan portfolio and evaluate the credit and risks under existing conditions. Try to ascertain whether the Mexican authorities will have policies that can change the adverse conditions. This requires the bank to have a view on what such policies could be. For example, is the decision to give wage compensation of 10–30 percent for the recent devaluation compatible with budgetary improvements? Will the minidevaluation policy work better in the future? Will the new members of the economic team do well?

The next step is to be in contact with the Mexican authorities. This step may be initiated by such Mexican authorities or by the banker. The Mexican authorities will be eager to give their explanation of what is happening and what is likely to happen. The banker must be prepared to evaluate what he hears and what he learns. He has no choice—too much is at stake. He does not know what his fellow bankers will do in the future; he is not even sure whether they share his views of the situation and how to correct it. Nevertheless, he can depend on certain common views on policies, like stricter budgets, realistic exchange rates, less inflationary monetary policy, wage restraint, avoidance of inconvertibility of the currency, and the like. His voice is added to others. The Mexicans can hear what the bankers are thinking and how they believe the difficulties could be handled in such a way as to defend Mexico's external creditworthiness. The Mexican borrower pays a great deal of attention. He will try to react in ways that will defend his critically important creditworthiness. Debt renegotiation, not to mention default, are ruled out. Mexico cannot afford an interim period of weak external creditworthiness. The views of private lenders weigh heavily in policy decisions at the highest levels.

In recent years we have observed similar cases. In countries like Brazil, Korea, and Argentina, damaged creditworthiness during periods of anxiety have been defended and overcome by policy changes *not* incorporated into formal agreements, but such changes were made with heavy weight given to maintaining external creditworthiness.

A different category of cases is that of private debt renegotiations—Peru, Jamaica, and Zaire. In these cases, banks came together for the purpose of renegotiation. Private banks' collective view of desired changes could emerge, instead of the separate views of individuals within banks. Conditions like a prior arrangement with the IMF could be agreed to more formally by the banks involved and implemented collectively. Banks in such situations create a system, which does not exist ordinarily or continuously. I have advocated more attention to the possibilities of creating some system that could operate under more ordinary conditions and have made some suggestions to this end. The official and private world has not yet been ready for such innovation.

The mechanisms used have worked—witness the major policy changes in Peru and Jamaica that have greatly improved the attitude of private banks toward borrowings from these countries.

The IMF has been helpful in this process. The IMF influence was strengthened by a country's knowledge of the importance given by the private creditors to the country's relations with the IMF. It is impossible to say who followed whom in the actions of the IMF and private banks, but a good deal of synergism came from the relationship. At no time, however, could the IMF take responsibility off the shoulders of the private banks. The IMF relationship increased or strengthened the progress being made in improving private banks' ability to assess country risk—the level of professional skills was heightened by this process. Similarly, I believe the process improves the Fund's skills. The process is not one of substitution but rather mutual reinforcement.

In the Mexican case, the president has said he will not go to the Fund. Other countries act differently. Whatever they do, the policy measures taken to defend their external creditworthiness must bring the comfort level of bank managers up to acceptable levels. Outsiders can help, but the crucial country evaluations and decisions for private bankers can be made only by the bankers, however uncomfortable the heavy burden of responsibility and accountability may be. It is being done and will continue to be done, for not only is the external exposure of private banks already very high, but it is going to become much larger.

Developing countries need a virtually certain source of external finance available in adequate amounts and when needed. Public sources of funds cannot provide these inadequate amounts. If private banks are to continue to provide an increasing portion of these needs, then such banks must be able to continue to enjoy the confidence of their shareholders, directors, depositors, and other lenders to banks as well as regulators and the public at large, despite their increasing exposure to developing countries. We need to assume that many developing countries will, in the forseeable future, continue to be plagued by grave social problems, economic difficulties and political instability. Risks and uncertainties are likely to be chronic. Lending to such countries by private banks requires the ability to manage risk and give the managers who are responsible and accountable sufficient comfort that they are acting prudently. Continued lending to developing countries will require: (1) careful credit examination; (2) professional country risk analysis and application to lending decisions; (3) portfolio management to avoid dangerous concentration; (4) skillful funding to avoid excessive costs of money to the bank, mismatching of maturities between assets and liabilities of the bank, and foreign exchange losses; (5) adequate returns on assets by achieving profitable spreads between costs and returns on lending; (6) growth in equity capital; (7) avoidance of frequent and widespread renegotiation of debt by insistence on fulfillment of contractual obligations and, unless due to fault of lender, insistence that delays in servicing and restructuring of debt will not result in losses to the bank, even if recoveries for the bank take time to achieve.

These preconditions for maintaining a major role for private banks in international lending drive the conditionality of the private banks. We are all aware of the vulnerabilities of creditors as well as debtors. I am encouraged to find that, in practice, debtors and creditors recognize these vulnerabilities of their business partners and act accordingly. Because they do, I remain optimistic that private banks will continue to be a major source of financing to developed and developing countries.

COMMENTS, CHAPTERS 4–6

Michael Bruno

In discussing the issue of International Monetary Fund (IMF) conditionality, it is easy to fall into one of two polar positions. One is to paint a caricature of the so-called standard IMF policy package that may have been valid in the 1960s and probably not even then. It is a view that puts exclusive emphasis on the short-term current account deficit and on inflation, attributes them entirely to pressures coming from the demand side, and suggests a standard remedy based on severe private and public credit restraint coupled with devaluation. According to this critical view of the Fund's procedures, emphasis is usually put on quick adjustment irrespective of social and political costs or realities. Obviously, this is far from a realistic description of the Fund's present day philosophy and procedures. But it is also easy to fall into the other extreme position. When one reads more recent IMF pronouncements on conditionality, considers all the new financing facilities (oil facility, extended Fund facility [EFF], and the like), and confines oneself only to examples in which the IMF has altered its procedures in the light of changing circumstances, one could paint an overly rosy picture of an institution that has always quickly adapted itself immediately to rapidly changing circumstances as they emerged.

Looking at both rhetoric and recent practice, one indeed sees impressive evidence of much welcome change during the last few years, but it is also clear that this process is very slow, that there is inertia in both theoretical and practical thinking, that past criticism may have played an important role in bringing this change about, and that there is a natural tendency to accompany an evolutionary process by saying "well, we have thought so all along."

Let me add a word about the changing world circumstances. It is not that previously only demand mattered and now it is also the supply side, usually interpreted to mean growth, that matters. Long-term growth has always mattered, and it was understood that there was a separate international institution, the World Bank, that took care of that. The main change that has taken place is in the nature of the major shocks to the world economy, coming from oil prices, costs of other raw materials, and related developments. The inherent difference with these supply shocks is that short-term adjustment and medium- and long-term structural change have become almost inseparable. Not only is the nature of stagflation (cost-push inflation coupled with a fall in output and unemployment of a partly classical rather than purely Keynesian character) different from previous inflation or recession episodes. The resulting effects on real wages, profit rates, investments, and savings call for a broader view of macroeconomic management on both the internal and the external balance.

Internal short-term macroeconomic policy can no longer be confined to conventional demand-management tools, and the view of the current account can no longer be confined to the short-term import-export balance, but it must consider savings and investment over a longer time perspective. The emergence of a massive private world capital market, coming from the recycling of petrodollars, is of particular relevance in this context because it is rapidly shifting the IMF's role from that of a major direct source of finance to that of an international arbiter providing a "seal of approval" to a more extensive flow of funds. The Fund's view of the nature of imbalance and of conditionality thus remains as important as it was—if not more important.

Along with the emphasis on the change in world circumstances, it is also important to stress that the new phenomena are only slowly being comprehended in the industrial countries. Diagnoses and cures differ widely. Pure Keynesian demand management has failed but so has pure monetarism, as some recent examples on both sides of the Atlantic seem to show. There is novel emphasis on wage and incomes policy and industrial and investment policy as legitimate tools of macroeconomic management. It is important to stress the slowness of response to the new circumstances because of the way an institution like the IMF is shaped; the winds in Washington may still be blowing in old ways, even though down in the field realities are conceived differently (for an example of slow filtering from the periphery to the center see Killick's interesting paper on Kenya, Chapter 16, this volume).

I will give a few examples relating to concepts and policy tools. If one looks at the current account imbalance in terms of savings and investment rather than imports and exports, a deficit per se cannot be pronounced to be undesirable, nor is a balance or a surplus on current account necessarily good. Most major industrial countries moved into surplus a couple of years after the first oil shock because they cut their investment sharply, while many developing countries moved into deficit while borrowing and investing very heavily. A rise in deficit that can be attributed to a fall in savings (in particular, government deficit on current account) is, of course, another matter where the conventional demand-management strictures hold. One must thus look at the imbalance in terms of structural change and within a longer time perspective. Another important and debatable issue is the list of legitimate tools of government intervention. One detects in David Finch's paper a softening of IMF attitude toward dual exchange rate systems and export subsidies as a short-term, transitory device. With a view to the possible harmful inflationary consequences of a flat devaluation in many rigid wage-price systems, such a second-best tool may prove quite effective, especially if used with specific time limits set by the IMF (which in turn can thus protect itself against unlimited pressure from domestic exporters).

Even in this case, however, one gets the impression that such a subsidy would only be half-heartedly approved, because subsidies, as a rule, are a "bad thing." I consider it important to stress that a subsidy or tax intervention in the price system, providing it is not abused, can often be fully justified on theoretical and practical grounds. Thus a case could be made, depending on circumstances, for a wage subsidy to promote employment in export industries or for a tax on interest rates for short-term capital inflow to prevent some of the undesirable short-term effects that have often accompanied such inflows in the process of financial liberalization. Even a food subsidy, so controversial an issue in this context, could at times be justified as a temporary second-best tool for a government that puts emphasis on distributional objectives and has no other tools at its disposal. Rather than expose itself to the blame that it is blind to social objectives, in such cases the Fund could confine its conditionality to being strict on overall government balance rather than on the specific choice of a subsidy or tax.

My final comment relates to a question raised in both David Finch's and Ernest Stern's papers—the role of Bank versus Fund. A visitor from outer space might now ask: is there any clear, inherent separation of functions left other than accidental institutional history? What is the difference between a Bank's structural adjustment loan (SAL) or a Fund's EFF if correctly interpreted? Would the Fund agree to adopt Bank conditionality on a SAL? Is it really the case, as seems to be claimed in Ernie Stern's paper, that the difference only lies in the "orientation and expertise of Bank staff?" That surely cannot be a viable and lasting reason for institutional separation. I would certainly not want to be misunderstood on this point. Having long been critical of the past lack of cooperation between these two great neighboring institutions, I have found the recent evolution of relationships (joint meetings of senior staff, increasing number of joint field missions, and so on) most welcome and would hope that this process will be continued and strengthened.

Finally, let me come back to the main point. The changing circumstances have called for an evolution of the nature of the adjustment process and of the concept of conditionality. It is not being implied that it should become a very loose concept within which anything could be legitimized, but rather that its scope should continue to be enlarged to suit the new circumstances of the 1970s and 1980s, both in the direction of allowing for adjustment with structural change and in respect of the time perspective allowed for such adjustment. How exactly this evolution actually takes place on the institutional and operational level matters less than the welcome reality of the change itself.

CHAPTER 7

On Judging the Success of IMF Policy Advice

John Williamson

This conference is intended to evaluate the operation of the high-conditionality facilities of the International Monetary Fund (IMF). The task requires that one form judgments on the success of the policy advice dispensed by the Fund and embodied in the conditional programs it approves. This immediately poses the question: success in terms of what? A possible answer would be: success in improving the balance of payments, so that the borrowing member can reimburse the Fund, repay its debts, and continue to honor its international obligations.

If this were the extent of the objective, however, it would have made no sense to set up an international organization designed as a mutual aid society tendering "grandmotherly" advice as opposed to a judicial organization armed with sanctions and threats. The Fund's Article I makes clear that the Fund is intended both to bring an international interest to bear on the decision-making processes of individual countries and to promote the economic well being of its individual members. In regard to some of the Fund's activities, notably with respect to surveillance, the first aspect is of dominant importance. But in the present context one can conceive of the Fund's role as being that of maximizing the economic self-interest of the member country in question, subject to the constraint that the member continue to honor its international obligations.

In principle, what is in the economic interest of a country depends upon the value systems of the citizens of that country. However, in

Note: The author is indebted to C. Fred Bergsten and William R. Cline for comments on a previous draft.

the absence of any articulation of different value systems or any persuasive evidence for believing that these differ radically from one country to another, it is natural to seek criteria of general applicability. There has been much discussion of this issue over the years, and accordingly the criteria suggested in this paper are not particularly novel. The purpose of advancing them is, rather, to test whether the content of the paper commands a consensus, in which case the conference will be able to proceed to discuss Fund policies knowing that differences of view must depend more on differing analytical models or factual judgments rather than on conflicting value judgments. To the extent that the paper proves controversial, the source of dispute should illuminate which value judgments are likely to be important in prompting different evaluations of the Fund's performance.

The plan of the paper is as follows. The first part identifies the comparison that is conceptually relevant in appraising the success of the Fund's role. The second section suggests the criteria that are relevant in appraising whether a country's economic interests have been promoted. The third section illustrates the inappropriateness of many of the comparisons and assertions that have traditionally been advanced to attack or defend the Fund.

On Relevant Comparisons

In a recent paper, Guitián (1981, p. 37) distinguished what he termed three "standards of measurement" for "assessing policy results and economic performance" as a result of Fund-supported adjustment programs:

(1) A "positive or practical standard would measure performance under adjustment programs by comparing their results to the situation that prevailed in the economy prior to the introduction of policy measures; this standard amounts to a measure of *what is* relative to *what was*."

(2) A "normative standard that would measure performance by comparing actual results under programs to the targets specified in those programs; this second standard compares, in a sense, *what is* with *what should be*."

(3) A "standard that might be called conjectural or judgmental and which would compare actual performance to the outcome that would have taken place in the absence of a policy program; this third standard focuses on a comparison of *what is* versus *what would have been*."

Discussion at the Croydon conference, where Guitián's paper was presented, revealed widespread agreement that the first comparison, despite its popularity, is conceptually inappropriate. The reason is that it implicitly assumes that, in the absence of the policy program, matters would have carried on as before. In fact, this type of comparison is likely to contain a systematic bias unfavorable to the Fund, inasmuch as countries frequently go to the Fund when confronted by a deterioration in their situation or a development that renders their previous situation unsustainable.

Guitián's paper alluded to a difficulty with the second comparison: that the targets themselves may be inadequate or unrealistic. The difficulty is, however, broader than this. It would seem conceptually more relevant to compare "what is" not with the targets, but with the best possible outcome that would have been feasible in the circumstances. Of course, that increases rather than diminishes the element of subjectivity in the comparison, but at the present stage we are inquiring into the nature of the conceptually relevant comparison.

In discussing Guitián's paper, I argued that there was a need for a further subdivision within the third comparison, and my argument appeared to be widely accepted. One comparison would involve "what would have been" had there been no policy changes, while the other would be what would have happened had the government changed its policies without any influence from the Fund.

We have distinguished five actual or hypothetical states of the economy. For ease of reference, these will be labeled as follows, where the underscoring indicates the mnemonic motivation:

- *A* The actual state of the economy in $(t + 1)$, after the program has been implemented.
- *P* The actual state of the economy in the previous period t, before adoption of the program.
- *N* The normative standard; the state the economy would have been in, in $(t + 1)$, had an ideal set of policies been implemented.
- *C1* The state of the economy in $(t + 1)$ under the conjecture that there were no policy changes.
- *C2* The state of the economy in $(t + 1)$ under the conjecture that the country had changed its policies without any influence from the Fund.[1]

[1] Actually, the Fund may at times exert an influence on the way in which a country changes its policies, even if the country does not negotiate a program with the Fund; this would suggest the possibility of further refining the conjectural alternatives.

Once one has made those distinctions, it is natural to define the measure of the Fund's success as the improvement (one hopes) in economic performance in the actual outcome (*A*), as opposed to the situation that would have occurred without Fund involvement (*C*1 or *C*2), as a proportion of the potential improvement from the state *C* (*C*1 or *C*2) to the best potentially feasible outcome (*N*). A finding that Fund involvement led to an improvement in performance would not suffice to justify endorsement of the role of the Fund: one also needs to consider whether the improvement came close to that potentially possible in the circumstances. But note also that it would not be enough to show that the outcome fell short of potential to condemn the Fund; one would also need to show that Fund involvement led to a deterioration in performance compared with what would otherwise have occurred. It is entirely possible for Fund involvement to have had some beneficial effects, but for these effects to have fallen well short of what was potentially possible, in which case one would not be justified in giving either a blanket endorsement or an outright condemnation of Fund performance.

On the Criteria of Economic Success

An evaluation of the success of economic policy demands a comparison among alternative states of the economy such as *A, C,* and *N*. Naturally, a comprehensive description of the state of the economy would be prohibitively complex. It is therefore customary to focus attention on a limited number of indicators, which are typically of a macroeconomic nature, to characterize the state of the economy. The indicators that are of relevance in evaluating the success of economic policy have been referred to as "targets."

The classic treatment of the targets of economic policy in an open economy was that of Meade (1951). He focused on two variables, a pressure of demand variable (unemployment) and a carefully defined concept of the balance of payments. State *N* demanded a particular value of each of those variables, described as internal balance and external balance, respectively. Internal balance was described as "whatever [pressure of demand] is considered on *domestic grounds* to be the best . . . for home production and for home employment," recognizing that "it is not at all certain that both general unemployment and . . . progressive inflation . . . can simultaneously be avoided" (p. 106). Although unemployment is frequently a poor indicator of the pressure of demand in developing countries, both because of the prevalence of disguised unemployment and the fact that output is limited more by a shortage of capital than of labor, the concepts of full capacity and an optimal demand pressure are as valid there as in developed countries. External balance was defined as a situation in which a country's "potential and continuing payments for autonomous trade and transfers" (p. 16) were in balance. (Meade included capital flows under the category of "transfers.") By "potential," Meade meant the flows that would occur in the absence of "exchange controls, import restrictions, or other governmental measures specially devised to restrict the demand for foreign currencies" (p. 15). By "continuing payments," he sought a concept of the underlying capital flow, ruling transitory capital movements to be "below the line." "Autonomous" flows were those that were not "accommodating"; i.e., that were not set in train by the specific need to finance some other item in the balance of payments.

Meade's framework is still a useful starting point for analysis. It indicates, for example, the inadequacy of judging the Fund's record by examining only the balance of payments, and it points to the need for combining expenditure-reducing and expenditure-switching policies in many adjustment programs. However, Meade's work was undertaken at the flood of the Keynesian tide, and it was representative of its epoch in ignoring certain issues that subsequent writers have argued demand explicit treatment as separate targets. Meade (1978) has himself argued that *inflation* needs to be treated separately. Once one abandons the Keynesian assumption that the supply capacity of the economy can be treated as exogenous, most would wish to add *productive potential,* or its *growth,* as an additional target. Finally, there is no longer the same easy optimism that issues of *income distribution* are orthogonal to macroeconomic policy, in which case it is natural to add the distribution of income to the list of critical variables characterizing the state of the economy. It would be possible to multiply indicators further (the investment ratio, as a determinant of future growth, would be a strong candidate), but it will mark considerable progress if policy evaluations cover the five variables already introduced.

In general, the ideal state of the economy (N) will not be characterized by any of the five variables achieving the value that might be judged individually optimal. If there were no trade-offs, one would presumably wish to operate the economy to achieve maximum output, maximum growth, zero inflation, and a relatively egalitarian income distribution. But the essence of the problem is, of course, that these objectives are in general mutually inconsistent, and it is therefore wise to seek a situation that represents a balance among the competing targets rather than to give absolute priority to any one. I proceed to advance a series of four propositions about the target values of the variables, based on my interpretation of current mainstream macroeconomics.

> *Proposition (1). Pursuit of microeconomic efficiency should be a major priority, ensuring that the economy is "on the frontier" of the trade-offs between egalitarianism and output, between consumption and growth, and between the pressure of demand and inflation.*

This proposition lists the three trade-offs that are most familiar to economic policymakers. The first is what Arthur Okun (1975) called the "big trade-off": that income redistribution tends to require high marginal tax rates, which blunt incentives and in this way cut the level of output. The second refers to the traditional focus of growth theory, that faster growth requires more investment and therefore higher savings which, given output, imply lower consumption. The third refers to the Phillips curve (which is nowadays usually assumed to take an "accelerationist" form in which a higher demand pressure induces an acceleration in the rate of, rather than simply a higher rate of, inflation).

Just as in microeconomics it is standard form to start off by establishing how to get to the production (or utility) possibility frontier before any question of making trade-offs arises, so is it suggested in Proposition (1) that the first test of the adequacy of economic policy should be whether the economy is "on the frontier." Presumably this proposition will be uncontroversial among economists; indeed, it may seem banal. But mounting evidence has accumulated in recent years to suggest that in fact most economies operate with elements of gross inefficiency. Foreign trade policies in many developing countries violate, often grossly, the elementary efficiency condition requiring that the domestic resource cost of acquiring or saving a unit of foreign exchange be the same over sectors and as between import saving and exporting. State enterprises are sometimes operated as though real resources were virtually without an opportunity cost. The social cost of commuting by automobile can be several times the private marginal cost, while the opposite situation may obtain with respect to off-peak public transport. Taxation systems frequently exhibit high marginal tax rates without achieving the income redistribution that might possibly justify the resultant endangering of incentives because of quite stunning exemptions. Some of us would argue that there exist possibilities of lowering the natural rate of unemployment through adoption of income policies. Clean water supplies are not provided to low-income communities able, willing, and even anxious to pay the economic cost. And so on.

Why are these sorts of inefficiencies allowed to persist? Sometimes, because of pure inertia. In other cases, because of the success of the lobbying of sectional pressure groups. In other cases still, because of ideological preferences for or against the public sector, or reliance on the price mechanism. And perhaps also at times because of an antipathy to dealing with foreigners. My first proposition urges economists to stick their necks out to the point of being prepared to say that these are inadequate justifications for practices that can and do lead to major inefficiencies.

Proposition (2). In normal circumstances inflation should decline whenever it is initially more than some modest level. High priority should be given to avoiding a major acceleration of inflation even under unfavorable circumstances. Favorable supply shocks (such as good harvests or improved terms of trade) should be exploited to achieve a significant reduction in inflation.

There is rather general agreement that inflation, especially variable and unpredictable inflation, is a bad thing. There are, however, two reasons for believing that the ideal (or asymptotically optimal) rate of inflation may be positive rather than zero. The first is that inflation acts as a tax on real money balances and can thus yield revenue to the government; developing countries with poor fiscal systems, in particular, may find it rational to exploit this revenue source. The burden of the literature seems to be that this factor cannot justify a very high inflation rate, although at times it might be rational to aim for as much as 10 percent a year.[2] The second reason for supposing that the asymptotically optimal rate of inflation may be positive is that an upward price creep can accommodate most needed changes in *relative* prices without requiring *absolute* wage reductions. This consideration might justify inflation of 1 percent or 2 percent a year, but not much more. The highest of those two rates, that justified by the inflation tax or that of value in lubricating relative price changes, determines the "modest level" of inflation referred to in Proposition (2).

There are still a few who would challenge the view that the asymptotically optimal inflation rate is an upward price creep. For example, Friedman (1969, Chapter 1) argued for a rate of price decline equal to the marginal productivity of capital, so as to induce the public to hold the "optimum quantity of money." This argument presupposes

[2] Estimates of the revenue-maximizing inflation rate have ranged as high as 30 percent, but, since no tax should be pushed to the point where its yield is zero, the optimal inflation rate is much less.

that resistance to absolute wage reductions is a form of money illusion that can be banished as easily as any other, which is not a presupposition that we would all find plausible. There also remain at least some traditional "inflationists," who believe that inflation is good for growth, helps to break bottlenecks, redistributes income, or whatever. The predominant view is that this ignores the distinction between anticipated and unanticipated price increases and confuses the *rate* of inflation with its *acceleration;* the dominant accelerationist view is that any continuing inflation will become anticipated, at which time relative prices—and the incentive effects and income distribution dependent on them—will return to the values characteristic of a position of price stability.

There is, paradoxically, probably less agreement about *why* inflation is a bad thing than there is about the judgment that it *is* undesirable. Indeed, the profession does not yet seem to have decided whether it is unanticipated or anticipated inflation that is the major evil. Since my own rationale for regarding inflation as an evil (as well as my interpretation of the evidence on the costs of combating inflation) has influenced the form of Proposition (2), it is necessary to explain that rationale even though I am not sure that the details are widely shared.

I would argue that unanticipated inflation has the ill consequences of disappointing the expectations on which actions were based and, more serious, of redistributing income in a way conceived to be capricious, and therefore particularly to be resented. Nevertheless, unanticipated inflation also performs the social function of acting as a shock absorber, and thus of allowing real activity to be maintained at a higher level than would otherwise be possible when shocks occur that are bound to disappoint expectations and to redistribute income. There are times, especially after unanticipated negative supply shocks, when a rise in the price level may be the most efficient way of absorbing the necessary adjustments.

The welfare consequences of anticipated inflation are quite different. A perfectly anticipated and neutralized inflation has rather trivial costs. Despite the effort invested in proving what a terrible thing inflation is, all that the literature reveals is the "shoe leather costs" of going to the bank more often and the "costs of changing price tags." As someone who has lived under three-digit inflation, I can attest that these costs exist, but also that they are rather modest. It seems increasingly clear that the major costs of inflation stem from the fact that it never is perfectly anticipated and neutralized; the stylized facts are that faster inflation brings with it greater uncertainty and variability of inflation and of relative prices. This leads to the distortion of investment away from productive projects and toward socially barren activities such as real estate speculation,[3] and it perhaps also lowers the utility value of a given expected income stream. Unlike unanticipated inflation, there are no benefits to trade off against these costs beyond the modest rate justified by the two factors discussed earlier (the inflation tax and the lubrication of relative price changes). Moreover, the attempt to reduce the costs of anticipated inflation leads to institutional developments, like indexation, that reduce the flexibility of the economy, undermine the ability of unanticipated inflation to act as a shock absorber, and hence result in adverse supply shocks leading to vastly more inflation.

The above account should explain why Proposition (2) refers to the need to give high priority to avoiding a major acceleration of inflation even under unfavorable circumstances: high priority because of the danger that faster inflation will be institutionalized, with a resulting locking-in of the costs of anticipated inflation and locking-out of future benefits from unanticipated inflation. Those benefits are too valuable to be squandered in meeting any single crisis.

The proposition also embraces the notion that, in general, anti-inflationary policy should be "gradualist" rather than abrupt. The underlying notion is that reducing inflation through demand restraint (i.e., monetary restriction) necessarily has a cost in lost output, and that this cost becomes progressively more onerous the more abrupt is the deceleration in inflation that is to be achieved. This view is not universally accepted, especially among monetarists, who are prone to argue that expectations can be sufficiently changed by binding commitments to monetary or exchange rate targets to avoid or to mitigate significantly the costs of reducing inflation. Harberger and Edwards (1980) claimed to have presented empirical support for the thesis that combating inflation need not be costly in lost output. They examined the characteristics of a number of cases in which there had been a sharp fall in inflation and found that these cases were typically associated with a sharp cut in monetary expansion, but not with a decline in output. In my view, the problem with this test lies in the

[3] For example, in Brazil even indexed assets are suspected as inflation hedges, in part because of the fear that the government will play with the indexation formula (as last occurred in 1980, when the government went through a phase of fighting inflation by influencing expectations, to which end it decreed a ceiling on monetary correction). This stimulates real estate speculation, which absorbs real resources (e.g., in the form of bulldozers to carve up beauty spots).

procedure of sample selection. Their sample consists of cases of *successful* stabilization programs. One would expect positive supply shocks, or a restoration of normal supply conditions following disruption, to reduce inflation as well as to increase output. My interpretation is that Harberger's criterion has picked up the cases in which such favorable supply effects coincided with a reduction in monetary growth, rather than represent a random sample of the cases in which countries restricted monetary expansion in the interest of restoring price stability.

My criticism of Harberger and Edwards may also help explain the final sentence of Proposition (2). Although fighting inflation purely by monetary restriction can be hideously costly, there are events—notably positive supply shocks—that can greatly aid in reducing inflation. The proposition urges that when these occur they should be utilized to that end rather than be frittered away in unsustainable demand expansion.

Proposition (3). Policy should always seek to avoid major departures from internal balance, conceived in a Meadean sense as a pressure of demand that balances greater output against the stimulation of inflation.

With endogenous inflationary expectations, "internal balance" will be largely determined by the "natural rate of unemployment" (or some analogous measure of demand pressure). In fact, Proposition (2) implies that internal balance is normally a somewhat lower pressure of demand (to provide scope for reducing inflation). The force of the proposition lies in the words "always" and in its juxtaposition with the "on average" nature of Proposition (4) regarding external balance. The logic of suggesting that countries should aim at *continuous* internal balance, while being content to ensure that external balance is satisfied *on average* over the medium term, is that departures from internal balance always involve a welfare loss. In contrast, variations in reserves (or foreign borrowing) provide leeway for departures from continuous external balance with a negligible welfare loss, under both pegged and floating exchange rates. Higher unemployment than that corresponding to internal balance involves a waste of resources that can never be fully recouped in the future, since today's unemployed cannot do today's work tomorrow. Lower unemployment risks an acceleration of inflation the reversal of which will cost more in lost output in the future than the benefits gained today. Thus, the founding fathers of Bretton Woods were profoundly wise in providing a Fund charged with assisting its members to finance temporary deficits, while insisting that exchange rate changes be directed to the correction of underlying ("fundamental") disequilibria, since this is exactly what is needed to support a policy of aiming for continuous internal balance but external balance only in the medium term.

The monetarist literature has not followed Meade in endorsing pursuit of an internal balance target. This does not, however, seem to be a result of a dismissal of the desirability of the objective, but rather because of contrasting views regarding the necessity for, or form of, policies directed specifically at such a target. One version of the monetarist school, led by Lucas (1973), assumes ubiquitous "flexprices" and rational expectations and argues that policy cannot systematically affect real demand or therefore contribute to the achievement of internal balance. A more familiar Friedmanian version argues that, because of lags, the most effective way of securing steady real demand at sustainable levels is to adopt a policy of constant monetary growth. One may or may not be persuaded by the intellectual force of these arguments, but they do seem to relate to the means of achieving an internal balance target more than to the legitimacy of measuring success by the extent to which such a target is achieved.

> *Proposition (4). External balance, interpreted as a current account balance calculated to maximize welfare in the light of national thrift and productivity and foreign borrowing and lending opportunities, should be a high priority but medium-term objective.*

The basic argument for making external balance a target to be pursued on average over the medium term, rather than continuously, has already been presented. Foreign borrowing or lending, or reserve variation, can provide a valuable way of insulating a national economy against many types of shock of external or internal origin. But, at the same time, honoring international obligations is indispensable to the maintenance of a global environment in which mutually beneficial capital flows are possible, which implies a requirement of payments adjustment over a reasonable time horizon. That business cycles are typically about four years in length, and that plans (which are, in a sense, programmed adjustment periods) are typically five years in duration, argue for thinking of five years as the sort of period over which a country ought normally to maintain external balance or achieve adjustment.

It will be noted that the concept of external balance embodied in Proposition (4) differs from that adopted by Meade, in that the reference to autonomous flows has been omitted and replaced by a criterion of the welfare-maximizing flow of capital. This is because Meade's distinction between autonomous and accommodating capital flows has become increasingly tenuous as capital mobility has developed. A capital inflow caused by a tightening of monetary policy would have to be defined as autonomous if the tightening were motivated by a domestic objective, and as accommodating if motivated by an external deficit. This is an unsatisfactory basis for a distinction in the best of circumstances, especially given the mixed motivations that often prevail in reality. In the limiting case of perfect capital mobility, where monetary policy cannot influence domestic objectives at all, all capital flows would by definition be accommodating, and this would point to the absurd conclusion that one would be forced to define external balance as a zero capital flow (current account balance). In reaction to this dilemma, McKinnon (1981, p. 541) has gone to the other extreme and argued that under perfect capital mobility the current account imbalance is irrelevant to the issue of whether there is an external imbalance or not. Apparently we are asked to accept that any current imbalance is consistent with external balance just as long as it can be financed. But would anyone argue that a firm or household should be indifferent to whether or how much it is borrowing or lending, just as long as it remains in sufficiently good credit standing to be able to maintain financial viability?

The alternative approach, which I have espoused for many years (Williamson 1973), poses the question of the current balance that would maximize the country's welfare, *given* its savings propensity and domestic investment opportunities ("thrift and productivity") and the terms on which it can borrow and lend vis-à-vis the rest of the world. What I define as external balance is the current balance that would be optimal in the light of these considerations, cyclically adjusted. Note that, by definition, this implies a current deficit no larger than the country can expect to be able to finance through sustainable capital inflows.

Summary and Implications

I have argued in this paper that in principle one should seek to evaluate the policy advice dispensed by the IMF by measuring the improvement (if any) in economic performance in the actual outcome (*A*) as opposed to the situation that would otherwise have occurred (*C*), as a proportion of the potential improvement from *C* to the best potentially feasible outcome (*N*). I have also suggested that comparisons between states of the economy *A, C,* and *N* should pay attention to the development of at least five variables: the pressure of demand, the current balance of payments, the rate of inflation, the expansion in capacity, and the distribution of income. Finally, I have advanced four propositions that I argue go a useful part of the way toward characterizing the ideal outcome *N:* efficiency; an effective but not necessarily rigid counterinflationary strategy; continuous internal balance; and medium-term progress toward external balance, interpreted as a current account balance appropriate in the light of national thrift and productivity and international borrowing and lending possibilities.

Acceptance of the preceding conceptual framework implies that quite a few of the comparisons that have traditionally been made to evaluate the Fund must be dismissed as irrelevant. Among them are the following.

- Reichman and Stillson (1978) evaluated whether the principal purposes of stand-by programs were achieved by examining the extent to which countries had satisfied agreed performance targets. Since performance targets relate to means, whereas success should be measured by what happens to the ends, this was in no sense a measure of success (which is not to say that the measures they developed were without interest in other contexts, nor that all their measures suffered from this criticism).
- Several analysts have sought to measure the success of IMF-sponsored programs by comparing the state of the economy prior to IMF involvement (*P*) with its subsequent state (*A*). As pointed out in the first section of this paper, this is not only a fundamentally irrelevant comparison but also one likely to be biased against the performance of the Fund.
- The Fund has often been blamed in the popular press, in left-wing circles, and even in the US Congress for many of the hardships that have befallen countries undertaking adjustment programs under stand-by arrangements. Many such criticisms have compared the state *A* with some alternative state of the economy that lay outside the feasible set, in the sense that real wages, absorption, and so forth were assumed to continue at their previous levels despite the fact that resource constraints required retrenchment somewhere if the adjustment needed to respect budget constraints were to occur.

The Fund's policy advice has an important impact on the policies adopted by many of its member countries. It is therefore right that the advice it dispenses should be subjected to critical scrutiny by the economics profession and the public at large—indeed, that is the purpose of the conference. The burden of this paper is, however, that such scrutiny needs to be a good deal more sophisticated than has been usual before it will be possible to place any confidence in the conclusions offered. Those conclusions will necessarily remain subjective, both because they involve value judgments about trade-offs among competing objectives and because they require comparisons involving hypothetical alternative situations. But it is surely better to make relevant but subjective comparisons rather than objective but fundamentally irrelevant comparisons. And to the extent that the value judgments articulated in this paper command a consensus, one of the two sources of subjectivity need not be an obstacle to the achievement of an agreed verdict on the performance of the Fund, or on measures that might strengthen the positive impact of the Fund's influence.

In concrete terms, my argument suggests that the authors of country studies (not to mention members of the Fund staff) should ask themselves the following sorts of questions. First, just what was the impact of the Fund in influencing the policies adopted in a particular country? Second, how did those policy changes affect the key variables of the pressure of demand, the current balance of payments, the inflation rate, capacity growth, and income distribution? Third, were those changes for better or for worse in terms of getting closer to the efficiency frontier, reducing inflation, moving the economy toward internal balance, and achieving an appropriate current balance target? Fourth, were there opportunities for doing better, and what policies would have given promise for a better outcome (in which dimensions)? My hope is that a disciplined treatment of such questions will yield more relevant comparisons, and therefore more trustworthy conclusions about the adequacy of past policies and the means for future improvements, than have been customary in past discussions.

References

Friedman, M. *The Optimum Quantity of Money*. London: MacMillan, 1969.

Guitián, M. *Fund Conditionality: Evolution of Principles and Practices*. Washington: International Monetary Fund, 1981.

Harberger, A. C., and S. Edwards. "International Evidence on the Sources of Inflation." Paper presented at the conference on World Inflation and Inflation in Brazil, Rio de Janeiro. Rio de Janeiro: Getulio Vargas Foundation, 1980.

Lucas, R. E. "Some International Evidence on Output-Inflation Tradeoffs." *American Economic Review,* vol. 63 (June 1973) pp. 326–34.

McKinnon, R. I. 1981. "The Exchange Rate and Macroeconomic Policy: Changing Postwar Perceptions." *Journal of Economic Literature,* vol. 14 (June 1981) pp. 531–57.

Meade J. E. 1951. *The Theory of International Economic Policy, vol. I, The Balance of Payments*. London: Oxford University Press, 1951.

———. "The Meaning of 'Internal Balance'." *Economic Journal,* vol. 88 (September 1978) pp. 423–35.

Okun, A. K. *Equity and Efficiency: The Big Tradeoff.* Washington: Brookings Institution, 1975.

Reichmann, T. M., and R. T. Stillson. "Experience with Programs of Balance of Payments Adjustment: Stand-by Arrangements in the Higher Credit Tranches, 1963–72." International Monetary Fund *Staff Papers* (June 1978).

Williamson, J. "Payments Objectives and Economic Welfare." International Monetary Fund *Staff Papers* (November 1973).

CHAPTER 8

The Adjustment Experience Of Developing Economies After 1973

Bela Balassa

This paper summarizes the results of the Organization for Economic Cooperation and Development (OECD) and the World Bank studies of external shocks and policy responses to these shocks in developing economies during the 1973–78 period.[1] External shocks, in the form of the deterioration of the terms of trade and the slowdown of foreign demand for the exports of developing economies, reflected largely the effects of the quadrupling of oil prices and the 1974–75 world recession. Policy responses, in turn, may have involved additional net external financing and domestic adjustment policies, including export promotion, import substitution, and macroeconomic policies affecting the rate of economic growth.

The OECD and the World Bank studies have employed a common analytical framework to estimate the balance of payments effects of external shocks and of policy responses to these shocks. In the OECD study, estimates have been made for 7 groups of non-Organization of Petroleum Exporting Countries (OPEC) developing economies, classified according to their level of industrialization and resource

[1] The bibliography to the chapter lists the author's publications that provide detailed estimates for the period under consideration as well as the findings of his earlier research for the 1960–73 period, when world market conditions were favorable. The figures presented in Chapter 6 of the *World Development Report 1981* (New York: Oxford University Press, August 1981) are based on these estimates, with modifications made in regard to the measurement of terms of trade effects as noted below.

base, as well as for 9 developing economies. The World Bank studies provide estimates for 24 developing economies that were adversely affected by external shocks and 4 developing economies that experienced favorable external shocks.

The balance of payments effects of external shocks have been estimated by postulating a situation that would have existed in the absence of these shocks. Terms-of-trade effects have been calculated as the difference between the current price values of exports and imports and their constant price values, estimated in the prices of the 1971–73 ("1972") base period.[2] This procedure reflects the assumption that price increases after "1972" were due to external shocks, in particular the direct and indirect effects of the quadrupling of oil prices.[3]

The effects of the slowdown of foreign demand on developing country exports have been calculated as the difference between the trend value of exports and hypothetical exports. The trend value of exports has been derived on the assumptions that the growth rate of foreign demand for particular export products and product groups remained the same as in the 1963–73 period and that the particular economy maintained its "1972' share in these exports. In turn, hypothetical exports have been estimated on the assumption that the economy in question maintained its "1972" market share in the actual exports of individual products and product groups during the period under consideration.

The balance of payments effects of adjustment policies undertaken by individual developing economies have also been estimated by hypothesizing a situation that would have existed in the absence of external shocks. Additional net external financing has been derived as the difference between the actual merchandise trade balance and the trade balance that would have been obtained if trends in imports and exports observed in the 1963–73 period had continued and import

[2] They have further been decomposed into a "pure terms of trade effect," calculated on the assumption that the balance of trade expressed in "1972" prices was in equilibrium, and an "unbalanced trade effect," indicating the impact of the rise of import prices on the deficit (surplus) in the balance of trade expressed in "1972" prices.

[3] The estimates presented in the *World Development Report 1981* took the rise of the price of manufactured goods exported by the developed countries as the benchmark, thereby largely excluding the unbalanced trade effect, with corresponding adjustments in the amount of additional net external financing.

and export prices had remained at their "1972" level. Nonfactor services and private transfers do not enter into the calculation of additional net external financing because they are assumed to be unaffected by external shocks.

The effects of export promotion have been calculated as changes in exports that resulted from changes in the "1972" export market shares of the particular national economy. In turn, import substitution has been defined as savings in imports associated with a decrease in the income elasticity of import demand compared with the 1963–73 period. Finally, the effects on imports of changes in GNP growth rates in response to the macroeconomic policies followed have been estimated on the assumption of unchanged income elasticities of import demand. This pertains to the impact of short-term policies, whereas long-term growth performance is affected by the allocation of existing and incremental resources and the rate of savings.

Particular policy measures may also have been taken independently of external shocks, or may themselves constitute an "internal shock." An excessively expansionary fiscal policy or a major transformation of political institutions come under this heading. The methodology applied does not, however, permit separating the balance of payments effects of policy changes taken in response to external shocks from the effects of autonomous policy changes, including internal shocks. Such a distinction necessarily becomes a matter of interpretation; it has been made in the studies of the individual developing economies.

External Shocks and Policy Responses in Seven Groups of Non-OPEC Developing Economies

The Classification Scheme

Non-OPEC developing economies have been classified according to their level of industrialization and resource base. The groups are: newly industrializing economies (NICs); agriculture-based, relatively industrialized developing economies; mineral-based, relatively industrialized developing economies; agriculture-based, less industrialized developing economies; mineral-based, less industrialized developing economies; and least developed economies. In view of their large size, and the impossibility of separating data for Pakistan and Bangladesh for the 1963–73 base period, these countries, as well as India, have been included in a seventh group.

Table 8.1 provides estimates of the balance of payments effects of external shocks and of policy responses to these shocks for the seven

TABLE 8.1 BALANCE OF PAYMENTS EFFECTS OF EXTERNAL SHOCKS AND OF POLICY RESPONSES TO THESE SHOCKS: RATIOS
(percentage)

Balance of payments effects	1974	1975	1976	1977	1978	1974–78	1974	1975	1976	1977	1978	1974–78
	Newly industrializing countries						*Relatively industrialized countries with economies based predominantly on agriculture*					
External shocks												
Terms of trade effects/average trade	43.0	59.8	43.8	29.5	32.9	41.2	10.7	48.8	33.7	33.1	40.4	33.8
Terms of trade effects/GNP	5.5	7.1	5.4	3.6	4.2	5.1	1.6	6.9	4.8	4.7	5.7	4.8
Export volume effects/exports	1.6	12.3	6.5	14.5	16.2	10.7	5.3	12.9	7.9	14.0	16.2	11.5
Export volume effects/GNP	0.2	1.2	0.7	1.6	1.9	1.1	0.6	1.5	1.0	1.6	1.8	1.3
External shocks/GNP	5.6	8.3	6.1	5.2	6.1	6.2	2.2	8.4	5.8	6.2	7.5	6.1
Policy responses												
Additional net external financing/average trade	50.0	48.1	21.4	−4.2	−8.6	19.9	36.6	76.4	54.1	68.5	72.8	62.4
Additional net external financing/GNP	6.4	5.7	2.6	−0.5	−1.1	2.5	5.4	10.8	7.7	9.7	10.3	8.9
Increase in export shares/exports	−4.9	−1.7	−2.7	0.5	5.1	−0.3	−4.9	−1.7	3.3	0.3	5.6	0.8
Import substitution/imports	−1.2	13.2	17.4	22.4	25.0	15.3	−13.4	−11.6	−10.5	−16.3	−15.6	−13.6
Import effects of lower GNP growth rate/imports	0.6	6.3	9.5	19.7	23.6	11.7	−1.4	−1.6	−3.7	−4.0	−4.4	−3.1

	Less industrialized countries with economies based predominantly on mineral production						Least developed countries					
External shocks												
Terms of trade effects/ average trade	−22.8	44.7	13.4	6.7	n.a.	10.1	29.9	55.6	20.6	−11.4	60.2	31.3
Terms of trade effects/ GNP	−7.0	13.1	3.7	1.8	n.a.	2.9	3.5	7.2	2.6	−1.3	7.3	3.8
Export volume effects/ exports	0.6	12.1	10.9	17.1	n.a.	9.8	10.2	10.8	9.1	24.9	22.3	15.0
Export volume effects/ GNP	0.2	3.9	3.5	5.1	n.a.	3.2	1.0	1.1	1.0	2.2	1.7	1.4
External shocks/GNP	−6.8	17.0	7.2	6.9	n.a.	6.1	4.3	8.3	3.5	0.9	9.0	5.2
Policy responses												
Additional net external financing/average trade	−32.4	39.5	−6.5	−1.7	n.a.	−0.6	49.4	75.8	26.4	14.5	107.3	55.2
Additional net external financing/GNP	−10.0	11.6	−1.8	−0.5	n.a.	−0.2	5.9	9.8	3.3	1.7	13.0	6.7
Increase in export shares/ exports	−3.8	−5.1	−11.2	−22.5	n.a.	−10.3	−35.2	−26.9	−24.3	−37.5	−67.5	−37.0
Import substitution/ imports	12.2	14.2	33.9	30.3	n.a.	21.9	15.8	6.8	16.3	13.6	−0.6	9.9
Import effects of lower GNP growth rate/ imports	4.4	13.1	22.8	29.7	n.a.	16.9	−1.2	1.7	4.3	3.7	8.6	3.6

n.a. Not available.
Source: Bela Balassa, Andre Barsony, and Anne Richards, *The Balance of Payments Effects of External Shocks and of Policy Responses to These Shocks in Non-OPEC Developing Countries,* OECD, 1981.

TABLE 8.1 Continued

	1974	1975	1976	1977	1978	1974–78	1974	1975	1976	1977	1978	1974–78
Balance of payments effects	*Relatively industrialized countries with economies based predominantly on mineral production*						*Less industrialized countries with economies based predominantly on agriculture*					
External shocks												
Terms of trade effects/ average trade	−1.7	47.9	41.7	41.9	47.4	35.9	14.5	28.1	−3.6	−34.5	6.4	1.5
Terms of trade effects/ GNP	−0.2	6.7	5.5	5.8	6.6	4.9	2.8	5.3	−0.7	−6.7	1.2	0.3
Export volume effects/ exports	0.9	11.3	9.1	12.9	15.2	10.0	6.2	11.2	8.4	19.8	20.3	13.0
Export volume effects/ GNP	0.1	1.5	1.2	1.8	2.1	1.3	1.2	2.1	1.5	3.2	3.1	2.3
External shocks/GNP	−0.1	8.2	6.7	7.5	8.7	6.2	4.0	7.5	0.9	−3.5	4.3	2.5
Policy responses												
Additional net external financing/average trade	−10.4	54.1	41.2	39.9	46.5	34.8	20.8	31.5	5.7	8.8	60.0	26.0
Additional net external financing/GNP	−1.4	7.6	5.4	5.5	6.5	4.7	4.0	6.0	1.1	1.7	11.6	5.0
Increase in export shares/ exports	10.2	12.3	5.4	12.2	14.6	11.1	−2.3	1.5	−5.5	−11.5	−17.5	−6.9
Import substitution/ imports	−0.8	−10.8	−2.4	−5.4	−9.0	−5.8	0.8	3.7	0.9	−17.7	−21.9	−8.4
Import effects of lower GNP growth rate/ imports	0.2	3.9	6.5	8.1	10.4	5.9	1.2	2.6	3.2	2.8	2.2	2.4

South Asian Countries

External shocks						
Terms of trade effects/ average trade	47.0	68.5	35.6	29.5	52.4	46.5
Terms of trade effects/ GNP	1.9	2.9	1.5	1.2	2.2	1.9
Export volume effects/ exports	2.1	13.2	8.5	16.1	22.3	12.7
Export volume effects/ GNP	0.1	0.5	0.4	0.6	0.8	0.5
External shocks/GNP	2.0	3.4	1.8	1.8	3.0	2.4
Policy responses						
Additional net external financing/average trade	75.7	114.2	69.2	92.0	135.8	98.7
Additional net external financing/GNP	3.1	4.8	2.9	3.8	5.6	4.1
Increase in export shares/ exports	−11.7	−2.7	−2.6	−13.7	−20.5	−10.3
Import substitution/ imports	−14.5	−30.1	−23.8	−34.6	−43.0	−30.1
Import effects of lower GNP growth rate/ imports	−0.2	1.9	1.4	2.1	2.1	1.5

groups of developing economies. Estimates for individual years between 1974 and 1978 and averages for the entire period are shown. The following discussion will concentrate on average results for the 1974–78 period.

External Shocks

The three more industrialized groups of developing economies suffered the greatest terms-of-trade loss in the 1974–78 period, reflecting largely the effects of oil price increases for these relatively energy-intensive economies. By contrast, increases in export prices, primarily coffee and cocoa, largely offset the adverse effects of higher oil prices in the case of the agriculture-based, less industrialized economies.

The mineral-based, less industrialized economies and the least developed economies occupy a middle position as far as terms-of-trade effects are concerned, while the low share of trade in GNP reduced the relative importance of terms of trade shocks in South Asia. The latter observation also applies to export volume effects. These effects were the largest in the mineral-based, less industrialized economies, with the other groups occupying positions between the two extremes.

All in all, the balance of payments effects of external shocks averaged 2.5 percent of the GNP in the agriculture-based, less industrialized economies and in South Asia during the 1974–78 period. These effects slightly exceeded 5 percent in the least developed economies and 6 percent in the remaining four groups.

With the exception of the agriculture-based, less industrialized economies, terms of trade effects exceeded export volume effects sevenfold in all the groups. Although export shortfalls acquired increased importance over time, terms of trade effects were still two to three times export volume effects in these groups at the end of the period.

Policy Responses

There were considerable differences among the seven groups as regards the policies followed in response to external shocks. The NICs offset three-fourths of the adverse balance of payments effects of external shocks through domestic adjustment policies of export promotion, import substitution, and deflationary measures, with additional net external financing accounting for the remainder. They were followed by the mineral-based, relatively industrialized economies, where additional net external financing exceeded in importance domestic adjustment policies three times.

In turn, in agriculture-based economies, including the least developed economies and South Asia, additional net external financing was one-and-a-half to two times as large as the balance of payments effects of external shocks, indicating that domestic policies aggravated the adverse effects of these shocks. However, limitations of external financing imposed wholly domestic adjustment on the mineral-based, less industrialized economies.

There are also substantial differences in the use of domestic policy measures among the individual groups. Only the relatively industrialized mineral producers increased their export market shares; the NICs and the relatively industrialized agricultural economies experienced little change; whereas the four less industrialized groups incurred substantial losses in market shares. In turn, there was import substitution in the NICs; the mineral-based, less industrialized; and the least developed economies. The first two of these groups also relied on deflationary policies to a considerable extent. The remaining groups experienced negative import substitution and made little use of deflationary policies in response to external shocks.

Comparing the four-year pattern of policy responses reveals important differences between the NICs and the rest. The NICs increasingly supplemented external financing by domestic adjustment while, apart from the mineral-based, less industrialized economies that were unable to obtain further financing, the remaining groups remained dependent on external financing to meet the combined adverse balance of payments effects of external shocks, losses in export market shares, and increased import shares. At the same time, the adverse balance of payments effects of domestic policies declined over time in the relatively industrialized, and increased in the less industrialized groups.

External Shocks and Policy Responses in Individual Developing Economies

The Classification Scheme

The differential pattern of policy responses to external shocks in national economies at different levels of development is also apparent

[4] The NICs have been defined as developing economies with per capita incomes between $1,100 and $3,500 in 1978 and a share of manufacturing in GDP of at least 20 percent or higher in 1977. The investigation includes every NIC other than Greece, Hong Kong, and Singapore. In turn, the LDCs cover the spectrum between the NICs and the least developed economies.

in the sample of 24 developing economies that experienced adverse external shocks. Of this total, 12 are NICs and 12 less developed economies (LDCs).[4]

The analysis of the individual countries allows a further distinction to be made between outward-oriented and inward-oriented economies. The former group provided, on the whole, similar incentives to domestic and export sales and to primary and manufacturing activities, while the latter biased the system of incentives against exports and discriminated in favor of manufacturing activities. Several inward-oriented economies also experienced internal shocks.

Among the NICs, the three Far Eastern economies—Korea, Singapore, and Taiwan—adopted an outward-oriented development strategy in the early 1960s and continued with this strategy after 1973. They were joined by Chile and Uruguay, which had earlier applied an inward-oriented strategy but turned outward following the external shocks of 1974–75. These countries devalued their exchange rate to a considerable extent, eliminated quantitative import restrictions, lowered industrial tariffs, and abolished price control.

After earlier efforts to lessen the bias of the incentive system against exports, Brazil, Portugal, Turkey, and Yugoslavia again increased the extent of inward orientation of their economies by raising levels of industrial protection during the period under consideration. Argentina, Israel, and Mexico maintained their relatively inward-looking policy stance, with little change in incentives to exports and to import substitution, and followed excessively expansionary policies that may be qualified as internal shocks. In Portugal, the 1974 revolution and the policies subsequently applied represented an internal shock.

Among LDCs, Kenya, Mauritius, Thailand, and Tunisia may be categorized as having followed outward-oriented policies. These economies have relatively low levels of industrial protection compared with the other eight LDCs that can be characterized as inward-oriented. Within the latter group, Jamaica, Peru, and Tanzania experienced internal shocks in the form of economic disruptions resulting from policy changes; such was not the case in the other five members of the group, including Egypt, India, Morocco, the Philippines, and Zambia.

Table 8.2 provides estimates of the balance of payments effects of external shocks and of policy responses to these shocks for the described groupings of developing economies. It should be noted that, whereas the NIC group includes practically all economies that belong

TABLE 8.2 BALANCE OF PAYMENTS EFFECTS OF EXTERNAL SHOCKS AND OF POLICY RESPONSES TO THESE SHOCKS (percentage)

	1974	1975	1976	1977	1978	Average 1974–78	1974	1975	1976	1977	1978	Average 1974–78	1974	1975	1976	1977	1978	Average 1974–78
	Newly industrializing economies						Less developed economies						NICs and LDCs					
External shocks																		
Terms of trade effects/average trade	35.8	47.5	31.5	26.1	26.7	32.9	11.3	50.1	38.8	39.4	57.4	40.3	29.5	48.2	33.4	29.6	34.5	34.9
Terms of trade effects/GNP	3.7	4.6	3.1	2.6	2.8	3.3	1.1	4.9	3.7	3.8	3.5	3.9	3.0	4.7	3.3	2.9	3.6	3.5
Export volume effects/exports	1.8	12.6	6.7	14.1	15.8	10.7	2.8	14.4	11.7	17.2	24.5	14.5	2.0	13.2	8.0	14.9	17.8	11.7
Export volume effects/GNP	0.1	1.0	0.6	1.3	1.5	1.0	0.2	1.1	1.0	1.4	1.9	1.2	0.2	1.1	0.7	1.3	1.6	1.0
External shocks/GNP	3.8	5.6	3.8	3.9	4.4	4.3	1.3	6.0	4.7	5.1	7.3	5.0	3.1	5.7	4.0	4.3	5.2	4.5
Policy responses																		
Additional net external financing/average trade	45.2	43.6	6.8	−2.1	−7.0	15.9	31.9	85.7	58.2	71.4	100.7	71.0	41.5	55.2	21.9	17.3	20.4	30.4
Additional net external financing/GNP	4.6	4.2	0.9	−0.2	−0.7	1.6	3.1	8.4	5.6	6.8	9.6	6.8	4.2	5.4	2.2	1.7	2.1	3.0
Increase in export market shares/exports	−2.9	−0.3	1.9	5.4	8.8	3.2	−10.5	−6.2	−1.9	−4.7	−7.0	−5.9	−5.0	−1.9	0.9	2.9	5.2	0.8
Import substitution effects/imports	−6.0	3.7	14.6	21.8	25.5	12.3	−0.1	−15.9	−6.9	−11.6	−15.6	−11.9	−6.5	−1.8	8.9	12.6	14.3	5.8
Effects of lower GNP growth rates/imports	1.3	8.9	10.1	11.5	11.8	8.6	0.0	−0.1	0.4	0.0	0.5	0.2	1.0	6.4	7.3	8.3	8.7	6.5
	Outward-oriented NICs						Outward-oriented LDCs						Outward-oriented NICs and LDCs					
External shocks																		
Terms of trade effects/average trade	28.8	35.7	16.3	11.8	15.4	20.3	9.5	32.8	26.1	35.6	55.0	33.1	25.4	35.2	18.1	13.0	21.4	22.5
Terms of trade effects/GNP	7.4	8.9	4.6	3.3	4.3	5.6	1.5	4.7	3.9	5.6	8.3	5.0	5.9	7.8	4.4	3.9	5.5	5.4

TABLE 8.2 Continued

	1974	1975	1976	1977	1978	Average 1974–78	1974	1975	1976	1977	1978	Average 1974–78	1974	1975	1976	1977	1978	Average 1974–78
Export volume effects/exports	0.1	12.9	4.8	12.2	13.3	9.2	2.5	13.8	6.3	9.4	12.6	9.0	0.5	13.0	5.1	11.8	13.2	9.2
Export volume effects/GNP	0.0	3.0	1.4	3.3	3.8	2.4	0.3	1.5	0.8	1.2	1.5	1.1	0.1	2.6	1.2	2.8	3.2	2.1
External shocks/GNP	7.5	12.0	6.0	6.6	8.3	8.0	1.8	0.2	4.7	6.8	9.8	6.1	6.0	10.4	5.6	5.6	8.7	7.5
Policy responses																		
Additional net external financing/average trade	20.8	13.6	−19.0	−26.7	−23.5	−10.0	10.0	32.2	8.8	20.7	47.4	26.6	19.0	16.9	−14.5	−17.4	−12.7	−3.9
Additional net external financing/GNP	5.4	3.4	−5.3	−7.4	−6.9	−2.7	1.7	4.6	1.3	4.5	7.1	4.0	4.4	3.7	−3.5	−4.3	−3.2	−1.0
Increase in export market shares/exports	4.1	7.7	15.5	10.9	23.0	15.2	1.8	1.3	11.9	15.2	15.5	10.0	3.7	6.7	15.0	18.4	22.0	14.4
Import substitution effects/imports	−1.7	10.1	13.6	22.8	25.2	13.3	−1.0	8.4	12.2	3.3	9.3	6.5	−1.6	9.7	13.4	19.1	22.5	13.7
Effects of lower GNP growth rates/imports	5.8	15.3	11.2	8.5	3.4	8.4	0.4	−0.1	−1.2	−1.4	−4.9	−1.6	4.7	12.2	9.0	6.6	2.0	6.5
	Inward-oriented NICs						Inward-oriented LDCs						Inward-oriented NICs and LDCs					
External shocks																		
Terms of trade effects/average trade	40.0	54.7	42.8	37.5	36.8	42.2	11.9	54.7	42.6	40.7	58.1	42.5	31.6	54.7	42.8	38.6	43.8	42.3
Terms of trade effects/GNP	3.0	3.9	2.9	2.5	2.5	2.9	1.0	4.9	3.7	3.4	4.9	3.7	2.5	4.2	3.1	2.8	3.2	3.1
Export volume effects/exports	3.0	12.7	8.4	15.9	18.2	12.0	2.8	14.6	13.2	19.7	28.4	16.0	2.9	13.3	10.0	17.2	21.3	13.4
Export volume effects/GNP	0.2	0.7	0.5	0.9	1.1	0.7	0.2	1.1	1.0	1.4	2.0	1.2	0.2	0.8	0.6	1.1	1.3	0.8
External shocks/GNP	3.2	4.5	3.4	3.4	3.6	3.6	1.3	6.0	4.7	4.8	6.9	4.9	2.7	4.9	3.7	3.8	4.5	3.9

Policy responses																		
Additional net external financing/average trade	59.8	62.0	30.0	17.6	7.7	35.0	38.4	100.0	73.3	85.6	118.3	84.7	53.5	74.4	44.1	39.8	43.8	50.9
Additional net external financing/GNP	4.5	4.4	2.0	1.2	0.5	2.4	3.3	9.0	6.3	7.2	10.0	7.3	4.2	5.7	3.2	2.8	3.2	3.8
Increase in export market shares/exports	−8.1	−6.4	−10.4	−7.1	−4.9	−7.3	−13.9	−8.1	−5.9	−10.8	−14.3	−10.6	−10.1	−7.0	−8.9	−8.3	−7.8	−8.4
Import substitution effects/imports	−8.2	0.3	15.3	21.0	25.8	10.4	−10.4	−22.6	−13.0	−16.8	−23.9	−17.8	−8.8	−7.0	6.4	8.7	8.9	1.6
Effects of lower GNP growth rates/imports	−1.0	5.5	9.3	13.7	18.8	9.0	−0.1	−0.1	0.9	0.5	2.4	0.8	−0.8	3.7	6.7	9.4	13.2	6.4
	NICs with internal shocks					LDCs with internal shocks						Economies with favorable shocks						
Internal shocks																		
Terms of trade effects/average trade	19.4	41.6	30.9	21.0	11.5	24.2	9.9	50.8	36.1	20.7	37.0	31.5	−142.0	−82.9	−99.6	−114.0	−77.2	−101.2
Terms of trade effects/GNP	1.3	2.5	1.8	1.3	0.8	1.3	1.4	8.1	4.9	2.7	3.2	4.5	−14.4	−9.2	−11.8	−14.3	−9.5	−11.0
Export volume effects/exports	2.2	12.8	4.6	11.4	12.1	8.8	5.8	18.5	23.0	28.8	34.0	22.3	4.4	19.0	15.2	24.2	30.1	18.8
Export volume effects/GNP	0.1	0.6	0.2	0.6	0.7	0.5	0.7	2.2	2.6	3.6	4.6	2.7	0.5	1.8	1.5	2.3	2.8	1.8
External shocks/GNP	1.4	3.0	2.0	2.0	1.5	2.8	2.1	10.3	7.5	6.3	9.9	7.2	−13.9	−7.3	−10.4	−12.0	−6.7	−10.0
Policy responses																		
Additional net external financing/average trade	42.7	67.7	33.7	10.4	−0.1	29.6	22.2	90.5	54.2	17.8	33.3	45.1	−133.4	−40.6	−49.8	−52.8	−14.8	−53.5
Additional net external financing/GNP	2.8	4.0	2.0	0.7	0.0	1.9	3.2	14.5	7.4	2.3	4.7	6.4	−13.5	−4.5	−5.9	−6.6	−1.8	−6.2
Increase in export market shares/exports	−10.4	−29.1	−34.3	−11.6	−10.1	−17.9	−17.4	−16.3	−25.7	−16.2	−11.3	−17.2	5.3	5.9	5.1	10.1	12.2	7.8
Import substitution effects/imports	−11.0	−6.6	7.6	7.9	3.2	−0.2	3.6	−17.4	4.5	27.2	17.8	5.2	−7.1	−27.9	−33.8	−35.3	−37.9	−31.8
Effects of lower GNP growth rates/imports	0.0	9.9	17.4	20.9	26.3	14.7	3.2	6.3	14.9	15.8	27.6	12.8	−3.1	0.4	−1.6	−1.5	−1.4	−1.4

Source: Bela Balassa, "Adjustment to External Shocks in Developing Economies," World Bank *Staff Working Paper* no. 472, 1981.

to this category, the coverage of the LDCs is necessarily limited. Also, while the distinction between outward- and inward-oriented economies was made on the basis of information derived from research studies and country reports, a binary classification scheme cannot reproduce the richness of country experiences.

Table 8.2 further includes the results for four developing economies that experienced favorable external shocks. Indonesia and Nigeria benefited from the rise in oil prices; in the Ivory Coast increases in the price of cocoa and coffee more than offset the adverse effects of higher oil prices; and Colombia enjoyed the rise in coffee prices without being burdened by the higher price of petroleum. The experience of countries with favorable external shocks is not considered in this section of the paper.

External Shocks

The LDCs covered by the investigation experienced somewhat larger adverse terms-of-trade and export volume effects than the NICs, irrespective of whether these effects are expressed as a proportion of trade or of GNP. Different considerations apply, however, if outward- and inward-oriented economies are compared.

Among the LDCs and, in particular, among the NICs, outward-oriented economies suffered substantially smaller terms-of-trade losses in relation to the average value of their exports and imports than inward-oriented economies. The opposite result is obtained in relating terms-of-trade losses to GNP; the differences are explained by the higher share of foreign trade in GNP under outward orientation.

Furthermore, outward-oriented economies experienced a smaller export shortfall, expressed as a percentage of export value, than did inward-oriented economies, largely because of relatively favorable changes in demand for manufactured goods, which account for a higher share in the exports of the former group. Thus, the ex post income elasticity of demand in the developed countries for the manufactured goods originating in the developing economies (defined as the ratio of the rate of growth of imports to that of GNP) increased over time and offset one-fourth of the export shortfall due to the deceleration of economic growth in the developed countries. Also, increases in the income elasticity of demand enhanced the favorable effects of the acceleration of economic growth in the developing economies, although this was in part offset by the adverse effects of decreases in GNP growth rates and in the income elasticity of demand in centrally planned economies.

Within the NIC group, however, the ratio of the export shortfall to GNP was higher in outward-oriented than in inward-oriented economies, because the share of exports in GNP was substantially larger in the former than in the latter. The difference between the results was reduced, but a reversal did not occur, in the LDC group.

Taken together, the balance of payments effects of external shocks represented a proportion of GNP more than twice as high in the outward-oriented than in the inward-oriented NICs. Among the LDCs, too, outward-oriented economies suffered larger external shocks than inward-oriented economies, although the difference did not exceed one-fourth in this case.

For the period as a whole, terms of trade effects exceeded export volume effects more than three times, with little difference shown between NICs and LDCs. And while the ratio of terms of trade effects to export volume effects showed a declining tendency over time, the average terms of trade loss was still about twice the amount of the export shortfall in the NICs and three times as high in the LDCs at the end of the period.

Policy Responses

Additional net external financing surpassed the adverse balance of payments effects of external shocks in the NICs in 1974. But this proportion declined over time and, toward the end of the period, additional net external financing turned negative as improvements in the balance of payments due to domestic policies came to exceed the adverse balance of payments effects of external shocks. This outcome reflects increased export promotion and import substitution as well as import savings at lower GNP growth rates.

After 1973 additional net external financing declined in importance in the LDCs as well. It continued to exceed, however, the balance of payments effects of external shocks, indicating that the adverse balance of payments impact of domestic policies aggravated the effects of external shocks. The LDCs lost export market shares, experienced negative import substitution, and their GNP growth rates changed little, on the average.

Within both groups, outward-oriented economies relied to a much greater extent on domestic adjustment than inward-oriented economies. The difference is particularly marked among the NICs. With greater reliance on external financing, debt-service ratios—defined as the ratio of interest payments and amortization to merchandise exports—rose on the average by two-thirds in inward-oriented NICs, while no change occurred in outward-oriented NICs.

Similarly, as outward-oriented LDCs relied to a large extent on domestic policies to adjust to external shocks, they experienced little change in debt-service ratios, while this ratio increased by one-half in inward-oriented LDCs. Notwithstanding reliance on external financing by the LDCs, however, their average debt-service ratios rose only slightly more than in the NICs as several LDCs received foreign grants and concessional loans.

Among the NICs as well as among the LDCs, by far the highest debt-service ratios were observed in economies that experienced internal shocks. This result occurred even though, due to liquidity problems, several of these economies had to cut back foreign borrowing to a considerable extent toward the end of the period.

Further interest attaches to differences in the pattern of domestic adjustment in the individual groups. The results indicate that, among the NICs as well as among the LDCs, outward-oriented economies not only gained export market shares but also did better in import substitution than inward-oriented economies. This result, at first sight surprising, may be explained by reference to the effects of the policies applied. On the one hand, the low extent of discrimination against primary activities, the relatively small degree of variation in incentive rates, and cost reductions through the exploitation of economies of scale in exporting contributed to efficient import substitution in outward-oriented economies. On the other hand, continued import substitution behind high protection brought diminishing returns in terms of net foreign exchange savings and entailed considerable costs under inward orientation.

Finally, import savings associated with the slowdown of economic growth declined after 1975 in economies pursuing an outward-oriented development strategy, whereas the opposite result obtained in economies characterized by inward orientation. The contrast is particularly marked in the case of the NICs, but it is observed in the LDCs as well.

Although outward-oriented NICs accepted a temporary decline in the rate of economic growth, their successful efforts in export promotion and in import substitution led to an acceleration of economic growth in subsequent years. In turn, inward-oriented NICs attempted to avoid a slowdown in economic growth through increased import substitution, but the rate of economic growth fell as import substitution proved to be increasingly costly. Growth rates declined even more in NICs experiencing internal shocks; these economies also incurred considerable losses in export market shares, whereas import substitution was nil.

Import savings associated with the slowdown of economic growth were nil in both outward-oriented and inward-oriented LDCs at the beginning of the period, but growth rates subsequently accelerated in LDCs characterized by outward orientation, whereas the opposite result obtained in inward-oriented LDCs. Within the latter group, the slowdown of economic growth was especially pronounced in countries experiencing internal shocks, reflecting economic dislocation that also led to substantial losses in export market shares. At the same time, increased protection and foreign exchange stringency gave rise to some import substitution in these economies.

Development Strategies and Growth Performance

Outward Orientation and Economic Growth

Table 8.2 indicates the effects of an acceleration or deceleration of economic growth on imports. Further interest attaches to the actual rates of economic growth. These are shown in Table 8.3 for the 1963–73, 1970–73, 1973–76, 1976–79, and 1973–79 periods. The separation of the 1973–76 and 1976–79 periods permits indicating the immediate and the longer-run effects of the policies applied in outward-oriented and in inward-oriented developing countries.

Among the NICs, the average annual rate of growth of GNP in economies pursuing an outward-oriented development strategy declined from 7.4 percent in 1963–73 to 5.9 percent in 1973–76 as several of them adopted deflationary policies, but it rose again to 9.7 percent in 1976–79. In turn, in inward-oriented NICs, rates of economic growth fell from 6.9 percent in 1963–73 to 5.0 percent in 1973–76 and remained at this level in 1976–79. At the same time, in NICs experiencing internal shocks GNP growth rates declined from 5.5 percent in 1963–73 to 1.9 percent in 1973–76, followed by an increase to 4.4 percent in 1976–79 as the internal shocks were increasingly overcome.

Among the LDCs, outward-oriented economies experienced a decline in their average GNP growth rate from 7.3 percent in 1963–73 to 7.1 percent in 1973–76, followed by an increase to 7.9 percent in 1976–79. By contrast, inward-oriented LDCs increased their rates of economic growth from 3.9 percent in 1963–73 to 5.1 percent in 1973–76, but experienced a decline to 4.4 percent in 1976–79. Within the inward-oriented group, an uninterrupted decline is shown for LDCs experiencing internal shocks, from 4.6 percent in 1963–73 to 3.0 percent in 1973–76 and, again, to 0.8 percent in 1976–79.

The favorable effects of an outward-oriented development strategy on economic growth are also indicated by a cross-section investigation

TABLE 8.3 EXPENDITURE SHARES, INCREMENTAL CAPITAL-OUTPUT RATIOS, AND GROWTH RATES

	1963–73	*1970–71*	*1973–76*	*1976–79*	*1973–79*	*1963–73*	*1970–73*	*1973–76*	*1976–79*	*1973–79*	*1963–73*	*1970–73*	*1973–76*	*1976–79*	*1973–79*
Savings ratios	Newly industrializing economies					Less developed economies					NICs and LDCs				
Domestic savings ratio	19.9	19.8	20.3	22.1	21.2	17.0	17.5	18.8	19.9	19.4	18.8	19.0	19.8	21.4	20.7
Foreign savings ratio	1.7	2.3	4.7	2.9	3.8	1.5	1.1	3.7	4.0	3.9	1.7	1.9	4.4	3.3	3.8
Incremental capital output ratios[a]	3.0	2.9	4.5	4.3	4.4	4.7	5.7	4.5	5.1	4.8	3.4	3.4	4.5	4.5	4.5
Growth rates (constant prices)															
Gross national product	7.1	8.4	5.1	5.8	5.4	4.3	3.2	5.4	4.7	5.3	6.2	6.8	5.2	5.5	5.4
Population	2.4	2.4	2.4	2.4	2.4	2.4	2.3	2.2	2.2	2.2	2.4	2.3	2.3	2.2	2.3
Per capita GNP	4.7	6.0	2.7	3.8	3.0	1.9	0.9	3.2	2.5	3.1	3.8	4.5	2.9	3.3	3.1
Savings ratios	Outward-oriented NICs					Outward-oriented LDCs					Outward-oriented NICs and LDCs				
Domestic savings ratio	16.9	19.0	21.2	25.8	23.5	20.3	21.4	23.3	21.5	22.4	18.2	19.6	21.8	24.7	23.3
Foreign savings ratio	3.2	2.6	4.6	1.5	3.0	2.4	1.0	2.2	5.7	4.0	2.9	2.2	3.9	2.6	3.2
Incremental capital output ratios[a]	3.0	3.3	4.9	2.7	3.4	3.2	3.1	3.4	2.9	3.1	3.0	3.3	4.4	2.7	3.3
Growth rates (constant prices)															
Gross national product	7.4	7.9	5.9	9.7	8.4	7.3	6.6	7.1	7.9	7.6	7.3	8.2	5.5	9.3	7.9
Population	2.1	1.9	1.9	1.7	1.8	3.0	2.9	2.9	2.6	2.7	2.5	2.4	2.3	2.1	2.3
Per capita GNP	5.3	6.0	4.1	8.0	6.6	4.3	3.7	4.2	5.3	4.9	4.8	5.8	2.3	7.2	5.[illegible]

	Inward-oriented NICs					Inward-oriented LDCs					Inward-oriented NICs and LDCs				
Savings ratios															
Domestic savings ratio	20.3	20.0	20.1	21.3	20.7	16.6	17.0	18.1	19.7	18.9	18.9	19.0	19.5	20.8	20.2
Foreign savings ratio	1.5	2.2	4.7	3.2	4.0	1.5	1.1	4.0	3.7	3.9	1.4	1.8	4.5	3.4	3.9
Incremental capital output ratios[a]	3.1	2.8	4.4	4.9	4.4	5.1	6.5	4.7	5.8	5.2	3.5	3.4	4.5	5.2	4.8
Growth rates (constant prices)															
Gross national product	6.9	8.5	5.0	5.0	4.9	3.9	2.7	5.1	4.4	4.9	5.9	8.3	4.9	4.7	4.8
Population	2.5	2.6	2.6	2.6	2.6	2.4	2.2	2.2	2.1	2.1	2.4	2.3	2.3	2.2	2.2
Per capita GNP	4.4	5.9	2.4	2.4	2.3	1.5	0.5	2.8	2.3	2.8	3.5	6.0	2.6	2.5	2.6
	NICs with internal shocks					LDCs with internal shocks					Economies with favorable shocks				
Savings ratios															
Domestic savings ratio	19.5	19.4	21.2	24.7	22.9	18.3	16.6	12.4	14.8	13.7	13.8	19.8	25.5	26.5	26.0
Foreign savings ratio	0.6	0.8	2.4	−0.9	0.8	0.6	1.9	7.3	0.5	3.7	1.2	−0.6	−4.5	−0.6	−2.7
Incremental capital output ratios[a]	3.4	3.0	9.5	4.5	6.1	3.8	3.7	6.6	28.6	10.1	2.1	2.1	3.0	4.4	3.7
Growth rates (constant prices)															
Gross national product	5.5	5.7	1.9	4.4	2.9	4.6	4.5	3.0	0.8	1.6	6.2	7.0	8.0	6.1	7.1
Population	2.6	2.6	2.6	2.6	2.6	2.9	3.0	3.0	3.0	3.0	2.3	2.2	2.2	2.2	2.2
Per capita GNP	2.9	3.1	−0.7	1.4	0.3	1.7	1.5	0.0	−2.2	−1.4	3.8	4.8	5.7	5.7	4.8

Source: Bela Balassa, "Adjustment to External Shocks in Developing Economies," World Bank *Staff Working Paper* no. 472, 1981.
a. Incremental capital output ratios have been calculated assuming one year lag between investment and output. For example, the 1970–73 ratio has been derived by dividing the sum of gross domestic investment in 1970, 1971, and 1972 by the increment in GNP between 1970 and 1978, both in constant prices.

of the 24 developing economies experiencing adverse external shocks. For the 1973–79 period taken as a whole, the Spearman rank correlation coefficient between the extent of reliance on export promotion in response to external shocks (defined as the ratio of export expansion associated with increases in export market shares to the balance of payments effects of external shocks) and the rate of growth of GNP was 0.60, statistically significant at the 1 percent level.[5]

A positive correlation between the extent of reliance on export promotion and the rate of growth of GNP was also observed for the NICs and for the LDCs, taken separately.[6] The Spearman rank correlation coefficients were 0.59 and 0.66, respectively, in the two cases, statistically significant at the 5 percent level. In turn, reliance on import substitution and rates of economic growth were negatively correlated in the case of the LDCs, with a Spearman rank correlation coefficient of −0.54 (statistically significant at the 5 percent level), while no correlation was shown for the NICs.

Outward-oriented developing economies thus had a more favorable growth performance after 1973, even though they experienced substantially larger external shocks than developing economies characterized by inward orientation. In the 1974–78 period, the balance of payments effects of these shocks averaged 7.5 percent of GNP in the first case and 3.9 percent in the second. Yet, between 1973 and 1979, cumulative GNP growth was 20 percentage points greater in outward-oriented than in inward-oriented developing economies. And, while the former group succeeded in increasing its average annual GNP growth rate by 0.6 percentage points compared with the 1963–73 period, the latter group experienced a decline of 0.8 percentage points.

The Determinants of Economic Growth

Intercountry differences in GNP growth rates may be decomposed into differences in incremental capital-output ratios and in domestic and foreign savings ratios. In the absence of data that would permit

[5] This result cannot be explained by differences in the extent of external shocks, market size, incomes per head, or the composition of exports (the share of manufactured goods in merchandise exports and the commodity concentration of exports). Thus, in a cross-section analysis, none of these variables has been found to be significantly correlated with reliance on export promotion in response to external shocks.

[6] The findings complement the author's earlier results for NICs concerning the favorable effects of outward orientation on economic growth in the 1960–73 period, when world market conditions were favorable.

estimating production-function type relationships, intercountry differences in incremental capital-output ratios may be taken as an indication of the efficiency of using existing and incremental resources. The relationship is not entirely unidirectional, inasmuch as variations in the rate of economic growth due to external causes will affect incremental capital-output ratios. Nevertheless, available information indicates that differences in these ratios reflect largely differences in policy performance in the developing economies under study.

Thus, outward-oriented economies that experienced greater than average external shocks had more favorable performance in terms of incremental capital-output ratios than inward-oriented economies. Between 1963–73 and 1973–79, incremental capital-output ratios rose from 3.0 to 3.4 in outward-oriented NICs and from 3.1 to 4.6 in inward-oriented NICs; they declined from 3.2 to 3.1 in outward-oriented LDCs and increased from 5.1 to 5.2 in inward-oriented LDCs.

Savings performance was also more favorable under outward than under inward orientation. Among the NICs, average domestic savings ratios increased from 16.9 percent in 1963–73 to 23.5 percent in 1973–79 in outward-oriented economies, whereas practically no change (from 20.3 percent to 20.7 percent) occurred in inward-oriented economies. And although outward- and inward-oriented LDCs experienced changes of a similar magnitude—from 20.3 percent to 22.4 percent in the first case and from 16.6 percent to 18.9 percent in the second—domestic savings ratios remained higher in economies characterized by outward orientation.

Among inward-oriented economies experiencing internal shocks, incremental capital-output ratios rose from 3.4 to 6.1 in the NICs and from 3.7 to 10.1 in the LDCs between 1962–73 and 1973–79. At the same time, domestic savings ratios rose from 19.5 percent to 22.9 percent in the first group and declined from 18.3 percent to 13.7 percent in the second.

In turn, economies experiencing favorable external shocks were not able to translate these gains into higher rates of economic growth in a sustained fashion. Although their average GNP growth rate increased from 6.2 percent in 1963–73 to 8.0 percent in 1973–76, it declined again to 6.1 percent in 1976–79. The results reflect offsetting changes in incremental capital-output ratios and savings ratios. Domestic savings ratios rose from 13.8 percent in 1963–73 to 26.0 percent in 1973–79, while incremental capital-output ratios increased from 2.1 to 3.7.

Finally, the net inflow of foreign capital averaged slightly below 4 percent of GDP in NICs as well as in LDCs in the 1974–78 period, with the averages being half a percentage point lower in economies characterized by outward orientation within both groups. In turn, developing economies experiencing favorable external shocks had, on balance, a net outflow of capital.

At the same time, there are differences among developing economies in the use to which the inflow of foreign capital has been put. This question will be taken up in conjunction with an examination of policies affecting the efficiency of resource allocation, savings, and foreign borrowing in the 28 developing economies.

Policy Response to External Shocks: An Evaluation

The Efficiency of Resource Use

The efficiency of using existing and incremental resources is affected by relative incentives to exports and import substitution, to manufacturing and primary activities, to traded and nontraded goods, and to capital-intensive and labor-intensive activities, as well as by credit rationing, investment incentives, and the choice of investment projects in the public sector.

As noted in the first section of this chapter, outward-oriented economies tended to provide similar incentives to sales in domestic and in export markets as well as to manufacturing and primary activities, while inward-oriented economies discriminated against exports and favored manufacturing over primary activities. Such discrimination lowers the efficiency of resource allocation because activities with higher domestic resource costs of foreign exchange are favored over activities where this cost is lower. Also, in the confines of small domestic markets, economies of scale are forgone, the extent of capacity utilization is limited, and there is little inducement for technological change.

By contrast, outward-oriented economies can ensure resource allocation according to comparative advantage, use large-scale production methods, and attain greater capacity utilization through exporting. Their exposure to foreign markets also provides incentives for technological change, and the experience acquired in changing product composition in response to shifts in foreign demand imparts a certain flexibility to their economies, enabling them to better respond to external shocks than is the case under inward orientation.

Policies favoring import substitution generally take the form of industrial protection that discriminates against primary activities. Price controls on primary products, applied to a much greater extent in inward-oriented than in outward-oriented economies, have a similar effect. In Tanzania, for example, fixing agricultural prices at low levels adversely affected production and exports. Also, failure to raise domestic energy prices *pari passu* with increases in world market prices discouraged energy savings, as well as the replacement of imported energy sources, in a number of inward-oriented economies.

Export promotion and import substitution are further affected by the exchange rate that governs the allocation of resources between traded and nontraded goods. In outward-oriented economies, the real exchange rate (the official exchange rate adjusted for changes in relative prices at home and abroad) depreciated or, in the event of an appreciation, its effects on exports were offset by promotional measures during the period under consideration.[7]

In turn, among inward-oriented economies, the appreciation of the real exchange rate led to losses in export market shares and to increases in import shares[8] in Colombia, Mexico, Egypt, Morocco, and Turkey. In the same group, the effects of currency overvaluation on exports were largely offset by measures of export promotion in Indonesia and the Ivory Coast, while measures of import protection led to reductions in import shares in Israel, Portugal, Yugoslavia, Jamaica, Tanzania, and Zambia.

Relative incentives to capital-intensive and labor-intensive activities are affected by the rate of interest. Among inward-oriented economies, only India had positive real interest rates. With the exception of Kenya, this was the case in all outward-oriented economies once the immediate effects of the quadrupling of oil prices had been absorbed.

On the whole, therefore, inward-oriented economies biased the system of incentives against labor-intensive activities; such a bias did not exist, or it was less pronounced, under outward orientation.[9] With negative real interest rates, credit rationing, too, was more prevalent under inward orientation than under outward orientation, and it tended to favor import-substituting activities, irrespective of whether rationing was done by the banks or by the government. In the first case,

[7] Toward the end of the period, Korea provides an exception inasmuch as the continued appreciation of its currency led to losses in export market shares in 1978.

[8] More accurately, increases in the income elasticity of import demand.

[9] Excessively high real interest rates would, however, adversely affect the private sector. This was not the case in any of the developing economies during the period under consideration, as real interest rates in no case exceeded 8 percent.

the lower risk of protected activities provided an inducement for lending; in the second case, credit rationing became part of the arsenal of protective measures.

Apart from credit rationing, governments may intervene in the choice of private investment projects through investment incentives in the form of credit and tax preferences. Inward-oriented economies generally used these measures to favor investments in import-substituting industries, while this was not the case in outward-oriented economies.[10]

Incremental capital-output ratios are further affected by the choice of public projects. The share of public investment was generally higher in inward-oriented than in outward-oriented economies, and there was a tendency to give less attention to efficiency considerations in the choice of public projects. The resulting deterioration in the efficiency of investment, with incremental capital-output ratios approximately doubling between 1963–73 and 1976–79, was particularly pronounced in countries that experienced rapid increases in investable funds. This was the case in Indonesia and in Nigeria, where the rise in oil prices, and in Morocco, where the (temporary) rise in phosphate prices, added to foreign exchange earnings. High-cost, capital-intensive investments in the public sector were undertaken, albeit to a lesser extent, also in the Ivory Coast, Portugal, Tanzania, and Turkey.

The Generation of Domestic Savings

Domestic savings consist of private (personal and business) savings and public savings. Personal savings are affected by the real interest rate and business savings by investment incentives, while the deficit in the budget of current revenues and expenditures indicates the extent of public savings or dissavings.

There is evidence that real interest rates and domestic savings tend to be positively correlated in developing economies. Various factors may explain the existence of this relationship. Negative real interest rates encourage the (often clandestine) outflow of capital, induce workers to keep their earnings abroad, provide incentives to holding gold, contribute to the accumulation of consumers' durables, and induce the use of borrowed funds to increase consumption.

Among individual economies, the effects of positive real interest rates are apparent in the high and rising domestic savings ratios in outward-oriented economies, the only exception being Uruguay. In

[10] Again, Korea provides an exception toward the end of the period.

turn, apart from countries experiencing favorable external shocks, domestic savings ratios were lower and showed a tendency to decline in inward-oriented economies, the exception being India, which had positive real interest rates after 1974.

Among the economies under study, Korea and Singapore experienced the largest increases in domestic savings ratios, with a rise by two-thirds between 1963–73 and 1976–79. They were followed by Taiwan, where domestic savings ratios increased by one-third during this period. In these instances, the effects of positive real interest rates on personal savings were reinforced by the impact of investment incentives on business savings, and the surplus in the government budget further raised the domestic savings ratio.

In turn, the adverse effects of negative real interest rates on savings were aggravated by government budget deficits in inward-oriented economies experiencing adverse external shocks. Thus, Jamaica, Israel, Egypt, and Tanzania, which experienced by far the largest budget deficits among the developing economies under study, had the smallest domestic savings ratios. In the 1977–79 period, average ratios of government budget deficits to GNP were 20, 18, 16, and 9 percent in the four countries respectively, while their domestic savings ratios averaged 12, 12, 12, and 9 percent.

Compared with the 1964–73 period, the domestic savings ratio declined by one-half in Jamaica and Tanzania, where budget deficits increased the most; the ratio fell by one-fourth in Israel, where these deficits rose to a lesser extent; and showed no change in Egypt, whose budget deficits changed little. By contrast, their improved budget position led to a near doubling of average domestic savings ratios in developing economies experiencing favorable external shocks.

The Inflow of Foreign Capital

All developing economies suffering external shocks increased their foreign borrowing in response to the deterioration of their balance of payments that resulted from the quadrupling of oil prices and the world recession. There were differences, however, as regards the extent of foreign borrowing and the uses to which it was put.

Among outward-oriented NICs, Singapore and Taiwan accepted a temporary decline in the rate of economic growth in order to limit reliance on foreign loans and used the proceeds of these loans in productive investments. They were thus able to maintain debt-service ratios at low levels throughout the period. Debt-service ratios stabilized at a higher level in Korea, which relied to a greater extent on foreign borrowing at the outset but was able to subsequently reduce external financing as the amounts borrowed were productively used. Finally, given the large external shocks they suffered, Chile and Uruguay could not forgo continued foreign borrowing but limited increases in debt-service ratios through the productive use of the amounts borrowed.

Among inward-oriented NICs, Brazil, Israel, Portugal, and Turkey utilized the proceeds of foreign loans in part to maintain the rate of growth of domestic consumption and channeled a substantial share of new investments into high-cost, import-substituting activities. The latter conclusion also applies to Mexico and Yugoslavia, where the rate of investment increased during the period under consideration. In the absence of rapid increases in exports, debt-service ratios rose to a considerable extent, the exception being Israel, which had a high ratio already at the beginning of the period and benefited from large unilateral transfers. Finally, Argentina, with negligible external shocks, experienced an increase in its debt-service ratio only toward the end of the period.

The inflow of foreign capital was used largely to avoid (Tanzania) or to minimize (Jamaica and Peru) decreases in consumption per head in LDCs experiencing internal shocks. In turn, with the exception of Zambia, foreign borrowing contributed to increases in investment shares in the other LDCs studied. However, with losses in export market shares, debt-service ratios increased in most cases. This ratio declined, or changed little, in outward-oriented LDCs that placed reliance largely on measures of domestic adjustment.

At the same time, in the 1973–79 period, there was a negative correlation between the debt-service ratio and the GNP growth rate, with the Spearman correlation coefficient of -0.35 (statistically significant at the 5 percent level). This result reflects the fact that increases in debt-service ratios eventually constrained economic growth in cases where the proceeds of foreign borrowing were not productively used.

Conclusions and Policy Implications

The estimates of the OECD study point to the conclusion that developing economies at higher levels of industrialization were more successful in overcoming external shocks through domestic adjustment than their less industrialized counterparts. This result appears to support the proposition that the objective conditions for adjustment were better for the more industrialized than for the less industrialized developing economies. An alternative hypothesis is that policy performance was superior in the first group than in the second.

The size of external shocks provides an indication of objective conditions, inasmuch as the magnitude of the task to be performed will affect the possibilities for successful domestic adjustment. According to the results of the OECD study, the balance of payments effects of external shocks represent a higher proportion of GNP in the three more industrialized groups, with the less industrialized, agriculture-based economies and South Asian countries experiencing the smallest external shocks. And, although in the World Bank sample external shocks appeared to get somewhat larger for the LDCs than for the NICs, there was no correlation between the extent of external shocks and economic performance.

Furthermore, the World Bank study indicates the differential performance of developing economies that followed different policies. Concentrating attention on domestic adjustment through increases in export shares and reductions in import shares in the 1974–78 period, on the average outward-oriented NICs fully offset—while outward-oriented LDCs offset two-fifths—of the balance of payments effects of external shocks through export expansion and import substitution. This ratio was only one-eighth in inward-oriented NICs, and reductions in export shares and the rise in import shares augmented the adverse balance of payments effects of external shocks by more than one-half in inward-oriented LDCs.

The differences in the performance of outward-oriented and inward-oriented economies are even greater if one considers export promotion alone, while the differences between the NICs and the LDCs are reduced as a result. Thus, increases in export shares raised export values by 15 percent in outward-oriented NICs and by 10 percent in outward-oriented LDCs, while declines of 7 percent and 11 percent, respectively, occurred in inward-oriented NICs and LDCs, reaching 17 percent in both the NICs and the LDCs experiencing internal shocks.

At the same time, the findings of the World Bank study indicate that export performance is closely linked to economic growth. This result was obtained both in a cross-section investigation and in a comparison of the results for the individual groups. Correspondingly, after a temporary decline, GNP growth rates accelerated in the two outward-oriented groups, whereas the decline in growth rates was maintained in inward-oriented NICs, and the increases experienced in the early part of the period were reversed in inward-oriented LDCs.

It appears, then, that domestic adjustment increasingly involved a rise in output through export expansion and import substitution in outward-oriented economies, boosting the rate of economic growth and providing the foreign exchange necessary to finance the imports associated with higher GNP growth rates. Such was not the case in inward-oriented economies, where the adjustment increasingly took the form of import savings associated with lower rates of economic growth.

The latter conclusion applies with particular force to economies characterized by internal shocks that experienced the largest decline in GNP growth rates, with the resulting import savings offsetting, on the average, 54 percent of the balance of payments effects of external shocks in the NICs and 29 percent in the LDCs during the 1974–78 period. The comparable figures for domestic adjustment through export expansion and import substitution were −48 percent and −18 percent in the two groups, thus reinforcing the adverse balance of payments effects of external shocks.

It should be emphasized that internal shocks reflected policy decisions in each particular case, including that of Portugal, where the policies adopted after the 1974 revolution had adverse effects on the national economy. In these economies, and in all the developing economies studied, the policies applied affected the allocation of existing and incremental resources, the amount of domestic savings, as well as foreign borrowing and its uses.

Outward-oriented economies provided, on the average, similar incentives to exports and import substitution and to primary production and manufacturing, while inward-oriented economies discriminated against exports and favored manufacturing over primary activities. Outward-oriented economies also placed less reliance on price controls and on interest rate ceilings than did inward-oriented economies. More generally, they gave greater scope to the market mechanism and tended to avoid "white elephants" in public sector investment that were often observed in inward-oriented economies.

Apart from affecting the efficiency of resource allocation, interest rates also influenced the amount saved. A further determining factor of domestic savings was the balance in the government budget. Except for developing economies benefiting from favorable external shocks, budget deficits tended to be high and rising over time in inward-oriented economies. In turn, outward-oriented economies reduced or eliminated their budget deficits, and several of them provided increased incentives to private investment.

Government budget deficits further contributed to inflation. Throughout the period under consideration, inflation rates were particularly high in Argentina and Israel. High inflation rates, in turn, gave rise to uncertainty, as exchange rates and interest rates fluctuated to a considerable extent in real terms for lack of simultaneous adjustments in these rates, and led to economic disruptions in general. By contrast, reductions in the budget deficit contributed to lower inflation and improved economic performance in Chile and in Uruguay.

By and large, outward-oriented economies were willing to accept lower rates of economic growth in the wake of the quadrupling of oil prices and the world recession in order to stabilize their economies and to avoid large foreign indebtedness. In turn, in inward-oriented economies, except for those experiencing internal shocks, foreign borrowing was used to accelerate economic growth. This proved temporary, however, as the proceeds of foreign borrowing were in part used to increase consumption and the efficiency of investment deteriorated under the policies followed.

These conclusions point to the importance of policies in effecting domestic adjustment in response to external shocks. While temporary retrenchment may be desirable to avoid the creation of economic imbalances and excessive reliance on foreign borrowing, the key to successful adjustment is to increase output through export expansion and efficient import substitution. This, in turn, requires taking measures that contribute to the efficient allocation of existing and incremental resources and to increased savings.

Bibliography

Bela Balassa, 1978. "Export Incentives and Export Performance in Developing Countries: A Comparative Analysis." *Weltwirtschaftliches Archiv,* (1), pp. 24–61. Spanish translation in *Politicas de Promocion de Exportaciones,* proceedings of a seminar on Policies of Export Promotion sponsored by ECLA, the World Bank, and the United Nations Development Programme (UNDP), Santiago, Chile, November 1976. Santiago: United Nations Economic Commission for Latin America. Vol. III, pp. 3–54. World Bank Reprint Series no. 59.

———. 1978. "Exports and Economic Growth: Further Evidence." *Journal of Development Economics* (June), pp. 181–89. World Bank Reprint Series no. 68.

———. 1981. "The Newly Industrializing Developing Countries after the Oil Crisis." *Weltwirtschaftliches Archiv,* Band 117, Heft 1, 1981, pp. 142–94. Portuguese translation in *Pesquisa e Planejamento Economico* (April 1981), pp. 1–77; Spanish translation in *Integracion Latinoamericana* (September 1981), pp. 3–46. Republished as Essay 2 in Bela Balassa, *The Newly Industrializing Countries in the World Economy.* New York: Pergamon Press, pp. 29–81. World Bank Reprint Series no. 190.

———. 1981. "Policy Responses to External Shocks in Selected Latin American Countries." *Quarterly Review of Economics and Business* (Summer), pp. 131–64. Also in *Export Diversification and the New Protectionism: The Experience of Latin America,* Werner Baer and Malcolm Gillis, eds. Proceedings of a Conference cosponsored by the National Bureau of Economic Research, the Bureau of Economic and Business Research, University of Illinois, and the Fundacao Instituto de Pesquisas Economicas of the University of Sao Paulo, Sao Paulo, Brazil, March 1980. Champaign, Ill: National Bureau of Economic Research and the Bureau of Economic and Business Research, University of Illinois, pp. 131–64. Portuguese translation in *Estudos Economicos* (April-June), pp. 11–50. Republished as Essay 3 in Balassa, *The Newly Industrializing Countries in the World Economy,* 1981, pp. 83–108.

——— 1981. "The Policy Experience of Twelve Less Developed Countries, 1973–78." World Bank Staff Working Paper no. 449. Washington, D.C. (April). To be published in a volume of essays in honor of Lloyd G. Reynolds.

———. 1981. "Adjustment to External Shocks in Developing Economies." World Bank Staff Working Paper no. 472. Washington, D.C. (July). To be published in the proceedings of the conference on Problem of Change in Relative Prices organized by the International Economic Association, Athens, September 1981.

———. 1981. "Structural Adjustment Policies in Developing Countries." *World Development* (January), pp. 23–38.

———. 1982. "Disequilibrium Analysis for Developing Countries: An Overview of Issues and Techniques." *World Development* (April), forthcoming.

———. 1981. *The Balance of Payments Effects of External Shocks and of Policy Responses to These Shocks in Non-OPEC Developing Countries* (with André Barsony and Anne Richards). Paris: OECD Development Centre.

CHAPTER 9

Economic Stabilization In Developing Countries: Theory and Stylized Facts

William R. Cline

In October of 1979 the Brookings Institution held a conference on economic stabilization in developing countries.[1] That conference focused on the theory and practice of economic stabilization (defined broadly as correcting inflation and balance of payments deficits) rather than on the issue of International Monetary Fund (IMF) conditionality, although analysis of IMF practices arose in the context of country studies. The purpose of this paper is to recapitulate the principal findings of the Brookings conference in both theory and stylized facts. Rather than repeat a paper-by-paper overview of the Brookings conference, this essay sets forth the issues thematically, drawing upon common strands in several of the conference papers to examine each issue and add the findings of more recent research where appropriate. As will become apparent, the state of the art as reflected in the Brookings conference contains considerable debate about the theory and policy strategy for stabilization.

The Orthodox Model

Orthodox stabilization theory focuses on excessive money creation and overvaluation of the exchange rate as the sources of inflation

[1] William R. Cline and Sidney Weintraub, eds., *Economic Stabilization in Developing Countries* (Washington: Brookings Institution, 1981).

and balance of payments deficits. The principal orthodox policy measures for achieving economic stabilization are reduction in the rate of growth of domestic credit and devaluation of the exchange rate. An influential formulation of the orthodox theory is that by Jacques Polak.[2] In the Polak model, income *equals* money supply *times* velocity (by the quantity theory); money supply *equals* domestic credit *plus* international reserves. In equilibrium, this year's income *equals* last year's. Therefore, this year's money supply must equal last year's. Any growth in domestic credit must therefore be offset by a reduction in reserves to hold money supply constant. Reduction in reserves means a balance of payments deficit. There is thus a monetary theory of the balance of payments: deficits exist because the rise in domestic credit must be offset by decreased reserves to maintain monetary and income equilibrium. Essentially, any expansion of domestic credit leaks abroad through balance of payments deficit and reserve loss. Accordingly, a balance of payments deficit may be corrected by reducing domestic credit. The model transposes to a growth basis as follows: if domestic credit is growing too fast for consistency with real output growth (and velocity trend), reserve losses will result, and stabilization can be attained by a reduction in the growth rate (rather than the absolute level) of domestic credit. This basic monetary model of the balance of payments has influenced IMF stabilization programs for years; typically these programs contain clauses specifying limits for expansion of domestic credit.

A more general version of the orthodox model of stabilization involves a package of three instruments: exchange rate, money supply growth, and government spending deficits. The package is designed to reduce inflation and the balance of payments (current account) deficit. For stabilization, the fiscal deficit is reduced following the absorption approach. From national accounts, $M - X = (I - S) + (G - T)$. The trade deficit (imports M *less* exports X) *equals* the investment-savings gap $(I - S)$ *plus* the fiscal deficit (government spending G *minus* taxes T). To the extent that the trade deficit corresponds to an investment-savings gap, there is no particular problem if foreign capital can be mobilized. But if the origin of the trade deficit is in excess government spending $(G - T)$, domestic absorption exceeds domestic output for reasons of excess current consumption, not capital formation, and the situation is remedied by reducing government spending (G) or by raising taxes (T).

[2] J. J. Polak, "Monetary Analysis of Income Formation and Payments Problems," *IMF Staff Papers,* vol. 6 (November 1957), pp. 1–50.

Figure 9.1 *Markets for tradables and nontradables in the orthodox stabilization model*

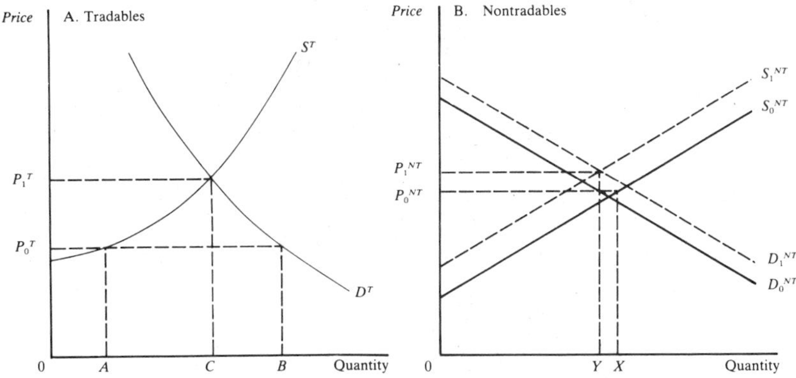

The monetary part of the general stabilization package stems from the quantity equation, $HV = PT$ (where H = money supply, V = velocity, P = price level, and T = transactions or real activity). To reduce inflation, money supply growth is decelerated. ($\dot{H}\downarrow \rightarrow \dot{P}\downarrow$, where the overdot indicates percentage change.)

The exchange rate component of the package is designed to address the trade deficit. Devaluation of the exchange rate should increase exports (as domestic producers receive more domestic currency per unit exported) and reduce imports (as consumers must pay higher prices for imports in domestic currency).

The three traditional elements of the policy package are complementary. Any recessionary impact of reduced fiscal deficits, and of a reduction in activity rather than price in response to monetary deceleration, tends to be offset by the stimulative effect of devaluation's impact on the trade balance. That is, in the national accounts the drag of imports is reduced, and the contribution of exports is increased, under the orthodox response of trade to devaluation.

Two of the more subtle aspects of the orthodox package concern reallocation of resources and induced inflation. To reduce the external deficit, resources must be shifted out of production of nontradables and into production of tradables, while consumption must be shifted out of tradables and into nontradables, so that the net exports of tradables may rise. This process requires a change in the price signals between the two groups: the price of tradables must rise relative to that of nontradables, to induce producers to shift resources into tradables and to induce consumers to shift consumption to nontradables. In Figure 9.1, panel A shows that, at the initial price of tradables $P_0{}^T$, the quantity of domestic demand exceeds that of supply (with the supply curve including foreign supply), and a trade deficit of AB exists. To eliminate the deficit, the price is raised to P_1^T, where excess demand for tradables disappears. The price of tradables rises from P_0^T to P_1^T as the direct consequence of devaluation.

Panel B of figure 9.1 shows the indirect consequences for the nontradable sector. Its initial equilibrium is at output X and price P_0^{NT}. As resources shift out of the sector because of reallocation to tradables, the supply curve shifts upward (to S_1^{NT}). Meanwhile, consumers discouraged by higher prices of tradables shift their consumption to nontradables, raising the demand curve (to D_1^{NT}). The new equilibrium is at a higher price (but lower quantity, because some resources have exited from the sector).

Taken together, the two panels of Figure 9.1 show the well-behaved case where devaluation raises the relative price of tradables ($P_1^T/P_0^T > P_1^{NT}/P_0^{NT}$). The figure illustrates the problem of induced inflation even in the nontradable sector as a consequence of devaluation; that is, the equilibrium price in the nontradable sector rises.[3] Harberger provided a classic early statement of the potential importance of induced inflation of this sort from devaluation in developing countries.[4] The problem of inflation induced from devaluation shows once again why the policy package has complementary components: if monetary restraint is missing, the effects of devaluation are likely to be inflationary, especially if supply and demand elasticities are low in the sector of nontraded goods and services.

Before turning to critiques of the orthodox model, it is important to consider the relationship of orthodox "stabilization" to the problem of "structural adjustment." In its simplest form, the orthodox policy package for stabilization is designed to correct short-term departures from equilibrium, usually departures precipitated by internal imbalances such as temporary loss of budgetary control. In the 1970s the problem was often the need for longer term structural adjustment to changes in the economic environment and, in particular, to terms of trade losses imposed by higher oil prices. While some elements of the orthodox stabilization package remain appropriate for such adjustment (especially devaluation), it has been increasingly recognized

[3] Technically, the rise in P_{NT} will in turn shift the demand and supply curves in the tradable sector once again, leading to a successive approximation of equilibrium but no change in the basic conclusion.

[4] Arnold C. Harberger, "Some Notes on Inflation," in Werner Baer and Isaac Kerstenetsky, eds., *Inflation and Growth in Latin America* (Homewood, Ill.: Richard D. Irwin, 1964).

that longer term development measures (such as development of alternative energy sources) are an important additional element in longer term adjustment as opposed to short-term stabilization.[5] The new orthodoxy (for example, the standard IMF approach in recent years) embraces the need for special developmental measures in achieving structural adjustment, as the lengthening of IMF lending maturities (and entrance of the World Bank into program lending for this purpose) testify.

A final element in the orthodox theory concerns the behavior of real wages under successful devaluation.[6] There is a tendency to assume that the orthodox model requires a decline in real wages for devaluation to be effective. However, a more careful reading of the standard analysis suggests that this rule need not apply generally. Indeed, in the case of the developing economy it might more often be the case that external stabilization through devaluation is possible without a decline in real wages (although a decline in wages relative to the price of traded goods would be required).

Following the absorption approach, lower real wages would facilitate external stabilization by reducing consumption, if consumption is wholly or primarily out of wages (the Cambridge assumption). The corresponding rise in saving would reduce the absorption-output gap represented by $(I - S)$ in the national accounts equation. Alternatively, if the economy were at below full employment because of excessive real wages and were operating inside its production possibility curve between traded and nontraded goods, devaluation together with a decrease in the real wage could raise activity to the production frontier, with the bulk of the rise in output coming in

[5] See Andrew Crockett, "Stabilization Policies in Developing Countries: Some Policy Considerations," IMF *Staff Papers* 28(1) (March 1981). Balassa has proposed an accounting decomposition of external adjustment in the 1970s into components: import substitution, export expansion, deceleration of domestic growth, and increase in external borrowing. Conceptually, to the extent that import substitution and export expansion result from devaluation, they lie within the more traditional stabilization approach; to the extent that they result from special developmental investments, they lie within the orthodoxy expanded to include structural adjustment; and to the extent that they result from new import barriers or export subsidies, they go beyond the expanded orthodoxy and enter into the area of trade distortions. Bela Balassa, "The Newly Industrializing Developing Countries after the Oil Crisis," *Weltwirtschaftliches Archiv,* Band 117, Heft 1 (1981), pp. 141–94.

[6] I am indebted to Rudiger Dornbusch and Jeffrey Sachs for comments prompting the discussion of real wages.

tradable goods so that external balance (as well as internal) could be achieved.

In Meade's early formulation, if money wages were flexible downward, the gold standard could achieve external (and internal) balance. If money wages were fixed, devaluation would accomplish the same goal, but only with "sufficient divorce between movements in the cost of living and movements in money wage rate." In Meade's terms, "this decline in real wages . . . must be accepted. Any offsetting rise in money wages . . . would prevent the terms of international trade from moving against [country] B and would therefore remove the whole inducement to shift demand back again from [country] A's more expensive products to B's relatively cheaper products."[7]

But Meade's specification of adjustment in the form of a decline in the terms of trade is a clue to the possible irrelevance of this approach to the developing country. For most developing countries, especially small exporters of raw materials, external terms of trade are set exogenously by the world market. External adjustment occurs not through orchestrating a decline in the terms of trade by devaluation, but through shifting the focus of activity from nontraded to traded goods. Similarly, the typical developing country is not operating inside its production possibility frontier because of excessive real wages, but is operating on that frontier, and needs to move away from nontraded and toward traded goods to achieve external balance.

The more recent orthodox literature focusing on the distinction between traded and nontraded sectors establishes the framework in which devaluation can correct external imbalances with or without a decline in real wages, depending on the circumstances. Essentially, prices and profitability of traded goods must rise relative to prices and profitability of nontraded goods. For profitability of traded goods to rise (inducing resources to shift to traded goods), nominal wages should lag behind devaluation (where tradable goods prices rise by the amount of the devaluation). That is, the ratio of wages to prices of traded goods must fall. However, prices of nontraded goods should not rise as much as nominal wages (assuming the country is on the production possibility frontier). Indeed, if resources are to be moved out of nontradables, profitability will have to decline in the sector, and the ratio of wage to price must rise.[8]

[7] James E. Meade, *The Theory of International Economic Policy, vol. 1: The Balance of Payments* (London: Oxford University Press, 1951), pp. 202–3.

[8] As Dornbusch puts it, "Corresponding to that equilibrium we have a reduction in the real wage in terms of traded goods and an increase in the

In this two-sector approach, the final outcome for real wages depends on the relative weights of tradables and nontradables in the consumption basket of workers and on the extent of induced price increases in nontradables. In particular, if d is the percentage devaluation, $\dot{w}$ is the percentage rise in nominal wages that accompanies devaluation (as the result of union pressures or indexing), ϕ_T the share of tradables and ϕ_{NT} the share of nontradables in worker consumption, and $\dot{P}_{NT}$ the induced price rise in nontradables (depending on elasticities as shown in Figure 9.1), then the percentage change in real wage w^* is:

$$\dot{w}^* = \dot{w} - \phi_T d - \phi_{NT} \dot{P}_{NT}.$$

Thus, if nontradables and tradables each account for half of the consumption basket (for example), and a 15 percent devaluation induces a 5 percent increase in prices of nontradables, a nominal wage increase of 10 percent will fulfill the condition that wages fall relative to prices of traded goods while holding real wages constant [$\dot{w} = 10 - (0.5)15 - (0.5)5 = 0$]. The smaller the induced price rise for nontradables, and the larger the share of nontradables in consumption, the easier it will be to hold real wages constant (or even to raise them) while achieving the necessary reduction of wages relative to prices of tradables.

In the developing country context it is unclear how large the role of tradables in consumption will be. While food is often traded, some forms of subsistence foods (such as manioc) may not be. Housing expenditures are in the nontradable sector. The broad point is that it may be possible to achieve external stabilization through devaluation without reducing real wages. And it should certainly be possible to achieve stabilization without a reduction of real wages by the full extent of the devaluation. This conclusion has major policy implications. Draconian reductions in real wages are not necessarily required for external stabilization, and the standard theory does not provide an automatic justification for the extent of real wage reductions that have often been observed in some of the more politically conservative stabilization efforts.

real wage in terms of nontraded goods, so that money wages rise relative to the price of home goods." Rudiger Dornbusch, "Real and Monetary Aspects of the Effects of Exchange Rate Changes," in Robert Z. Aliber, ed., *National Monetary Policies and the International Financial System* (Chicago: University of Chicago Press, 1974), pp. 77–78.

Neo-Structuralist Critiques

The old structuralist critique of orthodox stabilization is well known and need not detain the discussion here. Inflation was viewed as structural, not monetary; it was considered to be caused by structural phenomena such as rigid agricultural supply (attributable to archaic agrarian structures) and weakness of the tax system; monetary expansion was considered accommodative rather than causal in the inflationary process; and corrective measures were envisioned as active (increased investment to break structural bottlenecks) rather than passive (reduced investment to cut back the fiscal deficit). Neither side convinced the other in the structuralist-monetarist debate of the early 1960s. But the monetarists claimed that theory was on their side, and that the structuralists' arguments were ad hoc, lacking in any underlying theory comparable to the quantity equation of the monetarists.

Now neo-structuralism has struck back. Some of its practitioners employ sophisticated mathematical methods and forthrightly announce their intention to show that the theories of the earlier structuralists were right after all, even though they had not yet been rigorously formulated. Two neo-structuralist critiques were emphasized at the Brookings conference: (1) devaluation can be recessionary instead of expansionary; (2) monetary and credit restraint can cause more inflation rather than less. Thus, two fundamental components of the orthodox stabilization policy are called into question.

Devaluation may be recessionary for at least three reasons: (a) higher import (and export) prices may mean decreased consumption through the real balance effect (Pigou); (b) failure of export and import quantities to respond sufficiently to devaluation will mean that higher local currency prices of both will widen the trade deficit expressed in domestic currency, causing a recessionary increase in the net imports component of GNP; and (c) under plausible conditions devaluation may redistribute income from workers to owners, causing consumption to fall relative to savings (under the assumption that savings are mainly out of profits, not wages).[9] The greatest emphasis

9. Recessionary devaluation is discussed in detail in Montek S. Ahluwalia and Frank J. Lysy, "Employment, Income Distribution, and Programs to Remedy Balance-of-Payments Difficulties," in Cline and Weintraub, *Economic Stabilization,* pp. 149–88. Ahluwalia and Lysy cite the earlier work of Richard Cooper and Carlos Diaz-Alejandro (with respect to the domestic currency value of the trade deficit) and Taylor and Krugman (with respect to possible income distributional effects).

in the neo-structuralist critique is on the perverse trade-balance effect. To see this effect more clearly, consider an initial trade deficit of $P_0^x X_0 - P_0^m M_0 = -100$, where P_0^x and P_0^m are the initial peso prices of exports and imports, and X_0 and M_0 are export and import quantities. In the extreme case, trade quantities do not respond at all to devaluation. Doubling the peso price of the dollar causes P^x and P^m to double, so that $P_1^x X_0 - P_1^m M_0 = -200$. Devaluation has unambiguously caused a greater drain of net exports in the national accounts equation, $Y = C + I + G + X - M$ (in domestic currency).

Ahluwalia and Lysy develop a one-sector model that yields an equation showing the critical elasticity of demand for exports at which devaluation changes from being contractionary to expansionary:

$$e^* = mC/E\ (1 - m),$$

where e = export demand elasticity, m = the (fixed coefficient) ratio of imported inputs to production, and E = a term involving a scaling factor and the ratio of the (peso-dollar) exchange rate to the (peso) price of domestic output. The authors maintain that, under Malaysian conditions, the equation means that the elasticity of demand for exports must be at least 0.5 to avoid contractionary effects of devaluation.[10]

The Ahluwalia-Lysy model makes no allowance for substitution of imports by domestic supply (although in a subsequent five-sector model, substitution is permitted). Moreover, the authors' view that an export demand elasticity of 0.5 might not be unusual stands in question. In the traditional small country model, the elasticity is infinite.

In a less simple model the elasticities of export supply, import demand, and import supply all matter. The more dominant view at the Brookings conference (including that of Carlos Diaz-Alejandro, a charter member of the neo-structuralist school) was that experience had shown that trade-elasticity pessimism had been exaggerated; trade response to devaluation had typically been sufficient for the normal expansionary case to apply. Although there is a need for more empirical work on this point, numerous recent studies have tended to confirm that trade is relatively responsive to the exchange rate in

[10] $E = A(r/Px)$, where A is a scale factor, r is the exchange rate, and Px is output price; $Px = vPv + mPm$, where v is the ratio of value added to gross output and Pv is the price of value added, which depends on capital and labor prices. Ibid., pp. 158–63.

developing countries.[11] In short, the first plank of the neo-structuralist platform is a theoretically useful insight but one of dubious empirical relevance. Low elasticities combined with a prestabilization trade deficit may make devaluation contractionary, but (notwithstanding Ahluwalia and Lysy) in practice the trade elasticities are likely to be sufficient that this perverse effect of the orthodox stabilization package will not occur.

The second neo-structuralist plank is considerably more heterodox. Lance Taylor has developed a model concluding that monetary restraint causes more inflation, not less.[12] The heart of Taylor's analysis is the postulate that, because interest payments on borrowed working capital are typically a high component of production costs in developing countries, tighter money tends to raise prices by raising the interest rate and thereby raising production costs, which are passed on to product price on a mark-up basis. In particular,

$$P = f[(1 + i)w, (1 + i)eP_0, rP],$$

where P = product price, i = the interest rate, w = the wage rate, e = the exchange rate, P_0 = the external price of imported inputs, and r = the profit rate. The term $(1 + i)$ enters product cost (and price) because working capital is borrowed to cover operating costs of labor and imported inputs.

Taylor develops a series of IS-LM diagrams to analyze this system, although instead of the conventional interest rate-output labels the axes show price and output (because of the assumption that price varies positively with the interest rate). But the central idea is not complicated; in the United States, it has been called the "Wright-Patman effect" in honor of the congressmen who tirelessly complained that the Federal Reserve's tight money caused inflation by raising interest rates and, therefore, interest-sensitive prices such as mortgage costs.

[11] See Donal J. Donovan, "Real Responses Associated with Exchange Rate Action in Selected Upper Credit Tranche Stabilization Programs," *IMF Staff Papers* 28(4) (December 1981), pp. 698–727, and the reference therein to studies by Khan, Brillembourg, Teigeiro and Elson, Singh, and Okonkwo. In the Brookings Conference, Alejandro Foxley also maintained that export pessimism is unwarranted, based on recent experience in Uruguay, Brazil, and Chile. Alejandro Foxley, "Stabilization Policies and Their Effects on Employment and Income Distribution: A Latin American Perspective," in Cline and Weintraub, *Economic Stabilization,* p. 218.

[12] Lance Taylor, "IS/LM in the Tropics: Diagrammatics of the New Structuralist Critique," in Cline and Weintraub, *Economic Stabilization,* pp. 465–503.

Several participants in the Brookings conference criticized the Taylor model for capturing only the short-run effect of monetary restraint. Discussant Kemal Dervis noted that over a longer period the more conventional anti-inflationary effects of monetary restraint could take hold, but that before that time was reached political disruption in response to the short-run inflation could well scuttle the program.

It would appear that a major problem with Taylor's analysis is that it contradicts a large body of empirical evidence. Many studies have shown that money growth is positively, not negatively, associated with inflation in developing countries.[13] And it is insufficient to respond, as neo-structuralists tend to do, that the standard empirical studies misconstrue causation, that rising prices cause accommodative money expansion and not vice versa. That response is methodologically inadmissable because in the neo-structuralist formulation money supply is causal, so a fair test must allow a causal role in both cases. The only question is: is the sign relating (induced) prices to (causal) money positive or negative.[14] Although there are some isolated instances where empirical results purport to find a negative relation between money and prices,[15] the vast bulk of evidence supports the conventional (quantity theory) positive relationship. Moreover, where causality tests (of the Granger-Sims variety) have been conducted, they have tended to confirm causation from money to prices rather than vice versa.[16]

An important implication of the Taylor analysis, nonetheless, may be that the timing and severity of monetary restraint are crucial.

[13] See Robert Vogel, "The Dynamics of Inflation in Latin America," *American Economic Review* (March 1974).

[14] If the causation from prices to money is accepted, the neostructuralist model becomes garbled indeed. With P = prices and M = money, the following dynamics would result: (1) M P (Taylor-Patman); (2) P M (the "prices induce money" response to empirical correlations; (3) M P (by the logic of Taylor-Patman); and (4) P M (price induces money); at this point return to (1) and recycle. Any shock to money would cause an oscillating sequence of cycles, with money and prices rising and falling.

[15] S. van Wijnbergen, "Stagflationary Effects of Monetary Stabilization Policies: A Quantitative Analysis of South Korea," Washington: World Bank, 1981; restricted circulation). However, Wijnbergen's simulations show that the perverse inflationary effects of tighter credit dominate only in the first two quarters, lending support to the critique (by others) that Taylor's analysis focuses excessively on the short run.

[16] See Surjit S. Bhalla, "India's Closed Economy and World Inflation," in William R. Cline and associates, *World Inflation and the Developing Countries* (Washington: Brookings Institution, 1981), pp. 161–65.

Taylor himself does not conclude that the best solution to inflation is to increase the money supply (despite the logic of the model); instead, his main policy thrust is that the conventional IMF stabilization package can cause severe stagflationary results. Devaluation can cause recession, while monetary restraint can cause both recession and inflation. Broadly, Taylor prefers gradualism to shock treatment because of the danger of overkill from the orthodox policy package. But to reach this policy conclusion more rigorously, it would be necessary to develop a time sequence analysis, presumably one that would show the negative causal relationship (Taylor-Patman) causing higher inflation as the result of tighter money in the first quarter or two, followed by the conventional anti-inflationary consequences later. Analysis with specific time dimensions would be extremely helpful for policy formulation, especially in the choice between shock treatment (e.g., a massive initial reduction in money growth) and gradualism (e.g., a more moderate phasing-in of slower money growth).

Stabilization and Growth

A central issue in stabilization policy is the extent to which real growth must be sacrificed to reduce inflation to acceptable levels and to correct external disequilibrium. A related issue is whether any growth effects are likely to be transitory or extend to the medium- and long-run period. Anne Krueger has emphasized the long-run growth benefits from stabilization packages that correct previous distortions between the domestic and external sectors.[17] She identifies two dimensions of trade distortion: bias in the price ratio of tradables to nontradables, and bias in the price ratio of import substitutes to exports. An open trade deficit involves too low a price for tradables; an external imbalance with the deficit suppressed by import quotas or tariffs also involves bias toward import substitution and against exports. Krueger notes that the inflationary consequences of devaluation will depend on whether the external influence was open or suppressed. If it was open, devaluation will mean higher prices for imports and inflationary pressure; but if the influence had been suppressed by protection, higher import prices will already have affected the economy, and a package devaluing the currency while jointly

[17] Anne O. Krueger, "Interactions between Inflation and Trade Regime Objectives in Stabilization Programs," in Cline and Weintraub, *Economic Stabilization,* pp. 83–114.

removing protection need not worsen inflation. One might add, however, that, in the more severe cases where stabilization is required, there are open trade deficits that urgently require correction even though protection is also high.

Krueger also notes that inflation may be viewed as essentially separate from trade bias; indeed, the crawling peg exchange rate can be used to neutralize the external sector from domestic inflation and to ensure that trade bias does not arise solely because domestic inflation exists.

Eliminating trade bias in the application of a stabilization package has large benefits, according to Krueger. However, because correction of the bias alters resource allocation, it may also cause some temporary growth loss. Output will fall in the sectors formerly favored by the bias, while it may take some time for investment and activity to respond in the newly favored sectors, especially if economic agents do not consider the government's program to be credible. Nevertheless, Krueger holds that such growth losses are usually much smaller than the longer-run growth gains achievable by eliminating trade bias. Based on National Bureau of Economic Research studies, stabilization packages that include correction of trade bias can raise long-term growth rates by two or three percentage points annually, while reducing short-run growth by perhaps only one to two percentage points over 18 months. Moreover, the short-run losses may be ameliorated by special stimulus.

Considering anti-inflationary measures per se, Krueger maintains that, outside of a few exceptional cases, there typically has been some recessionary cost of reducing inflation. However, if external finance can be arranged, increased imports can help reduce inflation while reducing the trade bias at the same time.

Carlos Diaz-Alejandro presents a more adverse account of the growth effects of stabilization.[18] As applied in the Southern Cone of Latin America, past stabilization programs have often been so negative in their growth impact that, according to Diaz, one may ask whether the cure was worse than the disease. His stylized facts depict a sequence in which a populist government embarks on social and developmental spending that outstrips the tax base, while raising wages. The initial effects are a deceivingly buoyant economy, as the distortions only gradually wreak their eventual havoc. At that time increasingly harsh populist rhetoric alarms the private sector, and the

[18] Carlos Diaz-Alejandro, "Southern Cone Stabilization Plans," in Cline and Weintraub, *Economic Stabilization,* pp. 119–141.

military intervenes. The orthodox stabilization measures that then typically follow involve severe monetary contraction, devaluation, and sharp reductions in real wages. The results usually involve serious loss of production, and little progress against inflation; although the balance of payments improves, it does so mainly because of reduced income and import demand (although Diaz-Alejandro judges that trade elasticities typically have been adequate for devaluation to be effective). Contrasting the more favorable growth results during stabilization in Brazil with experience in Argentina and Chile, Diaz-Alejandro broadly favors an approach of gradualism rather than shock treatment. He favors price guidelines; less credit restriction with lower interest rates and less capital inflow; and greater use of taxes for equity. He also notes that the growth costs of stabilization will be smaller if the government's measures are credible; the worst stagflations tend to occur when, because of repeated failure to stick to stabilization programs in the past, new stabilization efforts lack credibility. Despite his general critique of the radical free-market stabilization strategy in the Southern Cone, Diaz-Alejandro applauds the long-overdue liberalization of trade.

Other participants in the Brookings conference more familiar with the Asian experience argued that there was scope for expansionary stabilization. Papanek cited the examples of Indonesia (1967–70) and Bangladesh (1974–76).[19] In Indonesia, a shock treatment reduced inflation from 1,000 percent to 10 percent. Output expanded as a result of improved efficiency in macroeconomic management, increased double-shift operation of industry, response of exports to devaluation, increased saving and reduced capital flight, and improved use of fertilizer and irrigation. Increased foreign aid, especially in food aid, was an important factor contributing to expansionary stabilization. Similarly, in his analysis of the case of Pakistan, Guisinger emphasizes the expansionary impact of government policy. However, for Pakistan in the mid-1970s the problem was not a classic stabilization problem but instead one of stagnation in the face of declining exports and investment, and Guisinger maintains that the stimulative government policy adopted was appropriate even though it had some cost in terms of inflation and balance of payments deterioration.[20]

[19] Gustav F. Papanek, "Comments," in Cline and Weintraub, *Economic Stabilization,* pp. 399–405; p. 233.

[20] Stephen E. Guisinger, "Stabilization Policies in Pakistan: The 1970–77 Experience," in Cline and Weintraub, *Economic Stabilization,* pp. 375–99.

Harberger and Edwards have recently conducted research indicating that substantial disinflation can be accomplished without cost in real growth rates (and, indeed, often in conjunction with accelerated growth). Using a selection criterion of initial inflation of 50 percent or more followed by a cut in inflation of at least one-half within seven years, the authors identified 10 disinflation episodes in seven countries and found that in the great majority of cases growth held steady or accelerated during the disinflation period.[21] The monetarist inference would be that monetary restraint can reduce inflation without loss of real output (a proposition put to test by the hybrid of rational expectations and supply-side economics dominating US policy in 1981 and, at least by the early election returns, found wanting). It is worth noting that the Harberger-Edwards sample is almost entirely composed of Latin American countries, suggesting that the contrasting views of Diaz-Alejandro and Papanek are not necessarily attributable to their respective focuses on Latin America and Asia. However, the Harberger-Edwards study makes no attempt to relate the disinflation experiences to actual monetary policy, and even if it did so the experience of seven countries would be a rather limited basis for concluding that monetarist stabilization is painless. Moreover, as Williamson has pointed out, by the nature of its selection the sample is likely to be biased toward cases where there were favorable exogenous supply developments; such exogenous factors would contribute to observed declines in inflation while biasing the test of the influences of monetary restraint on output.[22]

The stabilization-growth trade-off became more complicated in the 1970s because of the need for long-run adjustment to a changed external environment (the oil shock and slower growth in industrial country markets), as opposed to simple correction of internal disequilibria. At the aggregate level, the 1970s experience showed sur-

[21] Arnold C. Harberger and Sebastian Edwards, "International Evidence on the Sources of Inflation," paper presented at the Conference on Inflation, Rio de Janeiro, December 15–16, 1980, Getulio Vargas Foundation (Rio de Janeiro: Getulio Vargas Foundation, 1980).

[22] See Chapter 7, this volume. The logical implication of Williamson's critique is that not only should a proper test use a random sample to compare, among countries with high inflation, one group that imposed monetary restraint against another group that did not; but in addition, in evaluating the growth difference between the two groups, growth should be normalized to remove the influence of exogenous factors (weather, abrupt changes in international markets, etc.).

prisingly little growth cost of stabilization (and/or adjustment). While the average growth rate of industrial countries fell from 5.1 percent in 1960–70 to 3.2 percent in 1971–80, that of oil-importing developing countries only fell from 5.7 to 5.1 percent.[23] To the extent that developing countries did not adjust but merely borrowed abroad, this performance would not be particularly relevant to the growth costs of adjustment and stabilization. However, considerable adjustment and stabilization did take place. From 1974 to 1977 the real volume of imports of non-oil developing countries rose by only 2 percent while the real volume of exports rose by 23 percent.[24] There was less progress on stabilization of inflation: non-oil developing countries reduced average inflation only from 25 percent to 22 percent from 1974 to 1977 (although in Asia the reduction was from 28 percent to 9 percent).[25] Broadly, however, considerable adjustment cum stabilization appears to have taken place. Combined with the fact that growth fell very little, the aggregate experience of the 1970s suggests that the growth costs of stabilization need not be high.

In sum, the currently available analysis and evidence on the trade-off between stabilization and growth suggest the following: (a) In the short run, growth losses are likely to accompany stabilization, as the newly favored sectors take time to respond while newly disfavored sectors contract; (b) longer-run benefits of stabilization are likely to outweigh these costs, especially where trade-regime bias is eliminated; (c) despite this dominant pattern (and evidence of serious growth loss in some Southern Cone cases), a surprising amount of country-specific evidence seems to be emerging suggesting that the "exceptional" cases of stabilization without growth loss may not be so rare; and (d) at the aggregate level, the non-oil developing countries appear to have accomplished considerable adjustment in the 1970s at little cost in terms of growth. There is a need for more empirical work on the stabilization-growth trade-off, merely to clarify the stylized facts. Moreover, little work has been done on a broad empirical basis distinguishing between the growth effects of gradualist and shock-treatment strategies.

[23] World Bank, *World Development Report 1981* (New York: Oxford University Press, August 1981), pp. 15, 137.

[24] David P. Dod, "Bank Lending to Developing Countries: Recent Developments in Historical Perspective," *Federal Reserve Bulletin* (September 1981), p. 648.

[25] Excluding Argentina, Chile, and Uruguay. Cline and associates, *World Inflation*, p. 3.

Stabilization and Income Distribution

An important policy issue is whether stabilization measures as commonly practiced tend to cause a disproportionately heavy burden of adjustment on the poor, concentrating the distribution of income. The related theoretical issue is whether adverse distributional effects are necessary.

In the model developed by Ahluwalia and Lysy, income distribution depends on the elasticity of substitution and the direction of change of output. If the elasticity of substitution is less than unity, increased output (with capital fixed and labor variable) raises the share of capital, and reduced output lowers it; if the elasticity of substitution exceeds unity, the reverse occurs in each case (a standard neo-classical conclusion). The distribution thus depends on the direction of stabilization's impact on output, although the authors have no particular opinion on the likely size of the elasticity. They emphasize that factor shares are not likely to change much and that the important question is the absolute level of output (and therefore absolute income of the poor).[26]

Alejandro Foxley describes a more pervasive process of concentration of income during stabilization on the basis of Latin American experience.[27] He emphasizes that stabilization programs in Brazil in the 1960s—and in Argentina, Chile, and Uruguay in the 1970s—tended to reduce real wages (by 20 percent to as much as 40 percent in Chile in 1975) and the share of wages in GNP. Unemployment rose in at least two of the four cases. Where data are available, they show a decline in the share of low-income groups in the family distribution of income and a rise in the share of the top 20 percent of families.

The forces Foxley identifies as leading to income concentration are the following.

(1) Corrective price policies allow sharp price increases following repressed inflation, while controls are kept on wages. Nor do wages keep pace with inflation induced by devaluation. (However, in his comment on Foxley's paper, Fishlow noted that, although the critics have chronicled the adverse distributional consequences of stabili-

[26] Ahluwalia and Lysy, "Employment, Income Distribution," p. 169.
[27] Alejandro Foxley, "Stabilization Policies," pp. 191–225.

zation, they have not dealt with the question of whether the pre-stabilization wage level was unsustainably high.)[28]

(2) Financial reforms free interest rates, which reach high levels (40 percent in real terms over a three-year period in Chile). Returns to capital rise, along with its share in income. Assets tend to concentrate in large firms with access to foreign capital, which are well positioned to buy up undervalued assets of financially stressed medium-size firms.

(3) Reduction of the fiscal deficit through cuts in government spending can cut back labor-intensive public works and housing construction (as in Chile), contributing to unemployment. Spending cuts inevitably hit social programs: health, education, housing, social security. Tax increases can be either regressive or progressive; in the Chilean case, uniform value-added taxes were imposed while wealth and capital gains taxes were eliminated.

Adverse distributional consequences of stabilization may occur in practice but need not occur on the basis of theory, and even their predominance as a stylized fact is subject to dispute. My study on Peru for the Brookings conference suggested that the stereotype of stabilization on the backs of the poor had been overdrawn in the case of Peru.[29] Attention has focused on sharp decreases in real wages, but a closer examination showed that the most severe declines were for white collar workers well above the median income; higher food prices may have helped low-income farmers, and reduction of gasoline subsidies was almost certainly borne by the upper portion of the income distribution. In his study of Mexico, Sidney Weintraub emphasized that it is the poor who tend to be hurt by inflation, so that the alternative to a stabilization program may be even more inequitable. Moreover, income distribution data from Mexico indicate that the expansive government programs under Echeverria that eventually destabilized the economy did not achieve a more equal income distribution.[30]

There appears to be considerable scope for taking distributional considerations into account in stabilization programs. The extent to which distribution is considered depends fundamentally on the po-

[28] Albert Fishlow, "Comments," in Cline and Weintraub, *Economic Stabilization,* p. 232.

[29] Cline, "Economic Stabilization in Peru, 1975–78," in Cline and Weintraub, *Economic Stabilization,* pp. 271–326.

[30] Weintraub, "Case Study of Economic Stabilization: Mexico," in Cline and Weintraub, *Economic Stabilization,* pp. 271–92.

litical forces dominating government. In Malaysia, where the indigenous Malays have a majority population, dominate the government, but have relatively low income compared with the Chinese and Indians, policy response to external inflationary shocks in the mid-1970s was consciously tailored to achieve stabilization on an equitable basis that would not forfeit the socioeconomic goals of the New Economic Policy formulated in response to race riots in the late 1960s.[31]

Both internal and external factors caused Malaysia's inflation to surge from 4.3 percent at the end of 1972 to 21.4 percent in early 1974 before it was brought down again to 4.5 percent in 1975. The government employed severe monetary restraint as one measure, but it exempted loans to small borrowers and to the Malay community from ceilings on credit growth. Export taxes were increased, but through an increase in progressivity rather than on a neutral basis. At the same time, fiscal policy was designed to relieve the impact of price increases on the poor. Government subsidies were provided for rice, fertilizer, flour, milk, and school textbooks—belying the axiom that social spending is inevitably the first to be cut in fiscal restraint. To be sure, a relatively favorable external balance (given improved prices for rubber and other exports) facilitated the stabilization exercise. Terms of trade rose by 6 percent from 1972 to 1974, and Malaysia was actually able to obtain an anti-inflationary boost through floating and appreciating the exchange rate by approximately 20 percent. Nevertheless, the policy orientation toward "progressive" stabilization would probably have been followed even if external developments had been neutral or even unfavorable.

The sharp contrast between equity-oriented stabilization in Malaysia and the portrait of inequitable stabilization drawn by Foxley for Argentina, Brazil, Chile, and Uruguay suggests the dominance of the political orientation of the regime in determining the distributional consequences of stabilization programs (although the economic failure of the reformist variant of military rule in Latin America, the Velasco regime in Peru, and the economic mishaps of populist regimes described by Diaz-Alejandro, suggest that equitable orientation may be accompanied by technically unviable policies). Nevertheless, there are purely economic factors that also determine the distributional impact of stabilization.

[31] R. Chander, C. L. Robless, and K. P. Teh, "Malaysian Growth and Price Stabilization," in Cline, *World Inflation,* pp. 208–27.

Johnson and Salop have attempted to set forth the major economic forces determining distributional effects.[32] They note that direct effects of fiscal measures (such as a reduction in food subsidies) will be influenced by the political power of different groups. However, indirect effects associated with the transition to external balance will depend on economic structure. The authors stress the key role of raising relative prices of traded to nontraded goods. Factor rewards in the export sectors (and, by implication, import substitutes) will tend to rise at the expense of those in nontraded goods. The resulting distributional effect will depend on whether the export (and import-competing) sectors are dominated by upper or lower income groups (relative to the nontraded sectors). They note that, with capital fixed but labor mobile, these distributional effects through sectoral shift in demand are especially concentrated in capital income, so that the difference between concentrated capital income in some sectors and dispersed capital in others (for example, smallholder export crops) affects the distributional impact. They are relatively optimistic about distributional consequences of a market-oriented stabilization package. The alternative of controls invites allocation of windfall gains to the (rich and) powerful; export expansion often provides opportunities for employment growth; and reduction of inflation will tend to benefit the poor, whose assets are most likely to be in money rather than in other assets that keep pace with inflation.

To recapitulate, stabilization (including that along orthodox lines) does tend to affect the distribution of income, but not inevitably in the direction of concentration. In the range of discretionary measures, especially fiscal, stabilization can be progressive or regressive, depending on political choice of the regime. The more structural forces will be driven mainly by the distributional consequences of raising prices and activity in tradable goods relative to those in nontradable goods. To be sure, the overall level of economic activity will be important: if the stabilization package reduces output and employment (as the neo-structuralists fear, under the orthodox package) real income of the poor will decline, although it may be argued that, because profit share tends to be procyclical, the distribution of income will become more equitable during recession. As for the distributional outcome in practice, the variety of experience suggests that (ortho-

[32] Omotunde Johnson and Joanne Salop, "Distributional Aspects of Stabilization Programs in Developing Countries," *IMF Staff Papers*, vol. 27(1) (March 1980), pp. 1–23.

dox) stabilization can either concentrate or equalize the income distribution, for the reasons enumerated above.

Capital Flows and Exchange Rates

In addition to providing an update on new theories about old problems, the Brookings conference drew attention to new problems in stabilization. A broad new problem is the more hostile international economic environment that began in the 1970s (discussed in the next section). A more specific new development concerns interaction of the exchange rate and capital flows. Diaz-Alejandro notes that in the Southern Cone the new emphasis on liberalization of trade and exchange regimes and of domestic financial markets, combined with domestic credit restraint, has meant that large capital inflows have occurred in response to high domestic interest rates.[33] These inflows have caused appreciation of the real exchange rate, working at cross-purposes to the need to stimulate exports and adversely affecting the import-competing sector, already hard pressed by the dismantling of protection. In the process, large foreign debt is accumulated. Capital inflows also engorge reserves and expand the domestic money supply.

Diaz-Alejandro also criticizes the reliance on preannounced and decelerating exchange rate devaluations as the key instrument for reducing inflation. The logic behind the strategy is that preannouncing will reduce inflationary expectations. Moreover, domestic producers will be forced to reduce price increases in the face of foreign competition, and domestic inflation will necessarily fall to the international rate plus the (preannounced) rate of devaluation. But, as Diaz-Alejandro notes, persistent inflation in nontraded goods can lead to overvaluation. In his comment, McKinnon agrees with Diaz-Alejandro on the problem of excessive capital inflow in response to high domestic interest rates, and on the danger of overvaluation in the strategy of preannounced devaluation as an anti-inflationary device.[34] But McKinnon maintains that there is an unavoidable dilemma because the alternative of setting a crawling peg that wholly neutralizes domestic inflation destabilizes the monetary system if trade liberalization is complete; variations in the crawl induce fluctuations in the demand for money, causing inward and outward surges of capital.

[33] Carlos Diaz-Alejandro, "Comments," Chapters 11–14, this volume.

[34] Ronald McKinnon, "Comment" in Cline and Weintraub, *Economic Stabilization,* pp. 141–46.

McKinnon suggests that the complete liberalization of exchange rates should come last in the sequence of liberalization, and that trade and domestic financial liberalization should come first.

Blejer and Mathieson have analyzed the strategy of preannounced devaluation as an anti-inflationary device that was adopted by Argentina, Chile, and Uruguay beginning in 1978.[35] To the extent that the measure reduces inflationary expectations, it increases demand for real money balances, relieving inflationary pressure (reducing the excess of money supply over money demand). However, the gain in expectations occurs only if the preannounced schedule of devaluations is credible. On the side of product markets, the authors note that trade liberalization does not guarantee equalization of domestic and international prices (for traded goods) because of initial costs of organization and marketing in entering external trade. On capital flows, they note that, by reducing exchange rate uncertainty, preannouncement induces a once-for-all capital inflow until the previous divergence between domestic and external interest rates declines to reflect the now lower uncertainty. But after a long period of capital control, the domestic capital market is unlikely to achieve immediate integration with the world capital market (keeping the domestic interest rate premium relatively high). At the same time, the increased capital inflow puts pressure on money supply. Indeed, in so doing, it undermines the credibility of the preannounced schedule of devaluations. More generally, the authors conclude that preannouncement can be destabilizing when the other elements of the stabilization package, especially fiscal policy, are inconsistent with the deceleration of inflation implied by the preannounced crawl. Preannounced schedules that involve growing departure from purchasing power parity are destabilizing.

In practice, the instrument of preannounced devaluation led to a dramatic exchange rate collapse in Argentina in 1981, when there were three successive devaluations of 30 percent within three months following a break in confidence and large reserve losses. The mechanism had led to a wildly overvalued peso, sustained solely by the foreign capital inflow in response to high domestic interest rates and by mushrooming external debt. The same phenomenon appeared to be taking place in slow motion in Chile in 1981 under a fixed-rate version (fixed rates are a preannounced crawl at zero rate) as declining

[35] Mario I. Blejer and Donald J. Mathieson, "The Preannouncement of Exchange Rates as a Stabilization Instrument," *IMF Staff Papers,* 28(4) (December 1981), pp. 760–42.

copper prices and an overvalued exchange rate led to a current account deficit larger than exports, sustained only by large borrowing induced at the expense of real interest rates of 40 percent. The recent record on preannounced crawling for stabilization bears out the misgivings expressed by Diaz-Alejandro (and McKinnon) two years earlier.

The International Environment

The Brookings conference addressed the question of the role of external shocks in causing balance of payments and inflationary problems in the 1970s. Stanley Black has analyzed the relative weight of external and internal disturbances using discriminant analysis.[36] He classifies developing countries into five groups, from the most stable externally to the least, based on criteria such as their ability to issue international bonds or borrow abroad commercially, on the one hand, or their need to resort to IMF drawings, stand-by arrangements, or even default (debt rescheduling), on the other. By its nature, Black's classification scheme focuses on the external dimension of stabilization, omitting domestic price stability. Black identifies three sets of factors determining a country's classification: country characteristics (size, development, openness, concentration of trade); external factors (import prices, terms of trade, changes in reserves, export volume, oil prices, wheat prices); and internally determined factors (controls, debt service and maturity, consumer prices, reserves relative to imports, money growth, real interest rate, and real exchange rate).

Black's fivefold discriminant classification achieves good statistical explanation using these variables. Of the total distance separating the country groupings, 47 percent is explained by the country characteristics (especially development and trade concentration), and 35 percent is explained by the internal variables (the highest weight being on inflation). Only 17 percent is explained by external variables, of which terms of trade and exports are the most important. Black concludes that, although external factors have been important, internal factors have been dominant in causing stabilization problems. Accordingly, he advocates retention of meaningful conditionality in IMF lending, to ensure satisfactory domestic policies.

[36] Stanley W. Black, "The Impact of Changes in the World Economy on Stabilization Policies in the 1970s," in Cline and Weintraub, *Economic Stabilization,* pp. 43–77.

In his comment on Black's study, Sidney Dell draws upon his cross-country analysis for the United Nations' Development Program and Conference on Trade and Development in emphasizing that the bulk of stabilization problems in the 1970s were caused by external shocks: inflationary impulses from the industrial countries, followed by oil shock, followed by recession in industrial countries and contracting export markets.[37] Accordingly, Dell advocates much greater international financing to facilitate developing country adjustment, and less conditionality of this financing. Dell notes the precedent of the IMF's compensatory financing facility (CFF) for fluctuation in export prices.

Analysis of transmission of inflation into developing economies in the 1970s confirms the point made by both Black and Dell that international developments played a substantial role in the stabilization problems of this period. Cross-country regression analysis by Bhalla, using a basic monetarist model enhanced by variables for import prices and food supply, confirms the systematic process of inflationary transmission.[38] The transmission worked mainly through the monetary channel of reserve inflows (corresponding to US dollar outflows in the early 1970s) and expansion of the domestic monetary base (with a widespread and sharp acceleration in 1972), and through the channel of prices of imported goods (especially in the commodity price boom of 1973–74 and in the oil shock of 1974). A case study of Guatemala and El Salvador (by Gabriel Siri and Luis Raul Dominguez) illustrates the disruptive effect of world inflation on a traditionally price-stable country.[39] A case study of Brazil indicates that, even in a country with an inflationary tradition, the external shocks of the mid-1970s precipitated a reacceleration of inflation (in a three-stage sequence: reserve and money expansion; import price shock, especially oil; and price-push from Brazil's own increases in protection induced by balance of payments stress), and the world recession depressed export earnings. Both cross-country and case-study analyses thus support the common sense proposition that it was international transmission of inflation (not a simultaneous spree of fiscal irresponsibility) that swept developing country inflation from an av-

[37] Sidney Dell, "Comment," in Cline and Weintraub, *Economic Stabilization,* pp. 77–81.

[38] Bhalla, "The Transmission of Inflation into Developing Economies," in Cline, *World Inflation.*

[39] Gabriel Siri and Lewis Raúl Dominquez, "Central American Accommodation to External Disruptions," in Cline, *World Inflation.*

erage of 10 percent in 1967–72 to 22 percent in 1973 and to 25 percent in 1974.[40]

Even though the external sources of instability confronted a wide array of developing countries, internal policies were important, even dominant, in many cases. The choice of higher protection in Brazil probably heightened inflation (compared with the alternative of devaluation) by increasing distortions in resource allocation. In the case studies of Mexico and Peru for the Brookings conference,[41] Weintraub and I found domestic disequilibria to be considerably more important than external shocks in explaining inflationary and balance of payments problems in the mid-1970s.

Furthermore, even though the external shocks were common to many developing countries in the mid-1970s (at least those importing oil), the policy responses to them differed. Some developing countries succeeded in stabilization and adjustment, and others did not. A striking pattern of the subsequent policy response is that in Asia most countries succeeded in bringing inflation back down from its 1974 peak (from an average of 27.8 percent in 1974 to 8.8 percent in 1977) while those in Africa (18.6 percent in 1974 versus 25 percent in 1977), Latin America (25 percent versus 34 percent, excluding Argentina, Chile and Uruguay), and the Middle East (21.8 percent versus 24.2 percent) did not. A stylized fact from the 1970s is that Asia achieved price stabilization after external shock while other regions did not.

Given the differences in stabilization performance despite common external shocks, the implication is that different degrees of effectiveness in policy response were crucial in determining the outcome. Although it is a good debating point to cite the external shocks of recent years as grounds for increased unconditional financing from the industrial countries and the Organization of Petroleum Exporting Countries (OPEC), the logic of the recommendation of reduced conditionality depends on one's views of its effect on domestic policies. If conditionality is viewed as improving the chances that the right domestic policies will be adopted, it is a disservice to the developing countries themselves to couple a recommendation for increased financing with a recommendation for decreased conditionality. Removing conditionality will tend to cause a run-up in debt to sustain

[40] Cline, "Brazil's Aggressive Response to External Shocks," in Cline, *World Inflation*.

[41] Cline, "Economic Stabilization in Peru," and Weintraub, "Case Study of Economic Stabilization: Mexico," in Cline and Weintraub, *Economic Stabilization*.

poor policies. If conditionality is viewed as a nuisance that causes hardship for borrowing countries and that serves primarily to soothe international bureaucrats and bankers, then it makes sense to attach nonconditionality to the plea for more international financing based on the allocation of much of the responsibility for instability in the 1970s to international forces.

Another feature of the international economy in the 1970s represented an impressive response of market institutions to the new external shocks: private banks greatly increased their lending to developing countries. Irving Friedman has examined the role of private banks in international financial recycling.[42] Friedman emphasizes that banks consider the long-term development prospects of countries, not just short-term circumstances; that their portfolios are diversified among many borrowing countries; that indicators such as debt relative to exports or GNP do not show widespread deterioration, despite large growth in nominal debt; and that the IMF "seal of approval" for countries in difficult circumstances is an important signal for banks, magnifying the IMF's role far beyond provision of its own resources. Friedman contends that banks have seldom lent where the IMF would have preferred a prior agreement with the country (a view some IMF staff would probably dispute: "Why do countries wait so long before coming to the Fund?" is usually answered, "Because the banks let them.") He also urges that banks receive first priority in repayment. Yet the moral hazard problem suggests that this rule would be undesirable, and the experience of Peru and some other countries seems to show that the banks have sometimes exercised insufficient caution because they already assume they will be bailed out by the international community.

IMF Programs in Operation

The Brookings conference examined the theory and experience of stabilization rather than policies of the IMF. Nevertheless, the appropriateness of IMF conditionality practices is an issue implicit in several of the conference studies and in other recent literature on stabilization.

The Brookings conference included three case studies on countries where IMF programs had been applied (Mexico, Peru, and Tanzania),

[42] Irving S. Friedman, "The Role of Private Banks in Stabilization Programs," in Cline and Weintraub, *Economic Stabilization,* pp. 235–65.

as well as judgments by some of the other authors on the theory and practice of IMF conditionality.

Sidney Weintraub has examined Mexico's stabilization in the period 1977–79, which involved the IMF extended Fund facility (EFF) and conditionality.[43] Under Echeverria, expansive government spending unmatched by tax increases caused an average fiscal deficit of 5.7 percent of GDP (1971–76), rising to 9.5 percent in 1976. Money supply grew at an average of 19 percent annually in 1971–76, and wholesale prices rose at 14.5 percent compared with 2.9 percent in 1965–70. The fixed peso-dollar exchange rate—a fetish in Mexico, where the United States accounts for about two-thirds of trade and tourism earnings—meant that the peso became increasingly overvalued. In August 1976, massive capital flight precipitated a devaluation from 12.5 to 23 pesos to the dollar.

The IMF agreement involved a three-year program from 1977–79. Its conditions included a cutback on external borrowing from $4 billion to $3 billion yearly, reduction of the public sector deficit and targets for increased reserves, and limits to increases in the net domestic assets of the Bank of Mexico. Mexico was also committed to reducing import-licensing requirements and some tariffs. Thus, the package was conventional (considering that devaluations had already occurred), except that it covered three years rather than the more traditional one-year period.

Mexico achieved the various targets of the agreement. Economic performance was favorable except in inflation. Real output rose by 3.2 percent in 1977 and by 6.6 percent in 1978; the current account deficit fell from $4 billion in 1975 to $1.8 billion in 1977 (even though oil exports were still small); and the public sector deficit fell from 9.5 to 7.5 percent of GDP by 1978. However, inflation surged from 15.8 percent in 1976 to 28.9 percent in 1977 and remained at 17.5 percent in 1978; the sharp devaluation played a substantial role in the temporary acceleration of inflation.

Weintraub concludes that the IMF agreement was broadly successful except in its anti-inflationary objectives. It did involve a reduction in real wages, but the burden of stabilization was probably not greater than that of the destabilization period for the unemployed and underemployed. In his comment, Saul Trejo Reyes emphasizes the difficulty of achieving distributional objectives, rather than economic management, as the key to understanding the Echeverria pe-

[43] Weintraub, "Case Study of Economic Stabilization: Mexico," in Cline and Weintraub, *Economic Stabilization*.

riod.[44] He also suggests that the arrival of oil is the single most important factor in Mexico's economic turnaround. While this caveat is surely relevant in explaining the sharp improvement in growth in 1978, it does not explain the largely pre-oil recovery on the external current account, and it should not take away credit for a largely successful stabilization program with IMF participation.

The case of Peruvian stabilization in 1975–78 is one of the most controversial episodes of IMF involvement. My review of the case recounts the policy distortions under the military government that led to economic crisis: neglect of exports, growing overvaluation of the sol, mismanagement in state enterprises, increased government investment unmatched by taxes (leading to a fiscal deficit at 10 percent of GNP by 1975), and high expenditures on military imports.[45] Bad luck made matters worse: the anchovies disappeared off the coast, the price of copper plummeted in 1975, and expected oil discoveries failed to materialize. The current account deficit reached 123 percent of exports in 1975, and Peru rapidly accumulated external debt as private banks lent munificently in the expectation of bright oil prospects.

Sporadic stabilization attempts began in 1976 after an intramilitary coup, but the political onus of going to the IMF led Peru to conclude an unusual stabilization package with a syndicate of international private banks, on terms not very different from what the IMF might have advocated. The bank package failed within the year as Peru missed the targets, and the banks then insisted on IMF participation. Negotiations with the IMF from March to May 1977, and a false start at an actual agreement in November 1977, repeatedly failed for the essential reason that important segments of the government were unwilling to accept budgetary restraints. But by the second quarter of 1978 the country was near external bankruptcy, imports were freezing up for lack of trade credit, and there was little alternative to a firm stabilization program. The new economic team devalued the sol by 15 percent, imposed increases in prices of fuel and bread, eliminated most subsidies, raised interest rates, and restricted government spending. The measures precipitated strikes, riots, and some deaths.

The targets of a new IMF agreement negotiated in July 1978 were substantially met by Peru. Debt was successfully rescheduled. For 1978 as a whole the external deficit was down to only 10 percent of

[44] Saul Trejo Reyos, "Comment," Cline and Weintraub, pp. 292–95.

[45] Cline, "Economic Stabilization in Peru, 1975–78," in Cline and Weintraub, *Economic Stabilization,* pp. 297–334.

exports (although severe restrictions on imports early in the year played a role in the turnaround). However, inflation accelerated from approximately 35 percent in 1975–76 to nearly 60 percent in 1978. Strong export prices caused a large external surplus in 1979, and real growth averaged 3.5 percent in 1979–80 after a 1.8 percent decline in 1978, although inflation remained in the range of 60 percent.[46]

Regression analysis for Peru shows responsiveness of both exports and imports to the real exchange rate, contrary to the fears of some structuralists. And although Schydlowsky's comment criticized the IMF's (and government's) diagnosis of excess demand and recommended double shifting and export incentives as an alternative to demand restraint and devaluation, further examination tends to confirm the view that large fiscal deficits reflected excess demand, and a socioeconomic change in shifting patterns seems dubious as a feasible measure for cyclical adjustment.[47] The discussion earlier in this essay has addressed the common critique that the IMF package was disproportionately hard on the poor.

The Peruvian case illustrates the problems caused by excessive private bank lending followed by the wrenching outflows once banks lose confidence. It illustrates paradigmatically a widely recognized problem: countries that wait too long before reaching a stabilization agreement with the IMF typically reach a crisis of such proportions that there is little alternative to seemingly draconian measures. And the Peruvian case may also illustrate a political learning process by the IMF: the terms of the July 1978 package appear to have been more gradualist than those of the November 1977 package and those the IMF urged in March 1977. Broadly, however, the Peruvian case represents the more or less effective workings of the normal IMF stabilization package (once adopted) rather than a proof of structuralist criticisms of such programs, although (as in the case of Mexico) success on the external account and in growth was not matched by the results on inflation.

The case of Tanzania has also raised controversy about IMF policies; moreover, it raises questions about IMF policy approaches in socialist countries. Weaver and Anderson describe Tanzania's experience of relatively steady growth (5 to 6 percent) but intermittent

[46] IMF, *International Financial Statistics,* (Washington: January 1982).

[47] See the comment by Daniel M. Schydlowsky and my reply in Cline and Weintraub, *Economic Stabilization,* pp. 326–55.

balance of payments crises in the 1970s.[48] The current account deficit reached 50 percent of exports in 1971, over 70 percent in 1974–75, and 99 percent in 1978 (recovering between each episode). The study focuses on the 1974–75 crisis. Drought, the oil price shock, and world recession played an important role in that crisis. In addition, the Ujamaa process of villagization had disrupted food production, causing heavy imports of food.

The government's response to the crisis managed to reduce the external deficit while provoking critiques from right and left. Imports were strictly controlled. The government rejected devaluation on grounds of inelastic trade response. It abandoned communal farming efforts, raised agricultural prices, and carried out an ideological campaign to produce more food. It raised minimum wages by 40 percent but held higher wages to smaller increases. It increased prices on state services, raised taxes on cigarettes and beer, and tried to cut back government spending. Altogether, then, Tanzania's package was one of compromises that might be called socialist realism.

The package did not suit the IMF. Although the IMF responded to the 1974 crisis with loans averaging 10 percent of exports during 1974–76, these were in relatively unconditional programs: oil facility, first credit tranche, CFF. The IMF did not make disbursements of conditional second tranche funds, because the government failed to reduce government spending and money growth. For its part, the World Bank extended program loans in 1974 and 1977 amounting to 1 percent and 0.4 percent of exports, respectively.

Weaver and Anderson indicate that Tanzania overcame the balance of payments crisis in an equitable, if unorthodox, way. The rural-urban differential was probably reduced. The authors ask whether the multilateral institutions are sufficiently flexible to deal with socialist countries.

In his comment, Helleiner emphasized that, if the Tanzanian government did achieve equitable stabilization and the IMF did refuse to extend conditional support, the case would be an important instance where the IMF was proved wrong.[49] He highlights the point by citing the seeming conflict between the IMF and the World Bank; representatives of the latter reportedly were more favorable to the

[48] James H. Weaver and Arne Anderson, "Stabilization and Development of the Tanzanian Economy in the 1970s," in Cline and Weintraub, *Economic Stabilization,* pp. 335–69.

[49] Gerald K. Helleiner, "Comment," in Cline and Weintraub, *Economic Stabilization,* pp. 369–74.

government's strategy. But Helleiner raises doubts about the conclusion that stabilization was equitable and nonrecessionary. Stephen O'Brien of the World Bank clarified in the discussion that there was no disagreement between the Bank and the Fund; both had responded to Tanzania's needs in 1974, and the absence of second tranche IMF lending in 1975 was the result of Tanzania's failure to meet targets that the government itself had accepted.[50]

In view of the widespread documentation of the inefficiencies caused by import controls as a basic development strategy,[51] it would seem premature to conclude that the Tanzanian case shows the merits of controls over devaluation and other market-oriented mechanisms of adjustment, even accepting for the moment that Tanzanian results were at least temporarily successful (although that assessment is ambiguous). As a lender of revolving funds rather than grant aid, the IMF must calculate the likelihood of repayment in its decisions. In instances where the policy package involves import controls, a large minimum wage increase, and minimal exchange rate correction and spending cuts, there is a reasonable question whether the IMF would be meeting its fiduciary responsibility to the international community in making a loan, given the likelihood of future repayment difficulty. Indeed, many questions whether the much accelerated lending program of the IMF in 1980–81 did not involve several cases where the policy conditions were so weak and the underlying development strategies so questionable that the loans could de facto be turned into grant aid by the inability of borrowing countries to repay and by the lack of any alternatives to rolling over loans.

Two other authors in the Brookings conference had express views on IMF lending practices. While Diaz-Alejandro notes "modest" movement of IMF analysis "beyond the simplest versions of the monetary approach to the balance of payments," he indicates that the IMF still appears to favor outdated ideas (such as a preference for large, once-for-all devaluation rather than the crawling peg found effective in South America), and he criticizes IMF secrecy, pleading that at least documents older than 10 years be open to scholarly examination. He adds that in any event the large countries (Argentina, Brazil) are unlikely to place themselves at the mercy of IMF

[50] Cline and Weintraub, *Economic Stabilization,* p. 374.

[51] The extensive studies by the Organization for Economic Cooperation and Development, the World Bank, and the National Bureau of Economic Research have amply demonstrated the point. See Anne O. Krueger, *Liberalization Attempts and Consequences* (Cambridge, Mass.: Ballinger, 1978).

recommendations, however much modified (presumably, though not explicitly, because the game is not worth the candle in terms of available lending magnitudes, a view possibly now bypassed by the larger IMF quotas and higher multiples of quota for lending limits).[52] Lance Taylor is more abrupt, merely appending to his theoretical analysis a summary critique of the IMF's "draconian measures," "the fiscal stringency/credit contraction/devaluation/wage repression packages so beloved of orthodoxy and the IMF."[53]

Popular attacks on the IMF from the left are well known; the analytical critiques of the neo-structuralists have added a more sophisticated dimension to the attacks. However, two of the three country studies in the Brookings conference suggest that the IMF is miscast as the villain, and that the underlying ills of the patient have often been confused with the ministerings of the doctor. These case studies (Mexico and Peru) suggest that the IMF has not been guilty of violating the Hippocratic oath that the physician not make his patient worse off than he would otherwise be. It is worth adding, finally, that the most recent phase of the policy cycle has been toward an attack on the IMF from the right (in particular, from the Reagan administration) as being too soft in its lending conditions.[54]

Conclusion

It is evident from this survey that controversy remains abundant on the issue of stabilization. Several stylized facts have emerged, however. Balance of payments stabilization has proved easier than reducing inflation. Country experience in reducing inflation (after the shocks of the 1970s) has been considerably more favorable in Asia than in other regions. External forces caused considerable destabilization in the 1970s, but so did internal policies, and domestic policies were important in determining the degree of success in response to international shock. Countries have often waited too long before adopting stabilization measures, making adjustment more severe.

The perimeter around theoretical consensus would probably include the need to raise prices of tradables relative to nontradables in achieving external stabilization, with resulting resource shifts and

[52] Diaz-Alejandro, "Southern Cone Stabilization Plans," in Cline and Weintraub, *Economic Stabilization,* p. 140.

[53] Taylor, "IS/LM in the Tropics: Diagrammatics of the New Structuralist Macro Critique," in Cline and Weintraub, *Economic Stabilization,* p. 502.

[54] *Washington Post,* 28 September 1981.

income distributional consequences. Trade regime bias imposes heavy long-run costs, and its correction is usually a bargain despite transitional costs. Many income distributional effects of stabilization are determined more by the political choice of the regime than by any inevitable dynamic of stabilization.

The salient areas of dispute include whether trade elasticities are sufficiently robust to enable devaluation to work or whether they are so low that devaluation will have perverse contractionary effects. The mounting evidence is that the elasticities are sufficiently high for the standard case to hold. Also in dispute is the impact of monetary restraint on inflation, although the neo-structuralist assault on the issue seems chiefly relevant in the short run and consideration of longer run effects seems to vindicate the more traditional causal direction (from monetary restraint to reduction, rather than an increase, in inflation). Also in dispute is whether the IMF in practice has been overly rigid in the application of orthodox measures. New areas of analytical dispute include the relative merits of the crawling peg to offset domestic inflation as opposed to those of a preannounced, decelerating schedule of devaluations as an anti-inflationary device.

An area with high priority for more research is the time path of optimal stabilization policies. Despite the long-standing issue of the relative merits of gradualism versus shock treatment, and notwithstanding the modeling efforts of neo-structuralists, we have yet to see a carefully designed analysis of the alternative time paths of output, inflation, and external balance (for example, quarter by quarter) under alternative policy strategies (in particular, abrupt and severe credit restraint and devaluation as opposed to a gradual phasing-in of such measures). More generally, the neo-structuralists have yet to propose a viable alternative to the more traditional policy package. Although the logic of at least one version of their critique implies that in the face of stabilization problems governments should not devalue and should increase credit (and money expansion) rather than reduce it, they have (wisely) refrained from drawing the policy conclusion explicitly and have limited their policy conclusions to the negative stance that traditional policies have involved overkill. The less extreme among the neo-structuralists merely advocate more gradual doses of traditional medicine, but this approach implies again the need for analysis of the time paths of results under such policies. Similarly, some have advocated export subsidies as the alternative to devaluation, but, in view of the costs of trade regime bias and budgetary constraints, it is unclear how effective this alternative can be. (Moreover, if exporters will not respond to devaluation, why should they respond to subsidies?)

A new area of consensus on policy appears to be emerging. In the face of external shocks such as those of the 1970s, developmental adjustment may be more appropriate than short-term stabilization. New investment may be needed to expand production of exports and import substitutes. In this area the policy community has more than kept pace with the academic community. Without the aid of new theoretical models, the international financial institutions have sensibly extended the terms of IMF lending (up to five years for credit tranche borrowing and 10 years for the EFF), while the World Bank has introduced a modest amount of program lending for structural adjustment. Because developing country debt is high, external deficits are likely to remain high even if the OPEC surplus declines,[55] and because prospects seem likely for continued slow growth and high interest rates in the international economy, the need for these facilities is likely to increase over the medium term. Analytical understanding of stabilization policy is essential to the proper implementation of these international instruments. The extensive methodological work on stabilization issues in recent years, and the growing body of case studies, have done much to improve that understanding, but the task is far from complete.

[55] For a simple statistical analysis of the relationship of the OPEC surplus to the development country deficit, see William R. Cline, "External Debt, System Vulnerability, and Development," *Columbia Journal of World Business* 17(1), Spring 1982, pp. 4–14.

CHAPTER **10**

IMF–Developing Countries: Conditionality and Strategy

Samuel Lichtensztejn

It is almost impossible to analyze relations between the IMF and the underdeveloped countries without feeling that one is judging the Fund. There is undoubtedly a good deal of subjectivity in the stands taken. Most commentators either line up in defense of the Fund or adopt a rigidly critical attitude. The facts, the cases chosen or the very words that are used are influenced by an entrenched position that depends on the ideologies or interests of the nations and social groups at stake.

It must therefore be accepted that there can be no total objectivity or neutrality about the IMF's actions vis-à-vis borrowing countries. But it is at least possible to raise certain issues and questions about this matter, avoiding falling into simplifed visions or into easy generalizations. This is the intention and spirit of this critical paper.

Prologue: Two Methodological Hypotheses

The Fund's theoretical approach is well known. For short-term adjustment, it relies on monetary policy and global demand restriction. For the longer term, it believes that competitive market laws and the price system will permit stable and balanced growth. Despite its recent introduction of certain "supply-side" considerations and its admission of the need for projecting medium-term adjustments in the balance of payments, the Fund's interpretation of the working of the economic system has not changed fundamentally.

Conditionality, understood as being "the policies the Fund expects a member to follow in order to be able to use the Fund's general resources,"[1] has retained a great deal of formal similarity over time and vis-à-vis different situations. Fundamentally, these policies involve stablization programs encompassing budgetary, monetary-credit, wage, and foreign trade plans. In contrast with the World Bank (especially under McNamara's presidency), the IMF has developed a relatively rigid model of interpretation and of corrective policies for economic-financial imbalances.

The effects of the conditionality that this organization imposes on the economic policies of different countries are usually measured on the basis of the Fund's model. This might seem obvious if it were not that, as John Williamson emphasizes so well in his paper (Chapter 7, this volume) this evaluation is subject to different analytical alternatives. And what is even more important, the alternative chosen can change the sign and the character of the evaluation.

For example, it is very common to regard conditionality as a factor altering governmental policies which might otherwise have followed a different course. This is reflected in the conflicts in the relations between the Fund and certain governments.

However, at the other extreme, and not less important, there are cases in which economic policies are modified in the direction of the IMF's conditionality for basically domestic reasons. The evaluation criterion to be used in these cases is different to that to be applied to the earlier ones, although for tactical reasons many governments foster these policies under the label of "IMF pressures." In these circumstances, conditionality may at most precipitate a decision process that was already underway.

Both cases show the same problem: conditionality cannot be appraised by a formal analysis of efficiency — of congruence between objectives and instruments.[2] Any evaluation must pick up the heterogeneous internal social conditions of production and power, since

[1] Joseph Gold, "Conditionality," *Pamphlet Series* no. 31 (Washington: International Monetary Fund, 1979).

[2] This kind of analysis has been applied in numerous papers, such as those of the Winston Temple Seminar in examining the Polak and Robichek models as inspirors of IMF conditionality. See "¿Son severas las condiciones impuestas por el Fondo Monetario Internacional?" [Are the conditions imposed by the International Monetary Fund severe?] *Boletín del Centro de Estudios Monetarios Latinoamericanas* (CEMLA), Volume XXIII, No. 4, July-August 1977.

these may affect the very viability of IMF conditionality, or of its forms. These aspects have to do fundamentally with the governments' relative autonomy of decision and, therefore, must be contemplated in the judgment that one forms about conditionality. This is our first methodological hypothesis.

Seen in this way, one might argue on good grounds that the effects of any conditionality would, up to a certain point, be uncertain. This would suppose admitting that there is no regularity or reference pattern for the global evaluation of these policies. Consideration of this question leads us to our second methodological hypothesis.

If the IMF's conditionality were conceived as exogenous, the conditionality of economic policies would be an "indefinite process." However, our point of view is that one should consider the Fund as a part of the dynamics of an international economic and political system.

The recent internationalization, or transnational expansion, of capitalism tends to affect the relations between accumulation and domination within national frontiers. Internationalization is the contemporary way of changing social relations within countries; it is the more and more dominant way of reflecting economic speed-ups and slowdowns.

The IMF is one of the vehicles of this internationalization. As such it accompanies and contributes to the tendencies exhibited by this process in the post-World War II period. Internationalization has not followed a linear trend, but shows cycles and different forms of expansion. It nevertheless recognizes phases or common general characteristics at certain times. It is because of this fact that in the title of this paper we have incorporated another dimension that the concept of conditionality does not invoke, but which is inherent in its international projection: the existence of international strategies behind the policies that are being fostered.

The conditionality of the IMF is not exempt from these trends and the variations experienced by them. If this is true, one can deduce that, in spite of the rigidity of the theoretical scheme that backs it up, conditionality cannot, in practice, be exactly the same over time.

Consequently, the second premise that we defend is that the IMF's conditionality maintains a close coherence with the role that the institution has had to play in the growing process of internationalization of capital through its different stages.

The task of evaluating the "recommendations" proposed by the Fund makes it necessary to integrate the two hypotheses advanced above. They can jointly be summed up in the following way: the effects of conditionality depend on the type of relationships and contradictions between the national societies and international capital in its different cycles and forms of expansion. The nature of these relationships can be picked up in different abstract models; but finally it is a concrete historical product. Only a reasoning based on an historical background is of use in attempting to evaluate the consequences of IMF conditionality in different countries. Later on we shall attempt to make precisely this kind of an approach; to do so we shall draw from works that other colleagues and ourselves have carried out in the Latin American area.[3]

Phases of Conditionality: Some Experiences in Latin America

First Phase

When carrying out a comparative study on stabilization policies in Latin American countries, we had the opportunity of proving that as a general rule, from the mid-fifties to the mid-sixties, these policies were associated with the aims of controlling acute inflation and balance of payments deficits. The presence of IMF conditionality in those cases was fairly widespread in these first years.[4]

[3] See Samuel Lichtensztejn (in collaboration with Alberto Couriel): *El FMI y la crisis economica nacional* [The IMF and the national economic crisis]. Fondo de Cultura Universitaria, Montevideo, 1967. "Sobre el efoque y el papel de las politicas de establizacion en America Latina" [On the approach and the role of the stabilization policies in Latin America], *Economia de America Latina* (Latin American Economy), No. 1, CIDE, Mexico, September 1978. "Una perspectiva comparativa de las politicas de estabilizacion en America Latina (según un enfoque heterodoxo)" [A comparative perspective of stabilization policies in Latin America according to a heterodox approach], Latin American Program: The Wilson Center Working Papers no. 48, Washington, June 1980. "The IMF and the experience of Latin America's Southern Cone," ILET, June 1980 (presented at the Conference on the International Monetary System and the New International Order, which took place at Arusha, Tanzania). *Politicas economicas neoliberales en America Latina* (Neo-liberal economic policies in Latin America) CECADE, Mexico, April 1981. *Internacionalizacion y politicas economicas en America Latina* [Internationalization and economic policies in Latin America] ILET, Mexico, January 1982.

[4] The first experiences of Latin American countries with the Fund go back to the second half of the fifties. The following are some major examples: Chile (IMF participation started in 1955 with the Klein and Saks Mission);

The application of stabilization policies showed that the aim that was in fact promoted and that likewise characterized its instrumentation was that of promoting a greater opening-up of semi-industrialized economies, specially those of Argentina, Brazil, Chile, Mexico and Uruguay. In fact, the majority of the measures adopted at that time concentrated on foreign relations and it was in this area that it was recognized that there had been the greatest consequences. The principal measures were directed toward eliminating the mechanisms of trade protection (quotas or quota systems for imports and exports), achieving a significant devaluation of the national currency, unifying the foreign exchange system, abolishing trade and bilateral payments agreements, and encouraging the entry of foreign capital.

The economic and political trends emerging from the new international economic order under the leadership of the United States required the simultaneous external readjustment of those economies. The presence of the IMF in all of those countries demonstrated this common need for a redefinition of international relations.

Expressed in that way, one might think that the Fund's conditionality was decisive in the policies adopted in those economies. However, this inference merits some reserve.

On the one hand, in those first years, the experiences quoted demonstrate that the implantation of the conditions of that institution, rather than an imposition, was the result of the convergence of international trends and domestic interests. The degree of autonomy of decision that the state retained in each country depended on the level of development and on the crisis of the so-called import substitution process, and on the different forms of populist alliance supporting it. Although many countries were exposed to the same IMF conditionality, the reactions of their governments were not identical.

The case of Brazil is extremely informative in this respect. The internationalization of its economy was not submitted to the "me-

---

Bolivia (the Fund sent the Adair Mission in 1956); Paraguay (the first contacts were made in 1957 in connection with a monetary reform); Colombia (at the end of 1958 this country received assistance from the Eximbank which, in collaboration with the Fund, committed itself to undertake a stabilization program); Argentina (the first stabilization agreement was made in late 1958); Uruguay (its relations with the IMF grew closer in connection with the monetary and exchange reform of late 1959).

diation" and the rules of the Fund, in fact up to 1964 they were rejected head-on.[5]

Differences were also recorded concerning the type of role that international capital achieved in different countries. In this respect it is necessary to distinguish two types of situations: those of countries like Argentina, Brazil and Mexico, which predominantly encouraged direct foreign investment in new productive activities, or an enlargement of its share in those that were already in operation; and those countries like Uruguay and Chile (except for mining in the latter), which rather favored the opening-up to commercial and financial capital. For the first group of countries, their incorporation in the initial phase of transnational expansion affected the structure and dynamic of their manufacturing production systems. For the second group, on the contrary, the international opening-up was based in earlier productive structures and led to the growth of external debt.

In this first period, accumulation stimulated by a transnational expansion intervened in the domain of the main springs of the countries' economic functioning. Nevertheless, the property of already accumulated capital was not denationalized. There was a process of growing oligopolization but in relative terms. Internationalization redefined the importance of the sectors and the distribution assets and income. It tended to alter the balance of payments structure and to settle the deficits in the short run, without achieving equilibrium in the medium run.

An interesting aspect that is necessary to repeat is that where it intervened actively, the effect of the Fund's conditionality on the design of economic policies in those years was to change certain aspects of foreign trade regimes and the international movement of capital. In contrast, in the remaining areas of state regulation, such as subsidy mechanisms, industrial incentives, price control, wage policies and even credit policy, its repercussions were much less. This discrepancy between the theory and the practice of conditionality not only exhibited the Fund's flexibility, but also another phenomenon: the expansion of foreign capital in its new reproduction cycle in Latin America took advantage of, rather than disclaiming, the protectionist conditions of its domestic or regional markets. This permitted certain states to reconcile the different social interests at stake, to the point of preserving populist and reformist profiles of government.

[5] In other conditions, and more fleetingly, a similar attitude was adopted by the Illia government in Argentina, when it abruptly concluded a stand-by agreement with the Fund in 1965.

As the concentrating trends of the economy accelerated, the possibility of making a certain social and sectoral domestic structure compatible with a policy of opening-up to international capital encountered increasing obstacles.

The "stabilizing" takeovers in Brazil (1964) and Argentina (1965) demonstrate those limits, and also the relatively closer relations between the IMF's conditionality and some specific economic policies in Latin America. The adoption of stabilization measures to restrict domestic demand through wage, monetary, credit and fiscal constraints involved a fall in the share of wages in income, at the same time as generating critical situations for certain fringes of national capital involving their marginalization, elimination or absorption.

Although the so-called monetarist current gained an apparent victory in the sixties in the two countries considered to be most rebellious toward its recommendations, one cannot attribute the changes that their economic policies underwent solely to the IMF. Above all, the restructuring effects that followed the first phase of expansion of transnational capital and the internal contradictions that emerged in the political sphere, were the elements that took on a decisive role in the changes of orientation already mentioned. But even though its influence on this process was secondary, at this time the propositions of the IMF had more impact domestically. In addition to Argentina and Brazil, orthodox stabilization policy continued to characterize the Mexican strategy of "stabilizing development," won over the majority of the Central American economies, and regained strength in Uruguay, Peru, and partially in Chile. At this moment, the Alliance for Progress had already been left behind and reformist attempts, in general, seemed to be infeasible.

Second Phase

However, on the threshold of the seventies in Latin America there was an evident decline in the IMF's presence and in economic policies coherent with its model. Changes in power structures and new alternatives were opened up in economic policy. Governments such as those of Velasco Alvarado in Peru (1968–75), Ovando-Torres in Bolivia (1969–70), Allende in Chile (1971–73), Campora-Peron in Argentina (1973–74), Manley in Jamaica (1972–80), the heterodox forms assumed by the "Brazilian miracle" (1968–73) and Echeverria's "shared development" in Mexico (1970–76), exhibited a broader radius of maneuver for the Latin American states in the choice of their national policies.

There are many internal and external reasons explaining this new period which could be called a period of transition. The stabilization policies had neither brought down the rates of inflation nor reduced the deficits in the balance of payments as much as had been predicted. On the contrary, they had brought about recessive processes, and when they had positive effects on the growth rate, these were achieved at the cost of forced concentration of production and of income, and a higher social stratification. For all of these reasons, the criticisms of these policies, although directed toward the governments that adopted them, involved to a greater or lesser extent also the conditionality of the IMF and the predominance of US interests in its definition. In response to this, strategies of growth based on a progressive redistribution of income and nationalist claims to control basic resources and products prospered.

The international crisis also contributed toward these changes in economic policies. A crisis was brought about by the breakdown of the Bretton Woods agreement, involving the dollar, oil and the IMF itself, which proved incapable of controlling world liquidity, speculation and inflation. The breakdown of US hegemony, in addition to having economic effects, manifested itself in a more general contradiction whose origin was the maturity of power of the transnational companies: intercapitalist coordination (competition) at the international level no longer corresponded totally with the alliance (rivalry) between the governments of the central countries.

In this respect one must also take into account that some of the radical governments in Latin America (for example, the Peruvian one under Velasco Alvarado and the Argentinian one under Campora-Peron) were not against international capital, but basically opposed to the "old" monopolistic complexes or US enclaves. In the case of Brazil, even, the "miracle" years were characterized by a diversification of sources of foreign capital. For many countries, the drop in US bilateral aid and the conflicts with US-based firms did not prevent the solution of the balance of payments problem. Without the Fund's mediation, recourse was had to new expanding sources of financing (Eurodollar markets) and advantage was taken of rising world trade, with terms of trade that were conjuncturally favorable for various primary products.

Third Phase

Since the installation of military regimes in Chile and Uruguay (1973), and Argentina (1976), two modalities have opened up in these countries. We consider these to have dominated the conditioning actions of the IMF in the last few years: the changes in the stabilization proposals and their links to the expansion of private international banking; and the development of the political dimensions of this conditionality.

IMF—Private International Banking. Latin America's external financial liabilities rose from $10 billion in 1965 to more than $200 billion in 1982. Several analyses have focused on the theme of external debt and its effects on international policies and balances of payments as being of central importance. The ever greater share of the Latin American countries in the loans granted by private international banks and the obligations that the governments contracted as debtors or guarantors justify such preoccupation.

The exponential growth of these loans has not been the direct and exclusive result of a spontaneous increase in demand for international financing of production or trade. The external debt has also served to substantially enlarge the predominantly financial and speculative applications of such capital in foreign currencies. Such are the cases of Argentina, Chile and Uruguay, true paradigms of a speculative economy and of "wild" financial accumulation.

But, in addition to the phenomenon of indebtedness, the internationalization of finance has expressed itself in a worldwide projection and functional diversification of the banks. At the same time, in different Third World countries certain long-standing and also new national groups have prospered and acquired greater power. The connection between these local financial groups and transnational corporations and banks has endowed such groups with an economic and political power that is unprecedented in the modern history of these countries.

These phenomena are the product of structural crises that express themselves in a surplus of capital, on the one hand, and a search for profitable outlets of an essentially financial nature, on the other. To assure security, financial appraisal becomes, at a certain point, a necessary mechanism of protection against the ever imminent danger of an international collapse.

A corollary to this need is the rigid control of "critical" debtors and their economic policies. Closely linked to their interests, the private international banks have taken ever increased responsibilities in such control, in order to avoid a rise in, and the exaggerated dispersion of, "country risk." In spite of its weakening in other functions, the IMF supports this process by vigorously reconstructing its conditionality. Its presence has been extended from its traditional

Latin American "customers," with 25 or more years of close relations, to the newest African and Asian countries.

The ties that were established between the IMF and private international banking remain functional and have become institutionalized. Nevertheless, these relations have left behind the old picture according to which the Fund guaranteed and took the lead in negotiations with the underdeveloped countries. The initiative that the banks themselves are developing is many times more than that of the IMF. From 1976 to 1978 this showed up with countries such as Peru, Zaire and Gabon. On these occasions, the IMF's conditionality temporarily took second place.[6] The former government of Michael Manley in Jamaica went through the same experience on many occasions.[7]

It is also interesting to examine to what extent these new needs have been reflected in the IMF's conditionality, to back up the functioning of private financial markets. One of the Fund's most important recommendations at the present time is to stimulate the emergence of significant positive differentials between the real interest rates of the domestic market and those in force internationally. The object is to attract domestic savings and above all foreign savings, and at the same time foster the formation of larger international reserves as a guarantee for international creditors.

The "monetary approach to the balance of payments" rationalized in theoretical terms a policy which consists, among other aspects, of subordinating the exchange rate to interest rates and making the emission of money flexible to the entrance of foreign monetary capital. The restrictions on domestic credit that the IMF recommends as a supposed means of limiting the quantity of money and inflation stimulates the search for more foreign credits and capital. The entry

[6] See Samuel Lichtensztejn and Jose Manuel Quijano, *Deuda externa del Tercer Mundo y Capital Finaciero Internacional* [The Third World's External Debt and International Financial Capital], Centre International pour le Développement, Paris, 1979.

[7] "The agreements with the IMF, applied by Jamaica, have not been able to induce the transnational commercial banks to provide new funds and to accept a global refinancing or the postponement of payments," Richard L. Bernal, "La banca transnacional, el Fondo Monetario Internacional y la crisis capitalista de Jamaica" [Transnational banking, the International Monetary Fund and Jamaica's capitalist crisis], included in *Nueva Fase del capital Financiero: Elementos teoricos y experiencias en America Latina* [Financial Capital: a new phase. Theoretical elements and experiences in Latin America], Jaime Estevez and Samuel Lichtensztejn, eds., CEESTEM-ILET, Mexico 1981.

of such foreign capital is doubly favored according to the Fund's reasoning: as a "healthy" basis for the emission of currency, and as a factor permitting equilibrium of the balance of payments (understood as a deficit in the current account capable of being financed).

In addition to favoring international financial investments in the underdeveloped countries and improving their capacity for paying back their external debts, these conditions are responsible for strengthening inflationary trends in the different countries in which they have been adopted as policies. In fact, the spiral that is formed with high interest rates and their subsequent influence on the exchange rate and prices promotes the establishment of a minimum inflation ceiling. A similar result is already foreseeable with the extension of the practices of monetary correction and floating exchange rates. In its desire to "rationalize expectations" the Fund promoted this type of correction, setting up a kind of "institutionalization" of inflation within certain limits. What is important at the present time is that the reforms aimed at by the Fund for attracting and recycling financial surpluses end up by creating inflationary conditions which extraordinarily favor the banks, to the detriment of other business sectors and wage earners. In certain countries financial incomes now represent up to 10 percent of the national income.

These links that the IMF has created with the international banking system, and the priority it gives to the attraction of financial capital and the settling of external debts, affect the scope of this institution's conditionality. This conditionality is now combined with the conditionality, sometimes even greater, of the international banks in their negotiations with governments, which reflects an increasing power of banking organizations in general over economic policies. That process has, in practice, made the concepts of macroeconomic equilibrium, mainly those concerning the balance of payments, vary, and changed the emphasis between the spheres of financial relations, productive relations and anti-inflationary goals. In many of these aspects, the economic policies are directed toward favoring open "development" strategies with a strong speculative basis to the detriment of a greater internal integration and productive growth.

The Political Dimensions of Conditionality. When stabilization programs first began, unpopular policies were imposed in different underdeveloped countries, but they still allowed governments to reconcile conflicting interests to some extent, even without causing tensions with new foreign capital. Given the strong bargaining power of labor unions, these governments sought solutions based on "social pacts, contracts, agreements or arbitration" to diminish the struggle between the various classes.

On the whole, during the initial expansion of the international world economy, it became clear that stabilization policies did not necessarily have to be based on authoritarian regimes which required a collision of the economic pattern with existing democratic institutions. But a point was reached where the political structure could no longer resist its own contradictions, its lack of alternatives and its inability to control social antagonisms. Then conditionality went far beyond its traditional strict economic dimension, as described in the text books, and gained an unexpected and overwhelming political dimension. Milton Friedman used to say: "There is no technical problem as such in overcoming inflation. The real obstacles are of a political, not technical, nature."[8] For its part, a report of the Trilateral Commission affirmed that "inflation is the economic disease of democracy."[9]

Why did stabilization programs become fused with authoritarian political doctrines? In other words, how could authoritarian regimes make anti-inflationary policies a source of their legitimacy? Since an in-depth analysis of these questions is quite complicated, we will deal only with those elements which are most relevant in analyzing IMF policies.

One such element is the theory according to which inflation is progressively caused by the conflict between forces with monopoly control over labor (i.e. unions) and capital. The profits-wages struggle tends to increase costs and prices. With growing economic concentration and social contradictions, stabilization programs following this line will highlight wage and profit (i.e., incomes) policies.

Thus the emphasis on increasing wage costs as the cause of inflation also implicit in the IMF interpretation turns anti-labor policies into an equivalent of anti-inflationary efforts (for the benefit of the common interest, by definition). That is then one of the major economic justifications of authoritarianism.

Another element that contributes to make the fight against inflation a part of authoritarian theory is directly related to the conditions stipulated for an efficient implementation of economic policy. In particular, utmost importance was given to formal principles such as

[8] Milton Friedman, "Monetary Correction" in *Essays on Inflation and Indexation*, American Enterprise Institute, Washington, 1974.

[9] The "Governability of Democracy" report of the Trilateral Commission to the Executive Committee of the Trilateral Commission, May 1975.

"coherence," "compatability," and "consistency" — between anti-inflationary objectives and instruments. The implementation of stabilization policy became increasingly subordinated to those principles; however, its final success depended upon its maintenance. In fact, political changes or interruptions (due to elections, etc.) were pointed out as the source of a lack of continuity in anti-inflationary policy.

In our view, the IMF approach — and more recently that of Friedman and the Chicago School — had such a strong influence on the military regimes precisely because, besides "scientifically" supporting a specific stabilization policy and admitting all its negative effects as necessary, they make its success depend almost exclusively on a rigid discipline and on the continuity of implementation of their recommendations. Thus politics needed to be exempted from demagogical and populist practices, which are constantly invoked and criticized to justify and defend the need for an iron hand and a prolonged regime.

As time went by, stabilization experiences proved that, rather than being an improvement on preceding policies, they represented a link in a transformation and reorganization process undergone by the state and its functions. That is why it can be said that conditionality has contributed so much to destabilizing certain governments. In addition to the recent classical examples in the Southern Cone (especially Chile) we should also point out as examples the cases of Portugal, Peru, Turkey, Jamaica and Tanzania.

The Need for a New International Order

Controlling and handling the critical situation in the international financial system will be fundamental in the eighties. It is in this area that the real limits of the present crisis and its possible solutions will be permanently established. Those limits, in the first instance, as we have seen, refer to economic policy. But, in the final instance, those limits depend on more general political factors. Seen in this way, it is fundamental to reform the international financial order as a whole (including the role of the private banks), and not to limit oneself to particular institutions such as the IMF, the World Bank, and the regional development banks, which today constitute only a part of the system.

Perhaps only a world collapse or a new war will force this reform to be made. But it is our humble obligation as scholars of good will and partisans of the peaceful development of humanity to foster solutions by means of dialogue and agreement between nations.

In this sense we continue to make common cause with the Arusha Initiative, as an appeal in favor of a UN conference for solving the questions of international finance and monetary affairs. We believe that a new international monetary order must serve two basic objectives. First, it must be capable of achieving monetary stability, restoring acceptable levels of employment and sustainable growth, and checking the present strong inflationary and stagflationary tendencies and policies in the world economy. Secondly, it must be supportive of a process of global development especially for the countries of the Third World which contain the majority of the world's poor.[10]

Of course, what has been said above does not prevent transitional measures being adopted. As we stated in this paper, there are governments which by their own decision have adopted the orientation that at present characterizes the IMF. But many other governments, on the contrary, have chosen their own models of social and economic development and have clashed with the institution's strict criteria. That prevents their access to the higher credit tranches and to the extended Fund facility, because of the Fund's very restricted criteria. Changes in these criteria would help to bring about solutions with lower social cost than those that the IMF is at present fostering.

[10] The Arusha Initiative, *Development Dialogue*, 1980: 2, p. 18.

COMMENTS, CHAPTERS 7–10

Rudiger Dornbusch

The papers by Williamson, Balassa, Cline, and Lichtensztejn are stimulating, provocative, and diverse in their premises and conclusions. What do they tell us about desirable and essential features of conditionality and stabilization?

The Framework

A starting point is a categorization of beliefs as shown below where each box entry corresponds to a particular conjunction of views about successful trade and financial strategies:

WHAT IS TO BE DONE?

	Financial discipline	*Passive money*
Free markets	Harberger-Balassa	
Protection		United Nations Economic Commission for Latin America (ECLA), ca. 1960

One influential view holds that financial discipline is a long-run essential, but that it is also, in the short run, not "too" costly. This view has been forcefully advanced by Harberger (1981), who argues that monetary-fiscal stabilization in a number of Latin American instances was accompanied not by a collapse of activity but by growth. A tandem view to financial discipline is the case for free, undistorted markets of goods and factors. This view is represented and documented by Balassa in a number of contributions, including the work reported in this volume (Chapter 8). The Harberger-Balassa strategy for a developing country, then, is to consider monetary-fiscal control and elimination of discriminatory incentives as the cornerstone of a program for progress and stability. There is an alternative view, very influential in Latin America, which I characterize here as the ECLA-

1960 model, by which I understand elements of structuralism, anti-monetarism, and import-substitution as a basis for growth. It is a paradigm that is precisely the opposite of the Harberger-Balassa scheme of things. Money, in the ECLA-1960 view of the economy, is to be passive and accommodating—greasing the wheels of commerce—because the inflationary process is dictated by structural asymmetries and income-distribution issues. Protection is essential to avoid excessive exposure to the vagaries of world trade and the risks of a low-income dependency.

The problem of conditionality and stabilization policy is so uncomfortable and difficult because it forces us to take sides on the issues and choose a box. The economist, by training, is conservative and will opt for free markets and financial discipline as the presumptively better strategy. But as citizens and by force of common sense and experience, we are suspicious of the miracles of the market, recognizing that structuralism includes many sensible things both in economics and politics. We are therefore inclined to strike a balance, looking for a third dimension that captures the long-run advantages of open and financially stable economies without facing (or risking) the large economic and social costs of a disruptive, repressive transition.

Cline and Williamson in their papers (Chapters 9 and 7) take a middle ground, setting themselves up squarely in the middle of the box with a bit of each: no unreasonable protection, no excessive financial orthodoxy, certainly some monetary accommodation, and a genuine concern for income distribution. This is a serious position, but I do think it needs important reinforcement in the transition from a prestabilization disarray to the medium-term restoration of stability. I will discuss features of that transition after some specific comments on points raised in the papers.

Orthodoxy and Neo-Structuralism

Cline's discussion (Chapter 9) of the orthodox view rightly identifies the triplet—fiscal stabilization, monetary stabilization, and exchange depreciation—as the elements in conventional programs to stabilize inflation and correct external deficits. I would supplement his discussion, though, by making more forcefully two points: first, that *successful* devaluation almost always involves a cut in the real wage (certainly in terms of traded goods) and often a fall in real disposable income; second, that correcting the external imbalance requires a reduction in absorption relative to income, which frequently means a fall in the standard of living. In the orthodox model, stabilization and reduction in the standard of living are thought to be virtually tantamount.

The real wage must decline in most instances of successful devaluation because capital is internationally mobile, and therefore at best there is room for the short-term squeezing of quasi-rents of capital. That leaves labor to bear the burden of the decline in the real cost of domestic value-added that is required for enhanced competitiveness. It makes little difference whether we are in a situation in which the devaluation promotes exports by reducing the relative price of domestic exportables relative to those of our foreign competitors, or whether we have to lower the wage in terms of tradable goods, thus promoting domestic export supply. That will be a question of the particular domestic disequilibrium. But fall the real wage must, except in circumstances of pure overspending when labor can be transferred toward the traded goods sector with unchanging productivity.[1]

The need to cut absorption relative to income for an improvement of the external balance is a matter of identities and, thus, is beyond controversy. But it is worth emphasizing that external balance correction will most of the time involve a cut in the standard of living, the only exception being the case in which the initial situation is one of deficit/unemployment *and* the required expenditure-switching policy does not involve a terms of trade deterioration that more than offsets any employment gains. The burden of orthodoxy is that correcting an external imbalance hurts—almost always.

Cline discusses neo-structuralism, with its suggestion that tight money is inflationary and that depreciation causes adverse income distribution and employment effects. It is important to recognize these possibilities, but it is equally important to realize that these ideas have a distinguished intellectual tradition and discussion going back to the 1950s and 1960s, in the work of Keyserling, Hirschman, Cooper, Carlos Diaz-Alejandro, and others. It is worth recording the ancestry because it draws attention to long-standing discussion of the relevant evidence. I will comment on two points in this context. The first concerns the effect of real depreciation on output. It will be remembered that a terms of trade deterioration or a gain in home competitiveness exerts income (distribution) and substitution effects. The latter, if present, unambiguously raise demand for domestic goods. The former, adverse for the home country, will reduce demand. The

[1] Discussion of these issues can be found in the literature of the 1950s. See also Dornbusch 1974, 1980.

net effect, as we know from the Marshall-Lerner condition, is ambiguous. If there is no substitution, then demand and employment *must* fall. That is precisely the question elasticity-pessimism addressed in the late 1940s, and it is a question on which substantial evidence has built up. It is certainly not the presumption today, as Cline rightly notes, that there is no, or even insufficient, substitution. That must be considered the exceptional case. If it were the case, of course, there should be an export tariff the proceeds of which could be used to support domestic demand in a way that does not impair external balance. Inelastic demand should be actively exploited!

In the context of devaluation it is important to make another point, and that is the distinction between nominal and effective devaluation arising not only from adjustment of wages but especially from the presence of traded intermediate goods. Suppose the share of imported intermediates in the export sector were 50 percent. Then a 10 percent devaluation would increase the external competitiveness of exportables by only 5 percent because the devaluation works only on domestic value-added, not on the traded intermediates. This is important to bear in mind for two reasons. First, it obviously affects in an important way the algebra of what is the "right" depreciation. Second, it also is important in calculating the trade-off between the gain in competitiveness and the inflationary impact of devaluation as opposed to other instruments. Bruno's case for export subsidies[2] gains especially when it is borne in mind that, to gain 10 percent in competitiveness, it takes a 20 percent depreciation but only a 10 percent export subsidy. That amounts to an important difference in the price level impact of the tools.

Neo-structuralism also carries the message that interest rate increases are inflationary because, through the cost side, increased charges on working capital are passed on by firms to higher prices. The point can be put in terms of a cost-based price equation:

$$P_{t+1} = aw_t\,(1 + x)\,(1 + i), \tag{1}$$

where P, w, x, and i denote output price, wage, profit margin, and nominal interest, respectively, and a is the unit labor requirement. The idea is that a firm has a one-period lag between input costs and sales and that, therefore, the present value of price $P_{t+1}/(1+i)$ is

[2] Comments, Chapters 4–6, this volume.

equal to current costs. Decomposing nominal interest into real interest, r, and inflation, $\dot{p}$, the relation becomes[3]:

$$P_t = aw_t (1 + x)(1 + r). \qquad (2)$$

Neo-structuralists have emphasized that, as of given wages and capital, higher real interest rates lead to higher prices or transitory inflation. But that is, I believe, a negligible issue compared with two other channels through which increased *financial* interest rates adversely affect the supply side. The first is the recognition that, with nominal demand given, higher interest rates in equation (2) will not increase prices and lower output, but rather reduce profit margins, x. Higher financial interest rates reduce the profitability of firms. That, in turn, may imply only a reduction in rents. But, particularly if high real rates persist for any length of time, they mean reduction in investment and ultimately bankruptcy of firms. There is no question that in Argentina, Brazil, and Chile the serious controversy is about the decline in the profitability of operating firms because of the high real cost of working capital and the redistribution of income from operating firms to *rentiers* and banks. This is "intermediation" with a vengeance.

High real interest rates also adversely affect employment and output because firms that currently hire labor have to look at the *discounted* marginal product of labor in all industries, such as agriculture or construction where there are gestation lags. That means firms look at the real wage $w_t/[P_{t+1}/(1 + i)] = w_t (1 + r)/P_t$. The implication of this calculation is that, in the short run with given capital and the productivity of labor, higher real interest rates on financial capital lead to a decline in employment. Once again the need arises to identify the special role that financial, as opposed to real, capital plays on the production side.

Balassa's Findings

Balassa (Chapter 8) and his collaborators in the World Bank and Organization for Economic Cooperation and Development studies have made an important step in building up case material on adjustment policies and development strategies. Theory gives us an ambiguous answer when we search whether a reasonably protectionist

[3] $P_{t+1} = P_t (1 + \dot{p})$ by definition of the inflation rate, and $(1 + i) = (1 + r)(1 + \dot{p})$ by definition of the nominal interest rate. Using these relations in equation (1) yields equation (2).

or an overall free-trading country should perform better. The evidence Balassa reports, as he sees it, conveys a stronger message: countries that practice an outward-oriented, market-oriented strategy do better. There is little doubt that, as more evidence develops from further and different studies, we will gain a better understanding of precisely the weight to be placed on trade strategy. In the meantime, it is worth remembering that, in studies of the US sources of growth, liberal trade policy was given a nearly negligible significance.

What makes one skeptical of the strong findings Balassa reports is the example of Brazil, where trade policies by and large were exemplarily horrible. Yet the country has shown, during periods of political stability, an enviable, sustained growth record in large part because of extensive, systematic, large-scale public sector investment. It is also the case that 20 years of protection have carried the country to the point of being a competitive exporter of automobiles, small airplanes, and military hardware. So there certainly is an example that is exactly the opposite of what Balassa tells us is the rule. One would like to know whether there are more of these cases.

Two points of Balassa's paper call for comment. The first is the claim that positive real interest rates promote private saving. There is *no* evidence that has been found in an extensive search in industrialized countries for such a phenomenon. Episodic evidence, often comparing years of political upheaval with later stability, surely cannot be enough to support the view that stabilization should proceed by raising the return on *paper* assets relative to that of real capital. The foremost task of stabilization, on the supply side, is to create employment and to raise the productivity of capital, not to make financial capital expensive. The positive real interest binge is, in my judgment, a very misdirected and poorly founded wing of the free market school.

A second comment concerns the relation between budget deficits and savings rates. We are told that budget deficits lead to low savings rates. Surely that does not mean that budget deficits lead to reduction in private sector saving, but rather (identically) to reduced public sector saving. For were there any other interpretation, we should be hard pressed for an explanation. The only association one imagines is that recessions reduce both private and public sector saving.

Consensus on Conditionality

Williamson in his insightful paper (Chapter 7) has set out a menu for consensus. The agenda is uncontroversial and prudent. In my judgment it gives an excessive weight to inflation, but what concerns me more is a perhaps insufficient enthusiasm for stabilization policy as a concerted social program. In this respect, I find myself very much influenced by the perspective Lichtensztejn (Chapter 10) throws on the issues when he addresses the political dimension of stabilization. He asks:

> Why did stabilization programs become fused with authoritarian political doctrines? In other words, how could authoritarian regimes make anti-inflationary policies a source of their legitimacy? . . . In our view, the IMF approach—and more recently that of Friedman and the Chicago School—had such a strong influence on the military regimes precisely because, besides "scientifically" supporting a specific stabilization policy and admitting all its negative effects as necessary, they make its success depend almost exclusively on a rigid discipline and on the continuity of implementation of their recommendations.

The dimension Lichtensztejn brings to the debate is an uncomfortable one, but we cannot avoid taking sides on the issue. Financial discipline and reasonably efficient markets are quite desirable, even indispensable, in the medium term. But that does not mean, of necessity, that the transition should take a form hostile to society and progress. We therefore have to look to ways of shaping a broad social consensus supportive of stabilization. But this means, of course, that incomes policy is *the* cornerstone of effective, socially acceptable conditionality. Effective stabilization is, above all, not a technical issue but a political one.

There is another important dimension to stabilization that is raised by Cline and Williamson: shock treatment versus gradualism. It used to be the case that monetarists favored shock treatment, and people were on the side of gradualism. But here the sides are changing. If incomes policy can be mustered in a social consensus on the need for stabilization, then there is every reason to apply shock treatment: simultaneous and immediate, credible moves to rectify the entire disarray. That includes a combination of changes in real prices, fiscal and public sector sanitation, cuts in absorption, wage controls, and sharing rents, but it also includes, as an advantage, a full employment and growth policy. Such a package is much harder to engineer than 5 percent growth in the money supply, but unless we have the optimism and confidence to try, we might as well be plumbers.

References

Dornbusch, Rudiger. 1980. *Open Economy Macroeconomics*. New York: Basic Books.

———. 1982. "Stabilization Policy in Developing Countries: What Have We Learned?" *World Development* (Summer).

———. 1974. "Real and Monetary Aspects of the Effects of Exchange Rate Changes." In R. Z. Aliber, ed., *National Monetary Policies and the International Financial System*. Chicago: University of Chicago Press.

Harberger, A. C. 1981. "In Step and Out of Step with World Inflation." In J. Flanders and A. Razin, eds., *Development in an Inflationary World*. New York: Academic Press.

PART III

Country Studies

CHAPTER **11**

Economic Management And IMF Conditionality In Jamaica

Jennifer Sharpley

The economic management of the Jamaican economy and relations with the International Monetary Fund (IMF) have been major factors in domestic politics, and Fund conditionality was a central issue in the 1980 general election. Jamaica has borrowed under every IMF facility, and her experience with upper tranche stabilization programs received prominence at the North-South conference on "The International Monetary System and the New International Order," held in Arusha, Tanzania, in June 1980. Both domestically and internationally, the causes, cures, and consequences of Jamaica's economic instability have been the subject of much concern. In the first section of the paper I shall look briefly at the causes of instability and government attitudes toward stabilization in 1972–76. In the second section I shall examine relations with the Fund and national stabilization efforts in the period 1977–80. Details of the 1981 extended Fund facility (EFF) agreement are included in this second section for comparison. Some conclusions are presented in the last section.

Note: This study was undertaken while I was visiting research fellow at The Chr. Michelsen Institute, Bergen, Norway; it forms part of a collaborative project on the IMF and Economic Management in Developing Countries being conducted by Tony Killick (Overseas Development Institute, London). See his case study of Kenya, Chapter 16, this volume.

This chapter is excerpted from T. Killick, ed., *The IMF and Stabilisation: Developing Country Experience* (London: Heinemann Educational Books, forthcoming) by permission of the Overseas Development Institute, London.

The Causes of Disequilibria, 1972–76

In the eight years between 1972 and 1980, the overall economic performance of the Jamaican economy deteriorated dramatically compared with a record of aggregate growth throughout the previous decade. While the 10 years of Jamaica Labour Party (JLP) government until 1972 had been without any major economic disequilibria, the underlying structural weakness of the economy contributed to the economic difficulties facing the new People's National Party (PNP) government.[1] When the PNP government took office in February 1972 under the leadership of Michael Manley, Jamaica was already facing its first serious balance of payments deficit since independence, and rising domestic inflation. At the same time, the government was under pressure to raise employment, real wages, and government spending and to reduce social and economic inequalities. The responses of the authorities to the situation they inherited in 1972, and subsequent external and domestic events, were to plunge the economy into a prolonged recession and to produce disequilbria of major proportions. Some indicators of Jamaica's economic performance over this period are presented in Tables 11.1 and 11.2. For further discussion of the external and domestic causes of Jamaica's economic problems during the first term of the Manley administration, see Sharpley (1981).

The changing pattern of income distribution over this period—between factors, urban-rural sectors, unemployed, self-employed, and trade union members—is complex to unravel. Between October 1973 and October 1976, average real wages of those employed increased by approximately 30 percent. Although real GDP per capita declined by 15 percent between 1973 and 1976, the unemployment rate improved slightly, and the labor share of GDP recorded a rise. This apparent redistribution of factor shares from capital to labor is misleading, however, for the earnings of workers in cooperatives and those self-employed in farming and retail hawking form part of the capital share and are not included in the compensation paid to employees. The gap between rural and urban incomes (Stone 1980, p. 247) widened, partly because of higher levels of unionization in the

[1] The nature of these structural problems and the economic performance of the Jamaican economy during much of this earlier decade are discussed in Jefferson (1972) and Manley (1974, chapter 2). A comparison of the political parties and their public policies can be found in Stone (1980, especially chapters 4, 6, and 11).

TABLE 11.1 JAMAICA: ECONOMIC INDICATORS, 1970–79

Year	*Growth of real GDP (percentage)*	*Growth of real GDP per capita*[a] *(percentage)*	*Fixed capital formation/GDP (percentage)*	*Final consumption/ GDP (percentage)*	*Employees wages/GDP (percentage)*	*Unemploy-ment rate (percentage)*	*Consumer price increases*[b] *(percentage)*	*Real wage index (April 1974 = 100*[c]*)*
1970	12.1	10.6	31.4	72.6	50.1	n.a.	7.7	n.a.
1971	2.9	1.4	27.8	75.2	50.0	n.a.	5.1	n.a.
1972	9.6	8.1	25.5	81.0	52.4	23.0	8.2	n.a.
1973	0.9	−0.6	25.8	78.3	53.8	22.0	28.9	87.1
1974	−4.1	−5.6	22.0	86.1	54.0	21.2	22.1	103.4
1975	−0.7	−2.2	23.6	84.8	55.8	20.5	11.4	108.3
1976	−6.6	−8.1	16.7	90.4	56.6	22.4	8.3	109.9
1977	−1.6	−3.1	11.7	89.6	55.6	24.2	16.1	95.9
1978	−0.3	−1.8	13.4	83.5	52.2	24.5	47.0	79.3
1979	−2.0	−3.5	17.6	82.6	51.9	27.8	24.8	79.2

n.a. Not available.
Sources: Government of Jamaica, Department of Statistics, *National Income and Product 1979* and *Statistical Abstract of Jamaica 1979* (Kingston, 1979); Bank of Jamaica, *Statistical Digest* (Kingston, February 1981).
a. The average population growth rate of 1.5 percent annually has been applied throughout to avoid yearly fluctuations in the rate of emigration.
b. January to January.
c. Index of median weekly incomes (males) and consumer price index, October.

TABLE 11.2 JAMAICA: SELECTED BALANCE OF PAYMENTS INDICATORS, 1970–79
(million Jamaican dollars)

Year	*Merchandise exports (f.o.b.)* (1)	*Merchandise imports (f.o.b.)* (2)	*Balance on current account* (3)	*Net long-term capital* (4)	*Basic balance* (5)	*Change in reserves* (6)	*Total external reserves* (7)[a]	*Net external debt* (8)[a]
1970	285.1	373.3	−127.2	136.4	9.2	+17.6	95.9	80.3
1971	286.1	395.1	−143.1	157.8	14.7	−36.3	132.2	82.0
1972	302.4	423.4	−157.6	107.8	−49.8	−38.5	88.7	96.0
1973	357.2	518.4	−164.3	190.6	26.3	−17.5	76.1	150.4
1974	630.7	737.6	−151.8	205.0	53.2	+54.1	130.2	243.3
1975	714.3	881.5	−257.0	184.0	−73.0	−73.6	58.5	353.0
1976	596.7	719.6	−275.2	81.4	−193.8	−238.2	−181.4	421.5
1977	682.4	606.1	−31.4	−7.4	−38.8	−14.6	−196.0	452.4
1978	722.3	681.8	−78.8	−22.8	−101.6	−70.5	−447.0	1,138.4
1979	740.6	802.4	−129.9	−8.3	−138.2	−128.1	−758.5	1,328.1

Source: Bank of Jamaica, *Balance of Payments of Jamaica,* various issues, and *Monthly Statistical Digest,* various issues (Kingston).
a. Columns (1)–(6) are based on an accounting exchange rate of J$1 = US$1.1. Columns (7)–(8) are year-end figures using end-of-period exchange rate. As a consequence of repeated devaluations, these two sets of data no longer agree.

public service and manufacturing sectors than in agriculture. Government pricing and marketing policies also played a part. While price controls on basic food items and a fixed foreign exchange rate were aimed at protecting the costs of living of the urban poor, they also held down rural incomes and moved the domestic terms of trade against the agricultural sector. Many of Jamaica's poor are among the one-third involved in agriculture, but social unrest and violence among the poor were more likely to come from the urban areas than from the rural. It was those employed in the urban wage sector under trade union agreements that benefited most from rising real wages.

The events of one year, 1974, are crucial to understanding the deterioration of the economy and subsequent attitude of the authorities toward economic stabilization. In 1974, Jamaica's energy bill tripled following the recent announcement of higher oil prices, and then in May 1974 a bauxite production levy sharply increased tax revenue. Had the foreign exchange proceeds from this production levy been used for building up foreign reserves, and had the domestic value of these tax revenues remained in the Capital Development Fund to promote investment for structural adjustment or growth of physical production in the nonmining sectors as originally intended, the prolonged deterioration of the Jamaican economy and living standards might never have happened. Instead, the government spent these bauxite revenues on noninvestment activities aimed at providing greater social services, increased employment, and further public ownership and control of production. In keeping with the PNP's 1972 election campaign, many new social and economic programs had already been announced before Democratic Socialism was declared in late 1974 as the official PNP ideology. In the first two years of the Manley administration, social welfare programs introduced by the new government included free education, literacy and skill training, land reforms, food subsidies, and equal pay for women. After 1974 the political mood did not encourage fiscal restraint and a desire to live within the country's foreign exchange constraint.

Fiscal policy, or the rapid growth of government consumption expenditures, was the main cause of Jamaica's economic problems (Worrell 1980). The overall fiscal deficit (excess of domestic recurrent and capital expenditures over revenues) increased from 5 percent of GDP in 1972 to 24 percent of GDP by 1976, and up until 1975 much of the deficit was financed by external public borrowing. At the same time, domestic credit to the government sector expanded fivefold in 1971–1976, and the share of domestic credit going to the public sector doubled from 14 percent to 25 percent of total domestic credit over the same period. The growth and sectoral composition of this ambitious public spending program caused aggregate demand to far outstrip the supply of real resources from domestic production and available imports, and this added to the inflationary pressures from higher import prices and cost of living adjustments.

While government spending expanded dramatically in 1972–76, relatively little of this expenditure was for investment that would expand future production. Unpublished estimates of consumption and investment rates for the public and private sectors indicate that total public sector expenditures increased from 18.6 percent to 26.3 percent of GDP between 1973 and 1976, but that much of the increased government expenditures took the form of higher consumption, not investment. Public investment rose from 2.7 percent to 4.3 percent of GDP, but by 1976 the private investment rate had declined to only half that of 1973, a drop that vastly outweighed the small increase in the rate of public investment. Although government investment grew as a share of total investment, aggregate output declined, which suggests that the government's economic production strategy had the effect of replacing more productive private activities with less efficient public sector activities (Bourne 1980, p. 18). Income redistribution and short-term employment creation, rather than increased production, dominated government objectives, and the falling investment rate stemmed mainly from adverse private sector reaction to the political and economic policies of the Manley administration (Girvan, Bernal, and Hughes 1980, p. 144).

Jamaica's balance of payments crisis was not so much the result of external factors (higher oil prices, declining terms of trade, world recession) as of domestic politics and structural factors affecting the demand for non-oil imports, the supply of exports, and the net inflow of foreign finance. Among these domestic policies were import restrictions, exchange controls, and a fixed exchange rate. Overexpansionary fiscal and monetary policies (financed by the bauxite levy, foreign borrowing, and domestic money creation) encouraged the rapid growth of government consumption expenditures, which led to excess demand for local production and imported supplies. The decline in export supplies after 1974 was mainly due to policies affecting the ownership and profitability of bauxite and agricultural production. Policies such as the acquisition of land under the Land Lease Programme, government takeovers of sugar factories, and the greater use of cooperatives in production were designed to change the structure of production and the relative size of the private sector, but they also had the effect of discouraging agricultural export supplies. Over this period the production of all four major agricultural commodities declined, and Jamaica failed to meet its export quotas for sugar and bananas.

Macroeconomic stabilization was seldom afforded top priority among the goals of the administration. Social welfare, the living standards of the poor, unemployment, inflation, inadequate growth, and the shortage of foreign exchange were sometimes treated as separate short-run problems, although over the longer run they proved to be closely interrelated. The various corrective efforts undertaken by the authorities during this first term—including the introduction of tax measures, import controls, wage guidelines, and higher commercial bank lending rates—were inadequate to offset the disequilibria largely attributable to the rapid expansion of fiscal spending and domestic and foreign borrowing. In August 1975 an Economic Stabilization Committee was set up to advise as to how the economy should be run after the foreign exchange reserves were exhausted. However, these technical experts differed among themselves in their advice about the nature and urgency of stabilization measures, and the corrective efforts of the treasury, central bank, and planning agency were loosely coordinated. The PNP administration did not wish to usher in adjustment policies that required a reduction in real income to bring aggregate demand and supply into balance, and the attitude of the authorities toward stabilization was to delay any major adjustments in domestic demand and foreign exchange costs until after the 1976 elections.

If the general elections had been held early in 1976 and the government returned with a strong mandate, unpopular stabilization measures might have been introduced soon after net foreign reserves became negative in March 1976. As it turned out, a state of emergency was called in June 1976, and the elections were postponed until mid-December. In this election year, government spending rose by 20 percent, even though government revenues declined because of tax arrears and economic stagnation. Around 300 million Jamaican dollars (J$) of additional finance was required to cover the gap between government revenues and expenditures, and this was financed almost entirely by domestic money creation. In the general election, the PNP gained an overwhelming mandate, but the right- and left-wing elements within the party were divided on the policies to be followed and on the need for IMF assistance. This lack of consensus about Jamaica's economic strategy and wavering political commitment to stabilization were to persist throughout 1977–80.

Relations with the IMF, 1977–80

The financial flows between Jamaica and the IMF are summarized in Table 11.3. During the first term of the Manley administration, substantial use was made of the oil facility and the compensatory financing facility (CFF), particularly in 1976. Although discussion had taken place between the government and the Fund throughout the first term of the Manley administration, the government did not enter into any upper tranche stabilization agreement with the IMF until July 1977—nearly 18 months after net foreign reserves were exhausted. The Jamaican case may therefore be seen as that of a country which allowed conditions to deteriorate dramatically before a last-ditch recourse to the Fund. Jamaica had difficulty borrowing in the Eurodollar market because of its poor credit rating, and it had failed to obtain sufficient alternative sources of finance from foreign governments sympathetic to the Manley administration's policies.

In August 1977 Jamaica formally entered into a two-year stand-by agreement with the IMF that was soon suspended in December 1977. A three-year extended Fund facility (EFF) drawing was finalized in May 1978, and renegotiated in June 1979 to take advantage of additional drawings under the supplementary financing facility (SFF), but this collapsed in December 1979 when the performance tests were failed. In February 1980 the prime minister called for elections to decide the economic path the country should take and the role of the IMF, and in March 1980 negotiations for an interim stand-by agreement were discontinued. In the general elections held in October 1980, the PNP was defeated, and the new JLP government under Edward Seaga soon resumed negotiations with the Fund. In April 1981 an agreement was reached for SDR 236 million under the EFF, and this was increased to SDR 448 million when the enlarged access policy became operational. Although Jamaica has borrowed under every IMF facility, it is the economic management of the economy in 1976–80 and the size and conditionality of Fund resources under the stand-by and the EFF that are of prime concern in this section. Details of the 1981 EFF agreement are included below for comparison. Jamaica's relations with the Fund are also analyzed in Girvan, Bernal, and Hughes (1980), Bourne (1980), and Kincaid (1980 and 1981).

The 1977 Stand-by Agreement

Before the elections, the government and the Fund had worked out the broad terms of a two-year stand-by agreement that included

TABLE 11.3 FINANCIAL FLOWS BETWEEN JAMAICA AND THE IMF, 1972–80
(SDR milllion)

Item	*1972*	*1973*	*1974*	*1975*	*1976*	*1977*	*1978*	*1979*	*1980*
Gross inflows									
Reserve tranche	13.3	5.5	—	—	—	—	—	—	—
Credit tranches (stand-by)	—	—	—	13.3	—	19.2	—	—	—
Extended facility	—	—	—	—	—	—	42.0	35.1	—
Supplementary facility	—	—	—	—	—	—	—	77.9	—
Oil facility	—	—	—	—	29.2	—	—	—	—
Compensatory facility	—	—	13.3	—	26.5	—	15.8	31.7	—
Buffer stock facility	—	—	—	—	—	—	—	1.1	—
Total gross inflows	13.3	18.7	13.3	13.3	55.7	19.2	57.8	145.8	—
Repayments	—	5.5	−13.3	−13.3	—	—	−7.7	−18.1	−14.6
Net inflow	13.3	13.2	—	—	55.7	19.2	50.1	127.1	−14.6
Use of Fund credit (outstanding balance) at year-end)	—	13.2	13.2	13.2	68.9	88.1	138.2	265.9	251.3
Quota (year-end)	53.0	53.0	53.0	53.0	53.0	53.0	74.0	74.0	111.0
Credit as percentage of quota	—	25	25	25	130	166	187	360	220

— Zero or negligible.
Sources: Bank of Jamaica; and IMF, *International Financial Statistics,* various issues (Washington).
a. In January 1973 a stand-by agreement for SDR 26.5 million was agreed.
b. In 1974 and 1975 compensatory facility funds were both drawn and repaid.
c. In 1977 a two-year stand-by for SDR 64 million was agreed.
d. In 1978 a three-year extended Fund facility (EFF) of SDR 200 million was agreed.
e. In 1979 SDR 260 million over two years was agreed, with SDR 33 million under the EFF and SDR 227 million under the supplementary facility.
f. In March 1980 the Jamaican government decided to discontinue negotiations for an interim stand-by agreement.

a wage freeze, plans to curb the fiscal deficit, and a devaluation of 20–40 percent. The closure of the foreign exchange market on December 22, 1976, just after the election, was part of this tentative agreement, the architects of which were technocrats in the treasury and central bank. Although the PNP gained an overwhelming victory, it was felt that this owed much to the efforts of the left-wing politicians within the party who wanted an alternative to an IMF stabilization program, particularly the avoidance of a major devaluation. In his budget speech of January 19, 1977, the prime minister rejected the tentative agreement with the Fund and announced an alternative program for handling the crisis. There was to be no devaluation. Instead, the central features of the program were a sharp increase in import and exchange controls; strict foreign exchange rationing, which included a J$130 million reduction in the import target; and suspension of foreign loan repayments for 18 months. Demand restraint measures were announced, including a 6-month freeze on wages and prices, higher gasoline and income taxes affecting the middle and upper income groups, the reduction of tax arrears, a slower growth of government spending, and a rise in the liquid asset requirements of commercial banks.

Meanwhile, the government sought payments support from foreign governments—including Eastern European countries, Venezuela, Cuba, and Trinidad-Tobago—but it was unsuccessful in raising sizable sums. It was firmly advised to settle with the Fund before bilateral assistance would be reconsidered, and in April 1977 Jamaica had little option but to approach the Fund. The key issues delaying an agreement between April and July were the exchange rate and real wages.

The government argued that devaluation would provide little stimulation to the demand for exports, because bananas and sugar were sold under fairly inflexible negotiated agreements, but that it would reduce the foreign exchange required to cover the local costs of the bauxite/alumina companies. It was not believed that devaluation would stimulate domestic supplies and nontraditional exports. Instead, the higher cost of living of the urban poor, which surely would follow a devaluation, was of far more political concern than the benefits to the rural poor of higher incomes from agricutural exports and a possible switch in demand from imported to locally produced foods.

Devaluation was a precondition for the resumption of negotiations. As a compromise between the Fund's insistence on a major overall devaluation and the government's public stance that there should be no change, a dual exchange rate system was adopted in May 1977. The existing exchange rate, or basic rate, was applied to all government transactions, bauxite exports, and essential imports of basic foods and medicines, but for all other exports and nonessential imports a special rate was introduced that involved a 37.5 percent devaluation. Instead of a large overall devaluation, the authorities had undertaken a more limited exchange rate adjustment, and the dual system introduced multiple currency practices commonly outlawed in Fund agreements. Wage guidelines that would limit wage increases to J$10 per week were announced, but these were soon rejected by the trade unions and replaced by new guidelines that allowed wage increases in excess of J$10 when necessary to maintain real wages at their 1973 level. Hence, the exchange rate and wage measures went only part of the way toward meeting the IMF requirements.

Following these changes, it then took several months for Jamaica and the Fund to finalize an upper tranche program. Although Jamaica went to the Fund as a last resort, during these months the authorities persistently refused any further devaluations and a more restrictive wages policy. Girvan, Bernal, and Hughes (1980, p. 123) claim that the Fund finally settled largely on Jamaica's terms about the exchange rate and incomes policy because of considerable international support for Jamaica from the governments of Britain, Canada, and the United States and because of growing public criticisms of the general nature of Fund adjustment programs.

Under this agreement, a total of SDR 64 million was to be available to Jamaica over a two-year period, with the bulk of the money available in the first nine months. No conditions were attached to the first drawing of SDR 19.2 million once the agreement had been approved by the Fund Board in August 1977, and further drawings of SDR 9.2 million each were to become available in December 1977 and March 1978 if Jamaica passed the performance criteria. Each drawing under this stand-by was to be repaid within three years and not five years, the permitted maximum.

The Letter of Intent indicates that strict demand restraint was the underlying strategy, but the policy measures were not spelled out in detail:

> Jamaica's policies will be geared over the next two years to reducing gradually the Government's borrowing requirements and to building up the international reserve position of the Bank of Jamaica. To achieve this, the government plans to increase domestic production, to tighten further its demand management policies, to follow a restrained incomes policy, and to pursue a flexible exchange rate policy. ("Stand-by Agreement with Jamaica," August 1977.)

The agreement noted the tax, expenditure, and wages policy measures announced in January and called for a substantial reduction in tax arrears and for expenditure controls to be tightened. Jamaica was required not to introduce any new multiple currency practices or to intensify exchange and trade controls, but trade liberalization measures and devaluation were not included as performance criteria. The dual exchange rate system was accepted as a temporary measure, but it was to be reviewed if it appeared that the balance of payments targets would not be met.

The performance criteria set out in Table 11.4 required a sharp reversal in economic trends. Virtually no expansion was permitted in the net domestic assets of the Bank of Jamaica and in net bank credit to the public sector during the first six months of the agreement, whereas domestic credit had increased by 23 percent in 1976. Using the existing trade and exchange rate system, all outstanding arrears in foreign payments were to be eliminated in the first three months, and the net foreign assets of the Bank of Jamaica were to be stabilized after declining dramatically in 1976. The conditionality required under this agreement was clearly out of proportion to the size of resources directly available from the Fund.

The size of these resources from the Fund was far from adequate to cover the actual and projected size of the balance of payments deficit and elimination of arrears. The actual basic balance of the balance of payments and the current account deficit (Table 11.2) far exceeded the resources directly available from the Fund, and net foreign reserves were already negative. The Fund itself projected a current account deficit of J$137 million for 1977 and J$92 million in 1978, but it expected substantial foreign assistance to supplement the resources directly available from the Fund. It was projected that Jamaica would borrow J$175 million in foreign funds in 1977/78 and J$130 million in 1978/79.

In fact, the 1977 stand-by agreement failed to act as a catalyst, and the additional foreign funds did not materialize on the expected scale. In 1977, Jamaica's external borrowings totaled only J$40 million, or one-quarter of the sum projected by the Fund, and there was a net outflow of long-term capital of J$7.4 million. Directly and indirectly, insufficient resources were available to support the expansion of production and imports needed to improve the payments position. Even if substantial foreign funding had been forthcoming, it appears doubtful if the program would have been adequate to spread out the adjustment process. A two-year stand-by (120 percent of quota) was negotiated rather than a three-year EFF (240 percent of quota) when, by any definition, Jamaica's negative external reserves and declining GDP represented "fundamental disequilibrium." The short-term demand restraint strategy of this stand-by was inadequate to cure Ja-

TABLE 11.4 JAMAICA: 1977 STAND-BY AGREEMENT—PERFORMANCE CRITERIA AND OUTTURN

Indicator	1977 June 20	1977 Sept. 30	1977 Dec. 31	1978 March 31
Net foreign assets of Bank of Jamaica (million US dollars)[a]				
Ceiling	—	−162	−138	−138
Actual	−164	n.a.	−227	−317
Outstanding arrears (million US dollars)				
Ceiling	—	50.0	0	0
Actual	33.0	n.a.	27	82
Net domestic assets of Bank of Jamaica (million Jamaican dollars)				
Ceiling	—	345	355	345
Actual	342	n.a.	384	403
Net bank credit to public sector (million Jamaican dollars)				
Ceiling	—	745	745	735
Actual	730	n.a.	n.a.	841
Foreign borrowing authorization (million US dollars)				
1–5 years				
Ceiling	—	—	—	75
Actual	—	—	—	n.a.
1–15 years				
Ceiling	—	—	—	160
Actual	—	—	—	n.a.

n.a. Not available; — not applicable.
Note: The agreement was approved by the Fund Board in August 1977, and no conditions were attached to the September ceilings.
Source: Bank of Jamaica.
a. Including outstanding arrears.

maica's longer-term structural problems, and the meager Fund resources were insufficient to permit export-led growth.

Instead, the Fund appears to have viewed the tight fiscal and monetary targets under the stand-by as a test of the general willingness of the Jamaican authorities to undertake a stabilization program. Even if the major causes of disequilibria were largely the domestic policies under the control of the authorities, rather than temporary or permanent external factors, the speed and social costs of adjustment under a Fund stabilization program should be politically feasible; otherwise, social chaos may result if the expansion of fiscal spending and domestic credit is sharply and suddenly reversed. Although subsequent EFF agreements display greater awareness of the need for socially and politically tolerable adjustment costs and a longer adjustment process, insufficient attention was paid to these matters in 1977.

In December 1977 Jamaica failed the very first performance test, when at least three performance criteria were exceeded: the net foreign assets of the Bank of Jamaica, outstanding foreign arrears, and the net domestic assets of the Bank of Jamaica. The wide margin by which net bank credit to the public sector exceeded the March 1978 ceiling suggests that this ceiling was also exceeded in December 1977. Girvan, Bernal, and Hughes (1980, p. 124) incorrectly claim that only the net domestic assets of the Bank of Jamaica failed to be under the required ceiling and that Jamaica could have passed this test within a matter of days but for cash flow problems in reconciling new foreign loans and repayments.

In December 1977 the prime minister had announced retroactive wage increases for the police and military, and the technocrats were faced with a choice between refusing to honor checks for the additional public spending and failing the IMF tests. They honored the checks and expanded the domestic money supply to accommodate this increase in government spending. The Fund refused a waiver and a renegotiation of the December ceilings, arguing that the Bank of Jamaica and the treasury were unable to hold down government spending.

The 1977 breakdown illustrates both the lack of independence of the technocrats from their political context and the lack of flexibility of the Fund in view of changed external circumstances that had made the program unviable. The Bank of Jamaica and treasury officials responsible for administering the IMF program were unable to influence government spending announcements and failed to exert independent control over credit creation. Because it had been difficult for the Fund to negotiate a program with Jamaica, it is somewhat surprising that the stand-by was suspended so quickly, without showing more flexibility when net foreign borrowing fell far short of the Fund's projections and additional borrowing was needed to supplement the budgetary deficits. It would appear that the stand-by was never expected to work.

During 1977 there had been a noticeable improvement in the trade deficit as a result of the intensification of import restrictions and the recovery of world prices for alumina exports. Tighter exchange controls on private capital outflows and the accumulation of outstanding arrears helped temporarily to arrest the decline in international reserves. Real GDP per capita declined more slowly in 1977 (2.7 percent) than in 1976 (3.0 percent), but the investment rate dropped to only 11.7 percent of GDP because of the tighter import restrictions, a cut in bank credit to the private sector, and a lack of investor confidence. The growth of domestic credit to government was reduced sharply, and between 1976 and 1977 the overall fiscal deficit declined from 24 percent to 19 percent of GDP. With the introduction of the dual exchange rate system, domestic inflation reached 16 percent in 1977, or twice the rate of consumer price rises in 1976. While the nominal wage index remained constant, real wages declined between October 1976 and October 1977 by around 15 percent, and the unemployment rate increased despite heavy emigration.

The 1978 EFF Credit

The 1978 EFF agreement was signed at a time when Jamaica was in dire need of foreign exchange, to which the suspension of the IMF stand-by agreement had added by holding up other financial assistance already negotiated with the World Bank and foreign banking consortia. The economic strategy and conditionality surrounding the resumption of negotiations and use of resources under this credit reflect Fund views more fully than did the 1977 stand-by agreement, but once again the exchange rate and wage restraint were key issues in the negotiations:

> The message which came from the IMF in the first week of 1978 was short and to the point: (a) Jamaica must undertake a total weighted devaluation of 10 percent as a *precondition* to fresh negotiations; (b) the negotiations would only take place within a framework where Jamaica agreed that, in the first year of the programme, monthly devaluations would take place equivalent to the difference between the Jamaican rate of wage inflation and that of its main trading partners. The exchange rate was therefore firmly linked to wages policy; the greater the degree of wage increases allowed, the higher the devaluations would have to be; the lower the devaluations the government wanted, the more restrictive the wages policy it would have to impose. (Girvan, Bernal, and Hughes. 1980, p. 124.)

Accordingly, in January the basic rate was devalued by 13.6 percent, and there was a depreciation of 5.2 percent in the special rate, so that the differential between the rates narrowed slightly. While negotiations were in progress, the country's essential foreign exchange requirements were partially met with loans from commercial banks, intergovernment arrangements, and lines of credit. Foreign exchange shortages led to arrrears in foreign payments, and output and employment were affected by the lack of spare parts and raw materials.

When negotiations were finalized in May 1978, the IMF had agreed to provide SDR 200 million over a three-year period, credit which represented 270 percent of Jamaica's quota. Repurchases were to be completed within eight years—the maximum period permitted for repayment of the EFF. Unlike the earlier stand-by arrangement, the Fund recognized this time that the size of the resources directly available from the EFF had to permit an increase in imports consistent with the growth objectives of the program. Furthermore, the Fund sought more actively to mobilize additional external financing from commercial banks, international agencies, and foreign government. The adequacy of Fund and other foreign resources can be viewed in relation to the size of Jamaica's payments problems. In 1978 the gross inflows from the Fund totaled SDR 57.8 million, of which SDR 15.7 million was under the CFF and SDR 42.0 million (J$111 million) was under the EFF, which exceeded the actual deficit on current account J$78.8 million and the J$101.1 million deficit on the basic balance of payments. In 1978/79, J$400 million was raised in official funding from foreign governments, institutions, and commercial banks, compared with only J$40 million in the previous financial year. However, these net inflows of Fund and official foreign resources for balance of payments support were insufficient to cover the net outflow of private capital. In 1978 there was a net long-term capital outflow of J$22 million, and Jamaica's net international reserves declined by a staggering J$255 million.

The Fund and other official resources were to be used in support of a medium-term program, and the conditions involved major changes in the direction of government policies. To emphasize the political commitment of the government to these changes, the prime minister was required to accept the program publicly, including the proposed 25–30 percent cut in real wages. In general terms, the economic strategy envisaged a switch in resources from the public sector toward the private sector and from consumption to investment, and from reliance on administrative controls to the greater use of domestic market forces, although import controls were to retain a central role in balance of payments policy during the first year of the program.

Jamaica's deficits were to be cured in part by a major devaluation of the exchange rate, increased taxes, and slower growth of government expenditures. Income and price policies aimed to reduce real wages and to increase the share of profits in order to stimulate new investment. The speed with which the Jamaican authorities were

TABLE 11.5 JAMAICA: 1978 EXTENDED FUND FACILITY—PERFORMANCE CRITERIA AND OUTTURN

Indicator	*1977 (Dec.)*	*1978* *June 30*	*Sept. 30*	*Dec. 31*	*1979 (March 31)*
Net foreign assets of Bank of Jamaica (million US dollars)	(−227)				
Ceiling		−335.0	−300.0	−300.0	−280.0
Actual	(−227)	−318.3	−279.0	−289.5	−258.2
Outstanding arrears (million US dollars)					
Ceiling		80.0	60.0	40.0	20.0
Actual	(27)	79.2	48.8	30.4	18.9
Net domestic assets of Bank of Jamaica (million Jamaican dollars)					
Ceiling		440.0	445.0	480.0	473.0
Actual	(403)	405.2	393.6	424.6	413.1
Net bank credit to public sector (million Jamaican dollars)					
Ceiling		930.0	1,010.0	1,110.0	1,041.0
Actual	(841)	856.8	887.0	1,021.5	992.9
Foreign borrowing authorization (million US dollars)					
1–5 years ceiling		20.0	20.0	20.0	20.0
1–12 years ceiling		100.0	100.0	100.0	100.0

Source: Bank of Jamaica, *Balance of Payments of Jamaica 1978,* Ministry Paper no. 34 (Kingston, July 1978), p. 22.
a. Including outstanding arrears.

required to curb fiscal and monetary expansion was reduced, but there was little change in the mix between policies requiring demand restraint and those emphasizing supply considerations. The program reflected a preoccupation with aggregate monetary variables, the prices of traded goods, and the balance of payments, but little attention was given to structural constraints and disaggregated policy measures affecting output and investment in the major sectors of the economy.

The conditions attached to this agreement included the immediate unification of the exchange rate, and a weighted overall devaluation of 15 percent by May 1979. Two other conditions of the agreement, though not subject to quarterly performance criteria, were the eventual removal of import controls, trade restrictions, and multiple currency practices, and the repayment of arrears in amortization of private sector debt. The performance criteria set out in Table 11.5 reflect the Fund's emphasis on aggregate monetary variables. Under this IMF agreement, in nine months the net domestic assets of the Bank of Jamaica were permitted to increase by 16 percent (from J$405 million to a ceiling of J$473 million), and the net bank credit of the public sector was allowed to expand by 20 percent (from J$856 million to J$992 million), compared with virtually zero growth in the first six months of the stand-by agreement. However, this EFF credit required tight fiscal and monetary policy compared with the period from 1972–76, when total domestic credit rose by over 25 percent annually and net bank credit to the public sector expanded by around 40 percent annually.

During the first year of the program, the Jamaican government carried out every single aspect of the new agreement, and the implementation of these measures was made easier because of greater consensus and coordination between politicians and technocrats. All performance tests were passed. The net domestic assets of the Bank of Jamaica were well within the targets, and commercial banks were faced with excess liquidity as quantitative import restrictions restrained the demand for credit from the private sector. The balance of payments test (net foreign assets of the Bank of Jamaica and outstanding arrears in foreign payments) proved to be the most difficult performance test to pass. Despite the 30 percent devaluation, the supply response of investment, output, and exports was sluggish in 1978, but the demand for imports kept increasing. In the short run, devaluation was unlikely to lead to a significant reduction in the import bill because the major constraint on the volume of imports was the availability of foreign exchange rather than the Jamaican dollar cost of imports, and controls had already reduced import demand below the essential minimum. Bourne (1980, p. 24) argues that the response of domestic output was slight because of low investment rates in past years and because of the deterioration of the capital stock. The shortage of regular supplies of imported inputs and new equipment, plus uncertainties about future profits and the sociopolitical climate, also curbed the supply response. It was to be expected that agricultural output would be slow to respond because of institutional delays in passing on higher prices to farmers and because of lags in land preparation, crop maturation, and livestock gestation. Similarly, the demand responsiveness of traditional exports was delayed because of quota agreements for sugar and bananas.

The economic performance of the economy during the first year of the EFF program was not as good as the Fund had projected and the country had hoped for. Given the economy's high dependence on foreign resources, no immediate improvement of any significance was projected in the balance of payments. Instead of stabilizing, the payments deficit on current account and the basic balance widened further, by J$47.4 million and J$62.8 million, respectively. It is noteworthy that GDP in the export sectors (bauxite, alumina, agriculture, and tourism) recorded some growth in 1978, related in part to the exchange rate adjustments, but manufacturing and construction continued to decline because of the shortage of imported materials. Much of the additional foreign support was absorbed by debt service payments and foreign capital outflows, which, if not paid would have further undermined attempts to revive local and foreign investment.

Overall real GDP did not increase as projected by the Fund, but the decline in 1978 (1.6 percent) was less than in 1977 (2.7 percent) and 1976 (8.0 percent). The failure of the economy to recover as quickly as expected also affected tax receipts and, hence, fiscal performance. In 1978/79, the recurrent fiscal deficit was 2.5 percent of GDP, whereas the Fund had targeted a *surplus* of 2.8 percent, but this was not among the performance criteria. The size of the fiscal deficit in 1978 is reflected indirectly in the ceiling on net bank credit to the public sector, but this test Jamaica passed. Investment activity remained weak, despite efforts to reduce real wages and increase profits. There was a substantial drop in real wages, which declined by 20–25 percent between April 1978 and April 1979, partly as a result of the exchange rate adjustments, which contributed to the 47 percent increase in the consumer price index during 1978. By October 1980, the real wages of those employed were no higher than they had been in April 1973.

The 1979 EFF Credit

The adjustment costs of inflation, reduced government services, and lower levels of income caused immediate hardships, and the sacrifices seemed in vain because the economic benefits in the first year of the program were discouraging (Bourne 1980, p. 25). Public resentment was mounting against the EFF program, and there was a risk of social upheaval if it were not eased. Jamaica needed a more rapid resumption of economic growth, more jobs, less inflation, and some gradual improvement in living standards. In an effort to achieve these, there was a change in the mix of adjustment policies in the second year of the EFF. The Fund arranged for an expansion of its lending and permitted a stretching out of the adjustment process.

In the 1979 EFF, wage increases were to be limited to 15 percent while price controls on basic foods and rents were maintained. In 1979, the Social Contract between the government, private sector and trade unions called for wage increases to be kept to just 10 percent, and a norm for price increases of 10 percent was established. For the fiscal program, the authorities sought to improve the efficiency of the tax system and to reduce tax arrears, but taxation rates were not raised. The improvement in the recurrent deficit was to be achieved by reducing central government expenditures. Public sector pay increases were to be limited to 10 percent, and current expenditures were to be held at the nominal level of the previous year.

Under the new agreements, SDR 130 million was available in each of the two years, and 87 percent of these resources were provided under the SFF set up for countries in exceptional circumstances with large balance of payments needs relative to their quota. In May 1979, before this new arrangement, total Fund drawings (excluding purchases under the CFF and oil facility) were 221 percent of quota, and it was expected that by June 1980 total drawings would rise to 454 percent of quota, of which upper tranche drawings would amount to 378 percent of quota:

> In effect, the IMF opted to substitute direct Fund assistance for the commercial bank inflows which would normally have been expected to take place. The hope was that, through the additional resources provided, the basis for economic turn around would be created and eventually the commercial banks and foreign and local investors would be induced to support the programme. (Girvan, Bernal, and Hughes 1980, p. 128.)

In 1979 gross inflows from the Fund were SDR 145 million (J$340 million), of which SDR 78 million was from the SFF and SDR 35 million from the extended facility. Following this Fund program, Jamaica was able to renegotiate with foreign commercial banks an agreement to reschedule seven-eighths of all amortization payments on the government and government-guaranteed debt falling due before March 1981. While the Fund program may have helped to trigger pledges of foreign finance, official foreign borrowing in 1979/80 was J$100 million less than the year before,[2] and the net outflow of private capital continued (although it was J$80 million less than in 1978). Private net capital outflows would have been far greater, however, except that foreign exchange reserves were inadequate to meet debt obligations and arrears The net inflow of Fund resources in 1979

[2] Government of Jamaica, Ministry of Finance, *Financial Statements and Revenue Estimates*, Kingston. Between 1978 and 1979, the external debt service ratio declined slightly from 9.2 percent to 8.7 percent of GDP.

TABLE 11.6 JAMAICA: 1979 EXTENDED FUND FACILITY, PERFORMANCE CRITERIA, AND OUTTURN

Indicator	*1978 (Dec.)*	*1979*			
		March 31	*June 30*	*Sept. 30*	*Dec. 31*
Net foreign assets of Bank of Jamaica (million US dollars)					
Ceiling	n.a.	n.a.	−425.0	−425.0	−370.0
Actual	(−289.5)[a]	−319.1	−318.6	−419.6	−496.7
Net domestic assets of Bank of Jamaica (million Jamaican dollars)					
Ceiling	n.a.	n.a.	900.0	925.0	940.0
Actual	(424.6)[a]	708.2	866.9	924.5	1,064.1
Net banking system credit to the public sector (million Jamaican dollars)					
Ceiling	n.a.	n.a.	1,070.0	1,105.0	1,125.0
Actual	(1,021.5)	992.4	1,059.1	1,072.2	1,265.0
Foreign borrowing authorization (million US dollars)					
1–5 years					
Ceiling	n.a.	n.a.	60.0	60.0	60.0
Actual	—	n.a.	0.9	4.5	12.9
1–12 years					
Ceiling	n.a.	n.a.	110.0	110.0	110.0
Actual	—	n.a.	0.9	21.2	41.1

n.a. Not applicable; — Not available.
Source: Bank of Jamaica, *Balance of Payments of Jamaica 1979* (Kingston, 1979), p. 49.
a. There was a change in definition between Tables 11.5 and 11.6.

exceeded in size the deficit on current account and basic balance, but higher oil prices and higher external debt service payments meant that non-oil imports declined.

Just as under the 1977 stand-by and the 1978 EFF agreements, the performance criteria for 1979 reflected the Fund's usual emphasis on monetary variables. This time foreign borrowing ceilings were reintroduced, and outstanding arrears in international payments were included under the ceiling on net foreign assets of the Bank of Jamaica. The quarterly ceilings and outturn for the first nine months of the 1979 program are set out in Table 11.6, and a comparison with the 1978 performance ceilings shows these ceilings were more generous. In 1978 net domestic assets of the Bank of Jamaica actually increased by only 2 percent compared with the 16 percent maximum permitted by the ceilings because the demand for private sector credit was curbed by the inability to import raw materials, spare parts, and other items. The growth of credit to the private sector was emphasized in 1979, and the net domestic assets of the Bank of Jamaica were permitted to rise by 32 percent between March and December 1979. Net foreign assets and arrears of the Bank of Jamaica were required to improve under the 1978 program, but a further decline of 19 percent was permitted in the 1979 program. However, public sector credit was more restricted in 1979. In 1978 the permitted level of credit to the public sector implies an increase of 16 percent, but this was restricted in 1979 to only 13 percent above the actual level of March 1979.

It is interesting to contrast the size and conditionality of Fund resources under the 1977 and 1979 agreements. Over a two-year period the 1977 agreement provided SDR 64 million, whereas the 1979 credit was for SDR 260 million. The 1977 stand-by failed to act as a catalyst, and the additional foreign funds fell short of the Fund's projections, but in 1979 the IMF sought to substitute direct Fund assistance for foreign borrowing so as to improve foreign and local investor confidence and finance additional imports necessary for increased production. Although similar performance criteria were attached to both agreements, the 1977 stand-by required a quick improvement in the payments position, whereas the 1979 agreement permitted a further decline in the net foreign assets of the Bank of Jamaica. A sudden halt to the rapid growth of domestic credit was required in the 1977 credit, but scant attention was paid to the likely socioeconomic consequences that might have occurred if the politicians and technical experts had carried out the stand-by agreement and sharply reduced aggregate demand. Partly in response to mounting urban unrest, the Fund in 1979 permitted a stretching out of the adjustment process. The EFF emphasized the growth of credit to the private sector and the net domestic assets of the Bank of Jamaica were allowed to rise by 32 percent in nine months.

As to the economic performance of the economy in 1979, commodity exports and tourism increased by J$60 million because of the recovery of tourism and growth of minor exports, but severe floods in the middle of the year adversely affected agricultural exports, and in 1979 Jamaica drew J$73 million (SDR 31.8 million) under the CFF. Monthly devaluations were stopped, and a more disaggregated policy for stimulating exports—the Certified Exporters Scheme—was established. A loan of $30 million was obtained from the World Bank to establish an Export Development Fund to finance imports of raw materials specifically for the production of nontraditional industrial exports and their domestic suppliers. However, disbursements under this scheme were slow, and only $5 million had been approved by the end of 1979.

In 1979 Jamaica had to pay substantially higher oil prices and higher interest rates on external debt, and, instead of expanding, foreign exchange available for non-oil imports declined in nominal terms from $407 million in 1978 to $385 million in 1979. In real terms, however, there was a 13 percent decline, for the import price index rose by 9 percent over this period.

As a result of the shortage of foreign exchange and continuing social and economic uncertainties, the growth objectives of the program were not met, and real GDP per capita declined by 3.5 percent in 1979 compared with 1.8 percent in 1978. Partly as a result of the floods, real GDP from agriculture declined by nearly 7 percent, after increasing by 9 percent in 1978. Manufacturing, mining, and construction also declined, but to a lesser extent. Real gross fixed capital formation rose by 20 percent, but investment and foreign capital inflows were still far less than anticipated by the Fund. Limited foreign exchange for imports, and the poor response of GDP, resulted in fewer jobs in some sectors, and by October 1979 unemployment had officially reached 28 percent of the work force compared with 25 percent in 1978. After the monthly devaluations were ended, the inflation rate declined from 47 percent in 1978 to 24 percent in 1979, and real wages remained roughly the same as in the previous year.

The continued decline in GDP, together with tax arrears, reduced government revenues below their projected level. Government recurrent expenditures exceeded their 1978 levels because of higher interest payments on the government debt and public sector wage increases in excess of 10 percent. Although capital expenditures were within the initial estimates, recurrent expenditures between April–December 1979 were $50 million higher than in the comparable period in 1978 (Bank of Jamaica, *Balance of Payments of Jamaica 1979,* p. 38). These trends meant that the current account showed a deficit of J$177 million rather than being in balance. Instead of declining to 9 percent, the overall budget deficit expanded from 13.5 percent to 15 percent of GDP between 1978 and 1979, and some 80 percent of this expansion in the deficit was financed by the domestic banking system. Meanwhile, the demand for private sector credit remained depressed and expanded by even less than in 1978.

In December 1979, Jamaica failed to meet three of the major IMF performance criteria. The net foreign assets test was failed by $126 million, and the ceiling on credit to the public sector and the net domestic assets of the Bank of Jamaica were exceeded by J$140 million and J$124 million, respectively. Because of Jamaica's poor credit rating, only one-quarter of the foreign borrowing authorization was raised. Girvan, Bernal, and Hughes (1980, p. 128) argue that exogenous factors (higher interest rates, oil prices, and floods) were responsible for 60 percent of the breach in the ceiling on international reserves, but they are incorrect in claiming that government expenditures did not exceed the 1978 level or agreed targets. The inability of the authorities to monitor and control expenditures, plus arrears in taxes and recurrent payments, contributed to the failure to comply with the ceiling on the expansion of sector credit.

In September 1979 the program had already begun to run into trouble, soon after a speech by the prime minister to the Non-aligned Conference in which his references to a noncapitalistic development path effectively precluded private capital inflows. Discussions for new loans and for the refinancing of Jamaica's commercial bank debts falling due in 1980 were suspended, and around this time it became known that the government had been understating the size of its outstanding arrears in international payments. Furthermore, slippages in fiscal targets were apparent, but the government showed no signs of easing up on its spending. The Fund was willing to modify somewhat the December performance tests to allow for the effect of floods, higher interest rates, and oil price rises, but the Fund also required further tax changes, government expenditure cuts, and administrative controls to restrain and monitor the expansion of the fiscal deficit. The lack of consensus within the PNP about the country's economic strategy and need for foreign capital inflows and export earnings was reflected in a failure within the cabinet to reach agreement about the requested policy changes. Meanwhile further slippages occurred.

In February 1980, the government and the IMF were unable to arrive at an agreement about budget cuts, and the Jamaican authorities sought to apply directly to the IMF Board of Directors for a waiver. The prime minister also announced that general elections would be held as soon as feasible. It proved impossible for the Jamaican authorities to apply directly to the Board, without the endorsement of the Fund's management and negotiating team, and so fresh negotiations began for an interim stand-by agreement to tide the country over until the elections were held. These negotiations involved discussions of a further wage freeze and budget cutbacks in social programs and the number of government employees; and the finance minister reported in March 1980 that Jamaica would certainly fail the performance tests proposed by the IMF under this interim stand-by agreement. It was decided to discontinue negotiations with the IMF, but in March 1980 the prime minister reaffirmed that Jamaica would remain a member of the IMF and honor its obligations to the Fund. As a consequence, in 1980 the gross inflow of Fund resources was zero, and repayments totaled SDR 14.6 million.

The role of the IMF and the management of the economy were central issues in the 1980 general elections. The PNP campaigned on a platform of rejecting the IMF and its future participation in the economy and proposed an alternative path of economic development that would emphasize greater self-reliance. The PNP authorities blamed the economic crisis on external causes largely beyond their control, and party spokesmen condemned the Fund for the economic and social costs of adjustment that the country had suffered since 1977. The JLP, on the other hand, held that domestic policies and not external factors were the main cause of the economic crisis, that to cure the country's problems a massive injection of foreign exchange was required, and that Jamaica therefore had no alternative but to resume negotiations with the Fund.

The 1981 EFF Agreement

In the "IMF general elections" held in October 1980, the PNP was decisively defeated, and the JLP under Edward Seaga soon resumed negotiations with the Fund. In April 1981, agreement was reached with the Fund for SDR 236 million over the next three years from the extended facility, which resources were to be raised to SDR 447 million when the enlarged access policy became operational. In addition, SDR 37 million was agreed under the CFF because of a shortfall in receipts from exports and tourism in 1980. The Fund also approved a purchase in the first credit tranche equivalent to SDR 21 million.

Details are not available of the projected economic performance of the Jamaican economy, and it is too soon to evaluate the adequacy of these resources and effectiveness of the economic program. Some comparisons can, however, be drawn between the size and conditionality of resources under the 1981 EFF and earlier agreements. In the first 12 months, more resources were made available under the 1981 EFF (SDR 179 million), but, as with the 1979 EFF (SDR 130 million) and 1978 EFF (SDR 70 million) than under the 1979 agreement, around 60 percent of the resources in the first year of the 1981 EFF were to come from the more expensive supplementary facility with the remainder financed from the Fund's ordinary resources, which have a lower interest rate.

The economic strategy underlying this latest agreement emphasized the need to expand output and investment by relaxing the constraint imposed by the shortage of foreign exchange for raw materials, spare parts, and equipment:

> The strategy falls into two parts: firstly to put unutilized capacity to work with the emphasis on those sectors that will produce quick and substantial incremental foreign exchange earnings, secondly to initiate adjustments in industrial and agricultural policies and so provide a basis for expansion of production capacity with concomitant increases in employment opportunities. ("Extended Fund Facility Arrangement with the International Monetary Fund," Ministry Paper no. 9, April 1981.)

In the 1981 agreement it was recognized that Jamaica's extensive import controls could not be dismantled quickly without exacerbating the foreign exchange shortage, but the eventual liberalization of the import licensing system was called for. No further devaluation of the official foreign exchange rate was required. Instead, the informal or unofficial foreign exchange market was recognized, and imports financed by these informal (black market) channels were to be exempt from import licensing requirements. In essence, a dual exchange rate system (official and informal) was acknowledged and strengthened by this Fund program, notwithstanding the Fund's constitutional and other aversions to this type of arrangement.

The production program was expected to generate an early increase in foreign exchange from the growth of tourism, bauxite/alumina, sugar, and bananas. Steps to deregulate the economy and make greater use of market signals instead of controls were aimed at restoring investor confidence and encouraging private investment. As part of a World Bank structural adjustment lending program, a team was to examine Jamaica's industrial and agricultural pricing policies and identify changes that might help to promote production and provide greater incentives for investment. Many price controls were to be abolished and relaxed; "wage ceilings" and wage adjustments based on "comparability" between sectors were abolished. The new pay policy was to be based on market conditions, and wage claims were to be settled on the basis of the ability of the employer to pay. Unlike the 1977 and 1978 agreements, further devaluation and income policy measures to restrain real wages were not part of the 1981 program.

Fiscal policy changes were to constrain the growth of public consumption and shift the emphasis of government expenditures toward capital formation, whereas a review of the tax system was expected to increase tax buoyancy and reduce tax arrears and evasion. As a result of these expenditures and tax changes, over the three-year program, central government expenditures were to be reduced from around 40 percent to not more than 30 percent of GDP and the overall fiscal deficit reduced from 14 percent to 10 percent of GDP.

The performance criteria for the 1981 agreement include the customary ceilings on the net domestic assets of the Bank of Jamaica, net domestic credit to the public sector, and net foreign assets of the Bank of Jamaica. In addition, there was a ceiling on the foreign debt authorization, and the standard condition not to introduce any multiple currency practice nor intensify trade and foreign exchange controls. There was one major difference between the performance criteria in the 1981 EFF agreement and previous stand-by and EFF agreements—the 1981 performance criteria on domestic monetary variables and international reserves were all subject to automatic adjustments if there was either a shortfall or excess of non-IMF foreign loans and credits above or below the amounts set out in the Letter of Intent. At the end of the first 12 months of the 1981 agreement, this amount of foreign finance was $479 million, which was high in comparison with the amount of foreign borrowing in 1979/80. Hence, the 1981 ceilings appeared more flexible and more generous than those under the 1979 agreement. In the first 9–10 months of this program, the expansion permitted in net public sector credit without adjustments for the shortfall or excess in foreign borrowing was greater (J$310 million) than under the 1979 agreement (J$135 million), but less expansion was permitted in the net domestic assets of the Bank of Jamaica, and the decline permitted in international reserves was also less than under the 1979 agreement.

Conclusions

Without summarizing the details, some major conclusions about attempts to cure instability over the period 1979–80, and claims directed against Fund programs in Jamaica,[3] are as follows.

Jamaica's experience surrounding the 1977 stand-by agreement supports the conclusion reached in the Dell Report (Dell 1980, p.

[3] " 'Message from the Prime Minister of Jamaica,' Hon. Michael Manley to the South-North Conference on the International Monetary System and the New International Economic Order," *Development Dialogue,* vol. 2 (1980), p. 5. "Solidarity with Jamaica," Resolution adopted by the South-North Conference on the International Monetary System and the New International Economic Order, Arusha, Tanzania, June 30–July 3, 1980, *Development Dialogue,* vol. 2 (1980), p. 24.

10), that there is a relationship between the ability and willingness of developing countries to accept Fund conditionality and the amount of resources the Fund is able to make available. While the Jamaican authorities had allowed the economy to deteriorate dramatically before going to the Fund, the conditions for this agreement were out of all proportion to the resources the Fund made available. Even if the agreement was seen by the Fund as a test of the government's determination to implement tough stabilization measures, the size and conditionality of Fund resources provided little scope and encouragement for the government to adhere to this goal.

Whether or not factors outside the control of the authorities had been the main cause of Jamaica's stabilization problems, substantial foreign assistance was required to support a viable stabilization program and to reduce the social and economic costs of adjustment to a level that was not impractical. Although subsequent agreements display an increasing awareness of the need for adjustment costs to be politically feasible and for a longer period of adjustment, insufficient attention was paid to these matters in 1977.

While in 1977 the Fund's conditionality may have been politically impractical, the 1978 and 1979 EFF agreements illustrate that the Fund's conditionality was not applied in a rigid fashion, and that there was "constrained" flexibility in response to mounting social tensions and changed external circumstances. In the 1978 EFF agreement, the speed with which the Jamaican authorities were required to curb fiscal and monetary expansion was reduced compared with the conditions of the 1977 stand-by agreement. In 1979 the Fund permitted a stretching out of the adjustment period so as to ease the costs of adjustment, and there was a change in the mix of demand and supply policies—with more emphasis given to structural constraints and disaggregated supply policies aimed at increasing output in key sectors of the economy. In December 1979 the performance criteria were adjusted to the extent of allowing for unforeseen external events, such as the damage to export supplies caused by Hurricane Allan, higher foreign interest rates, and oil price increases—but not for slippages in domestic fiscal targets.

Overall, Fund stabilization programs for Jamaica do reflect a promarket bias and do assume the economic efficiency of market forces rather than regulations and controls. The eventual liberalization of the import licensing system was called for in the 1978, 1979, and 1981 EFF agreements, but it was recognized that Jamaica's extensive import controls could not be dismantled quickly without exacerbating the foreign exchange shortage. Claims of an antisocialist bias in the Fund programs for Jamaica are questionable. The 1978 EFF program did call for a switch in resources from the public to private sectors, but this Democratic Socialist government, with its left-wing interventionist policies, was the largest recipient of IMF resources on a per capita basis in 1979, and the total outstanding balance of Fund credits to Jamaica was 360 percent of its quota, against developing country average of 64 percent.

The Jamaican experience shows clearly that a Fund agreement may help to reschedule old debts and to trigger pledges of additional foreign finance, but that the IMF "seal of approval" may not always act as a catalyst providing the desired size of international borrowing because foreign bank loans are also influenced by evidence of government adherence to the Fund program and by risk of arrears in debt service payments. Recognizing this, the performance criteria under the 1981 EFF agreement were automatically adjusted for fluctuations in official external borrowing.

In the case of Jamaica, Fund agreements after 1977 could not quickly dispell the uncertainty surrounding the domestic policies of the PNP, which earlier had been the main cause of the decline in real GDP and international reserves. The ambivalent attitude of the authorities toward the implementation of stabilization measures persisted throughout 1977–80, and the inadequate and irregular supply of imports continued to restrain the recovery of the domestic economy. Hence, Fund stabilization programs proved to be far from sufficient to revive local and foreign investor confidence and to promote export-led growth. A sharp change in government policies and more attention to stabilization measures were required to arrest the decline in real income and foreign reserves. The experience of the Jamaican economy supports the view that there are fundamental laws and constraints for socialist and other developing countries alike; namely, that "a country that raises wages and vastly increases the government's budget at a time when productivity and aggregate supply are falling will get itself into a first-class economic mess" (Morawetz 1980, p. 361).

References

Bonnick, Gladstone. 1980. "The Experience of Jamaica." In Dell Report (1980), vol. 1.

Bourne, Compton. 1980. "Jamaica and the International Monetary Fund: Economics of the Stabilization Programme." *Studies in Rural Finance.* Occasional Paper no. 729. Columbus, Ohio: Department of Economics and Rural Sociology, Ohio State University (May).

Dell Report. 1980. *The Balance of Payments Adjustment Process in Developing Countries.* UNCTAD/MFD/TA/5. New York: United Nations Conference on Trade and Development. Also published as: Sidney Dell and Roger Lawrence. 1980. *The Balance of Payments Adjustment Process in Developing Countries.* Oxford: Pergamon.

Girvan, Norman, Richard Bernal, and Wesley Hughes. 1980. "The IMF and the Third World: The Case of Jamaica, 1974–80." *Development Dialogue,* vol. 2.

Jefferson, Owen. 1972. *The Post-War Economic Development of Jamaica.* Kingston: Institute of Social and Economic Research, University of West Indies.

Kincaid, G. Russell. 1980. "Fund Assistance to Jamaica." *IMF Survey* (December 15, 1980).

———. 1981. "Conditionality and the Use of Fund Resources: Jamaica." *Finance and Development,* vol. 18, no. 2 (June 1981).

Manley, Michael. 1974. *The Politics of Change.* London: Andre Deutsch.

Morawetz, David. 1980. "Economic Lessons from Some Small Socialist Developing Countries." *World Development* (May-June).

Sharpley, Jennifer. 1981. "Economic Management and the IMF in Jamaica: 1972–80." DERAP *Working Paper* no. 235. Bergen, Norway: The Chr. Michelsen Institute (September).

Stone, Carl. 1980. *Democracy and Clientilism in Jamaica.* New Brunswick, NJ: Transactions Books.

Worrell, DeLisle. 1980. "External Influences and Domestic Policies: The Economic Fortunes of Jamaica and Barbados in the 1970s." Paper presented at the Caribbean Studies Association, Curaçao, May 1980. Bridgetown: Central Bank of Barbados.

CHAPTER **12**

Economic Performance Under Three Stand-by Arrangements: Peru, 1977–80

Adolfo C. Diz

This paper describes the performance of the Peruvian economy under three successive stand-by arrangements with the International Monetary Fund (IMF), during the period November 1977 to December 1980.

The main purpose of this analysis is not Peruvian economic performance per se. That is why the analysis is not carried on in full detail, since it would then miss the purpose of this conference. Rather, the main objective is to utilize the Peruvian case to show the difficulties involved in trying to arrive at a judgment on the success or failure of either the authorities' decision making or the IMF's policy advice. Although widely diverging results were observed in this particular experience, covering more than three years and at least two economic administrations, IMF advice was present throughout. Political circumstances, and favorable or unfavorable external and internal factors beyond the control of the authorities, make it extremely difficult to arrive at such judgments.

The November 1977 stand-by was the seventeenth arrangement made between the Peruvian authorities and the IMF (including the first ever made by the Fund), and the first made since the expiration of a stand-by in 1971.

Although the last of the three arrangements here considered expired on the date originally planned, both of the first two were originally intended to cover more than two years but were canceled prior to their termination dates and immediately replaced by new arrangements involving higher sums. This peculiarity suggests that the three arrangements be considered together (Table 12.1).

TABLE 12.1 PERUVIAN STAND-BY ARRANGEMENTS

Amount (SDR million)	*Initial date*	*Expiration date*	*Date canceled*	*Duration (months)*	
				Planned	*Effective*
90	Nov. 1977	Dec. 1979	Aug. 1978	26	9
184	Aug. 1978	Dec. 1980	Aug. 1979	29	12
285	Aug. 1979	Dec. 1980	Expired	17	17

Source: Central Reserve Bank of Peru.

Background

By 1977 the Peruvian economy was in a difficult situation. Since the early 1970s the government had followed an expansionary demand management policy, particularly in increased public sector spending. The current account of the public sector, which had shown a surplus in 1974, turned to a deficit of approximately 1 percent of GDP in the next two years and reached almost 4 percent of GDP during 1977. The overall (current and capital) public sector deficit increased from 6 percent of GDP in 1974 to 10 percent of GDP in 1975 and remained at that level for three years, until 1977. The financing of these deficits required large foreign borrowing, equivalent to about 6 percent of GDP in both 1974 and 1975, and substantial net domestic bank borrowing averaging 5 percent of GDP in the years 1975–77. Peru's public external debt doubled from the end of 1974 to the end of 1977 as it went from a level of $2.3 billion to $4.6 billion. Excessive monetary expansion affected prices and the balance of payments. The annual average cost of living index increased 17 percent in 1974 and 38 percent in 1977. Net foreign assets of the banking system fell from a level of $700 million at the end of 1974 to a negative $1.1 billion at the end of 1977, a shift of $1.8 billion in three years.

The 1977 Stand-by

In November 1977 the Fund approved an SDR 90 million stand-by arrangement with Peru in the upper credit tranches. The main aim of the program was reduction of the public sector deficit. This objective was to be achieved by: reducing expenditures, especially for investment; increasing revenues through tax increases; improving tax administration; and eliminating operating deficits of public enterprises. The program also included the floating of the exchange rate for the sol and a considerable liberalization of import-related operations in the foreign exchange market.

TABLE 12.2 PERU'S PERFORMANCE UNDER THE 1977 STAND-BY ARRANGEMENT

Item	*Dec. 31, 1977 (S/. 85 = $1)*	*June 30, 1978 (S/. 110 = $1)*
Net domestic assets of the banking system (billion soles)		
Ceiling	302	344
Actual	313	393
Excess over ceiling	11	49
Net credit of the banking system to the public sector (billion soles)		
Ceiling	152	163
Actual	149	198
Margin under ceiling (−) or excess	−3	35
Net international reserves of the banking system (million dollars)		
Target	−1,088	−1,060
Actual	−1,101	−1,212
Shortfall from target	13	152
Contracting of new external debt (million dollars)		
1–10 years		
Ceiling	300	300
Actual	104	240
Margin under ceiling (−)	−196	−60
1–5 years (million dollars)		
Ceiling	115	115
Actual	18	93
Margin under subceiling (−)	−97	−22

Source: Central Reserve Bank of Peru.

The stand-by established a set of ceilings on: net domestic assets of the banking system, net credit of the banking system to the public sector, and the contracting of new external debt by the public sector (with a subceiling for short- and medium-term public external debt). In addition, there were a set of targets for the net international reserves of the banking system.

Table 12.2 shows these quantitative limits and targets and the economic performance under the stand by up to June 30, 1978. With the exception of the ceilings on the external debt, compliance with the ceilings only occurred for a brief period at the beginning of the agreement, between December 7 and December 29, 1977, when Peru was able to purchase SDR 10 million under the stand-by arrangement. These were all the resources that the authorities drew under this particular agreement.

By June 30, 1978 the monetary ceilings had been exceeded by a margin of 15–20 percent, and the target for net international reserves showed a shortfall of 15 percent. The contracting of new external debt showed a margin of 20 percent under the ceilings for both the short- and medium-term debt and the total debt.

During this period, and despite some improvement, the public sector current and overall deficits remained the most important source of excessive credit expansion, as a consequence of both loose expenditure control and a significant shortfall of tax revenues. The intensified demand pressures implied further losses of international reserves, despite the virtual rationing of foreign exchange and new and extended delays in payments abroad. Internal prices accelerated, and inflation reached a 96 percent annual rate during the first semester of 1978. The exchange rate rose approximately 90 percent from October 1977 to May 1978 (an annual rate of 200 percent), when a system of frequent devaluations was reestablished.

In terms of the specific aims of the program, there was a reduction in the overall deficit of the public sector. It fell from 10 percent of GDP in 1977 to 6.8 percent of GDP during the first semester of 1978. This decline combined a 3 percent of GDP fall in the current deficit and a 1.2 percent of GDP decline in investment expenditures. The results were negative in the area of tax revenues, where there appeared a shortfall. During the first semester of 1978 there was some improvement in the current account of the balance of payments, but the overall balance continued to show reserve losses, contrary to what had been programmed.

The 1978 Stand-by

In September of 1978 the IMF approved a new SDR 184 million stand-by arrangement for Peru, covering the period through December 1980, in support of a new economic program started some months earlier. At the same time the 1977 stand-by arrangement, due to expire in December 1979, was canceled. At the time Peru was facing an acute foreign exchange crisis and the risk of having to default on its external debt obligations.

The objectives of the new program were to restore balance of payments equilibrium, achieve a deceleration of inflation as quickly as possible, and revive production in strategic sectors of the economy—mainly agriculture and export-oriented activities.

The IMF staff is believed to have argued that the restoration of balance of payments equilibrium would be the objective of the Peruvian authorities that would prove easiest to achieve. The deceleration of inflation was likely to be a more elusive objective, mainly because the requisite price, wage, exchange, and interest rate adjustments were thought bound to impart new inflationary impulses. Of the three declared objectives of the program, the one whose early attainment was most in doubt was a revival of production.

The performance criteria included a set of ceilings on the net domestic assets of the Central Reserve Bank (instead of the banking system, as before), bank credit to the public sector, and the value of new public foreign debt contracted. In addition, there were targets on the net international reserves of the Central Reserve Bank. The dates for these tests were extended through December of 1979. The agreement also included a timetable for reduction of the basic minimum financing requirements for private imports, and injunctions against the introduction of any new multiple currency practice or other restrictions on payments and transfers for current international transactions.

The basis of the intended adjustment effort was a significant improvement of the public sector finances. The current account of the public sector was programmed to shift from a deficit of 1 percent of GDP in 1978 to a surplus of 5.75 percent of GDP in 1979. The overall deficit was programmed to be reduced from 7 percent of GDP in 1978 to less than 2 percent of GDP in 1979.

All this implied an improvement of tax administration, a drastic reduction of current expenditures, and frequent adjustments of tariffs, prices, and fees for goods and services marketed by the public sector. There was a decision to maintain a tight control of monetary expansion during 1978, particularly of credit to the private sector, until the lower public sector financing requirements were able to allow an easing of private sector credit. Rates of interest on deposits were raised by 12 percentage points in August 1978, but they were still almost 20 percent negative in real terms.

Table 12.3 shows the quantitative limits and targets of this agreement compared with actual performance under the stand-by until June 30, 1979.

Peru's observance of the quantitative criteria was very good. On each testing date (including some other intermediate dates not shown in the table), the performance criteria were met by a substantial margin. Generally speaking, the monetary expansion left a margin

TABLE 12.3 PERU'S PERFORMANCE UNDER THE 1978 STAND-BY ARRANGEMENT

Item	*Nov. 15, 1978 (S/.160 = $1)*	*June 30, 1979 (S/.200 = $1)*
Net domestic assets of the central reserve bank (billion soles)		
Ceiling	200	280
Actual	182	187
Margin under ceiling	18	93
Bank credit to public sector (billion soles)		
Ceiling	271	340
Actual	261	286
Margin under ceiling	10	54
Net international reserves of the central reserve bank (million dollars)		
Target	−747	−918
Actual	−634	−350
Margin	103	568
Contracting of foreign debt (million dollars)		
1–5 years		
Ceiling	135	135
Actual	39	81
Margin under ceiling	96	54
1–10 years (million dollars)		
Ceiling	300	300
Actual	65	213
Margin under ceiling	235	87

Source: Central Reserve Bank of Peru.

of 10 percent under the ceilings. The expected further deterioration of net international reserves changed to a significant improvement, and the contracting of new short-, medium-, and long-term foreign debt by the public sector reached only 60 percent of the amounts allowed under the agreement. All the nonquantitative performance criteria of the program were also observed.

With respect to the declared objectives of the program, the turnaround of the balance of payments was dramatic. Already during the second half of 1978 the balance of payments showed a surplus, while the current account deficit was virtually eliminated. The current deficit of the public sector was almost eliminated and the overall deficit was further reduced. The figures for the second half of 1978 were 0.2 and 5.4 percent of GDP, respectively. The inflation rate was halved from the first to the second semester of the year, to a monthly rate of 3.5 percent. The reactivation of the economy proved to be a more difficult target to reach. During 1978 as a whole, GDP fell more rapidly, although there were positive reactions in the mining and fishing sector.

The 1979 Stand-by

In August 1979, the IMF approved an SDR 285 million stand-by arrangement with supplementary financing for Peru and, again, the previous one was canceled. This new stand-by was requested in support of the same economic program initiated in 1978, and the testing dates and limits for the remainder of 1979 were identical to those approved earlier. Performance criteria for the year 1980 were to be determined before the end of 1979.

The Letter of Intent stated that "notwithstanding these encouraging developments, the disposable gross international reserves of the Central Reserve Bank of Peru remain low in relation to the level of external payments. In addition, the Central Reserve Bank has sizable short-term obligations to central banks in the Western Hemisphere that were contracted prior to July 1978." It also mentioned that the stand-by would "strengthen the gross reserve position of the Central Reserve Bank of Peru and provide support for the liberalization of the exchange and trade system at a faster pace that would otherwise be possible."

Table 12.4 shows performance under this stand-by for December 1979 and June and December 1980. Compliance with the performance criteria was very good throughout the whole program. The most striking result continued to be the improvement in the balance of payments, which moved from a deficit of $350 million in 1977 to a surplus of $1.5 billion in 1979, followed by a further surplus of $600 million in 1980. These figures reflect a strong rise in the prices of Peru's principal export commodities as well as the benefit of an important external debt renegotiation, but also the flexible exchange rate policy adopted and the fiscal effort made. During 1979 the current account of the public sector showed a surplus of 4.1 percent of GDP and an overall deficit of 1.9 percent of GDP, with increased investment expenditures.

Judging Economic Performance

It is extremely difficult to judge from actual or conjectural situations the success or failure of IMF policy advice in the Peruvian case.

TABLE 12.4 PERU'S PERFORMANCE UNDER THE 1979 STAND-BY ARRANGEMENT

Item	*Dec. 31, 1979 (S/.250 = $1)*	*June 30, 1980 (S/.288 = $1)*	*Dec. 31, 1980*
Net domestic assets of the central reserve bank (billion soles)			
Ceiling	329	209	166
Actual	70	-25	-77
Margin underceiling	259	234	243
Bank credit to public sector			
Ceiling	324	313	358
Actual	209	202	346
Margin underceiling	115	111	12
Net international reserves of the central reserve bank (million dollars)			
Target	-833	-24	293
Actual	387	937	1,315
Margin	1,220	961	1,022
Contracting of foreign debt (million dollars)			
1–5 years			
Ceiling	200	150	150
Actual	163	116	133
Margin underceiling	37	34	17
1–10 years (million dollars)			
Ceiling	450	350	350
Actual	345	251	349
Margin underceiling	105	99	1

Source: Central Reserve Bank of Peru.

In the preceding description, the economic performance has been judged according to the usual IMF's normative standard (i.e., stated in the program). Judging solely according to these criteria, one could conclude that the first stand-by was a failure and the others a success. Such judgment, however, would leave too many important questions without an answer: How realistic were the targets agreed upon for the first stand-by, if they could only be complied with during 20 days at the beginning of the agreement? How adequate were the targets for the second and third stand-by agreements, in the light of the IMF staff's initial opinion on the balance of payments outlook? Is it really a success to overshoot the balance of payments targets so significantly under such inflationary conditions? And so on.

One can easily agree with Williamson (Chapter 7, this volume) that these are not appropriate criteria, even though the IMF uses them as the operational criteria for judging economic performance. Williamson's paper presents an alternative procedure. His proposal is to measure the Fund's success as "the improvement (one hopes) in economic performance in the actual outcome (*A*), as opposed to the situation that would have occurred without Fund involvement (*C*1 or *C*2), as a proportion of the potential improvement from the state *C* (*C*1 or *C*2) to the best potentially feasible outcome (*N*)" (Chapter 7, under "On Relevant Comparisons"). The suggestion is conceptually valid, but the difficulties involved in arriving at such judgments in a particular situation are almost insurmountable. First, with the exception of the actual outcome, the other three are conjectural, nonobservable situations. Second, in the first comparison, implying no policy change, the suggested measure would not provide information on the authorities' and IMF's separate contributions to the progress (if any) implied by the actual outcome. One should not forget that the IMF advises the authorities but that the authorities are responsible for the execution of the policies envisaged in the agreement, which usually are based on the original proposals of the same authorities. It would not be fair to give credit for any progress solely to the IMF policy advice. The first comparison carries with it, as it were, a problem of identification. Third, the second comparison, assuming a policy change without IMF influence, does not have a similar problem. It represents that part of what the authorities would have failed to achieve in the absence of the IMF, that its presence helps to achieve. Further, it operates in the right direction: the relative contribution of the IMF policy advice varies directly with the conjectural shortfall of the authorities acting alone. The problem is to estimate situation *C*2.

An alternative could have been to consider what fraction of the total distance between *A* and *C*1 is represented by the distance between *A* and *C*2 and what fraction is represented by the distance between *C*2 and *C*1. One could then attribute the first portion of the improvement to the IMF's presence and the second portion to the authorities' conception and execution. This would eliminate the problem of defining *N*, but the other difficulties would remain unsolved.

No attempt is made here to judge the Peruvian experience in the light of these conjectural criteria. If we try to survey the behavior of the economic variables suggested in Williamson's paper throughout the entire period of those stand-by arrangements, we could briefly summarize as follows.

Output, as measured by GDP, fell initially in 1978 and then recovered to a rate (3.8 percent and 3.6 percent, in 1979 and 1980) close to the population growth rate (3 percent per year). The fall in 1978 affected most sectors, and the same was true of the recovery—with the exception of agriculture in 1980, which declined by 6.3 percent.

The balance of payments began to turn around in the second half of 1978 and it showed a significant surplus in 1979 and a smaller surplus in 1980. From 1977 to 1979 the current account shifted from a deficit of 7.4 percent of GDP to a surplus of 5.2 percent of GDP and registered again a small deficit in 1980 (0.9 percent of GDP).

The overall public sector deficit was reduced from an unsustainable level of 10 percent of GDP to a level of 1.9 percent of GDP in 1979 but increased again to a level of 5.7 percent of GDP in 1980.

The inflation rate initially rose from 32 percent to 74 percent from 1977 to 1978 and then remained high, although slightly declining, registering 67 and 61 percent levels in 1979 and 1980, respectively.

The rate of unemployment improved only slightly at the beginning, moving from 8.7 percent to 8.0 percent from 1977 to 1978, and then recorded 6.3 percent and 7.1 percent in the next two years (at mid-year). Finally, real wages, with all the statistical difficulties involved, appear to have fallen through 1979 (17 percent from 1977) and recuperated during 1980 (9 percent).

Generalizing even more broadly—at the risk of oversimplification—one is tempted to say that the figures appear to show an initial worsening of the economic situation, particularly in the areas of growth and inflation; an abrupt turnaround for the better, beginning in 1978 and extending through 1979, in the areas of growth, balance of payments, government finances (despite the little progress made in the area of inflation); and, finally, a weakening of government finances, while still maintaining acceptable levels of growth and balance of payments figures, in the midst of a stubborn, almost intractable inflationary process.

On the basis of Williamson's four propositions, the task may be a little less difficult.

Proposition 1. The Peruvian authorities appear to have strived for microeconomic efficiency. They removed many administrative and other controls on the making of payments for international current transactions. Corrections were also introduced in the prices of products and services subject to price controls or marketed by the public sector, but these corrective adjustments seem to have lost momentum toward the end of 1979. Nominal interest rates in the banking system were also adjusted upwardly, but they remained significantly negative in real terms.

Proposition 2. The problem of inflation was the one that clearly worsened during the period under consideration. When the stand-by started in 1977, Peru was already facing an annual 32 percent inflation, which was not a "modest level." There was a sharp acceleration of prices during 1978 and a slight deceleration afterwards. Inflation became a difficult problem to deal with because people tended to anticipate it and to adopt an inflationary mentality. In the light of the significant improvement in the terms of trade and the balance of payments that occurred during 1979 and 1980, it is difficult to understand why the authorities did not exploit these benefits to open up the economy more rapidly and thus significantly reduce the rate of inflation.

Proposition 3. There was continued departure from internal balance, and the pressure of demand persisted throughout the whole period. Output was finally increased, but unemployment and underemployment remained relatively high.

Proposition 4. The external balance, and even the surplus, was the one goal that was achieved first, as correctly anticipated by the IMF staff. External prices helped considerably, but the internal policies pursued, both fiscal and monetary, went a long way to reach this goal fairly soon. There was no need to wait for the medium term for results to begin to show.

Conclusion

One could probably conclude that the 1976–77 situation was unsustainable and that the corrections introduced at the end of 1977, and particularly during the second half of 1978, significantly improved the economic situation in Peru. But it is extremely difficult to say which part of such progress was due to the IMF policy advice and which part to the handling of the difficult decision making by the authorities concerned.

CHAPTER 13

IMF Conditionality: The Experiences of Argentina, Brazil, and Chile

Jorge Marshall S.
José Luis Mardones S.
Isabel Marshall L.

This paper reviews the experience of International Monetary Fund (IMF) stabilization programs in three Latin American countries: Argentina between 1958 and 1977, Brazil between 1964 and 1972, and Chile between 1958 and 1975. The first part describes conditions and targets contained in the agreements. The second reviews the countries' compliance with the programs, their relations with the IMF, and the origin of Fund involvement. In the third part, macroeconomic performance after the implementation of the agreements is analyzed. General remarks on conditions of stabilization programs are presented in part four. Drawings by the three countries under IMF stand-by agreements, and selected economic indicators, are given in Tables 13.1 and 13.2.

Policy Targets in Stand-by Agreements

Programs with quantitative policy targets supported by IMF stand-by credits started in Latin America during the late 1950s in agreements with Peru, Chile, Paraguay, Argentina, and Bolivia. Noncompliance with the targets implied automatic suspension of further drawings.

Note: This paper is based on research supported by a Ford Foundation grant.

TABLE 13.1 DRAWINGS UNDER STAND-BY AGREEMENTS, ARGENTINA, BRAZIL, AND CHILE
(million SDR)

Year	Amounts granted	Drawings	Reasons for not drawing full amount
		Argentina	
1958/59	75.0	42.5	No need
1959/60	100.0	100.0	—
1960/61	100.0	60.0	Not eligible for more
1961/62	100.0	—	Not eligible
1962/63	100.0	100.0	—
1967/68	125.0	—	No need
1968/69	125.0	—	No need
1976/77	260.0	159.5	No need
1977/78	159.5	—	No need
		Brazil	
1958	37.5	37.5	—
1959	—	—	—
1960	—	—	—
1961	160.0	60.0	No need for more
1962	—	—	—
1963	—	—	—
1964	—	—	—
1965	75.0	75.0	—
1966	125.0	—	No need
1967	30.0	—	No need
1968	87.5	75.0	No need for more
1969	50.0	—	No need
1970	50.0	—	No need
1971	50.0	—	No need
1972	50.0	—	No need
		Chile	
1956	35.0	—	No need
1957	35.0	31.1	No need
1958	35.0	10.7	Not eligible for more
1959	8.1	0.7	No need
1961	75.0	60.0	Not eligible for more
1963	40.0	40.0	—
1964	25.0	20.0	Not eligible for more
1965	36.0	36.0	—
1966	40.0	40.0	—
1968	46.0	43.3	Not eligible for more
1969	40.0	29.0	No need
1974	79.0	79.0	—
1975	79.0	20.0	Not eligible for more

— Not applicable.
Source: International Financial Statistics.

TABLE 13.2 SELECTED ECONOMIC INDICATORS, ARGENTINA, BRAZIL, AND CHILE

Year	Real GDP growth rate (percentage)	Manufacturing production growth rate (percentage)	Rate of inflation[a] (percentage)	Balance of payments (million dollars)	Current account (million dollars)
			Argentina		
1958	6.3	9.8	50.8	-214	259
1959	-6.6	-8.0	101.6	119	11
1960	8.0	9.3	12.1	173	-204
1961	7.1	9.7	18.8	-140	-583
1962	-1.4	-4.5	31.7	-315	-273
1963	3.3	-4.6	23.8	-175	255
1964	8.3	15.1	18.2	43	-36
1965	8.4	12.7	38.2	180	137
1966	0.2	-0.2	29.9	104	305
1967	2.3	0.7	27.3	372	174
1968	4.7	7.4	9.6	65	-19
1969	6.6	7.2	6.7	-147	-224
1970	4.8	6.0	21.7	254	-137
1971	3.7	7.1	39.1	-541	-389
1972	3.8	7.2	64.1	-111	-205
1973	6.1	6.4	43.7	621	721
1974	6.5	6.1	40.1	51	127
1975	-1.9	-2.8	334.9	-1,107	-1,285
1976	-3.3	-4.5	347.6	-35	650
1977	5.2	4.2	160.4	2,214	1,.290
1978	-4.1	-7.9	169.8	3,246	2,078
			Brazil		
1963	1.6	0.7	81.3	-89	-171
1964	3.1	5.1	86.3	87	81
1965	3.8	-4.9	36.8	295	283
1966	4.4	11.8	40.8	139	-33
1967	4.8	3.0	24.6	-148	-277
1968	9.3	15.5	24.9	93	-503
1969	9.0	10.8	20.1	732	-364
1970	9.5	11.1	19.3	552	-663
1971	11.4	11.2	19.5	530	-1,418
1972	11.0	13.8	15.7	2,439	-1,494
1973	11.9	15.0	15.5	2,228	-1,715
1974	9.6	8.2	34.5	-1,145	-7,147
1975	4.0	4.2	29.4	-1,235	-6,964
			Chile		
1955	4.7	3.8	83.8	55	7
1956	-5.6	-5.9	37.7	-10	8
1957	3.8	4.4	17.2	-49	-100
1958	3.8	3.0	32.5	45	-77
1959	1.7	11.6	33.2	27	-25

TABLE 13.2 Continued

Year	Real GDP growth rate (percentage)	Manufacturing production growth rate (percentage)	Rate of inflation[a] (percentage)	Balance of payments (million dollars)	Current account (million dollars)
			Chile (continued)		
1960	2.9	−4.1	5.5	−28	−148
1961	6.0	8.6	9.6	−109	−241
1962	5.3	11.5	27.7	−49	−182
1963	4.4	4.2	45.3	−28	−158
1964	4.9	6.0	38.5	23	−132
1965	6.5	6.4	25.8	47	−57
1966	9.9	8.6	17.0	120	−82
1967	1.3	2.8	21.9	−23	−127
1968	3.5	2.5	27.9	118	−135
1969	5.5	3.0	29.3	175	−6
1970	3.5	1.3	34.9	114	−81
1971	5.2	13.7	22.1	−300	−189
1972	−0.6	2.8	163.4	−231	−387
1973	−1.1	−6.5	508.1	−112	−295
1974	4.2	−0.9	375.9	−45	−211
1975	−14.3	−25.5	340.7	−285	−491
1976	3.8	6.9	174.3	450	148
1977	9.7	7.6	63.5	−15	−551
1978	8.3	9.3	30.3	654	−1,088
1979	8.2	6.9	38.9	1,049	−1,189
1980	6.5	5.0	31.2	776	−1,597

Note: For the "real GDP growth rate" and "production growth" of Chile (first and second columns), due to changes in the methodology of national accounts. figures up to 1960 are not directly comparable with those from 1961 onwards. Some attempt at securing compatibility has been made, though the results are clearly not completely satisfactory.
Sources: For Argentina, central bank of Argentina and IMF (several bulletins); for Brazil, Getulio Vargas Foundation, central bank of Brazil, and *International Financial Statistics;* for Chile, National Accounts, Corfo, central bank of Chile, Economic Institute of the Catholic University.
a. Cost of living in Buenos Aires.

The variables subject to ceilings were not always the same, but their aim was almost always to restrict the expansion of credit and money; to ensure a noninflationary behavior of the public sector; and to promote a multilateral system of trade, exchange, and payments free of restrictions, discrimination, and of multiple currency practices, and where the exchange rate should play a central role in achieving balance in the external accounts. With time, and probably more at the urging of creditors (governments and bankers), control of foreign indebtedness—mainly of the public sector—was also incorporated. Other fields of policy—wages and salaries, prices, tariffs of public services, and sometimes economic development—were also touched upon, but the commitments on these aspects were of a more general or vague character, and noncompliance did not imply suspension of drawing rights under the stand-by.

By the middle or late 1960s, the variables subject to ceilings were pretty well defined, and differed only with respect to specific characteristics of the country concerned or of its economic circumstances. These variables were as follows:

(1) Policies on restrictions, payments, and the exchange system: These vary according to the specific system and regulations existing in each country, but are always directed at liberalization.

(2) Certain targets on net international reserves, by quarters, were required as a test of proper exchange rate policies.

(3) Net domestic assets of the banking system (it used to be of the central bank) should not exceed certain specified values, generally for each quarter. The purpose of this control is to prevent the domestic component of the monetary base growing by more than necessary to provide a supply of money equivalent to the demand, assuming no change in central bank foreign exchange holdings. Unexpected increases or declines in foreign services should be worked out through inflation or deflation of the internal economy. As the amount of expansion allowed is dependent on a foreign exchange target and an estimate of the demand for money, net domestic credit control is properly an instrument of control of the balance of payments.

(4) Net bank credit to the public sector (and sometimes government expenditures or the deficit) was subject to quantitative limits, also stated by quarters.

(5) The same type of limitation was imposed on new foreign indebtedness, generally of the public sector. It should be stressed that the first and second variables are not under the direct control of the authorities.

In this section of the paper the main conditions involved in the stand-by agreement between the IMF and Chile, Argentina, and Brazil will be summarized, in order to follow their evolution through time and to observe the differences by country.

Credit Limits

All IMF programs for the three countries contained quantitative targets of credit growth, and after the end of the 1950s noncompliance with the targets automatically deprived the country of the right to further drawings.

In the years before the early 1960s, the variable subject to limit does not appear to have been established. In Chile (1958) two ceilings were imposed: on central bank loans and investments and on its issue of notes and coin. The same limits were repeated in 1959. In 1961 the ceiling was on gross domestic assets (including those denominated in foreign exchange). In Argentina (1959) the controlled variable was central bank domestic assets. This was repeated in the stand-by agreements for the years 1960, 1961, 1962, and 1963.

After 1963 the target variable was, in general, the net domestic credit of the central bank, defined as the difference between its monetary liabilities and its net external assets. This was the case of Chile in 1963, 1964, 1965, 1966, 1968, and 1969; Argentina in 1967, 1968, 1976, and 1977; and Brazil from 1965 to 1972.

Some specific definitions of the variable were spelled out in many instances. Ceilings would be increased by the local currency product of foreign loans for balance of payment reasons from sources other than the IMF (Argentina: 1958–59, 1959–60, 1960–61). Central bank loans and rediscounts to the banking system should not increase (Argentina, 1958–59). Ceilings should cover secondary money expansion due to reduction in minimum legal reserves (Argentina, 1961–62 and 1962–63). Ceilings should cover losses on exchange operations and would be increased by the profits (Argentina, 1959–60; Chile, 1963). Excluded were accounting gains and losses produced by revaluation of foreign assets and liabilities of the central bank and capital subscription payments to international organizations (Chile, 1963). Interest accrued but not paid was counted against the ceiling. Credits and investments that were the counterpart of foreign loans received by the central bank were excluded (Chile, 1964). Financing of price support programs of farm products should be kept within the overall financial program (Brazil, 1966).

In some of the most recent cases (Chile, 1974 and 1975), the credit control was shifted from net domestic credit of the central bank (a balance sheet variable) to net domestic banking credit (a statistical variable implying a consolidation of central, state, and commercial banks balance sheets).

Most of the agreements have provided for a quarterly expansion of the variable under control in order to take into account seasonal factors and the need of a smooth expansion during the year.

In several agreements specific provisions were made about *banks' reserve requirements*. They were increased, and a marginal requirement was imposed on bank demand deposits, in the 1958 agreement with Argentina. Compliance with the requirements was a performance clause in the 1959 program with the same country, and they were authorized to be reduced in the following year to allow for more credit to the private sector. The same provision was repeated in 1961 and 1962. In 1968 a drastic reform was contemplated in the existing complex system of bank reserve requirements, with a view to reducing basic and marginal requirements, to promote bank regionalization and certain types of credit.

Maintenance of bank reserve requirements was a provision of the 1965 stand-by with Brazil, and they had to be increased in 1966 if strong net foreign purchases continued.[1] In 1967 they were to be maintained, and any reduction would have to be counted against the allowed margin of credit expansion. At the end of 1967 reserve requirements were raised, and in March 1968 there were changes in basic and marginal requirements, with an increase on the average. During the rest of 1968, requirements were going to be gradually reduced to reach the level of December 1967 by the end of the year. In the 1969 stand-by, reductions in reserve requirements were to be counted against the credit ceiling.

In Chile, changes in the reserve requirements of the banks could not be authorized without the consent of the managing director of the Fund (1963). This was also included in the 1964 agreement, together with a provision that any reduction should be counted against the credit ceiling. The agreements for the years 1965, 1966, 1968, and 1969 provided that bank and private sector deposits were to be subtracted from the variable "net domestic credit of the central bank" that was subject to limit. In this manner, any changes in reserve requirements would be absorbed by the permitted margin of central bank credit expansion.

Only rarely were interest rates mentioned in the agreements: Chile (1975) and Peru (1978, 1979).

The government or the public sector was subject, in several stand-by agreements, to limitations on its borrowing from the central bank or from the banking system. In some cases, bank financing was entirely barred; in other cases, it was authorized in specified quantities; and in others, seasonal financing was allowed. Stand-by credits with Chile (1974 and 1975) established quarterly limits on the net credit of the banking system to the public sector.

In the experiences analyzed, compliance with credit ceilings was not clearly linked with decreases in inflation. In the Brazilian case, credit ceilings were generally surpassed; notwithstanding, inflation

[1] This was an attempt to control a monetary aggregate as compared to a pure credit control.

systematically decreased between 1964 and 1973, although the level reached continued to be higher than the desired one. In Chile credit ceilings were generally complied with, but this was not an obstacle to rising inflation, as in 1957–59, 1963–64, and then again in 1967–70.

In the Argentine experience noncompliance with the credit limits was associated with increased inflation (1961, late months); compliance with very generous credit ceilings in 1967 and 1968 was simultaneous with reduced inflation; and compliance in 1976–77 was associated with an initial decrease in inflation, although the rate later ran at a very high level. Obviously, other elements, such as expectations in 1967–68, played an important role.

If the credit variable under control is defined as notes issued by the central bank minus net foreign reserves, unexpected increase in foreign exchange revenues will create more margin for credit expansion. This will last longer the greater the lag in expenditures. Although it would be difficult to defend policies aimed at fully compensating external shocks, more restrictive policies during the upswing can prevent inflation from getting out of hand in the boom and facilitate adjustment during the downswing, allowing for some compensation (expansion of domestic credit) when the balance of payments gets into deficit.

Setting up credit ceilings assumes a forecast of the demand for money. In fact (as in Chile, 1960, 1965, 1966, and 1971 and Argentina, 1967 and 1976), demand for money is subject to large changes in the short run (one, two, and perhaps three years) that may not be obvious at the time or easy to explain.

The best case for a credit ceiling is in a small open economy with a fixed exchange rate, where there is no central bank control of the nominal money supply. This is not the case in many developing countries. Without a well-integrated capital market, including short-term funds, credit ceilings may produce drastic and very troublesome fluctuations in domestic interest rates (Chile, 1981).

If the monetary authorities have control over monetary aggregates, implicit to establishing the IMF type of bank credit ceilings is the assumption that expenditures—and consequently, aggregate demand and financial stability—depend on the stock or the rate of change of that stock called money. As the relevant components of that stock are not well defined and may change over time, inclusions and exclusions of items show attempts made to identify the variable properly. It is difficult to be sure that this has been achieved.

Fiscal Performance

Since early times, IMF stabilization programs have included provisions on revenues, expenditures, and the financing of the government and the public sector in general. This was a recognition of the paramount importance of public finances for reducing inflation and attaining equilibrium in the balance of payments. Policy conditions were directed to different targets: sometimes to reinforce taxation, reduce expenditures or both; at other times to the size of the global deficit, or to the amount of savings generated by the government or the public sector. In many stand-by agreements, limits were established to bank financing of the government and the public sector, or bank financing was barred altogether. Also price policy and expenditures of public agencies and enterprises were included in the commitments.

In Chile (1957) it was stated that it was the firm purpose of the government not to have recourse to central bank financing. In 1958 ceilings were imposed on fiscal expenditure authorizations in domestic and foreign currency as a performance criterion. In 1959 it was said that central bank credit to the government would not exceed the amount outstanding in 1958, except when the bank was channeling loans granted abroad. The same performance criterion was repeated in 1961, except for an advance of $25 million during the first part of the year, to be repaid during the second half.

In Argentina (1959) a very drastic reduction of the public deficit was required, and what remained should be financed with foreign loans. Several measures to increase revenues and reduce expenditures (including large dismissals of employees and a reduction in public works) were contemplated. The following year, the central bank was barred from granting loans to the government. The deficit was to be covered with foreign loans and direct foreign investments for projects included in the budget and the issue of treasury bills to be placed in nonbanking sectors. Efforts were going to be made to improve revenues and reduce expenditures of the main public enterprises with large deficits (railroads, oil, urban transportation, and water and electricity supply). Similar commitments were made under the 1961 stand-by. In 1962 no central bank credit was to be given to the government, although this agreement was never put into effect. A new stand-by for 1962–63 contemplated several measures to increase revenue and reduce expenditure. About 60 percent of the credit expansion authorized for that year could be lent to the government.

In Brazil (1965) there was a commitment to cut the treasury's cash deficit in half. To this end, reductions of the deficits of the railroads and the merchant marine and a limitation to wage readjustment in the public sector were programmed. In 1966 several measures were proposed on the revenue and expenditure sides of the budget. The deficit was programmed at nearly half of the previous year (8 percent of expenditures), and deficit targets were set up for each quarter. Fifty percent of the financing of price support programs should be absorbed within the programmed deficit, which was to be covered through the issuance of treasury bonds (indexed by price changes) and limited central bank financing (set out by quarters). From 1967 to 1972, the agreements established programmed deficits by quarters that reduced the maximum permitted deficit in relation to expenditures from 7 percent in 1967 to 11 percent in 1968, to 3.4 percent in 1971, and 2.4 percent in 1972. The maximum amount of central bank financing was stipulated.

Agreements with Chile for the years 1963, 1964, 1965, 1966, 1968, and 1969 required current account surpluses (difference between total revenues and current expenditures) for the fiscal budget, and after 1964 for the rest of the public sector as well. Targets were stated by quarters. Any deficiency should be compensated by long-term external loans or a reduction of investment. Ceilings on government borrowing from the central bank were set up in 1966 and 1969.

One of the main objectives of the financial program with Argentina for 1967 was to reduce the fiscal deficit, which in 1966 had reached 33 percent of expenditures. Fiscal revenues were reinforced, mainly through foreign trade taxes, which partly offset the impact of devaluation. It was the government's purpose to improve efficiency in public enterprises, and several of their tariffs were adjusted. Salary increases were limited to 15 percent for public employees, and a freeze was established until the end of 1968. There was also to be a reduction of some 80,000 public employees. The 1967 agreement provided for a limit to the total treasury deficit to an amount about half the actual previous years' deficit.

The 1974 stand-by with Chile established, as a performance criterion, a limit on net credit of the banking system to the public sector (including all state enterprises and the large mining companies). In the 1975 stand-by, a limit on total central government expenditures, excluding capital expenditures financed with foreign loans, was added.

In Argentina, under the stand-by of 1976, it was expected that the fiscal deficit would be reduced by more than 60 percent in the second half by eliminating excess personnel and by new taxes and increases in public sector tariffs. The following year the needs to improve public sector efficiency and to reduce the deficit by half in real terms were recognized.

Measures to limit the increase in public expenditures, the size of the deficit, and bank financing of the deficit are clearly a part of any financial stabilization program. But there are surely also other objectives, concerning the structure and level of public revenues and expenditures, that are as important as financial stability, and they should be considered in any program. Targets on current public sector surpluses are very commendable inasmuch as they attempt to use foreign help, in addition to domestic public savings, to bolster investment, but they are clearly outside the competence of the IMF.

Balance of Payments Tests

Maintenance of realistic rates of exchange has been a basic objective of all stand-by agreements. In cases where financial stability was not in sight, fluctuating rates (although never practiced as clean floating) were allowed, or a system of periodic adjustment of the rate was encouraged. Dual markets were tolerated as temporary devices on the grounds that the second market was useful for some invisible trade and capital transactions that were too difficult to control. Nevertheless, it was always provided that not a very wide spread appear between the two rates and that the monetary authority did not intervene in the financial market as a net seller of foreign exchange. On occasion, pegged rates were accepted (as in Chile, 1959–61 and after 1979; in Brazil from 1968 onwards; and in Argentina from 1967 to 1970).

In Argentina in 1959 a single fluctuating rate replaced the dual market previously in existence. Market forces would determine the rate until economic conditions warranted the establishment of a new fixed rate of exchange. It was in fact stabilized by mid-1959 and defended by the central bank until March 1962. The same system was repeated in 1960, 1961, 1962, and 1963, with no balance of payments tests.

Early agreements with Chile (1956, 1957, and 1958) were based on a dual exchange market system with no central bank action allowed to counteract basic market tendencies. In January 1959 both markets were unified, and although the government stated its purpose of letting the rate move according to market forces, in fact it was pegged for more than three years. In 1963 the dual market system was reestablished, and the government committed itself to relying mainly on the exchange rate for any balance of payments adjustment that was necessary. The same system was maintained for several years.

Until 1964, exchange rate determination, or central bank intervention in the market, was a matter of continuous controversy between the IMF and some of the countries concerned. Starting in 1965, the Fund required, as a condition for drawing under any stand-by, compliance with certain targets on foreign exchange reserves as an indicator that the "right exchange rate policies" were being pursued. Targets were generally drawn by quarters.

In Brazil (1965) the test was that net external assets of the monetary authority should not fall below their level on October 31, 1964. Maintenance of the reserves, with an increase if the sales of exchange to the monetary authorities exceeded a certain quantity, was the target test in 1966. Also for that year, the stand-by agreement specified that the difference between the official exchange rate and the nonofficial rate could not exceed 2.5 percent. The following year the test provided for a surplus in the balance of payments, stated as quarterly increases in net international reserves, and similar targets were repeated from 1968 through 1972.

In Argentina (1967 and 1968) net official foreign exchange reserves were required to increase by certain specified amounts in both years.

Maintenance of the net foreign exchange position of the country was an objective in the 1965 stand-by with Chile. It was defined as the difference between the net foreign exchange position of the banking system and the amount of import arrears (without letters of credit) exceeding the 120-day compulsory waiting period for import payments in existence in Chile at that time. Exceptions were contemplated to meet seasonal fluctuations and reductions in the compulsory waiting period. Similar tests were set up in 1966, 1968, and 1969. After October 1973 a big devaluation of the exchange rate took place and the authorities readopted the policy (abandoned in 1970) of adjusting the rate by small amounts at frequent intervals. Targets for the net international reserve position of the banking system were established under the 1974 and 1975 stand-by agreements.

In Argentina (1976) a limit was established to the decline in foreign assets of the monetary authorities. Minimum increases were stipulated in 1977.

Observation of the net foreign reserve targets would be an easy matter if the central bank bought or sold foreign exchange in the market in the amounts necessary to meet the quarterly targets. The exchange rate would then be determined by market forces. But no central bank has been prepared to pursue that policy, and it does not seem that the IMF expected it. Rate fluctuations can easily overshoot what could be considered reasonable levels, especially in countries beset with financial instability and speculation of a destabilizing nature. This will have serious consequences for the allocation of resources and the reduction of price inflation, which was also an objective of the programs.

Management of the rate to attain the targets leaves out of consideration the reactions of the markets to relative price changes and the considerable and unknown lag that makes it impossible to predict the timing of any rate change on the current account. This is aggravated by the unpredictable response of capital movements to exchange rate adjustments and the existence of unforeseen shocks that may affect the supply or demand of foreign exchange.

Limits on Foreign Debt

Commitments on foreign borrowings up to about 1965 were generally relegated to medium-term supplier's credits (defined as those with initial maturities of more than 180 days and less than 8 years), and in most cases were not binding. Those credits expanded greatly during the 1950s as the industrial countries desired to promote their exports. The IMF, and even more the World Bank, were concerned, because that expansion could reduce the capacity of developing countries to assume credit more suitable to their development needs, applied to well-studied projects and with terms tailored to their ability to pay. After the middle of the 1960s, control of foreign indebtedness seems to have been more directed to the protection of creditors, who were induced to several debt renegotiations (13 during the 1960s, and 11 in the period 1973–78). Scope of the controlled credits was widened, and commitments were made a performance criterion. Control was generally exercised on new debt authorizations. Credits with maturities of less than 180 days (trade finance) and over 12–15 years (development concessional credits) were excluded. Credits to the private sector without public guarantees and to banks have very seldom been included, although the latter have been controlled through balance of payments tests.

Early stand-by agreements (Chile, 1956 and 1957) had no commitments on foreign indebtedness. In 1958 medium-term supplier's credits (defined as the ones with maturities of more than 180 days and less than 8 years) were to be limited, and the country had to avoid payment arrears. In 1959 the government stated its purpose of prohibiting all its agencies and other public entities incurring medium-term foreign debts and credits to the private sector with the same maturities were not to be guaranteed by the central or the state bank. Letters of Intent for the year 1961 said that "the authorities were aware that external financing was reaching a high proportion of total investment and also that there was a need to increase the share of long term in the total debt." The 1963, 1964, and 1965 agreements had no provisions about foreign debts.

In Argentina, medium-term supplier's credits contemplating amortization in the years 1959 to 1962 (with the exception of some special cases) were forbidden in the stand by for 1959. The same policy was stated in 1959–60, with special reference to the government and its agencies and enterprises; and in 1960 it was added that the government was not going to guarantee supplier's credits in favor of the private sector. A very restrictive use was to be made by the authorities of medium-term supplier's credits in 1962, and they would not, in general, guarantee credits to the private sector. In the second 1962 stand-by, the amounts of those outstanding credits were stabilized and commercial banks were restricted in guaranteeing obligations in foreign exchange. Furthermore, official banks should maintain the level of foreign borrowing and guarantees to foreign borrowing and public sector imports financed with credit had to be previously approved by the central bank and the Ministry of Economy.

An important aspect of the 1965 stand by with Brazil was regularization of the service on foreign debts that were in default. This was accomplished by April 1965, partly through repayment and partly through debt rescheduling. In the 1966 stand-by it was provided that no authorization was going to be given to Banco do Brasil or other commercial banks to guarantee short or medium foreign credits other than external trade financing and supplier's medium-term credits to the private and the public sector would be limited to the amount of gross amortization of existing credits of those maturities. Similar limits were included in 1967 and 1968, but in the latter year, only for the public sector. In 1968 it was also agreed that surveillance would be exercised over commercial banks and other financial institutions that had been authorized to contract short-term foreign credits in order to relend at home. Domestic debtors should assume exchange risks, and they should be limited as soon as they started to grow too fast. Similar commitments were enforced in 1968 and 1969. The 1970 agreement stated that a commission would be formed to study foreign debt controls. In 1971 measures were taken to increase the maturing period of credits, and in 1972 the maximum of foreign credits with maturity under a year was limited to the outstanding amount existing on November 30, 1971.

Commitments similar to those for Brazil in 1967 were incorporated in the stand-bys with Chile in 1966 and 1968 (with the limitation covering the private sector as well in 1968). The Argentine stand-by for 1967 provided for a freezing of medium-term supplier's credits to the public sector, while in 1968 a net expansion was allowed.

The stand-by with Chile in 1969 established a limit on the authorization of external debt of the public sector, and the private sector with public guarantee and with initial maturities of more than 1 year and less than 15 years, according to a schedule stating amounts by periods or initial maturity of loans. Central bank borrowings were excluded. The 1974 and 1975 stand by agreements repeated the same limits on external debt as those from 1969 to 1970, though with schedules differing in amounts and periods.

External debt of the public sector and the private sector with public guarantee was defined as the sum of: (1) all external obligations of the public sector (including the banking system) other than those arising from any renegotiation of the debt or those arising from the nationalization of foreign firms; and (2) all external obligations of the private sector that carry the guarantee of the government or any other public agency (including central and state banks).

Furthermore, the Chilean authorities were committed that the banking system's foreign liabilities with maturities of less than one year should not increase by more than $45 million over the level of November 1973 during 1974.

In Argentina (1976 and 1977) the purpose was stated to be moderation of the rate of increase of external debt and improvement of its profile. The central bank was seeking credits for $900 million, but strict control was to be exercised on other borrowing or guarantees of the public sector.

Control of foreign borrowing shifts responsibility in determining how much external credit a country can get from the creditors to the IMF. It implies a judgment over the optimum size of the current account deficit, about which very little can be said objectively. If control is extended to private sector borrowing, it inconsistently forces the authorities to a quantitative control of one item of the balance of payments, while they are denied the possibility of exercising the same type of control over other items (current imports or other current payments abroad).

Exchange Systems

All stand-by agreements pushed countries in the direction of eliminating exchange restrictions on current payments, quotas, licensing, multiple exchange rates, advance import deposits, bilateral payments agreements, arrears of import payments, etc. In some cases, measures were undertaken drastically: Chile (1956); Bolivia, Paraguay, and

Argentina (1959); and Brazil (1965, only with respect to paying its arrears). But in most cases gradual advances were allowed, and the conditions were of not intensifying existing restrictions or imposing new ones for balance of payments reasons.

Elimination of import prohibitions—or agreement not to increase the number of items prohibited—was also a part of some programs. There was also an encouragement to reduce the level of customs tariffs.

The Chilean request for a stand-by in 1956 was based on the introduction of a new exchange system: all quantitative restrictions and import licenses were eliminated. All commodities included in a permitted list could be imported by any person in any quantities. Different import and export rates were eliminated. Trade, official transactions, and certain specified private transactions were conducted through a banking market, with the exchange rate being determined by supply and demand. Other authorized invisible and capital transactions were made through a broker's market, with the exchange rate also subjected to supply and demand. Import advance deposits could be established in percentages from 1 percent to 400 percent of the value of imports of specified commodities. Export proceeds had to be surrendered within specified periods.

Central bank intervention was limited to the correction of temporary excessive variations in the rate, without countering fundamental trends. This system was maintained practically until the end of 1961, except that in 1959 the two markets were unified and the exchange rate pegged. Import surcharges started to replace import deposits, and there was an effort to eliminate existing bilateral payments agreements.

Exchange reform in 1959 unified the two existing exchange markets in Argentina, and licensing and quantitative restrictions were eliminated. Market forces were to determine the exchange rate until economic conditions allowed the establishment of a fixed rate. Export controls were also eliminated, except for the compulsory surrender of foreign exchange within six months. Import deposits were maintained, but their volume should be no more than 5 percent of the stock of money. Exchange insurance by the central bank was discontinued. The government expressed its intention of eliminating bilateral payments agreements, which channeled about 20 percent of Argentinian trade. Export and import taxes at different rates were imposed to reduce the impact of devaluation on profits, to discriminate according to essentiality of imports, and to reinforce fiscal revenues. The tax structure on external trade was modified on various occasions in 1959. From 1960 to 1963, stand-by agreements with

Argentina provided for maintenance of the same system, with changes mainly in the direction of gradual elimination of advanced import deposits and bilateral payments agreements and a reduction in import taxes.

Commitments were made in the stand-by agreements with Brazil (1965 to 1972) to simplify and liberalize the exchange system and to eliminate multiple currency practices and restrictions on current international payments and transfers. Bilateral payments and other swap arrangements were to be discontinued, and also restrictions that could prevent the establishment of an internationally competitive exchange rate. In 1967 it was provided that if an export tax introduced to offset internal repercussions of sudden external fluctuations should become a multiple rate practice, it would be replaced by some tax not affecting the exchange system.

The 1970 agreement mentioned the need to favor production in those sectors with comparative advantage, like agriculture, by decreasing the protection given to intermediate industrial goods used by this sector. The 1971 program advanced this idea by proposing a tariff reform that would decrease intermediate good costs of agriculture and industry. In view of some deterioration in the current account in 1971, the following year's program established that the tariff reduction should continue, although closely watching its effects on the balance of payments.

The two exchange markets were reestablished in Chile in 1962, and after October both rates fluctuated according to market forces (1963 stand-by). A compulsory waiting period for import payments, established in January 1962 as an emergency measure, should not be increased and was to be eliminated as soon as conditions warranted. Restrictions on imports were allowed only for social and political reasons, and not for balance of payments support. Advance import deposits were to be gradually eliminated. None of the existing rates would be raised, nor could transactions from lower rate categories be shifted to higher rates. Additional import surcharges imposed in October 1962 should be eliminated after March 31, 1963. No net sales of foreign exchange by the central bank in the broker's market were authorized. All these commitments were repeated with only minor changes in the agreements for 1965, 1966, 1968, and 1969.

In Argentina (1967) the peso was devalued by 40 percent, but export taxes at different rates were established for traditional exports, thus reducing the effect of devaluation on export earnings. Export subsidies for nontraditional exports were eliminated. Import taxes were reduced within the framework of a tariff reform, which had the effect of increasing import costs in different degrees, according to the type of commodity. The same system was maintained in 1968: import duties were to be kept constant, although afterwards a tax of 20 percent on certain capital goods was imposed. Export taxes were reduced during the second half of the year.

An adjustment of the exchange rate that took place in October 1973 in Chile was accompanied by a major simplification of the exchange system. Two markets (as in most of the time prior to 1970) replaced a complex system of multiple rates, and the government was planning to move gradually to a more liberal system of trade and exchange. All commitments in previous agreements with the Fund on waiting periods and payments arrears, multiple rates, advance deposits, prompt processing of import applications, and maintenance of the items in the permitted import list were repeated in 1974. During the year prior to March 1975, several important steps were taken to liberalize the exchange and trade system, e.g., the 10,000 percent deposit requirement for certain goods was eliminated.

The Argentine authorities announced in 1976 their intention to eliminate the existing multiple exchange rates and various restrictions on trade and payments. These included import financing requirements and an obligation to purchase Foreign Trade Investment Bonds in the amount of the financed part of imports. Remaining restrictions were to be eliminated before the end of 1977.

Measures undertaken with respect to the exchange system were almost always positive. They tended to eliminate or reduce enormous distortions created by the previous systems. In some cases, however, one has the impression that the Fund attempted to force formal compliance with the agreement, depriving the country of policy instruments that could have been useful in an emergency with no great damage to the international community.

Salaries and Prices

Commitments on salaries—not a performance criterion—were aimed at reducing nominal wage readjustment in order to reduce inflation. Prices, in general, were freed; if controls were maintained, they were to be administered in such a way as to approximate market conditions. Public agencies and enterprises were urged to fix tariffs and prices of their services in order to cover costs and leave a surplus to meet investment needs.

Before requesting the 1956 stand-by credit, wage and salary adjustments in Chile were set by law to half the cost-of-living increase between December 1954 and January 1956. Adjustment of controlled prices during 1956 could not exceed 40 percent, unless they were for imported goods or used imported inputs. The program also made reference to creation of conditions propitious to more competitive markets, eliminating monopolistic situations.

In 1957 private sector employees were given a salary readjustment equivalent to 80 percent of the cost-of-living increase in 1956. Public sector workers were granted a 25 percent increase. Goods of general consumption could not have their prices increased by more than 25 percent in 1957. No commitments were made in 1958 on wages and prices, and salary readjustments exceeded the cost-of-living increase in 1957. A complex formula was used in 1959 for salary increases, which on average were higher than the rise of the cost of living in 1958. In requesting the 1959 stand-by agreement, the government declared that it intended to attain, by the end of 1959, a maximum of price stability in order to eliminate general legislation on wage and salary readjustment at the beginning of 1960. No commitments were made on salaries or on price in the 1961 agreement.

The 1959 IMF program with Argentina contemplated abolition of price control and subsidies, elimination of the overvalued exchange rate, and a limitation of wage increases. Several public service prices—like those of urban transportation, railroads, oil, and electricity—had to be increased in order to reduce the deficits of the enterprises. Price controls were going to be maintained for about 10 basic goods in order to prevent speculation on them during the first period of the exchange reform. Wage negotiations in the public sector would imply increases between 20–30 percent, and for the private sector there would be no automatic readjustments, except for banking employees. Wage agreements were extended to a two-year period. In the 1960 stand-by, price controls over a small list of essential goods had diminished during the year; only rents continued to be controlled. Sugar imports were prohibited to protect internal production, except when domestic prices surpassed a certain amount fixed by the government. Salary increases in the public sector were not going to be granted as long as the fiscal deficit persisted.

In railroads, wage negotiations were going to imply some increases, despite the huge deficit. As far as the private sector was concerned, there was not going to be bank financing for payment of wage increases. Automatic adjustments had been eliminated for most sectors in 1959. Wage increases in 1961 were to be maintained in step with increases in productivity. Previous settlements in the electric power sector (15 percent increases, plus a retroactive 10 percent and a reduction in working hours) had been exceptional and were granted, as it was then said, in view of an important increase in productivity.

No provisions on wages or prices were in the 1962 and 1963 agreements.

In Brazil (1965) public sector salary adjustment was considerably below the cost-of-living increase since the last readjustment. There was a tendency toward price liberalization, but direct and indirect government controls were maintained.

In June 1965 the government enacted guidelines to settle wage controversies in the private sector that were similar to the wage adjustment formula being applied in the public sector. Salary adjustment should aim to recover the average purchasing power of wages during the last 24 months, with two small adjustments to take into account increases in productivity and expected price rises. The guidelines would be kept in force during 1966. Also, the guidelines for price adjustments in 1965 remained in force in 1966. In the 1967 and 1968 agreements, wage controls implemented in previous years were maintained. A realistic price policy, mainly for public services, would be kept.

In 1969 the wage increase formula was revised, due to the decline in real wages in previous years. Additional compensation was provided when the inflation rate was higher than had been anticipated when the initial adjustment was made. This revised formula was maintained in the stand-by agreements through 1972.

From 1963 to 1969, all the agreements with Chile had policy commitments on salaries and prices—sometimes called incomes policies—and on the tariffs of public services. References were made to "reasonable readjustments," maintenance of a law requiring adjustments according to the cost-of-living increases in the previous year, prevention of other social groups increasing their share in the national income and the possibility of financing public salaries and their impact on the private sector settlements. In all of the agreements, reference was made to a final goal of relating wage adjustments to gains in productivity. Any price controls should avoid distortions, and public service tariffs should cover more adequately their costs and capital requirements.

In order to keep cost pressures under control in Argentina in 1967, wages and salaries were to be adjusted by law and not by collective bargaining. At the same time, certain public tariffs and the exchange rate were going to be increased, and they would be kept frozen until the end of 1968.

In the industrial sector, agreement was sought to limit price increases. Prices should be maintained, except for increases in imported inputs. Public sector purchases should be limited to enterprises participating in the agreement, and the same limitation was established for a bank line of credit for personal consumption. For basic foodstuffs (the main export products in Argentina), export tax management was considered an appropriate instrument to control prices.

Although salaries were not readjusted in 1968, there was a reduction in employees' social security contributions implying an increase of 7 percent in disposable earnings, and some family allowances were improved.

The program of controlling inflation depends critically on the implementation of a careful wages policy, it was said in the 1974 agreement with Chile. It was the objective of the government to provide a substantial improvement in real wages and salaries over the level at the end of 1973. Public sector wage increases in January 1974 were of 60 percent, and additional adjustments in 1974 were going to take place only to the extent that they were consistent with the public sector credits committed in the stand-by. Private sector adjustments would follow the same guidelines. Prices had been liberalized on a massive scale, relying on control over aggregate demand through monetary and fiscal policies to reduce the rate of price increase over the coming year. A more effective antitrust law was being adopted. Public enterprise prices had been, or were being, increased and were going to be kept at economic levels in the future.

In 1975 wages and salaries were adjusted at three-month intervals in line with past consumer price increases. Notwithstanding this indexation—essential for social reasons—it was considered possible to decelerate inflation through strict implementation of the fiscal and credit policies outlined in the Letter of Intent. To deal with the problem of unemployment, insurance and other forms of assistance were going to be provided.

In Argentina (1976) the stand-by agreement stated that the government would be cautious in granting new wage adjustments to the public or private sectors. During the year, four wage increases were decreed, but of amounts lower than the huge existing inflation. In 1977 wage policy was based on the belief that a permanent improvement of real salaries would depend on a lower rate of inflation and productivity increases. Price controls were eliminated in 1976, but surveillance would be exercised over monopolistic powers. A policy of control over industrial prices was implemented during four months starting in March 1977, with the object of cooling off inflationary expectations. In the 1977 agreement the policy was oriented toward increasing external competition via lowering import tariffs.

Efficiency in resource allocation is the main argument for liberalizing prices that appear in stand-by agreements. In some experiences, as in the stabilization program in Argentina in 1967 and 1968, it was possible to freeze prices by voluntary, although government stimulated, arrangements. But in cases of gross distortions in the structure of relative prices, corrective inflation may be needed, as in Argentina in 1976 or in Chile after 1973.

Control of nominal wages was often justified by the authorities with the argument that real wages are out of line. In addition, cost pressures due to wage increases are a source of inflation. Although the approach of stabilization programs designed or backed by the Fund is one of excess demand, and hence measures to control it are emphasized, it has been argued that wage control policies included in stand-by agreements demonstrate that cost pressures are not neglected. Nevertheless, adjustments of the exchange rate, the interest rate, or public service tariffs, also cost-pushing factors, are generally viewed from an external equilibrium or budget balance perspective, instead of considering their impact on inflation.

If a trade-off exists between salaries and employment levels, the goal of maintaining employment during economic recessions, as in Argentina in several periods, is easier if real wages are sharply reduced. The wage control may imply income redistribution toward sectors of the population with higher propensities to save; the reallocation of income and spending from consumption to savings and investment may be seen as beneficial from the point of view of capital accumulation and development.

Another implicit argument in favor of wage control is that it may break the distributive conflict between salaries and profits, a mechanism of the propagation of inflation. The costs, in this case, are put on the shoulders of wage earners.

Depending on the structure of the economy, the effects of wage control may be quite different. In the case of Argentina, which in the past has based its development policy on creating a highly protected manufacturing industry, the drop in real wages will reduce the demand for industrial goods, thus inducing a recession. In other cases, the resulting income distribution may dynamize certain industrial sectors through the increase in the demand for certain goods by medium- and high-income groups, as was the case in Brazil. In a small, open economy, the drop in real wages will improve the competitive position of the country, and the reduced domestic demand will only affect the nontradable activities and the level of imports. Low real wages improve the prospects of an export-oriented strategy.

Fulfillment of Stand-by Commitments

It is difficult to make a general statement on the degree of fulfillment of the commitments made in stand-by agreements undertaken by Argentina, Brazil, and Chile.

To start with, there are marked differences in the experiences of the three countries. But also, within each country there were variations over time in the degree to which commitments were achieved. Finally, a stand-by agreement is not generally fulfilled in all or none of its goals: some will be attained while others are not.

In the following pages a brief survey of the degrees of compliance in the various stand-by agreements covered by the analysis is presented. At the same time, the reasons for calling on the Fund and the tensions and difficulties between the institution and the countries will be pointed out, where known.

Argentina

The expansive policies taken at the beginning of the Frondizzi government in 1958, including wage increases and a sharp rise in public investment, gave rise to an acceleration of inflation and a balance of payments crisis, which led the administration to seek assistance from the IMF. The stabilization program aimed at putting a quick end to inflation and external imbalances as necessary conditions for a later expansion of the country's production capacity with recourse to foreign resources.

An extensive exchange reform duly took place in December 1958. Foreign trade was freed from quantitative controls and bilateral agreements were gradually reduced and eventually disappeared. The commitment that the central bank would only intervene in the exchange market to smooth seasonal variations was not strictly complied with: the limit to central bank intervention during 1959 was not complied with, and in 1961 and the first quarter of 1962 the central bank sustained the exchange rate acting as heavy seller of dollars.

Although a serious effort was made to limit the fiscal deficit and credit expansion, the deficits weighed heavily on fiscal performance, and when limits were fulfilled, payment arrears increased. Drawings were suspended in 1961 due to an excessive increase in central bank domestic assets, a consequence of a liberal rediscount policy. Compliance was good with respect to wage policies and foreign debt limits, although in a lesser degree during 1961. Borrowing from external private sources, which was desired by the government to boost investment and an important reason to ask for stand by agreements, was sizable during that period. Relations with the Fund were good, although the credit ceiling was not complied with during 1961 and drawing rights were suspended.

None of the limits agreed to in the stand-by entered into in December 1961 was complied with, and a new agreement was signed in mid-1962 with Guido's military administration; it was later extended until October 1963. Under this stand by, the full amount ($100 million) was drawn. The large current account deficit in 1961 led to a number of measures to restrict imports. Massive salary adjustments given in December 1961, increased debt service, lower import levels, and severely reduced tax collection (due to political instability), were the main elements behind the huge deficits recorded in 1962 and 1963.

Under the Illia government, from 1963 to 1966, understandings with the IMF were rather difficult, and no agreement was signed. The abrogation of oil contracts at the beginning of the administration was regarded as demonstrating a hostile attitude toward the international financial community, and this fact weighed heavily during this period.

After economic stagnation in 1966 (the end of the Illia government and first months of the Ongania military administration), partly due to bad winter harvests, a stabilization program aimed at reducing inflation was carried out in 1967, obtaining a satisfactory balance of payments and reducing fiscal deficit and wage pressures on costs. The Argentinian government was able to obtain IMF support for a program with ample expansion of credit to the private sector, on the grounds that price stability would quickly increase money demand. A new stand-by was entered in 1968, of which approximately one-third was drawn. The active limits in both years were those on the fiscal deficit. In the first year the deficit was 99 percent of the ceiling, and in 1968 it surpassed the ceiling by 48 percent. All other targets were largely complied with, except for the balance of payments test in 1968, which fell 25 percent short of the agreed figure. Relations with the Fund were good, although the IMF pointed out that monetary expansion during 1968 was excessive, due to a sharp reduction in legal bank reserves, and that the abundant placement of bonds to finance the deficit was a weak aspect of the program. No drawings were made under these arrangements.

During 1972 (Lanusse government) a $284 million credit was given under the compensatory financing facility and in connection with quota increases. In the last months of 1975 (Mrs. Peron's government) negotiations were carried out in order to utilize again the compensatory facility and the first credit tranche. The IMF was not enthusiastic about the economic plan because it avoided limiting wage increases and was soft in relation to the public sector deficit. The US State Department aided to finally obtain IMF support, and $311 million were drawn.

Further compensatory financing was negotiated in 1976. A stand-by agreement was also signed, aimed at avoiding external debt default and a substantial reduction of the very high inflation rate. Liberalization of the economy and correction of distortions in relative prices to favor the agricultural sector were also objectives of the program. A second agreement was signed in 1977. The general trend was one of gradual liberalization of the exchange and payments system. Other limits were generally respected. The fiscal deficit was slightly higher than authorized in the second half of 1976. No limits were suggested by the government for the rest of the first stand-by period, and in consequence no further use of the credit was made, although targets were later agreed upon for May and June 1977. The first credit was partially used, and the second one was not used at all.

Fund resident representatives were stationed in Buenos Aires from December 1958 to May 1960 and during the late 1960s. Argentina's total drawings up to 1981 were SDR 1,295 million and repurchases SDR 1,142 million.

Brazil

Brazil entered two stand-by agreements prior to 1964, in 1958 and in 1961. In both cases the country was facing strong external deficits and lack of external credibility with private and official agencies. To gain balance of payments relief and win the confidence of the international financial community, Brazil sought IMF aid. The IMF conditioned its assistance on introduction of a stabilization program. In the first case, although Brazil immediately drew the whole credit, negotiations with the Fund were interrupted and the program abandoned in mid-1959 due to internal pressures against the measures undertaken, coming from industrial entrepreneurs and other social forces. Results were better in 1961. The country received external credits that together with a better situation in other accounts of the balance of payments, led to an overall surplus, the only one between 1957 and 1963.

With the change of government in 1962, a better external situation, and no clear economic program for that year, Brazil did not request a new stand-by credit agreement.

In March 1964 there was a military coup, and toward the end of the year a third stand-by credit was signed with the IMF. The country was in a situation of heavy payment arrears, continuous external deficit, high indebtedness, and strong inflation. It again needed external credits and international credibility. Thus the agreement with the IMF was not only important as a source of actual financing, but also as a guarantee for other possible lenders. Of the eight stand-by credits from 1965 to 1972, Brazil actually drew on only two. In 1965 it drew the whole credit, although successive renegotiations with the Fund had to take place during the year to keep the credit in operation, since many of the targets were exceeded. The IMF, however, seems to have shown a good disposition in understanding the problems the government was facing. In 1968 Brazil drew around 85 percent of the credit.

Brazil seems to have used the IMF stand-by credits in the other years as a guarantee for the availability of credits from other international agencies, as a means of keeping international credibility, and to remain in compliance with the US requirements for assistance under the "Alliance for Progress" program.

The effective negotiations on the economic policy put in practice by the government, however, were apparently not carried out so much by the IMF as by certain US agencies, like the Agency for International Development (AID) and the US Export-Import Bank. During this period, the Fund's role seems to have been more formal than effective. From 1968 on, restrictions were no longer put on the size of credit drawings, or on their timing.

Compliance with stand-by credit agreements from 1965 to 1972 was, in general, not bad. Targets were surpassed more in the initial years of the program (1965–67), probably because of the magnitude of previous imbalances. The poorest performance tended to be in credit expansion, a key variable that successive governments used to stimulate economic growth.

Ceilings for fiscal deficits tended to be met. Only in one year, 1967, was it surpassed by large amount, and this mainly because the government used fiscal expenditure to reactivate the economy, which was entering into a recessive cycle. Fiscal deficit ceilings were also surpassed in 1966 and in 1969, though moderately. The rest of the years, specifically from 1970 onward, goals were met and the deficit tended to decrease further.

Monetary and credit expansion was always higher than planned. Only in 1966 was an effective constraint put on these variables, due to the still high inflation and the strong monetary expansion of the previous year. The limits were almost met. Although from 1969 onwards there was compliance with ceilings on growth in net domestic assets of the monetary authority, and outstanding amounts were even reduced in 1970 and 1972, credit and monetary expansion was high through growth in private bank credit and big surpluses in the balance of payments.

Limits on legal reserve requirements of commercial banks and on rediscounts and loans from the central bank were generally not met. After a year of strong credit expansion because of financing of the coffee program in 1966, limits to this expansion in following years tended to be relatively successful.

Except for 1967, in which international reserves declined instead of increasing, and 1968, in which they increased but less than planned, targets on foreign reserves were met. Moreover, from 1969 onward the actual increases in reserves surpassed by far the objectives stated in the stand-by agreements. Though this was partly because of a better situation in the commercial account due to the crawling peg exchange rate policy, the main reason was the huge inflow of external capital during these years.

Progress was made in trade liberalization. The exchange rates were unified; swap agreements, certain taxes on imports, taxes on buying foreign currency and the special list of goods that had quantitative restrictions were all eliminated; bilateral payments agreements and guarantee deposits for imports were reduced; and a program leading to tariff reduction was proposed and started to be implemented. All these steps, however, were taken very slowly, with extreme caution and pragmatism. Every time balance of payments problems were sensed, steps toward foreign trade liberalization were stopped or even reversed.

Though restrictions and controls were put in place, short-term debt grew in 1967, in 1968, and very sharply (much more than planned) from 1970 to 1972. Only in 1966 and 1969 did it not grow.

The application of the wage formulae was always effectively implemented. In general, price liberalization (though with authorized increases for certain products) and the adjustment of public tariffs and the prices of public enterprises to cover costs were put in practice, though with flexibility.

In recent years Brazil has made no drawings from the Fund, and although pressure has been put upon it, it has resisted entering a stand-by credit agreement.

Chile

Stand-by credits for the years 1956–58 were obtained in order to overhaul the exchange system as a part of a stabilization program. Compliance was good in fulfilling commitments on exchange arrangements, quite good in credit and wage policies (although ceilings were exceeded in 1958, they were nearly attained in the two previous years) but very little was achieved on fiscal reform. Relations between the

Fund and the government were good, except for disagreements about the way in which the exchange rate was readjusted, and, at the end of the period, over the effects of the program on economic activity and unemployment. At this time the Fund started to be criticized in academic circles and in the United Nations Economic Commission for Latin America for having a monetarist approach to inflation and balance of payment problems in Latin America.

In the period 1959–61, IMF assistance was sought to bolster a weak balance of payments and to get other official and banking loans. Credit ceilings were met in 1959 but exceeded in 1961. Fiscal deficits persisted, despite the efforts to improve fiscal revenues. The exchange system was further liberalized but the rate of exchange was pegged, and this led to the exchange crisis of 1961. Commitments on the exchange system were complied with, except those related to foreign indebtedness. Equally met were the objectives on salaries and prices—except for the reinforcement of price controls after May 1960, the date of two big earthquakes in Chile—but public service tariffs were not increased as proposed.

The exchange crisis of 1961 marks the end of this stabilization effort, with a resurgence of exchange controls, restrictions on imports, a dual foreign exchange market, payments arrears, and, by the end of 1962, considerable price increases.

From the end of 1961 until October 1962, relations between the IMF and Chile were severed. The country's exchange system remained unapproved, because the Fund considered the measures introduced by the authorities to meet the 1961 crisis as inappropriate, specifically the nondevaluation of the exchange rate for trade.

Stand-by agreements entered by Chile from the end of 1962 to 1969 were under the aegis of the Alliance for Progress, which required Latin American countries to make an internal effort to qualify for soft American loans. One of the requirements was to follow Fund advice to attain financial stability and to streamline the exchange system. At the beginning of the period (1962–66), Chile was having serious external payments difficulties, but by the end, large foreign surpluses made Fund assistance unnecessary.

Relations between the Fund and the authorities were very good; differences arose only in connection with the specific targets that were incorporated in the agreements. Commitments on the exchange system were met during this period, except for some intervals in which the authorities did not adjust the rate and the overcautious reduction of restrictions during periods of strong external surpluses. Balance of payments targets were surpassed. Credit ceilings and the projected current account of the government and public sector were complied with. Control on foreign indebtedness was not very effective, and in several years ceilings were exceeded. Wage increases were more liberal than agreed in 1963–64, and again in 1968–69, and the pricing of services of public sector services and enterprises were not made in accordance with agreed policies.

During the years 1970–73 (Unidad Popular), Chile did not request any stand-by credits from the Fund, but it kept good relations with that institution, which provided assistance under the compensatory financing facility and also played a very helpful role in obtaining the foreign debt rescheduling of 1971–72.

During 1974 and 1975 Chile requested two stand-by agreements in order to finance the huge deficits in its external payments and obtain further rescheduling of its foreign debt service payments. The whole amount of the stand-by granted for 1974 appears to have been drawn, although bank credit expanded much more than the targeted ceilings. The rate of inflation, projected at 80–100 percent for the year, was in fact 375 percent (although down from 650 percent in 1973). In 1975 credit ceilings were greatly exceeded, and the same happened with limits to the net credit of the banking system to the public sector. The balance of payments target was almost fulfilled, and the external position was improving strongly during the second half of 1975 (due to a big contraction in economic activity). Commitments on the exchange system were largely met, as were policies on prices and tariffs of public enterprises. Chile did not draw under the 1975 stand-by, but made use of the compensatory and oil facilities.

Relations between the Fund and Chile since 1974 have been very good, and there were IMF representatives in Santiago from 1974 to 1979. During the last few years Chile has repaid practically all its indebtedness with the Fund, excepting a small balance still due under the oil facility.

Macroeconomic Developments

In this section the empirical evidence as to the effects of stabilization programs in bringing about price stability and external equilibrium will be analyzed. An attempt will be made to show the effects on growth rates, economic activity, employment, and income redistribution.

Inflation and Relative Prices

Argentina. The increase in the cost of living (in Buenos Aires) doubled in 1959 in relation to 1958. The devaluation of the peso, public sector tariff adjustment, and the liberalization of prices brought about an acceleration of inflation and drastic changes in relative prices in favor of agriculture. In mid-1959 the exchange rate was stabilized, and in 1960 the same happened with prices. Massive salary increases were granted in 1961, and bank credit, mainly to the private sector, greatly expanded, but it was largely absorbed by central bank sales of exchange.

Prices grew moderately until April 1962. The devaluation of the peso was followed by an acceleration of inflation, which moderated by the end of the year as a consequence of restrictive measures, and the same tendency was maintained during the first three quarters of 1963.

Relative prices tended to move in favor of the export sector—agriculture and livestock—each time and devaluation took place (beginning in 1959 and April 1962), but as the exchange rate was maintained after each devaluation, inflation gradually eroded this effect.

The strategy of adjusting wages, the exchange rate, and tariffs, and subsequently freezing prices and salaries, led to a moderate reduction of inflation in 1967, but significant successes in 1968 and 1969. Price restraint was obtained by agreements with the business community, with some stimulus in the form of easier credit access. At the same time fiscal deficit was curtailed. Relative prices were maintained by simultaneous adjustments in wages, the exchange rate, public tariffs, and several other prices. But excessive bank credit and a change in expectations, related to political disturbances in 1969, led to an inflationary outburst in 1970.

One of the main objectives of the government that took office in early 1976 was to drastically reduce inflation and to change relative prices, which were seen as grossly distorted. Partial success was obtained, inasmuch as inflation was cut from 335 percent in 1975 and 348 percent in 1976 (cost of living in Buenos Aires) to 160 percent in 1977. But no further progress has been made. A sharp real wage drop in 1976, of approximately 35 to 40 percent, and reductions in the fiscal deficit helped to slow down the rate of inflation. Nevertheless, price decontrol, devaluation of the peso, and public sector tariff increases implied that in 1976 prices actually rose faster than during 1975.

Several measures were taken to improve relative agricultural prices. The effective exchange rate for primary products was raised, agricultural export taxes were reduced, and minimum support prices were set for corn, sorghum, and wheat. Temporary price controls, wages adjusted by decree, and indexation of public tariffs and of the exchange rate were used in order to break inflationary expectations. Although agricultural prices increased in relation to other prices during 1976 and 1977, declines in international prices in 1978 eliminated the advantages obtained.

Brazil. The policies put in practice in Brazil under the stand-by agreements between 1964 and 1972 were relatively sustained and coherent, although there were changes of emphasis.

Inflation fell during these years, though rather gradually. From a level of over 80 percent in 1963 and 1964, it fell to around 40 percent in 1965 and 1966, took a second step downward in 1967–68 to around 25 percent, and in 1969 moved down to the 20 percent area and stayed there until 1971. Finally, in 1972 and 1973, inflation was further reduced to around 15 percent. In 1974, two years after the last stand-by agreement was signed, inflation went up to over 30 percent, and has kept on climbing since then, to some extent due to increases in the price of oil.

Brazilian authorities took a gradualist approach in fighting inflation. Although they were worried by the problem, especially in the initial years, after 1966 they generally tended to give first priority to high rates of growth, and any recessive tendencies in the economy were quickly compensated. The level of inflation was also sustained due to a very high degree of indexation, which was a useful mechanism to avoid big distortions while inflation was high, but later contributed to maintaining inflation rates.

Although the Brazilian authorities kept a large measure of control over prices in general, they tended to end large price distortions. Thus industrial prices were allowed to rise in correspondence to increases in costs, and no great distortions seem to have been created. Price support schemes for coffee and other agricultural products and subsidies to internal consumption tended to decrease and eventually end. After a period in which the exchange rate was kept too low, it was finally increased in 1968 toward its equilibrium value, and from then on it was adjusted periodically to maintain a competitive foreign trade position.

Interest rates were also allowed to rise to values better reflecting the cost of capital. Public service tariffs and prices of public enterprise goods were also increased to at least cover costs.

Chile. To analyze the Chilean experience we shall differentiate four basic periods, which run from 1956 to 1958, 1959 to 1962, 1964 to 1970, and from 1974 to 1975.

During 1956 to 1958, inflation fell sharply from a very high 84 percent in 1955, to 38 percent in 1956, and 17 percent in 1957. In 1958, however, it increased again to 33 percent. The initial decrease was possible due to a tough policy in controlling wage increases, a change in expectations, and a decrease in the rate of expansion of money supply. But due to the recessive impact that this program had, pressure was put on the government to alter the policy, increase wages in excess of the rate of inflation of the previous year, and expand the money supply. This was done in 1958, and inflation increased again. Distortions in relative prices were not corrected substantially, although some advances were made, specifically in relation to interest and exchange rates.

In 1960, a year in which no stand-by agreement was subscribed, inflation fell abruptly to 6 percent. This was again due to drastic controls on wage increases, changes in expectations that increased the demand for money, a balance of payments deficit that compensated credit expansion, and a freezing of the rate of exchange. In 1961 inflation went up to 10 percent, although this level was still very low by Chilean standards. That year, money demand did not grow at the same rate as the previous year, while internal credit grew at a very high rate. With a fixed exchange rate, this resulted in a balance of payments crisis. In the following two years, inflation grew to 28 percent and 45 percent, respectively.

From 1965 to 1970, inflation was first lowered from 38 percent in 1964 to 17 percent in 1966, but then gradually went up again until it reached 35 percent in 1970. Its fluctuations were, in general, moderate and smooth. Influencing the rate of inflation were contradictory forces: a declining fiscal deficit, despite a high level of fiscal expenditures; important increases in real wages through adjustments in nominal wages; a more conservative rate of credit expansion; a large surplus in the balance of payments; and changing expectations.

During 1974 and 1975, inflation remained extremely high: 375 percent and 340 percent, respectively. These rates were in great part determined by high rates of expansion in the money supply and frequent large increases in nominal wages. Also affecting price increases were a generalized liberalization in prices, which had been subjected to widespread control in previous years; cost pressures due to important increases in interest rates, and in the exchange rate; expectations of high inflation which decreased money demand; the oligopolistic structure of internal markets; which permitted high markups and generalized indexation.

Notwithstanding the very strict and drastic stabilization program put into practice in 1975, and maintained during the following years, inflation fell very little in 1975 and to around 175 percent in 1976. It kept on falling gradually in the following years.

External Sector Balance

Argentina. After trade deficits recorded in previous years, in 1959 the trade account was balanced due to the devaluation of the peso and import surcharges. The investment boom of 1960 and 1961 led to growing imports, financed by foreign capital inflows, although there were not enough to prevent a decline in reserves in 1961. Capital flight due to political disturbances was recorded in 1962, and repayments of previous loans began to weigh on the balance of payments. As a result, the capital account was roughly balanced that year. Export increases, based on a new devaluation and good harvests, balanced the trade account.

The trade balance recorded a huge surplus in 1963, and, although the capital account was in deficit, reserves increased. The trade surplus was due to a drastic drop in imports after new surcharges were applied, and the effect of the 1962 devaluation and economic recession were felt. The devaluation of the peso in early 1967 was compensated with other measures affecting trade but not capital movements. As a result, short-term capital inflows were recorded in 1967 and 1968. In both years imports maintained the 1966 level, and exports diminished, mainly due to unfavorable international conditions.

Reserves built up in 1967 and in 1968, although moderately. In 1967 capital outflows, produced by a lack of confidence and overvaluation of the peso, led to a decline in foreign reserves.

The devaluation of the peso, and further measures taken to raise agricultural relative prices, made exports jump in 1976 and 1977. At the same time, imports went down in 1976, due to the devaluation and a decline in economic activity, but they recovered to their previous level in 1977. As a result, the trade balance passed from a deficit of nearly \$1 billion to a surplus of \$880 million in 1976 and \$1.5 billion in 1977.

Large repayment of import credits and swaps took place in 1976, giving a near equilibrium for the balance of payments. Sizable capital inflows in 1977 led to an increase of international reserves of \$2.2 billion.

Brazil. Brazil started off 1964 with a very weak external position. International reserves were low, the country had large payments arrears, and the current account and the balance of payments had been in deficit in 1963. During the period running from 1964 to 1972, Brazil's external position strengthened. First of all it payed off all its arrears. Except for 1967, its balance of payments was always in surplus, and from 1969 to 1972 these surpluses were very large and much higher than planned. This meant that Brazil accumulated large foreign reserves.

From 1968 onward, the balance of payment surpluses were helped by a relatively realistic exchange rate that favored a positive trade balance. But the main reason for the surpluses was the very large inflow of foreign capital that swept into the economy after 1968. Although this inflow was partly due to the credibility achieved by Brazil as a result of its sound policies, including the stabilization programs, it was also favored by an excess of liquidity in international financial markets.

The capital inflow had a negative side, however, in that it strongly increased Brazil's foreign debt. In particular, short-term debt grew more than planned or desired. This put strains on the country's external position in later years.

Brazil's balance of payments ran into deficit in 1974, and its external position became weaker from then on. As in the case of price stabilization, this situation was influenced by the increase in oil prices.

In the stand-by agreements, emphasis was put on the need to liberalize foreign trade and to end restrictions. Although the Brazilian economy continued to be rather protectionist during the whole period, with strong barriers aimed at promoting its industrial development, steps were taken to liberalize. They were taken with great caution, however, and were reversed every time the government felt they were having a negative effect on some sector. All in all, Brazil advanced toward being a more open economy in comparison to what it was in 1963.

Chile. From 1956 to 1958, the balance of payments showed little improvement that could be attributed to the stabilization program. Notwithstanding a better trade account because of higher copper prices and greater physical exports, in 1956 the balance of payments was in overall deficit ($10 million). In 1957 it was in deficit ($49 million), mainly because of a strong drop in the international price of copper and an increase in imports due to some trade liberalization. Although in 1958 imports decreased as restrictions were renewed, the trade balance was in deficit as a result of further declines in copper prices. However, the current account deficit was reduced because of smaller profit repatriation of copper companies, and the balance of payments as a whole again attained a surplus ($45 million) as a consequence of investments of the copper companies due to a more favorable tax policy. During these years there was little net advance in liberalizing foreign trade, although progress was made in decreasing restrictions and rationalizing the foreign exchange system.

From 1959 to 1961, the deficit on all accounts of the balance of payments grew continuously. Starting from relative equilibrium in 1959, the situation became explosive and ended in a balance of payments crisis, with large losses of international reserves and an overall deficit of $110 million. This was due to the combination of a policy of a fixed and very overvalued exchange rate, important liberalization of the exchange market and foreign trade restrictions, and an expansionary credit policy. Although in 1962 the balance of payments (and all its accounts) was still in deficit, it was smaller, because of the increase in restrictions on trade and payments and a big backlog in import payments.

From 1965 to 1970, the balance of payments was in almost permanent surplus, except for 1967 when there was a small deficit. During the first two years, $167 million of international reserves were accumulated, mainly due to high copper prices and a strong inflow of external credits to the public sector. In 1967 the deficit was the result of a lower copper price, bigger interest payments, and a decrease in the inflow of external capital. Then again, from 1968 to 1970, over $400 million of international reserves were accumulated due to the maintenance of restrictions on imports, the implementation of a crawling peg, and very high copper prices. The very strong position of the balance of payments in this period permitted some liberalization in foreign trade (although this was done with caution), the quick repayment of arrears and some very costly foreign debts, and a very large accumulation of international reserves.

Both in 1974 and 1975, the balance of payments was in deficit. In 1974, however, the deficit ($45 million) was significantly smaller than in the previous year, while in 1975 it increased steeply ($285 million). In 1974 the trade account was in surplus, which explains the reduction in the overall deficit. Although there was a big increase both in imports and in exports, the latter grew at a higher rate due to the much higher value of copper exports and some increase in nontraditional exports because of the strong devaluation of the currency. In 1975 imports fell significantly because of an internal recession, but exports decreased even more, principally due to a dramatic fall in the copper price. This led to a deficit in the trade balance that, added to an increase in interest payments, explains the high deficit on the current account. From 1976 to 1980, however, with the exception of 1977 in which there was a small deficit, the balance of payments showed large and successive surpluses. The period also combined important measures of foreign trade liberalization and decreases in restrictions in the foreign exchange system. These measures were continued and intensified in the following years.

Economic Activity and Growth

Argentina. In the first year of the Frondizzi government (1958), very expansive monetary and fiscal policies were carried out and wages were sharply increased. As a consequence, GDP rose strongly, but inflationary pressures built up and balance of payments difficulties arose. A new economic policy was applied at the end of 1958, the time at which the government signed a stand-by agreement with the IMF.

A sharp contraction of liquidity resulted from the budget restrictions and credit ceilings adopted, although a prolonged bank strike implied that minimum legal reserve requirements were not fulfilled for a certain period. Payment of central bank exchange guarantees provided some liquidity, and foreign capital inflows operated in the same direction. A drop of 5 percent in GDP was registered in 1959. In the following two years GDP recovered strongly, stimulated by direct foreign investment, official development loans and suppliers' credits. Investment and growth were significant in the oil sector, petrochemical industry, and durables. Manufacturing industry grew at healthy rates, and domestic investment boomed.

Toward the end of 1961, the economy stagnated. Balance of payments problems arose as a consequence of a poor harvest due to bad weather and because of a drop in the foreign capital inflow. The contractive effect of the latter was somewhat mitigated by a reduction in legal banking reserves, inducing an increase in liquidity exceeding the IMF limits.

A loss of confidence developed mainly due to widespread strikes and salary increases, the violation of a performance clause of the stand-by agreement, and poor results in the balance of payments. Adverse capital movements occurred, partly because much of the foreign debt was very short term.

The crisis was followed by contractive measures in 1962. Money supply was drastically restrained as a means of preventing speculative foreign currency sales financed by bank credit. GDP dropped in 1962 and 1963, to recover in 1964.

Industrial activity followed the same pattern as GDP. Agriculture and livestock did not respond to the stimulus provided by the devaluation of the peso, but the mining sector grew continuously, due to the rise of oil production.

The stabilization program for 1967 and 1968 included the expansion of private credit and public investment, the latter until private investment recovered in 1968. After the stagnation of 1966, and based on existing unused capacity, the economy grew moderately in 1967, accelerating in 1968 and 1969. The expansive monetary and fiscal policy was accompanied by a devaluation compensated with other measures affecting trade but not capital movements, and by adjustments in, and then the freezing of, prices and wages. Manufacturing production and private investment remained sluggish during 1967, but rose sharply in 1968. Agricultural production, on the other hand, fluctuated inversely.

In 1976, the time of signing a new stand-by agreement, the government of Argentina faced a recessive economic situation, gross financial disequilibrium, and balance of payments difficulties. The recession deepened that year, as the drastic drop in real wages resulting from the stabilization program depressed the demand for consumer goods, and private investment was restrained by the prevailing economic situation.

Exports led the recovery in early 1977. Good crops and an increase in manufacturing activity, mainly in intermediate and final goods, were recorded during the first half of the year. But, as a result of measures taken in the monetary field to control inflation, economic activity fell from the end of 1977 until the end of 1978.

Brazil. On average, Brazilian gross domestic product and industrial production grew around 4 percent a year in real terms during the first half of the 1960s. In 1965, the first year of the stabilization program, gross domestic product grew 4 percent in real terms, strongly favored by agricultural growth (about 14 percent) due to an excellent crop; industrial production fell nearly 5 percent that year.

In 1966 economic growth picked up, despite a decline in agriculture, but growth again slowed the following year. From 1968 until 1973, the Brazilian economy grew at very high rates: around 9–10 percent a year from 1968 to 1970, and over 11 percent a year from 1971 to 1973. Rates of industrial growth were even higher, fluctuating between 11 and 16 percent. During this period, the share of industry and commerce in the gross domestic product increased, while that of agriculture declined. Within the industrial sector, capital goods and durable consumer goods had the highest levels of growth, while non-durable consumer goods grew at the lowest rates.

Summing up, stand-by agreements with the IMF had no obvious negative effect on Brazilian rates of growth. Only in the first years could some effects be noted, although they were mild. In no year was the rate of growth of GDP negative, and only once, in 1965, did industrial production decrease.

These results were to a great extent due to the emphasis that the Brazilian authorities put on growth over other goals, like price stabilization. Since 1968, together with the stabilization program, the authorities put in practice a long-term development plan that was followed with a rather high degree of continuity. The plan included a great deal of government coaxing of the economy, especially in certain areas, like the manufacture of capital and durable consumer goods, and exports. Brazil also took advantage of conditions in the world economy, which was in a phase of growing trade and plentiful capital supply.

Chile. In 1956, the year of the first stand by agreement subscribed by Chile, GDP fell 5.5 percent in real terms. Industrial production and construction also fell strongly (−6 percent and −29 percent, respectively). In 1957 and 1958, GDP grew by 4 percent each year. Industrial production also grew (4.5 and 7 percent respectively), but construction again fell by 1957 (−9 percent), and then grew in 1958 (5.5 percent). In sum, although in 1956 there was an important fall in GDP, in the two following years its growth was the same as the average from 1940 to 1959. Hardest hit by the stabilization program would seem to have been the industrial and construction sectors.

Between 1959 and 1962, GDP grew 2 percent, 3.6 percent, and 6.5 percent, respectively. Though these growth rates were higher than those registered between 1956 and 1958, they were, on the average, near the historical rate. Economic growth in these years must be mainly attributed to fiscal investments that were specially programmed to stimulate development, and to the reconstruction of a region devastated by two earthquakes in 1960.

The 1965–70 period can be divided into two subperiods. In 1965 and 1966 GDP grew at high rates (6.5 and 10 percent, respectively), with high growth of industrial production (6.5 and 8.5 percent) in response to higher real wages and fiscal spending on construction, and by significant rates of growth in agriculture and the mining sector in 1966 (the latter having been favored by high copper prices). In contrast, the period running from 1967 to 1970 was rather recessive. GDP percentage growth rates were 1.5, 3.5, 5.5, and 3.5, respectively, rates much lower than planned by the government, and lower than the country's historical rates. An important factor explaining this lower growth was an erratic policy on public investment, especially in construction. Also, public investment in the industrial sector concentrated on buying enterprises that were already producing. With regard to other productive sectors, investments in the mining sector matured only after 1970, while in agriculture they were mainly directed at the land reform program, which did not increase production. Finally, it must be added that the general environment of reform and social change was not favorable to private investment and growth.

In 1974 GDP grew a little over 4 percent. Industrial growth in 1974 was negative as the first effects of the stabilization and reallocation policies were being felt. However, GDP was favored by a large increase in agricultural output due to a readjustment in internal relative prices and the devaluation of the currency, both of which stimulated production and exports from this sector. Also favorable was the big increase in the mining sector due to a higher value of copper exports. In 1975, however, the stabilization program became drastic. The decrease in fiscal expenditures was especially harsh. GDP fell over 14 percent according to official figures, and according to some economists by more than 15 percent. Industrial production declined more than 25 percent. The outcome was also influenced by a lower value of production of the mining sector due to very low copper prices.

Employment

Argentina. The unemployment rate was more or less constant during the period 1958–61. In 1962 and 1963 it rose somewhat, but in the whole period it fluctuated within a very narrow range. The government expected an important increase in private sector employment after the stimulus provided to investment, but it did not materialize.

Unemployment rose by one percentage point in 1967, declining to its previous level in 1968, and further declined in 1969. The 1967 increase reflects the industrial recession of that year.

Unemployment in Buenos Aires went up by two percentage points in 1976, declining steadily in 1977 and 1978. The huge drop in real wages prevented a more drastic effect of the economic slowdown of 1975–76 on employment.

Brazil. In Brazil, the recessive impact of the stabilization program in the initial years, 1965–67, led to an increase in unemployment.

According to an index of industrial employment in São Paulo, employment systematically decreased in the first three quarters of

1965, reaching a fall of around 13 percent. In the fourth quarter of 1965 and the first three of 1966, employment increased to a level higher than any period in 1964. However, in the last quarter of that year, and the first two of 1967, a recessive trend again overtook the economy, and employment fell around 9 percent.

As in the case of economic growth and activity, the negative effects of the stabilization programs on employment were not harsh.

Chile. Unemployment seems to have been adversely affected during the 1956–58 stabilization programs. However, it is difficult to make precise statements, since systematic information on the subject began only in late 1956. According to the 1952 census, unemployment in April of that year had been 5 percent. A survey carried out in Santiago in October 1956 indicated that the existing level of unemployment was 7 percent. This figure was 6.5 percent for June 1957 and a high 9.5 percent for June 1958.

From 1959 through 1961, unemployment in Santiago started from a very high 10.5 percent, went down to 8 percent in June, and stayed around 7 percent from then until September 1961. In December 1961, it again fell to around 5 percent, the smallest figure since the initiation of the employment surveys.

Over the 1965–70 period, unemployment in Santiago tended to grow, although the increase was relatively moderate. In 1965 and 1966, the unemployment rate was a little over 5 percent. In 1967, together with the more recessive economic conditions, it jumped to 6 percent, and was 6.5 percent in 1968 and 6 percent in 1969. Again in 1970 it gave another jump to 7 percent. This was a result of a change in the structure of public investment already noted, and of tight credit policies to prevent additional inflationary pressures.

In 1974 and 1975, unemployment increased dramatically. From a rate of 5 percent of the total working force in 1973, it grew to 10 percent in 1974 and then jumped to 16 percent in 1975. Very high unemployment rates remained during the following years. This rate of unemployment was a consequence of the strong economic contraction that the country suffered, especially in 1975. However, later increases in production did not lead to an equivalent decline in the rate of unemployment.

Income and Wealth Distribution

Argentina. Although employment approximately maintained its level during the 1959–63 period, real wages dropped drastically in 1959, recovered somewhat in 1960 and 1961, and declined in the following two years. Participation of salaries and wages in national income followed the same pattern.

In contrast, during the 1967–68 period there was no clear regressive effect on income distribution. Real wages declined in both these years, but moderately.

From 1976 to 1977 stronger recessive effects occurred. Real wages fell drastically in 1976, around 35–40 percent; and remained approximately constant the two following years.

Brazil. Several indicators tend to show that during the 1965–72 period income and wealth in Brazil suffered a regressive redistribution.

The wage adjustment formula was meant to restore wages their average purchasing power during the previous 24 months. Small additions were allowed in order to cover increases in productivity and the expected rise in prices during the next year. Between 1964 and 1968, however, this last factor was always underestimated. Thus, in the face of much higher than planned inflation rates, real wages decreased rather systematically. Real minimum wage fell around 20 percent from 1964 to 1967, and average wages fell almost 15 perent in that same period.

Due to these decreases, in 1968 additional wage increases were given and the wage formula applied in 1969 was modified. If real inflation surpassed the estimate previously used to adjust wages, additional wage increases would be given in order to prevent further declines in purchasing power.

Between 1968 and 1971 real minimum wages became relatively stagnant, with small, occasional falls. Average wages grew moderately in 1968. Only in 1972 and 1973 did minimum real wages begin to grow again, and this increase was moderate, 3.5 percent in 1972 and 1 percent in 1973. In contrast, profits seem to have increased and real interest rates rose remarkably over this period. The spread between the rate charged to borrowers and that paid to lenders was very high, which permitted large earnings and a strong expansion of the financial sector.

Other evidence shows that participation in national income of the poorest 50 percent of the population fell from 18 percent in 1960 to 15 percent in 1970, and to 12 percent in 1976. The next 30 percent of the population also decreased their income participation, from 28 percent in 1960, to 23 percent in 1970, and to 21 percent in 1976. Meanwhile, the richest 5 percent of the population increased their participation in national income from 28 percent in 1960, to 35 percent in 1970, and to 39 percent in 1976. The next richest 15 percent of the population also increased their participation in income, but moderately, from 26.5 percent in 1960, to 27 percent in 1970, and to 28 percent in 1975.

Summing up, there are indications of wealth concentration and regressive income redistribution in Brazil between 1964 and 1972. This effect can be partially attributed to the wage adjustment policy, which contrasted to the policy applied to other prices.

Chile. There is no evidence to draw unambiguous conclusions regarding the effect of the stabilization programs between 1956 and 1958 on income and wealth distribution. But there are some indicators, like the increase in unemployment during this period (which mainly affected unskilled labor) that point toward a more regressive distribution of income. According to existing statistics, real minimum wages fell 5.5 percent in 1956 and 5 percent in 1958, although they went slightly up in 1957 (1 percent). However, it must be noted that real minimum wages had been falling since 1953, due to increasing rates of inflation and lagged wage adjustments. Average real wages of public employees, which had risen remarkably between 1951 and 1955, fell drastically from 1956 to 1958 (21 percent, 18 percent, and 9 percent each year, respectively).

For 1959–61, there is again only partial evidence of the effects on income and wealth distribution. The real purchasing power of minimum wages seems to have fallen in 1959 in relation to 1958. In 1960, however, it grew slightly, even though wage adjustments were lower than past inflation.

It seems possible to conclude that the stabilization programs between 1959 and 1961 did not contribute to a regressive effect on income distribution. Real wages rose steeply in 1965 (13.5 percent), in 1966 (12.1 percent), and in 1967 (15.3 percent). This was principally achieved by high increases in nominal wages in excess of the previous rates of inflation. In 1968 real wages were practically stagnant (they grew less than 1 percent); in 1969 and in 1970 their rate of increase went up again (9 percent and 10.5 percent, respectively).

The government was conscious that these increases, which surpassed by far any gain in productivity, were not compatible with maintaining internal stability. But it lacked the political power and will to exert a stronger control in wage adjustments. To the previous figures it must be added that a series of structural changes, like the land reform and the nationalization of certain enterprises, tended to deconcentrate wealth from the traditional capitalist groups or classes.

In 1974 and 1975, the stabilization program put in practice seems to have had a negative effect on real wages. These fell 11 percent in 1974 and 3 percent in 1975. It must be noted, however, that due to increasing inflation, real wages had also been falling in previous years. After 1975, due mainly to decreasing inflation, they tended to grow at relatively high rates. Probably more important than the impact of the losses in real wages on income redistribution was the enormous increase in the rate of unemployment.

Other factors that contributed to a concentration of wealth during these years was the massive sale of state enterprises to private groups at extremely low prices, the restoration of large areas of land that had been affected by the land reform to their previous owners, the sharp increase in real interest rates that favored the relative income of capital vis à vis other productive factors, and a large increase in relative prices of property and other real assets.

General Remarks on Conditionality

Control of the IMF over policies and performance of member countries entering into stand-by agreements is much less effective than is generally thought both by partisans of conditionality and by its detractors. The chances of adequate implementation of agreed policies are much greater when the authorities present programs formulated by themselves than when they accept programs without being convinced of their appropriateness, because they are seeking some other objective (e.g., foreign assistance) or because they are facing a crisis they do not know how to deal with. In most cases countries have tried to live up to their commitments, and when they did not do it, it was because of compelling internal reasons. In the latter case, the loss of drawing rights was almost always minimal, because violations occurred when a large part of the credit had already been utilized and the objective of attaining other credits had been fulfilled.

A second and important point about policies is that on many occasions they have not been maintained long enough, either because the general line of a new government has been different, (in inspiration and goals, or both) or because an expected rapid success has not been forthcoming, or perhaps because programs gave little importance to structural conditions that, in many cases, were at the root of the imbalances. These stop-go policies may have had a negative effect on general economic performance. Successful experience appears to have been correlated with continuity of policy, as in the case of Brazil.

Taking a long-term view of the results of the IMF involvement with the southern Latin American countries, the balance is rather niggardly. None of them appears to be better off in terms of growth, income distribution, and financial stability at the beginning of the 1980s than they were at the end of the 1950s, except for Brazil (in terms of growth). And in the case of Brazil, exogenous factors—like the amount and diversification of productive resources and the international environment—were basic for the country's economic performance. These results are clearly not the fault of the IMF, but they could well be a sign of its impotence.

The best outcomes were probably achieved in the simplification and rationalization of the exchange and payments systems and the reduction of some blatant distortions that were inherited from the depression and war years. In general, less was achieved in the effort to establish equilibrium in the finances of the public sector and to maintain control over credit expansion.

However, in most periods achievements and failures were combined with respect to the main targets. They had much to do with exogenous circumstances (demand and prices for export products, import prices, inflow of foreign credits and investments) or with the degree of existing imbalances that were the result of social or development policies pursued without a proper regard to the availability of resources.

Performance and judgment on performance are strongly hindered by the loose relation between instruments and targets of policy, and also by the time lags and the variability of lags between the use of the instrument and the achievement of a goal. Compliance with the credit ceilings was not an obstacle to high and increasing rates of inflation, as in Chile in 1957–59, 1963–64, and again in 1967–70. Nor was little credit control an obstacle to decreasing inflation, as in Brazil from 1965 to 1968 and in 1971 or in Argentina, 1967–68. Effects of exchange rate changes on the results of the current account of the balance of payments, if they existed, are difficult to identify in magnitude and in time, except, perhaps, in the case of Argentina. Exogenous variables may change in ways difficult to predict at the time of the stand-by inception, and they can influence performance much more than the instrument variables that have been the subject of an agreement with the Fund.

It is not possible to say that a program has failed because any of the ceilings set up as performance criteria have been surpassed or because any prohibited restrictive practice has been put into effect. That judgment can only be the result of an assessment of the whole set of policies (quantitative as well as qualitative) that the country is pursuing.

As an example, one can take the Chilean experience of 1975. Demand restrictions went far beyond what the IMF could have reasonably expected from any country in order to reduce inflation and improve its balance of payments. The exchange rate was devalued by 25 percent in real terms. This was at the cost of a 15 percent decrease in production and an increase in unemployment from 9.7 percent of the labor force of Santiago at the end of 1974 to 18.7 percent at the end of 1975. Despite that tremendous and costly effect, Chile did not comply with several of the performance criteria set up in the stand-by for that year. In a less extreme case, like Brazil from 1965 to 1972, the general direction of economic policy and compliance with IMF targets could be said to be satisfactory, macroeconomic performance was quite good, but on many occasions individual targets were surpassed.

On the other hand, it seems reasonable that the Fund should provide its resources in support of a well-conceived and consistent program tending to correct financial imbalance. But even if drafted in the form of quantitative targets, both its progress and the continuity of its stabilization policies should be judged on a global basis, taking into account changing circumstances that may not have been contemplated at the time of initiation of the program. This could be achieved by a process of consultations between the country and the Fund (at present provided for in all stand-by agreements), with drawings suspended if it were concluded that the country had strayed from the purposes of the agreement. This would impose a burden on the Fund, but it appears more reasonable than obliging the country to make an advance statement of failure if some variable surpasses a predetermined value.

Fund resources would be well protected because: (1) drawings are made in installments during the stand-by period; (2) there are provisions guaranteeing repurchases (as if drawings were loans) in periods agreed upon between the Fund and the member, or when the Fund so decides, according to the agreement; and (3) it can reasonably be expected that relations between the Fund and its members will be conducted in good faith.

In designing programs the Fund should take into consideration basic aspirations and goals of the country concerned, while taking care that basic macroeconomic balances are reasonably observed or that steps are taken to reach balance. Criteria set up in Chapter 7 of the present volume seem to be quite acceptable; the only problem is to give them an operational meaning. Special care should be taken about the macroeconomic imbalances that may be the result of policies aiming at changes in social and economic structures. In those cases, exceptional measures could be authorized even if they may collide with some provisions of the agreement. Emphasis then should be that *policies* should not affect legitimate interests of other countries or produce financial disruption that would jeopardize the objectives of the reforms (e.g., reduce the rate of growth of the economy, worsen the wealth or income distribution).

The most important aspect of all programs is the reconciliation of financial stability and of high and sustained employment and economic growth. Relevant to this question is the timing of the adjustment; the amount of finance needed; the role of other credit institutions, particularly the World Bank; and the priorities in objectives, if there are conflicts among them.

Various criticisms of the Fund, which have sometimes caused conflicts between the Fund and member countries, have been voiced: Fund models that are too monetarist and rely excessively on the workings of the market mechanism; the lack of consideration of structural problems that may affect developing countries; excessive intervention or monitoring of economic policies in the interest of developed countries; and the secondary interest of problems of employment and growth, implying that if they were produced by stabilization policies they will take care of themselves in due time.

From the experience of the countries reviewed, IMF programs seem to have had, on occasion, some negative effects on growth. In general, however, except for Chile in 1975, this effect was moderate and brief. This was partly due to a not very strict compliance with agreed targets in the face of even a mild recession. The magnitude of a recessive outcome was related to the size of previous imbalances, and economic growth seems to have been closely tied to international economic conditions.

Lack of emphasis on instruments and policies geared to influence expectations was quite costly, as for example in the experience of Chile in 1975. In Brazil, where the government used price controls and other less orthodox instruments to influence expectations, and at the same time stimulated investment, economic policy between 1964 and 1972 was much more successful.

Another factor that in some cases led to costs that could have been avoided was the joint implementation of stabilization and liberalization measures. Where distortions were too great this may have been unavoidable, but when this was not the case the increase in the costs of the policies endangered their continuity.

Criticism of excessive intervention in domestic policies by the IMF could perhaps be somewhat reduced if the idea of regionalization of the Fund materialized. Specific provisions of stand-by agreements would then be implemented through regional Fund boards where the countries of the region would have more weight than they have now in the Board of Executive Directors of the institution.

Conflicts have arisen because of the variables selected for control and because of the precise figures chosen as targets. In early times, programs were more monetarist in content, but near the middle 1960s more consideration was given to gradual approaches, and departures from principles were accepted (although on a temporary basis). Recently there have been announcements of more interest in structural and development needs, which should be welcome, but there is not yet enough experience to make a judgment.

Inasmuch as the new policies are directed to measures enhancing the country's productive capacity—and this is not limited only to measures implying more freedom in the working of markets, price policies, or elimination of obstacles, controls, taxes, or subsidies that improve the allocation of productive resources but also to structural or institutional changes that eliminate hindrances to a better economic development—those policies may be much more difficult to formulate and implement.

Criticism on the precise levels of targets and ceilings are much more difficult to judge, and it may well be that in many instances the Fund has not been unreasonable; but because of the very fact that there is haggling on them, Fund officials tend to be too tight, and the countries' authorities too loose.

Fund judgments on the performance of countries tend to be excessively negative when there is no agreement with them, and excessively positive if there is agreement. Also, financial stability is given great weight, but at the same time serious imbalances in other important macroeconomic variables, employment, level of activity, amount and composition of investment, although mentioned, are sometimes not stressed enough.

The Fund has been, and certainly will be, a catalyst for moving resources from other institutions or countries to its members. This is all to the good, provided it remains a by-product. The main Fund activity should be helping countries to formulate policies and providing finance to aid a proper and smooth working of the adjustment process. Adjustment policies and finance should be adequate to the circumstances, and no correlation should exist between toughness of policies and amount of financing. At present the Fund follows the rule that the higher the amount of finance sought, the tougher the policies. But actually, the tougher the policies, the less finance is needed.

CHAPTER 14

Vicissitudes of Recent Stabilization Attempts in Brazil And the IMF Alternative

Edmar L. Bacha

This paper describes recent macroeconomic events and policies in Brazil, and attempts to evaluate the Brazilian government's decision to implement a stabilization policy like those of the International Monetary Fund (IMF) in 1981, after deciding not go to the Fund in 1980.

Selected political events since 1968 are introduced in order to provide a frame of reference for a description of the wage policy applied by the military regime through November 1979. There follows a discussion of inflation acceleration in 1979, leading to a delineation of the new wage policy implemented by the government late that year. Delfim Netto's unbalanced growth strategy through mid-1980 is presented. This leads to an analysis of the foreign exchange shortage that caused a sharp reversal of government policies at the end of 1980. Consideration of the industrial slump of 1981 completes the descriptive part of the paper.

Evaluation of the government's decision not to go to the Fund starts with a statement concerning conflicting views on appropriate stabilization policies for Brazil. Two scenarios for a counterfactual IMF involvement in Brazilian policy making are developed, the first for mid-1979 and the second for late-1980. Estimates are presented

Note: Advice from Paulo Batista, Jr., Dionísio Carneiro and Pedro Malan; comments on a previous draft from other colleagues at PUC/RJ; research assistance from Demosthenes de Pinho Neto; and financial support from PNPE/IPEA are gratefully acknowledged. The usual caveats apply.

of possible foreign exchange savings, derived from lower spreads on international loans, that the Brazilian government would have enjoyed as a consequence of an IMF "seal of approval" over its economic policies. The paper concludes with considerations relating to possible economic costs for the country that would have derived from a three-year commitment to an IMF stabilization program.

Political Prelude

The Institutional Act no. 5 (AI–5) of December 13, 1968 suspended constitutional guarantees and allowed an authoritarian state to prevail in Brazil during General Medici's administration (1969–73). General Geisel took over in 1974, determined to follow a path of "political decompression," which culminated with the abolition of AI–5 toward the end of his term in 1978. Swearing "to bring democracy to this country" by the end of his mandate in 1984, General Figueiredo began his term in 1979 decreeing a complete political amnesty, which cleared Brazilian prisons of political prisoners and brought back to the country all who had been chased away by the post-1964 military regime.

With the end of AI–5, long-repressed wage demands were unleashed, and the labor union movement marked its rebirth with a series of strikes and street demonstrations.

Under an uncertain climate, newly formed political parties are now preparing to face in November 1982 a critical general election that should alter in a fundamental way the power balance maintained since 1964.

Post-1964 Wage Policy

The hallmark of post-1964 stabilization policy was the introduction of a mandatory wage policy, laying down a precise mathematical formula that had to be followed in all collective wage readjustments in the country. These overlapping wage contracts traditionally are signed at regional labor courts, once every 12 months, at a specific date for each industry grouping. According to the formula, the wage readjustment would result from the sum of three parcels. The first one provided for a wage hike equal to 50 percent of the cost of living increase in the previous two years. This would bring the real value of the wage at the time of the readjustment to its average real value during the previous two years. The second part consisted of an additional wage hike equal to 50 percent of the inflation predicted for the coming year. If the prediction were fulfilled, this would ensure the maintenance in the following year of the same average value for the real wage as in the previous two years. The third part consisted of a wage bonus corresponding to the yearly increase in aggregate labor productivity. This was meant to guarantee the constancy of the wage share in GNP.

Such was the theory. In practice, during the 1964–68 period, the government prediction of inflation consistently fell short of the realized level. Eventually, as the inflation rate receded, an adjustment factor was added to the formula to compensate for the previous year's underprediction of inflation. After November 1974, the formula started allowing for the reestablishment of the average real wage in the previous 12 months, instead of the previous 24 months. However, the labor productivity allowance continued to be authorized with much lower values than the growth of GNP per capita. According to one calculation, a fair application of the mathematical formula up to 1973 would have resulted in a minimum wage rate 38 percent higher than the value that was in fact decreed by the government.[1] Some wage drift did occur, but not at a sufficiently high rate to compensate the wage earners for their real income losses under the government wage policy.[2]

1979: Inflation Acceleration and New Wage Policy

A deep fiscal reform was put into effect in 1964–67, allowing the federal government to balance its regular budget without expanding the money supply. Rather than taking this opportunity to force inertial inflation down, the government chose to pursue a passive monetary policy, using the "inflation tax" to provide cheap credit for additional public and private sector activities. The mandatory wage policy previously described made this growth-oriented policy compatible with a significant reduction of inflation after 1964. In fact,

[1] See Livio de Carvalho, "Politicas salariais brasileiras no periodo 1964–81," *Revista Brasileira de Economia* 36, no. 1 (January-March 1982): 51–84.

[2] For an attempted measure of the wage drift above the minimum wage and a discussion of the role of the wage policy on income concentration in Brazil during the 1960s, see Edmar Bacha and Lance Taylor, "Brazilian Income Distribution in the 1960s: 'Facts,' Model Results and the Controversy," *Journal of Developing Countries* 14, no. 3 (April 1978); reproduced as chapter 10 in Lance Taylor, et al., *Models of Growth and Distribution for Brazil* (Oxford: Oxford University Press, 1980).

inflation was brought under control and kept at a rate of about 20 percent a year during the "Brazilian economic miracle," when GNP growth rates averaged 11 percent a year. The first oil shock hit the Brazilian economy at the top of the boom. The increase in the prices of oil and other tradable products interacted with the domestic indexation schemes, forcing Brazilian inflation toward a new plateau of 40 percent a year in the 1974–78 period.[3]

During 1979 the Brazilian economy suffered a series of adverse cost pushes. Under the pressure of the US government, early in 1979 the Brazilian government started phasing out its industrial export subsidies program. As a compensation to exporters, this was accompanied by an acceleration of the rate of minidevaluations. In mid-1979, the second oil shock started hitting at a time when a third consecutive poor annual harvest made its way to local markets. As inflation began accelerating, labor unrest became more pronounced. Mario Simonsen, since March 1979 the minister in charge of economic affairs, concluded that he did not stand a chance of implementing a stiff monetary policy under such conditions, and resigned his post in August. The animal spirits of the local bourgeoisie reached euphoria when General Figueiredo announced that Delfim Netto, the architect of the "Brazilian economic miracle," would replace Simonsen. Entrepreneurial delirium became manifest when Delfim Netto suggested that he would fight inflation by raising production, and buried his predecessor's plans for monetary control.

Meanwhile, in order to appease the labor movement, Labor Minister Murilo Macedo conceived a new wage policy that received congressional approval and was put in practice by the government in November. The new wage law encompassed several changes. First, the system of annual wage adjustments was replaced by one of half-yearly wage changes. Second, the wage formula was eliminated, and wage indexing started to be based on a new price index, the National Index of Consumer Prices, using a nationwide sample. This meant that projected inflation ceased to have an effect on legal wage readjustments. Third, the new wage law introduced an element of income redistribution by guaranteeing higher adjustments for lower wage

[3] For an overview of the period, see E. Bacha, "Selected Issues in Post-1964 Brazilian Economic Growth," in L. Taylor et al., *Models of Growth and Distribution for Brazil* (Oxford: Oxford University Press, 1980), pp. 17–48. Relevant econometric evidence is presented in Francisco Lopes and André Lara-Resende, "Causas da recente aceleracão inflacionária," *Pesquisa e Planejamento Económico* 11, no. 3 (December 1981).

groups.[4] The new law also provided for an additional adjustment for productivity increases, to be negotiated annually between management and labor. Finally, in order to speed up the transition to half-year indexing, an immediate 22 percent wage bonus (corresponding to one-half of the annual wage adjustment of November) was decreed for workers whose annual settlement dates fell between December 1979 and May 1980 (at the corresponding dates, these workers now would receive a six-month wage adjustment).

This form of switching over to six-month wage indexing gave an additional impetus to inflation. But that still was not the end of the story. For in December, Delfim Netto decided on a 30 percent maxi-devaluation, accompanied by an elimination of tax credits granted to industrial exports and of advance import deposit requirements.

The resulting effective trade-weighted devaluation was on the order of 16 percent, hence providing a final boost to inflation.[5] At year-end, the 12-month inflation rate reached the 80 percent mark. A quickening of monetary expansion in December guaranteed ample liquidity to validate the doubling of the inflation rate between 1978 and 1979.

Delfim Netto's Strategy Through Mid-1980

There has been no unambiguous statement of short-term economic policy coming from Delfim Netto since he began his term as economic czar in August 1979. In retrospect, his initial policies do not seem to add up to a consistent package, but an attempt can be made at

[4] Initially, the wage law guaranteed adjustments of 110 percent the rate of inflation for earnings up to 3 minimum salaries; earnings above 3 but below 10 times the minimum salary were to be adjusted by the rate of inflation; those above 10 but lower than 20 minimum salaries by 80 percent of the inflation rate, and those above 20 minimum salaries by one-half the inflation rate. As the average adjustment implied by this formula was somewhat above the inflation rate, in December 1980 there was a modification to the law. Two brackets were created, from 10–15 and from 15–20 minimum salaries, to which adjustment factors of 80 percent and 50 percent, respectively, were to be applied. Adjustments for wages in excess of 20 minimum salaries were left to free negotiation between employer and employee.

[5] Calculated from data in Alkimar Moura, "A política cambial e comercial no período 1974–1980," *Relatório de Pesquisa,* no. 16. São Paulo: EAESP–FGV, 1981.

understanding what his intentions were, prior to steering toward a monetarist course in the second half of 1980.

Delfim Netto seems to have diagnosed correctly the reasons why inflation *began* to accelerate in 1979, namely, the speeding up of the minidevaluations and the continuing poor performance of domestic agriculture. He seems to have hoped to reduce inflationary pressures by slowing down the rate of devaluation *after* December 1979 and by promoting a "super-harvest" in 1980, mostly through minimum price guarantees and an extended subsidized agricultural credit program. Betting on this possibility, in early January 1980 he prefixed the rate of devaluation through December at 40 percent.

Attempting to influence inflationary expectations, he further prefixed the annual rate of "monetary correction" at 45 percent.[6] In anticipation of these measures, Delfim Netto used jawboning techniques to force private banks to reduce lending rates to the tune of 10 percentage points per year. Money supply targets and credit limits were also established, but at the same time open market policies were directed at keeping market interest rates at the level of about 45 percent per annum.

Apart from his contradictory attempt at simultaneously controlling the growth rates of money and credit and fixing interest rates, Delfim Netto's strategy was marred by a misjudgment of the behavior of critical variables that were not under his control. The first was the strength of the inflationary pressures built into the economy in 1979. In spite of interest rate controls and the slowing down of the devaluation rate, by mid-year Delfim Netto's prediction of 12-month inflation had already been reached at the wholesale price level. The government also seems to have underestimated the Organization of Petroleum Exporting Countries' resolve to increase oil prices and Volcker's intent and ability to reduce US money supply growth, with its consequences for the level of dollar interest rates. As a result of these events, by mid-year Brazil had accumulated a $6.8 billion current account deficit in spite of a good export showing.[7] Finally, Delfim Netto overestimated his trump cards with the international banking community—and it was their unwillingness to bank his unorthodox policies that finally forced him into a complete policy reversal.

[6] "Monetary correction" is an indexing scheme for a number of financial assets: housing rents and mortgages, tax debts, etc.

[7] This compares unfavorably with a $4.5 billion deficit during the first half of 1978.

1980: Foreign Exchange Shortage and Policy Reversal

Early in 1979 Brazil still had an oversupply of foreign exchange, and the central bank was busily trying to keep foreign financial capital from flowing into the country. Official foreign reserves then began to fall as the minidevaluations accelerated after March, and domestic interest rate controls were imposed after August. Over the year the central bank lost some $3 billion in convertible foreign exchange, but in December it still displayed a foreign reserve balance of $9.7 billion, more than enough to pay for a half-year's import bill.

As described in *Euromoney,*[8] the Brazilian government then started playing "a cat and mouse game" with foreign bankers, refusing to accept the higher spreads that the market demanded, as Brazil's economic situation deteriorated and confidence in Delfim Netto's policies disappeared. As shown in Figure 14.1, convertible foreign exchange reserves fell abruptly during the first half of the year, from $8.3 billion in December 1979 to $4.8 billion in June 1980. The sharp reserve losses harmed the creditworthiness of the country, reinforcing the banks' desire to hold back from Brazilian loans. The feeling spread in the market that Brazil would be forced to reschedule its commercial debt in 1981, and in private meetings US bankers started urging Brazilian officials to go to the IMF to clear the air.

Rather than going to Washington, Delfim Netto chose to undo in Brasilia his past policies. New "monetary correction" (of 50 percent) and devaluation targets (of 45 percent) were announced for the July 1981–June 1982 period as a means of loosening the values previously fixed for December 1981 without losing much face. Interest rates were allowed to creep upward and controls over money and credit tightened. A 25 percent tax on domestic borrowing was introduced in May with the triple purpose of restricting credit demand, inducing local firms to borrow abroad, and diminishing the size of the budget deficit. Centralized controls were established over the expenditure plans of state enterprises.

These measures of mid-1980 proved insufficient for the task at hand: during the third quarter, inflation continued to accelerate and the current account to deteriorate. When foreign exchange reserves threatened to dry up, officially nearly going under the $4-billion mark in November, Delfim Netto gave up, decontrolling domestic interest

[8] Peter Field and Steplen Downer, "Brazil's Rescheduling: This Year, Next Year, Sometime, Never?" *Euromoney,* October 1980, pp. 89–98.

Figure 14.1 *Brazil: International and Foreign Exchange Reserves, 1979–81*

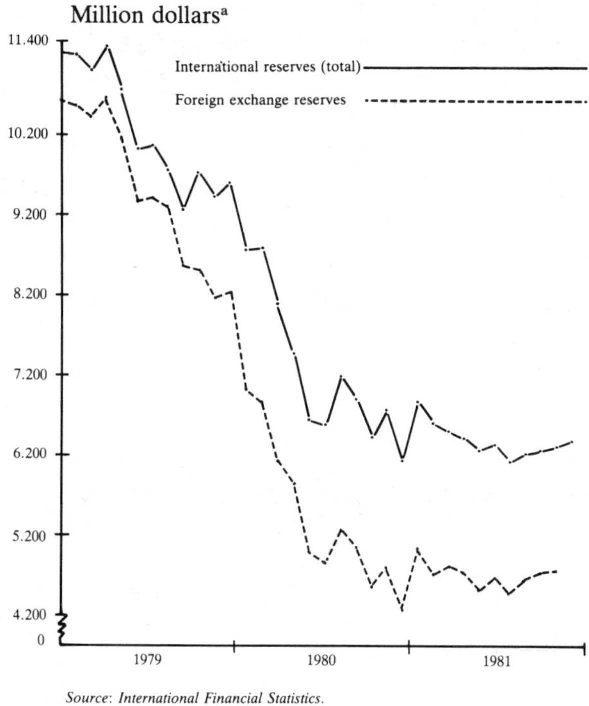

Source: *International Financial Statistics*.
a. End-of-period balances.

rates and canceling the prefixation of monetary correction and devaluation rates.

1981: Industrial Recession

During the following months, Delfim Netto implemented the tightest monetary policy that the country has experienced since Joaquim Murtinho failed in his utopian attempt at reestablishing the pre-Republican sterling parity at the turn of the century. Correspondingly, Brazil witnessed one of the deepest industrial slumps in its statistically recorded history.

The evolution of real money supply, real ex post interest rates, and industrial output are displayed in Table 14.1 on a quarterly basis for 1979 to 1981. The behavior of interest rates clearly indicates the alternating pattern of Delfim Netto's monetary policies: very loose from mid-1979 to late 1980, followed by extreme tightness until the

TABLE 14.1 BRAZIL: MONEY, INTEREST, AND INDUSTRIAL PRODUCTION, 1979–81
(quarterly averages)

Year and quarter		Real money supply (1978 = 100) (1)	Real ex post annual interest rates: 3-month government bills (annual percentage) (2)	Real ex post annual interest rates: 6-month consumer credit (annual percentage) (3)	Industrial production (1978 = 100) (4)
1979	I	100.0	− 6.8	11.5	100.0
	II	98.4	−16.6	− 5.4	106.9
	III	97.3	−35.6	−14.9	111.2
	IV	98.1	−36.9	−13.5	110.9
1980	I	89.8	−41.7	−20.4	107.9
	II	89.8	−47.7	−21.7	111.8
	III	79.4	−39.1	−14.1	122.6
	IV	77.0	−26.9	6.6	117.8
1981	I	65.5	−18.1	43.7	106.0
	II	62.1	0.7	46.6	104.4
	III	59.9	1.5	52.6	106.4
	IV	65.8	2.0	n.a.	99.2

n.a. Not available.
Note: Column (1): quarterly averages of M1 deflated by the wholesale price index of *Conjuntura Econômica* (column 2). Column (2): obtained as quarterly averages of $[(1 + i_t)/(1 + p_t)]^4 - 1$, where i_t is the three-month interest rate on LTNs auctioned in the primary market at month t and $p_t = P_{t+3}/P_t$, where P_t is the wholesale price index for month t. The interest rate on LTNs is calculated from the discount rates, d_t, published by the central bank according to the formula $i_t = [1/(1 - 0.25d_t)]$. Column (3): quarterly average of $[(1 + i_t^*)/(1 + p_t^*)]^2 - 1$, where i_t^* is the six-month lending interest rate of São Paulo finance companies at month t, and $p_t^* = P_{t+6} + 6/P_t$, where P_t is the wholesale price index for month t. Column (4): "general indicator" of industrial production from the Brazilian Institute of Geography and Statistics (IBGE).

end of 1981. The differences between 1980 and 1981 in real interest rates on consumer credit are astonishing, although the rates for 1980 may understate true costs for the borrower, as controls prevailed and thus the rate reported to the central bank may have been biased downward. The magnitude of policy reversal is indicated by the behavior of real interest rates on three-month government bills. From a negative 40 percent in the first half of 1980, they rose steadily to become positive in the second half of 1981.

The real money stock, which was kept constant during 1979, was already falling in the first half of 1980. But this did not affect short-term interest rates, as inflation acceleration certainly reduced real money demand. The liquidity crunch picked up toward the end of 1980 to acquire unheard-of proportions halfway through 1981. At the

TABLE 14.2 BRAZIL: INFLATION RATE INDEXES, 1979–81

Year and quarter		Wholesale prices (overall index)	Aggregate supply Industry	Aggregate supply Agriculture
1979	I	44.5	43.0	47.4
	II	46.9	47.0	46.3
	III	56.0	56.8	54.0
	IV	72.1	71.5	73.3
1980	I	86.5	84.1	91.3
	II	99.0	98.8	98.3
	III	113	112	115
	IV	119	113	134
1981	I	122	118	132
	II	121	117	130
	III	106	108	101
	IV	94.0	102	77.0

Note: yearly rates: quarter of present year over same quarter of previous year. These indexes are derived from columns 3, 17, and 26, respectively, of *Conjunctura Econômica*, various issues.

height of the crunch, in the second quarter of 1981, the money stock in real terms was made nearly 30 percent lower than a year before. The response of industrial production to such powerful money contraction, and accompanying sky-high interest rates, is shown in the last column of the table. Yearly industrial growth rates, already null in the beginning of 1981, became increasingly negative during the year. The last recorded figure, for the last quarter of 1981, showed a value 16 percent lower than in the previous year.[9]

On a 12-month basis, inflation rates peaked in the first quarter of 1981 and then started to decline, as shown in Table 14.2. A two-way decomposition of the aggregate index indicates that inflation reduction was associated with a significant deterioration of the agricultural terms of trade; in the last quarter of 1981, industrial price inflation was only 10 percent lower than in the corresponding period of 1980. Ironically, Delfim Netto obtained the inflation deceleration that he

[9] An ongoing revision of industrial statistics suggests that the above figures may exaggerate the extent of the industrial slump in 1981. On the basis of the data in Table 14.1, the Brazilian national accounts reported initially that industrial output had fallen by 8.4 percent between 1980 and 1981. In a recent revision, this negative change was reduced to 5.4 percent. *Cf. Conjuntura Econômica* 36, no. 5 (May 1982).

had hoped for through the "super-harvests" that he had planned—but one year too late to justify his heterodoxies.[10]

The resilience of industrial price dynamics, in face of such a deep reduction in real aggregate demand, testifies to the rigidity of markup pricing rules in modern Brazilian industrial structures.[11]

This inflexibility is compounded in the Brazilian case by a mandatory wage readjustment scheme at fixed intervals, which is now entirely dependent on past, not future, inflation. Additionally, according to some calculations, the redistributive principle built into the 1979-80 wage policy implies that the average wage readjustment is mildly over 100 percent of past cost-of-living increases.[12]

If the impact of tight money on industrial wage and price dynamics was tenuous, its effect on the balance of payments was much clearer. In 1981 the import quantum was 13 percent lower than in the previous year, whereas the export quantum was 20 percent higher. Thus, in spite of a 15 percent terms of trade loss, the trade balance turned from a negative $2.8 billion in 1980 to a positive $1.2 billion in 1981. Higher domestic interest rates also induced the private sector to go abroad for funds, thus lessening the burden on the public sector to generate through its state enterprises the financial inflows required to cover the current account deficit.

This confirms that a recession at least temporarily improves the trade balance; but the question remains whether such improvement can be maintained once the economy recovers. For a primary exporting country, the traditional structuralist answer is in the negative. But for a semi-industrialized country like Brazil, it may be that the unused capacity generated by lack of domestic demand under pressure can be made suitable for import substitution and/or export expansion. In this case, a temporary recession may permanently improve the

[10] According to the national accounts, the growth rate of agriculture was 6.3 percent in 1980 and 6.8 percent in 1981.

[11] For alternative tests of the hypothesis of markup pricing in Brazilian manufacturing, see A. Lara-Resende and F. Lopes, "Sobre as causas da recente aceleração inflacionária," and C. Considera, "Preços, mark-up e distribuição funcional da renda na indústria de transformação," both in *Pesquisa e Planejamento Econômico* 11, no. 3 (December 1981).

[12] See A. Baumgarten, Jr., "A aritmética perversa da política salarial," *Revista Brasileira de Economia* 35, no. 4 (October-December 1981).

balance of payments. Empirical evidence for this optimistic hypothesis is scanty.[13]

Two Views on Stabilization Policies

We proceed to evaluate Delfim Netto's decision not to go to the IMF and whether this was sensible. As a starting point, a short statement needs to be made to distinguish in a necessarily stereotyped fashion between two visions of stabilization policies in a semiclosed economy like Brazil. For brevity, one is identified as "neoclassical" and the other as "heterodox."

Neoclassical orthodoxy on stabilization policies asserts that: (1) inflation and current account deficits are symptoms of excess domestic demand over full-employment output; (2) over the medium haul, a contraction of domestic demand does not affect the level of real output; and (3) with adaptative expectations and short-term rigidities in the price mechanism, it is inevitable that a contraction of domestic demand will temporarily reduce the level of employment. Within the orthodox field, "Keynesians" see gradualism in demand contraction as the best way to deal with the last set of problems, whereas "monetarists," on a number of grounds, still prefer a shock treatment type of stabilization package. Both camps, however, tend to view the reluctance of domestic residents (who previously enjoyed excess absorption) to live within their means as the basic political difficulty faced by a stabilization program.

At least in Brazil, heterodoxy would diverge on three counts: (1) full employment is not the natural state of the economy, but a consequence of the level of aggregate demand; (2) imports are mostly complementary to domestic production, and the growth of exports is limited by price-inelastic foreign demand, not so much by the pressure of domestic demand on capacity; and (3) Brazilian inflation is mostly inertial—the result of markup pricing and wage reaction functions—and it fluctuates mainly according to the direction and intensity of the supply shocks experienced by the economy. According to this view, a contraction of domestic demand affects mostly the level of employment, and thus the current account as it reduces complementary imports, but it does not directly change the rhythm of inflation

[13] For a theoretical discussion, see E. Bacha, "Growth with Limited Supplies of Foreign Exchange: A Reappraisal of the Two-Gap Model," in M. Syrquin, L. Taylor, and L. Westphal, eds., *Economic Structure and Performance* (New York: Academic Press, forthcoming).

or improve the current account at a full employment level. This view implies that money should be passive during a stabilization program, with its rate of growth declining *pari passu* with, but never anticipating, the reduction of inflation. The active stabilization policies supported by the heterodox are necessarily more structurally oriented and state-interventionist than the neoclassical accept. To make the full employment trade balance more sensitive to domestic demand controls, domestic production and exports need to be made more similar to foreign supplies, and this presumes both maintenance of investment and a movement toward industrial diversification. Inflation reduction can be achieved by productivity increases or by income policies, the specification of which would vary according to the political milieu.

Delfim-I: IMF Would Be Better?

The evidence is abundant that Delfim Netto's conception of stabilization policies is much closer to heterodoxy, as previously defined, than to neoclassical orthodoxy.[14] IMF thinking, on the other hand, even under its recent conversion to gradualism, clearly classifies as orthodox.[15]

In the case at hand, however, it can be argued that an early intervention of the Fund might have avoided the policy blunders that Delfim Netto committed in 1979–80, and thus prevented a foreign exchange shortage from occurring in mid-1980. Delfim Netto entered the Planning Ministry with an apparent carte-blanche from the military establishment and the Brazilian entrepreneurial elite. But in fact he had to do something not only different from Simonsen, but spectacular too. He then made the regrettable choices of rigidly controlling interest rates, maxidevaluing in November 1979, and unrealis-

[14] See, for example, his critique of the Campos-Bulhões 1966 stabilization measures in "*Análise do Comportamento da Economia Brasileira*," mimeographed (Rio de Janeiro: Joint Advisory Group to the Ministries of Finance and Planning, 1967); partly reproduced as an appendix to Ministério do Planejamento, *Diretrizes do Governo, Programa Estratégico de Desenvolvimento* (Rio de Janeiro: Departamento de Imprensa Nacional, 1967).

[15] As a recent paper by Crockett makes clear, when the IMF staff worries about the supply side, their concern is with getting the prices right and promoting savings. This is not necessarily bad, but has little to do with the problems with which the heterodox are concerned. *Cf.* A. D. Crockett, "Stabilization Policies in Developing Countries: Some Policy Considerations," IMF *Staff Papers* 28, no. 1 (March 1981):54–79.

tically prefixing the monetary correction factor and the devaluation rate for 1980.

The IMF presence might have forced Delfim Netto to be more modest in his policy objectives, maintaining the economy in slow gear as export promotion efforts progressed and import substitution projects matured. He then might not have embarked on a selective price control program at a time when most other prices were getting out of hand. This, plus the IMF "seal of approval," might have preserved foreign bankers' confidence, even as inflation inevitably accelerated and the current account deteriorated in 1980. A foreign exchange shortage might not have occurred, and consequently the shock treatment implemented in 1981 might not have been necessary.

But this is just a daydream. First, because no one in Brazil was pressing (or even suggesting) Delfim Netto to go to the Fund when he entered the Planning Ministry in August 1979. In fact, except for the financial sector, everyone that counted in the country was quite happy to see Simonsen's policies knocked out by Delfim. Second, because the odds are that the Fund would not have approved the adoption of a passive monetary policy in 1979–80, and this was required to accommodate the underlying inflationary pressures without provoking an earlier recession. Most likely the Fund would have wanted to see Simonsen's monetary control policies put into effect as a precondition for a loan application. And this would only have brought forward to 1979–80 the economic crisis of 1981. The loss of production might have been less, but, politically, a voluntarily adopted contractionary policy would have been interpreted as a right-wing reaction against the new wage policy. This undoubtedly would have jeopardized a pacific transition toward a more democratic order in Brazil. Delfim Netto's contractionary policies are not similarly stigmatized, apparently because the body politic interprets them as being adopted out of necessity rather than as an act of choice.

Delfim-II: A Scenario for the IMF

These considerations relate to policy decisions taken from mid-1979 to early-1980. A different picture emerges when late-1980 policies are considered. The country then was about to face a foreign exchange crisis and international bankers were pressing the government to go to the Fund. It was Delfim Netto's decision not to do this that needs an evaluation.

Adopting the Guitián-Williamson standards of measurement approach for assessing policy measures and results,[16] we need to imagine what actions would have taken place as a result of a Fund-supported adjustment program. According to informed sources, the IMF board was quite happy with the monetary policies adopted by Delfim Netto in 1981, considering that this was exactly what the country needed. There is no question of their judging monetary stringency in 1981 to be excessive. However, the Fund would apparently have liked stiffer fiscal policies implemented, particularly concerning the subsidized credit programs. Additionally, the new wage policy is considered to be an impediment to inflation abatement and it is likely, for example, that the IMF staff would have pressed for a reduction of the wage readjustment currently benefiting lower salaries, from 110 percent to 100 percent of past inflation.

The fiscal deficit and wage policy are two complicated and sensitive issues with which the government is unlikely to deal before the November 1982 elections. In order to simplify the alternative scenario, perhaps unrealistically we will assume that the Fund would have accepted a postponement of these two problems, and would have accepted Brazil's loan application on the basis of the stabilization policies actually implemented in 1981.

The unemployment and output losses would then be the same. The balance of payments on current account, however, might have been favorably affected: first, because the interest charges on Fund loans are lower than market rates; and second, because spreads on Eurodollar loans to Brazil might have been less than the country is currently paying. It is hard to know how much less, but a start can be made in this direction by calculating how much higher the Eurodollar spreads on Brazilian loans became between 1979–80 and 1981. According to the central bank, in 1981 the average spread on syndicated loans to Brazilian state enterprises was 2⅛ percent over London interbank offered rate (Libor) or 2.0 percent over US prime, with a flat fee of 1½.[17] At the end of 1979, *Euromoney* reported that Brazil was paying a spread of ⅝ percent over Libor with a flat fee

[16] See M. Guitián, *Fund Conditionality: Evolution of Principles and Practices* (Washington: International Monetary Fund 1981); and J. Williamson, Chapter 7, this volume.

[17] Banco Central do Brasil, *Informativo Mensal,* 2, no. 18 (January 1982), p. 12.

of 11/16 percent.[18] By mid-1980, according to this source, spreads had risen to 1½ percent over Libor plus a front-end fee of 1⅛ percent.

We will assume the following: (1) the spread increases from 1979 to 1980 would have occurred with or without the Fund presence, as a result of inflation acceleration and balance of payments deterioration; (2) the spreads of 1980 would have been kept constant in 1981 if Brazil had gone to the IMF as bankers wanted; and (3) the rate differentials quoted above for syndicated loans apply to all Brazilian deals in the Eurodollar market.

Two important qualifications due to Batista, Jr., need to be added before figures are presented.[19] First, it was only in 1981 that the US prime rate started to appear frequently as an optional reference rate for banks to charge their spreads on Brazilian loans. During that year, the US prime (Citibank) on average was 2⅛ percentage points above Libor.[20] Second, in some recent deals, Brazilian state enterprises have accepted the payment of interest charges on a quarterly basis, rather than on a semiannual basis as before. With annual interest rates in the neighborhood of 20 percent, this practice increases the yearly spread by about 1 percentage point.

Ignoring these two qualifications, in 1981 Brazil would have paid spreads over Libor ⅝ percentage points higher than in 1980. When they are taken into account, the difference rises to 3⅝ percentage points. Unfortunately these cost estimates are far apart, but we are unable to tell how much of the gap between them is due to an effective increase of the "Brazil risk" or to a general worsening of credit conditions in the Euromarkets in 1981. For lack of more precise information, we will consider the shift to three-month compounding of interest as a reflection of a general worsening of credit conditions in 1981, and will take one-half of the difference between Libor and prime as reflecting an increase of the "Brazil risk." This means taking the value of 1 11/16 (percentage points per year) as our estimate of the

[18] *Cf.* P. Field and S. Downer, *op. cit.*, pp. 91–92.

[19] *Cf.* Paulo Nogueira Batista, Jr., "O custo financeiro da dívida externa em 1981"; processed (Rio de Janeiro: Centro de Estudos Monetários e de Economia Internacional, Fundação Getúlio Vargas, September 1981).

[20] For lack of information, we ignore the problem posed by the fact that Libor seems to be charged at its value at the beginning of the period, whereas the prime tends to be computed at its value at the end of the period (with the relevant period varying from three to six months, depending on the credit contract).

spread improvement that would have taken place had Brazil gone to the Fund in 1981.[21]

On a balance of payments basis, Brazil contracted $16.7 billion in the Euromarkets last year. The size of Brazil's quota and the recent Indian deal suggest that $1.5 billion could have been borrowed from the Fund at an interest rate of 12 percent a year, or 7 percentage points less than the market rate.[22] The remaining $15.2 billion would have cost Brazil 1¹¹⁄₁₆ percentage points less in spreads. Savings on the IMF loan would amount to $105 million, and on market loans to $256 million—adding up to a difference of $361 million in total interest costs.

This represents only 1.7 percent of Brazilian exports in 1981, but one needs to take into account that economic activity in the country clearly was constrained by the supply of foreign exchange. This means that the marginal social value of one dollar was much higher than its market value. How much higher is anybody's guess, but a rough idea can be obtained as follows. Consider the expression:

$$B = NX(Y) + F,$$

where B is the balance of payments; Y is national income; NX is the trade balance; and F stands for all other autonomous international transactions. If B is constrained to be equal to zero, then:

$$\left.\frac{dY}{dF}\right|_{B = 0} = 1/n,$$

where n is the marginal propensity to import minus the "marginal propensity to export" (presumably, a nonpositive value). Now, n is considerably lower than unity, in fact, it is difficult to imagine it to have a value higher than ¼ in Brazil. Hence, we need to multiply the $361 million by a factor of 4 to get a figure comparable to Brazilian national income, which was about $250 billion in 1981. The conclusion is that the savings in interest charges would have been worth something like ½ percent of Brazil's GNP in 1981. This balance of payments gain has to be weighted against its cost for the government, i.e., the loss of flexibility in changing economic policies at will during

[21] This figure should be multiplied by the ratio 1.0150/1.0125 = 1.002 to reflect the deterioration in flat fee charges between 1980 (when that fee was 1⅛) and 1981 (flat fee equal to 1½). Due to our rounding procedures, this correction does not show up in the results.

[22] The market rate is calculated as the sum:
16⅝ (average value of Libor in 1981) + 2⅛ (nominal spread over Libor) = 18¾ × 1.015 (correction for the flat fee of 1½) = 19.

a three-year period. From a heterodox point of view, this may be deemed a real cost, as the Fund would want to keep monetary stringency far longer than Delfim Netto, because for him the 1981 monetary package is an emergency measure, whereas the IMF would want to implement it on the belief that this was the best policy course for the country to take. The nature of the impasse is previewed by the current debate on "excessive" monetary expansion in the first quarter of 1982. This debate will become hotter as the November elections approach. It is certainly to the benefit of all concerned that the IMF is not openly involved in this particular imbroglio.

Things may change after the election, if—following the example of Spain—the government negotiates a Moncloa Pact with the opposition. Terms could then be worked out to ensure that the 1964–74 wage crunch would not be repeated. In this case, labor leaders might be willing to accept changes in the new wage policy leading to disinflation.[23] A political compromise regarding the degree of public sector intervention in the economy also needs to be worked out, providing adequate financing for government expenditures. Brazilians would then have to make up their minds whether they want to face the Herculean task of convincing the Fund that a passive monetary and credit policy is a necessary ingredient of a correct stabilization policy for their country.

[23] The endogenization of the wage settlement period, making it dependent on the accumulated rate of inflation, is a politically attractive alternative, since it is part of the economic program of the main opposition party. For a theoretical analysis, see Persio Arida, "Reajuste salarial e inflação: uma sugestão de política econômica," *Pesquisa e Planejamento Econômico* 12, no. 2 (August 1982).

COMMENTS, CHAPTERS 11–14

Carlos F. Diaz-Alejandro

Two strands are running through our discussions that should be kept distinct. One refers to the "correct" macroeconomics one should use when giving policy advice to different species of economies. Another is the proper role for the International Monetary Fund (IMF),and the optimum conditionality for its lending. Perhaps the following mental experiment will help to delineate the two strands: Would one's view of the proper role for the Fund change depending on whether its managing director were Arnold Harberger or Lance Taylor? Mine would not. Others may prefer a more or less interventionist (paternalistic) IMF depending on whether they like the prevailing macroeconomics at that institution. So before commenting briefly on the Western Hemisphere papers, I would like to discuss possible Fund roles and argue for a modest one that would be, on the whole, independent of fashions in macroeconomics.

The purposes of the IMF could include:

- overseer of international macroeconomic stability, warning countries of threats of slump and inflation, of excessive or insufficient national and international liquidity, and engaging in countercyclical lending
- promoter of trade liberalization
- overseer of international financial markets, a role that could be limited to encouraging freer capital flows and harmonizing central bank regulations over them, or extended to the "planning," jointly with private and public banks, of international capital movements
- supplier of short-term credit, at financial charges more favorable than going market rates, to countries with temporary balance of payments difficulties
- dispenser of advice on banking organization, central bank regulation, debt management, and other economic policies;
- overseer of exchange rates.

Both international economic conditions and the "clients" of the Fund have changed considerably since the 1940s, influencing both the demand for and supply of its services. The international capital market of the 1970s and 1980s, to give the most dramatic example of changed circumstances, has provided an environment not contemplated by those meeting at Bretton Woods in 1944. It is a safe bet that the name Zaire meant nothing to at least 90 percent of those delegates.

A first group of today's IMF members, more patrons than clients, include the economically healthier industrial countries, such as France, Germany, Japan, and the United States. These and other industrialized countries have a number of favorite fora preempting possible Fund roles listed above. Thus, the Organization for Economic Cooperation and Development, summit meetings, and other ad hoc arrangements, excluding Third World and socialist countries, handle the major tasks listed under the first item. The more international General Agreement of Tariffs and Trade (GATT) is in charge of the second item, and one has to strain to argue that this item should be a major responsibility of the IMF. The founding fathers of the Fund did perceive that international financial turbulence contributed to the decline of international trade during the 1930s, so the maintenance of financial and exchange rate orderliness was deemed to promote trade liberalization. But to argue that Keynes, White, et al. charged the IMF with the task of seeking free trade is silly. There are many things wrong with the GATT today, but they will not be corrected by making the IMF its militant vanguard.

The Bank for International Settlements handles for the industrialized countries the more modest tasks listed under the third item. The stronger industrialized countries do not see themselves on the demand side for possible Fund services listed under the fourth and fifth items, leaving the last item as their major interest for an IMF presence, beyond their creditor interest in the more ambitious tasks listed under item three.

The economically weaker industrial democracies remain potential clients for IMF services listed under the fourth and fifth items. Their use of the Fund as not just a provider of short-term credit, but also as a specialized consultant is due not to their lack of technical expertise, but to the hope that an outside consultant may play a catalytic role in reaching a consensus among conflicting domestic groups. Apparently the IMF has been successful in playing this role in countries such as Italy and Britain, suggesting that for the catalyst to work one needs a home-country chemistry involving a good deal of free discussion and open political debate, removing the mists of suspicion around the presence of an outside consultant (a point suggested to me by Winston Fritsch). If this conjecture is correct, the IMF catalytic role could also be useful for another rather small group of clients, i.e., less developed countries (LDCs) with relatively open political systems. Costa Rica and India come to mind in this context.

Semi-industrialized countries whose past relations with the Fund have been sticky, and who may be attempting a transition toward a more open polity under authoritarian tutelage, are unlikely to want the IMF's services under either the fourth or the fifth category. As policy autonomy for those countries is enhanced by an unregulated international capital market, they will be suspicious of a possible Fund role as described by the third item. Brazil is the archetype of such reluctant clients.

Under the circumstances of the 1980s, and given past history, the steadiest and largest group of Fund clients for services under the fourth, fifth, and sixth items is likely to be drawn from the economically weakest and most authoritarian developing countries. Little wonder, then, that during 1979–80 efforts were made by the Fund to broaden its appeal to other types of potential clients, such as India.

Finally, among the list of potential clients, one has Organization of Petroleum Exporting Countries nations with persistent surpluses, and some socialist countries. The former, together with other major creditors, have an interest in services under the third item and also under the last. The latter appear to view IMF membership mainly as a stepping-stone toward World Bank membership and also, in ironic contrast with much of the Third World, as a symbol of independence.

The Fund is a supplier of short-term credit at financial charges more favorable than those of loans available from private lenders, who are concerned about sovereign and other risks relevant for private agents. In distributing the limited pool of such credit, it is allocating real resources from the rest of the world. This provides the fundamental justification for some form of nonprice rationing, and therefore conditionality. The international community represented by the IMF has the right to expect when the loan is made that the chances of repayment on time are high. In general equilibrium, everything depends on everything else, but how much do prices for public utilities, food subsidies, or agricultural credit have to do with expected balance of payments deficits or surpluses? It is the expected balance of payments situation that will determine the chance of repayment of the IMF loan, and balance of payments targets may be achieved using a large number of instruments, which one may regard as more or less efficacious or efficient. It is the business of the Fund to insist on balance of payments targets consistent with loan repayments, to closely monitor performance in this area, and to suspend credit to countries that do not repay promptly without good reason, such as unexpected exogenous shocks. It is *not* the business of the IMF to make loans conditional on policies whose connection to the balance of payments in the short or even medium run is tenuous. It was a brilliant administrative stroke for the IMF staff to develop "the monetary approach to the balance of payments" during the 1950s, allowing the translation of balance of payments targets into those involving domestic credit, but the assumptions needed for such a translation cannot be sustained for all countries at all times.

Given the present lack of consensus on "correct" macroeconomics, not just among academics but also among major Fund patrons (contrast macroeconomic policy in France and the United States), the case for IMF conditionality focused narrowly on balance of payments targets is strengthened. It is true that observed performance in the balance of payments is the result both of domestic policies and factors beyond the country's control. Yet a number of indicators, such as staple prices and market shares, could be used to evaluate performance and failures to meet agreed targets. Note that the compensatory facilities of the IMF have accumulated experience in this area.

Focusing on balance of payments targets would remove IMF conditionality from the more political aspects of short-run macroeconomic policy making. Countries that feel that they want to use Fund services under the fifth item could of course request such help, and under those circumstances the IMF staff could give full expression to its views on inflation, optimal trade regulations, food subsidies, and the like. If the Fund were to adopt this modest role, the composition of its active clientele might change over time, and the numbers might decline, but only those with a bureaucratic vested interest will want to argue that work must be found to maintain full employment at the IMF.

What about the more ambitious role listed under the third item? Is not the Fund a natural overseer of international capital markets full of imperfections and prone to instability? Those of us skeptical of the accuracy and fruitfulness of conceptualizing international markets of any kind as pure and perfect have no trouble admitting that financial markets are far from textbook ideals, and cannot help but to be amused that, nearly 10 years after the first call for a New International Economic Order, so many northern observers are discovering imperfections and dilemmas in international financial markets, some arguing that banks lend too little and others that banks lend too much. Both, of course, could be right for different countries and at different times, perhaps in a cyclical pattern. But let us remind newcomers of an old neoclassical point: in the process of correcting one imperfection, there is the danger that we may introduce a bigger one. To make the IMF a kind of central committee of an international credit cartel would be a remedy worse than the disease, at least from the viewpoint of many LDCs and perhaps from a more cosmopolitan viewpoint. (This complex matter is discussed in more detail by Edmar Bacha and myself in *International Financial Intermediation: A Long and Tropical View,* Princeton Essays in International Finance no. 147, May 1982).

Given my viewpoint on the proper IMF role, not to mention space limitations, my comments on the papers on Argentina, Brazil, Chile, Jamaica and Peru will focus on points related to the previous discussion. Marshall, Mardones, and Marshall, in their thorough paper (Chapter 13), trace the decline of IMF influence in Argentina, Brazil and Chile, from the 1950s to the present. The expansion of international capital markets plus import substitution of economists contributed to such a trend. Whether one likes their brand of macroeconomics or not, it would be difficult to argue that the technocrats in those three countries have much to learn from the Fund staff regarding how to run their own economies. Under the often paranoid political circumstances of those countries, the catalytic role played by the IMF in Italy and the United Kingdom is unlikely to be reproduced; rather, the Fund's presence is bound to acquire, whether unfairly or not, mysterious and somewhat sinister overtones. Chapter 13 also reminds us how much and how often views on optimum exchange rate policy have changed, both inside and outside the Fund. Fixed exchange rates, come hell or high water, were associated with structuralists in the 1950s, who argued that "devaluation does not work and is simply inflationary." Similar conclusions have been preached by the Chilean authorities during 1979–82, and it would be interesting to know the Fund's position on this matter. Someday, if IMF archives are opened to researchers, it would also be interesting to trace the evolution from support of fixed rates, with periodic large and abrupt devaluations, to tolerance of crawling pegs. From research on the Colombian experience, my impression is that the Fund staff was unsympathetic to crawling pegs in the late 1950s and early 1960s, regarding sporadic and massive devaluations of fixed pegs as the only method of exchange rate adjustment compatible with the IMF Articles.

Bacha carefully estimates the high price the Brazilian authorities are paying to keep the Fund at arms' length (Chapter 14). One imagines that the gifted technocrats in Brasilia must have done similar calculations; the resulting high cost is not a measure of their irrationality, but an appalling indictment of the Fund's record over the past 35 years in dealing with Brazil. The Fund during 1979–80 seemed to be on the way toward a more sensible approach to conditionality. Had those trends continued, a Brazilian use of Fund resources over the next few years could have been foreseen, perhaps after a more open political situation developed allowing a freer discussion of economic alternatives within Brazil. The outlook, after all, is for Brazilian macroeconomic policies that are fairly austere. But during 1981 the Fund had second thoughts regarding the flexibility promised during 1979–80; just like the Supreme Court and the Federal Reserve of the United States, the IMF may not be totally insensitive to election results. While Brazilian borrowing now appears less likely, perhaps Bacha could extend his calculations to different scenarios with longer horizons, some involving eventual Brazilian use of Fund credit. Another topic for further research is the determinants of the "spread" charged to Brazil: how much do Brazilian macroeconomic policies influence it, independently of the Fund's explicit "seal of approval"? During 1981 and early 1982, the "spreads" have been singularly unresponsive to the new Brazilian austerity, signaling, perhaps, a lack of credibility.

Peruvian generals were as reluctant as those in Brazil to submit to the Fund's conditionality until private credit dried up. In a curious contrast with Southern Cone experience of the 1970s, the incompetence of military governments in macroeconomic management eventually led to a civilian administration. Diz (Chapter 12) emphasizes the difficulties in evaluating the post-1977 stabilization plans; more discussion of the exogenous shocks suffered by the Peruvian economy during the 1970s should help to delineate the role of policy in aggravating or improving economic conditions both before and after 1977.

Finally, the Jamaican paper (Chapter 11) documents a case where the Fund appears to have been more flexible than usual in its dealings with a populist government, although it remains unclear the extent to which this was due to the then prevailing political winds in the United Kingdom, Europe, and the United States. But for someone used to Ibero-American circumstances, the most intriguing aspect of the Jamaican story is the dog that did not bark. Suffering from crippling external shocks and, apparently, from gross macroeconomic mismanagement, Jamaicans settled their differences at the ballot box. Where were the Jamaican generals?

CHAPTER **15**

Political-Economic Adjustment And IMF Conditionality: Tanzania, 1974–81

Reginald Herbold Green

A man who has inherited a tumbledown cottage has to live in even worse conditions while he is rebuilding it and making a decent house for himself.

—President Julius Nyerere

But it is surely better to make relevant but subjective comparisons rather than objective but fundamentally irrelevant comparisons.

—John Williamson

Mistakes are mistakes.

—President Julius Nyerere

Situation, Goals, Performance: An Introductory Sketch

Tanzania is a very large territory in respect to geographic size, a moderate-size polity in respect to population (approaching 19 million

Note: Dr. Green is a professorial fellow of the Institute of Development Studies at the University of Sussex. He was associated with two studies on the adjustment process carried out by the United Nations Conference on Trade and Development for the Group of 24 and with the 1980 Arusha Conference on the International Monetary System. Over 1966–74 he was economic advisor to the Tanzanian Treasury and since 1980 has been part-time advisor to the Tanzanian treasury, central bank, and ministry of planning. The views expressed and suggestions made are his personal responsibility and are not necessarily those of any Tanzanian institution. While he has been involved in past Tanzanian negotiations with the International Monetary Fund (IMF) and the 1981 Bank of Tanzania Exchange Rate Study, this paper does not use information considered confidential by Tanzania.

in 1980), and a very poor economy (about $250 per capita and $4 billion overall at the official exchange rate in 1979).[1] It is one of the "least developed economies," albeit at the upper end of that range, with the manufacturing sector contributing about 10 percent of GDP and adult literacy near 70 percent. In 1974 it was "ranked" third in the list of "most severely affected" economies, and over 1979–81 was buffeted by exogenous shocks of greater aggregate magnitude than those of 1973–74. In the earlier case, the shocks were primarily related to bad weather drastically affecting food import requirements, but also to oil price increases, rapid growth in other import prices, and a halt to increases in real per capita aid.[2] In the past few years, the major shocks were the 1979–80 oil price increases, the 1978 invasion of Tanzania by Idi Amin and the consequential liberation war in Uganda and its aftermath,[3] poor weather in 1979–81 (exacerbated by disastrously bad storage of 1976–78 food crop surpluses), and the 1978–81 coffee price collapse.

As of the end of 1981, the economy was characterized by extreme external imbalance (exports of the order of 50 percent of imports, payments arrears of over $300 million, negligible gross foreign ex-

[1] The background to 1974–81 is presented in much greater detail in: B. Mwansasu and C. Pratt, *Towards Socialism in Tanzania* (Toronto and Dar es Salaam: University of Toronto and Tanzania Publishing House, 1979); and R. H. Green, D. Rwegasira, and B. Van Arkadie, *Economic Shocks and National Policy Making: Tanzania in the 1970s*, Institute of Social Studies, Research Report no. 8 (The Hague, 1981). The latter presents a summary, interpretation, and evaluation of 1974–78 adjustment. So, from a different point of view, does R. Liebenthal, *Adjustment in Low-Income Africa, 1974–78*, World Bank Staff Working Paper no. 486, August 1981, pp. 29–39. More recent data and evaluations are drawn from Bank of Tanzania, "Exchange Rate Study, 1981," processed (D. Rwegasira and R. H. Green, eds.) and Bank of Tanzania, "20-Year Political-Economic Review, 1961–81 (in press; title tentative; relevant chapters largely by Van Arkadie, Green, Kamori, Rwegasira, and Mwansasu).

[2] Over 1972–75 up to two-thirds of aid was Chinese (of which over a quarter was de facto balance of payments support), whereas after 1976 this flow was minimal. Development Aid Committee members' and multilateral aid per capita has risen significantly since 1975.

[3] The post-liberation costs total over $250 million, those of the war period over $400 million, plus $100 million adjustment and demobilization costs. Of this, approximately $150 million represents loans in principle recoverable from Uganda, but in practice beyond Uganda's present and foreseeable capacity to repay.

change reserves), rapid inflation (probably in the 30–35 percent range in both 1980 and 1981), substantial recurrent budget deficits (nearly 5 percent of GDP in 1979–80 and perhaps 3.5–4 percent in 1980–81 and 1981–82), and massive underutilization of capacity. The output of the industrial sector was down from an estimated 65–70 percent of capacity in 1977 to, at most, 35 percent in 1981. A backlog of unprocurable, unprocessable, or unshippable exports related to transport and processing bottlenecks was by the end of 1980 in excess of a quarter of actual 1980 visible exports, although 1981 export performance suggests some subsequent improvement.

Political-Economic Goals and Strategic Approaches

Tanzania has had a political-economic strategy with relatively clearly identified goals, instruments, and evolutionary pattern since 1967. It can be presented under four main items: overcoming poverty and approaching equality, economic restructuring, participation and public sector leadership, and growth and balance.

Overcoming poverty and approaching equality comprises:

- increasing productive employment and self-employment, including health, education, and output for one's own consumption, with the emphasis on investment in these sectors and supporting infrastructure (including extension services)
- provision of basic services (notably primary and adult education, basic curative and preventative medicine, pure water) with universality to be achieved within a defined time period (early 1980s for primary education and literacy, and the early 1990s for access to pure water and basic health care)
- reduction of inequalities in wages and salaries through public sector practice, legislation, price management, and fiscal policy with centrally financed regional expenditure substantially less uneven than revenue as well as growth pole policies to combat regional inequalities, and higher producer prices and extension of services to rural areas to reduce urban/rural inequalities
- increasing control over, or reduction of opportunities for, exploitation, for example, by nationalization of rental housing; controls on wages, salaries, and working conditions; creation of workers' and village councils, and investment and surplus use allocation (particularly, but not solely, in respect to the public sector).

Economic restructuring comprises:

- increasing national economic integration through extending the range of goods produced and the sectoral linkages from raw materials through finished products, primarily by public sector investment, acquisition of technology and personnel, and price incentives

- the consequent reduction of the imbalance in domestic production, though with no goal of autarky[4]
- reduction and diversification of external economic dependence, partly by reducing the ratio of imports (of goods, personnel, knowledge, and capital) to GDP, and partly by increasing control over production and external trade by nationalization and creation of new business entities, as well as by foreign exchange budgeting and import price vetting
- seeking to develop effective economic regionalism (through 1976, primarily in the East African Community [EAC] context, since 1979 primarily in that of the Southern African Development Coordination Conference [SADCC][5]) and South-South economic cooperation.

Participation and public sector leadership comprises:

- planned intervention, with annual plans in respect to recurrent and capital budgets, foreign exchange, bank credit, and personpower allocation, and wage, salary and peasant income
- managed markets plus public investment, with substantial decentralization but no serious commitment to material balances planning or physical directives, except in respect to a limited number of scarce resources and/or emergencies[6]
- broadened participation in decision making and implementation focused on village and workers' councils and party and governmental bodies.

Growth and balance (which are in a sense means rather than goals per se) included:

[4] This approach is broadly similar to that of Ragnar Nurkse's "Istanbul Lecture."

[5] For a concise introduction to EAC and SADCC, see *Africa Contemporary Record*, Africana, New York, chapters on EAC (1975–76, 76–77, 77–78) and Southern Africa Economic Cooperation (1978–79, 79–80, 80–81, 81–82) by the author.

[6] Credit and foreign exchange budgeting are intermediate cases; they are clearly not material balances planning, but involve quite selective market management.

• substantial growth of real GDP—in principle[7] at about 6 percent per annum
• expansion of domestic savings toward 20 percent and net external transfers toward 10 percent of GDP to allow an investment ratio of at least 25 percent
• limited inflation (implicitly under 5 percent before 1970 and below the rate of growth of import prices since)
• a goods and services account deficit financeable out of concessional transfers, World Bank loans, and specific project-related finance in normal years, and these plus IMF low-conditionality facilities in external shock years.

Tanzania has pursued these goals by what might be described as a sequential, unbalanced approach. At any one time resource allocation and attention is focused on a limited number of problems (secondary contradictions) believed to be soluble at that time. Subsequently, the effects of this concentration create or make soluble other problems (exacerbate other secondary contradictions?) leading to an alteration of allocations, which over time may lead to a more balanced trend than at any particular moment.

This approach places emphasis on pushing the possibility frontier outward (structural change). In principle (and, less evenly, also in practice) it is paralleled by concentration on approaching closer to the attainable frontier (microefficiency via incremental change) in areas in which structural changes have been achieved. On occasion the two overlap; for example, the 1980–81 emphasis on restoring rationality among agricultural prices, raising them at least as rapidly as the cost of living (and, therefore, relative to wages and salaries), was a macro or structural priority, but also a microefficiency one.

In practice this approach has led to sustained lacunae in respect to two critical areas not subject to handling by secondary allocations on an incremental basis, nor particularly suitable for once for all structural shifts: development of export earnings and of basic food storage capacity. These gaps have had, and continue to have, disastrous consequences, even though the former (though not, to date, the latter) has become an identified priority area.

Tanzania has overtly denied that in its context there is any clear evidence of a trade-off between growth and equality (at least within the range of policies actually pursued), but also indicated that, subject

[7] Target rates have usually been about 6.5 percent, and achieved rates 4–6 percent, which is considered dangerously low.

to a growth performance adequate to sustain the strategy, some loss in growth would be acceptable. When the option has existed,[8] trade-offs between consumption and investment have tended to be biased heavily toward the latter, subject to attempts to maintain the real minimum wage and peasant incomes. In principle (and until 1977–78, in practice) a relatively austere view was taken in respect to restraining inflation.[9]

Performance

Performance has been marked by a definite periodicity: 1967–69 was relatively favorable; 1970–72 was marked by an endogenously generated (and reversed) bank credit–external reserve crisis; 1973 was again relatively favorable; 1974–76 was characterized by a major set of shocks and their overcoming; 1977–79 was marked by a more lax policy than before or since, and a sharp deterioration of the underlying position; while 1980–81 has been a period of crises.

Productive employment, including self-employment, has grown about as rapidly as population—wage employment distinctly faster. Unemployment[10] remained relatively low (8–10 percent urban). Until 1974 real incomes of wage earners rose, while those of salary earners were probably static, with promotions offsetting the inflationary erosion of basically static scales. Thereafter, real wages fell—sharply until 1980 and 1981, but relatively little in these years. Real salaries fell sharply, with the rate slowed but not halted by a 20 percent salary increase in 1981.

Peasant household real incomes (on average about two-thirds those of minimum wage households) have fluctuated sharply with weather, real producer prices (which have fluctuated with no trend from 1967, and in 1980 were 5 percent above 1975), and crops (with staple foods, on balance, doing better than export and industrial crops). The peak

[8] In the absence of adequate foreign exchange, ex post domestic savings cannot readily exceed one-third of gross investment, because the direct and indirect import content of investment is of the order of two-thirds.

[9] Domestic credit formation targets have been set at or below real output growth projections plus exogenous inflation, and include government bank borrowing.

[10] The landless rural population is very small. Seasonal unemployment associated with rain-fed agriculture is high, although the increased command investment (buildings, public works, small-scale irrigation, afforestation) made possible by villageïsation has reduced it marginally.

was probably in 1977 or 1978, since in 1979–81 strong terms of trade for agriculture have come in relatively poor crop years.[11]

Service provision has improved radically. For example, only 5 percent of the rural population had access to pure water in 1961, against nearly 50 percent in 1981. Primary school enrollment rose from 20 percent to 90 percent, with the biggest gains for rural residents and women (who benefit disproportionately from the approach to universality in education and from improved access to water).

Regional production and service inequalities have been reduced, although partially and unevenly. Some secondary towns' positions have been strengthened, or at least preserved, vis à vis Dar es Salaam. In both respects this represented "evening up" and not "cutting down" until 1980–81 when fiscal and import constraints made "all boats sink lower." The tax incidence seems to be relatively progressive, because basic foods are exempt from sales tax, and amenities relatively highly taxed.

Control of exploitation worked to a degree to 1979, but since then general economic decline has created opportunities for "entrepreneurs of adversity" in housing, goods, and in the extorting bribes for public service provision. Surprisingly, both rent control and price management designed to manage moderate and/or temporary shortages continue to have some impact under conditions for which they were not designed.

On balance, intraurban and urban/rural income distribution has become less unequal since 1967.[12] Intrarural change is less clear. Service distribution has become more equal. However, since 1977 (and since 1974, for the urban population) this has been in the context of falling average real purchasing power, and from 1979–80 of, at best, static per capita real public services.

Economic restructuring has been substantial. Almost all consumer goods used in Tanzania, except cars, light bulbs, and refrigerators, can now be produced there, and the direct import content of the industrial sector is down to 20 percent. Substantial progress has been

[11] Because of a record coffee crop and substantially increased "parallel market" food sales, 1981 rural real incomes might have approached 1977 per capita levels in the absence of growing shortages of urban manufactured goods.

[12] The World Bank (cited in Leibenthal, *Adjustment*) draws gloomier conclusions, but these are open to question. The Bank of Tanzania's *20-Year Review* and a recent Ph.D. thesis by J. Wagao present the case for the position stated here in much greater detail.

made in respect to intermediate goods and contruction materials, and a quite limited but real base exists in capital goods.[13] Similarly, in respect to food imports, dependence has been reduced on the production side, albeit failure to develop storage adequate to serve a 15 percent urban population and to handle reserves to cope with harvest cycles has limited the value of this achievement.

Import dependence for goods (especially investment goods) has not been reduced. Rising proportions of fixed investment (and machinery within it) and of industry, which have higher import ratios than agriculture and nontransport services, combined with negative terms of trade shifts, have meant that all the running Tanzania could do left it in the same macroratio position. Expatriates have declined from 90 percent (4,500) to perhaps 20 percent (4,000) of high level personpower over 1961–81, but remain very high in respect to each novel undertaking or function in its initial years.

External dependence has certainly been diversified—there is no dominant trading partner or source of resource transfers. However, with exports falling from over 100 percent of imports in 1966 to under 45 percent in 1980 (a trend arguably correct to 1973 because an export surplus for a developing country is hardly optimal, but thereafter exacerbated by terms of trade shifts and a continued export decline temporarily masked by the 1976–77 beverage price boom) and still only marginally above 50 percent in 1981, external dependence has clearly increased, and now applies to basic economy operation as well as to fixed investment.

Regional and South-South coordination has progressed erratically. The results and potential are not insignificant, but their size and the time scale meant that they are more relevant to averting or limiting crises in the 1990s than to overcoming the present one.

Planning and managed market intervention has operated with mixed efficiency. Until 1981 its chief macro weakness was a failure to give priority to exports. A reversal in 1980–81 was paralleled by, and in part caused, a volume increase of the order of 20 percent. Micro efficiency has varied both in government and in parastatals, with one (National Milling) a combined Chrysler Penncentral, and two others

[13] For more detail see chapters by M. A. Bienfeld and R. H. Green in M. Fransman, *Industry and Accumulation in Africa*, Heineman, 1982. The low direct import content in consumer goods results in severe problems when import cutbacks are needed: goods availability at retail prices falls $8–9, tax revenue $2–2.50, and domestic value added over $3.50 for each dollar of forced import savings.

(National Bank of Commerce, Tanzania Petroleum Development Cooperation) having profits equal to National Milling's losses—and a claim to efficiency in resource use and service provision under severe handicaps.

Decentralization and participation have had mixed but, on balance, positive macro- and microefficiency results. However, this does not hold for regional and district parastatals, which, unlike villages,[14] present a nearly unbroken vista of financial and physical inefficiency—and as a result have been radically downgraded.

Growth through 1979 averaged just under 5 percent. However, terms of trade deterioration (1961–71, 1973–75, 1977–81) has been very severe, reducing the "real purchasing power" growth to perhaps 4 percent, versus population growth of perhaps 3 percent. From 1977 the terms of trade deterioration, forced reallocation of resources to defense, and abnormal waste of food through inadequate storage have reduced per capita real consumption power perhaps 15 percent (little on public services and housing, about 5 percent on food, around 30 percent on manufactured consumer goods and private services).

Saving, which had approached 20 percent at the beginning of the 1970s, fell sharply over 1974–76, and again after 1977, because ex post only one-third of fixed investment can be financed from domestic sources, and foreign exchange was barely available above "operating inputs" over 1974–76 and 1977–81. Real foreign resource transfers on concessional and quasi-concessional terms approached 10 percent in the early 1970s and over 1979–81, but in a context of crisis and of total foreign exchange availability, it was inadequate to allow maintenance and operation of existing capacity[15] or to prevent a build up of commercial payment arrears. Low-conditionality IMF facilities have been fully utilized.

Except for a deliberate structural adjustment to 1973–74 changes in world oil and grain prices, Tanzanian prices rose by less than import

[14] Village operations relate primarily to investment, marketing, and commerce, with some transport and small-scale manufacturing. Ninety-five to ninety-seven percent of peasant agricultural production is individual, *not* communal, a pattern unlikely to change rapidly, nor one in which radical, rapid change is a public goal.

[15] This suggests a serious overallocation of resources to investment in *new* capacity from 1979 onward—a misallocation supported by rigidities in the use of concessional finance and unwise use of supplier credit over 1979–81 to sustain investment without adequate regard to forward foreign exchange requirements.

prices until 1979. Over 1979–81 the inflation rate skyrocketed from perhaps 8 percent to over 30 percent—still not significantly above the African average, and below that for all developing countries. This resulted directly from inability to utilize existing capacity because of import strangulation.

Tanzania and the IMF

Prior to 1974, Tanzania made no use of Fund facilities.[16] Fund missions' advice was therefore precisely that—indeed it was viewed as advice from a conservative, rather academic research body that might be of use in identifying weaknesses in Tanzanian policy implementation, albeit its political economic ideology posited means that were often unacceptable. Since Tanzania maintained a recurrent budget surplus and—except for a brief period in 1970–72—relatively low rates of growth of domestic credit formation, as well as fairly adequate reserve levels with external debt financed largely by concessional transfers, the IMF missions, while somewhat quizzical, were not sharply critical.

From 1974–75 to 1976–77, Tanzania utilized its special drawing rights (SDRs), "gold tranche," first credit tranche, oil facility and compensatory financing facility drawings and trust fund credits totaling about $75 million, or 7 percent of total external resource transfers over the period (but about 17.5 percent in 1974–75). These were all low-conditionality facilities available on demonstration of a balance of payments need. Substantial exogenous shocks contributed to those pressures. Plausible programs of import compression (including domestic credit expansion [DCE] control) and selective production increases helped restore balance. A 10 percent devaluation in 1975, like earlier ones, was designed to facilitate domestic price adjustments (particularly higher producer prices) and avoid revaluation against major trading partners, rather than as an IMF condition or an attempt to use devaluation to alter the external balance.

Negotiations over 1975–76 toward a second credit tranche drawing petered out early in 1977, when the impact of the beverage boom

[16] The earlier programs are discussed in Green, Rwegasira, and Van Arkadie, *Economic Shocks*, and those through 1980 in the balance of payments and international economic relations chapters of Bank of Tanzania, *20-Year Review*. An earlier discussion of the 1979 and 1980 negotiations (before the collapse of the 1980 program was known) by the present author appeared in *Bulletin of Tanzanian Affairs*, no. 11, December 1980.

(and the lagged response of concessional finance sources to the mid-1974 requests) set reserves on an upward course to almost five months' imports at the end of the year. There were differences over appropriate DCE ceilings, with Tanzania arguing that the proposed IMF trigger level would abort sustained recovery of real output by preventing adequate expansion of productive working sector capital.[17]

The period of 1977–78 was marked by relatively relaxed relations, but also by IMF (and World Bank) advice to relax foreign exchange budgeting (import allocations by category and major user). This advice was adopted in 1977 as the beverage boom began to recede, and the relaxation was maintained through much of 1978 although the external balance turned sharply negative. The period of 1974–76 had been marked by severe import compression (perhaps 30–40 percent in relation to GDP in real terms). Some import relaxation was needed—and some was begun in 1976 in respect to industrial and agricultural inputs and spares. But the 1977 advice was for import levels that could not possibly have been sustained unless the beverage price boom was viewed as the new norm; across the board liberalization frittered away substantial sums on nonpriority consumer goods imports.

In early 1979 an interim program was agreed, involving use of the balance of the first credit tranche, compensatory facility drawings, and trust fund resources. It included a devaluation of about an eighth, and a set of targets. As the explosive evolution of oil prices was not foreseen, and the war-related deficit quite unguessable,[18] it is hardly surprising that none of the targets were met. The devaluation was viewed by some Tanzanians (with scant evidence[19]) as a substantial contributory cause to inflation (which rose from 8–10 percent to over 20 percent by the year's end) and to erosion of the purchasing power of the poor.

An attempt to negotiate a major program led to a sharp breakdown in the fall of 1979. The program proposed was a fairly standard one,

[17] In fact the beverage boom also radically increased government revenue and reduced net bank lending to government (which declined for several quarters), so that the ceiling might have been met because both sides' projections of foreign exchange and tax revenues were too pessimistic.

[18] The negotiations were three months before the end of the war, at a time when no projection of that period could be made.

[19] The war costs and dislocations and import bottleneck constraints on output, combined with the direct and indirect impact of petroleum price increases, appear to have been much more significant.

involving a substantial devaluation, a nominal wage freeze, abolition of price management, higher interest rates, reduction of real government expenditure (at least implicitly centered on health, primary education, and water[20]), and relaxation of import controls. It was clearly unacceptable to Tanzania, but the timing and acerbity of the breakdown did not result primarily from that, as further negotiations would normally have ensued. Rather, the appearance of an IMF intent to present a "take it or leave it" package, which included the dismantling of several key economic management tools, a sharp worsening of the income distribution, and a reversal of the extension of basic services was created by two factors:

- Proponents of a quasi-orthodox line (somewhat similar to the IMF's) were perceived to be allying themselves with the IMF, rather than negotiating with it or seeking to convince their colleagues by reasoned argument.
- At a stage when they were presumptively still negotiable, the IMF proposals were presented to the president as if they were a "final offer."

The 1980 program was significantly different. In the first place it was negotiated *after* the annual budgetary, wage, and price exercise, and therefore could hardly be seen to be causing major policy changes. Minimum prices had been raised selectively to improve urban/rural terms of trade and cross-product rationality, and the recurrent budget deficit had been targeted for a reduction of 80 percent, to 1 percent of GDP. There was no immediate devaluation or interest rate adjustment, nor any significant commitment to dismantle price control or foreign exchange budgeting.

The key conditions for a three-year stand-by totaling SDR 195 million (including SDR 15 million from the compensatory facility) were:

- a coordinated Bank of Tanzania–IMF exchange rate study by early 1981 leading to agreed action by mid-1981
- conclusion of a Bank of Tanzania interest rate review, already scheduled by the end of 1980 with a view to raising deposit and lending rates (in the event by about 1 percent)

[20] The issue was not fiscal austerity—1977–78 to 1979–80 had been the laxest budgets in Tanzanian history and the incoming minister of finance predictably (on his record in two previous terms at the treasury) tightened expenditure control.

- a ceiling on additional government borrowing of about SDR 200 million and on total DCE of about SDR 300 million over 1980–81 (22.5 percent and 19 percent, respectively, against an implicit projected rate of inflation of about 20 percent and increase in real output of 4–5 percent)
- a reduction in external commercial arrears from about SDR 185 million to about SDR 150 million over 1980–81.

The program fell apart in November for four reasons:[21]

- While dated from July, it did not become effective until October, creating a lag in possible use of the proceeds with effects on imports, production, tax revenues, and exports.
- The estimate of arrears "in the pipeline" proved seriously inaccurate.
- The IMF Tanzanian assumption that a World Bank structural adjustment credit of about SDR 80 million would be concluded and disbursed in 1980–81, beginning in the last quarter of 1980, proved totally wrong. A much smaller credit, excluding the industrial sector, was negotiated in 1981, but drawings were negligible during the fiscal year.
- In terms of actual 1980–81 outturn, the loss of the IMF facility caused import strangulation that reduced revenues by forcing a fall—instead of the posited recovery—in manufactured goods output, and thus radically increased DCE.

If Fund and Bank finance had been available (some 1,155 million Tanzanian shillings, T Sh), the clearing of transport bottlenecks would have allowed some T Sh 500 million higher exports for a net availability gain of SDR 200 million. Half of this would have allowed arrears to be held to target levels, and the other half would have generated tax revenues from additional imports of SDR 80–100 million, thus reducing government borrowing from SDR 300 million to SDR 200–220 million (around the SDR 210 trigger).

Thus the program would probably have succeeded had the projected Bank and Fund resources been available despite several adverse factors:

[21] The following section is based on the 1980–81 budget speech and analysis of preliminary 1980–81 fiscal, credit, and balance of payments outturns. It may or may not correspond exactly to official estimates of impact and causation.

- the World Bank's insistence on export tax abolition, which reduced revenue by perhaps SDR 20–25 million
- the collapse (unanticipated by the IMF or Tanzania) of tobacco and coffee prices
- relatively poor weather affecting cotton and maize output
- the limited (20 percent in real terms) cut possible in defense and related expenditure because the Uganda security situation required continued involvement on a substantial scale to mid-1981 (at least six months longer than anticipated), with a budgetary cost of perhaps SDR 20–40 million.

Negotiations in 1981 toward an extended facility loan of the order of $400 million reached deadlock relatively quickly, where they have remained. They took place against the background of two exchange rate studies (one by the Bank of Tanzania, the other by the Fund) that could not be reconciled.

The Tanzania study concluded that devaluation and interest rate adjustment were irrelevant to the current account balance in real terms, as import reduction was undesirable and barriers to increasing exports, at least in the short and medium term, turned on quite specific bottlenecks, requiring imports to break them. It doubted the fiscal gain from devaluation because its analysis suggested rapid cancellation by inflation and a potential built-in spiral effect. Finally, it argued that managing devaluation would divert key personnel from more hopeful policy measures related to specific resource reallocation measures to raise export.

The IMF study was a superficial summary of recent events followed by a "standard" IMF package. Its elements appear to have included:

- 66⅔ percent–75 percent devaluation
- 35–40 percent nominal interest rates
- no increase in nominal wages or salaries
- dismantling of price controls
- reductions in real government recurrent and capital expenditure
- DCE limits such as to require reduction in productive sector inventories that were already at levels totally inconsistent with significant output expansion
- 50 percent–75 percent increases in export and 25 percent increases in staple food crop grower prices (the latter below Tanzanian estimates of the predevaluation inflation rate).

These features could be deduced from the initial March discussions and became clearer in July and Annual General Meeting dialogues. While the acerbic 1979 breaking of discussions has been avoided, the present dialogue is one of the deaf. Ironically, the chief policy result of the IMF's proposals seems to have been to delay internally proposed Tanzanian action to restore the mid 1980 Tanzanian shilling–SDR parity (and peg to the SDR), reversing the 15 percent revaluation over 1980–81 resulting from Tanzania's dollar-pound reference basket. This technical adjustment would probably have been agreed much sooner than March 1982 in the absence of perceived IMF pressures for a much larger devaluation.

The IMF and Tanzanian Analyses, Policy Debates, and Decisions

The IMF has interacted with an ongoing process of analysis, discussion, debate, and decision in Tanzania. It has had rather different priorities in respect to items on that agenda and a somewhat narrower agenda. The most evident impact (which the author would view as a negative one) has been to focus a substantial amount of attention on devaluation and interest rates at the expense of micro and structural issues.

In respect to prices, the IMF's argument that *relative agricultural prices* had, over 1975–79, become radically inconsistent with output, equity, or export criteria reinforced the position of those who pushed through substantial rationalization in 1980 and 1981. For the target crops, the increases were, if anything, above the IMF's suggested norms.

The debate on the *elimination of subsidies* has been on timing. Tanzania was, and basically is, opposed to consumption subsidies. Those in grain arose because bad accounting concealed the losses. The 1980 consolidation left only one product, maize, subsidized (partly from sugar surplus, and partly from a budgeted treasury payment), and the 1981 maize price increase reduced the subsidy (to perhaps 1.5 percent of GDP), with a view to phasing it out. The difference of opinion was on whether it would be prudent to eliminate the subsidy at one go, at the cost of almost doubling the cost of a staple urban wage good (i.e., a 300 percent increase in 1981 versus the 100 percent actually made).

Price management is an area of contention. Policy is to limit it to a manageable number of basic items and improve the analysis underlying the acceptable return on assets, given attainment of target levels of output/efficiency (modified cost plus). Tanzania views price management as critical, especially in conditions of shortage and for—to a degree—keeping surpluses in manufacturing, wholesaling, and finance (where they can be taxed and are likely to be productively reinvested), as opposed to subwholesaling/retailing (where neither condition applies). The IMF disagrees—apparently on principle—with price management on the basis that free markets would work smoothly and effectively in Tanzania.

The debate on *industrial strategy* has been largely implicit. Tanzania perceives industry as relatively integrated, relatively efficient (prior to import strangulation), and a critical source of surplus, incentive goods and inputs, reduction of import dependence, and (less agreed within Tanzania) exports.[22] The average capacity utilization and profit ratios of both public and private sectors vary widely, but among firms, rather than on public/private lines. Since the average public sector performance is better, most Tanzanians perceive criticism of the role of public industrial enterprises as showing ideological bias or lack of knowledge of the facts. The IMF appears to view the Tanzanian industrial sector as inherently weak and featherbedded on a fairly simplistic, static comparative advantage model. It clearly does not place equal importance on restoring capacity utilization as a means of providing incentive goods or raising exports,[23] albeit it does acknowledge its relevance to closing the recurrent budget deficits.

In respect of *agriculture*, the IMF has stressed price adjustments and public corporation efficiency. The first is not an area of disagreement, except that Tanzania perceives the main changes as already made (urban goods–rural goods terms of trade improved sharply over 1979–81, and relative prices among crops were rationalized). On the public corporations, the debate is partly internal to Tanzania (with the Ministry of Agriculture/Marketing Development Bureau at least until 1982 relatively unwilling to plan for, or enforce, efficiency reforms sought by the treasury, and the central and commercial banks and planning), and partly between Tanzania and the World Bank plus the Marketing Development Bureau (which wished to reform

[22] The National Economic Survival Program (NESP) represents a partial consensus that, given import allocations tied to subsequent exports, certain industries can generate substantial exports at prices above their incremental costs. The emphasis on the Morogoro shoe, Mufindi pulp and paper, and Kilwa ammonia urea plants also reflects a reorientation of sectoral priorities to export generation.

[23] The IMF appears to view substantial manufactured exports from Tanzania as inconceivable because it is thinking of labor-intensive (low-wage export) industries rather than natural resource-intensive and/or specialty (for example, khanga and kitenge prints) products.

by increased centralization and administrative fiat, as opposed to decentralization and managed market/managerial responsibility approaches). However, Tanzania argues that the key bottlenecks are transport, storage, production and processing inputs, and "incentive goods," which can be broken only by increased import capacity and detailed micro programs. This does not get much sympathy from the Fund—apparently being seen as irrelevant, whereas, if correct, it makes much of the present devaluation/price controversy a dangerously attention-misallocating primrose path (for both opponents and proponents). The Fund's pressures for public enterprise reform may have strengthened the hand of the internal advocates of reform—how much is unclear.

Export expansion seems to be viewed by the Fund as both necessary, and, in the short term, virtually impossible. The Tanzanian debate has shifted radically from no active priority to export expansion (1961–72), to a verbal priority not matched by action (1973–79), to central priority (1980) backed by an articulated program (1981). The National Economic Survival Program (NESP), backed by articulated export targets with ways and means relevant to achieving them, results from external reality giving powerful support to the internal proponents of export expansion as vital to political economic room for maneuver and sustained growth, who were as of 1969–70 an isolated minority. The IMF has made surprisingly few proposals (beyond devaluation, which it admits seems likely to have little impact), but the Exchange Rate Study by the Bank of Tanzania laid the foundations for the NESP. In that indirect sense, IMF intervention was critical—but toward producing a Tanzanian alternative to the IMF's own adjustment proposals.

Arrears reduction is not an area of IMF-Tanzania or intra-Tanzania disagreement. The faster the better, consistent with partial and sustainable restoration of real import levels, is the common target, and differences in ideas as to timing reflect optimism or pessimism rather than ideological or analytical divergences.

The related issue of *supplier credit* has received surprisingly little Fund attention. Its use rose over 1979–81 to the level of perhaps SDR 200 million, largely to sustain fixed investment in low foreign exchange generation: long payoff projects and became the topic of an intense debate in Tanzania. The year 1981 saw new guidelines drastically limiting the use of supplier credit to major export developments, interim spares and replacement capital goods, and the final tranche of otherwise financed bottleneck-breaking projects. However, here, where IMF advice might have achieved an earlier correction,[24] there was little Fund interest.

On uses of *foreign resources*—i.e., reallocation from creating new, unusable capacity to rehabilitation and maintenance of existing capacity, bottleneck breaking, and restoration of capacity utilization—the IMF and Tanzania appear to have had parallel internal debates. The preservation of gross fixed investment rates—come what may—has had strong proponents in Tanzania and the Fund. But in the present crisis—if it is expected to be more than transient—maintaining and utilizing existing capacity, plus selective new investment aimed at debottlenecking, generating significant net exports, or reducing present import needs seems a better allocation of resources. That view came to prevail in Tanzania (spearheaded by the treasury) over 1979–81 and is embodied in NESP. One major obstacle (not the only one—domestic project–defenders abound too) is that many resource transfers are not fungible. Over 1979–81 the Fund and Bank have come to endorse such a reallocation of resource use in respect to Tanzania—possibly in part as a result of their dialogue with Tanzanians. They did not take the lead, however, as the shift began with treasury balance of payments support fund raising in 1979–80.

Credit ceilings are not a matter of disagreement in principle, nor have target levels proved contentious. There are disagreements on how rigid targets should be if events are significantly more adverse (reducing government revenue and production and thereby increasing government borrowing) or more favorable (allowing economic expansion, but requiring more productive sector working capital) than projected.

Because of credit allocation and import constraints, productive sector credit has grown slowly, well below implicit IMF or Tanzanian targets. But with relaxation of the import constraint, it would need to rise to finance inventories to allow greater production, and so reduce inflationary pressure directly and by generating tax revenues. The IMF missions accept this in principle but not, it seems, in selecting performance criteria.

In respect to the *government deficit*, the first divergence is in definition. Tanzania (unlike the Fund) sees a sharp difference beween the recurrent budget deficit and the public sector investment borrowing requirement which—so long as financed from long-term sources

[24] The inadvisability of sustaining gross fixed investment at the cost of mortgaging future export earnings was fairly rapidly accepted once an internal analysis was done as a by-product of the Exchange Rate Study.

or within an overall ceiling on DCE consistent with economic balance—it sees as no more a deficit than, say, International Business Machine's (IBM's) external borrowing requirement. In respect to the recurrent budget, Tanzania (and to a degree the Fund) sees the only route to regain balance as restoring manufactured goods production, and therefore sales and company tax. Secondary gains are coming from phasing down defense costs now that the Uganda support operation is concluded. There is, equally, no divergence on the need to raise maintenance and repair expenditure. Where there is a divergence (both Fund-Tanzania and within Tanzania) is on what savings, if any, on real recurrent expenditure are obtainable. The treasury, while forceful in imposing tighter micro control, doubts that these can be significant, given the real cuts already made, the global price uncertainties leading to supplementary estimates, and the well-known difficulties in collecting enough candle ends to have a macro impact. The Bank of Tanzania and Ministry of Planning (whose capital budgets' average cost overrun per project of over 25 percent *may* offer greater scope for real savings) are more optimistic as to the potential. The Fund apparently is advocating program cuts, but, barring reduction of services supporting directly productive sectors, the only candidates large enough to have a macro impact would appear to be education, health, and water. While Tanzania has accepted curtailed growth (and some real per capita cuts) in these sectors, major cuts are so inconsistent with government, party, and public priorities as to be virtually inconceivable.[25]

Devaluation has become a central focus of disagreement—probably out of any relation to its possible use in any stabilization and reconstruction program. The Fund accepts that its short-term impact on the external balance would be near nil, its impact on inflation substantial (albeit, less than Tanzanian analysis suggests and—apparently—seen as self-limiting, which is contrary to the Tanzanian evaluation of probabilities), and its effect on income distribution substantial, inegalitarian, and uncertain. But it contends that devaluation would allow substantial relative price adjustments, enhance government revenue relative to expenditure (which Tanzanian calculations suggest is highly doubtful), and improve agricultural enterprise surpluses (which

[25] Because certain Tanzanians would find cuts of this type desirable, but would be in a position to enforce them only by a coup and a highly repressive regime, sustained pressure for such cuts (however intended) is perceived by many of the Tanzanian leadership as political interference and *not* economic advice.

Tanzania sees as simplistic—unnecessary in several cases, for example, coffee, and hopelessly insufficient in others, for example, tea, tobacco, and cotton). It is difficult to escape feeling that the basic thrust is moral: "devaluation is good for your soul."

Tanzanian positions are split. A minority but growing view favors a limited and phased devaluation, so as first to reverse the 1980–81 de facto revaluation—as was finally done in March 1982—and to subsequently make marginal steps to limit adverse unexpected consequences on prices or income distribution and restore the 1967–75 position, when small devaluations were seen as one among many policy instruments. The dominant position views large devaluations as inequitable, leading to uncontrollable inflationary spirals and reducing or destroying the efficiency of economic planning and management. This view also tends, in the end, to make the issue a moral one of good and evil.

The impact of Fund pressure for massive devaluation on Tanzanian debate is clear. It has cut the ground from under the feet of those proposing lagged, phased, limited devaluation and prevented rational consideration of devaluation as one policy instrument among many.

On *wages and salaries*, the Fund clearly believes a greater reduction to be desirable than most Tanzanian opinion (spearheaded by State House and—surprisingly—the treasury) considers economically efficient, politically wise, or morally acceptable. Tanzania has compressed real minimum wages about 25–30 percent since 1973, and real salaries by over 50 percent, and believes serious personal hardship, productive inefficiency, problems of morale, and corruption would flow from any further sharp reductions, such as would flow from a wage freeze accompanying a large devaluation and its consequential inflation. Neither side appears to have convinced the other: 1980 and 1981 minimum wage and grower price changes were designed to protect real purchasing power, and 1981 salary increases (the first since 1974 and the second since before independence) partially offset the impact of 1980–81 inflation on real salaries.

The *interest rate* dialogue appears to have been theoretical and ideological on the Fund side (moving to a 5 percent *real* interest rate at one stroke) and structural and pragmatic on the Tanzanian. Given credit budgeting, it is doubtful that allocation by use would change much. Given the actual holders of deposits in Tanzania and their past nonresponsiveness to interest rate changes (admittedly relatively small ones), there is no real reason to suppose much higher rates would increase savings.[26] But the Tanzanian side perceives large increases as having a major inflationary impact, as they would fall on domestic trade (raising consumer prices) and export marketing (creating deficits for the marketing boards unless, as neither the IMF nor Tanzania proposes, grower prices were reduced). Much Tanzanian opinion sees the solution in reducing inflation so that the 9–12 percent nominal short-term rates become positive in real terms, and perhaps raising long-term (fixed investment financing) rates to, say, 12–15 percent. A harder line sees any increase as both inflationary and negative in income distribution implications (a point which is somewhat doubtful; but, as with devaluation, the deadlock in the interest rate debate has led some participants to abandon analysis and resort to moral reasoning of good versus evil at best tenuously related to reality).

It is agreed that there is a *need to adjust*, whatever the balance of external and internal causes of the crisis, given that there has been a structural worsening of the external balance position that external events (for example, a new beverage price boom) cannot be expected to reverse speedily and sustainably. On the Tanzanian side this is a change, in the sense that over 1974–76 the permanence of the shift was not fully recognized, and in 1977–78 the temporary relaxation of external constraints caused by the beverage boom was not seen as transient. The potential of that boom for financing structural improvements to build up new export potential was frittered away, partly through IMF-pushed import liberalization. But the IMF appears to view its lending as primarily bridging finance to ease demand contraction, while Tanzania regards it as primarily bridging finance to allow supply expansion, with priority to export supply via rehabilitation and new exports (for example, pulp and paper; ammonia urea; processed forms of existing primary exports, such as shoes, twine, and specialty textile prints; and manufactures more generally).

Nor is there real divergence on the need for austerity—Tanzania's 1979–81 program (arguably precisely because of the absence of IMF support) has been harsh in the extreme, with real government spending (excluding debt service and funding past parastatal deficits), real wages and salaries, real imports, and real availability of manufactured goods (except agricultural inputs) all sharply compressed. The differences are on who should bear the costs of adjustment and receive the gains of recovery and whether a sustained recovery to a growth

[26] It might cause some shift from currency to deposits, but this has no macro meaning, i.e., it alters asset holdings, not savings rates.

rate consistent with development is a daydream (the apparent IMF view—which on global projections may be analytically valid) or essential to maintain support for and implementation of any program (the Tanzanian position, whose psychological and political economic force is substantial).

The *basic differences* between Tanzanian and IMF perceptions are fivefold:

- whether the present imbalances came largely from artificial monetary expansion of demand (implicit IMF position) or external shocks
- therefore, what the cumulative and sustainable, as well as the short-term, result of more import capacity would be (Tanzania seeing much more scope for internal and, to a degree, export expansion being triggered by such an injection)
- whether the balance of emphasis should be on domestic demand compression (IMF) or domestic supply enhancement with a bias toward exportables (Tanzania)
- combined with a parallel difference in perspective as to the merits of "free" versus "managed" markets, and a sharp difference in balance of emphasis on macro, standard model elements (IMF stress) versus micro, articulated, structural, context-based approaches (Tanzanian position).

The *technical* debate on trigger targets (performance criteria) has turned on three points:

- What are appropriate quarterly ceilings given the sharp—but not very stable—quarterly variations in foreign exchange and government account balance, and commercial credit requirements, over the fiscal year?
- Are official (and publicly known) government, foreign exchange, and credit budget estimates appropriate performance criteria, and what margins should be allowed?
- Given external uncertainties and data weaknesses, do precise figure "triggers" (as opposed to ranges) make sense, and should certain alterations be allowed quasi-automatically if external events are very different from agreed Fund Tanzania projections?

These are not per se issues of principle, but in practice they are critical to the sustainability of any program. The remarkably high mortality rate of 1979–81 multiyear facility programs suggests present Fund procedures are objectively unsatisfactory under present conditions of stress and uncertainty.

Tanzanian and IMF Adjustment Strategies: Notes Toward Evaluation

Tanzania's structural adjustment strategy, as prepared in 1981, turns on six priorities:

- raising domestic food production and—at least equally important—improving storage and rehabilitating transport
- developing new export sectors based on present unprocessed exports (for example, shoes), newly exploited renewable raw materials (for example, pulp and paper), and newly discovered mineral and hydrocarbon resources (for example, ammonia urea)
- completing and initiating projects to break bottlenecks preventing use of existing capacity (for example, transmission lines for electricity to secondary industrial centers, local phosphate and barley production to cut the import content of fertilizer and beer production)
- completing or rehabilitating productive enterprise and infrastructure units with significant export potential or impact (for example, Morogoro shoe plant, khanga and kitenge textile production, main rail lines and lorry fleet)
- raising existing primary product and manufactured goods exports through loosening production procurement and processing and shipping constraints
- restoring domestic manufactured goods output by making additional imported inputs and spares available, and plant rehabilitation.

These priorities—of which the fifth was seen as the most urgent in the short run, and the most workable until the foreign exchange constraint is eased—imply a shift away from generalized promotion of fixed investment. In real terms, 1981–82 capital budget estimates were 20–25 percent below 1980–81. The shift required is not to consumption, but to maintenance, rehabilitation, working capital, and selective fixed investment.

Elaboration of means to achieve these "operational goals" was perceived as necessarily starting at the micro or sectoral level with macro requirements aggregated upward. The discovery that for many manufacturing firms, exports at world prices would be profitable (i.e., above incremental cost), but were prevented by imported input constraints, led to a column in the foreign exchange budget for import allocations tied to export target performance. But simply increasing allocations to potential exporters was not seen as a solution because, while export sales from additional output would be profitable, additional domestic sales would be more so.[27]

In a majority of cases, quite specific constraints and opportunities were identifiable. These varied from case to case, but imported raw material and spares availability, fuel and power network gaps, and transport availability were the most common. Cost reduction also appeared to require case by case approaches: raising output to spread overheads was in most cases the most logical approach, and in many almost "all" that was needed. Where serious internal inefficiencies existed, these required enterprise changes (in extreme cases like National Milling, total institutional restructuring) not particularly related to macro instruments like devaluation or interest rates. Certain crops face serious problems—of a technical agronomic nature in the case of cotton, of sustainability in the case of cotton and (because of fuel requirements) tobacco, and of dismal real global price trends in the cases of coffee, tea, and probably tobacco. These problems require specific measures, such as reduction of acidity in cotton soils, cutbacks in production support overheads, and interim subsidies either during restoration or phasing out. Macro demand-management and price level measures are either irrelevant or expensive ways of approaching such problems.

The NESP has directed attention to these priorities. It has had some results in the production, procurement, processing, and transport of exports, which appears to account for much of 1981's substantial export increase. However, it is clearly operating within too tight real resource (and especially import) constraints and requires an injection of new resources to produce substantial results (including reducing external imbalances, clearing arrears, and maintaining debt service) over an acceptable time period.

Evaluation on Uniform Criteria

Because there is not, and has not been for any period long enough to analyze, a Tanzanian program under the Fund's high-conditionality facilities, this evaluation is necessarily somewhat speculative. It centers on the Tanzanian 1981 NESP and—where it appears clearly divergent from Fund advice—is contrasted with IMF proposals.

[27] This is not unique to Tanzania—unit profits on domestic sales normally exceed those on exports. However, given the domestic imbalance, it will be especially severe in Tanzania, at least until external and internal balance are closer.

Microeconomic efficiency[28] is clearly central to the NESP's approach more than it is to the excessive macro concentration and somewhat blind faith in market efficiency under conditions of extreme scarcity and uncertainty of the Fund. It has been reflected both in the 1980–81 rationalization of agricultural prices and in the operation of the Prices Commission.

Whether there is an egalitarianism/growth trade-off in the present Tanzanian context is open to question. One may argue that more food, incentive goods, and basic services (especially pure water, health facilities, education) for low-income workers and peasants, and continued constraint on middle and upper incomes has, *in this context*, a positive link to growth.

The consumption/growth trade-off has certainly been pushed heavily to the growth (investment) side by Tanzania. The NESP change is in stressing working capital, maintenance, rehabilitation, debottlenecking (including, above all, raising exports), and improved capacity utilization, in contrast to general fixed investment.

The employment-inflation trade-off is also complex. Given underutilization of capacity, the most plausible route to restoring mid 1975–mid-1980 rates of inflation (6–10 percent) would appear to be increased production (through fuller "employment" of existing plant and labor forces), not demand compression. In fact the latter seems more likely to generate hyperinflation and sustained falls in output than stability.

The more general problems arise in applying micro criteria. The first is that expanding the production frontier often requires imbalances, structural changes, and nonmarginal measures that have microefficiency costs justified by allowing higher levels of production, even with temporarily reduced microefficiency. The NESP's export development priority is a case in point: albeit in a broad sense it is also a move toward microefficiency, given the past de facto bias against exports. Similarly, total institutional reconstruction (as needed in National Milling) has interim micro costs, but may be necessary both for macro gains and for creating a context in which significant micro gains are possible and sustainable. Second, there is a time frame problem. For example, few production diversification moves anywhere (especially industrial sector creation) have been microefficient over the short term. Much of the debate on Tanzanian industry turns on this point. Third, for microefficiency, account must be taken of

[28] These criteria are drawn from J. Williamson, "On Judging the Success of IMF Policy Advice," Chapter 7 of this volume.

alternative uses, scarce resource requirements, and market price rigidity, not only of profit and loss results. Failure to do so can lead to generalized recommendations[29] to shift from domestic food production to massive increases in coffee, tea, and cocoa production on asserted static comparative advantage and (preshift) terms of trade projections—a prescription more likely to accelerate starvation than development if it leads to action by a majority of sub-Saharan African economies.

High priority to *avoiding inflation* is a Tanzanian goal. Indeed, much of the opposition to a front-end loaded, massive devaluation turns precisely on this point. The NESP strategy seeks to reduce excess demand by reactivating capacity to increase supply (at the same time balancing the recurrent budget through revenue increases).

The desire to achieve the reduction rapidly underlies both the objection to a large devaluation, which would raise and lengthen the 1980–81 period of high (30 percent) inflation and build in expectations inconsistent with regaining stability,[30] and to the attempt to shift existing foreign resource transfers to maintenance, rehabilitation, and operating input uses.

Tanzanian managers, officials, and technocratic decisionmakers have an objection to high inflation in addition to those outlined by Williamson. In the context of managed market economic policy instruments, lagged and uncertain data and no capacity to run detailed, generalized material balances checks, inflation has serious macro and micro policy efficiency costs because decisionmakers (presumably in the private as well as the public sector) do not know where they are.

To seek to *avoid major departures from internal balances* in the Tanzanian context means attempting to reduce present imbalances rapidly. To compress demand further would be perverse. Systematic debottlenecking and capacity utilization restoration (à la NESP) are

[29] As in the World Bank's *Accelerated Development for Sub-Saharan Africa—An Agenda for Action*, Washington, 1981, especially pp. 21, 65.

[30] Admittedly in 1974 major price and wage adjustments were made to pass on the world grain and oil price increases and to achieve a rapid shift to a new price plateau. This did work—very rapid price increases in two quarters were followed by restoration of inflation rates under 10 percent. But in 1974 past inflation was lower, the starting point was of internal and external balance, and the attention mobilized for a coherent forward projection of consequences was much greater than would be the case in 1982. An attempt to repeat 1974 would run a very high risk of collapsing into hyperinflation on an enduring basis.

called for. Balance restoration seems unlikely to be facilitated by major initial cost-raising shocks—this is the argument for delayed and phased exchange rate and interest rate adjustments. Whether the NESP targets are sustainable in the absence of "front-end loaded" or "bridging" additions to external resource transfers is, however, open to grave doubt, as such transfers are critical to a rapid reduction of inflation and to sustained export growth, as well as to a restoration of manufactured goods production and recurrent budget balance.

External balance as a high priority but medium-term objective is again a priority within the Tanzanian adjustment strategy. Whether it is for the Fund—or can be, given the IMF program and drawing repayment schedule constraints—is open to some doubt: three years is not medium term for the forty- or fifty-odd economies with external imbalances as severe as Tanzania's.

Given the present import strangulation, no gains can be seen from further absolute import reduction—*au contraire*. The focus in the short run needs to be—and is—on restoring exports (25 percent below peak levels in physical terms in 1980) and carrying out those import substitution possibilities with low import content and quick results (for example, barley growing?). In the medium term, investment in new exports (including processing of existing ones and pushing the manufacturing sector to a ratio of exports to output much nearer to operating import requirements) and selective import substitution (especially backward integration to intermediate goods and raw materials and lateral to spares and construction inputs) requires sustaining current attention and more articulated priorities for specfic products and plants.

The main NESP-IMF divergence is on the relative weights to be given to specific, contextual, micro measures (often physical and requiring allocation either by nonmarket instruments or market intervention) and to macro, "free play of market forces" oriented measures. Especially in the short term, the weight of evidence[31] appears to be on the side of the Exchange Rate Study–NESP approach.

Influence, Impact, and Results

IMF *influence* on Tanzanian action has, to date, been fairly modest. Direct impact since 1976 has, arguably, been negative. Indirect effects are hard to assess.

[31] As identified in much greater detail in the Exchange Rate Study, NESP working papers, and *20 Year Review*.

Positive direct influence since 1974–76 has been limited to underlining (in 1979–81) how serious Tanzania's external balance and domestic surplus flow position were, and were likely to remain, and, marginally, strengthening the position of advocates of certain subsidy-reducing or surplus-enhancing measures. In 1974–75, however, IMF resource transfers were essential to allowing Tanzania to hold out until other, very lagged, transfers actually arrived.

Negative direct influence has had two main aspects. First, the 1977–78 general import liberalization wasted resources (especially since, predictably, it could not be put into reverse rapidly) and bolstered Tanzania's erroneous perception that the 1976–77 external balance recovery was based on something more stable than the 1975 Brazilian frost. Second, the 1979–81 calls for major interest rate boosts and devaluation have made rational discussion of these policy instruments in Tanzania almost impossible, and totally blocked the Tanzanian proponents of their use on a smaller scale and over a different time frame as supportive instruments within the Tanzanian economic survival strategy.

The indirect positive influence centers on the 1981 Exchange Rate Study. Work done in connection with it provided the base from which the NESP—the first coherent, comprehensive, medium-term response[32] to the 1978 crisis—was built. While this was hardly the IMF's intent, it is a fact that without its pressure there would have been no Exchange Rate Study and—at least in 1981—no NESP.

Indirect negative impact includes very high 1979–81 allocations of analytical, professional, and decisionmakers' time to working and negotiating with the IMF. IMF disagreement has also hampered Tanzania's attempts to fund alternative approaches. (Over 1974–76 IMF "approval" may have had a positive effect.)

Impact flows from influence. The IMF facilities of 1974–75 were crucial to allowing the success of the 1974–76 adjustment strategy. Equally, denial of substantial resources over 1979–81 has made attempts to devise and implement any stabilization and structural adjustment strategy more costly and less successful.

The 1980 agreement breakdown had a particularly high cost. The year's foreign exchange and revenue budgets were drawn up, assuming both the IMF drawings and World Bank structural adjustment credit. As a result, second-half 1980 foreign exchange allocations were made at levels which—when neither flow materialized—both added

[32] Previous action was certainly substantial, but not coordinated and largely centered on import compression.

to arrears and forced draconian cutbacks in first-half 1981 allocations, below what would have been possible had the whole year's budget been made on the basis of funds actually available.

These measures of impact do not relate to the particular IMF targets in actual, suspended, and debated programs with Tanzania. The trigger clause figures are tests of means, *not* of ends (for example, external balance, internal balance, capacity untilization, growth, income distribution). Nor would it be valid to treat the costs of adjustment as the impact of the IMF. In 1974–76 the causes of adjustment costs were primarily drought and fuel price increases and, secondarily, increases in other import prices. The IMF facilities, by providing bridging finance, mitigated the impact on production and public services and therefore permitted prompter recovery in 1975–76 than would have been possible without them.

In 1979–81 the primary causes were again external, with secondary domestic inefficiencies caused by attempting to manage with radically reduced real resources. Difficulties were exacerbated not by IMF-imposed measures or IMF funding, but by the inability to negotiate IMF facilities on terms Tanzania considers consistent either with economic stabilization or adjustment leading to renewed development. As the present finance minister has observed, it is bitterly ironic that failure to agree to IMF proposals for demand compression because of commitment to supply expansion is forcing Tanzania to undertake even more drastic initial demand compression in order to free at least some real resources for supply (especially export supply) bolstering—an exercise that is both high cost and high risk.

Whether the "post IMF" situation is better or worse than it would have been in the absence of IMF program/transfers[33] is answerable only for 1974–76. For that period it is clearly better. Equally for that period, no better strategy was evident to Tanzania (the internal opponents of the actual strategy in fact advocated a classic IMF demand compression as a response to drought), nor is any such alternative visible now to the author looking back. The failure to move more promptly in reducing import intensity in manufacturing and in raising exports were deviations from the strategy, not components of it, and were certainly not the result of IMF influence. Without the IMF facility, that strategy would not have been viable (i.e., *P* was better

[33] The two can be evaluated only ex post as a package. However, conceptually the transfers might have produced better results if linked to a different program—indeed in one sense that is precisely Tanzania's argument.

than *C2* in terms of Professor Williamson's comparisons (Chapter 7, this volume).

Over 1979–81 *P* does not exist, since there have been no significant IMF transfers. One is therefore in one sense still at "*A*"—the pre-IMF state of affairs—or, more realistically, at *C2*, given the radical initial demand compression and policy reshaping of 1977–80 and the new strategic formulation in NESP of 1981.

The question then is whether *C2** (i.e., *with* IMF facilities) would be better than the present and better than *P** (the results of the program proposed by the IMF). *C2** would include:

- the NESP strategy elements outlined above
- continued price management to ensure that reductions in excess demand pressure lead to reductions in effective prices
- rehabilitation and consolidation of basic services and their gradual expansion
- a more flexible approach to bank working-capital lending linked to expansion of production so as to finance increased needs for inventories
- "rear-end loaded," phased, and probably relatively limited exchange and interest rate adjustments following supply boosting to avert generating new inflationary pressures
- maintenance—and subsequent restoration—of real wages, real peasant incomes and—once recovery has become rooted—some restoration of real salary levels.

The author's belief that this strategic package would have more positive impact in Tanzania than the IMF proposals is presumably evident, and is—or is not—convincing on the basis of the whole previous line of argument that obviates both the need for, and value of, any closing peroration. However, it may be worth pointing out that the external and material (if not necessarily the political economic goal and policy) contexts of Tanzania are similar to those of many other low-income economies, especially in sub-Saharan Africa. If the criticisms of IMF proposals and approaches in respect of Tanzania are valid in this case, they are probably (as the author has argued elsewhere[34]) more generally relevant.

[34] "Low Income Countries and the International Monetary System," paper for the Group of 24 Expert Group Meeting of the same title, New York, February 1982, publication pending. An earlier perspective is "Aspects of the World Monetary and Resource Transfer System in 1974: A View From the Extreme Periphery" in G. K. Helleiner, *A World Divided: The Less Developed Countries in the International Economy*, Cambridge, 1976.

TABLE 15.1 BALANCE OF PAYMENTS, TANZANIA, 1965–80

1	2	3	4	5	6	7
	Merchandise trade					
Year	Exports (million Tanzanian shillings)	Imports (million Tanzanian shillings)	Balance (million Tanzanian shillings)	Balance on services	Col. 4 as percentage of current GDP	(Col. 4 + Col. 5) as percentage of current GDP
1965	1,475.9	1,410.0	65.9	—	1.07	—
1966	1,889.9	1,694.9	195.0	−72.9	2.77	1.73
1967	1,796.9	1,637.6	159.0	—	2.15	—
1968	1,719.0	1,833.7	−114.7	—	−1.45	—
1969	1,756.5	1,710.1	46.4	177.3	0.55	2.67
1970	1,797.2	2,274.2	−477.0	225.9	−5.21	−2.74
1971	1,913.1	2,725.6	−812.5	208.8	−8.11	−6.03
1972	2,312.7	2,882.9	−570.2	256.0	−9.99	−3.7
1973	2,581.1	3,478.9	−897.7	190.1	−6.85	−5.4
1974	2,878.1	5,377.0	−2,498.9	181.7	−15.6	−14.49
1975	2,764.0	5,709.4	−2,945.4	480.9	−15.49	−12.96
1976	4,108.0	5,349.5	−1,241.5	466.4	−5.3	−3.3
1977	4,464.2	6,161.3	−1,697.1	155.7	−5.8	−5.2
1978	3,670.6	8.797.7	−5,127.1	210.1	−15.3	−14.72
1979	4,484.3	9,073.2	−4,588.9	306.0	−12.2	−11.37
1980	4,702.2	10,261.9	−5,559.7	156.1	−15.6	−15.1

— Not available.
Sources: Bank of Tanzania, *Economic and Operations Reports*, various issues, National Accounts, various issues; Green, et al. (1980).
a. Revised estimates.

TABLE 15.2 PUBLIC FINANCE/GROSS DOMESTIC PRODUCT RATIOS, 1961–80
(percentage of GDP)

Item	*1960/61*	*1963/64*	*1966/67*	*1969/70*	*1972/73*	*1975/76*	*1977/78*	*1978/79*	*1979/80*
Recurrent revenue	13.0[a]	14.2	15.5	20.1	22.8	20.9	21.7	21.6	22.6
Recurrent expenditure[b]	13.6	13.7	15.5	19.5	21.1	19.8	19.8	26.0	27.5
Capital expenditure	2.6	2.9	4.5	7.8	7.0	12.0	11.8	15.1	15.8
Total expenditure	16.2	16.6	20.0	27.3	28.1	31.8	31.6	41.1	43.3

Sources: Adapted from "Twenty Year Review" Annex Tables on Gross Domestic Product and Trends in Government Finances; *Financial Statement and Revenue Estimates* (various years); World Bank, *The Economic Development of Tanganika*.
a. Excludes Colonial Welfare and Development Payments.
b. Includes debt service in full. Technically, debt redemption should not be included.

TABLE 15.3 ANALYSIS OF BUDGETARY FINANCING REQUIREMENT, 1963/64–1979/80
(percentage)

Ratios to GDP	*1963/64*	*1966/67*	*1969/70*	*1972/73*	*1975/76*	*1977/78*	*1978/79*	*1979/80*
Capital budget	2.9	4.5	7.8	7.0	12.0	11.0	15.1	15.8
Plus recurrent budget deficit or minus surplus	(0.5)	(0.0)	(0.6)	(1.7)	(1.1)	(1.9)	4.4	4.9

Budgetary financing requirement	2.4	4.5	7.2	5.3	10.9	9.9	19.5	20.8
External finance[a]	1.0	1.9	1.6	3.3	5.5	4.2	8.0	10.5
Domestic finance[b]	1.4	2.6	5.6	2.0	5.4	5.7	11.5	10.3
Grants/transfers/etc.[c]	(1.4)	(2.6)	(0.7)	(0.2)	(0.5)	(0.5)	(0.4)	(0.3)
Non-bank borrowing	(—)	(—)	(2.2)	(1.8)	(1.8)	(2.5)	(1.4)	(1.4)
Bank borrowing	(—)	(—)	(2.7)	(0.0)	(3.1)	(2.0)	(9.7)	(8.6)
Ratios to financing requirement								
External finance	39	43	22	63	50	42	41	51
Bank borrowing	—	—	38	1	28	19	49	41
Ratios to capital budget								
External finance	33	43	20	47	45	36	54	67

— Not available.
Sources: Adopted from "Twenty Year Review" Annex Tables on Public Finance, GDP; *Financial Statement and Revenue Estimates* (various years).
a. Includes grants, loans to government. Some small private agency grants may be misclassified under domestic. Includes counterpart Funds from food aid and balance of payments support finance in year paid into Development Revenue account.
b. Excludes domestic counterpart funds from external aid (see note 1).
c. Early year figures appear to include some borrowing, e.g., from Cotton Authority, East African Currency Board. Later years include resources from special funds in year allocated/paid over to development revenue.

TABLE 15.4 GROSS BANK LENDING, 1966–79
(million Tanzanian shillings)

Year	Central government: Bank of Tanzania	Central government: Commercial banks	Total	Nongovernment borrowing
1966	72.5	98.0	170.5	806.9
1968	64.9	80.1	145.0	819.8
1969	75.6	168.3	243.9	964.1
1970	291.3	164.7	456.0	1,141.3
1973	484.9	558.6	1,043.5	1,566.9
1974	863.3	671.2	1,534.5	2,456.4
1976	1,477.2	1,895.1	3,372.3	3,513.6
1977	1,445.6	1,878.7	3,324.3	3,847.7
1978	2,041.3	1,898.2	3,939.5	5,153.1
1979	4,515.6	2,589.3	7,104.9	6,418.2

Note: The figures are given in quarterly averages.
Source: Bank of Tanzania. *Economic and Operations Report* (various years).

CHAPTER 16

Kenya, the IMF, and The Unsuccessful Quest For Stabilization

Tony Killick

This paper is extracted from a somewhat fuller study of the International Monetary Fund (IMF) and economic management in Kenya. The paper starts with a very brief statement of background information; the second section goes on to consider the possibilities of short-term economic management in the Kenyan context; the third section examines a succession of higher conditionality credits negotiated with the Fund from 1975 onwards; and the last section takes up some of the issues arising.

Background

While Kenya is not a country where IMF involvement has hit the headlines, there are factors that make it a particularly interesting case to study. For a country with a record of political stability under a rather conservative government and with an essentially market-oriented economy, we might predict that there would be a natural con-

Note: This chapter is excerpted from T. Killick, ed., *The IMF and Stabilisation: Developing Country Experience* (London: Heinemann Educational Books, forthcoming) by permission of the Overseas Development Institute. The author is currently directing a broader research project at the Overseas Development Institute (London) on the IMF and economic stabilization in developing countries. He was formerly a visiting professor of economics at the University of Nairobi.

TABLE 16.1 KENYA: SELECTED BALANCE OF PAYMENTS INDICATORS, 1970–80
(million Kenyan pounds)

Year	*Balance on current account* (1)	*Net long-term capital inflows* (2)	*Basic balance (1 + 2)* (3)	*External reserves*[a] (4)	*External debt*[b] (5)
1970	−17.5	30.9	13.4	73.3	n.a.
1971	−39.9	15.2	−24.7	51.8	n.a.
1972	−24.3	30.6	6.3	66.4	186.9
1973	−66.8	48.1	1.3	76.3	223.0
1974	−112.0	71.0	−41.0	68.4	258.6
1975	−83.9	57.4	−26.5	70.6	285.1
1976	−51.9	90.7	+38.8	114.0	350.3
1977	11.4	84.9	96.3	208.6	458.5
1978	−255.3	168.0	−87.3	133.3	542.6
1979	−178.3	181.0	2.7	234.5	713.7
1980[c]	−332.8	215.0	−117.8	187.0	835.9

n.a. Not available.
Sources: Government of Kenya, *Economic Surveys* and *Statistical Abstracts;* debt data from World Bank.
a. Year-end figures. There is a break in the series between 1971 and 1972, so figures for those years are not strictly comparable.
b. Year-end figures. Converted from dollars at K£0.5 = $1.
c. Provisional.

gruence between the type of stabilization program favored by the IMF and the preferences of the Kenyan government. Moreover, the government's relationships with the IMF have never been the subject of acute political sensitivity—neither within the government nor with public opinion—in the way that it has been in other countries. There have been no ideological barriers to cooperation with the IMF. It seems, then, that if successful stabilization and good working relations with the Fund are not feasible in Kenya, it is unclear where else in Africa they might be achieved.

Key balance of payments indicators are set out in Table 16.1. Prior to 1974, deficits on current account were generally modest, and little difficulty was encountered in meeting these with inflows of long-term capital. In fact, the basic balance showed a surplus in most years prior to 1974, and from 1966 (when national records of reserves were first compiled) until 1973 the official foreign exchange reserves increased during all except two years. At the end of 1973 reserves were equivalent to about five months' imports; the exchange rate had been stable; with certain exceptions, exchange and import controls were either not restrictive or not enforced; and external debt-servicing costs were equivalent in 1973 only to about 3 percent of that year's export earnings. Partly because of this absence of a foreign exchange constraint, the economy had a good growth record, averaging 6.5 percent a year in 1964–73. There was also a virtual absence of inflation.

Although there had been a brief alarm in 1971, and some economists had begun to draw attention to underlying weaknesses, no one could have forecast the abrupt deterioration in the balance of payments that occurred in 1974. The import bill shot up, the current deficit more than doubled to a record size, and the basic balance moved from approximate equality into a deficit of 41 million Kenyan pounds (K£). Despite substantial use of IMF resources and other short-term borrowings, reserves were run down, so that by the end of 1974 they were equivalent to only 2.7 months of imports, compared with 5.1 months a year earlier. The payments indicators in Table 16.1 show the worsening in 1973–74 but then a recovery in the following three years. By 1977 the current account was actually in surplus (for the first time in 12 years), and foreign exchange reserves were so large as to be an embarrassment to the government in its requests for continuing development aid. This did not last, however. There was a second dramatic deterioration during 1978, a diminished but still large current deficit in the following year, and a huge one in 1980. Another deficit of about K£275 million was forecast for 1981, with scarcely less bleak prospects for 1982. Exceptionally large inflows of capital in 1978–80 cushioned the impact on the basic and overall balances so that reserves were quite well protected. By September 1981, however, net reserves had become negative and were only restored by utilization of a Euromarket loan. By the end of 1981, the country was confronting a full-scale payments crisis.

The inevitable price of increased dependence on capital receipts, of course, was an accelerated accumulation of external debt, all the more serious because the Kenyan government data seriously underreported the extent of this. According to World Bank data, the foreign-owned public debt rose from K£223 million at end-1973 to K£836 million seven years later (Table 16.1, col. 5), while the cost of servicing it rose from K£15 million to an estimated K£79 million by 1980. With a debt-service ratio in 1980 estimated at nearly 13 percent and rising fast, the size of the external debt was emerging as a source of major concern.

The year 1973–74 was also a watershed for other aspects of economic performance. The growth rate slowed down and averaged only a little over 4 percent a year in 1974–80. The inflation rate moved abruptly into double figures, where it has stayed ever since.

The deterioration of the balance of payments from 1974—in an economy heavily dependent on imported sources of energy—was obviously related to the quadrupling of oil prices and associated increases in other oil prices. But it would be a mistake to attribute the problem entirely to these causes. Analysis of the sources of payments weakness suggests the following conclusions.

• Movements in the commodity terms of trade account for about 70 percent of the deterioration in the balance of trade in 1973–74 and all the deterioration in the current account. The country was, however, a massive gainer from the world coffee and tea booms of 1976–77, so there were swings as well as roundabouts. And while movements in the terms of trade provide a strong proximate explanation of payments trends they by no means tell all the story.
• Some analysts have, in fact, attributed all or most of the troubles to monetary causes. Along the familiar lines of the monetarist models, strong connections have been found between changes in domestic credit and external assets. These analyses can be criticized as too narrowly conceived, overly argued, and as neglecting the impact of both exogenous and "real" domestic factors. They are nevertheless correct to draw attention to the constraints imposed by the balance of payments in an economy such as Kenya's on domestic credit expansion. In particular, the Kenyan authorities can be criticized for mishandling the 1976–77 coffee/tea boom by passing virtually all the windfall gains on to the farmers and by making no attempt to offset the expansionary monetary effects.
• Structural factors—particularly the slow growth in the volume of exports and weaknesses in the underlying performances of the agricultural and industrial sectors—have also contributed to the seriousness of Kenya's current payments situation, although they probably played a minor role in the wild swings that have occurred since 1973. Structure helps us to understand the trend but not the fluctuations.

The Possibilities of Short-Term Economic Management

Despite the general conservatism of government economic policies and public assertions to the contrary, it is not at all clear that the Kenyan government gave much priority to short-term economic management during the 1970s. One could interpret the post-1973 period as revealing a failure to come to terms with the new policy challenges posed by the emergence of financial constraints.

Government Attitudes to Stabilization

It is useful in this context to draw a distinction between fiscal and monetary policies that are conservative in their general thrust and policies of active economic management. King (1979, pp. 60–62) has shown, for example, that the finance minister of 1962–69, James Gichuru, pursued conservative policies designed to reduce the government's dependence on outside budgetary support, which involved tight restraints on the spending ministries and substantial increases in taxation, but that the corollary of these policies was that "aggregate fiscal policy could not be and was not used for short-term stabilization measures" (p. 62). In 1969 Gichuru gave way as finance minister to Mwai Kibaki, who has held the post ever since (also becoming vice president in 1979). Kibaki proved more expansionist, and King (pp. 65–67) blames the 1971 budget for causing the foreign exchange crisis of that year by opting for expansion when reserves were already falling, prices had begun to rise, domestic credit was already expanding fast, and there was little Keynesian-type excess capacity in the economy. The adverse consequences of this led to more cautious budgets in 1972–74, giving greater emphasis to control over government expenditure. During this period, the treasury widened the tax base, and—despite the increasing difficulty of controlling the spending ministries (resulting in substantial overruns against budget estimates)—it made only modest use of borrowing from the banking system.

The first half of 1975 saw a potentially important landmark in the history of Kenyan economic management with the publication of Sessional Paper no. 4 of 1975: *On Economic Prospects and Policies* (Government of Kenya 1975). This was issued in response to the worsened world economic climate that had emerged with the oil crisis and it attempted to state how the government intended to adjust. It could be described as the first serious public attempt to reconcile the objectives of long-run development and short-term stability, and it contained explicit recognition of the desirability of using fiscal policy as an instrument of stabilization. Unfortunately, in this as in other respects, the implementation of the admirable policies set out in that document left much to be desired.[1] The budget of 1975, announced a few months after the issuance of the Sessional Paper, was sensible, but by the 1976/77 fiscal year the beneficial effects of the coffee/tea

[1] See Killick (1981, pp. 113–14) for a brief general evaluation of the implementation of the Sessional Paper; see also Killick (1980, pp. 41–42).

boom were already large and the treasury chose to exceed the credit ceilings agreed with the IMF, forfeiting access to the extended fund facility (EFF) credit that had been negotiated in the previous year, in favor of a more expansionary budget. The result was a record budget deficit on current account, although other forms of borrowing limited the government's recourse to the banking system.

If the 1976 budget gave forewarning that the government was not serious in its statements about the use of fiscal policy for stabilization, the next one proved the point to the hilt. When it was obviously only a matter of time before world coffee and tea prices fell back to more normal levels, when the turnaround in the balance of payments was already leading to large increases in the domestic money supply, and when the economy was already awash with the spending power resulting from the export boom (which the government refused to tax), the 1977 budget opted for large increases in government spending and a record amount of deficit financing.[2] The 1978 and 1979 budgets were more moderate but both could be—and were—criticized for accurately identifying the reemergence of a balance of payments problem without proposing any solutions.[3] The new development plan issued in 1979 was criticized on the same grounds.[4] In short, if during the 1970s the government ever was serious about the importance of stabilization, it abandoned this priority as soon as the commodity boom allowed it off the hook.

There were signs, however, that the 1980s might usher in a more genuine change of attitude. In the first half of 1980 a new Sessional Paper was issued (Government of Kenya, 1980) for purposes exactly analogous to the 1975 paper. Like its predecessor, it included a strong assertion of the need for more effective economic management, for

[2] In a newspaper article at the time of the budget, the author criticized it as ill-advised, as based on a misreading of the economic situation, and as adding fuel to an already overheated situation. See Tony Killick, "Kenya's Budget: Expansion or Inflation," *Sunday Nation* (Nairobi), June 19, 1977. In the event, an unforeseen upsurge in tax revenues resulted in a much improved budgetary out turn, but what is most relevant for present purposes is that in its fiscal planning the government should favor what it intended as an expansionary budget in circumstances where short-run management clearly indicated the desirability of moderation.

[3] On these budgets, see articles by Tony Killick in the *Sunday Nation* (Nairobi), June 18, 1978 and June 17, 1979.

[4] Killick (1981, pp. 104–10) criticizes the plan for the weakness of its balance of payments policies, especially its silence on exchange rate policy and its failure to offer adequate incentives for improved export performance.

measures to adjust the economy in the face of a payments constraint, and other sensible things. Its specifics included the replacement of quantitative import restrictions by tariff equivalents, and the standardization and reduction in levels of industrial protection—all designed to strengthen the ability of the manufacturing sector to achieve a better export record. A higher interest rate structure was promised, although not for the first time. The crucial question, of course, was whether these good intentions would be carried into effect, and the 1980 and 1981 budgets made a good start to their implementation.[5] On the one hand, the program of import liberalization and of rationalizing protection was being carried out, and the interest rate structure was indeed being raised.[6] On the other hand, the government was having more modest success in carrying out its stated income policies, it was reluctant to introduce major new tax measures, and, as we will see, no end was in sight to the difficulties of containing government spending.

There were other signs of change, too—for example, on exchange rate policy. Since independence and until 1980, the central bank had consistently acted as if it agreed with the first managing director of the IMF that devaluation was a form of confiscation, and it had sought to "maintain the integrity of the Kenya shilling." This it interpreted as entailing a fixed exchange rate (but not, curiously, as entailing the control of domestic credit as a safeguard against domestic inflation). There was, it is true, a 14.5 percent devaluation in October 1975, undertaken in collaboration with the Tanzanian and Ugandan governments (the three currencies were at that time fixed at par with each other as part of the East African Community arrangements) under pressure from the IMF.[7] Thereafter, by word and deed, the government set its face against overt use of the exchange rate, even though the effect of the 1975 change was gradually eroded by differential inflation,[8] and despite the fact that the government tacitly admitted the existence of overvaluation by fiscal measures—an import

[5] See Rupley and Finucane (1981) for a detailed examination of the 1980 budget.

[6] By October 1981 the interest rate on bank savings deposits was up to 10 percent, against only 5 percent at end-1979, and maximum bank lending rates were up from 10 percent to 14 percent.

[7] See Maitha, Killick, and Ikiara (1978, pp. 50–51) for a discussion of this.

[8] Estimates by the United Nations Conference on Trade and Development show the real exchange rate, after adjustment for differential rates of inflation, to have reverted to the pre-1975 devaluation level by early 1978.

duty surcharge and export subsidy, etc.—which amounted to a partial devaluation.

The logic of the 1980 Sessional Paper pointed clearly to a devaluation, and while in 1979–80 the government expicitly declined to employ this policy instrument, a change occurred in 1981 when there were two devaluations with a combined effect of raising the shilling price of SDRs by nearly 24 percent. Whether these changes reflected a fundamental change in government thinking is unclear, however. The prompting of the IMF and World Bank was important in motivating the second, larger, devaluation of 1981, as well as interest rate changes, import liberalization, and the rationalization of industrial protection. It remained unclear whether there would be a more active use of monetary policy in economic management than had previously been the case, and whether the commitment to stabilization would weigh heavily enough when the government was faced with specific spending decisions attractive on their own merits but tending to widen the budgetary gap.

But whatever weaknesses there may have been in the past, it is important to keep them in proper perspective. For example, while there has been a case for currency depreciation, the official rate of exchange has never been allowed to move hugely out of line with a national "equilibrium" rate, as has occurred in other developing countries. Similarly, while the budget has not been used effectively as an instrument of short-run management, in other respects the fiscal record has been good.[9] While there has been a massive increase in state spending since independence, current revenues have generally kept pace and, in almost all years (including the most recent), have financed 75–80 percent of total spending. Budgetary reliance on external grants and loans is much below the immediate postindependence situation, and in recent years it has generally fluctuated around 10 percent of total spending (although this went up to an average of 15 percent in the 1978/79–1980/81 fiscal years). Large-scale financing of deficits by bank borrowing has been confined to a few years (mainly the mid-1970s, 1978/79, and 1980/81). International comparisons of tax effort among developing countries show Kenya with an above-average and improving record,[10] and another comparison shows the overall budgetary deficit to have been slightly better in recent years

[9] See Brough and Curtin (1981) for a general review. See also Killick (1981, pp. 6–7, table 3, and text).

[10] Tait, Gratz, and Eichengreen (1979) compute international tax comparison indices for 47 developing countries for 1969–71 and 1972–76. By this

than the African average.[11] Kenya could not be accused of the fiscal irresponsibility which has marked some other countries.

Similarly, while we have criticized the weak implementation of the 1975 Sessional Paper, it would be wrong to leave the impression that nothing has been done to adjust the economy to the post-1973 economic realities. There have been useful improvements in the structure of price incentives, taxation, government spending, and industrial protection. The government has proved itself more willing than some to increase its taxation of petroleum products, and the indications are that its policies are resulting in some diminution of the economy's dependence on oil-based energy sources. Moreover, the signs are of a better implementation record on the 1980 Sessional Paper.

The main criticism, therefore, is not that the government has acted irresponsibly, but rather that the fiscal and monetary authorities have failed to adapt to the need for more effective short-run economic management necessitated by the financial constraints that first emerged in the earlier 1970s and reemerged a few years later. The stabilization of an economy such as Kenya's is bound to be most difficult, however, so we turn next to examine some of the technical difficulties that the authorities would encounter in attempting this task.

Problems of Stabilization

The earlier analyses of the causes of the inflationary and balance of payments disequilibria placed considerable stress on the influence of unpredictable changes in world prices, as well as on the secondary influence of weather conditions, with the strength of external factors particularly large on the balance of payments in 1974–77 and again in 1979–80. Were these exogenous forces to remain as unruly in the future as they were then, it must be doubted whether stabilization would be an attainable objective, although the relative stability of an extended period prior to 1973–74 indicates that exogenous disturbances are not inevitably unmanageable. Nevertheless, to maintain equilibrium in such an economy must be a demanding task necessitating the use of powerful policy instruments with which to counter

---

comparison, Kenya ranked eighteenth and eleventh for the two periods, respectively. Chelliah, Bass, and Kelly (1975) also rank Kenya with above-average tax effort indices in 1966–71.

[11] Data in *IMF Survey* (September 7, 1981, p. 276) show an average overall deficit for 1973–78 equal to 19 percent of expenditures for Kenya, against 20 percent for Africa as a whole.

TABLE 16.2 VARIABILITY AND BIAS IN KENYAN BUDGETS, 1973/74–1980/81

Item	Coefficient of variation[a] (1)	Direction of bias[b]	
		Over-estimate (2)	Under-estimate (3)
1. Current revenue	13.2	1	7
2. Recurrent expenditure	12.5	0	8
3. Current account surplus	119.3	6	2
4. Capital expenditure	39.6	5	3
5. Receipts of external grants and loans	28.6	6	2
6. Remaining deficit for domestic financing	258.7	2	6
7. Deficit for financing by bank borrowing	152.5	4	4

Sources: Central Bank of Kenya, *Annual Reports;* Government of Kenya, *Economic Surveys*.
a. In percentages of original budget estimates.
b. Number of observations.

the exogenous forces. How potent are the conventional fiscal and monetary instruments of economic management in Kenya?

As a first approach we can enquire into the extent to which fiscal variables are sufficiently predictable to be capable of short-run manipulation. A study was undertaken of the eight budgets of 1973/74 to 1980/81, comparing actual outcomes with the values that were predicted in the budgets, with the results summarized in Table 16.2. Column (1) provides a measure of the extent to which actual outcomes differed from the budgeted amounts, and columns (2) and (3) together reveal the direction of bias in the budgets.

Take variability first. All the items show significant average deviations of actual from budgeted values. As might be expected, the residual balances (entries 3, 6, and 7) display the largest deviations from budgeted estimates. Strong systematic biases are also revealed. On current account, both revenue and expenditure are generally underestimated, but the absolute difference is largest with expenditures, so that there is a persistent tendency to overestimate the current account surplus (line 3). External aid almost always falls short of budgeted amounts, but the potential for nonbank domestic borrowing tends to be underestimated, as can be inferred from a comparison of lines 6 and 7. Interestingly, there is no particular bias in the estimates of bank borrowing, although the proportionate deviations from budgeted values are very large.

Particular interest attaches to this last fact, for bank borrowing by the government is generally regarded as the chief fiscal variable available to be manipulated for short-term management and is the main ingredient of the domestic component of the high-powered money base featured in monetarist models. But since it is a residual, meeting whatever deficit (or absorbing whatever surplus) happens to result when all the other entries in the budget have been completed, can it rightly be treated as a *policy instrument* at all? As one Kenyan adviser complained, it is a "residual of a residual"; i.e., that part of residual item 6 which is left over after the treasury has made its decisions about nonbank borrowing. Since the total deficit to be filled by domestic borrowing has a coefficient of variation of 259 percent and bank borrowing of 153 percent, it is not at all clear that manipulation of deficit financing is a practical way of trying to maintain the macroeconomic balance of the economy.

To this it can reasonably be retorted that it should be possible to improve the accuracy of budget forecasting, as the IMF staff has urged. A reduction in the eccentricity of the tax on company profits, which yields almost all its revenue in the fourth quarter of the fiscal year, would ease the task of prediction and reduce the present large degree of seasonality in government revenues. Imperfect information inevitably means that there will be some—possibly quite large—deviations from budget forecasts, but the biases revealed in Table 16.2 are presumably capable of reduction because other African governments have managed to avoid the severe sources of unpredictability that characterize Kenya. It should be possible for the treasury to adjust for the tendency to underestimate revenues and current spending and to correct for the overestimation of current savings, capital spending, and aid receipts. Were this achieved, it would undoubtedly bring greater predictability to items 6 and 7 of the table. Whether there would be sufficient improvement for deficit financing to become a practical instrument of stabilization policy must nevertheless remain in question, although this has been the chief item upon which the IMF has focused in stand-by negotiations.

There are further difficulties, concerning the transmission mechanism between deficit financing on the one hand and the performance indicators it is intended to influence on the other: the GDP growth rate, the balance of payments, and the price level. For one thing, variations in government indebtedness to the banks may be offset by contravariations in credit to the private sector, as tended to happen in 1974, 1975, and 1978. It is thus necessary to look at the total credit scene. There are also the questions of the magnitude of the impact and of time lags. King (1979, p. 100) expresses doubts about the practicability of a workable contracyclical stabilization policy (1) because his financial flows model indicated that "budgetary policy has a relatively small effect upon economic activity at the best of times," and (2) because of "the eighteen-months delay between the Kenyan authorities' decision to borrow in 1970 and the impact of this decision on the economy." In this context, we should also report Adongo's finding (1978) of a two-year time lag between changes in money supply and the price level.

When we turn from fiscal to more purely monetary factors, there are further technical complications. The Polak-type model utilized by King (1979) treats the marginal propensity to import (m) and the marginal income velocity of circulation (k) as constants. The monetary model employed by Grubel and Ryan (1979) analogously required stable relationships between the money supply, on the one hand, and time (as a proxy for income?) and high-powered money on the other, as well as stable elasticities of demand for money with respect to prices and interest rates. Calculations of the coefficient of variation of m and k yield the following results (as a percentage of the mean values for each period):

	m	k
1968–71	8.3	4.7
1972–80	12.1	10.6

The estimate for k can be compared with a similar calculation by Park (1970, Table 1, col. V_3) for 14 developing countries that had an average coefficient of variation of 7.1 percent in 1953–68. On the basis of his estimates, Park was pessimistic about the practicability of monetary models for short-term forecasting and management, yet the Kenyan figure for 1972–80 is half as large again. The variability of m is even greater, of course.[12] It is true that the above calculations are for the *average* propensity and velocity, whereas King (1979) merely assumes constant *marginal* values, but it is surely the case that the variability revealed above is also inconsistent with assumptions of constant marginal values.

[12] The variability of both parameters is much smaller for the 1968–71 period, which may explain why King (1979) obtained reasonable predictions from his model.

This leaves us to examine the stability of the money multiplier, *b*. This was investigated by Bolnick (1975) for 1967–73, who concluded that:

> (1) Variations in the "money multiplier" on a quarter-to-quarter basis have been relatively large, implying instability of the behavioural parameters affecting the money stock.
>
> (2) The major source of variation in the money multiplier has been commercial bank liquidity behaviour. Our analysis suggests that the liquid asset ratio is neither fully predictable nor fully controllable. . .

Bolnick's analysis thus casts doubt on the feasibility of effective monetary policy, but Grubel and Ryan (1979, p. 27) obtain less negative results. Utilizing annual (as against quarterly) data, they derive a money supply function that provides a good statistical explanation, with the high-powered money base and a time trend as the independent variables ($R^2 = 0.98$). They think their result is consistent with Bolnick's because, by using annual data, they abstract from intrayear variations, and "it is well known that in most countries the money multiplier is much more unstable in the short than in the long run. But relevant for policy is the long-run stability observed in our data." This latter point is questionable, however. In the context of economic management (and negotiations with the IMF!), it is most important to be able to predict for the short run.

We must conclude this section, therefore, on a note of skepticism concerning the feasibility of effective short-term stabilization. Against the potentially large exogenous destabilizing forces are arrayed a set of fiscal and monetary instruments of dubious reliability. It is unclear:

- whether the government could be in a position to manipulate the volume of its deficit financing for stabilization purposes in more than a very approximate manner
- how much impact deficit financing will have on total domestic credit, money supply, or both
- whether the key parameters are sufficiently well behaved to permit the short-run forecasting accuracy needed for stabilization policy
- whether the time lags are short and predictable enough to allow the manipulation of instrument variables to achieve desired short-run macroeconomic results.

It seems clear that there can be little hope of effective "fine tuning" in such circumstances and that the most that can be hoped for is a rough-and-ready avoidance of the worst extremes of economic fluctuations.

Having thus laid an analytical foundation, we turn next to examine the role of the IMF in the quest for stabilization in Kenya.

Relations with the IMF

A number of considerations make a study of Kenya's relations with the IMF of more than normal interest. First, being wholly dependent on imported supplies, Kenya has been one of the countries most seriously affected by the large relative rise in crude oil prices and by the oscillations in world economic conditions associated with that.[13] Second, even though the economic philosophy of the government is closer to that of the Fund than is true of many developing countries, being essentialy pragmatic, conservative, and market-oriented, Kenya-IMF relations have had a troubled recent history, and it is thus particularly interesting to enquire into the reasons for this. Third, while we have seen that Kenya has had major payments difficulties since 1974, it is not a country that has allowed economic conditions to deteriorate dramatically before a last-ditch recourse to the Fund, as demonstrated by its good Euromarket credit rating. In general, the government has been fairly prompt in commencing negotiations and might therefore expect to have received more favorable policy conditions than the late appliers. Finally, Kenya has been the subject of collaboration between the IMF and the World Bank and was the first country to reach an agreement under the Fund's EFF which came into operation in 1975.

Financial flows between Kenya and the Fund are summarized in Table 16.3. As can be observed, credits were used under the 1974 and 1975 oil facilities, and substantial use was made of the compensatory financing facility (CFF) in 1976 and 1979. There were also credits from the higher conditionality facilities (recorded in lines 2–4 of the table) in 1975 and 1979–81, and it is on these that we focus below. Line 9 reveals significant net inflows from the Fund in 1974–76 and 1979–81, with a relatively large net return flow in 1977. Lines 13–15 record the balance of certain other receipts as at mid-1980, not included in the remainder of the table.

What follows will concentrate on the higher conditionality credits of 1975–76 and 1979–81, most notably the EFF credit of SDR 67.2

[13] According to the World Bank (1981, p. 148), petroleum imports represented 95 percent of total Kenyan commercial energy consumption in 1978, a figure among the highest recorded in Africa.

TABLE 16.3 FINANCIAL FLOWS BETWEEN KENYA AND THE IMF, 1974–80
(million Kenyan pounds)

	1974	*1975*	*1976*	*1977*	*1978*	*1979*	*1980*
Gross inflows							
1. Reserve tranche	5.4	—	—	—	3.2	—	—
2. Credit tranches	—	5.8[a]	—	—	—	8.4	8.2[b]
3. Supplementary facility	—	—	—	—	—	—	20.8[b]
4. Extended facility	—	3.7[c]	—	—	—	—	—
5. Oil facility	14.0	13.9	1.5	—	—	—	—
6. Compensatory facility	—	—	11.6	—	—	33.3	—
7. Total gross inflows	19.4	23.4	13.1	—	3.2	41.7	29.0
8. Repayments (repurchases)	—	−5.8[b]	−5.1	−18.1	−1.2	−14.8	−3.4
9. Net inflow	19.4	17.6	8.0	−18.1	2.0	26.9	25.6
Memorandum items							
10. Use of Fund credit (outstanding balance at year-end)	14	33	41	23	25	52	94
11. Quota (year-end)	21	23	23	23	33	33	64
12. Credit as percentage of quota	67	144	177	100	75	157	147
Other receipts, at mid-1980							
13. SDR allocations							14.5
14. Profits from gold sales							2.8
15. Loans from Trust Fund (gross)							22.6

—Not available.

Note: Flows are converted from SDRs at the year-end exchange rate. There were no transactions of the types recorded in lines 1–6 prior to 1974.

Sources: IMF, *Annual Reports* and *International Financial Statistics*.

a. A net credit tranche drawing of K£5.8 million was both effected and paid back during 1975.

b. During 1980 a two-year stand-by credit was agreed for total amounts of K£27.6 million of ordinary credit tranche drawings and K£89.1 million from the supplementary facility.

c. During this year an extended Fund credit totaling K£29 million was agreed, intended to be drawn during 1975–78.

million (equivalent at that time to K£29 million) intended to be drawn down during 1975–78, and two-year upper tranche stand-by credits negotiated successively in 1979 and 1980. These were of SDR 122.45 million and SDR 241.5 million (K£59 and K£117 million), respectively, which latter amount was equivalent to approximately 350 percent of Kenya's IMF quota. We choose this focus because these are the credits that raise the issues of economic management and Fund conditionality that are the prime concern of this conference.

The 1975 EFF Agreement

The EFF was established in September 1974 to give medium-term assistance to countries in "special circumstances of balance of payments difficulty" whose solution would require a longer period than that for which normal credit tranche facilities are available.[14] Requests for EFF credits may be approved "in support of comprehensive programs that include policies . . . required to correct structural imbalances. . ." Credits may be drawn over a three-year period. They were originally repayable over a maximum of 8 years, since extended to 10 years.

Kenya's request for assistance was the first to be received and approved (in July 1975) under this scheme and was thus regarded as of particular interest. The credit was approved on the grounds that the economy was "suffering serious payments imbalances relating to structural maladjustments in production and trade and where price and cost distortions have been widespread." The request was in support of a three-year program covering the 1975/76 to 1977/78 fiscal years, spelled out in the Sessional Paper on economic prospects and policies referred to earlier (Government of Kenya 1975). According to Bhatia and Rothman (1975, p. 40—hereafter, B & R),"the program reflects, in part, extensive discussions by the Kenyan Government with staff members of the Fund and of the World Bank who have made coordinated policy recommendations to the Government." The credit was payable in six half-yearly installments, with the bulk of the money becoming available during 1976 and 1977, subject to six-monthly reviews of progress. It was repayable over a maximum eight years. Performance criteria were established, satisfaction of which would govern continued access to the credit. The total value of the credit of SDR 67.2 million was then equivalent to 140 percent of Kenya's IMF quota. At approximately the same time, the World Bank approved a programme loan for $30 million (K£11 million).

Given that this was the first use of the EFF, particular interest attaches to the extent to which the policy conditions for this credit differed from those associated with conventional stand-by credits. Unfortunately, different answers are provided, according to the source of information. Two facts can be asserted with some assurance, however. First, the existence of a medium-term adjustment program, of

[14] This and the following paragraph are based upon Bhatia and Rothman (1975) who provide a useful account of Kenya's EFF credit.

the type set out in the 1975 Sessional Paper, was a precondition for agreement on an EFF credit. The Fund essay describing the agreement (B & R) includes an account of the longer-term factors contributing to the payments difficulties (although it rather remarkably fails to mention the payments impact of higher oil prices and other exogenous factors analyzed above) and gave prominence to the program set out in the Sessional Paper. The paper sent by the IMF staff to the Executive Board recommending the credit similarly spent 16 pages on medium-term degelopments and policies, against only 3 pages on the financial program.

Second, however, it appears to be the case that the Fund staff were content to play a secondary role in the formulation of the Sessional Paper's policies for structural adjustment, although they did press for a tariff reform in support of a restructuring of the manufacturing sector, for more credit to agriculture, and for some other measures. The World Bank made most of the running, initiating the idea that the government should prepare a paper in support of its application for a program loan. The Bank particularly pushed for the inclusion of measures that would limit the (previously very rapid) growth of spending on education, increase the share of government spending on agriculture, and introduce a more active use of interest rates (although in the event the paper was notably noncommittal on this latter point). The IMF and World Bank coordinated their respective contributions, and the Bank's decision to approve the program loan was influenced by the government's willingness also to comply with the additional conditions accompanying the EFF credit.

It is more difficult to provide a firm judgment about the extent to which the substance of the conditionality for this credit differed from the policy conditions normally attached to short-term stand-bys. While it probably incorporated a less abrupt (and hence lower-cost) adjustment, at a formal level the similarities appear greater than the differences.

Letters of Intent from member governments to the Fund identify certain "performance criteria," satisfaction of which governs continuing access to the credit. The performance criteria written into Kenya's 1975 EFF agreement related only to government borrowing from the banking system and to total domestic credit, both of which were restricted to specified ceilings. In these respects, the agreement was identical to an ordinary stand-by. And, on at least some descriptions, when it came to the crunch of detailed negotiations it was as if the government were negotiating a stand-by: demand management primarily through credit restrictions, with the usual provisions concerning performance criteria, six-monthly reviews, and so forth—although admittedly set within a three-year framework—and with the detailed discussions largely focusing on the rival merits of government and Fund forecasts for the 1975/76 budget and the resulting requirements for deficit financing. The Fund was thus apparently emphasizing policies of short-run demand management to deal with problems that the Fund itself identified as longer-term structural weaknesses. As shown earlier, they were also problems substantially created by external forces entirely beyond the control of the Kenyan authorities.

However, these criticisms should be qualified by two other considerations. This credit, it must be remembered, was the first to be negotiated under the EFF arrangements, and it was understandable that the Fund should tread carefully in consenting to major innovations in its conditionality. Further, the nature of the negotiations was no doubt conditioned by the fact that an acceptable medium-term adjustment program was already in place. Had this not been the case, discussions between the Fund and the government would probably have been taken up more with putting such a program together and would hence have appeared rather less like a stand-by negotiation. The fact stands, however, that the performance criteria were the strictly conventional ones of credit control.

Although it seems that the Fund took little active interest in the contents of the Sessional Paper, had it done so and if the EFF credit would not have been agreed in the absence of some such medium-term policy commitments, it follows that any such conditions were *additional* to the Fund's conventional short-term monetary conditions. Careful reading of the Board decision setting up the EFF confirms this because

> A member making a request for an extended arrangement must, *in addition to* presenting a program "setting forth the objectives and policies for the whole medium-term period . . ." present "a detailed statement of the policies and measures for the first twelve months . . . of the program" (B & R, p. 41; italics added).

This new form of support provided by the EFF, while undoubtedly valuable in permitting a more gradual adjustment, thus provided an occasion for increasing the scope of Fund conditionality. By retaining the conventional demand management programs for which the Fund is well known, it places an exceedingly ambiguous gloss on the extent to which the Fund's policies were adapted to take account of structural or supply-side considerations, or of externally caused disequilibria.

Whether the actual credit ceilings written into the agreement were reasonable is a question taken up shortly, but we should also ask about the adequacy of the EFF credit in relation to the size of Kenya's

TABLE 16.4 FINANCING GAPS AND KENYA'S EXTENDED FUND FACILITY CREDIT, 1974–76
(million Kenyan pounds)

Year	*Sums available from EFF*[a] *(1)*	*Actual deficit on basic balance* *(2)*	*Expected financing gap*[b] *(3)*	*EFF target*[c] *(4)*
1974	0	41	35	n.a.
1975	3.7	27	50	37
1976	13.0	n.a.	60	17

n.a. Not applicable.
Sources: Government of Kenya, (1975), p. 4, and other official sources.
a. A further amount of K£15.7 million was scheduled to become available during 1977.
b. Expected gap after "normal" inflows of aid and other capital.
c. Targeted deficit on overall balance.

payments imbalances of that time. Relevant data are summarized in Table 16.4, from which it appears that the value of the credit was substantial in relation to past and expected future payments deficits, especially when viewed as part of a package which also included the World Bank loan, possibly increased aid from bilateral sources (which did, in fact, increase—see Maitha, Killick, and Ikiara 1978, p. 45), and any additional private inflows that might result from agreement with the Fund. In the event, the EFF targets and the value of the credit itself were quickly rendered obsolete by the coffee/tea boom, but what is important for present purposes is the size of the assistance in relation to the payments deficits experienced in the immediate past and anticipated at that time for the immediate future. Even taken by itself, the EFF credit would in 1976 have been equal to about half the actual previous year's deficit on basic balance, about a quarter of the government's estimate of the financing gap and nearly all of the targeted deficit on the overall balance.

As things turned out, coffee export prices began a rapid rise in the second half of 1975, standing at the end of the year 69 percent above the June level, although it was not until April 1977 that the price peaked, and it was not until 1977 that the export prices were strongly influenced. The favorable movement in the commodity terms of trade took pressure off the government and probably explains why the government quickly borrowed from the banks in excess of the ceiling agreed with the Fund, forfeiting continued access to the credit. This failure by the government to observe the terms of the agreement was not allowed to stand in the way of reaching new understandings at the time of the 1976 budget, but by then much of the rationale for the loan had disappeared, and the ceilings were again breached. This first experiment in the use of the EFF thus fizzled out. Only the initial installment of K£3.7 million was drawn, and the actual impact of the demand management package associated with it was negligible, although that was scarcely the fault of the IMF.

The 1979–81 Stand-bys

As was shown in the first section, major improvements occurred on the balance of payments in 1976–77, followed by a drastic deterioration in 1978. Toward the end of that year, the government applied for a stand-by loan within the first credit tranche, to which, of course, it had nearly automatic access. This credit of K£8.4 million was drawn down in the first half of 1979, as recorded in Table 16.3. The government anticipated financing needs additional to this sum and thus initiated a number of further moves. First, it approached commercial banks and agreed a Eurodollar loan of $200 million (K£74 million). This was arranged prior to the budget in June 1979, although it was not signed until July, and a substantial part of it was almost immediately utilized. No policy strings were attached but the commercial terms (1.5 percent) above the London interbank offered rate Libor, repayable over 7 years) were expensive.

This loan gave the government an assurance that it would not be forced into a devaluation during the politically sensitive period of a presidential election and the settling-in of the president's new cabinet. Simultaneously, however, the government began negotiations for a two-year upper tranche stand-by credit of SDR 122.5 million (K£59.2 million), and agreement was finalized in August 1979. Finally, negotiations were also commenced with the World Bank for a loan under its new "structural adjustment" program, totaling $70 million (K£28 million),[15] agreement on which was finalized in February 1980. We are particularly concerned here, of course, with the stand-by, especially because it was negotiated after the Fund had reviewed its guidelines on conditionality in March 1979. Since this review was heralded as ushering in some relaxation in the stringency of the Fund's policy conditions, it is instructive to enquire whether as a result the

[15] Of this sum, $55 million was to come from the International Development Association, the World Bank's "soft-loan" window, to be supplemented by a $15 million Special Action Credit from the European Economic Community.

conditions put to the Kenyan government showed signs of a greater liberality.

It would be difficult to assert that they did. In fact, they were arguably tougher than in 1975. The program presented by the government for the two-year period of the loan included provisions for improvements in tax revenues, real reductions in government recurrent and development spending in 1979/80, a 15 percent expansion in bank credit to the private sector, a study of the potential value of interest rate adjustments as a policy instrument (again!), a policy of wage restraint that would reduce real wages, and careful control of new additions to the external public debt. As always, however, what was of greatest importance were the items included as performance criteria. These were (1) ceilings on the net domestic assets of the central bank; (2) ceilings on net government borrowing from the banking system; (3) an "understanding" with the Fund on exchange rate policy, to be reached by the end of 1979; and (4) another "understanding" by the same date on the early elimination of an advance import deposit scheme which had been introduced at the end of 1978 and had proved highly effective as a means of achieving a once-for-all reduction in the volume of imports.

The import deposits scheme was, in fact, relaxed in November 1979 (which contributed to the larger volume of imports experienced in 1980), and no difficulties were experienced with the agreed ceilings on the domestic assets of the central bank. An IMF report recommending a devaluation was quietly pigeonholed and the official exchange rate remained unchanged. However, the ceilings on bank credit to government proved unworkable. These were greatly exceeded during July-December 1979 and, although the government was able to reduce its indebtedness to the banks in the final three months, it was only at the very end of the fiscal year that the amount came within the agreed ceiling and the government seemingly became eligible to draw upon the credit. In retrospect, the Kenyan government and IMF officials recognize that the intrayear ceiling was excessively restrictive.

When in mid-1980 its bank borrowing eventually fell within the ceiling and the government sought to draw upon the credit, it was astonished to be told that it was ineligible on technical grounds. The Letter of Intent had contained the standard undertaking not to introduce multiple currency arrangements. In his 1980 budget, however, the minister of finance announced certain changes intended to make the long-standing export subsidy scheme more effective. The rate of subsidy was doubled, and, to speed up payments of the subsidies, its administration was to be transferred from the customs department to the central bank. The Fund was notified of the intention to make these changes and offered no objection. After they had been announced in the budget, however, the Fund's lawyers ruled that this administrative transfer (which in the event was never implemented) converted the scheme into a multiple currency arrangement and that the government thus stood in breach of its undertaking. This left a hapless Fund mission to break the news to annoyed Kenyan officials and to advise them that the best course was now to scrap the 1979 agreement and negotiate a new one. Strong views are still held by some about what was regarded as the malign influence of remote lawyers whose inflexibility revealed scant sensitivity to local problems, but whose opinions on this issue prevailed in Washington over the objections of the Fund mission.

The end result of these events was that the credit negotiated in 1979 was never utilized, even though there is no question that the country was faced with major payments difficulties, monetary expansion was fairly moderate, and bank credit to government by the end of the fiscal year was actually lower than at the beginning. In compensation for the difficulties created by the breakdown of the 1979 agreement, however, a new two-year stand-by was quickly agreed, worth considerably more than would have been due under the 1979 agreement. The new credit was for SDR 241.5 million (K£117 million) and received IMF approval in October 1980.

It was believed in official Kenyan circles that the ceilings agreed for government bank borrowing in 1980/81 were less draconian in amount and form than those for 1979/80 and, more generally, that the Fund mission displayed flexibility during negotiations, departing substantially from their initial brief in response to the case presented by Kenyan representatives. In fact, Kenyan officials suspected that the IMF mission chief was under instructions to reach an agreement at any reasonable cost: the 1980 IMF and World Bank annual meeting was imminent, and it was desired to minimize allegations of Fund harshness and rigidity on policy conditions. Whether or not this is the case, members of the Executive Board in Washington expressed disquiet about what was regarded as the laxity of the policy conditions in the agreement, although it was eventually approved.

In one respect, however, the 1980 agreement incorporated a widening of the scope of conditionality, for it required the government to reach agreements with the Fund on import policy *as a performance criterion*. Specifically, this was intended to ensure the implementation of the government's policy of replacing quantitative import restrictions by tariff equivalents and represented a most interesting innovation because it is rare for the Fund to include unquantified policy commitments as performance criteria. This could be seen, perhaps, as a move in the direction of paying greater attention to medium-term structural adjustment, because the import policy was seen as an important aspect of the strategy of industrial restructuring. This strategy was, in turn, the hard core of the policy conditions attached to the World Bank's February 1980 structural adjustment loan; viewed as complementary to the Bank's conditions, the new IMF credit terms could be seen as paying greater attention to medium-term adjustment. The IMF press release announcing the 1980 credit emphasized this aspect.[16] In the nitty gritty of detailed negotiations, however, the focus was again largely on short-term credit ceilings and on the underlying fiscal projections.

As regards the adequacy of these credits, what can be said is that the amounts agreed upon in 1979 and (especially) 1980 were quite large in relation to the country's payments magnitudes. Had they been fully utilized, the 1979 agreement would have provided K£59 million over two years and the 1980 agreement was for K£117, also over two years. These sums may be compared with the deficits recorded in columns (2) and (3) of Table 16.1 and with the government's expectation of an overall financing gap of K£139 million in the 12 months beginning July 1980. Although the increase in Kenya's quota was modest between 1975 and the times of the 1979 and 1980 negotiations (see Table 16.3, line 11) and indeed diminished in real terms (when deflated by an index of the country's import prices), policy changes allowed the IMF to grant larger credits relative to quotas, so that the amount of assistance agreed in 1979 and 1980 was substantial relative to the likely size of the payments deficits. The

[16] The relevant part of the press release read as follows (*IMF Survey*, October 27, 1980, p. 339):

> The Government has formulated a set of medium-term policies designed to strengthen the balance of payments and establish a high rate of growth of output and employment. These policies address the restructuring of the economy with greater emphasis on agricultural growth and a reorientation of the manufacturing sector away from import substitution and toward exports. This medium-term strategy will be complemented by short-term demand management policies designed to contain inflationary pressures and the external deficit while the reallocation of resources in the economy is taking place. The Government also intends to take firm action to restrain the consumption of petroleum-based energy by making optimal use of imported fuels and by accelerating the development of alternative energy sources.

TABLE 16.5 TARGETED AND ACTUAL BANK CREDIT TO KENYAN GOVERNMENT, SELECTED YEARS
(million Kenyan pounds)

Item	*1975/76* *(1)*	*1976/77* *(2)*	*1979/80* *(3)*	*1980/81* *(4)*
1. Amount of additional credit during year[a]				
Ceiling	17.5	30.8	45.0	53.5
Actual	26.6	9.5	−6.3	114.7
Ceiling as percentage of:				
2. Amount of government credit at year-beginning[b]	32	38	31	41
3. Money supply at year-beginning[b]	5.8	8.3	6.2	6.7
4. Domestic credit at year-beginning	6.3	9.7	7.2	7.5
5. Total budgeted government spending	4.9	8.0	6.2	3.4
6. Monetary GDP[c]	1.9	3.1	2.7	2.7

Note: The years selected are those for which upper tranche or extended facility credits were negotiated. The figures do not agree with published data because of differences in the definition of credit to government.
Source: Author's own computations.
a. On a June-to-June comparison. Ceilings were also agreed for various dates within the fiscal year, which are not shown above.
b. "Year-beginning" refers to the balance as at end-June 1975, 1976, 1979, and 1980, respectively.
c. As a percentage of monetary GDP at factor cost and in current prices, in the last calendar year before commencement of the fiscal year in question.

assistance was still relatively short term, however, being repayable over a maximum of five years.

In the event, the 1980 agreement proved even less workable than its 1979 forerunner. With considerable difficulty, the Kenyan treasury managed to remain within the agreed ceiling on its bank borrowing until the first benchmark date of December 31, 1980, thus entitling it to utilize the second installment of the credit, but thereafter the amount of deficit financing far exceeded the agreed total, as can be judged from Table 16.5. That the actual level of government bank borrowing was more than double the agreed ceiling for the fiscal year as a whole was, as is candidly admitted by the treasury, due to unforeseen government spending rather than to any intrinsic unreasonableness in the height of the ceiling. There was an unbudgeted 30 percent increase in civil service salaries—an increase which only partially restored a past erosion in the real value of salaries but which nevertheless was not anticipated in the 1980 budget. There were also unexpected calls on the revenues resulting from the food shortages of that year, and there were a number of other spending increases, some of which reflected inadequate expenditure control by the treasury over other ministries.

Attempts by the government and Fund staff during the second half of 1981 to rescue the remainder of the two-year program and to agree ceilings for 1981/82 ran into a number of difficulties, and in the end it was decided to abandon that program and to put in its place a 12-month stand-by for SDR 151.5 million (K£90.5 million). This was finally approved in January 1982. It was a tougher agreement than that of 1980. The Fund was anxious to safeguard against a repetition of the 1980/81 failure. It had had similar recent experiences of agreements breaking down in several other African states, and this further increased its determination to close any remaining loopholes. And the cold wind blowing from the Reagan administration, which was first felt at the 1981 IMF and World Bank annual meeting, added greatly to the pressures on the Fund mission not to come back with an agreement that could be branded as soft. In consequence, the Kenyans, with a major balance of payments crisis on their hands, (see "Background," above), found themselves obliged to enter into a wider range of commitments than in 1979 and 1980—on external debt, on government spending, and on import liberalization. Moreover, the largest installment of this credit was reserved to the end, until satisfaction of the performance criteria at the conclusion of the agreement period, thus raising the Fund's effective leverage during the full span of the agreement. It remained to be seen whether this agreement would work better than its predecessors, but there seemed to this observer a probability that the government would once again be unable to stay within the agreed ceiling on government bank borrowing. The government was reluctant to introduce major revenue-raising measures, so all the burden of an improved fiscal balance was falling on a limitation of expenditure that was bound to prove most difficult for the treasury to enforce.

Evaluation of the Credit Ceilings

We have seen that bank credit to the government was a key—*the* key—performance criterion in all the higher conditionality credits negotiated.[17] Evaluation of the policy conditions attached to these credits therefore involves forming a judgment about whether the credit ceilings were reasonable. Evidence on this issue is summarized in Table 16.5 for each of the fiscal years for which higher conditionality agreements were negotiated up to 1980/81. These statistics are based on June-to-June comparisons (the fiscal year runs from July to June) and thus ignore the additional ceilings for intermediate dates within the year.

On the basis of the evidence in Table 16.5, it would be impossible to characterize the ceilings as very restrictive. They generally envisage total government borrowing increasing annually by between 31 percent and 41 percent (line 2), which, when compounded, are rapid rates of increase. Lines 3 and 4 record the amount of the ceilings as percentages of money supply and total domestic credit, but this understates the monetary expansion that would result because much state borrowing from the banking system takes forms that increase the high-powered money base, thus permitting a secondary round of credit expansion to other borrowers. Bolnick (1975, Table 1) found a money multiplier with an average value of 2.3, so the figures in lines 3 and 4 might be roughly doubled to obtain a better grasp of the degree of expansion implicit in the deficit financing ceiling. (In fact, the Letters of Intent also contained explicit or implicit targets for the expansion of total domestic credit, which were 19 percent for 1975/76, 21 percent for 1976/77, 19 percent for 1979/80, and 23 percent for 1980/81.)

In the light of information then available and reasonable forecasts of the immediate future, there was a case for some monetary expansion in mid-1975, to offset the deflationary forces then emanating from the outside world, even though the government had set itself the objective of reducing inflation to "no more than half of the increase in import prices" (Government of Kenya 1975, p. 7), and the emergence of the coffee boom in the second half of 1975 soon changed the situation. But any case for expansion had disappeared by the time of the 1976 budget, and the ceiling for that year could be criticized as *too high* for the purposes of economic management. Perhaps 1979/80 was an intermediate case, but, given the underlying weakness of the balance of payments situation, it would be difficult to argue that a ceiling permitting a 31 percent increase in government bank bor-

[17] The ceilings on the net domestic assets of the central bank never created any difficulties, and this item was dropped as a performance criterion in 1980, when total domestic credit was added.

rowing (and a 19 percent increase in total credit) was excessively restrictive. The same general judgment also holds for the 1980/81 ceiling, which actually envisaged a 41 percent increase in credit to government (and a 23 percent increase in total credit). The fact is, of course, that in two of the four years actual deficit financing was well below the agreed ceiling, which increases the difficulty of viewing the ceilings as too low.

The matter no doubt looked different to Kenyan treasury officials, concerned more with the fiscal situation and how to balance the accounts. Line 5 of Table 16.5 shows the ceilings as proportions of total budgeted government spending. These were relatively modest, especially in 1980/81. The treasury was being buffeted by competing pressures—from the IMF to limit the deficit, from the public not to raise taxes, and from the spending ministries to raise their budget allocations. Its authority over the spending ministries was also far from unquestioned and was tending to weaken over time. The ceilings were also modest in relation to GDP (line 6). It was through the monetary system, rather than through its direct impact on aggregate spending, that the deficit financing would have its main impact on the economy. But, to repeat, it is difficult to think that the monetary impact of the ceilings would have been deflationary.

Matters Arising

We have analyzed three higher conditionality agreements between the Kenyan government and the IMF, all of which quickly broke down. Generally, the relationship has not worked smoothly. It was the Kenyan government (and the improving payments position) that was responsible for the breakdown of the 1975 agreement, although the government may have been less inclined to go its own way had it not perceived the Fund terms as onerous. In 1979/80, however, intrayear credit ceilings proved unworkably tight, so that the government was unable to use this credit, for which it was finally declared ineligible in mid-1980 on a legal technicality. This was immediately followed with another stand-by that was more generous both in value and policy conditions, but this too broke down, largely because of unplanned increases in government spending.

These difficulties must be seen in the context of an economy that has rarely been grossly mismanaged—no hyperinflation, no hugely overvalued currency—with a rather conservative, pragmatic, and generally market-oriented government. The government's dealings with the IMF have not been of any great political sensitivity, and there has been no great ideological divide. Ministers and senior officials in the treasury and central bank are by no means heedless of the importance of economic stability, and the treasury does not disagree with the thrust of the IMF's policies. The principle of conditionality is not contested by them, and they see the Fund staff as potentially useful allies in strengthening the hands of the treasury and central bank in their efforts to impose financial discipline. It is thus worth repeating what was said earlier: if successful stabilization and good working relations with the Fund are not feasible in Kenya, it is unclear where else in Africa they might be achieved.

It is all the more significant, therefore, that things have worked badly, even though personal relations have been generally cordial. While they are by no means hostile to the basic task of the Fund, Kenyan officials dislike the way in which that role is played. They contemplate an application of an IMF credit with reluctance and regard negotiations with it as unnecessarily taxing. They also point to the considerable costs of a Fund credit because of (1) interest charges that are not now very far below commercial rates and because of (2) what is regarded as the excessive amount of high-level manpower tied up in the preparation of a credit application, the subsequent negotiations, and the monitoring of results.

One reason for their reservations about the Fund is that they view it as being too concerned with the short term, too anxious to achieve quick results. We have shown earlier that, in addition to short-run monetary factors, Kenya's payments difficulties stem from basic structural weaknesses and from the effects of rising oil and other import prices. In truth, the increase in real oil prices will not be reversed, and Kenya must adjust to it. But such adjustment cannot be expected quickly, and in the interim there will remain large financing needs. One of the most interesting results to emerge from our research has been the uncertain importance attached by the IMF to medium-term restructuring, even in the context of the EFF, with negotiations and performance criteria being largely confined to conventional, short-term concerns. When Kenyan negotiators urge the need to take a longer-term view and to go beyond the scope of demand management, the response from Fund missions has sometimes been to the effect that they are personally sympathetic, but that IMF headquarters is looking for a conventional financial program and that longer term adjustment is more a concern of the World Bank. On the Kenyan evidence, the EFF is perceived as making few concessions to the case for structural adjustment when it comes to binding policy conditions, and to the extent that "structural" measures are included, they are additional to the usual Fund performance criteria. This not only opens the Fund to the criticism that the limitation of aggregate demand is far from being a sufficient condition for adjustment to major disequilibria, but also leave it appearing always to require rapid action when a gradual approach might achieve an equal result at a smaller cost.

Comparison with the World Bank invites itself because Kenya was among the first countries to obtain a structural adjustment loan, early in 1980, with another likely to be agreed in 1982. The Bank's conditionality for the 1980 loan was quite stringent, involving a rather wide range of specific commitments, largely on industrial protection, and a detailed program of action, progress with which would influence access to further Bank project and program loans. The loan planned for signature in 1982 was expected to widen the range of conditionality to agricultural and energy policies. In no sense did the Bank's conditions represent a soft option, but they differed from those of the Fund both in taking the form of agreed policy actions (rather than numerical outcomes) and in relating to longer-term variables. What is more, the 1980 agreement was regarded as working fairly well, with the Bank reportedly satisfied with implementation and the Kenyan authorities apparently more comfortable in their policy commitments to the Bank than to the Fund.

Another point of interest in the Kenyan case is that there is no evidence that Kenya has obtained an easier deal from the IMF than have other major governments because it has asked for assistance at relatively early stages of its crises. It was also difficult to perceive any softening in conditionality as a result of the guidelines review of March 1979. The general scope of the conditions in August 1979 was no less extensive than in 1975. The Fund ceilings on government borrowing at various dates within the 1979/80 fiscal year were regarded in Kenya as harsh and, in the event, proved unworkable. Consistent with more general changes occurring in Fund policies at that time, there were signs of some relaxation in 1980, but this was turned sharply around in 1981, again as a reflection of policy changes at IMF headquarters. This said, however, we should bear in mind the conclusion drawn from Table 16.5 that, year on year, the ceilings on government credit were not generally deflationary nor particularly restrictive.

But even though they were not excessively restrictive, and though we have shown that domestic credit is among the important influences on the balance of payments, the credit ceilings are open to the criticism of being inadequate instruments of macroeconomic management. For reasons given earlier, we suggest that:

- Monetary forces are only partly responsible for the payments difficulties and inflation.
- The relevant parameters are not sufficiently stable, and the time lags not sufficiently understood, for the outcome of any given credit restriction to be predicted with reasonable confidence.
- The uncertainties surrounding budget planning are too large, and the diffusion of political authority too great, for the deficit financing residual to be readily manipulated as an instrument of macroeconomic management.[18]

Deficit financing is important, of course, and, as we suggest shortly, the government could certainly improve its policies in this regard. But the precise quantities of deficit financing and of private credit are weak reeds upon which to place so much of the burden of macroeconomic management. A Fund response to this complaint would be that these ceilings should be viewed as monitoring devices rather than as policy instruments, but there are reasons for doubting whether they can be expected actually to perform such a function.

Not the least of the practical drawbacks of a focus on deficit financing ceilings is the attention bias it causes in negotiations between the government and Fund missions. Much time and effort is spent arguing about the merits of rival forecasts of government spending and revenue, about how best to define credit to government and other concepts,[19] and about other minutiae of minimal importance

[18] The 1975 EFF agreement provides a revealing illustration of the uncertainties and the resulting difficulties of treating government bank borrowing as a variable to be consciously manipulated as a policy instrument. This set a ceiling on bank lending to the government in the July 1976/June 1977 fiscal year of K£30.75 million. In a draft communication to the Fund of May 11, 1977 (i.e., only about seven weeks before the end of the fiscal year), the government wrote that it now expected government borrowing to exceed the ceiling by the end of the year and to amount to K£42.5 million: "It appears that the budgetary situation has become more intractable than we had anticipated." In the end, however, there was a large reduction in government indebtedness in the last weeks of the year, and the net increase in government borrowing was only K£9.5 million. A year later a Fund staff evaluation wrote of "growing uncertainties surrounding budgetary prospects which have led the authorities to produce varying estimates of likely budget deficits and, correspondingly, their requirements of bank financing."

[19] There was, for example, much concern in 1976–77 within the Fund and the Kenyan treasury about precisely what item should be included in calculations of net credit to the government from the banking system, and there appears to have been considerable confusion about the application of this.

to balance of payments adjustment. The arguments tend to be about numbers and may thus be a distraction from a serious discussion of the nature of the problems and how best to solve them. Government officials tend to find this particularly irksome and to make adverse comparisons with what they see as the more fundamentally relevant policy negotiations for World Bank structural adjustment loans.

This type of attention bias adds force to the common complaint of developing countries that the Fund has a doctrinaire tendency to focus narrowly on a small number of monetary variables. This is particularly unfortunate because, however falteringly, the Fund has sought to adopt a wider, longer-term approach in recent years. Depending on the personality and interests of the mission chief (an important factor in Fund-country relations), staff reports on Kenya have reflected this change. We have already cited the 1974 report that suggested a relaxation of credit policies; this report also urged the government to begin to give thought to the medium-term adjustment problem. Over the years, other reports have concerned themselves with tariff reform, agricultural policies, energy conservation, and so forth. We have found it more difficult to tie down the extent to which such longer-term, supply-side concerns have influenced the course and content of concrete credit negotiations—a factor made elusive because of the concurrent existence of agreements or negotiations with the World Bank based on policies of structural adjustment that may otherwise have featured more prominently in agreements with the Fund. What remains undoubtedly true is that (with an interesting exception in 1980, noted in the third section, above, under "The 1979–81 Stand-bys") the hard core of the EFF and stand-by agreements—the performance criteria—have retained the Fund's traditional concern with demand management. Had the Fund been able and willing to substitute improved supply-side policies for credit ceilings in its performance criteria, the relationship might have been more successful.

It would, in any case, be wrong to conclude on a note that suggests that all the difficulties have stemmed from the Fund's approach. This is not at all the case. The Kenyan government has yet to demonstrate a *steady* adherence to the objective of economic stability, especially when such adherence would necessitate politically unpopular measures. It is important here not to confuse the conservatism and responsibility that had generally characterized Kenyan government policies with the conscious pursuit of policies for short- and medium-term economic management. The government has not yet set in place the data base and reporting procedures necessary for monitoring short-run economic trends.[20] There is need for further studies of key macroeconomic relationships and for the development of an econometric model designed to meet the needs of economic management. Experiences in 1980/81 revealed serious weaknesses in the Kenyan treasury's ability to monitor the ongoing budgetary situation and in its knowledge of the true extent of external debt. The poor record of fiscal forecasting shown in Table 16.2 could, and should, be improved. Although we have drawn attention to the limitations of monetary policy, we would add that monetary policy has been weak in Kenya, partly because the central bank has usually interpreted its role in ways that have been incompatible with the increasingly urgent need for effective economic management.

Above all, it seems that, during the period surveyed here, the Kenyan government had not fully come to terms with the unwelcome implications for its economic policies of a world environment that worsened drastically in 1973 and shows every sign of remaining sharply adverse. Left to itself, a simple inability to import would impose its own payments solution, but one that would levy a heavy cost upon the economy and, perhaps, on the country's political fabric. There were encouraging signs in the early 1980s that the government was increasingly coming to the conclusion that the adoption of a more planned approach to payments adjustment was an urgent necessity.

[20] See Murugu (1978) for a survey of short-run economic indicators in Kenya and suggestions for improvement.

References

Adongo, J. I. 1978. *Inflation in Kenya, 1964–77.* M.A. research paper. Nairobi: University of Nairobi (June).

Bhatia, Rhattan J., and Saul L. Rothman. 1975. "Introducing the Extended Fund Facility: The Kenyan Case." *Finance and Development* (December).

Bolnick, Bruce R. 1975. "Behaviour of the Determinants of Money Supply in Kenya." *Eastern Africa Economic Review* 7(1) (June).

Brough, A.T., and T.R.C. Curtin. 1981. "Growth and Stability: An Account of Fiscal and Monetary Policy." In Killick, ed. (1981).

Chelliah, R.J., H.J. Bass, and M.R. Kelly. 1975. "Tax Ratios and Tax Effort in Developing Countries, 1969–71." *IMF Staff Papers* 22(1) (March).

Government of Kenya. 1975. *Sessional Paper no. 4 of 1975: On Economic Prospects and Policies.* Nairobi: Government Printer.

———. 1980. *Sessional Paper no. 4 of 1980: On Economic Prospects and Policies.* Nairobi: Government Printer.

Grubel, Herbert G., and T.C.I. Ryan. 1979 (ca.). "A Monetary Model of Kenya's Balance of Payments." Nairobi: University of Nairobi. (Mimeo.)

Killick, Tony (with J. K. Kinyua). 1980. "On Implementing Development Plans: A Case Study." *ODI Review,* no. 1. Also published in Killick (1981).

———, ed. 1981. *Papers on the Kenyan Economy: Performance, Problems, and Policies.* Nairobi and London: Heinemann.

King, J. R. 1979. *Stabilization Policy in an African Setting: Kenya, 1963–73.* London: Heinemann.

Maitha, J. K. Tony Killick, G. K. Ikaiara. 1978. *The Balance of Payments Adjustment Process in Developing Countries: Kenya.* Nairobi: University of Nairobi.

Murugu, John K. 1979. *Requirements for Short-Term Economic Management in Kenya,* M.A. research paper. Nairobi: University of Nairobi (January).

Park, Yung Chul. 1970. "The Variability of Velocity: An International Comparison." *IMF Staff Papers,* XVII (3) (November).

Rupley, Lawrence A., and Brendan P. Finucane. 1981. "Kenya's 1980 Budget." *International Bureau of Fiscal Documentation Bulletin* (January).

Tait, A. A., W. L. M. Gratz, and B. J. Eichengreen. 1979. "International Comparisons of Taxation for Selected Developing Countries, 1972–76." *IMF Staff Papers* 26(1) (March).

World Bank. 1981. *Accelerated Development in Sub-Saharan Africa: An Agenda for Action.* Washington, DC.

COMMENTS, CHAPTERS 15–16

Stanley Please

These are two markedly different papers—not surprising, given the differences in both their authorship and in the two countries whose experience with International Monetary Fund (IMF) conditionality they examine. Yet, in relation to the concerns of this conference, the two papers carry virtually the same message—the limited significance of the approach and of the component parts of Fund programs to the needs of either Kenya or Tanzania. Moreover, both authors go on to assert that this conclusion can be generalized for the whole relationship of the IMF to sub-Saharan Africa. Tony Killick, right at the beginning of his paper (Chapter 16, under "Background") puts it this way: ". . .If successful stabilization and good working relations with the Fund are not feasible in Kenya, it is unclear where else in Africa they might be achieved." Reginald Green raises a similar point at the end of his paper (Chapter 15, under "Influence, Impact, and Results"): "If the criticisms of IMF proposals and approaches in respect of Tanzania are valid in this case," he asserts, "they are probably . . . more generally relevant."

These assertions of the continent-wide implications of their individual country analyses permit me to leave for subsequent comment any discussion of the details of the Kenyan and Tanzanian cases, thus enabling me to focus my comments on the sub-Saharan problem more generally. In so doing, I hope that more perspective can be given to the role of the IMF and World Bank in Africa. Needless to say, in making my comments, I will be leaning heavily on the analysis and conclusions contained in the Bank's recent report on *Accelerated Development in Sub-Saharan Africa: An Agenda for Action* (Washington: World Bank, 1981).

Bela Balassa (See Chapter 8 and the bibliography therein) has defined structural adjustment programs as those policy actions required to return a country to its preshock growth path. Even in those instances (e.g., Korea, Thailand) in which this definition of structural adjustment is most relevant and useful, many of the component parts of the adjustment package are policy changes that were desirable for the achievement of growth and development objectives even before the external shock. The external shock simply makes these policy changes even more desirable.

In the case of sub-Saharan Africa, however, Balassa's definition is markedly less relevant and useful. First, a return to a preshock growth path for many countries in Africa would mean a continuation of the downward trend of per capita incomes that many of them experienced in the 1970s—hardly an objective acceptable to African governments or to international institutions such as the Fund and the Bank. During the 1970s, if Nigeria is excluded, per capita incomes of low-income Africa declined by 0.3 percent a year, and those of middle-income Africa by 0.5 percent a year. Second, for many African countries during the 1970s, the external shocks of oil prices, high interest rates, and stagflation and protectionism in developed countries were far less important than for the newly industrialized countries (NICs), although since 1980 the external circumstances which they confront have been very adverse.

The African problem is, in fact, overwhelmingly a fundamental development problem in relation to which adjustment to the changed global environment is of less importance. It is a problem of formulating and implementing the deep and pervasive changes in policies required to stop per capita incomes from falling and to get them moving upward, in contrast with the problem in many of the NICs, which is to maintain preexisting annual per capita growth rates of 4–5 percent or more.

It is not surprising, therefore, that both Green and Killick have concluded that the typical Fund programs are inadequate and badly designed for the needs of Africa in general, and of Tanzania and Kenya in particular. Both of them concentrate their criticisms on the failure of Fund programs to address the policy and institutional issues that are relevant for generating a greater supply response from African countries. Killick makes this point by referring favorably to the stringent conditionality implied in the approach and content of the Bank's structural adjustment lending to Kenya, in contrast with the conventional emphasis of the Fund's program on demand management issues. The Bank has not made a structural adjustment loan to Tanzania; therefore, even had he wished to do so, Green was not able to make such a comparison. The major shortcoming of Fund programs and proposals for Tanzania, in his view, are that they emphasize "demand contraction," whereas the approach of the government, with which he agrees, emphasizes "domestic supply enhancement," particularly to increase export supply.

I doubt whether there is any member of the Fund staff who would dispute the overwhelming desirability of all possible policy and institutional measures being taken to increase supply in the short run from existing productive resources. Where the dispute arises is: first, on the nature of the policy and institutional measures that are required to increase domestic production; second, on what macroeconomic measures are required to make the sectoral and microeconomic measures feasible and effective; and, third, on the focus and role of IMF conditionality (and, I would add, of World Bank conditionality) in relation to these issues. I would like to structure my comments around these three issues.

On the first issue, the Bank's views have been set out in its report on sub-Saharan Africa. The long-term constraints on African growth and development are formidable—rapid population growth; inadequate cadres of educated and trained people; the need for a healthier population and, therefore, one that can both more fully enjoy the fruits of greater per capita production and more fully contribute to production; improved infrastructure; more productive and relevant technologies developed through increased agricultural research; and so on. Many African countries, including Kenya and Tanzania, have records of addressing some of these basic constraints on development, particularly in the areas of education, health, and infrastructure development. However, all these longer term programs are in danger of being cut back unless the production underpinnings of African economies, on which the financing of these long-term programs depends, are reinforced. It is the Bank's belief that during the 1980s per capita production can be markedly increased—we suggest by over 20 percent by 1990—even within the present human, infrastructural, and other basic constraints. This will require, in our view, a significant change in domestic policies, together with a doubling of aid in real terms. Each without the other will be of markedly less effectiveness.

It is clearly impossible in this comment to present the more detailed recommendations on domestic policy reform set out in the Bank's report. However, two themes are central. First, that governments have inadequately recognized the importance of pricing policy for the achievement of their national objectives; second, although "getting prices right" is important, that the institutional framework of input supplies, market outlets, transport, etc., is equally important for enabling producers to take advantage of price opportunities. In this regard, the Bank's report believes that the public sector's administrative and managerial capacity is, in general, overextended in African countries—in some countries, grossly overextended (Tanzania is a prime example). Governments in these countries must, in the Bank's view, ask themselves (as other socialist countries have done—e.g., the Soviet Union in the 1920s, some Eastern European countries since 1945, and possibly China in the 1980s) how governments can limit their own direct management of the use of resources and rely more on market prices, decentralized public agencies, and the private sector, while at the same time ensuring that their long-term objectives of structural change, poverty redressal, provision of basic needs, and avoidance of economically powerful elites are achieved. It is the failure of the Tanzanian government to address these issues that is of concern when one starts examining the government's "supply enhancement" approach, which Green outlines: there is no recognition by the government of the withdrawal of agricultural producers from the organized output market and the widespread development of illegal markets; of the breakdown of efficient input supply services; and of the unreliability of transport services. Relief from the immediate foreign exchange constraint to augment the supply of imported inputs to deal with critical bottlenecks is certainly required in Tanzania, as he asserts, but this is not sufficient, as the experience of the 1970s bears witness. Kenya has similar problems with its agricultural marketing and other support institutions, but not of the same severity as in Tanzania. The problem of the inadequate use of pricing and the overextension of the public sector is, however, a pervasive one in Africa.

On the second issue—the macroeconomic framework within which domestic policy reform must take place—the Bank's report is emphatic that the exchange rate must be treated as a more active component of policy reform to achieve appropriate structural change and development in African economies. It is critical for inducing a switch of income-earning opportunities from the nontradable to the tradable sectors, and in particular for inducing a switch in the internal terms of trade toward agriculture. Contrary to Green's conclusion, the Bank also believes this will be in the interests of poverty redressal policies, and probably also of income distribution objectives.

Green is certainly correct when he regrets the time that ministers and officials in Tanzania have devoted in recent years to the exchange rate issue at the cost of adequate attention to other aspects of economic policy. However, the implication that can be drawn from this experience is that the exchange rate issue should be depoliticized and left to reflect the prospective scarcity value of foreign exchange. I am, in this regard, impressed by the Kenyan policy, which during 1981 resulted in a devaluation of over 40 percent of the shilling against the US dollar by a combination of two small, formal devaluations and the tying of the shilling to a depreciating currency basket against the dollar.

This leads me to the third issue—the content of IMF programs. My own view is that the pervasive importance, from a development point of view, of what can be called strategic prices—such as the exchange rate, interest rates, and related issues of taxation policy and financial institution development—makes it highly desirable for the IMF to concentrate its efforts on those critical variables. This should, wherever possible, be attempted well before crisis situations develop. Increased efforts are required by the Fund to explain more convincingly to governments in Africa the significance of exchange rate policy for structural change, development, and poverty redressal. Furthermore, such relevance needs to be emphasized as a part of more comprehensive programs of import liberalization, such as those Reg Green criticizes as being imposed on Tanzania during the period of high foreign exchange earnings in 1977–78, and also as a complement to programs of industrial incentive reform (as in Kenya since 1980) and of agricultural pricing. Rather than seeing the Fund being drawn further into involvement in sectoral and subsectoral issues of policy reform and institutional change, as Killick and Green would at times seem to be suggesting, I would wish to ensure in the first place that the Fund is giving pride of place to ensuring the implementation in African countries of a developmentally oriented exchange rate policy and other strategic prices such as interest rates, tax policy, and financial market development.

Which leads me to my final point—the role of the World Bank in relation to policy formulation and monitoring. The Bank undertakes a large amount of economic and sector work—for instance, 20 percent of the manpower in its Eastern Africa Regional Office is engaged in economic and sector work, as against regular operational activities such as project appraisal and supervision. However, as the paper by Mr. Ernest Stern emphasized (see Chapter 5), until the introduction in 1980 of the systematic use of nonproject lending in the form of structural adjustment lending, the Bank's involvement in policy issues was essentially through the gentle persuasion implied in the dialogue with each government—based on the Bank's country, sector, and other economic reports—plus the indirect and limited policy conditionality associated with project lending, which is particularly difficult in practice to monitor and to follow up.

The Bank's report on sub-Saharan Africa emphasizes that deep and pervasive domestic policy reform is essential in Africa during the 1980s if the declining trend in per capita incomes is to be reversed. Assistance to governments in formulating these policy reform packages is overwhelmingly assistance requiring the staff specializations to be found in the Bank. What is required, therefore, is not the extension of the range of Fund involvement into these areas, as suggested by Killick and Green, but the rapid development by the Bank of structural adjustment lending and other operational modalities by which the Bank can take on this responsibility more effectively. Beyond the applications to Africa, I would hope that in the conference's synthetic discussion the combined roles of the Bank and of the Fund in relation to the whole range of stabilization, adjustment, and development policies will be addressed. I would also hope that the final report on the conference will draw conclusions and make recommendations in respect of the Bank's responsibilities in changing or strengthening policy formulation and implementation.

CHAPTER **17**

High-Conditionality Lending: The United Kingdom

Malcolm Crawford

The United Kingdom enjoys (if that is the apt verb) a unique relationship with the International Monetary Fund (IMF), in that no other country has remotely approached it in the magnitude of its usage of the high conditionality tranches of the Fund's lending facilities. It used to be said in Washington, at the time the Fund's present headquarters building on H Street, NW, was nearing completion in the early 1970s, that it was built with the interest earnings on the British drawings that had been continuously outstanding since 1964. Whether or not that statement is accurate in an accounting sense, it is certainly true that no other country has been so lavish in its provenance of interest payments to the Fund.[1]

In July 1961, a drawing equal to 100 percent of quota was negotiated, but not wholly drawn. Drawings were made in 1965 and 1968 under stand-by agreements, in the fourth credit tranche in each case, and in June 1969 a further drawing was agreed. Since a substantial part of the 1965 drawing remained outstanding at the time of that of 1969, the then prevailing terms of repayment applicable to IMF drawings were being stretched to the limit, if not beyond. In the event, there was continuous use of Fund credit from 1964 to 1972, when the last repayments of credit drawings were made.

[1] This does not necessarily mean that the United Kingdom was the ultimate provider of the resources that financed the building. The incidence of the cost of Fund expenditures thus financed would depend on the terms on which the currencies drawn were provided to the Fund, and by the Fund to the United Kingdom.

Early in 1976, the United Kingdom drew on the first oil facility. At the beginning of 1977, drawings commenced on a new loan that, at its peak level of usage, brought UK drawings outstanding (including that on the oil facility) to $5 billion of which $4.1 billion was use of Fund credit—easily the largest use of Fund credit by any country.[2] Total drawings, excluding that on the oil facility, were then 109 percent of quota. Credit tranche drawings were repaid in 1978 and 1979, ahead of schedule.

Scope of This Paper

The intention herein is to expound and appraise the developing and final form of the conditions attached to the UK drawings, and to consider the consequences of the attendant policies as implemented. Finally an attempt will be made to evaluate the role of the Fund as a large-scale lender of international resources to a diversified and relatively wealthy economy such as the United Kingdom.

Little can be said about the conditionality attached to the 1961 drawing, as no Letter of Intent was published, nor was any statement made by either party concerning conditions. A set of fiscal and monetary measures was taken immediately. A recession began before the measures could conceivably have had any impact: the trend corrected peak of real GDP occurred in the first quarter. The balance of payments current account showed a small surplus for the year, on revised data. Repayment of the drawing commenced before the end of the year.

The Drawings of 1965–69

In order to limit the length of this paper, only a compressed account will be given of this episode. Owing to the beliefs and monetary arrangements of the time, especially the prevailing view that maintenance of a fixed sterling-dollar parity was essential to the international monetary system, with its two reserve currencies (which made the United Kingdom something of a special case), the period is perhaps richer in historical interest than relevance to present international economic problems.

[2] India has recently negotiated a larger drawing that, if fully disbursed, will exceed $5 billion. See the paper by Catherine Gwin, Chapter 20 of this volume.

The broad policy from 1963 to 1966 was one of deliberate creation of growing demand designed to induce a demand-led, long-term increase in the growth of output and productivity. The conservative Government that held office until October 1964 had in 1963 endorsed a plan for 4 percent annual growth from 1961 to 1966 (compared with 2.7 percent between 1953 and 1963) and in 1965, the Labour government introduced its National Plan for 3.8 percent annual growth from 1964 to 1970. While the balance of payments was recognized as a constraint in both these plans, it was hoped that temporary external payments deficits could be financed externally until productive capacity had grown sufficiently to turn the deficits into surpluses.[3]

After the election in October 1964, a run on sterling occurred, to deal with which a $3 billion credit line was arranged by central banks which, by convention, expected repayment within three months. It was only on the understanding that Britain would seek a drawing from the Fund that the central banks agreed to rollover the short-term debt for a further three months.[4]

On April 29, 1965, the United Kingdom requested a drawing from the IMF of $1.4 billion (having drawn its first tranche of about $500 million late in 1964). In this way the United Kingdom finally came under IMF conditionality five months after taking recourse to international credit to replenish losses of reserves. Precisely the same pattern was to be repeated in 1976.

A set of monetary measures was taken (special deposits by banks and limits on bank loan growth) the same day as the formal request for the drawing. Two weeks before, there had been a moderately restrictive budget (a contractionary effect of 0.7 percent of GDP). Three months later, a second run on sterling provoked further measures, including a panoply of exchange controls, consumer credit controls, and cuts in government expenditure designed so as to take a quick effect. A third and larger run in June and July of 1966 led to a package of deflationary fiscal measures, this time aggregating some 1.5 percent of GDP. On this occasion, ministerial anxiety over sterling was reinforced by a consensus in the treasury that unemployment, which had averaged 1.4 percent in 1960–65, should be raised to about

[3] Expenditure switching (a rise in the exported proportion of manufactured output from 25 percent to 27 percent was anticipated. See *The National Plan*, Cmnd 2764 (London: HM Stationery Office, September 1965, ch. 7).

[4] Susan Strange, et. al., *International Economic Relations of the Western World, 1959–71, Part 2 - International Monetary Relations*, ch. 5 (Oxford: Oxford University Press, 1976).

2 percent to achieve a lower growth of wage earnings, which by then had risen above 10 percent. There was no direct involvement of the IMF in this set of measures. Use was, however, made of central bank credit lines.

During the following year, a start was made to repayment of the drawings, but a fourth run on sterling led to devaluation in November 1967. Again the Fund was asked to provide finance, because the balance of payments was expected to worsen temporarily owing to the well-known *J*-curve. A stand-by of $1.4 billion was quickly agreed, and this time a Letter of Intent was published requiring a limit to the "exchequer's borrowing requirement" (CGBR, central government borrowing rate) of £1 billion in 1968–69, and a reduction in the growth of the money supply. Fiscal measures taken at various times in the succeeding year caused the borrowing limit to be met easily. Monetary growth came narrowly within the limit, after a bad start in the first half of the year.

Unexpectedly heavy intervention in the exchange markets contributed to this success with the money supply, however. To have pitched the monetary clause in the letter in terms of money supply rather than domestic credit expansion appears to have been a mistake, from the Fund's standpoint. Confidence was slow to recover, despite the deflationary fiscal measures, and the officially held overseas sterling balances, which had remained fairly stable between 1964 and 1967, declined sharply after mid-1967. An agreement was devised in September 1968 to shore them up and also reduce them by agreed amounts.

In large part, the problem lay with the official statistics, which indicated a patchy recovery, at best, in the trade balance and the current account deficit. Revised data reveal, however, that the current account deficit peaked in the fourth quarter of 1967, improved steadily through 1968, and swung into surplus in the first quarter of 1969, during which year both the current account and the overall[5] balance of payments were in surplus in every quarter. Downward bias in the initially published payments figures has been a persistent feature of British economic statistics then and subsequently.

Early in 1969, it appeared unlikely that debt repayments due on the 1964–65 drawings could be made. Soundings for extension or refinancing were made before the April budget. A stand-by of $1 billion was applied for, and the Letter of Intent, published in June, makes it clear that conditionality was much more stringent this time.

[5] The balance excluding UK government financing. Balance of payments figures are from *Economic Trends*, annual supplement, 1981 edition.

A limit of £400 million was imposed on domestic credit expansion (DCE), while the central government borrowing requirement was to be negative to the extent of £800 million. Both figures relate to 1969–70. Public expenditure was also subjected to a limit of 1 percent above the planned level for the previous year in real terms. Half the stand-by was held back subject to interim review of performance. Use of IMF credit reached 94 percent of quota in the summer of 1969, having peaked at 100 percent in mid-1968.

The rapid turnaround that was already in train enabled rapid repayment, so that by the end of 1969, use of Fund credit was reduced to 84 percent of quota and by end-1970, 58 percent. Following tax increases of a further 0.5 percent of GDP in the budget, the central government was in surplus of £900 million in 1969–70 and domestic credit actually fell by £540 million. Reconstruction of the British drawings was completed in 1972.

Growth of GDP, which had been the underlying objective of the governments during this period, averaged 3.1 percent per annum between 1961 and 1968, and abated in the succeeding three years to 2.4 percent, 2.0 percent, and 1.5 percent. Unemployment rose each year from 1969 to 1972, and inflation escalated in each successive year from 1967 to 1975. The Labour government was ejected from office in June 1970.

The September 1976 Application

Following the oil price explosion of 1973–74, the Labour Government elected in February 1974 decided, on the basis of forecasts of a deep recession to come, upon a policy of counter-recession expenditure, to be financed by borrowings both internal and (so far as the balance of payments required) external. In the financial year 1974–75, public sector expenditure equivalent to 6.0 percent of GDP was added with respect to the current year and 3.8 percent (of GDP) to plans for 1975–76. In the latter year, a further amount equal to 1.8 percent of GDP was added to expenditure in that year.[6] In the summer of 1974, value-added tax was reduced, yielding a revenue loss of 0.4 percent of GDP, and in November the burden of corporate profit tax was reduced.

[6] Calculated from tables headed "Analysis of changes" in *Public Expenditure to 1978–79*, Cmnd 5879, 1975; and *Public Expenditure to 1980–81*, Cmnd 6393, 1976.

A program of external borrowing was begun in 1974, on the premise that the oil price increase had shifted income temporarily from industrial to oil-exporting countries, and that the latter would need to invest a large proportion of this windfall in financial assets. Accordingly, Her Majesty's Government raised loans through banks, and in one case bilaterally with an Organization of Petroleum Exporting Countries (OPEC) member country, and tolerated a large increase in sterling balances owned by overseas official holders. The current account balance of payments deficit rose to 4.2 percent of GDP (£3.4 billion) in 1974, subsiding to 1.7 percent in 1975, when economic activity in the United Kingdom declined abruptly. At the end of 1975, official indebtedness in foreign currency amounted to $8.9 billion compared with official reserves of $5.4 billion, and official sterling balances were $8.2 billion at the prevailing exchange rate (£4.1 billion). These official balances had in fact reached their peak early in 1975, at nearly £5 billion. In January and February 1976, indications from commercial banks suggested that further credit for the United Kingdom would not be available on the scale utilized in 1974 and 1975, and that the terms on such credit as would be available would be inferior to that on those outstanding.

Exchange rate policy during this period consisted of management of the rate both by intervention and by manipulation of short-term interest rates, with a view to securing gradual depreciation of the effective (weighted average) index of the exchange rate, broadly in line with the difference between the rates of change of export unit values of manufactures in competing countries and those in the United Kingdom. It was not implemented as a precise crawl against this statistic, partly because domestic considerations affected decisions at times, and partly because of differences of view among those implementing the policy.

This policy was never officially announced, although the prime minister (Harold Wilson) did say, in March 1976, that "our inflation rate is still above that of other important countries and it was inevitable that the market should at some stage exert downward pressure on the exchange rate."[7] Later, his press secretary (who had resigned in the meantime) wrote in a book that from early in 1974, the government had expected the exchange rate to decline gradually in a way that would reflect the higher rate of inflation in the United Kingdom than in other countries.[8]

[7] *Hansard*, House of Commons, 11 March 1976, col. 640.
[8] J. Haines, *The Politics of Power* (London: Cape, 1977).

TABLE 17.1 INTEREST RATES AND DIFFERENTIALS, JANUARY–MARCH 1976
(three-month deposits, annual percentage)

Date	*Sterling interbank*	*Eurodollars*	*Difference*
Jan. 2	10.56	5.81	4.75
Jan. 9	10.69	5.56	5.13
Jan. 16	10.00	5.59	4.41
Jan. 23	9.94	5.56	4.38
Jan. 30	9.44	5.37	4.07
Feb. 6	9.09	5.53	3.56
Feb. 13	9.19	5.62	3.57
Feb. 20	8.87	5.66	3.23
Feb. 27	8.78	5.62	3.16
Mar. 3	8.69	5.75	2.94

Source: Bank of England *Quarterly Bulletin.*

Between October 1975 and January 1976, the exchange rate remained virtually unchanged, and the real exchange rate was rising (on data not then available, it rose 2 percent between the two quarters). Intervention virtually ceased in January and February, and short-term interest rates were lowered, with the effect summarized in Table 17.1.

The exchange rate (both weighted and dollar) remained virtually unchanged during that period. Then on March 4, the authorities sold sterling while the Nigerian monetary authority almost simultaneously made a sale from its sterling balances. The same day, the treasury bill tender produced a further fall in minimum lending rate (effected the next day), which the chancellor chose not to override. Sterling fell 5 percent against the dollar in just over a week. Soon after, the chancellor admitted in the Commons that errors had been made. Such highly uncustomary promptness in admitting mismanagement can only point to a desire to conceal the aims that were actually being pursued.

In subsequent published writings, much importance has been attached to the coincidence of these two official sales of sterling on March 4. In view of the fact that the official sterling balances had been declining since early in 1975, the Nigerian disposal must be seen not as an isolated event that triggered a crisis, but as part of a continuous process that reduced the official balances from nearly £5 billion to £4 billion at the end of March 1976. It was also suggested that the events of that day generated a crisis by depressing sterling below the "psychological barrier" of $2. If that was indeed the case,

TABLE 17.2 MAJOR UK PAYMENTS AGGREGATES, 1974–77
(million pounds sterling)

Year and quarter		Current account	Change in official sterling liabilities	Private capital
1974	I	-894	232	303
	II	-873	231	392
	III	-764	555	-63
	IV	-848	262	-242
1975	I	-625	228	-125
	II	-391	-303	424
	III	-572	-380	719
	IV	-86	-162	-274
1976	I	-125	-80	-425
	II	-375	-921	-925
	III	-341	-349	-338
	IV	-274	-57	-85
1977	I	-675	190	1,049
	II	-499[a]	-398	-337
	III	495	74	956
	IV	395	115	948

Source: Central Statistical Office. *United Kingdom Balance of Payments*
a. The decline in official sterling balances in the second quarter of 1977 resulted from the arrangements to fund part of these balances.

the round number of $2 could only have been a psychological barrier if the markets did not correctly comprehend the policy that was being pursued. If there is a policy of gradual depreciation, and the rate stands slightly above a particular number, then inevitably it must fall below that number. It is hard to avoid the conclusion that if such a policy is to be pursued, it should be done openly, with target rates known to the markets.

Although the rate fell only 5 percent against the dollar during March, intervention to support it was very heavy in relation to existing reserves. Use of reserve assets totalled $1.3 billion in March, and $3.3 billion in the three months March to May. Nevertheless, the rate fell to $1.76 by the end of May and by 9.5 percent in weighted average terms between February and May. Reserves totalled $5.4 billion at the end of May, including $2 billion drawn from the IMF under low-conditionality arrangements entered into the previous autumn.

The official sterling balances fell by £827 million between mid-February and mid-June, the biggest declines occurring in March-April and May-June. There were also large outflows of private short term capital (see Table 17.2).

Monetary and Fiscal Policy

Growth of the money supply was low, owing partly to these external flows. Broad money (£M3) rose only 4.7 percent in the six months to mid-June, much the same as in the United States. Domestic credit expansion was more rapid, at 8.2 percent, mostly in the second quarter, although a large part of this comprised credit flows abroad. Throughout the period March to October there was a large covered arbitrage discount on three-months sterling (generally at least 2 percent) that provided nonresidents who could borrow domestic sterling (through a loophole in the exchange controls) a guaranteed profit from selling the sterling proceeds spot and swapping forward. (The unwinding of such transactions, of course, provided powerful strength to sterling once the period of speculation ended.)

Policy measures taken during this period included tax reductions in the April budget, equivalent to about 2 percent of GDP, tightly drawn terms for a second year of wage restraint, and two increases in minimum lending rate, raising it from 9 percent in March to 11.50 percent at the end of May. Less well known were efforts made by the UK treasury to regain control over public expenditure, with the result that the outturn for 1976–77 fell below planned levels (most unusually) by 4 percent.[9] In short, fiscal policy appeared superficially a good deal more lax than it really was.

The $5.3 Billion Central Bank Credit

Sterling was subjected to heavy selling in the markets again at the beginning of June, and a multilateral central bank credit line totaling a dollar equivalent to $5.3 billion was hastily arranged. Half of the US contribution of some $2 billion was subscribed by the US Treasury, reportedly because the Federal Reserve Board was unwilling to go to that figure[10]; the consequence (whether intended or not) was to inject an element of government-to-government conditionality. The credit was to be available for six months, with the presumption that drawings on it would be repaid from further drawings on the IMF, should the United Kingdom be unable to repay from reserves. A package of fiscal measures was recommended by the US treasury

[9] *The Government's Expenditure Plans, 1978–79 to 1981–82*, vol. 1, Cmnd 7049-1, 1978.

[10] A potential credit availability of $3 billion was reported to exist under Federal Reserve reciprocal currency arrangements with the Bank of England by the Federal Reserve Bank of New York in its winter 1976 issue.

secretary,[11] and this duly emerged on July 22, when cuts in expenditure programs and a new payroll tax, in all equivalent to a little under 2 percent of GDP, were announced. This total of some £2 billion related wholly to the following financial year, however. Also announced was a target for the money supply (M*3*) of 12 percent growth through the financial year.

Heavy use was made of the central bank facility as soon as it was available. Reserve assets of $1.5 billion were used during the month, and just over $1 billion of the new facility was drawn down. In the process, the exchange rate was driven up from $1.71 to $1.79 during the month.

A further run on sterling began early in September, and after a week, in which a further $500 million was drawn on the credit line (and largely used) intervention ceased. Sterling fell to $1.64 on September 28, and the chancellor decided to apply for the maximum IMF drawing. The application was announced the next day. This was the latest it could have been left, in view of the expiry of the central bank credit on December 7 (in fact, the Letter of Intent was not finalized until December 13). Yet even as late as mid-September, the chancellor and some other ministers were hopeful that such an application could somehow be averted. In this context, the Labour Party annual conference, which started on September 27, was most unfortunately timed.

At the conference, the chancellor gave a public assurance that his application to the Fund would not entail further deflationary measures. British ministers made a series of attempts to avoid conditionality, through bilateral contacts in Washington and Bonn, over a period of weeks. They also sought arrangements to limit and support the official sterling balances, regarding this scheme as an alternative to high-conditionality drawing from the IMF.[12]

The United States and Germany did of course have a legitimate interest in the UK drawing, in that activation of the General Arrangements to Borrow would be required, and these two countries were the largest potential contributors. On November 27, a large team of US economic officials arrived in London to take part in the discussions. According to press reports, they endorsed the IMF view-

[11] S. Fay and H. Young, *The Day the £ Nearly Died* (Times Newspapers, 1978).

[12] This was the subject of a visit by Harold Lever, a cabinet minister with financial responsibilities, to Washington the week of November 15, and is reported in detail in Fay and Young, *op. cit.*

point on conditions, and agreed to cooperate with measures concerning the sterling balances after accord had been reached on an IMF drawing. According to Fay and Young,[13] it was not until a meeting between the prime minister, James Callaghan, and the managing director of the Fund, Johannes Witteveen, on December 1, a month after the IMF mission arrived in London, that the former admitted the need for conditions.

In the meantime, minimum lending rate had been raised to 13 percent on September 10 and to 15 percent on October 8. Sterling fell to its lowest point in history, $1.555, on October 28. The IMF mission arrived on November 1. As is customary, loan conditions were not discussed at an early stage in the talks. On November 18, the treasury announced measures to control the growth of interest bearing bank deposits, and to close the exchange control loophole whereby sterling could be lent from the United Kingdom to nonresidents for trade finance other than the purchase of goods from the United Kingdom. At the time, the treasury estimated that this measure would improve capital flows by £1.5 billion once for all. Subsequently officials regarded this figure as an underestimate. Spot sterling recovered steadily from the end of November through December.

The Loan Conditions: Fiscal and Monetary

The Letter of Intent, published on December 15, revealed fiscal targets in the form of an "aim to hold the PSBR (public sector borrowing requirement) to £8.7 billion" in 1977–78, and to £8.6 billion in 1978–79. To achieve this, measures were taken as follows: £1 billion in expenditure cuts,[14] plans to sell government shares in British Petroleum to yield £500 million, and other mutually offsetting changes, in 1977–78; and £1.5 billion in expenditure cuts in 1978–79.[15] In addition, a further fiscal adjustment of £500 million was promised for that year, but does not appear to have been implemented, and further deflationary measures in 1978–79 were promised, contingent upon a growth forecast in that period in excess of 3.5 percent per annum. (No such forecast emerged, nor any such growth rate.)

It would be rash to describe these measures as IMF conditions, for the fiscal situation was politically complicated. Informal soundings in

[13] *Op. cit.*, ch. 3.

[14] In survey prices, or about £1.3 billion at outturn prices, 0.9 percent of GDP.

[15] In survey prices, or about £2.1 billion at outturn prices, 1.25 percent of GDP.

October indicated a provisional PSBR target in the minds of IMF staff of about £8 billion,[16] which was not far from the forecasts emerging from private institutes at the time, or from the treasury's midsummer forecast of £9 billion. On November 6, however, the *Financial Times* leaked a report that the treasury's new PSBR forecast was over £11 billion. This forecast was reduced to £10.5 billion by December 15, after discussions with the IMF mission. A quotation from a recent book by the then chief secretary of the treasury is relevant: "I thought I had done a fair amount of juggling with figures as an accountant, but when it came to the sort of sophisticated 'massaging' and 'fudging' I learned as chief secretary to the treasury, I realized I had been a babe in arms by comparison. It was a case of changing this and that assumption, and—abracadabra—the PSBR is about the figure you first thought of."[17] On this occasion, there is circumstantial evidence that the forecast was massaged upwards; for example, the usual provision for shortfall in the execution of expenditure programs was omitted. In consequence, the treasury's forecast enhanced the case for measures to reduce the PSBR.

There were two reasons. One was that there was a potentially heavy majority in cabinet against acceptance of IMF conditionality. Opposition consisted of two groups, Social Democrats and traditional Socialists. It was essential to the chancellor, who had applied for the loan, that these two groups did not coalesce. In the event, the social democratic group was won over by various means, including persuasion that the PSBR was rising too rapidly. The other motive (which also helped in the first aim) was a desire on the part of the chancellor, the prime minister, and some others to reduce income tax. The cabinet was divided as to whether expenditure should be cut for this purpose, however. In his Letter of Intent, the chancellor said: "If, at the time I plan my budget for 1977–78, I judge that without increasing the PSBR above £8.7 billion there is scope for tax reliefs and if, as I hope, a satisfactory agreement has been reached . . . on pay arrangements, then I would plan to use the available margin to reduce the present burden of direct taxation."

In the event, such an "available margin" was found, and tax reductions of £1 billion were made in the spring. This operation was repeated later in the year to yield another £1 billion. Nevertheless, the outturn PSBR for 1977–78 was £5.6 billion, some £3 billion below the figure given in the Letter of Intent.

[16] *The Sunday Times*, 24 October 1976.

[17] Joel Barnett, *Inside the Treasury* (London: Andre Deutsch, 1982).

Although the cuts in expenditure for 1978–79 were presumably implemented (apart from the "further cuts"), actual expenditure increased by 6 percent in real terms in that year,[18] and the PSBR was £9.2 billion. IMF conditionality appears to have weakened, if not lapsed, at least in regard to fiscal policy, some time during 1978.

Ceilings on domestic credit expansion were promised of £7.7 billion in 1977–78 and £6 billion in 1978–79. In the event, DCE was £3.8 billion in 1977–78 and £7.3 billion in 1978–79. As with the PSBR, DCE was unduly low in the first year of surveillance and overshot in the second. The undershoot of DCE in the first year was remarkably large, a fact that may have been partly attributable to the unwinding of speculative positions against sterling taken up in 1976 through the lending of domestic sterling abroad. It is not clear that the IMF, or other scrutineers of United Kingdom financial policy during this period, took adequate account of this influence, either during the crisis or in its reversal.

The Loan Conditions: Exchange Rate Policy

During the period of fixed exchange rates, maintenance of a fixed exchange rate was an important, and usually explicit, element in conditionality connected with drawings from the Fund. It was indeed the main purpose of the drawing. After the breakdown of the fixed rate system, this primacy of place became less clear, but exchange rate conditions continued to appear in Letters of Intent. There are two reasons why this should be so. First, a country drawing from the Fund does so because it requires foreign exchange to support its exchange rate. The Fund, as lender, has an interest in ensuring that the borrowing country does not dissipate the loan proceeds by defending too high a rate. Second, the borrowing country must subsequently repay the drawing together, quite commonly, with other foreign currency loans raised for the same purpose. The Fund, as lender, has an interest in ensuring that an exchange rate policy will be pursued that will enable the country to accumulate sufficient nonborrowed foreign exchange to repay the drawing and other loans, and still have sufficient reserves to implement whatever exchange rate policies it then aims to pursue. International monetary theory would suggest that the appropriate instruments in this connection

[18] *The Government's Expenditure Plans, 1980–81 to 1983–84*, Cmnd 7841, 1980.

would be a suitably low ceiling on domestic credit expansion and a suitably low exchange rate target, either fixed or crawling.

During negotiations for the UK 1976 drawing, an exchange rate condition was proposed in two versions, each advocated by one of the two senior members of the mission. One proposed a target of $1.55, which was approximately the low point reached in the markets, and the other proposed a managed depreciation related inversely to the rate of change of UK export unit values of manufactures (in sterling), less the change in an index of those other countries. This proposal was, in effect, a fixed crawl based on export unit value purchasing power parity, with the exchange rate keyed in on a base of third-quarter 1976. Had this policy been implemented, and had cross rates of other currencies against the dollar remained unchanged, the dollar sterling rate would have been reduced to $1.57 by the end of 1977. In the Letter of Intent, the relevant clause said: "Intervention will be designed to minimize short-term fluctuations in the rate and to maintain stability in the exchange markets consistently with the continued maintenance of the competitive position of UK manufactures both at home and overseas." This was a promise to maintain a target exchange rate, or trend of rates, subject to minimal fluctuations, and selected so as to maintain the recent or existing level of international competitiveness of UK manufactured goods, and could be construed as a slightly generalized statement of the second proposal.

The target rate was, in the event, fixed in dollar terms, at $1.70–$1.72, by the prime minister, who was (according to guidance given the media from Downing Street) "taking charge of the exchange rate."[19] This range was held between January and July 1977, when it was converted to the then prevailing equivalent weighted average rate. This revised target was maintained until October, when strong market pressures obliged the authorities to let the rate float upward.

Although this policy was widely criticized at the time, because the abandonment of the fixed peg gave the appearance that the policy had failed, it must in retrospect be judged a great success. At the end of 1976, the United Kingdom possessed only $4.1 billion of reserves, and had $14.2 billion in official short- and medium-term foreign currency debt outstanding. At the end of 1977, reserves had risen to $20.6 billion, while the corresponding debt total was $18.0 billion. This increase in reserves was a matter of some urgency, be-

[19] Inter alia, the *Financial Times*, 13 January 1977.

cause $16.2 billion of official foreign currency borrowing[20] was due for repayment within five years (i.e., by the end of 1982). By March 1979 this latter figure had been reduced to $11.3 billion, while the reserves were slightly higher due to revaluation of the gold content.

The Loan Conditions: The Economy

The Letter of Intent stated that the measures were taken with the expectation that real GDP would rise by about 2.0 percent in 1977–78, and about 2.5–3.0 percent in 1978–79. The balance of payments current account, which the chancellor estimated would be in deficit by £2 billion in 1976:–77, would improve to a deficit of about £1 billion in 1977–78, and then move into a surplus of £2–£3 billion in 1978–79.

In the event, the GDP forecasts proved remarkably accurate: output rose 1.8 percent in the first year and 3.1 percent in the second. The balance of payments deficit in 1976–77 was £1.6 billion, and improved to a mere £100 million in 1977–78. The surplus in the following year did not, however, emerge, or rather was cut short by the strike-ridden first quarter of 1979, when the surplus of the preceding three quarters (£1.1 billion) was wiped out. The pay restraint policy collapsed at about that time too.

Conclusions

Errors by the British Treasury between July and November allowed the crisis to develop to a greater extent than it need have. Prior to the fiscal measures in July, remarkably heavy use of reserves made for exchange market intervention; yet the July measures related exclusively to the following year. No short-term measures were taken at that time (apart from announcement of the money supply target, which the markets did not know whether to take seriously). Interest rates remained pegged at end-May levels until September, with the result that money supply escalated in the third quarter. There is no obvious explanation, moreover, for the delay in taking the measures announced on November 18, which were crucially important.

The delay in dealing with the official overseas sterling balances (for which a support package was announced in January 1977) was of minor importance, as the reduction of official holdings, cumula-

[20] This figure includes repayments due on long term debt. Data on reserves and foreign currency debt are from Bank of England *Quarterly Bulletins*.

tively £1.75 billion between April 1975 and June 1976, ceased thereafter to be such a powerful, depressing influence on the markets (see Table 17.2). After mid-November, the level of official holdings began to rise again. This observation, of course, benefits from hindsight—it could not have been apparent in the summer and autumn of 1976. But in any case, the holders of sterling balances would have wanted a conditionality package.

Judged in terms of the needed improvement in reserves in relation to debt repayments falling due, the policies implemented during and after the negotiations for the IMF loan proved a signal success. It is more doubtful whether a drawing of the magnitude that was agreed ($3.9 billion at the time) was actually necessary, given the sharp turnaround that occurred in external monetary transactions, and in the official reserves. What was clearly needed, at the time the Letter of Intent was being negotiated, was a part, if not all, of the fiscal measures subsequently taken, together with short-term credit. Inadequate attention seems to have been paid to the effect of speculative outflows of domestic sterling (and their subsequent reversal) on the monetary aggregates.

Even on the basis of existing policies, the exchange markets drove the rate to irrationally low levels between September and November 1976. Actual rates were exceptionally low during this period compared with those calculated (retrospectively) from models based on so-called "fundamentals," whether relative excess money supply models, asset market models, or flow models. In this sense, the market got it badly wrong during those months, and a correction was inevitable. The views of Fund staff on this at the time are unknown to outsiders, but some other participants took market behavior as an endorsement of particular, strong policy prescriptions.[21] This would seem to be an error to be avoided. In fact, on this occasion, the recovery in the rate began before the announcement of the Letter of Intent and the measures therein.

Little account seems to have been taken of North Sea oil, either by the markets or by those framing the policy conditions. It was given only one brief passing mention in the Letter of Intent, and was not

[21] For example, a news report in the *Washington Post*, 26 October 1976, containing attributions to Dr. Arthur Burns, then chairman of the Federal Reserve Board, said that Federal Reserve "officials" believed that an increase in minimum lending rate to 18 percent (it was then 15 percent), cuts in government expenditure, and other such measures were necessary to stabilize the exchange rate.

TABLE 17.3 DIRECT CONTRIBUTION OF UK OIL AND GAS TO UK BALANCE OF PAYMENTS, 1973–77
(million pounds sterling)

Item	*1973*	*1974*	*1975*	*1976*	*1977*
Value of oil and gas sales	134	168	248	903	2,543
Direct import of goods (f.o.b.)	−100	−125	−351	−554	−532
Direct import of services	−60	−227	−490	−648	−686
Interest, profits, and dividends due abroad	−10	−10	−23	−24	−367
Direct contribution to current account	−36	−194	−616	−323	958
Direct contribution to capital account	64	307	1,111	1,192	1,349
Direct contribution to balance for official financing	28	113	495	869	2,307

Source: Central Statistical Office. *United Kingdom Balance of Payments 1967–77.*

mentioned in any of the numerous quotations of foreign officials (mainly American) in Fay and Young (see note 11). Yet oil production was already rising rapidly, and was a strong influence on the balance of payments turning from negative to positive (Table 17.3).

The improvement in the balance of payments was greater than forecast, and the fiscal measures were much greater than needed to meet the stated targets. Internally, the main effect of the IMF's involvement, and of the Letter of Intent, was to enable the British chancellor to make large reductions in income tax, following reductions in public expenditure, that might not otherwise have been possible because agreement in cabinet on the latter would not otherwise have been forthcoming. This is not normally one of the purposes of the Fund. The tactical maneuvering at the political level would, however, have been extremely difficult for the Fund to predict, and once involved, the IMF mission probably had little option but to support the chancellor in this domestic political struggle.

The use of the PSBR as a catch-all for fiscal policy is of dubious merit. Not only is it highly susceptible to "massaging" and "fudging," it also fails to make the necessary distinction between ex ante aggregate measures and their effects. The PSBR may, moreover, be raised or lowered by measures that have no effect on economic activity, domestic credit expansion, or (in some cases) the balance of payments. Such measures, on this occasion, included the shifting of fixed rate export credit from the government to the banks, and the sale of

British Petroleum shares (which did, however, increase the reserves, insofar as they were sold to foreigners, and a fixed exchange rate was being held). A better procedure might be to fix the DCE limit and then approve or reject, the measures proposed to meet it.

Even making due allowance for the fact that British ministers mistakenly sought US involvement in an attempt to avoid conditionality, this involvement was most unfortunate. It is the Fund's mission—not the US treasury secretary, or even his undersecretary for monetary affairs, nor the chairman of the US Federal Reserve Board—that is in a position to assess the outlook, drawing requirements, and necessary conditions pertaining to the applicant country. Such involvement can place pressure on the Fund's managing director, even if the advice of another government is not directly made to him, and could wrongly influence his decisions. It should be strictly avoided in future.

The package caused no serious damage to the real economy of the United Kingdom in aggregate: real GDP fell for only one quarter (1977–II) and its growth for the year deviated little either from the forecast or from the trend for the 1970s. This was in marked contrast to the 1969–71 period, when a second high conditionality package during the same prolonged crisis either caused or aggravated a prolonged slowdown. Subsequently, as in 1972–73, so in 1978–79, an upswing in economic activity generated (or encountered) severe inflationary conditions that had undesirable consequences, not least for the government in office.

IMF high-conditionality packages have, on at least two occasions, helped the United Kingdom to resolve difficulties in sustaining sterling on the exchanges—difficulties encountered after effective devaluations in both cases (or three, if one includes July 1961). In the process, external payments deficits have been turned into surpluses rather dramatically. The net foreign reserves position was at least adequately improved, if anything more rapidly, once the exchange rate was suitably low and domestic credit expansion was sharply reduced. Given a financial market structure such as that of the United Kingdom, the responsiveness of capital markets and their openness to foreign participants appears to facilitate the restoration of net reserves, once such policies are visibly in place.

It is at least plausible, however, that there are characteristics of IMF high-conditionality lending that are systematically destabilizing in the long term. To argue this in detail would be outside the scope of this paper; in any case the proposition cannot be tested by the UK experience along. One can, by way of hypothesis, tell the following story. The IMF, in discussions with the applicant country, sets a suitably low ceiling on DCE, and agrees on a suitably low exchange rate target. The balance of payments and the reserves improve as desired, while internal growth slows down. IMF surveillance then weakens, because the country is under no constraint upon its ability to repay IMF drawings and other debt. It is not necessary to assume the introduction of profligate new policies: deferment of capital and essential current expenditure (e.g., maintenance) normally produces some rebound after a period of restraint. Simultaneously, the improvement in the balance of payments, combined with adherence to an exchange rate target, produces an externally induced expansion of the money supply, which is aggravated by a rebound in DCE. The more successful is the adjustment on the external side, the greater is the subsequent monetary expansion. Success on the external side is essential for the Fund's role as international banker, but may lead to a renewal of the excess monetary expansion that, some might maintain, is the root cause of the kind of crisis that leads to an application for IMF assistance.

In the case of the United Kingdom, excess monetary expansion was identified quickly in the autumn of 1977 and choked off by the upward float of the exchange rate. By that time, money supply targets had effectively superceded the DCE ceilings in the Letter of Intent. Whether or not the subsequent pursuit of money supply targets was a success is another story. Clearly, however, the monetary policies, together with the rapid transformation of the United Kingdom from an importer to net exporter of oil, have obviated any necessity for the United Kingdom to become a client of the Fund once again.

CHAPTER **18**

Two Letters of Intent: External Crises and Stabilization Policy, Italy, 1973–77

Luigi Spaventa

In his background paper (Chapter 7, this volume), John Williamson poses four questions, setting them as guidelines to appraise the success (or lack thereof) of International Monetary Fund (IMF) policy advice: (1) what was the impact of the Fund in influencing the policies actually adopted? (2) how did the policy changes affect some key variables (output, current balance of payments, inflation rate, capacity growth, income distribution)? (3) were such changes efficient, in the sense of moving the economy closer to its (multidimensional) efficiency frontier? (4) were there better policies, which both should and could have been pursued?

These are precise and relevant questions, but I doubt that they can all receive straightforward and unambiguous answers. There is, first, a problem regarding the validity of the model on which the policy recommendations are implicitly or explicitly based: major theoretical issues aside, the costs and benefits of a recommended policy course depend on the accuracy of the underlying forecasting model and of the projections regarding the behavior of external variables (world demand, export markets and prices, prices of imported inputs), which

Note: The author is grateful to the Bank of Italy for the help he obtained in preparing this paper and is particularly indebted to Antonio Fazio, Cesare Caranza, Franco Cotula, Stefano Micossi and Fabrizio Saccomani for their suggestions. He is also grateful to Bruno Ingrao for research assistance. The entire responsibility of the paper, and of any errors and omissions, is of course the author's own.

are of crucial importance for a small, open economy. There is next the question of the time horizon chosen for appraising the results of a policy program. Is the effectiveness of IMF *operational* recommendations (apart from the inevitable lip service to some broad objectives of equilibrium and growth) to be judged with the criteria of first aid surgery or with reference to some more ambitious goals? Are its recommendations designed to remove the most acute symptoms of imbalance, or are they meant to affect the deeper causes?

A third and more important point is one which has received growing attention in the theory of economic policy. One does not need to go all the way with rational expectations theories to recognize that the success of an economic policy program depends not only on its intrinsic technical merits, but also on whether it is believed to be a lasting change of course, on the degree of consensus it can elicit and, as a result, on the extent to which it affects expectations (Sargent 1981; Spaventa 1981). On the one hand, unless expectations and agents' behavior are influenced, even a consistent implementation of the program may become difficult, since the agents' learning process reduces the effectiveness of specific measures that appeared perfectly adequate on paper. The effect on expectations and behavior, on the other hand, also depends on the readiness by social and political forces to accept the program and its implications—hence, on the social and political situation of a specific country in a specific period. History no less than economics is relevant to answer Williamson's questions.

All these problems loom large when appraising Italy's dealings with the IMF (and with the European Economic Community, EEC) in the period 1974–77. In that period Italy turned to the Fund twice to request a stand-by arrangement. Negotiations for the first arrangement—of SDR 1 billion—began in February 1974, and the Letter of Intent was signed, after an internal political crisis, on March 27, 1974 (Annex 18.A). The Letter of Intent for the second arrangement, for SDR 450 million, was signed, after lengthy negotiations, on April 6, 1977 (Annex 18.B). The amount granted under the first arrangement was entirely drawn, but no drawings were made under the second. In the same period Italy was granted over SDR 1.7 billion under the IMF oil facility, $1.885 billion as EEC support, and a $1 billion EEC loan (Table 18.1). Italy further obtained $2 billion from the Bundesbank, against a gold guarantee, and $500 million in a swap operation with the US Federal Reserve.

Both the IMF and EEC loans were accompanied by a policy program (with the EEC following the lines set by the IMF); the performance targets and the forecasts of the programs are reproduced in Table 18.2, together with the actual outcomes.

TABLE 18.1 ITALY: OFFICIAL BORROWING, 1974–77

Date		*Million SDR*	*Million dollars*
March 1974	EEC: short-term support (transformed into medium-term support in December 1974, with the exception of the UK share; UK share of 486 million reimbursed in December 1976, then replaced early in 1977 by EEC support for the same amount).		1,885
April 1974	IMF: first stand-by arrangement (drawn in August and September 1974 and in March 1975).	1,000	1,235
August 1974	Bundesbank, with gold guarantee (500 million reimbursed in March 1975, drawn again in March 1976, then reimbursed in September 1976; further 340 million drawn in December 1976 and at the beginning of 1977 as a result of the rise in gold prices).		2,000
September 1974	IMF: oil facility	262.5	312
November 1974	IMF: oil facility	412.5	514
September 1975	IMF: oil facility	780.2	920
First quarter 1976	Federal Reserve: swap (extinguished in third quarter 1976).		500
March 1976	EEC loan under EEC recycling (drawn in March and April).		1,000
April 1977	IMF: second stand-by arrangement (never drawn).	450	530

Source: Banca d'Italia.

The two stand-by arrangements with the IMF cannot be considered as two separate episodes, each susceptible of separate analysis. The two crises which led Italy to turn to the Fund and the two stabilization operations, although different in their origins and outcomes, belong to the same story. This paper will divide the story into four phases: the inflationary boom which led to the 1974 crisis, and the negotiations on the first Letter of Intent; the stabilization program of 1974–75 and its effects; the policy engineered inflationary recovery of 1975–76 and the resulting currency crisis; and the wide-ranging 1976–77 stabili-

TABLE 18.2 INTERMEDIATE TARGETS AND FORECASTS IN CONDITIONAL LOANS TO ITALY AND OUTCOMES, 1974–77

	Target or forecast		*Outcome*	
IMF 1 (1974–75)				
Total domestic credit (billion lire)				
April 1, 1974 to				
June 30, 1974	6,000[a]		4,130	
Sept. 30, 1974	11,000[a]	10,700[b]	7,110	
Dec. 31, 1974	19,500[a]	19,050[b]	16,500	
March 31, 1975	22,400[a]	21,800[b]	19,540	21,500[c]
Financing needs of treasury, 1974 (billion lire)	9,200		8,650	
Current external balance (billion lire)				
"Oil," 1974	−3,600		−3,600	
Total, 1974	−5,300[d]	−4,600[e]	−5,210[f]	
"Non-oil," end-1975	0		−4,270[g]	
Exchange rate, effective, (percentage change)	level of 1974/I		−8[h]	
GDP (growth rate)				
Constant prices	4–5		3.4[i]	4.1[j]
Current prices	16–17		20.6[i]	23.4[j]
Gross fixed investment (growth rate)				
Constant prices	4–5		4.2[i]	3.3[j]
Current prices	22–23		34.1[i]	32.8[j]
EEC 1 (1975–76)				
Total domestic credit (billion lire)				
April 1, 1975 to				
December 31, 1975	20,500		27,940	
March 31, 1976	24,700		35,360	
Financing needs of treasury, 1975 revised, (billion lire)	11,000		24,130	
Current external balance, 1975 (billion lire)	−1,100		−377[f]	158[g]
EEC 2 (1976)				
Total domestic credit (billion lire)				
January 1, 1976 to				
March 31	5,800		7,420	
June 30	11,200		12,860	
September 30	16,800		22,450	
December 31	29,500		33,280	
Financing needs of treasury, 1976 (billion lire)				
Original	14,000		14,230	
Revised	15,000			
Monetary base for treasury, 1976 (billion lire)	5,700		11,745	

TABLE 18.2 Continued

	Target or forecast		Outcome	
IMF 2 (1977–78)				
Total domestic credit (billion lire)				
April 1, 1977 to				
June 30, 1977	8,200		8,190	
Sept. 30, 1977	14,500		14,700	
Dec. 31, 1977	24,500		28,320	
March 31, 1978	30,000		38,520	
Year 1977	30,600	32,050[k]	35,800	
Year 1978	30,000		49,020	
Financing needs of treasury, 1977 (billion lire)	13,400		17,720	
Financing needs of "enlarged" public sector, 1977 (billion lire)	16,450		21,000	
State budget cash expenditures, 1977 (billion lire)	55,350		55,542	
World demand (growth rate)	8		4	
Export prices in dollars (percentage increase)	7			
Exchange rate, effective (percentage change)	level of 1977/I		−3[h]	
Export quantities (growth rate)	9		5.8	
Import quantities (growth rate)	3.5		−1	
Current external balance, (billion lire)				
1977	0		2,175	
12 months ended March 1978	500		3,400	
Internal demand (growth rate, constant prices)	1 to −2		0.1[i]	0.5[j]
GDP (growth rate):				
Constant prices	2 to −3		1.7[i]	1.9[j]
Current prices	22		20.3[i]	21.3[j]
Inflation rate during 12 months ended				
December 1977	16		13.1	
March 1978	13		12.5	
Number of points of cost-of-living escalator index in 1977	27		24	

Source: Banca d'Italia.

a. Original.
b. Revised to allow for a presumed smaller oil deficit.
c. Adjusted to discount the effects of commercial banks' window dressing.
d. Fund staff's estimates.
e. Italian estimates.
f. Unadjusted.
g. Adjusted for concealed capital movements.
h. End-year.
i. Old series.
j. New series.
k. Adjusted to account for the consequences of the end of the import deposit.

zation program. A final section of the paper is addressed to a consideration of Williamson's questions in the Italian case, bearing in mind the problems mentioned above.

The Inflationary Boom and the 1974 Crisis

As the world economy began cooling off, around the first half of 1973, Italy's long-awaited recovery, after two years of near stagnation, gathered strength (Izzo and Spaventa 1981). At the beginning of 1973, a wave of industrial strikes accompanying the national wage negotiations caused a fall in industrial production. The loss of output affected mostly exports, with lasting consequences on Italy's share in world markets (which fell from 6.7 percent in 1972 to 5.9 percent in 1973 and regained the 1972 level only in 1977), but did not prevent a rapid and accelerating growth of internal demand. Such acceleration was partly the natural result of cyclical evolution and of a desirable pickup in investment demand; domestic policies, however, transformed the recovery into an uncontrolled inflationary boom.

The decision taken in February 1973 to let the lira float led to a depreciation in the effective rate, in the first month of the float, of 5.6 percent. This development was probably inevitable[1] and perhaps desirable. What was neither inevitable nor desirable was the combination of policies that accompanied depreciation. Monetary policy was very permissive: the growth of monetary and credit aggregates reached record values in the course of 1973, and so did almost all the indicators of monetary and financial ease.[2] Fiscal policy became definitely expansionary: demand was boosted by a steep rise in current public expenditure (especially for civil servants' salaries and for pensions), which caused an increase of 1.7 points in the ratio of public sector (general government) deficit to GDP. At the same time, industrial wages rose by over 25 percent between the end of 1972 and the end of 1973.

Thus, in 1973 Italy offered an extreme textbook example of a wrong policy mix: a "remarkable combination of expansionary fiscal and

[1] The lira had been subjected to heavy speculative pressures since 1972 (see Bank of Italy 1973, pp. 377 ff.) and was considered too weak to participate in the joint float on the conditions offered by the other partners. What happened later to the French franc provides an ex post justification for Italy's decision.

[2] The degree of liquidity of the economy and, in particular, of the enterprise sector had already increased remarkably since 1971 and increased further in 1973. See Caranza and Micossi (1979).

monetary policy, negative real interest rates, negative covered interest rate differentials, currency devaluation and a situation of booming internal demand, sharply rising labor costs, and rising inflationary expectations" (Izzo and Spaventa 1981, p. 91). The result was a heavy, and worsening, external imbalance. Exports, hit by the strikes at the beginning of the year, were later affected by the slowing of world demand and were crowded out by booming domestic demand—their quantity barely increased year on year. Imports grew in quantity by 11 percent while, under the influence of the lira depreciation and the rise in raw material prices, their unit value grew twice as fast as that of exports. Adverse capital movements affected tourism and emigrants' remittances, and the current balance went heavily into the red. Meanwhile, in spite of intervention in the exchange market to the tune of $2.7 billion between February and December, the depreciation of the lira reached 15 percent in July and settled around 11 percent in the following months. Since June 1972, intervention had totaled $7.6 billion, while compensatory borrowing contracted by state agencies to replenish official reserves reached $6 billion at the end of 1973.

The first oil shock thus caught Italy in the worst possible shape: moving countercyclically with respect to the other major industrial economies, heavily indebted and with a high non oil-deficit. The situation, moreover, grew worse at the beginning of 1974. Domestic demand kept growing at high rates; the attempt to restrict credit expansion by setting ceilings to bank loans proved ineffective both because of the existence of large loopholes and because of the liquidity of the economy; the balance of payments deteriorated further under the impact of the oil price rise. The exchange rate fell, in spite of intervention amounting to $3.16 billion in the first quarter of 1974. Under these conditions—faced with the prospect of paying an additional oil bill amounting to some 3 percent of Italy's GDP, and with borrowing in the private capital markets becoming increasingly difficult—the Bank of Italy and the treasury decided to turn to the Fund for a stand-by arrangement.

This decision and the terms of the negotiations, which started in Washington in February, were kept very secret: not only, as was natural, from the press and the public, but also, as was less natural, from the other economic ministers of the Italian government.[3] This proved to be a mistake for at least two reasons. First, in a coalition government, presenting one's political partners with a *fait accompli*

[3] The negotiations took place in Washington at the same time as the energy conference called by the United States. It was the Italian treasury's wish that

causes a great deal of unnecessary discussion. Second, the gravity of the situation at the beginning of 1974 was fully known to the monetary authorities, but not, owing to information lags and lack of communication, to other economic ministers in the government.

Lack of communication and lack of timely factual and technical information explain the somewhat reserved attitude taken by the Socialist budget minister, Mr. Giolitti, and his ministry, toward the terms of the arrangement negotiated in Washington. Mr. Giolitti's reserve arose from the opinion that the limits to credit expansion of the Letter of Intent were too tight and such that they would cause an undesirable recession. There were two major points involved in the dispute: whether the possibility of a growth target more ambitious than that set in the projections for the stand-by arrangement should be left open; and whether the credit target was compatible with the given projections. On the second issue, plausible and implausible arguments were advanced on both sides: the credit targets, as we shall see presently, proved more restrictive than was intended, mostly because the underlying projections turned out to be wrong. On the first issue, the budget ministry's position underestimated the gravity of Italy's external imbalance and neglected the problems arising from her relative cyclical position, but they were also motivated by the opinion, shared at the time by the Organization for Economic Cooperation and Development (OECD) secretariat, that generalized recession was the least desirable reaction to the oil price rise.[4] Such reservations found expression in a letter to the treasury minister, Mr. La Malfa (of the Republican Party), dated February 27. Mr. La Malfa replied by resigning on February 28, thereby causing a government crisis.

The reaction of the Fund's officials was one of dismay. First, they did not like an arrangement with the Fund becoming the object of, or being used as an occasion for, an internal political row. Second, they attributed considerable importance to the arrangement with Italy, which was the first with a major developed country after the oil price rise: such an arrangement would establish the Fund's role in

---

representatives of another Italian economic minister to the conference be prevented from meeting and from being informed of the presence of members of the delegation dealing with the IMF. This proved impossible, or at least too embarrassing.

[4] See Izzo and Spaventa (1974 and 1981, pp. 95 ff.) and the literature cited therein; see also Bank of Italy (1973, pp. 405 ff.).

the new situation of imbalance caused by the oil shock.[5] Third, and no less important, the Fund's officials thought that they had gone a very long way toward meeting Italy's requirements and that the conditions agreed upon, far from being too restrictive, might be considered too lax if compared with the Fund's usual standards.[6]

It looked for a moment as if the arrangement might be canceled. But a new government expressed its intention of accepting the Fund's original terms, and the Letter of Intent signed on March 27 was the same as that originally drafted on February 16. In one of those paradoxes which make Italian political life so predictably varied, Mr. La Malfa and his party, although remaining in the majority, left the government, while Mr. Giolitti remained at his post.

The 1974 Letter of Intent: Stabilization Through Recession

The projections and assumptions on which the Fund's program (which embodied that proposed by the Bank of Italy) was predicated are reproduced in Table 18.2. This program had one, and only one, precise final target: a sizable reduction of the non-oil current deficit in 1974 and its elimination by 1975. It was openly recognized that this would imply a considerable slowing down of the growth of final demand and of domestic product. Owing to the rapid growth in the second half of 1973, 4 percent growth for 1974 implied a near stagnation between the last quarters of the two years. It was not, however, either the Bank of Italy's or the Fund's intention to engineer a recession, which would cause a new decline in capital formation.[7]

[5] In the Fund staff's analysis prepared in connection with Italy's request, it was noted that the arrangement "would not only be the largest Fund transaction since 1969 but also the first made in an international environment dominated by the increase in oil prices."

[6] In the document cited in note 5, the huge size of the effects of the oil shock on the Italian economy was considered, and it was stated that, although an effort had been made to keep the analysis "free from any sort of shock reaction to these large changes in statistical magnitudes. . . . the difficulty of doing so may well have colored much of the exposition."

[7] The Fund's document cited above repeatedly emphasizes the necessity of not interrupting the investment recovery which was taking place in Italy after years of decline or stagnation. See for instance the following passage:

The intermediate target selected to achieve first the reduction and then the elimination of the non-oil current imbalance was total domestic credit (TDC), for which quarterly and annual limits were set. These limits were complemented by a ceiling on the state sector's financing needs, to prevent an excessive squeeze on the productive sector's financing requirements. TDC represented an innovation in Fund practice, which has traditionally been based on targeting domestic credit expansion (DCE).[8]

DCE is the flow of domestic credit which results in money creation. In the Italian case it is therefore defined as the sum of the credit by the banking system to the private and public sectors, in the form both of loans and purchases of bonds and treasury bills, and of the financing of the treasury by the central bank.[9] TDC is, instead, the total flow of domestic financing to domestic sectors, inclusive of the nonbanking public's net purchase of bonds and bills (but not of equities). TDC is therefore the domestic counterpart of the creation of total financial assets, excluding shares, and is thus a wider aggregate than DCE. Its introduction, instead of DCE, was justified by at least two, related, reasons: the peculiarities of the Italian financial system, where the high substitutability between deposits and other assets is a cause of instability of the money demand function[10]; and the necessity of achieving a more direct control of domestic demand.

Given the flow of direct foreign financing, a target for TDC should ensure creation of domestic financial assets compatible with a level of money income consistent with the desired current balance. Of course, a correct estimate of the relationships between TDC and total financial assets and between the latter and money GDP, the stability

---

"The staff believes that any slower rate of growth would be inconsistent with the international need to avoid a general spread of deflation and the urgent national need for improvements in productive investment and social infrastructure."

[8] On the choice of intermediate targets in the Italian case, with particular reference to the introduction of TDC and its merits and limits also relative to DCE, see Vaciago (1975 and 1977), Cotula and Micossi (1977), Cotula and de' Stefani (1979), Arcelli (1978), Caranza and Cotula (1980), Sarcinelli (1981).

[9] In other words, DCE is equivalent to the change in the liabilities of the public and the private sectors to the consolidated banking system.

[10] Such instability is, however, questioned by Caranza, Micossi, and Villani (1982), especially with reference to a later period.

of such relationships, and a reliable projection of the evolution of internal and external prices are crucial for a correct assessment of the degree of restriction that will result. The neglect of stock factors in the flow model used for the TDC approach, the difficulty of assigning a value to the amount of borrowing from the foreign sector (assumed to be exogenous), the development of other financial instruments escaping the control of the authorities, and the increase in assets available to the nonbanking public are all factors that affect the stability of the relationship between TDC, financial assets, and money GDP—factors that help to explain the change of objectives and techniques of monetary policy in Italy in the late 1970s and early 1980s. In 1974–75, however, stock movements mostly affected the relationship between financial assets and the money supply,[11] whereas other factors that reduce the significance of TDC as an intermediate target became relevant only in later years. Errors in the projections underlying the IMF-Bank of Italy program are more important in explaining why implementation of the conditions set forth in the Letter of Intent resulted in a higher degree of restriction, caused a deeper recession, and produced a more rapid (though ephemeral) adjustment than either the Italian authorities or the Fund had bargained for. The final outcome was more instability as the excessive restraint and the rapidity of adjustment provoked the extravagant recovery policy of 1975–76, which precipitated another crisis.

In the first half of 1974, as the other major industrial economies (with the exception of France) were slowing down or entering a recession, growth of final demand and income seemed to go on unabated in Italy. Inflation became rampant, with wholesale prices rising at an annual rate of 76 percent in the first quarter and consumer prices rising at 26 percent. The total cash deficit of the balance of payments reached 650 billion lire in March and 1,000 billion lire in April and May. In spite of intervention in the exchange market of the order of $5 billion in the first five months, the effective exchange rate of the lira fell by five more points between January and early June. Actually, the economy had already begun to slow down in the second quarter, and the current non-oil deficit (which reached a peak between the first and the second quarter) was now largely the result

[11] A rise in interest rates tended to cause a massive switch from bonds to deposits.

of price factors, also connected with the *J*-curve effects of past depreciation.[12]

In these conditions, the authorities took stringent monetary measures to comply with the conditions of the stand-by arrangement. In March the discount rate was raised from 6.5 percent to 9 percent, the policy of sustaining bond prices was abandoned, and the whole structure of interest rates was allowed to rise. At the same time the two-tier exchange rate system (which had proved of little use, especially after the float) was discontinued, and restrictions on the import and export of Italian bank notes were introduced, complemented in May by stricter limits for expenditure on travel abroad.[13]

The truly important measures were taken in April, May, and July. In April the ceilings to the expansion of bank loans were made more stringent and, by removing the possibilities of exemptions dictated by allocation considerations, more effective: the overall expansion of each bank's loans could not exceed 8 percent in the 6 months ending September 30, 1974, and 15 percent in the 12 months ending March 31, 1975, with the latter limit applying also to individual loans to local authorities and to larger borrowers. In May, the introduction of a 50-percent, 6-month, noninterest-bearing deposit with the Bank of Italy on the c.i.f. value of most imports proved to be a powerful instrument for controlling the creation of liquidity: the absorption of the monetary base because of this measure averaged 235 billion lire per month between May and October and 1,237 billion lire for the year as a whole, and the 12-month growth rate of the stock fell from 18.6 percent to 15.4 percent. A further step to control liquidity was a prohibition on commercial banks' increasing their net foreign liabilities above the level of July 19.

In July the effects of monetary policy were belatedly reinforced by fiscal policy—with increases in car and property taxes, indirect taxes,

[12] According to Bank of Italy estimates, between the last half of 1973 and the first half of 1974 import volumes fell by 0.7 percent, with prices rising by 41 percent; export volumes rose by 1.2 percent, and export prices by 22 percent (Bank of Italy 1974, p. 164).

[13] Tourism was (and still is) a much used channel for illegal capital movements. According to Bank of Italy estimates, capital export concealed under "tourism" in the current balance peaked at the beginning of 1974, reaching 700 billion lire for the year as a whole, against 440 billion in 1973 (Bank of Italy 1974, pp. 182–83).

social security contributions (amounting to approximately 1 percent of current GDP) and the tariffs of public utilities.

All available indicators confirm that monetary policy in Italy in the course of 1974 acted brusquely and in a highly restrictive manner. All the relevant ratios (between financial assets, M2, and liquid assets of enterprises on the one hand and GDP on the other) fell sharply and to an unprecedented extent over the 12 months (Caranza and Micossi 1979); the growth of monetary aggregates suddenly decelerated between the second and third quarter; the banking system, and especially the enterprise sector, became highly illiquid; and interest rates rose sharply.

In a situation of declining world demand, when a downturn would have occurred in any event (as shown by the leading indicators and the level of orders), the drastically restrictive stance of credit and monetary policy precipitated a severe recession, the worst since the war. Industrial production fell by over 10 percent between the second and the last quarter of 1974 and by another 6 percent between the first and the third quarter of 1975. GDP and total domestic demand declined for four consecutive quarters and gross fixed investment for six, by 5.9 percent and 14.6 percent, respectively.

Along with the fall in demand and output, there was an equally rapid adjustment of the foreign account. By the third quarter of 1974 the non-oil trade balance went into the black, and a huge non-oil surplus developed in the following 12 months. The turnaround of the Italian current balance between 1974 and 1975—$7.5 billion, or 4.4 percent of 1975 GDP—was proportionally by far the most sizable of all the industrial countries.

Considering the depth of the recession, there was not much ground for complacency about overshooting the external objective to such an extent. Nor, as we said, were such developments intended by the Fund: that the 1974 outcomes for the real growth of income and investment were not much below the program's forecast (Table 18.2) is not significant, considering the unexpected strength of the first half and the severity and length of the following recession.

What went wrong then? A first, but only partial, explanation points to the failure, common to all industrialized countries and to international organizations at the time, to appreciate fully the joint effect on world demand of the restrictive policies pursued almost everywhere long after the cyclical downturn and of the recessionary impact of the oil price rise: each country neglected the consequences on its export market of a behavior of other countries similar to its own.[14] The Fund expected Italian exports to rise in 1974 by 11 percent in volume and imports to rise by 6.5 percent; the actual changes were, respectively, 8.5 percent (with zero growth between the second halves of 1973 and 1974) and −0.8 percent.

There was, however, a more important cause of the gap between intentions and results: the policies adopted turned out to be far more restrictive than had been intended. One evident reason for this was the gross underestimation, in the program, of the strength of inflation which, at least for consumer prices, accelerated in the course of the year. As is apparent in Table 18.2, the GDP deflator grew by 17 percent and fixed investment prices by 29 percent, instead of the projected 12 percent and 17 percent. As a result the economy, and especially the enterprise sector, hit the ceilings set in the program much earlier than expected (Fazio 1979, p. 302). Enterprises—compelled to finance the investment in progress, but deprived of access to credit—were obliged to reduce drastically their financial assets and their liquidity, with a heavy deterioration of their overall financial position.

The comparison between the forecasts underlying the program and the outcomes (Table 18.3 B, row 5, on financial requirements of the private sector) shows clearly the extent and the effects of the credit crunch. On top of forecasting errors on prices, and hence on the ratios between credit expansion and the growth of demand at current prices, there were wide errors (again evidenced in Table 18.3) in assessing the effects of inflation and of a restrictive monetary policy on the financial markets: bond and share issues were severely curtailed, and this contributed to increasing the financial difficulties of the productive sector.

There may still, however, be a missing element in the picture. A perusal of Table 18.3 seems to suggest that, in implementing the program, the Italian authorities were *plus royaliste que le roi.*[15] In the conditions of early 1974, they may have decided that it was better to err on the side of excessive severity than of excessive laxity. The crucial factor was perhaps the drain of liquidity caused by the 50 percent deposit on top of the effect of the ceilings to bank loans.

[14] A comparison betwen national forecasts and outcomes for domestic demand and exports is in Izzo and Spaventa (1981, Table 6): "The major cause of the forecasting errors appears to be the gross overestimation of the growth of markets and exports" (p. 101).

[15] Vaciago (1975), expresses such doubts.

TABLE 18.3 FINANCIAL PERFORMANCE UNDER THE 1974 STAND-BY

A. *Credit expansion: flows from April 1, 1974, to March 31, 1975* (billion lire)

	Targets	*Outcomes*
Financing business sector and housing from		
Credit system	12,800	9,048
Government	1,800	2,129
Direct bond issues	1,000	346
Total	15,600	11,423
Balance on current account	−4,200	−4,148
Treasury and other agencies	6,800	7,764
Overall total	18,200	15,039

B. *Monetary and financial aggregates, 1974* (billion lire)

	Forecasts	*Outcomes*
Bond issue	11,200	3,473
Treasury	6,400	1,226
Special credit institutions	3,800	2,153
Others	1,000	94
Banking system		
Loans	8,200	7,305
Bonds	2,600	5,355
Deposits	13,000	11,653
Special credit institutions, loans	4,600	3,225
Creation of monetary base	5,000	4,104
Foreign sector	−5,000	−3,115
Treasury	8,200	7,670
Enterprises and housing, financial requirements		
Gross investment	19,300	21,245
Financial assets	4,500	2,538
Capital transfers	−1,450	−642
Subtotal	22,350	23,141
External financing	15,350	12,604
Gross savings	7,000	10,537

Source: Banca d'Italia.

Certainly, while prices and money demand were underestimated, the growth of the finance available to the productive sector remained substantially below the targets and forecasts of the program.

An Extravagant Recovery and a New Crisis, 1975–76

Italy's recession between 1974 and 1975 was worse than in any other industrial country. The current external deficit fell drastically in the first quarter of 1975 and turned into a surplus in the second and third quarters; the effective exchange rate of the lira tended to appreciate in the first half, though the Bank of Italy intervened in the market to purchase almost $1 billion. The progress made with regard to inflation appeared even more dramatic: the wholesale price index, after rising by 33.7 percent between December 1973 and December 1974, remained constant in the first six months of 1975, and the rate of growth of consumer prices was halved in the course of the year.

The discount rate was reduced at the end of 1974, and interest rates were allowed to fall. In March 1975, the ceilings to bank loans were removed altogether. Meanwhile, the end of the import deposit made a further 1.2 billion lire available to enterprises. In the Bank of Italy's view, control over the creation of monetary base would be sufficient to ensure respect of the TDC target set by the EEC Commission.[16] This was a risky assumption, especially in view of the behavior of the treasury: a gradual relaxation of the credit ceilings would have been preferable to their hasty elimination.

As 1975 went by, however, the general atmosphere became one of justified preoccupation for the depth of the recession, of less justified impatience for the fact that the more permissive stance adopted at the beginning of the year was not producing immediate effects, and of even less justified euphoria for the results achieved on the stabilization front.

True, there had been some real improvement in the external balance, but, after allowing for the effects of the recession on the trade account (which in Italy are particularly quick and strong) and of the monetary and currency measures on capital movements, the situation was still very fragile, with extremely high foreign liabilities and extremely thin foreign currency reserves. As for inflation, the speculative component, so important in 1973–74, had been eliminated by the monetary squeeze and by recession, while falling raw material prices and a stable exchange rate were contributing to disinflation. Domestic underlying inflation, however, was going up, not down: while productivity fell substantially for cyclical reasons, wages rose rapidly, as a result both of contractual agreements and of a new system of indexation agreed upon in March 1975, so that labor costs per unit

[16] See Bank of Italy (1975, p. 251). With the purpose of making such control more effective, the Bank of Italy and nonbank operators were admitted to the auctions of treasury bills, reserved until then only to banks. On the monetary developments of this period, see Vaciago (1977) and Fazio (1979).

of output in the industrial sector rose by 33 percent. Thus, 1975 was a year of repressed inflation.

By the late spring, when some recovery was already under way, the pressures for more definite, and more effective reflationary measures mounted, finding some support also internationally: the EEC Commission in July, the EEC finance ministers in September, and the EEC Council in December all recommended that Italian economic policy should take a more expansionary course. On paper, the prescription was to stimulate the recovery by increasing public investment. In practice, the major impact of reflationary policy was on consumption, on inventory accumulation, and on rekindling inflationary expectations.

Bank interest rates were reduced twice in the spring, also as a result of pressures on the part of the authorities. The official discount rate was lowered in May and again in September, while the rate on treasury bills fell even more rapidly. The limits to banks' net foreign indebtedness were removed in June, while, as a result of some measures in the field of credit and taxation, compulsory reserve requirements were in fact reduced by over one-third.[17] The rate of creation of monetary base was stepped up in the third quarter by allowing 50 percent of export credits to be automatically refinanced by the Bank of Italy. The economy, and especially the banking system, quickly became very liquid again.

Fiscal policy was even more expansionary than monetary policy in the second half of the year. With expenditures increasing by 23 percent and revenues by only 15 percent, the ratio of public sector deficit to GDP doubled, reaching 13 percent. This was not merely the result of cyclical factors, but also of legislative measures, especially in the field of pensions, and of conscious efforts on the part of the treasury to accelerate disbursements. Further, at the end of the year personal income tax rates were reduced, and enterprises were allowed to revalue their assets to offset the fiscal drag of past inflation. The treasury deficit was particularly huge in the last quarter—3,000 billion lire higher than the October forecasts—and had to be financed largely by the creation of monetary base.

The rebound of economic activity, which would have occurred in any case in the second part of the year, was magnified by this remarkable combination of expansionary monetary and fiscal policies. In the last quarter total domestic demand grew at an annual rate of some 12 percent: there was a sizable export recovery, but the main

[17] See Fazio (1979, p. 305) and Bank of Italy (1975, p. 269).

thrust came from consumption and inventory accumulation, as shown by the much steeper rise of import volumes.

There followed familiar consequences: an acceleration of the inflation rate; a deterioration of the balance of payments; renewed pressures on the lira; loss of reserves in the attempt to defend the exchange rate, while the commercial banks rapidly reduced their foreign liabilities. On January 20, 1976, the authorities, unable to resist further attacks for sheer lack of foreign currency reserves (which had fallen to some $600 million), decided to close the exchange market, which reopened only 40 days later.

As noted above, economic policy was to a considerable extent responsible for this new crisis. The underlying condition of the economy had not improved, and a sudden recovery fed by monetary expansion and accelerating treasury cash expenditures was bound to cause trouble. Other factors, however, contributed to the violence of the currency crisis: the upward movement of the dollar in the second half of 1975; the realization by the markets that it would now be more difficult for Italy to find new international credit; leaks about the size of reserves and rumors as to the attitude of the US comptroller of the currency towards loans to Italy; finally, but no less important, a government crisis that opened the way to new elections and caused increased uncertainty.

While the market was closed, economic policy started backtracking on its previous expansionary course, but too slowly and too timidly to reverse expectations. The official discount rate was raised twice by one point to mop up excess liquidity, the automatic refinancing of export credits (a major cause of the quick monetary expansion of the last quarter of 1975) was suppressed, and compulsory reserve requirements were increased. At the same time, $500 million was borrowed on the swap line with the Fed and $500 million reborrowed (after it had been reimbursed in March 1975) from the Bundesbank, while in March the EEC granted a $1 billion loan under the recycling arrangement.

As the market reopened on March 1, the exchange rate fell steeply: the effective rate dropped from 77.3 in January to 66.5 in March, to 62.7 in April, to below 62 at the beginning of May. To cope with the new crisis, the official discount rate was raised by four points, and a number of measures were taken to reduce leads and lags and restrict speculative movements. Further, in May, a 50 percent noninterest-bearing deposit on all purchases of foreign currency was introduced, with the twofold purpose of encouraging commercial credits from foreign exporters and draining liquidity. The whole structure of interest rates was pushed up again, at levels higher than in 1974.

As conditions of monetary stringency prevailed again, there followed a period of tranquility in the summer months. It ended in September, with renewed international currency turbulence and the seasonal deterioration of the Italian current balance. There were pressures on the lira and a further depreciation in September, in spite of intervention of over $500 million. The observer's impression, on the basis of the available evidence, is that this was not the worst and the gravest crisis. It is, however, the one that was followed by the most drastic short-term measures and, especially, that opened the way to the most complete and organic stabilization program adopted in the Italian economy for over a decade. Even if the authorities somewhat overplayed the currency crisis, they were right to have done so.

The stabilization program will be examined in the next section. The emergency measures were a further increase of compulsory reserve requirements, an increase in the share of export credits to be financed with foreign currency, a three point rise in the discount rate, the reintroduction of ceilings to the expansion of bank loans, and the introduction of a special 10 percent tax on the purchase of foreign currency. This tax, the purpose of which was to delay payments in currency until the situation was under control, was initially to last for a fortnight only; a week after it expired, on October 23, it was introduced again until February 21, 1977, with a gradual phasing out.[18]

The 1977 Letter of Intent: A Success Story

The possibility of going to the Fund for a new stand-by arrangement had been considered by the Italian authorities since early in 1976, and there had been several formal or informal meetings with the Fund's staff. The last such meeting took place in Paris in October,[19] at the worst possible moment. By imposing a tax on the purchase of foreign currency on top of the 50 percent deposits, Italy had gravely sinned against the principle of avoiding restrictions on current payments and transfers, and the Fund took a severe view of both this and of the policies, or lack thereof, that had caused the new predicament. A complete breakdown of the negotiations was avoided but, unlike in 1974, negotiations dragged on for months. Only in April,

[18] The effect of such a tax on the cost of foreign currency "is in many ways similar to a devaluation of the exchange rate (but, unlike the latter, is both unilateral and reversible)": Bank of Italy (1976, p. 188).

[19] It should have been secret, but news of it leaked to the press.

after a protracted exchange of proposals and counter proposals,[20] and possibly also as a result of some political pressure,[21] was the approval of a stand-by arrangement recommended to the IMF executive directors.

The sterner attitude taken by the Fund is evidenced by a comparison of the staff's analysis on this occasion and in 1974. Now, the argument that Italy could not be expected to balance its current account in a world of massive oil surpluses was rejected, because "the Italian deficit is at least in part due to deficient economic policies and because there is no plausible answer to the question as to how continuing Italian deficits can be financed year after year." Further, the program explicitly allowed for some recession, stating that "another year of low growth . . . is inevitable if Italy is to break free from constrictions, self-imposed though many of them may be, that presently hamper economic policy." Finally, the arrangement extended over a period of 20 months, far more than the norm: "its duration reflects the belief that the nature of the disequilibrium in Italy is such that correction in a short period of time is not possible."

A lengthy and detailed Letter of Intent outlined the stabilization program, of which monetary and credit policy this time was only a part, and not the most important. Greater emphasis was placed on the reduction of the public sector deficit, in the short and the longer run. Specific targets were, moreover, set for a deceleration of inflation, which, under the influence of steeply rising labor costs and a depreciating exchange rate, had climbed again to 31 percent for wholesale prices and 22 percent for consumer prices in the 12 months ending December 1976. The importance of the indexation system in the price-wage relationship was stressed in this connection. For the exchange rate, the prescription was that intervention should be confined to avoiding disruptive fluctuations in the market.

Most of the measures required by this program were implemented before the Letter of Intent was signed. It was an impressive list.

In March 1976, in the middle of the worst of all currency crises, there had been an increase in taxes yielding no more than 1,000 billion lire, little more than offsetting the decrease in the personal income

[20] And after a sudden trip of the treasury minister to Washington to persuade the Fund to accept the changes to wage indexation agreed upon with the unions instead of those on which the Fund had insisted.

[21] The necessity of granting the stand-by was pressed on the US administration by its ambassador in Rome, Richard Gardner.

tax rates.[22] In the six months between October 1976 and March 1977, discretionary measures for direct taxation yielded 4,900 billion lire; another 1,400 billion were raised by increasing the tariffs of public utilities, while disposable income was further reduced by 1,100 billion by allowing the rise of some prices under public control. Altogether, the revenue from higher taxation and tariffs represented 3.3 percent of GDP in 1977. Moreover, in October 1976 it was decided that for two years the increase in the cost of living allowance to higher income earners should be paid wholly or partly in special nonnegotiable bonds rather than in cash.

In the first months of 1977 the unions agreed to a change in the climate of labor relations and accepted a number of specific measures aimed at increasing productivity and reducing the rise in labor costs: the elimination of all escalator systems providing higher indexation than that prevailing in industry; complete deindexation of the funds set aside by enterprises for severance pay; and reduction of the weight of some public utility tariffs in wage indexation. The unions further made concessions on overtime and internal mobility of the work force.

In the monetary field, interest rates were kept at a high level at the beginning of the year, and the ceilings to lira-denominated bank loans were renewed for a year. At the same time, the deposit on currency purchases ended on April 15, while the special tax was abolished on February 18.

The abolition of the deposit and the tax was also the result of international pressures: the governor of the Bank of Italy warned that "the international community" would not allow them to be reintroduced. The situation, however, was now under control, and the removal of such temporary protection caused litle harm: in spite of the flow of delayed payments for imports, only moderate intervention ($850 million) was required in February and March. From April on, the Bank of Italy became a massive buyer of foreign currency to prevent an appreciation of the lira effective rate: foreign currency reserves rose by $3 billion between December 1976 and June 1977 and by another $1.8 billion between June and December 1977.

These favorable, and not wholly expected, developments were due to two factors. The first was a quick and remarkable improvement of the current balance: the year ended with a 2,100 billion lire surplus

[22] The public sector deficits, however, fell steeply in 1976 both in absolute terms and relative to GDP. This was mostly the result of fast growth of tax revenues, due to the introduction of a new system of self-assessment and to shorter terms of payment by the banks of the witholding tax on interest.

(2,100 billion more than the Fund's target). Second, there occurred a sudden reversal of expectations on the external stability of the lira: with covered interest rates much higher at home than in international markets, and under conditions of domestic tightness, enterprises, through the commercial banks, borrowed massive amounts of foreign currency in the first half of the year. The improvement in the current balance was this time not only due to the fall in economic activity, which lasted only two quarters and was far more limited than in 1974–75. In spite of the disappointing growth of world demand (4 percent instead of the 8 percent assumed in the Fund's program), exports rose quite fast (so that Italy's share of world exports returned to its 1972 level), as a result both of the effect of past depreciation and of improved productivity at home. The terms of trade, moreover, improved substantially in the course of the year. Toward the end of the year, as the dollar fell with respect to the stronger European currencies, management of the exchange rate ensured some appreciation of the lira against the dollar, Italy's major import currency, and a depreciation towards the Europen currencies, to keep exports competitive; this policy was pursued for the rest of 1978, allowing a huge increase in reserves and laying the ground for an export-led recovery. In the course of 1977 inflation fell to 9.5 percent for wholesale prices and 14 percent for consumer prices.

The success of the 1976–77 stabilization plan was no doubt helped by favorable external factors that had not been present on earlier occasions: the international currency conditions and stable or falling raw material prices helped a great deal, and world demand started recovering in 1978. Such factors, however important, cannot by themselves provide a satisfactoy explanation of the change in the Italian economic situation in 1977, and other more relevant elements should be considered.

The Italian government acted with decision on many fronts between the fall of 1976 and the spring of 1977, with measures that public opinion could immediately perceive as implying a change of regime. While the monetary situation was brought under control, and in the pause afforded by the artificial protection erected around the lira, a tough fiscal policy not only freed resources for export but also gave a sense of urgency to the need for stabilization that monetary policy alone would not have been able to provide. If the entire burden of stabilization had fallen on monetary policy, the process of adjustment would have been slower, more uncertain, and far more costly. That sense of urgency was of utmost importance in inducing the unions to adopt a new and cooperative attitude and to accept officially that they should make concessions in the field of labor relations, productivity, and the cost of labor. Such concessions were not only intrinsically relevant but also contributed to the reversal of expectations.

The stabilization program thus succeeded not only because the individual measures went in the right technical direction, but also because of their overall impact on expectations and confidence. A tough program, however, also requires widespread political support, so that it can be enacted rapidly in parliament, accepted by the unions, and interpreted as reflecting substantial agreement on the objectives and instruments of policy. The peculiar political situation prevailing in Italy at the time made this possible. After the elections in mid-1976 a minority Christian Democratic government was formed with the abstention of all other parties (including, for the first time, the Communist party), representing 33 percent of the electorate. Though there was no formal partnership in a majority, the abstaining parties were kept informed of major economic policy decisions (including the dealings with the Fund): they all shared the view that urgent action was required and explicitly or implicitly agreed on the whole strategy. With a powerful opposition party capitalizing on the unpopularity of some of the measures adopted, the program would probably have failed.

Italy never used the loan of the second stand-by arrangement because the improvement in the external balance and the increase in reserves made it unnecessary. Had Italy wished to use the loan, would the Fund have allowed her to draw the tranches due after December 1977? The question arises because further purchases under the arrangement were conditional in respect of all the targets set, in the Letter of Intent, for credit expansion, treasury and public sector deficit, and the rate of inflation. As shown in Table 18.2, in the last quarter of 1977 the financing needs of the treasury overshot by some 4,000 billion lire the Fund's target, and this caused an overshooting of the credit expansion target by a similar amount. The overshooting was even greater in 1977. In spite of this, the inflation target was respected, and the external objective was overrealized in both years.

The Italian Experience and Williamson's Questions

The narrative of the preceding pages perhaps conveys the difficulty of providing straightforward answers to John Williamson's questions (Chapter 7, this volume).

Even at a superficial level, the answers can only be ambiguous. As to the first question (the impact of the Fund in influencing the policies actually adopted), on both occasions the Italian authorities, when turning to the Fund, clearly had in mind that they should adopt the policies eventually outlined in the letters of intent. In 1974, the stand-by arrangement, besides being essential for financing the external deficit, provided the pressures necessary to win acceptance of a tight monetary policy. In 1977 the stabilization program was implemented before the arrangement: the latter served perhaps to obtain some futher concessions from the unions, but the loan was not used, nor were the intermediate targets respected. As to the second question (the effect of the policy changes on key variables), in both cases there was an improvement of the current external balance and a reduction in the rate of inflation, but these were short-run results in the first case and long-lasting consequences in the second. Further, capacity growth was badly impaired in the first case, but only temporarily affected in the second, while income distribution changed in favor of dependent labor income in the first case and in favor of profits in the second. Finally, the policy changes of the Fund's programs appear to have been relatively "inefficient" in the first case and relatively "efficient" in the second, so it can be surmised that better policies were available in the first case, but not in the second.

All this, however, does not lead us very far, for the Italian case (and I suppose not only the Italian case) shows how important, and how difficult, are the problems mentioned at the beginning of this paper.

First, the Italian experience, both in 1974 and 1977, shows how much one's judgment must depend on the forecasts underlying the policy program. Gross errors in the projection of inflation caused the 1974 program to be overrestrictive, which was in turn a cause of the extravagant reflationary policy of late 1975. In 1977 the final objectives were achieved (or overachieved), but the intermediate targets were not.

Some relaxation of the intermediate targets would have been desirable in 1974 in view of the forecasting errors. In 1977, strict adherence to the credit target would have caused an unnecessary degree of restriction, nipped the incipient investment recovery in the bud and further increased an already huge current surplus. But insistence on adherence to the targets for the public deficit, although not essential for the success of the program in the shorter run, would have induced a much needed structural adjustment and perhaps would have avoided considerable trouble in later years.

This brings me to the question of the time horizon of the policy program. The Fund's interventions *are* normally conceived as operations of first aid surgery (or were so conceived in Italy). The 1974 program was explicitly and particularly unambitious in this respect, and the result could be seen in 1975–76. The 1977 arrangement instead took a longer view, which was reflected in the policies adopted. The paradox is that, if the program is immediately successful (as was the case in 1977), the Fund loses any leverage in respect of longer term conditions of a more structural nature (such as the reduction of the public sector deficit), while pressure can be kept on only if the program is unsuccessful.

Finally, the Italian experience proves to what extent the degree of success of an economic policy program, measured in terms of its contents as well as of its benefits, depends on a very complicated interaction between technical considerations, effects on expectations and confidence, social reactions and political conditions. The impact of the whole program on expectations is as important as correct definition of the targets, and its efficiency can be enhanced or reduced by a greater or lesser degree of social and political consensus. Such a consensus is not a problem the Fund can be expected to solve, but neither is it a problem the Fund can afford to neglect.

References

Arcelli, Mario. 1978. "Obiettivi intermedi e obiettivi finali della politica monetaria." *Banche e Banchieri* (September).

Bank of Italy. 1973, 1974, 1975, 1976. *Relazione Annuale*, Rome.

Caranza, C., and F. Cotula. 1980. "Targets, Indicators, and Techniques of Monetary Policy." Processed.

Caranza, C., and S. Micossi. 1979. "Indicatori aggregati e settoriali della politica monetaria." *Moneta e Credito*, no. 126 (June).

Caranza, C., S. Micossi, and M. Villani. 1982. "La domanda di moneta in Italia, 1963–81." Processed.

Cotula, F., and P. de' Stefani, eds. 1979. *La politica monetaria in Italia: Istituti e strumenti*. Bologna.

Cotula, F., and S. Micossi. 1977. "Riflessioni sulla scelta degli obiettivi intermedi della politica monetaria nella esperienza italiana." *Contributi alla recerca economica*. Servizio studi della Banca d' Italia (December).

Fazio, Antonio. 1979. "La politica monetaria in Italia dal 1947 al 1978." *Moneta e Credito*, no. 27 (September).

Izzo, L., and L. Spaventa. 1974. "Some Internal and External Effects of the Rise in the Price of Oil." Banca Nazionale del Lavoro *Quarterly Review* (March).

———. 1981. "Macroeconomic Policies in Western European Countries, 1973–77." In H. Giersch, ed., *Macroeconomic Policies for Growth and Stability: A European Perspective*. Tuebingen: J.C.B. Mohr (Paul Siebeck).

Sarcinelli, Mario. 1981. "Il ruolo della Banca Centrale nell'economia nazionale." *Economia Italiana*.

Sargent, Thomas. 1981. "Stopping Moderate Inflation: The Methods of Poincaré and Thatcher." Processed.

Spaventa, Luigi. 1981. "Comments on 'Stopping Moderate Inflation: The Methods of Poincare and Thatcher' by Thomas Sargent." Processed.

Vaciago, Giacomo. 1977. "Investimento finanziario e controllo della liquidita." *Rivista internazionale di scienze sociali*, pp. 1–2.
———. 1975. "Credito totale interno e offerta di moneta."
Rivista internazionale di scienze sociali, pp. 5–6.

Annex 18.A 1974 Letter of Intent

Annex to Stand-by Arrangement
Rome
March 27, 1974

Dear Mr. Witteveen:

1. The Government of Italy hereby requests the International Monetary Fund for a stand-by arrangement under which the Government of Italy will have a period of one year the right, after making full use of any gold tranche that it may have, to purchase from the Fund the currencies of other members in exchange for lire up to an amount equivalent to SDR 1,000 million. Before making purchases under the stand-by arrangement, the Government will consult with the Managing Director on the particular currencies to be purchased from the Fund.

2. The purpose of this stand-by arrangement is to support the policies that the Government of Italy proposes to follow in order to strengthen the balance of payments position and moderate domestic inflationary pressure while having regard to the need to maintain a high level of employment of domestic resources.

3. In 1973 the current account deficit of the balance of payments is estimated at Lit 1,300 billion (after making an adjustment of Lit 600 billion for under-recording of net current receipts). Recent increases in oil prices will add substantially to the deficit. It is the firm intention of the Italian Government to reduce substantially in the course of 1974 and eliminate before the end of 1975 the "non-oil" current account deficit, that is, the part of the current account deficit that is not directly attributable to the increased deficit on oil trade consequent on the rise in oil prices above their average level in 1973. The Government intends to adapt its economic policies with the objective of greatly strengthening the private capital account.

4. In order to achieve the aim for the current account, it will be necessary to follow certain domestic financial policies which will help to ensure that the necessary capacity be made available to produce an appropriate growth of exports and that the demand for imports is restrained. For these purposes the Government will rely on consistent budgetary and credit policies and on selective measures affecting the composition of internal demand.

5. The Government will take measures to ensure that the internal prices of refined oil products rise by an amount that is at least equal to the rise in the cost of oil imports. This will reduce private disposable incomes by an amount which is at least equal to the burden of the increased oil price. The Government intends to introduce measures which will secure the payment in 1974 of certain taxes presently due in 1975. It is estimated that this will reduce the financing needs of the Treasury by Lit 500 billion. It is not only the intention of the Government to endeavor to restrict the size of the financing needs of the Treasury but also to select forms of financing that will minimize the inflationary consequences for the economy.

6. It is expected that the financing needs of the Treasury will in any event not exceed Lit 9,200 billion in the period January 1, 1974–December 31, 1974. This total would be consistent, allowing for seasonal factors, with an amount of not more than Lit 4,600

billion in the period January 1, 1974–June 30, 1974, and an amount of not more than Lit 6,800 billion in the period January 1, 1974–September 30, 1974.

7. Credit policy will be consistent with the achievement of an expanding volume of fixed investment in line with the Government's policy of significantly increasing the nation's productivity. The policy will be to reorient the flow of new capital expenditure toward exporting industries in order to strengthen the balance of payments. The Government is fully aware that over the medium term the economy will have to be restructured in order to offset the consequences of the deterioration in the terms of trade.

8. The authorities' objectives and policies imply an expansion of total domestic credit in the 12 months ending March 31, 1975 of not more than Lit 22,400 billion. This total would be consistent, allowing for seasonal factors, with an amount of not more than Lit 6,000 billion in the period April 1, 1974 to June 30, 1974; of not more than Lit 11,000 billion from April 1, 1974 until September 30, 1974; and of not more than Lit 19,500 billion from April 1, 1974 until December 31, 1974. The credit ceiling assumes an oil deficit of Lit 3,600 billion. It is agreed that if this part of the deficit turns out to be lower or higher, the credit ceiling will be adjusted correspondingly. This position will be determined in the course of July 1974 and any such adjustment that may be required will be made at that time.

9. In the field of credit and interest rate policy, the authorities will take steps to keep short-term interest rates in line with those prevailing on foreign and international markets. The credit and interest rate policies described above will contribute toward the desired improvement in international private capital flows. However, it is expected that, for the time being, they will need the support of measures controlling capital outflows, including the maintenance of the existing dual exchange market arrangements. The adequacy of exchange controls to limit unauthorized capital outflows will be kept under review, but it is the firm intention of the Government not to introduce new restrictions on payments and transfers, or new multiple currency practices, for current international transactions, or new restrictions on imports.

10. The Government of Italy believes that the present effective exchange rate of the lira, which on a trade-weighted basis has depreciated by about 17 percent since early 1973, is in present circumstances sufficient to maintain Italy's competitive position and is not inconsistent with the achievement of its external and internal objectives. However, under present circumstances, the Government is of the view that it is necessary to continue the flexible exchange rate policy which Italy has pursued since February 1973. The Italian authorities stress their support of the Executive Board Decision of January 23, 1974 on Consultations on Members' Policies in Present Circumstances, and reiterate their desire to collaborate with the Fund in accordance with the provisions of Article IV, Section 4(a). The Italian authorities will, during the life of the stand-by agreement, consult with the Fund on their exchange policies at any time on the initiative of the Managing Director.

11. The Government believes that the policies set forth in this letter are adequate to achieve the objectives of the program but will take any further measures that may become appropriate for this purpose. During the period of the stand-by arrangement the Government of Italy will consult the Fund on the adoption of any measures that may be appropriate at the initiative of the Government of Italy or whenever the Managing Director requests consultation because any of the criteria in paragraphs 6, 8, and 9 above have not been observed or because he considers that consultation on the program is desirable. In addition, after the period of the stand-by arrangement and while any Fund holdings of lire above the first credit tranche include currency resulting from purchases under the stand-by agreement, the Government of Italy will

consult the Fund from time to time, at the initiative of the Government or at the request of the Managing Director, concerning Italy's balance of payments policies.

Yours sincerely,

/s/ Emilio Columbo
Minister of the Treasury

Mr. H. Johannes Witteveen
Managing Director
International Monetary Fund
Washington, D.C. 20431

Annex 18.B 1977 Letter of Intent

Rome, April 6, 1977

Dear Mr. Witteveen:

1. The Government of Italy hereby requests from the International Monetary Fund a stand-by arrangement under which the Government of Italy will have, for a period ending December 31, 1978, the right to purchase from the Fund the currencies of other members in exchange for lire up to an amount equivalent to SDR 450 million. Before making purchases under the stand-by arrangement, the Government will consult with the Managing Director on the particular currencies to be purchased from the Fund.

2. The purpose of the stand-by arrangement is to support the policies being followed by the Government of Italy, designed to curtail domestic inflationary pressures and to strengthen the external position. In this way, a basis can be laid for a steady and sustainable rate of growth of gross national product and for rising levels of employment. A lasting improvement in the economic outlook will depend to some extent also on a satisfactory growth of world trade assisted by adequate policies of economic expansion in countries presently enjoying strong external positions.

3. The maladjustments in the Italian economy have been recognized for a number of years. The structure of the labor force and of the stock of capital have adapted only with a lag to the constantly shifting requirements of rapid economic and social change. The results have shown themselves most starkly in a weakening of investment and in undesirably high levels of unemployment and underemployment. Italy's difficulties were compounded in 1973 and 1974 by a sharp deterioration in its terms of trade and by the subsequent recession in world trade. Until these maladjustments have been corrected, attempts to achieve a faster rate of economic growth will, as recent experience has again shown, be quickly dissipated in a rapid acceleration in the rate of inflation and an unsustainable deterioration in Italy's external position. Adjustment will require a diversion of resources from consumption, private and public, to investment and exports. That is what we intend to achieve.

4. The Government has chosen to follow a step-by-step approach to adjustment and intends to continue building a comprehensive program to cover the next two or three years, which is designed to restore the possibility of higher rates of growth and employment in conditions of relative price stability and a sustainable external position. In Italian circumstances it is essential that a consensus on the constituent parts of this program be reached if it is to be successfully implemented. This letter describes the policies the Government will follow in the 12 months to end-March 1978 and, subject

to a review with the Fund by the end of April 1978, those it plans to follow in calendar 1978 as a whole and beyond.

5. In formulating their economic strategy for the period ahead, the Italian authorities have no doubt that priority needs to be given to four interrelated initiatives:

First, a reduction in the deficit of the Government, defined so as to embrace a much broader coverage of the public sector than that of the Treasury alone, combined with additional measures to secure a sharp decline in the recent rates of increase in expenditures of this enlarged public sector through a more effective control.

Second, a sustained reduction in the rate of increase in prices. The Government has stressed its view that the successful implementation of such a policy will require further modifications in the present system of wage indexation, which undermines the effectiveness of important policy instruments and hampers efforts to create conditions in which investment and exports can lead to a revival of economic growth. The Government has actively sought modifications of the system and intends to ensure that further changes will be made.

Third, a tight control over the rate of domestic credit expansion in order to protect the balance of payments position and thus help to defend the external value of the currency.

Finally, the authorities are determined to ensure the continued competitiveness of the Italian economy. Intervention in the exchange market will therefore have the purpose only of smoothing disruptive short-term fluctuations in the exchange rate for the lira. The Italian authorities are determined to reach a reasonable degree of exchange rate stability through the underpinning of appropriate domestic policies.

6. In 1976, the current account of the balance of payments is estimated to have been in deficit to the extent of Lit 2,380 billion. It is a firm intent of the Italian Government to achieve a small surplus of not less than Lit 500 billion in the 12 months to end-March 1978 and to ensure that a sizable surplus of some Lit 1,000 billion or more is achieved during 1978 as a whole. The Italian authorities also intend to safeguard the position on private capital account by means of the credit policies described below, by the continued enforcement of administrative regulations against unauthorized capital exports, and by ensuring that both long-term and short-term interest rates are appropriately related to those prevailing abroad. The resulting surplus should be largely sufficient to provide for repayments falling due on Italy's official external indebtedness, which at the end of 1976 amounted to some $14 billion. In addition, commercial banks were indebted for a further $3 billion at that date.

7. The objectives and policies of the authorities imply an expansion of total domestic credit in the 12 months ending March 31, 1978 of not more than Lit 30,000 billion. The Italian authorities intend to keep this total under continuous review during the next 12 months, taking into account the prospective financial requirements of industry for investment and expansion. This total would be consistent, allowing for seasonal factors, with an amount of not more than Lit 8,200 billion in the period from April 1, 1977 to June 30, 1977, of not more than Lit 14,500 billion from April 1, 1977 to September 30, 1977, and of not more than Lit 24,500 billion from April 1, 1977 to December 31, 1977. Subject to the review set in paragraph 4, the Italian authorities further intend that domestic credit expansion should not exceed Lit 30,000 billion in the period January 1, 1978 to December 31, 1978. Quarterly ceilings for 1978 will be established during the same review.

The authorities will ensure that these ceilings are observed through the use of appropriate monetary instruments, including those designed to bring about adequate levels of interest rates. In pursuing their monetary policies the authorities do not intend to make further use of measures which involve external restrictions.

8. It is a major objective of the project to limit the deficit of the Government and its associated institutions in order that adequate room should be left to accommodate the credit requirements of productive enterprises on whose investment the prospects for a resumption of balanced growth in Italy depend. Between 1974 and 1976 the Treasury deficit (excluding funding operations and lending to specialized credit institutions) rose from Lit 8,300 billion to Lit 13,200 billion or from 8.4 percent to 9.5 percent of GDP. The authorities had previously committed themselves to limiting the Treasury deficit so defined to Lit 9,800 billion for the year 1977, which included an amount of Lit 2,400 billion for the financing of the local authorities. As part of the process of reforming the financial position of the local authorities, as described in paragraph 12, it has now been decided that to finance their deficits in calendar 1977 the Treasury will disburse an amount of Lit 5,700 billion, so that the revised Treasury deficit now amounts to Lit 13,100 billion for 1977. If comparable adjustments were made to the 1976 figures, the equivalent deficit would have been Lit 15,000 billion. Allowing for seasonal factors, this total of Lit 13,100 billion would be consistent with an amount of not more than Lit 8,700 billion in the period January 1, 1977 to June 30, 1977; and of not more than Lit 11,200 billion in the period January 1, 1977 to September 30, 1977. Quarterly ceilings for the calendar year 1978 will be established during the review referred to in paragraph 4.

9. However, as mentioned in paragraph 5, it has become increasingly obvious that decisions on fiscal policy need to be taken not only by reference to the position of the Treasury but also by focusing attention on a number of other agencies, whose rising deficits in recent years have seriously weakened the public finances. The Government therefore intends to place ceilings on the consolidated deficit of the Treasury, the local authorities, the social security institutions, the health institutions (including the Hospital Fund), and ENEL. While this extended coverage is still not comprehensive, it does include the main agencies whose deficits have required substantial Treasury financing in the recent past. In 1976 the deficit of this enlarged public sector amounted to Lit 18,700 billion and the Government has concluded that it should not exceed Lit 16,450 billion for the period January 1, 1977 to December 31, 1977. This intention implies a reduction of the deficit from 13.4 percent of GDP in 1976 to 9.7 percent in 1977. In order to make this ceiling fully effective as an instrument of operational control it will be necessary to introduce improvements in the collecting and reporting of information, and it is intended that this be done in time to allow reviews on a quarterly basis during 1978. Subject to the review referred to in paragraph 4, the Italian authorities intend that in calendar 1978 this enlarged public sector deficit should not exceed Lit 14,450 billion, which is estimated to be the equivalent of some 7.6 percent of GDP.

10. The Italian authorities regard the attainment of these targets as a minimum requirement both for their policy of reallocating resources to investment and exports and of maintaining a sound domestic monetary position. The Government has therefore in recent months taken a wide range of measures to increase revenues and to raise administered prices. Together, these measures are expected to increase the current revenues of the public sector by a total of Lit 6,300 billion in 1977, equivalent to 3.7 percent of GDP. The Government has further concluded that the ceilings specified in paragraphs 8 and 9 for 1977 cannot be assured without additional restraints on expenditure and/or further increases in revenue of approximately Lit 2,000 billion. Some Lit 1,000 billion of this sum is to be used to cover the cost of extending the fiscalization of employers' social security contributions throughout 1977. The Government still has under consideration the measures it will need to take in the near future in order to ensure that the deficits are kept within the ceilings. It is intended that an effective

restraint on the growth of expenditures will play a major role in ensuring adherence to the limits in 1978.

11. The Government has also concluded that it is necessary to undertake a thoroughgoing reform of the methods of and instruments for controlling public expenditure. Since this reform will require time for implementation, the Government believes that in 1977 the purpose it has in mind can be served by placing a ceiling of Lit 55,350 billion (including Lit 1,400 billion on account of fiscalization) on the cash expenditures in the State budget together with a Lit 3,500 billion ceiling on the deficit of what are known as "other Treasury operations."

The Government is planning to require in the future the annual submission of cash budgets not only for the State but also for each of the main entities in the public sector in order to secure an improved control. If the new system is in operation at the time of the review specified in paragraph 4, then the limit on expenditures in 1978 will be specified in that context. If the new system is not in operation, then the approach used for 1977 and described in the previous paragraph of this section will again be used.

In order to control the growth of public expenditure in the medium term, the Government also intends to limit the rate of increase of expenditures in the competenza budget for the State in 1978 to 7 percent, and to a lower rate of increase in 1979. These figures imply a fall of some 3 percentage points in each year in real terms; the sharp deceleration compared with previous rates of increase will be partly absorbed by a reduction in the outstanding amount of unspent appropriations (residui passivi). The rates of increase in expenditures will be reviewed under the terms of paragraph 4. In achieving these objectives the Government will ensure that so far as possible fixed investment is not constrained below present plans. As a result, the cuts will bear most heavily on planned current expenditures.

The Government wishes to underline the strength of its intention of strictly controlling the rate of increase in cash expenditure of the total public sector in 1978 and 1979.

12. The control of the Government over the finances of the public sector has, as noted earlier, been greatly weakened by inadequate surveillance over important components of the sector. The Government has initiated the preparation of specific reforms designed to bring under the effective control of the Central Government the financial operations of various bodies. As part of the reform of local authorities' finances, the access of municipal and provincial authorities to short-term bank credit has been cut off. Furthermore, the Government intends to restore certain revenue-raising powers to the local authorities, to allow them to raise fees and charges on services rendered and through a system of centralized accounting in the Treasury to exercise, in addition, surveillance on the aggregate of their total expenditures.

The reforms of the finances of the social security institutions will aim to establish, in agreement with the Ministry of the Treasury, annual cash budgets which will set specific expenditure limits to their operations and will control the means of their financing. The Government intends to introduce immediately legislation to prohibit access by the health institutions, including the Hospital Fund, to short-term bank credit. When the legislation has been enacted, the ceilings under paragraph 8 will be subject to review with the Fund. The Government will also consider raising contributions to the social security schemes and extending the "ticket system" proposed for purchases of pharmaceutical products to other health benefits and to hospitalization charges. A full review will also be made of the pension system to eliminate abuses and prevent unjustified claims.

13. The Government is also determined to secure a continuing reduction in the rate of price inflation so as to avoid a degree of reliance on credit restraint that would lead to unnecessary delays in the growth of employment and productivity. The rate of increase in consumer prices, as measured by movements in the indice sindacale which forms the basis for the scala mobile system of wage indexation, reached an estimated 22 percent in the 12 months to March 15, 1977; it is to be brought down to a maximum of 13 percent in the 12 months to March 15, 1978. This index averaged 143 in the three months to January 15, 1977 on a base of 100 in the three months to October 15, 1974. The authorities intend that the average for this index will not exceed 150 in the three months to April 15, 1977, 156 in the three months to July 15, 1977, 161 in the three months to October 15, 1977, 165 in the three months to January 15, 1978, and 169 in the three months to April 15, 1978. The Government is determined to achieve these targets without imposing new price controls or preventing required increases in administered prices. If at any time these targets are not achieved, the authorities will, on the basis of an immediate review of economic policies, put forward appropriate proposals for the realization of their price objectives. At the time of the review provided for in paragraph 4 above, the Italian authorities will set additional ceilings on the permissible increase in the indice sindacale to October 15, 1978 designed to reduce the Italian rate of inflation in as short a time as practicable to that of the major industrial countries that are price setters in world trade. The Government presently intends that the rate of increase in prices during the year 1978 will not exceed 8 percent and it believes that the thrust of the present program is compatible with this intention.

14. The present system of almost complete indexation of wages has the avowed purposes both of effecting a degree of income redistribution and of protecting wage-earners from the effects of rising prices, irrespective of their cause. It has now become clear that the deterioration in the terms of trade, increases in indirect taxes which were an essential element of fiscal policy, and increases in contractual wages have, as a result of the scala mobile, accelerated inflation sharply, squeezed profits, and thus put such severe pressure on investment that the growth of employment has been jeopardized. In these conditions the present scala mobile system is increasingly recognized as an instrument that threatens the employment opportunities of the mass of the Italian people. The Government has therefore continuously stressed the need to mitigate the impact of price adjustments on the wage level and has also insisted on the need to modify the system itself. It has already proved possible to take a series of steps which, in combination, will have a significant impact on cost and price developments. The three main changes are:

First, legislation was adopted in October 1976 requiring payment in specially issued nonnegotiable Treasury bonds of all index-linked wage increases on incomes in excess of Lit 8 million and of 50 percent of such increases on incomes between Lit 6 million and Lit 8 million.

Second, an agreement between labor and management on various arrangements to increase productivity and reduce wage cost was enacted into law in early 1977, including the abolition of special arrangements favoring special groups.

Third, a change in the method of computation of the indice sindacale has been made with respect to daily newspapers, urban transport, and electric energy. These changes will result in the indice sindacale showing, when it is next published, an increase which will be 1.5 points less than it otherwise would have been. It is the intention of the Italian Government to make use of the resulting increase in flexibility to raise public sector tariffs in order to increase public sector receipts by an additional Lit 500 billion during the next 12 months and thus contribute to the reduction in the public sector deficit foreseen in paragraphs 9 and 10.

15. A prerequisite for any further modification of the existing system of indexation is a broad consensus with labor and management, but the Government is aware that the realization of its objectives may require further modifications of the system. Until the system can be modified in a significant manner, the deterioration in Italy's relative labor costs can be partly offset by the transfer from enterprises to the State budget of a proportion of employers' liabilities for social security contributions. A reduction in social security contributions by employers has already been agreed until January 31, 1978, and financing by increased taxation for the first six months of 1977 has been approved. The Government intends to obtain parliamentary approval for any additional financing that may be required to cover the cost of this provision over the remainder of the period.

16. Despite the reduction in the rate of increase in costs and prices now foreseen and the temporary alleviation of the rise in labor costs due to the measures referred to in paragraphs 14 and 15, it will take some time before the rates of inflation and of increases in labor costs in Italy are brought into line with those of its major competitors. The Italian authorities are fully aware, however, that the competitive position of the economy cannot be allowed to deteriorate if Italy is to secure a lasting improvement in its balance of payments. In these circumstances they are determined, without the imposition of restrictions, to maintain a competitive position, both at home and abroad, of internationally traded goods and services produced by Italy. They will not use intervention to contain the increase in the domestic price level. While the proposed stand-by arrangement remains in force, intervention in the market will be confined to operations designed to minimize disruptive short-term fluctuations in the market.

17. The Italian authorities stress their support of the Executive Board Decision of January 23, 1974 on Consultation on Members' Policies under Present Circumstances, and reiterate their intention to collaborate with the Fund in accordance with the provisions of Article IV, Section 4(a). The Italian authorities will, during the life of the stand-by arrangement, consult with the Fund on their exchange policies at any time on the initiative of the Managing Director.

18. During the period of the proposed stand-by arrangement, the Government of Italy does not intend to introduce any multiple currency practices or impose new or intensify existing restrictions on payments and transfers for current international transactions. Furthermore, the Government of Italy does not intend to introduce new or intensify existing restrictions on imports for balance of payments reasons during the period of the stand-by arrangement. Exchange controls now in effect limiting capital outflows will be strictly enforced, and new controls for this limited purpose will be introduced as required.

19. The Government believes that the policies set out in this letter are adequate to achieve the objectives of its program, but will take any further measures that may become appropriate for this purpose. The Government of Italy will consult the Fund in accordance with the policies of the Fund on such consultations on the adoption of any measure that may be appropriate. In any case, the Italian authorities will reach understandings with the Fund before the end of April 1978 on their policy intentions for the remaining period of the stand-by arrangement.

Yours Sincerely,

/s/ Gaetano Stammati
Minister of the Treasury

CHAPTER **19**

IMF Conditionality: the Stand-by Arrangement With Portugal, 1978

José da Silva Lopes

The change of the political regime in Portugal in April 1974, from a dictatorship that had lasted more than 40 years, was followed by a period of about one- and-a-half years of political turbulence and revolutionary economic transformations. That change had far-reaching effects on the balance of payments, which was simultaneously hit by the first oil shock and by the effects of the decolonization of Angola and Mozambique. In face of the difficulties of external equilibrium which thus arose, Portugal concluded in May 1978 a stand-by arrangement with the International Monetary Fund (IMF) covering the period of 12 months up to March 1979. The improvement in the balance of payments during that period and in the following year went far beyond expectations. The current account deficit, which had reached $1.5 billion (about 9 percent of GDP) in 1977, came down to $826 million in 1978 and $52 million in 1979. In spite of the size and the speed of that adjustment, the growth rates of GDP, of 3.4 percent in 1978 and 4.5 percent in 1979, exceeded the average of the Organization for Economic Cooperation and Development (OECD) countries during those years.

Yet there are also some less favorable aspects in the Portuguese stabilization experience: the improvements in the pattern of income distribution that had taken place just after the revolution were to a large extent reversed; the rate of inflation remained, on average, above 20 percent; and the current account reverted to a large deficit in 1981, reaching almost 10 percent of GDP, despite an increase of output of only 1–2 percent in that year. The deficit of 1981 was a consequence of the second oil price shock, of the dollar appreciation, and of the recession in the industrialized countries, but it also reflected the structural weakness that persisted in the economy and the partial return to inadequate short-term economic policies.

The present paper analyzes, in the second section, the buildup of the balance of payments crisis during the period 1974–77; in the third section, the main characteristics of the arrangement concluded with IMF in 1978; and, in the fourth through the ninth sections, the most important instruments on which the policy package of that arrangement was based: exchange rate devaluation, reduction of import controls, increases in interest rates, overall credit ceilings, and ceilings to public sector borrowing from the banking system. The concluding section comments briefly on structural aspects of the economy and on the resurgence of balance of payments difficulties in 1981.

The Balance of Payments Crisis of 1974–77

During the 1960s and up to 1973, the balance of payments of Portugal remained exceptionally strong. The current account showed a surplus in every year of the period 1961–73, despite the increase of both domestic demand and GDP at an average annual real rate of 7 percent.

Such a favorable development was essentially due to the rapid growth of exports and to the spectacular increase in emigrants' remittances. The volume of exports of goods and services rose at an average annual rate of 10.7 percent from 1961–1973, mainly as a consequence of the participation of Portugal in the European Free Trade Association (EFTA) and of the dynamism of import demand in OECD countries. At the same time, the outflow of Portuguese workers attracted by the booming conditions in the economies of Western Europe produced such an increase of emigrants' remittances that in 1973 they covered 30 percent of total imports of goods and nonfinancial services.

At the beginning of 1974, this situation changed abruptly and drastically. By an unfortunate coincidence, the Portuguese economy was struck simultaneously by three exogenous shocks: the first oil price increase; the revolutionary transformation of the political regime; and the independence of the former colonies in Africa.

A large proportion of the worsening of the current account deficit in 1974 and 1975 was due to external causes. The terms of trade deteriorated by about 18 percent in those two years, causing a loss of approximately 6 percent in the real purchasing power of GDP. In addition, both exports of goods and services and emigrants' remittances were strongly affected by the international economic crisis of 1974–75.

As a consequence of the independence of the former colonies in Africa, their share of Portuguese total exports declined from 15 percent in 1973 to 5 percent in 1976. More important, however, were the effects of the forced return to Portugal of more than 600,000 settlers of Angola and Mozambique. This sudden population increase, of about 7 percent in one year, created serious difficulties for the balance of payments, for the budget, and for the unemployment situation because of the additional needs for food imports, budgetary support, and jobs for the returnees.

During the period of political instability from April 1974 to the end of 1975, several important economic and social transformations took place: banks, insurance companies, and many of the largest enterprises of the manufacturing and transportation sectors were nationalized; most of the large farms in the southern part of the country were taken over by peasant workers; the trade unions, which had been severely repressed under the previous regime, became highly militant and achieved increases in wages, which from 1973 to 1975 amounted to 93 percent in nominal terms and to 25 percent in real terms, despite the losses in per capita income that had been caused by the deterioration of the terms of trade, the fall of output in 1975, and the influx of refugees; a severe system of price controls, designed to protect the purchasing power of wage increases, was imposed on a large variety of goods and services; many enterprises, including medium and small ones, found themselves squeezed between tightly controlled prices and rapidly increasing costs of labor and imported inputs and, in order to survive, had to be taken over by the state or had to be run by groups of workers with state assistance; and the budgetary deficit of the administrative public sector rose to 5.5 percent of GDP in 1975 (Table 19.1), reflecting mainly the objectives of income redistribution that led to important increases of government consumption and government transfers.

These changes had a considerable impact on the balance of payments. On the one hand, they produced, as would be expected, substantial increases in private and public consumption, although these were largely offset by reductions in investment in fixed capital and in inventories, which have a high import content. On the other hand, there were important losses in the competitive power of Portuguese industries, both in the domestic and in external markets, due to large wage increases and declines in productivity that were not compensated by corresponding adjustments in the exchange rate.

TABLE 19.1 PORTUGAL: PUBLIC SECTOR ACCOUNTS, NATIONAL ACCOUNTS BASIS
(billion escudos)

Item	*1973*	*1974*	*1975*	*1976*	*1977*	*1978*	*1979*	*1980*
Current receipts	64.5	78.5	94.0	132.0	168.0	212.2	264.3	361.8
Current expenditure	55.5	77.3	103.2	145.1	180.6	238.5	302.2	407.0
Current balance	9.0	1.2	−9.3	−13.0	−12.6	−26.3	−37.9	−45.2
Capital balance	−5.0	−6.7	−11.3	−19.8	−30.2	−39.1	−42.7	−65.0
Overall balance	4.0	−5.5	−20.6	−32.9	−42.8	−65.4	−80.6	−110.1
As percentage of GDP								
Current balance	3.2	0.4	−2.5	−2.8	−2.0	−3.4	−3.8	−3.8
Overall balance	1.4	−1.6	−5.5	−7.0	−6.9	−8.4	−8.1	−9.1

Source: Banco de Portugal.

TABLE 19.2 PORTUGAL: ANNUAL CHANGES IN THE BALANCE OF PAYMENTS ON CURRENT ACCOUNT
(million dollars)

Item	*1974*	*1975*	*1976*	*1977*	*1978*	*1979*	*1980*
External factors	−0.56	−0.19	0.34	0.24	0.27	0.09	−0.45
Effects of price changes on	−0.58	−0.10	0.16	0.14	0.14	−0.11	−0.60
Imports of goods	−1.28	−0.33	0.32	−0.10	−0.35	−1.07	−1.87
Exports of goods	0.56	0.01	−0.21	0.07	0.11	0.49	0.78
Receipts from tourism	0.03	0.04	0.01	0.07	0.11	0.12	0.12
Emigrants' remittances	0.11	0.18	0.04	0.10	0.27	0.35	0.37

Effects of volume changes in	0.02	−0.09	0.18	0.10	0.12	0.20	0.15
International trade of goods	0.00	−0.13	0.16	0.06	0.09	0.15	0.10
International tourism	−0.02	0.02	0.00	0.02	0.01	0.03	0.02
Number of emigrants abroad	0.04	0.02	0.02	0.02	0.02	0.02	0.03
Internal factors	−0.62	0.04	−0.75	−0.32	0.57	0.87	−0.26
Effects of changes in volume of domestic demand on volume of imports of goods	−0.05	0.62	−0.49	−0.39	0.09	−0.03	−0.37
Private and public consumption	−0.14	0.01	−0.09	−0.03	−0.02	−0.05	−0.15
Fixed capital formation	0.05	0.10	−0.01	−0.11	−0.04	0.01	−0.12
Stockbuilding	0.04	0.51	−0.39	−0.25	0.15	0.01	−0.10
Effects of changes of competitiveness on	−0.57	−0.58	−0.26	0.07	0.48	0.90	0.11
Import volume	−0.16	0.10	−0.17	−0.04	0.08	−0.01	−0.08
Export volume	−0.18	−0.05	−0.08	−0.01	0.12	0.34	0.04
Volume of tourist receipts	−0.05	−0.21	−0.04	−0.02	0.05	0.19	0.07
Volume of emigrant remittances	−0.18	−0.42	0.03	0.14	0.23	0.38	0.08
Unclassified causes	0.01	0.16	−0.03	−0.15	−0.17	−0.19	−0.31
Interest on debts and other capital revenues	0.04	−0.14	−0.12	−0.05	−0.15	−0.11	−0.18
Nonspecified services and transfers	−0.03	0.30	0.09	−0.10	−0.02	−0.08	−0.13

−*Note:* For definitions, sources, and methods see annex, Silva Lopes (1982).
Volume changes in each year are expressed in prices of the preceding year.
Source: Silva Lopes (1982).

To make the situation worse, there was also a large reduction of the remittances of emigrants, due to the situation of political instability, the lack of confidence on the exchange rate, and the strongly negative real interest rates paid to time deposits, in which emigrants place a large proportion of their savings. There are indications that capital flight increased enormously, for the same reasons, in spite of exchange controls that could be easily circumvented by underinvoicing, overinvoicing, leads and lags, and black markets.

The effects of all these changes in the balance of payments are roughly quantified in Table 19.2. The methods used for the calculation of the figures of that table are briefly described in the annex to the chapter.

In 1976 Portugal entered a period of political stabilization. After the presidential and parliamentary elections of that year, the democratic regime became fully normalized. The first priority of the government was to stimulate the recovery of the productive sector and restore the economic and financial equilibrium of numerous enterprises that had been badly shaken by the troubles of the preceding two years.

The measures introduced with that objective included: the elimination of price controls and increases of controlled prices; the return of many enterprises to their former owners; the subsidization of firms that were facing great difficulties of survival; the establishment of ceilings to wage increases; and the revision of some clauses of the labor legislation that had created difficulties for employment.

The expansion of domestic demand was an essential component of that policy of economic recovery. The overall budgetary deficit rose to 7 percent of GDP both in 1976 and 1977. Up to the middle of 1977, interest rates were kept at very low levels and no effective limits were imposed on the expansion of bank credits, although many enterprises had difficulty in getting all the loans they needed because of problems of creditworthiness.

The expansion of domestic demand produced the desired recovery of output (Table 19.3), but it was associated with enormous difficulties in the balance of payments. The current account deficit increased to about $1.3 billion in 1976 and $1.5 billion in 1977, corresponding roughly to 9 percent of GDP.

With less reflation, the external deficits could have been lower, but it would have been more difficult to fight the crisis of productive activities and to avoid faster increases in unemployment, which in 1976 already exceeded 7 percent of the labor force. Table 19.2 shows that the effects of the expansionary demand policies were concentrated mainly in stockbuilding. The increases in inventories that took

TABLE 19.3 PORTUGAL: ANNUAL CHANGES IN NATIONAL EXPENDITURE
(percentage)

Item	*1974*	*1975*	*1976*	*1977*	*1978*	*1979*	*1980*	*Value, 1980 (billion escudos, current prices)*
Private consumption	9.7	−0.9	3.5	0.6	0.4	1.7	4.5	889.4
Public consumption	17.3	6.6	7.0	11.8	6.0	5.2	5.6	186.2
Fixed capital formation	−7.0	−11.3	0.8	12.0	4.0	−1.0	9.0	252.5
Stockbuilding[a]	5.0	−3.2	1.7	5.6	3.2	3.1	4.1	50.0
Domestic demand	6.0	−9.0	8.1	7.2	0.0	1.5	6.1	1,378.1
Exports	−15.7	−15.6	0	5.9	14.6	28.0	8.2	338.8
Aggregate demand	1.9	−10.2	6.9	7.1	1.9	5.5	6.5	1,716.9
Imports	4.7	−25.2	3.4	12.0	−1.8	7.9	9.6	511.6
GDP at market prices	1.2	−4.3	6.9	5.6	3.4	4.5	5.5	1,205.3

Sources: 1973 to 1975—Organization for Economic Cooperation and Development (OECD), *National Accounts of OECD Countries* (Paris, 1979). 1975 to 1980—*Annual Report of the Banco de Portugal* (Lisbon, 1980).

a. Changes in inventories at the prices of the previous year, expressed as percentage of GDP of previous year.

place in 1976 were an essential prerequisite for the recovery of the output of most productive sectors, since stocks had been severely run down in the preceding period. In 1977 there was, however, some speculative accumulation of stocks.

The figures of Table 19.2 suggest also that the most important causes of the deterioration of the balance of payments in 1976 and 1977 are related not to the expansion of domestic demand, but to the failure to recover the competitiveness lost both in the domestic and in external markets, and to attract a larger proportion of emigrants' savings. In particular, if the exchange rate had depreciated earlier and faster, both the balance of payments and the level of output would have gained, as was confirmed by the experience of subsequent years.

The IMF Stand-by Arrangement

During the period from 1974 to 1977, Portugal had little access to international financial markets, apart from short-term bank borrowing in 1976 and 1977. There were, accordingly, few alternatives to finance the large balance of payments deficits of those years but to draw heavily on the central bank reserves. The currency reserves, which amounted to about $1,600 million at the end of 1973, had been almost totally spent by the last quarter of 1975. Since then, and until the middle of 1977, the Banco de Portugal was forced to pledge practically half of its gold reserves as collateral for loans obtained from the Bank for International Settlements and from several European central banks. From 1975 to 1977, Portugal drew SDR 274 million from the IMF under its gold tranche, the oil facility, the compensatory financing facility, and the first credit tranche. In addition, some loans were received from the European Investment Bank, from the EFTA Industrial Fund, from the World Bank, and from various bilateral sources, mainly as export finance. In spite of all these loans, and of a substantial increase in short-term borrowing from international private banks, Portugal was forced to sell 111 tons of its gold reserves in the course of 1977.

The critical foreign exchange situation that thus emerged required not only a decisive effort of balance of payments adjustment, but also substantial external loans, with maturities long enough to avoid the economic costs and political risks of a shock treatment. Such loans were not available from international private banks, and the IMF could contribute with only SDR 57 million on the basis of an arrangement in the second credit tranche. Fortunately, Portugal was assisted by a consortium of 14 countries, which agreed in Paris, in June 1977, to grant medium-term credits amounting to $750 million. But several of those credits required, as their only condition, that the Portuguese authorities negotiate a stand-by arrangement with the Fund in an upper credit tranche.

The arrangement was concluded in May 1978. The policy package established in the Letter of Intent, for the period ending in March 1979, followed closely the typical model of IMF programs (Letter of Intent 1978). It involved: ceilings to the increase of net foreign liabilities of the banking system; faster depreciation of the exchange rate; increases of interest rates; ceilings to the expansion of overall net domestic bank credits; subceilings to public sector borrowing from the banking system; increases of some controlled or subsidized prices; restraints in wage increases; reduction of the surcharge on imports; and relaxation of quantitative restrictions on imports. The relative emphasis given to these different instruments, however, was adapted to the particular circumstances of the Portuguese economic situation.

The most important objective of the program was to reduce the current account deficit from $1.5 billion in 1977 to $1 billion during the 12-month period ending in March 1979. The actual current account deficit in that period turned out to be only $520 million. This result was achieved with a growth rate of GDP in 1978 of 3.4 percent, instead of the 2 percent that had been forecast.

The success of the program, proved by these figures, can be attributed to several factors.

First, international conditions were clearly favorable. The figures of Table 19.2 and 19.4 show that the effects of both international price changes and the growth of international demand were substantially positive. But the same had happened in 1976 and 1977, when the external deficit reached dangerous levels.

Second, the availability of the Paris credits made it possible to envisage a more gradual adjustment and to fix a target for the current account deficit requiring a less drastic contraction of domestic demand than would otherwise have been the case.

Third, the program had judiciously recognized the scope for achieving a large part of the intended improvement of the balance of payments through expenditure-switching policies. In consequence it put great emphasis on exchange rate depreciation and increases in interest rates, although measures to restrain domestic expenditure were also considered. Some important measures involving devaluation and increased interest rates had already been taken before negotiation of the IMF program, especially when the crawling peg was introduced

TABLE 19.4 PORTUGAL: IMPORTS AND EXPORTS OF GOODS AND TOURISM AND EMIGRANTS' REMITTANCES
(percentage)

Item	*1974*	*1975*	*1976*	*1977*	*1978*	*1979*	*1980*
Imports of goods							
Average unit value	45.3	11.0	−6.7	1.9	7.8	20.9	27.8
Volume	6.5	−23.4	17.7	12.7	−2.1	6.7	9.0
Exports of goods							
Average unit value	28.8	3.2	−12.0	5.5	6.1	16.0	20.5
Volume	−6.8	−15.8	5.0	5.9	12.0	28.6	7.1
International trade							
Average unit value of exports from OECD countries	28.7	11.7	1.0	7.9	12.8	15.4	12.7
Weighted average of the volume of imports into OECD, former Portuguese colonies, and rest of world	1.6	−6.4	10.3	4.9	5.7	8.0	3.9
Tourism							
Prices in Europe	7.2	14.1	2.6	19.6	23.3	14.4	11.3
Volume in Europe	−4.8	6.4	1.7	7.9	4.2	4.5	2.3
Volume in Portugal	−13.6	−39.4	−10.0	1.5	19.1	38.9	9.9
Emigrants' remittances							
Wages in countries of residence	11.4	25.7	5.0	9.1	19.0	17.0	14.5
Number of emigrants	4.9	3.1	2.0	1.6	1.2	1.2	1.0

Note: Percentages are annual changes in volume and average unit values expressed in dollars.
Sources: Banco de Portugal; OECD *Economic Outlook,* OECD *Statistics of Tourism;* IMF *International Financial Statistics.*

in August 1977, but that program required additional and faster depreciation of the exchange rate and higher interest rates.

Fourth, the adjustments in the exchange rate and in interest rates were exceptionally effective because of a combination of specific circumstances that are not likely to be easily repeated, and that included: the acceptance by the trade unions of large declines in real wages; the quick response of exports of goods and tourism to the exchange rate policy due to the high proportion of unused capacity in the export sector; and the large sums of emigrants' remittances abroad awaiting better conditions for transfer into Portugal.

Finally, the Portuguese authorities applied much less restrictive budgetary and credit policies than those that had been established in the program, in part because it soon became evident that exports and money demand were increasing much more satisfactorily than had been projected.

These factors and circumstances are explained in more detail in the following sections dealing with the main instruments fixed in the Letter of Intent: exchange rate and wage ceilings; import controls; interest rates; overall credit ceilings; and subceilings on credit to the public sector.

Exchange Rate Devaluation

The effective exchange rate of the escudo depreciated by about 10 percent in the course of 1976. However, the policy of unannounced, gradual devaluation that produced that result had to be abandoned because, in combination with the low interest rates that were then in force, it led to speculative outflows of capital.

In 1977, after a step devaluation of 17.6 percent, an attempt was made to keep the effective exchange rate stable. However, the real exchange rate (nominal exchange rate corrected by the ratio between consumer price indexes in Portugal and in her main trading partners) and the unit labor costs in manufacturing (as determined by changes in wages, productivity, and the exchange rate in relation to the main foreign partners and competitors) were still far less competitive than in 1973. Besides, inflationary expectations were strong, and interest rates were kept very low. In such conditions the speculative pressures on the escudo remained unabated.

When the foreign payments difficulties became particularly acute in the summer of 1977, additional exchange rate moves had to be contemplated. On the basis of recommendations made by a group of Massachusetts Institute of Technology (MIT) advisors (Dornbusch 1981 and Dornbusch and Taylor 1977), and after consultations with the IMF, the solution chosen by the Portuguese authorities was that of introducing, in August 1977, a crawling peg, with a preannounced rate of devaluation of the effective exchange rate of 1 percent a month. That solution involved also a system of forward quotations of foreign currencies by the Banco de Portugal, based on the preannounced rate of monthly depreciation and the forward quotations in the London foreign exchange market. The rate of crawl corresponded approximately to the projected differential between the domestic and the OECD rates of inflation.

The adoption of the crawling peg required the adjustment of interest rate policy in order to avoid speculative capital movements like those that had taken place in 1976. But at the same time, it was feared that high interest rates would have undesired contractionary effects on domestic production. Given this conflict, there were some interesting discussions about the maximum differential between domestic and world market interest rates, adjusted for the programmed exchange rate devaluation that could be tolerated without providing incentives to capital outflows (Dornbusch 1981). A compromise was finally adopted. On the one hand, it was decided to increase domestic interest rates, but to maintain a negative differential of the order of 3–4 percentage points between their level, adjusted for the programmed rate of exchange depreciation, and the interest rate in the Eurodollar market. It was assumed that capital was not perfectly mobile and, consequently, a narrower differential was not necessary. On the other hand, the required interest rate increase was reduced by fixing a lower monthly rate of depreciation of the exchange rate than would have been needed to achieve a rapid improvement of competitiveness. That improvement was obtained, however, by making an unannounced initial devaluation of 4 percent in the course of the week preceding introduction of the crawling peg.

The new exchange rate policy immediately started to produce the benefits that had been expected from it. It restored confidence and quickly eliminated speculation. However, in the negotiation of the stand-by program of May 1978, the IMF required two changes in the system. First, the rate of monthly depreciation of the exchange rate was stepped up to 1.25 percent, after a new devaluation of about 7 percent. The purpose was to achieve faster gains in competitiveness. Second, the forward quotations were eliminated in order to avoid the danger of losses to the Banco de Portugal if it proved necessary to accelerate the depreciation rate again in the future. These modifications were supported by new increases in interest rates of the order of 4 percentage points, which kept approximately the same differential vis à vis interest rates abroad.

The new monthly rate of depreciation was in force for about one year, but, in view of the strengthening of the balance of payments and a moderate decline in inflation, it was reduced to 1 percent in April 1979 and to 0.75 percent in July 1979.

This exchange rate policy was accompanied by a system of ceilings to wage increases imposed by the government, which implied a progressive reduction of real wages of about 17 percent from 1976 to 1979. The combination of both policies produced a depreciation of the real exchange rate of about 22 percent from 1976 to 1979, and a reduction of relative labor costs vis à vis a weighted average of industrial countries for 45 percent (Table 19.5).

ABLE 19.5 PORTUGAL: ANNUAL CHANGES IN EFFECTIVE EXCHANGE RATE AND COMPETITIVENESS
(percentage change of annual average)

em	*1974*	*1975*	*1976*	*1977*	*1978*	*1979*	*1980*
ffective exchange rate, nominal	−2.3	−3.3	−9.1	−21.8	−21.1	−15.3	−3.5
abor earnings in manufacturing industries							
Nominal	45.4	32.9	18.7	16.4	14.2	20.2	25.7
Real	13.7	10.3	0.5	−8.7	−6.4	−3.2	7.8
Relative labor costs in manufacturing industries[b]	19.5	15.1	−0.9	−22.6	−21.3	−10.1	5.4

ources: Banco de Portugal; OECD *Economic Outlook.*
. Nominal effective exchange rates corrected by the ratio between the increase of domestic consumer prices nd the weighted average of the consumer prices in the main trading partners.
. Changes in the ratio between domestic labor costs (taking into account changes in productivity) and the eighted average of labor costs in the main trading partners, corrected by changes in the effective exchange ate.

The effects of those changes on the balance of payments appeared with some lags, which are apparent from the comparison of the figures of Tables 19.4 and 19.5, but they exceeded all expectations. The volume of exports of goods increased by 52 percent between 1976 and 1979, as against an increase of about 20 percent in external demand. On average, the market shares of 1973 had been fully recovered in 1979 (Schmitt 1981, chart 1, p. 3). The improvement in receipts from tourism was even faster. On the other hand, the figures of Table 19.2 suggest that in 1978 there was a significant reduction of the import content of domestic expenditure.

In the light of these results, it will be interesting to review some of the issues raised in the discussions on exchange rate policy that took place in 1977 and 1978.

One of the arguments was that most of the effects of the exchange rate depreciation would be dissipated in internal inflation after a few months, and that, consequently, improvement in competitiveness would be only temporary. The changes of the real exchange rate and relative labor costs show that this did not happen. But it must be recognized that if the trade unions had tried to recover fully the increased domestic prices in wage rates, the inflationary impact of devaluation would have been much higher and the positive effects of the balance of payments would have been much weaker. Surprisingly, they accepted without resistance the wage ceilings imposed by the government in 1976, 1977, and 1978, in spite of the substantial declines in real labor earnings involved. That behavior is partly explained by the fear of more unemployment, and partly by the strategies of the political parties with influence on the trade unions. Also, the sharp increase of real wages in 1974–75 made it easier for workers to accept a subsequent reduction. But it is not possible to count on similar reactions in all episodes of devaluation under democratic regimes.

The effectiveness of exchange rate policy in the adjustment of the balance of payments was thus closely linked with its effects on income distribution. There is no doubt that devaluation was a main factor contributing to the decline of the wage share in national income. It has been argued (Modigliani and Paddoa-Schioppa 1978) that with full employment output there is a unique warranted real wage consistent with external balance. If real wages exceed the warranted level, the balance of payments or the level of unemployment, or both, will suffer. On the basis of this model, it has been remarked (Krugman and Macedo 1981) that in Portugal the deterioration of the terms of trade and the increased supply of labor resulting from the arrival of returnees reduced the warranted real wage and that the decline in real wages was consequently unavoidable, particularly after the unsustainable increases of 1974 and 1975. These arguments are based on a model assuming that prices are fixed on the basis of a constant mark-up over costs. While this assumption may be disputed in a short-term analysis, it appears realistic enough in a medium-term framework. If this is so, a strategy of bringing the current account deficit to a sustainable level without reducing the real wage of 1975 would have implied an enormous increase in unemployment. But the distributional inequities would certainly have been worse, with fewer people keeping their jobs at higher wages rather than more employment and lower real wages.

Another controversial issue was the contractionary effects of devaluation. It was feared that the positive impact from devaluation on the production of export- and import-competing industries would be dominated by the negative effects of lower real wages on domestic demand and by the deflationary effect of a probable increase of the balance of payments deficit expressed in domestic currency (Krugman and Taylor 1978 and Taylor 1979, p. 55–59).

The price increases caused by devaluation and the wage controls did indeed exert a depressive influence on domestic demand. In view of the decline of the wage share in national income and of the higher savings propensity of nonwage earners, private consumption increased only 0.6 percent in 1977, 0.4 percent in 1978, and 1.7 percent in 1979. But the slowing down of private consumption was more than offset by the expansionary effect of the rapid rise of exports and, to a smaller extent, of import substitution stimulated by the exchange rate depreciation. As mentioned above, GDP increased by 3.4 percent in 1978 and 4.5 percent in 1979.

The main explanation for the favorable result is to be found in the quick response of exports to the depreciation of real exchange rate and the decline in relative labor cost. Pessimistic views about export elasticities were very common, but they were not borne out by the facts. However, it must be recognized that the results would have been different if there had not been so much idle productive capacity in the export sector, and if market shares abroad had not previously declined. In fact, between 1973 and 1977 the volume of exports of merchandise had fallen by 13 percent, while the number of nights spent by foreign tourists had declined by about a half.

Import Controls and Export Subsidies

The agreement with the IMF required the elimination—in three steps, by October 1979—of the 30 percent import surcharge that had been introduced in 1975 and modified in 1976. That surcharge, levied on imports competing with domestic production, covered about 30 percent of total imports. Portugal was nevertheless allowed to keep a surcharge of 60 percent on luxury goods, covering about 2 percent of total imports, although it was established that the government should study alternative tax measures to replace it, beginning in 1979. Similarly existing import quotas on a few consumer durables and nonessential goods were maintained temporarily with the proviso that they should be reviewed in 1979, with a view to reducing or eliminating their restrictiveness. The Letter of Intent also contained the usual clauses of IMF arrangements under which Portugal could not introduce new import restrictions or intensify existing ones for balance of payments reasons.

These provisions ran against the views of those who maintained that the tightening of import restrictions would be a better policy to improve the balance of payments than devaluation and domestic demand contraction. It was argued that import controls would be more effective than exchange rate adjustment in shifting demand from foreign goods to domestic production. It is also argued that their inflationary effects would be much weaker than those of devaluation, and that they would stimulate domestic production, thus avoiding the need for reducing real wages and improving the unemployment situation.

Apparently, the views of those who supported an import control strategy were inspired by the proposals of the Cambridge Economic Policy Group with respect to the United Kingdom (Stallings 1981). But even if it was accepted that such proposals are correct for the United Kingdom, it is highly doubtful that they could be valid for Portugal. Given the small size of the domestic market and the insufficient industrialization of the Portuguese economy, production covers a much smaller share of total demand than in the United Kingdom, particularly as regards intermediate and capital goods. If the restrictions were concentrated only on those imports that could easily be replaced by domestic production, the saving of foreign currency would fall far behind the amount needed. Moreover, since in the preceding years exports had fallen much more than domestic sales, there was much more idle capacity in the export sector than in import-competing industries. The introduction of tighter import controls would therefore have tended to be quickly reflected in higher prices, rather than in higher output or employment. Such controls would in no way have contributed to easing the crisis of export industries, whose production, in a country with the characteristics of Portugal, can only to a very small extent be shifted to the domestic market. On the contrary, they would have reinforced the bias against exports. In addition, one should mention other usual arguments against quantitative import restrictions: the inefficiency in the allocation of scarce resources; the negative effects on income distribution resulting from the protection of monopoly positions in the domestic market, from the scarcity rents awarded to the holders of import licenses, and from risks of corruption in the distribution of those licenses, etc. Finally, as well as the IMF's hostility to the adoption of balance of payments strategies based on import restrictions, the links of Portugal with EFTA and the European Economic Community (EEC) precluded recourse to such strategies.

In spite of all these arguments against a generalized system of import restrictions, some specific controls deserve a special comment. To begin with, it is widely accepted that in a situation of foreign exchange scarcity, the consumption of luxury goods with a high import content should be restricted. Of course, heavy indirect taxes levied not only on imports but also on the domestic production of luxury goods are in principle the better solution, because they will not encourage the use of scarce foreign currency in importing inputs for the production of domestic substitutes for such goods. However, because of practical problems of implementation and supervision, surcharges and other restrictions against imports may be needed as a second best solution. As mentioned above, in the arrangement with the IMF, Portugal was allowed to keep temporarily the 60 percent surcharge on luxury imports and a few quotas on the imports of some less essential consumer goods. The most important difficulty in this regard has been that the heavy charges and the tight restrictions on the import and domestic sale of luxury goods have strongly encouraged smuggling and evasion of indirect taxes.

Another area where there may be justification for control is that of foreign currency expenditures by the government and public enterprises. The reactions of the public sector to devaluation tend to be much weaker than those of the private sector. On the other hand, the import content of the investments of public enterprises is usually very high in Portugal. The planning of such investments and of other public sector expenditures in such a way as to take into account the short-term balance of payments constraint may be an effective method of reducing the import content of domestic expenditure. This solution was discussed in Portugal (Dornbusch and Taylor 1977), but it was never implemented seriously because of the shortcomings of the planning apparatus and the pressures of special interests in the public sector.

A strategy of import controls would require a system of export subsidies to offset the bias against exports resulting from those controls. It has been argued that a system of export subsidies based on value added could replicate the effects of devaluation on exports, while at the same time reducing the negative consequences on inflation and real wages (Bruno 1978). Even ignoring the financial difficulties that a system of export subsidies would create in view of the existing budgetary deficits, Portugal could not contemplate that solution on a large scale because of its links with the EEC and EFTA. Nevertheless, the usual arguments for the protection of infant industries have special relevance with regard to the introduction of temporary export subsidies, based on value added, in a semi-industrialized country like Portugal, to help the development of new exports or the penetration of new foreign markets (Bruno 1978).

Interest Rates

From 1974 to 1976 there had been some increases in deposit and lending interest rates, but they fell far short of what was required in view of the existing level of inflation and the adjustment needed in the exchange rate (Table 19.6). In August 1977 the introduction of

TABLE 19.6. PORTUGAL: INTEREST RATES AND MONEY DEMAND
(percentage)

Item	*1974*	*1975*	*1976*	*1977*	*1978*	*1979*	*1980*
Interest rates in Portugal[a]							
6–month time deposits	6.7	8.5	9.5	12.1	17.6	19.0	19.0
6–month credits	7.5	9.3	10.0	13.3	18.8	20.0	20.0
Changes in the price of the dollar[b]	−4.8	11.2	15.3	26.3	15.4	8.8	6.0
Interest rates in Portugal expressed in dollars[c]							
6–month time deposits	12.0	−2.4	−5.1	−11.3	1.9	9.4	12.3
Average 6–month interest rates in the Eurodollar market[a]	11.0	6.7	5.6	6.0	8.7	12.0	14.4
Increase of consumer prices in Portugal[b]	29.3	17.5	25.7	20.8	25.2	22.4	13.1
Real interest rates in Portugal							
6–month time deposits	−17.5	−7.7	−13.7	−7.2	−6.1	−3.8	5.2
Money demand as percentage of GDP[d]							
M1	48.0	51.3	48.4	40.7	35.5	32.6	33.6
M2	95.2	96.9	89.2	80.8	81.2	83.3	93.3

Sources: Annual Reports of the Banco de Portugal; IMF *International Financial Statistics*.
a. Annual averages.
b. From the beginning to the end of the year.
c. From $1 + i_d = (1 + i_e)/(1 + c_d)$, where i_d is the interest rate expressed in dollars, i_e is the interest rate expressed in escudos, and c_d is the increase of the price of the dollar.
d. The average money stock for each year was calculated as the weighted average of the values at the end [of] the last quarter of the preceding year and the four quarters of the year for which the calculation was ma[de] with weights of 0.5, 1.0, 1.0, 1.0, and 0.5, respectively.

the crawling peg was accompanied by a more substantial rise of interest rates. Thus, for instance, the interest rate on 6-month time deposits increased from 11 percent to 15 percent. As a result of the negotiation of the stand-by agreement with the IMF, those rates had to be further increased by 4 percentage points. In spite of such sharp increases, interest rates remained moderately negative in real terms and, taking into account the projected crawling devaluation, their expected escudo yields remained lower than those of Eurodollar deposits (Table 19.6).

The effects of the interest rate adjustments on the balance of payments were quick and powerful. As explained in the fourth section, they were an essential component of the crawling peg policy. They improved the capital account of the balance of payments by elimi-

TABLE 19.7 PORTUGAL: BALANCE OF PAYMENTS
(billion dollars)

Item	*1973*	*1974*	*1975*	*1976*	*1977*	*1978*	*1979*	*1980*
Imports	2.76	4.28	3.61	3.94	4.53	4.79	6.18	8.61
Exports	1.86	2.29	1.94	1.81	2.00	2.38	3.55	4.59
Trade balance	−0.90	−1.99	−1.67	−2.13	−2.53	−2.41	−2.63	−4.02
Tourist receipts	0.55	0.51	0.36	0.33	0.40	0.59	0.94	1.15
Emigrants' remittances	1.08	1.05	0.82	0.91	1.17	1.68	2.45	2.93
Capital revenues (net)	0.09	0.13	−0.01	−0.13	−0.18	−0.33	−0.44	−0.62
Other services and transfers	−0.47	−0.52	−0.32	−0.24	−0.35	−0.35	−0.37	−0.51
Current balance	0.35	−0.82	−0.82	−1.26	−1.49	−0.82	−0.05	−1.07
Capital balance	−0.02	0.19	−0.19	0.12	0.06	0.99	1.41	1.93
Overall balance	0.32	−0.63	−1.01	−1.13	−1.44	0.16	1.36	0.86
Percentage of GDP								
Current balance	3.0	−6.0	−5.5	−8.0	−9.2	−4.4	−0.02	−4.4
Overall balance	2.7	−4.6	−6.0	−7.2	−8.9	1.2	6.7	3.5

Source: Banco de Portugal.

nating a large part of the benefits expected from speculative capital outflows and by making foreign borrowing more attractive.

But their effects on the current account were even more important. Part of the capital movements were, in fact, affecting the recorded current account through the underinvoicing of exports, the over-invoicing of exports, the black market for tourist receipts and emigrants' remittances, and the accumulation of stocks of imported goods. In addition, the increase of interest rates played an important role in stimulating the transfer of emigrants' remittances that had been retained abroad, especially during the years of 1974–76 (Table 19.7). The sharp increase of those remittances from $914 million in 1976, to $1,687 million in 1977, and $2,246 million in 1979 was a major factor behind the spectacular improvement of the balance of payments on current account in 1978 and 1979.

The effects of interest rates on domestic financial savings were also very important. In the absence of a diversified supply of financial assets, those effects were reflected mainly in the growth of time deposits. It had been expectd that, given the persistence of inflation, the demand for broad money (M2), which had fallen from 96.9 percent of GDP in 1975 to 80.8 percent in 1977, would continue to decline, but what actually happened was that it rose to 81.2 percent of GDP in 1978 and to 83.3 percent in 1979. This increase of money demand reversed the trend of the previous years toward the replacement of domestic money assets by the accumulation of consumer durables, smuggled gold, and foreign currency, all of which affected, legally or illegally, the current account.

The contractionary effects of higher interest rates on the demand for credit, and consequently on investment, provided an additional important contribution to import saving. A substantial part of that effect was concentrated in inventory accumulation, which, in volume terms, fell from 5.2 percent of GDP in 1977, to 3.2 percent in 1978, and 3.1 percent in 1981 (Table 19.3).

The interest rate increases and credit ceilings also had negative consequences on fixed capital formation, which, at constant prices, increased by only 4 percent in 1978 and declined by 1 percent in 1979.

Ceilings to Overall Credit Expansion

It is not easy to establish a comparison between the quarterly ceilings to the overall expansion of domestic credit established as a performance clause in the Letter of Intent and the actual outturn, because of adjustments introduced in the Portuguese monetary statistics. A rough idea can nevertheless be obtained about the compliance by the Portuguese authorities with that clause by mentioning that, according to the Letter of Intent, net domestic credit of the banking sector should not expand by more than 23 percent of the initial money stock during the program year, and that the actual increase was 29.6 percent. The discrepancy is almost entirely due to the fact that bad debts were inadvertently classified outside the credit ceiling. The program thus had some unintended flexibility, provided by the transfers of loans under the ceiling, in which arrears had appeared, to bad debts. However, compliance by the Portuguese authorities with the credit ceiling in a strictly formal sense, i.e., leaving bad debts aside, was reasonably satisfactory. In fact, due to a system of monthly limits to credit expansion imposed by the central bank on each commercial bank, the increase in net domestic credit from March 1978 to March 1979 was 23.9 percent of the initial money stock, as compared with the 23 percent ceiling. But it became clear after some months that without the flexibility provided by the exclusion of bad debts, full compliance with the ceilings would have resulted in serious difficulties for the productive sector that were not required by the balance of payments situation.

As usual in IMF programs, the credit ceilings established in the stand-by arrangement with Portugal were framed on a performance clause, in the sense that if they were not observed, the quarterly installments of the Fund loan could be drawn. In spite of that, the role of such ceilings was certainly less important than in other Fund programs. It has been explained (Schmitt 1981, p. 10) that, in principle, the interest rate and exchange rate policies established in the arrangement with Portugal should have been sufficient to produce the desired balance of payments results, but that in view of the uncertainties concerning the efficacy of the instruments chosen, traditional limits on credit expansion were also deemed desirable as a fallback position.

There are several reasons why less weight was apparently attached to overall credit ceilings in the Portuguese case than in other IMF arrangements. But it may be argued that if interest rates had remained low, bank deposits would have grown much less and, in consequence, tighter ceilings to the expansion of domestic credit would have been necessary. Such ceilings would have squeezed working capital and fixed investment even more than higher interest rates (Fry 1976 and Schmitt 1981).

In any case, the deflationary effects of the increase in interest rates on fixed investments, which on average have a high import content, helped the balance of payments. To the extent that the investments affected had a social rate of return below the interest rate, which remained negative in real terms, there was no loss. On the contrary, there was a contribution toward rationalization of the selection of investments and the improvement of their productivity. There are, however, at least two cases to which this conclusion does not apply.

One is that of the investments of the public sector, including public administration and public enterprises. The level and composition of investments in the public sector are not very sensitive to the interest rate. They should therefore be regulated essentially by planning and careful project evaluation. Unfortunately, no substantial progress has been made in Portugal in this area. Some big projects of the public sector, with high import content and extremely doubtful rates of return, continued to be carried out during the period of balance of payments difficulties, largely on the basis of foreign export financing and of borrowing in private international capital markets.

Another case requiring special comment is that of the strongly adverse effects that high nominal rates of interest may have on long-term investments, because of the cash flow difficulties for borrowers resulting from the element of real amortization included in the high nominal interest rates in situations of inflation. These difficulties tend to be especially acute in the financing of housing, a key sector from the point of view of sustaining the level of employment, and one with a comparatively low import content. The authorities tried to reduce those cash flow difficulties by two methods. One was that of interest rate subsidization of housing credits and long-term industrial credits meeting some minimum standards of social profitability. The other consisted in refinancing part of the initial interest rate payments. It may be said that the second solution corresponded to a disguised and incomplete indexation of the principal.

First, the improvement programmed for the balance of payments was much less drastic than would have been the case had Portugal not received the Paris credits mentioned in the third section. It has been argued that in a country with substantial unemployment and idle capacity, like Portugal in 1977, the solution for the external disequilibrium should be based on the stimulation of additional savings from additional income, rather than on forcing down consumption to create savings, or reducing investment to the level of existing savings (Eckaus 1977). Such a solution would be more favorable from the point of view of the level of output and employment achieved, but it would be feasible only if very large amounts of external finance were available. The Paris credits fell short of those amounts, but without them a much tighter domestic demand policy would have had to have been applied, and the restrictions on the expansion of domestic bank credit, consistent with the same behavior of money demand, would have been much more severe. This remark emphasizes the need to support IMF stabilization programs with substantial loans. The Fund has made considerable progress in this respect since 1978, but it may be argued that larger amounts of official external finance may still be necessary in acute cases of balance of payments disequilibrium, particularly when they are predominately due to external shocks.

Second, it was correctly recognized in the Portuguese case that there was ample room for improving the balance of payments on current account by means of expenditure-switching policies. Although considerable progress had been made in those policies before the negotiation of the Fund program, particularly when the crawling peg was introduced in August 1977, that program put more emphasis on additional exchange rate and interest rate adjustments than on tighter credit ceilings. It seems that in this respect, the experience in many other IMF arrangements was different, either because there was less scope for effective expenditure-switching or because a greater preference was shown for expenditure-reducing measures.

Third, the credit ceilings were fixed without excessive ambitions with regard to the reduction of inflation. Such ceilings were based on a projected real growth of GDP of 2 percent and on an inflation rate of 25 percent through the year ending in March 1979. That projected inflation rate, which should be compared with the increase of consumer prices of 21 percent through the year of 1977, duly took into account the effects of the exchange rate depreciation, and the wage policy, and the impact of the increases that had taken place in several important controlled prices. If greater weight had been attached to achieving a substantial reduction of inflation, the contractionary effects of the credit ceilings on output and employment would have been far stronger. In principle, countries negotiating stand-by arrangements with the Fund are free to choose, in accordance with their social and political preferences, between alternative programs, involving different combinations of inflation and unemployment consistent with the required balance of payments target. This principle was acknowledged in the case of Portugal, but it seems that in some other stand-by arrangements the difficulties of compliance with the credit ceilings can be attributed, to a significant extent, to unrealistic objectives concerning the reduction of inflation.

In spite of all these considerations, the credit ceilings fixed in the stand-by agreement with Portugal proved to be more restrictive than was needed. This is because the projections on which they were based had underestimated substantially both the increase in exports of goods and services and the effects of interest rates in stimulating the inflow of emigrants' remittances in reversing capital movements and in increasing the demand for money.

Two alternative methods were used by the Portuguese authorities to escape the unnecessary restrictiveness of the ceilings: first, the recourse to foreign borrowing by the government and by public enterprises, as a substitute for domestic credit; second, the creation of some room for expanding credits under the ceiling, by the transfers to bad debts mentioned above. However, the possibility of using such methods is not open in most stand-by arrangements. The recourse to foreign credits was not limited in the Portuguese case, but very often ceilings on foreign debt are performance clauses of Fund programs, and, as mentioned above, bad debts were excluded from the ceilings only by inadvertence.

Another possibility of avoiding the restrictiveness of credit ceilings that could have been contemplated would have been to stimulate the issue of short- and medium-term bonds by the government and large enterprises as a substitute for bank credit. The issue of such bonds would, of course, have resulted in an increase of the income velocity of money and would therefore have produced approximately the same effects on aggregate demand and on the balance of payments as an expansion of credit above the ceilings, but the formal compliance with those ceilings would have been easier.

It must be stressed that in the consultations with the IMF that took place about six months after the stand-by agreement entered into force, the Fund staff recognized that the ceilings had been calculated on the basis of overly pessimistic assumptions concerning the behavior of the income velocity of money and the recovery of exports. In principle, it would have been possible during those negotiations to revise the ceilings and to increase them to more realistic levels. That was not done, because at that moment there was a change of government in Portugal and there was no pressing need to draw on the Fund loan.

The above description shows that although credit ceilings may be an important device in situations where expenditure reduction is required to improve the balance of payments, there is the risk that very often they will be a very blunt instrument. The analysis of the Polak model (Polak 1957 and IMF 1977), on the basis of which the credit ceilings of Fund programs are explicitly or implicitly calculated, shows that the level of those ceilings depends crucially upon assumptions and projections about quite a large number of variables or parameters, the most important of which are: nominal GDP, which in turn depends, among other things, upon cost-push factors affecting the inflation rate; the demand for money; the behavior of exports; the import content of domestic expenditure; and the inflow of foreign transfers, loans, or direct investments. It is extremely difficult to make sufficiently accurate projections of these variables, particularly in countries that have reached an advanced stage of internal and external disequilibrium. And even small errors in a few of them can be reflected in large variations of the desirable credit ceilings.

Of course, when a credit ceiling proves to be excessively and unnecessarily restrictive, it will be possible to change it after consultation with the IMF. But the difficulties and uncertainties related to the outcome of such negotiations may push the national authorities that are endeavoring to comply with the limits into more contractionary policies than would be required by the balance of payments situation. It is true that such contractionary policies will at least offer the advantage of producing lower than projected balance of payments deficits. But if the political and social costs of reductions of output and increases in unemployment become unbearable, there are serious risks that the stabilization effort will be entirely abandoned, and that the attainment of a sustainable balance of payments situation will become more difficult than would be the case with a less ambitious program.

For these reasons, there have been demands for more flexibility in the IMF's credit ceilings. One possible solution would be to establish those ceilings on a quarterly or half-yearly basis, although with indicative targets for the quarters ahead. It seems that in some individual cases the IMF has made significant moves in that direction.

Subceilings on Credit to the Public Sector

The subceilings on credit to the public sector, which were a performance clause of the stabilization arrangement, were substantially exceeded, and because of that Portugal was not able to make any drawing from the Fund loan. They allowed for an increase of public sector borrowing from the banking system of 44 billion escudos during the program period, but the actual increase was 56 billion escudos. In addition, the government borrowed $450 million from the Eurodollar market, corresponding to about 20 billion escudos, which had not been anticipated in the calculation of the subceilings. These results reflect the fact that the overall budget deficit for 1978, which had been forecast at 6 percent of GDP (as compared with 7 percent in 1977), reached 8.4 percent of GDP. The discrepancy was found mainly in the current account of the public sector, whose deficit increased from 2 percent of GDP in 1977 to 3.4 percent in 1978, instead of being transformed into a small surplus as had been projected.

There has been an animated controversy between those who argued that the budget deficits of the years 1974–77 had played a useful stabilization role by compensating the deflationary impact of the balance of payments deficit, and those who argued that fiscal policy had contributed to, rather than compensated, the external deficit (Schmitt 1981, p. 19).

The budget deficits certainly resulted more from internal political pressures than from a clear and conscious policy of stabilization of output and employment. But the pressures for increased public investment, subsidization of prices of mass consumption goods, higher social security transfers, more employment in the public administration, financial assistance to the returnees from Angola and Mozambique, and budgetary support to public and private enterprises in a difficult situation, while resulting in part from objectives of income redistribution, reflected to a large extent the hardships created by external shocks.

As explained above, the contribution of the expansion of domestic demand to the external imbalance was comparatively modest. That demand had risen by 11 percent in volume between 1974 and 1977, which corresponds approximately to stagnation on a per capita basis, given the sharp increase in the population after the return of the settlers from the former colonies. In itself, that increase would not have been a cause of concern if the negative impact of external factors and the loss of competitiveness had not been so serious.

In any case, since there were doubts that expenditure-switching policies would be sufficient to produce the balance of payments objective of the stabilization program of 1978, the adjustment in public finances was considered as one of the important components of that program. Such adjustment was justified by the familiar crowding out argument: in view of the overall credit ceilings, the fiscal deficit had to be restrained in order to safeguard an adequate supply of credit to private exporters and investors. In addition, if the public sector was to make a contribution to the increased savings on which a reduction in the external current deficit depended, the fiscal balance on current account would also have to be improved (Schmitt 1981).

Nevertheless, the failure of the Portuguese authorities to keep the public sector within the programmed targets did not preclude a better than expected improvement in the balance of payments. Rather, it contributed to reducing the contractionary effects of the stablization program and to avoiding a more marked deceleration of output growth (Cavaco Silva 1980). Of course, it may be pointed out that if the public sector had borrowed less from the banking system, more credit would have remained available for the productive sector within the overall credit ceiling. But unless interest rates had been significantly lower (thus creating problems for the crawling peg policy), it is questionable whether the additional private investment demand resulting from less credit stringency would have been sufficient to compensate more than a small part of the squeeze of the public deficit. The credit ceilings imposed on commercial banks in order to comply with the performance clauses of the IMF program were restrictive, but only moderately so, in view of the flexibility provided by bad debts.

But the true reasons why the budgetary deficits went far beyond the programmed targets are not to be found in an intentional manipulation of aggregate demand. The authorities were just unable to collect as much tax revenue as had been projected, or to avoid new increases in public expenditure. It must be recognized that the fiscal performance not only in 1978, but also in subsequent years has indeed been one of the most disappointing features of recent economic developments (de Fontenay 1982). The very high deficits that persisted in the public sector have been an important source of inflationary pressures, of rigidity in adapting domestic demand to the requirements of external equilibriums, and of reduction of the domestic savings rate. These consequences are linked to some of the structural aspects analyzed in the following section.

Supply and Structural Aspects

The Letter of Intent recognized that the balance of payments problems of Portugal had been complicated by serious structural maladjustments in the economy and that a policy to overcome those maladjustments would be indispensable to correct the external imbalance on a more permanent basis.

Since the program was only for one year, it did not require structural adjustments, but one of its objectives was to stimulate the expansion of supply by eliminating price distortions with a negative impact on the efficiency of production or on the pattern of expenditure. Thus, it restored the international competitiveness of the economy, which relaxed the balance of payments constraint on the growth of output. It improved domestic resource mobilization by increasing the private savings rate; attracting emigrants' remittances; and redirecting savings to domestic financial assets rather than foreign assets, consumer goods, and other inflation hedges. Finally, it stimulated the efficiency of investment by correcting cost-price distortions and relative profitability rates, particularly in the following cases: sectors submitted to price controls; production of tradable goods vis à vis nontradables; export industries vis à vis import-competing industries; projects that would not be feasible without highly negative interest rates; choices of appropriate technologies and combinations of productive factors; and the like.

The correction of price distortions should, in principle, play an important role in encouraging the growth of aggregate supply. But although it was a necessary condition, it could not be considered as a sufficient one. Price incentives offer the advantage of being quickly implemented without raising great administrative difficulties, once the political resistance to their introduction has been overcome. But they may be easily reversed. This means that very often they are not perceived by economic agents as being sufficiently stable, and therefore do not lead to drastic changes in investment behavior.

The experience of Portugal in the last two years provides a good illustration of this point. After 1980 the system of price controls was tightened again, although subsequently there was a partial relaxation. The controls of imports through licensing became more widespread. The level of interest rates remained practically stable in nominal terms, in spite of significant variations of the domestic inflation rate and large swings in interest rates abroad. The exchange rate policy was modified substantially with the revaluation of the escudo by 6 percent in February 1980 and the slowing down of the rate of monthly depreciation shortly afterwards, while at the same time there was an acceleration in the growth of nominal wages and of money supply.

As a consequence of the new exchange rate policy, relative labor costs in manufacturing vis à vis main foreign trading patterns increased by about 5 percent in 1980, and probably by at least as much in 1981. In 1981 Portugal repeated the experience of the prestabilization period of losing market shares for its exports and for tourism. It had been a disappointment that the devaluations of the 1977–79 period and the corrections of other price distortions had not produced a significant increase of private investment, particularly in the export sector. But the changes of policy after 1980 suggest that investors had valid reasons for their hesitations.

All these changes took place when the balance of payments was hit again by a marked deterioration of the terms of trade resulting from the second oil price shock and the consequences of international economic recession. Domestic demand was reflated substantially in 1980, but it proved impossible to maintain the same momentum in 1981. In such circumstances, it is not surprising that the ratio of the current account deficit to GDP was even higher in 1981 than it had been in the years preceding the IMF arrangement.

A more difficult problem is that not much progress has been made in the last decade in correcting the structural weakness of the economy with a view to relaxing the balance of payments constraints on growth. The productivity of agriculture remained very low, and the high proportion of imports in food consumption did not decrease. The dependence on imported oil has not been significantly reduced either by energy conservation or by domestic production, although the scope for sizable results in this field is limited. The capacity and the diversification of the export sector did not improve very much. The difficulties of ensuring adequate efficiency in the investments of the public sector, including public enterprises, persisted. The tax system became progressively more distorted, and tax evasion has increased. The budgetary deficits continued to grow, and the negative savings of the public sector have reached almost 4 percent of GDP.

It is easily recognized that structural reforms are far more difficult than the implementation of the usual measures of IMF programs. The experience of Portugal in this area is certainly common to many other countries at different levels of economic development. But the examples given illustrate the limitations of Fund programs in correcting some of the deep causes of external imbalances. It would not be realistic to expect that such programs, even when established under three-year extended arrangements, could correct the most important structural rigidities and bottlenecks in countries with balance of payments problems. Apart from other reasons, most governments would certainly resist the idea of deeper Fund involvement with their economic policies. Therefore, it should at least be concluded that one should not expect more from Fund programs than they can provide. In the case of developing countries, closer coordination with the World Bank, and in particular with its structural adjustment programs, may be particularly useful.

Annex: Methods of Calculation of Table 19.2

The calculations of Table 19.2 were made as described below. The annual changes of the main items of the balance of payments on current account were split into a component resulting from price changes and another resulting from volume changes. The price indicators used for emigrants' remittances and for tourist receipts were, respectively: the weighted average of the indexes of wages converted into dollars in the main countries of work of Portuguese emigrants and the ratio between the index of the dollar value of tourist receipts in European countries and the index of the number of nights spent by foreign tourists in hotels in the same countries.

The changes between any two years in the volume of exports of goods and tourism, net of their estimated import content, and of emigrants' remittances were split into a component explained by foreign demand and a residual related to competitiveness. The indicators for foreign demand were: (1) for exports of goods and services, the weighted averages of the real growth rates of imports into Portugals' main trading partners; (2) for tourism, the number of nights spent by foreign tourists in hotels in Europe; (3) for emigrants' remittances, rough estimates of the rates of increase of the number of emigrants abroad.

The changes in the imports of goods (less the import content of exports and tourism) were split into a component related to changes in the volume of domestic demand and another related to competitiveness. The import content of private and public consumption, of fixed capital formation, of stockbuilding, and of exports of goods and services was estimated on the basis of the coefficients of the input output table for 1974 and the assumption that the changes of such coefficients from year to year are proportional to each other and reflect changes in competitiveness.

For most details about the sources, the methods, and the assumptions of the calculations of Table 19.2, see Silva Lopes 1982.

References

Bruno, M. 1978. "Short-term Policy Trade-offs under Different Phases of Economic Development." In *The Past and Prospects of the World Economic Order* (Symposium, Saltsjobaden, August).

Cavaco Silva, A. A. 1980. "A política orçamental portuguesa em 1974/78." 2a. *Conferencia International sobre Economia Portuguesa.* Vol. I. Lisboa: Fundação Calouste Gulbenkian and German Marshall Fund of the United States.

Dornbusch, Rudiger. 1981. "Portugal's Crawling Peg." In J. Williamson, ed., *Exchange Rate Rules: the Theory, Performance, and Prospects of the Crawling Peg.* London: MacMillan.

Dornbusch, Rudiger, and Lance Taylor. 1977. "Economic Prospects and Policy Options in Portugal." Lisboa: Banco de Portugal.

Eckaus, R. S. 1977. "Is the IMF Guilty of Malpractice?" *The Institutional Investor* (September 1977).

de Fontenay, P. 1982. "Adjustment Policies: The Case of Portugal." Washington: IMF (January).

Fry, M. J. 1970. "Financial Instruments and Markets." *Conferencia Internacional sobre Economia Portuguesa.* Vol. I. Lisboa: Fundação Calouste Gulbenkian and German Marshall Fund of the United States.

International Monetary Fund (IMF). 1977. *The Monetary Approach to the Balance of Payments.* Washington.

Krugman, P., and J. B. Macedo. 1981. "The Economic Consequences of the April 25 Revolution." In J. B. Macedo and S. Serfaty, eds., *Portugal since the Revolution: Economic and Political Perspectives.* Boulder, Colo.: Westview Press.

Krugman, P., and Lance Taylor. 1978. "Contractionary Effects of Devaluation." *Journal of International Economics,* vol. 8.

Letter of Intent (Government of Portugal). 1978. "Carta de Intenções do Governo Portugues ao FMI." *Economia,* vol. 2, no. 2 (maio).

Modigliani, F., and T. Padoa Schioppa. 1978. *The Management of an Open Economy with 100% plus Wage Indexation.* Essays in International Finance no. 130. Princeton, NJ: Princeton University.

Polak, J. 1957. "Monetary Analysis of Income Formation and Payments Problems." IMF Staff Papers, vol. 6 (November). Washington.

Schmitt, H. O. 1981. "Economic Stablization and Growth in Portugal." *IMF Occasional Paper no. 2.* Washington.

Silva Lopes, J. 1982. "Fatores Explicativos da Evolução do Saldo da Balança de Transações Correntes." *Economia* (forthcoming).

Stallings, B. 1981. "Portugal and the IMF: The Political Economy of Stabilization." In *Portugal since the Revolution: Economic and Political Perspectives.* Boulder, Colo.: Westview Press.

Taylor, Lance. 1979. *Macromodels for Developing Countries.* New York: McGraw-Hill.

COMMENTS, CHAPTERS 17–19:

Jeffrey Sachs

The papers by Crawford, Silva Lopes, and Spaventa offer a fascinating group portrait of International Monetary Fund (IMF) dealings with high-income member countries. While the papers are valuable as individual case studies, I will focus my comments on some common themes that can be gleaned from the studies taken together. Very broadly speaking, the four IMF agreements studied in these three papers (two for Italy [1974, 1977—Chapter 18], and one for Portugal [1978—Chapter 19] and the United Kingdom [1976—Chapter 17]) illustrate several facets of macroeconomic management: (1) in all countries, external problems resulted partly from poor aggregate supply conditions, and not merely excess demand; (2) monetary mismanagement added to weak export performance in generating a balance of payments crisis; (3) the most effective policies in the IMF package were those aimed at stimulating aggregate supply and at restoring domestic interest rates to world levels; (4) IMF policies to restrain demand were either downplayed or unsuccessful (with Italy, 1974, an exception), but without major cost to the overall success of the programs; and (5) the IMF was most important in its roles as policy advisor, lightning rod for political fallout, and "bond-rating agency," but almost irrelevant as a direct provider of funds. Let us examine these themes in turn.

Nature of the Crises

Many discussions of Fund policies start from the premise that balance of payments crises are prima facie evidence of excess demand, with the corresponding symptom of excess production of home goods relative to tradables. The debate based on this view revolves around the appropriate mix of policies to achieve expenditure switching and expenditure reductions. A decline in money growth is often seen as a vehicle for reducing official reserve losses while simultaneously restraining aggregate demand.

TABLE 1 INDICATORS OF MACROECONOMIC PERFORMANCE: ITALY, PORTUGAL, UNITED KINGDOM, 1972–78

Item	*1973*	*1974*	*1975*	*1976*	*1977*	*1978*
Output: manufacturing sector						
Italy	105.4	110.0	100	112.4	113.6	115.8
Portugal	84	108	100	104	117	125
United Kingdom	109.4	105.1	100	102.0	105.9	109.8
Unemployment rate						
Italy	6.2	5.3	5.8	6.6	7.0	7.1
United Kingdom	3.0	2.9	3.9	5.5	6.2	6.1
Inflation: CPI growth						
Italy	10.8	19.1	17.0	16.8	17.0	12.1
Portugal	12.9	25.3	15.2	21.1	27.3	22.5
United Kingdom	9.1	16.0	24.2	16.5	15.9	8.3
External balance: current account/GDP						
Italy	−1.7	−4.7	−0.3	−1.5	1.1	2.4
Portugal	3.0	−6.0	−6.0	−8.0	−9.0	−5.2
United Kingdom	−1.6	−4.0	−1.6	−0.9	−0.1	0.4
Monetary policy: M2 growth						
Italy	23.5	15.7	24.5	21.0	22.2	23.0
Portugal	28.4	13.6	12.6	20.9	16.9	20.8
United Kingdom	27.5	12.9	7.1	11.6	9.8	14.6
Profitability: labor share in income						
Italy	0.58	0.59	0.64	0.62	0.63	0.62
Portugal	0.45	0.50	0.60	0.58	0.53	0.51
United Kingdom	0.65	0.70	0.73	0.71	0.68	0.68
Profitability: relative wage						
Italy	100	93.3	107.1	94.1	95.0	93.0
Portugal	100	119.5	137.5	136.3	105.5	83.0
United Kingdom	100	104.3	111.2	103.2	100.1	106.7

CPI Consumer price index.
Sources and definitions: Output: industrial production, 1973 = 100, from International Financial Survey unemployment rate: standardized unemployment rate, *OECD Economic Outlook,* Dec. 1981; profitability labor share in national income, from *OECD National Income Accounts;* relative wage: unit labor costs in manufacturing relative to index costs for other industrial countries. For UK, Italy: from IFS; for Portugal from J. Silva Lopes, converted to levels from rates of change from table 19.5. Monetary growth: percentage change in M2, year-end over year-end, IFS; Inflation: CPI growth, year over year, IFS.

In fact, only one of the four cases in the papers (Italy, 1974) seems to be well captured by the model, as Table 1 indicates. From the data on output and unemployment, we see that while 1974 was a boom year for Italy, the other IMF programs took place during periods of high unemployment and low output relative to potential.

(Unemployment data are not readily available for Portugal, although Silva Lopes makes clear the high levels of unemployment and excess capacity in Portugal during 1974–78.) Because of the large excess capacity, there was the potential for improvements in the current account without the classic dose of demand deflation. This lesson is particularly evident in Portugal during 1977–80.

The data on profitability give a hint as to the supply difficulties in these economies. In all three cases, there is a sharp shift in the distribution of income toward labor after the 1973 oil shock (again, for Italy, the shift is not present until after the 1974 IMF program). Silva Lopes provides a rather detailed account of the profit squeeze and the attendant unemployment in Portugal, pointing out that:

> The trade unions, which had been severely repressed under the previous regime, became militant and achieved increases in wages, which from 1973 to 1975 amounted to 93 percent in nominal terms and to 25 percent in real terms, despite the losses in per capita income that had been caused by the deterioration of the terms of trade, the fall in output in 1975, and the influx of refugees.

The wage shocks in Italy and the United Kingdom were not so dramatic, but were strong just the same. Unfortunately, Crawford and Spaventa only mention the wage issue in passing, so we do not get a good sense for Italy and the United Kingdom of the forces behind the shift in income distribution.

Michael Bruno and I,[1] along with many others, have studied the role of excess real wages in external and internal imbalance. Perhaps the main message for the present context is that poor export performance and high unemployment may be sharply reversed without demand contraction if real wages can be reduced relative to productivity. Of course, exchange rate depreciation may be a principal tool for real wage moderation, if unions agree to forgo wage increases as tradable goods prices rise. All three authors mention the moderation of wages as an underlying target in the stabilization programs, although, again, Silva Lopes is most explicit. The success in moderating the profit squeeze (at least in the short run) is evident from the decline in labor share of income in Italy after 1975, in Portugal after 1976, and in the United Kingdom after 1976. A similar story is evident from the data on relative wages (measured as home unit labor costs

[1] M. Bruno and J. Sachs, "Supply versus Demand Approaches to the Program of Stagflation," in H. Giersch, ed., *Macroeconomic Policies for Growth and Stability,* Kiel: Institut fur Weltwirtschaft, 1981

relative to competitors' unit costs). In all three countries we see a deterioration in international competitiveness in the years leading up to the IMF program, and an improvement after.[2]

Monetary Aspects of the Crises

While the IMF program in Portugal was in large part directed toward Portugal's unsustainable current account deficits, the programs in Italy and the United Kingdom were more importantly geared to the capital account. In Portugal, it was crucial to improve competitiveness as well as to reverse a private speculative outflow of capital. In Italy and the United Kingdom, both sets of goals were again important, but the latter was probably paramount. For Italy and the United Kingdom, the issue was not primarily one of creditworthiness in the face of looming current deficits, but rather the correction of fiscal and monetary policies that had contributed to a deterioration on the capital account and a run on central bank reserves. Each of the authors describes how interest rates were allowed to fall sharply below (covered) world levels in their respective countries, through a combination of interest rate ceilings and expansionary monetary policies, in the period before the Fund programs were put in place. Given a high degree of capital mobility, de facto if not de jure, the interest differentials were quickly converted into sharp official reserve losses. In all cases, the IMF program called for a restoration of interest rates to world levels (on a covered basis).

The rise in domestic interest rates provided a simple and effective fix to the reserve losses in every case. Once the covered differentials were eliminated, the private capital outflows were reversed and reserves rose sharply in all three countries. Indeed, two remarkable points stand out on the monetary side of the Fund programs. In the United Kingdom in 1976, Italy in 1977, and Portugal in 1977–78, the reflow of private capital was so great that actual borrowing from the Fund became superfluous. The IMF credit lines remained largely untouched in Italy and Portugal. In the United Kingdom, a large drawing was made, but it was repaid well ahead of schedule. The second remarkable point is that this restoration of private capital inflow occurred even though the IMF performance criteria on do-

[2] Again, Italy in 1974 is an exception. Also, the improvement in Portugal begins in 1977, with the adoption of the crawling peg, a year before the Fund program.

mestic credit expansion and public deficits were almost always exceeded, and in some cases by a large margin. Ironically, for all three countries, the failure to meet performance criteria might have precluded borrowing from the Fund—at the same time that the final objectives of the programs were being more than met! In the event, the rise in official reserves obviated the need for continued IMF credits.

Evaluating the IMF Role in Italy, Portugal, and the United Kingdom

The three authors pronounce the Fund programs as short-run successes, with the exception of Italy in 1974. They suggest as well, however, that some of the short-run improvements were certain to deteriorate over time, because of deeper underlying difficulties in their economies that were not reached by short-term IMF stand-by arrangements. The programs are most successful, according to the authors, along the dimensions of external balance, official reserve accumulation, and (perhaps) employment; little credit is given for any significant dent in inflation in any of the economies.

In each of the cases, the Fund helped to galvanize support to pursue appropriate credit and exchange rate policies, but played little or no role in actually supplying credit to the economies. This is strongly consistent with the view that for high-income countries (including Portugal), the IMF is probably most important in helping a country to reestablish creditworthiness with private creditors, rather than in acting itself as a substitute source of credit.[3]

Finally, the demand-management aspects of the four Fund programs seem to get the lowest marks, both in their importance and efficacy. Spaventa severely criticizes the 1974 Italian stand-by arrangement as too contractionary. Silva Lopes similarly argues that the 1978 Portugal stand-by was successful, in part, because "the Portuguese authorities applied much less restrictive budgetary and credit policies than those which had been established in the program . . ." With remarkable regularity, the specific demand-side elements of the programs were exceeded, with little effect on overall performance.

[3] This is not to deny that the existence of the high-conditionality credit tranche provides a very direct form of reassurance to the credit markets. The point is rather that the actual flow of credit from the Fund to the country was either small (Italy, Portugal) or quickly reversed (United Kingdom).

In each of the cases here, the matters of predominant importance were a realignment of real wage rates with world levels; and a similar realignment of interest rates to levels in world markets. Details of domestic credit expansion rank far behind in significance.

CHAPTER 20

Financing India's Structural Adjustment: The Role Of the Fund

Catherine Gwin

On November 9, 1981, the International Monetary Fund (IMF) approved an extended arrangement for India authorizing purchases up to $5.75 billion over a three-year period.[1] The arrangement is the largest in the Fund's history and perhaps one of the most controversial. While some of the controversy has focused on the arrangement's conditionality, the case raises, as well, a broader question of when to use Fund resources for financing structural adjustment.

India approached the Fund for extended financing after its economy suffered a sharp setback in 1979/80. Although the economy began to show moderate signs of recovery in 1980/81, the balance of payments position continued to weaken. Anticipating that its payments position would remain under pressure for several years to come, India brought to the Fund a "supply-side" adjustment program. As spelled out by the government, the program seeks to resolve India's medium-term balance of payments problem primarily by measures to promote higher

[1] Under the arrangement, purchases up to the equivalent of 291 percent of India's quota will be financed in part (48 percent) from the Fund's ordinary resources and in part (52 percent) from resources borrowed by the Fund under the policy of enlarged access. If fully drawn, the loan will carry, therefore, an average annual rate of interest of 12 percent. Of the total amount, not more than $1,035 million can be purchased before June 30, 1982; not more than another $2,070 million in the second year; leaving $2,645 million for the remaining period of the program.

export growth and import substitution, especially in the energy sector. In other words, the aim is to achieve adjustment through growth.[2]

Obviously, it is too soon to judge the success of India's arrangement with the Fund. Nevertheless, it should be possible to arrive at some preliminary conclusions about how good the extended arrangement looks at the outset, in light of India's economic problems and prospects; how important the Fund was, at the margin, in getting India's commitment to a sound set of policies; and what the implications of this case are regarding the Fund's role in promoting balance of payments adjustment.

This paper addresses these questions by examining India's economic situation; its negotiations with the fund; and the criticisms of the program that have been raised within and outside India. The main conclusions the paper draws are the following.

- The IMF was right to agree with India that the country faced serious structural problems and needed to concentrate its adjustment effort on certain supply-side problems.
- The principal impact of the Fund's policy advice in this case has been to hold the government of India to its own supply-side adjustment program.
- More specifically, IMF pressure on Indian officials, which focused on the mobilization of domestic resources for investment, seems (at least preliminarily) to have enhanced the chances of successful adjustment without having imposed undue sacrifices on India's growth or distributive objectives—largely because India came early to the Fund.
- Existing performance criteria do not, however, provide adequate means for monitoring India's adherence to the central savings and investment features of its adjustment program and, thus, to the overall goals of the program.
- Moreover, it remains to be seen how much of an effect the IMF will have on the further liberalization of the Indian economy, and it is this issue that, in the final analysis, will determine the success or failure of the Indian case as a Fund initiative.
- Although IMF-World Bank cooperation worked well in this case—with the Bank playing a key role in the assessment of India's invest-

[2] One might compare India's approach with what is referred to as "expansionary stabilization" in William Cline and Sidney Weintraub (eds.), *Economic Stabilization in Developing Countries* (Washington: Brookings Institution, 1981).

ment program—there are no procedures that ensure such cooperation in other cases. Nor can such cooperation be an adequate substitute for greater Fund expertise on the processes of structural adjustment.

• In India's case the Fund has served as a lender of "first" resort. If it is to play this same role in other cases, it will need additional resources.

India's Economic Situation

India's economy is continental in scope; highly industrialized and extremely poor; centrally planned—some would say overly planned; administratively encumbered and rampant with corruption; caste-bound and socialist-inspired; determinedly self-reliant; and, though guided by principles of social democracy, protective of the interests of politically powerful, propertied groups. The dilemmas and paradoxes in this situation have been written about in great depth by those seeking to understand why the country—with sources of strength many other developing countries would envy—has failed to make a greater impact on its problem of massive poverty. All these factors have to be taken into account in understanding the economic policies and programs that set the context for India's extended arrangement. However, the description that follows of India's economic situation will focus largely on the problems that directly led the government of India to turn to the Fund.

Briefly stated, following several years of strong economic performance marked by sustained growth in output, internal price stability, and a healthy external payments position, India entered the 1980s faced with uncertain medium-term growth prospects and a large balance of payments gap brought about by a sharp deterioration in the terms of trade and by domestic supply shortfalls. The situation confronts its decisionmakers with the difficult challenge of how to adjust without sacrificing growth or distributive goals, for given the country's low level of per capita income ($190) and its pervasive poverty, efforts to increase the level of income and to improve its distribution remain at the center of India's development effort.

The most immediate source of the country's economic woes was the triple blow dealt to the economy in 1979/80. First, a severe drought triggered substantial power shortages, associated shortages of coal and transport services, and related deep cuts in agricultural and industrial production. The drought, the worst since independence, received only little attention in the international press because newly attained agricultural resiliency spared the society the human drama that had previously accompanied poor monsoons. In economic terms, however, the drought took a heavy toll, contributing in 1979/80 to declines of 16 percent in agricultural production and 4 percent in national income. Resulting shortages of basic inputs and cuts in production contributed also to a decline in export performance at a time when India's external economic environment was also deteriorating.

The second blow, unrest in Assam, cut into domestic production of crude oil and thus led to a $1 billion increase in India's oil import bill. Concomitantly, India along with others was hit by the 1979/80 sharp rise in world oil prices, which contributed significantly to a terms of trade loss equivalent to 3 percent of GDP.

The result was a sharp rise in inflation to a rate of nearly 20 percent by the end of 1980. Also, India's current account fell from a $413 million surplus in 1978/78 to a deficit of $850 million in 1979/80 and $3.5 billion by 1980/81. This then led, for the first time since the mid-1970s, to the start of a steep decline in India's foreign exchange reserves that continued through 1981, leaving India at the end of that year with reserves equivalent to only three months' imports.

From a political point of view, the jump in the rate of inflation was the government's greatest concern. As a prominent Indian economist stated in an essay supporting India's request for an IMF loan, "inflation redistributes command over resources in favor of the well-to-do and of the parallel economy, and against the poor and the unorganized;" it "does not benefit employment, production, or savings at the macro-level." This view of inflation has traditionally been a major factor in the government's economic policy making and was, in 1979/80, a principal reason for deciding to turn to the Fund.

By the end of 1979/80, there was related widespread concern that the country was beset with certain deep structural problems that were impeding full economic recovery and threatening future growth.

First, as already indicated, India suffered a structural deterioration in its terms of trade due largely to the increase in world oil prices. Although the government plans to double domestic oil production by 1985 and to act to curb the growth of demand, India's oil imports will continue to rise through the next two decades.

Second, India is faced with basic infrastructural and supply constraints whose alleviation will depend on substantial domestic investment and imports requiring an unprecedented mobilization of foreign resources. According to all reports, the country is caught in a vicious circle of power, coal, steel, and rail shortages that have exacerbated each other and have contributed to a substantial rise in imports of several important products in which India has an apparent comparative advantage. There is substantial scope for improved capacity utilization in a number of these key industries—notably fertilizer, steel products, and cement—as well as the potential for increased domestic oil production, but only if the interlocking constraints of power, coal, and transport are eased.[3]

Third, India's economy is constrained by major inefficiencies, particularly in the operations of its large public sector. Although India has made enormous capital investments, particularly in the public sector, it has a capital-output ratio of about 6:1. The public sector, which now accounts for about 50 percent of total capital investment, provides only 15 percent of total domestic savings. Moreover, while total saving as a proportion of GNP has now climbed to about 24 percent, which is high for a poor country, average annual growth in output has never risen for any length of time beyond 3.5 percent a year. As one Indian analyst has recently noted, the major preoccupation of successive governments has been with attempting a more equitable distribution of wealth, with controlling inflation, and with preventing a concentration of economic power in the hands of large industrial houses. This has resulted in a complex system of controls, most of which have operated to restrain initiative, particularly by the private sector. Hence, "there are plenty of levers to stop action," but "relatively too few to push things forward."[4]

In times past, when the country faced balance of payments difficulties, the government responded by cutting back imports and thereby slowing growth. This time, the government has decided not to close up but rather to pursue a different course, i.e., to adjust to a deteriorated external environment while simulataneously bringing about improvements in the use of internal resources and high rates of investment to maintain growth. Both political and economic considerations seem to be driving India's policymakers along this course. For one, the economy today, despite current problems, is in an overall

[3] Inadequacy of railway transport services is now the greatest problem. In 1967–77 the railways carried 212.6 million tons of revenue-earning traffic. This level has not been exceeded in the subsequent four years. Center for the Monitoring of the Indian Economy, *Basic Statistics Relating to the Indian Economy*, vol. 1, table 5.2 (September 1981).

[4] L. K. Jha, *Economic Strategy for the '80s* (New Delhi: Allied Publishers, 1981). In this most recent Indian treatment of the country's economic problems, the author contends that the country is passing through "not just a bad patch in our economic progress but a deeper social, political, and moral malaise, the seeds of which lie in the malfunctioning of the economic system as a whole." Quoted in David Housego, "Economic Basic Premises Attacked," *Financial Times,* section III, p.1, January 19, 1981.

stronger position than it was during previous periods of serious external imbalance. The agricultural sector, which accounts for over 72 percent of the labor force, has achieved a level of growth such that, barring some extraordinary conjunction of unfavorable weather conditions, the society is freed of heavy dependence on imports of staple foods. The country's industrial base is significantly larger and more diversified than a decade ago. Its saving and investment rates are much higher. Its level of indebtedness is low, and it has a substantial capacity to borrow. Furthermore, in the period 1975–79, when its economy was growing at a rate of more than 6 percent and it was accumulating sizable foreign exchange and food grain reserves, the government introduced a series of liberalization measures to spur production and promote exports.

In addition, there are strong political pressures on the government to "get the economy moving"; there has been a change in the composition of Indian imports (now roughly 85 percent basic commodities and capital goods), which makes it harder now than ever to "close up" without significantly reducing growth; there is no escaping the structural nature of the deterioration in the terms of trade; and there is recognition that the country cannot continue to count on growing amounts of concessional aid[5] and will therefore need to increase both its exports and its foreign commercial borrowing to sustain imports of capital goods and essential raw materials.

There is some reason to doubt that the government will actually carry through on the politically difficult decisions that adjustment requires. Politicians, bureaucrats, and entrepreneurs do well under the present licensing system. However, political tolerance in India for inflation and recession is low, and, with state elections in 1982 and a national election in 1985, the political situation seems now to be putting considerable pressure on the government to make adjustments that will encourage accelerated noninflationary growth.

To this end, in April 1980 the government announced that it would continue rather than turn back from the import liberalization steps taken by the Janata government in 1977 (when India's reserves were high). In July 1980, an industrial policy statement was issued that eased restrictions on private enterprise and announced plans to "re-

[5] The foreign aid point, discussed in India's Sixth Five-Year Plan, was borne out in early 1982, when the World Bank announced that it was reducing both the total lending to India (from $2.1 to $1.9 billion in 1982) and the amount of that lending provided by the International Development Association on highly concessional terms.

structure" money-losing state-owned industries to bring about more efficient management. At several points throughout the year, administered prices on key commodities (e.g., cement, petroleum, and fertilizer) were raised. Toward the end of 1980, the government took several steps to promote an expansion of exports—allowing production units exporting 100 percent of their output relief from import duties; relaxing restrictions on capacity expansion where the expansion was for export; and setting up an export-import bank. Furthermore, the government invited the participation of foreign oil companies in a program of domestic oil exploration and development.

The overall framework for these policies is India's Sixth Five-Year Plan, released in early 1981 for the period 1980/81–1984/85. The plan, which was a year in drafting, aims at an overall rate of growth of 5.2 percent and a reduction of the number of people below the poverty line from 48–30 percent of the population; estimates total investment on the order of $190 billion (53 percent of which would be in the public sector); focuses heavily on alleviating infrastructure constraints; seeks to replace certain key imports with domestically produced goods and to promote exports; and anticipates an increase in foreign borrowing on commercial terms to help meet an expected current account deficit projected to peak at about 2.2 percent of GNP in 1983–84 before declining to 1.8 percent in 1984–85 and gradually thereafter throughout the decade.

In accordance with this plan, the government went to the private capital markets for several large project loans,[6] approached the Asian Development Bank for the first time for a $2 billion nonconcessional loan, and began negotiations with the IMF for extended financing.

Negotiations with the Fund

India's decision "to go early" to the Fund—in anticipation of persistent pressures on its balance of payments and well in advance of exhausting its access to the private capital markets—reflected the government's view that its deteriorating balance of payments position gave it a legitimate claim to Fund resources; that in the absence of foreign aid increases it needed to expand and diversify its sources of

[6] For example, India approached the market in 1980 for a $680 million syndicated credit as part of the financing for a $2.1 billion aluminum complex to be built by Pechiney of France. A second major commercial offering that year involved a $200 million credit for the Oil and Natural Gas Commission.

foreign borrowing[7]; that by drawing from the Fund in support of a strategy of adjustment through growth it could hold down the cost of immediate increases in international borrowing and maintain its strong credit rating for future borrowings; and that it would have little difficulty with Fund conditionality, given both recent changes in Fund lending policy and the overall thrust of its own Sixth Plan.

In fact, in the negotiations between India and the IMF, the Fund was quick to agree with the Indian government that the adjustment problem the country faced was of a structural nature. The actions needed, the Fund concurred, were not primarily in the area of demand management. Nor did India's exchange rate appear out of line.[8] Rather, the Fund shared the view of Indian authorities that, as a matter of priority, the country needed to increase domestic production of oil and certain other imported items, take a variety of measures to step up its export earnings, and improve efficiency in the utilization of existing capacity. The Fund was also of the opinion that, while the deterioration in India's current account balance was large relative to the country's level of exports, reserve position, and record of foreign borrowing in the past, it was not particularly large in terms of the economic adjustments required to achieve a sustainable balance of payments.[9]

In addition, the Fund was willing to acknowledge a difference in point of view on the usefulness of certain economic instruments and therefore to accede, in particular, to the government of India's strategy on interest rates, at least at the outset of the extended program. While having taken some limited measures to raise interest rates, the government stated that it intended to act to reduce inflation and thereby return to a situation like that of the mid-1970s, when the rate

[7] India's disbursed external debt at the end of 1980/81 (excluding the Fund) amounted to about SDR 14 billion, which is equivalent to about 11 percent of GNP. Of this total only about 2 percent related to loans from supplier credits, commercial and financial institutions, and bonds; the rest involved bilateral and multilateral loans.

[8] From 1974–79 the rupee-dollar rate remained stable, and the real value of the rupee fell relative to the currencies of Japan, Germany, and the United Kingdom because of price stability in India. In 1980–81, the value of the rupee depreciated against the dollar and at the same time appreciated against the major European currencies.

[9] This opinion was expressed, in interviews, by those sources who felt that some of what the critics of the Indian loan wanted involved changes in the basic organization of the Indian economy, and that this went far beyond the appropriate concern of the Fund in applying conditions to extended financing.

of saving was high. The Fund accepted this policy (with the clear understanding that India's interest rates and its exchange rate would be among a number of issues given close attention in subsequent six-month reviews). The Fund also got from the World Bank, whose involvement it sought, a general endorsement of the overall thrust of India's economic plan.

The Fund was not initially satisfied, however, with the government of India's commitment to the measures necessary to "get it from here to there." In the words of one person on the staff, "India had a plan but not enough up-front action." The Fund, therefore, pressed the Indian government hard for specific commitments, particularly in the area of domestic resource mobilization.

Part of the history of Indian economic development has been that resources for investment fall short of plans. In the Fund's view, there was a danger of history repeating itself. The Sixth Plan addressed this issue by indicating a number of tax and nontax measures that would have to be taken to meet ambitious investment goals. Specifically, given that the nominal tax rate and rate of private sector saving were already high,[10] the plan emphasized the need to increase public sector saving by raising administered prices (e.g., for petroleum, coal, and steel), reducing subsidies (e.g., for fertilizer), and fostering greater efficiency in the utilization of existing capital. The Fund urged India to break down this five-year program into annual components with commitments to saving and investment targets. This kind of commitment in advance was impossible, the Indian authorities argued, because the government was obliged to take expenditure and revenue-raising measures to parliament on a yearly basis.

For a time, negotiations between the Fund and India were at a stalemate. The Fund, therefore, advised India to come in with commitments for a one-year program. This India resisted doing; instead, the government took a number of powerful revenue-raising actions. Most importantly, in July 1981, it raised the price of domestic crude oil from an average of $46.92 to $141.84 per ton (an increase of 200 percent), and it further reduced its subsidy burden by over $900 million by increasing fertilizer prices for the second time in just over one year. The government also raised the price of most petroleum products, including kerosene, by 9–13 percent (after a rise of similar magnitude six months earlier). In addition, the tariffs of electricity boards in a number of states were raised.

[10] Central government taxes amounted in 1981 to about 20 percent of national income.

Three things should be noted about these actions. First, they followed quickly on similar actions taken by the government before coming to the Fund. Together, the tax and nontax measures that the government took over this period should cover over 90 percent of the anticipated domestic resource needs of the Sixth Plan. Second, the type of measures taken are all foreseen in the Sixth Plan. Third, by taking these measures "in advance," the government not only avoided the appearance of submitting to Fund conditions, but it also took the teeth out of the arrangement it eventually submitted to the Fund. In place of public sector saving targets, India's arrangement with the Fund lists actions already taken that will have the effect of raising public sector savings.

Reduction of external restrictions in the Indian economy was a second and even more sensitive issue that figured prominently in India-IMF negotiations. On this point, about all that can be said is that any real coming to terms was deferred to the first and subsequent program reviews.

Thus, the text of the extended arrangement and accompanying documentation commit the Indian government to a set of performance criteria and economic policies that mirror the policy approach and broad objectives of its Sixth Plan, refer to measures already taken, and indicate in broad terms an intention to continue with more of the same. Specifically, the performance criteria are as follows.

- In the first year of the extended arrangement India will (1) hold to stipulated ceilings on domestic credit to the banking system and on net credit to governments[11] and (2) limit its contracting or guaranteeing of medium-term loans of maturity of 1–12 years to no more than SDR 1.4 billion (and within this ceiling, new commitments of between 1 and 5 years will be limited to SDR 400 million).
- Second and third installments will be dependent on subsequent consultations and additional performance clauses.
- Throughout the duration of the extended arrangement, India will not impose or intensify import restrictions for balance of payments reasons; impose or intensify restrictions on payments and transfers for current international transactions; introduce multiple currency

[11] The ceiling for total domestic credit expansion is placed at 19.4 percent. Net credit to government is limited to a rise from 258.06 billion rupees in March 1981, to 294.29 billion rupees in November 1981 and 309.81 billion rupees in March 1982. Overall, growth of total liquidity is limited to 15.7 percent.

practices; or conclude bilateral payments agreements inconsistent with Article VIII of the Fund.

In its statement of economic policies and objectives, the government further commits itself to a wide-ranging adjustment effort that includes, along the lines suggested above, a massive investment program with emphasis on energy production, production of certain other bulk imports, and alleviation of infrastructural constraints; policy adjustments to encourage production, investment, and economic efficiency in the private sector; continued flexibility in pricing policy (following the upward adjustment in prices made prior to the start of the extended fund facility, EFF): monetary and financial policies aimed at "containing inflationary pressures" while "supporting rapid growth and supply-side policies"; pursuit of "a realistic policy in regard to exchange rates"; "further measures," in addition to those taken prior to the start of the EFF, to strengthen the export effort; and "the intention to carry forward the progress achieved over recent years toward liberalization of imports of raw materials, intermediate and capital goods needed by the economy."

In defending this program before parliament, the Indian authorities stated that: (1) they had not agreed to anything other than what was in the official plan; (2) if pushed too hard by the Fund on any issue, they would not continue the program; (3) if the rate of growth of output was not sufficiently high to enable them to afford the program, they would not continue to draw resources from the Fund; or (4) if economic conditions improved sufficiently, they would not draw.

The Impact

Today, at the end of the first three-month period of India's extended program, economic indicators suggest that the adjustment effort is, generally, on course. Indeed, in most areas the economy is doing better than expected. Inflation is down from its high of almost 20 percent in 1979/80, to below 10 percent, and is expected to average under 8 percent for the year. Expansion of credit has stayed well within the specified ceilings. Most subsectors of the industrial sector have continued to expand, and performance in key infrastructural sectors has recovered from the decline of the last few years, although problems remain for the longer term. Agricultural production, which was up in 1980/81, has continued to improve, although less dramatically than industrial production. Overall, the rate of growth for 1981/82 will be about 5.5 percent—which means that it is back to the predrought trend. The weakest area, however, is the trade sector, with foreign exchange reserves falling more rapidly in the first half of the fiscal year than expected. Nonetheless, in this area as well there are signs of some improvement: e.g., imports grew, in volume, at a rate of 10 percent.[12]

That having been said, it is obviously still too soon to draw any real conclusions about the effectiveness of India's extended program. Instead, it might be useful to explore, at least preliminarily, the major criticisms that the program has evoked in India and from member countries of the Fund.

In India, opposition has come principally from the left, but also from others skeptical of the government's capacity to manage the economy. According to these critics, the IMF loan was *unnecessary;* its policy conditions *intrusive* and their impact *inequitable;* and the outcome of the program likely to be *ineffective* as a means of closing the country's balance of payments gap.[13] Each of these points warrants brief review.

The seriousness of India's balance of payments problem, some critics argue, does not itself constitute a case for borrowing from the Fund. Rather, the decision to borrow is seen as a "soft option" that allows the government to postpone politically more difficult, but socially and economically more desirable, alternative actions. Specifically, it is argued that the imbalances in the economy could be significantly reduced by further curbing oil consumption, reducing slack in the import bill created by previous years of liberalization, limiting military spending, instituting major tax reforms, and achieving much greater efficiency, especially in the public sector. For the left, the preferred alternative is, in a word, to return to a more inward-looking, self-reliant strategy. For others, the preferred option (with or without the IMF loan) is a more rapid and more extensive freeing-up of the economy.

The response of the government to criticism from the left is that a major cutback in imports and a sharper reduction in oil consumption would cause a significant decline in the rate of growth, with all the attendant consequences, especially for the poor, that recession entails. (The significance of the resource savings that might result from reduced military spending is perhaps a calculation worth making, but

[12] This paragraph is based on interviews.

[13] These views are expressed in a collection of articles published by the West Bengal government in a widely distributed book entitled *The IMF Loan: Facts and Issues* (November 1981). Some were also expressed in interviews conducted in India in February 1982.

there has been no indication that the government would have made cutbacks in this area even in the absence of the IMF loan.)

Perhaps a retrospective look at India's EFF program will prove its leftist critics right. At this point, however, the government's aim of achieving adjustment with growth seems entirely appropriate given the nature of the current adjustment problems facing India, the longer-term economics of a more outward-looking policy (discussed further below), and the overwhelming accumulation of evidence suggesting that faster economic growth in India is a necessary condition for achieving distributive as well as other development objectives.

A second point made by the critics in India is that, even if some external financing is required, the country need not have gone in for so large, and thus so highly conditional, an IMF loan. India could have borrowed less from the Fund (thereby staying within the lower and less conditional credit tranches) and borrowed more from the commercial markets (whose conditions are profit oriented, not ideologically oriented). Instead, by accepting IMF conditions—which emphasize credit stringency, price decontrol and elimination of subsidies, import liberalization, and a greater role for the private sector both foreign and domestic—India loses economic sovereignty and forfeits the social objectives of its economic policy.

In response to this charge, the government has insisted that no conditions have been accepted that depart from national policy as set out in the Sixth Plan. Although it is impossible to say whether or to what extent "anticipatory conditionality" has a bearing on that plan, it is quite clear that, in comparison to most other IMF stabilization programs, the Indian EFF involves a less severe reduction in aggregate demand and less stringent credit controls, a longer term perspective on regaining a sustainable balance of payments, and more emphasis on government investment in infrastructural bottlenecks and other supply-side problems—an approach that critics of traditional IMF stabilization programs have long been recommending.[14]

No adjustment process is, however, cost-free. Having suffered a terms of trade loss of some 3 percent of GDP, and having faced a rate of inflation nearing 20 percent, India had to adjust. But it is legitimate to question where the burden of adjustment should fall. Critics of the IMF loan argue that the program is inequitable and

[14] See, for example, Sidney Dell and Roger Lawrence, *Balance of Payments Adjustment in Developing Countries* (Elmsford, NY: Pergamon, 1980); and Carlos Diaz-Alejandro, "Southern Cone Stabilization Plans," p. 119–47 in Cline and Weintraub, *Economic Stabilization.*

that the burden of adjustment has been allowed to fall too heavily on the poor. In particular, they oppose the rise in indirect taxes and prices of public goods and services and the curtailing of public welfare expenditures. As argued by one of the leading critics:

> Since expenditure on infrastructure development cannot be cut and since export subsidies are deemed necessary for reversing the relative attractiveness of the domestic market vis-à-vis exports, the axe has to fall on salary increases and welfare and relief expenditures, including food subsidies. At the same time, to "encourage investment and production in the private sector," prices of agricultural and key industrial products have to be revised upwards. The logic of the IMF package therefore is such that its net result must be an "engineered" inflation, an "engineered" recession and unemployment, a squeeze on money wages and salaries and a cut in public expenditure on welfare relief and subsidies on essential consumption items. Each of these measures adversely affects the low- and middle-income groups; together their impact can be disastrous. And if a devaluation is additionally thrown in, the impact is even greater via its inflationary consequences.[15]

Several points might be made in considering this argument. First, it is hard to believe that fiscal conditions would be less stringent without the IMF loan. Second, the government has acknowledged that, while the margin for consumption will be tight given the Sixth Plan's focus on massive investment requirements, there will be continued spending on key antipoverty efforts. The government also argues that it is making an effort to cushion the impact of adjustment on the poor by, among other things, maintaining food subsidies and by increasing prices on items of particular importance to the poor (e.g., kerosene) by far less than the increase of other import prices. It is also argued by supporters of the program that among those most affected by price and subsidy changes are the relatively large commercial farmers, who currently contribute little to the tax revenue of central and state governments.[16] Reducing subsidies on products consumed by them (e.g., fertilizer, power, irrigation) and increasing in-

[15] Prabhat Patnaik, "Implications of Borrowing from the Fund," in the West Bengal government publication, *The IMF Loan: Facts and Issues* (November 1981).

[16] Although agriculture accounts for about 40 percent of India's total national income, its share of total tax revenues is about 1.4 percent. Indeed, agricultural income is wholly exempt from income taxes levied by the central government.

direct taxes on products such as electric pumps is seen as "the only way to extract due contributions" from those few and politically powerful.[17]

It can be reasonably argued, nevertheless, that the burden of adjustment in India today is falling most heavily on the poor. The point is argued even by some who are strong supporters of the IMF loan. Hannan Ezekiel, editor of the Bombay *Economic Times,* agrees with the left that the poor ought not to be made to bear so much of the burden of adjustment; but he suggests that the right policy response is not price controls and subsidization, but rather more deliberate moves to generate additional employment. Other supporters of the loan argue further that a greater effort should be made to discriminate between "socially relevant subsidies" that ought to be maintained and dysfunctional subsidies for other than basic welfare purposes (e.g., export subsidies) that ought to be cut. Many argue, moreover, that more direct taxation through reform and stronger efforts to stop tax evasion ought to accompany indirect tax measures.

These points raise the question of whether, in advising governments on adjustment policies, the Fund should not only be sensitive to governments' concerns to avoid measures that place a disproportionate burden on the poor but also should take some initiative in proposing policy approaches that would favor the poor. My own view is that the Fund should not. What is important is that, by accepting a medium-term perspective on adjustment and early and expanded access, the Fund allows for flexible responses to this issue by governments on a case-by-case basis.

A fourth criticism that has been raised in India, however, is that the government does not even have a viable program for reducing its balance of payments deficit. The government, it is argued, is "mortgaging the country's future," leading it into an all too familiar "debt-trap," since it does not have the capacity to make the adjustments necessary to ensure the ability to repay the Fund. Of concern to the left are both the dangers of nonconcessional borrowing and the threat of pressure from the Fund for too rapid import liberalization. Of concern to others in India are the absence of Fund criteria that will force the government to deal effectively with inefficient management in the public sector and to accelerate a freeing-up of the economy—both actions being seen as essential to the achievement of faster, sustainable growth.

[17] Center for the Monitoring of the Indian Economy, *Basic Statistics,* table 7.10.

India, I was told in numerous interviews, must not let itself get into a situation like that of Brazil: in the face of great uncertainty in today's climate for world trade, there is a danger of becoming captive to a large, potentially unmanageable debt. And if this were to happen, the fear of some is that the country would lose its freedom of action. In other words, the IMF arrangement is perceived by some as only the first step on a slippery slope. The government's answer to this charge is that the country can no longer depend on increasing amounts of foreign aid, and that entry into the arena of nonconcessional borrowing is being handled prudently. The evidence seems to bear this out. India's debt service ratio in November 1981 was between 10 percent and 12 percent. It will go up with the IMF loan. Except for its arrangement with the Fund, however, all major official external borrowings are for project financing, including, in particular, oil-related projects. Partly for this reason, India is now able to borrow at a rate of interest of one-half to three-eighths of a percentage point above the London interbank offered rate (Libor). The arrangement with the Fund is expected to maintain, if not to improve, this exceedingly good credit rating even as India's imports rise. Moreover, supporters of the Fund program within India and outside believe that there is considerable scope for a sustained moderate rate of growth, for domestic substitution of major bulk imports as well as for expansion of Indian exports.

Certain critics disagree. They claim that the IMF arrangement, which prohibits new or tighter import restrictions, threatens India's self-reliance and its chances to regain external equilibrium. Born out of the colonial experience and reinforced by relations with major donors in the 1960s, the concept of self-reliance has received high priority in India over the last several decades, limiting foreign trade and foreign investment. For many, today's IMF deal arouses bitter memories of the devaluation of 1966, which failed to produce desired economic consequences and had a disastrous political impact. Even among those critics who recognize the difference between 1966 and today's arrangement, there is nonetheless a fear that to "open up" the economy is to make India "vulnerable." Those who oppose a further liberalization of trade and industrial policy argue that there is particularly good reason to be apprehensive in a world of rising protectionism that will make it difficult for India to balance a rise in imports with an expansion of exports. But the issue is a long-standing one that has been debated continuously throughout the quarter century since Indian independence.[18] Positions on the issue are deep-rooted, and the interests well entrenched.

Obviously, this paper cannot give adequate coverage to this particular issue, which is central not only to Indian economic policy but also to the policies of many other developing countries. I would submit, however, that the evidence seems to be overwhelmingly on the side of those who argue that India can hasten its development by accepting greater exposure to the world economy and by making greater use of its comparative advantage. As convincingly argued by Lawrence Veit:

> Whether India's foreign trade policy is evaluated (1) according to technical economic criteria such as efficiency (allocation of resources and ability to minimize costs) and impact on domestic savings or (2) from the vantage of India's triad of growth, equity and self-reliance, the conclusion is that India has gone well beyond what "infant industry" logic would justify. Through its extreme protectionist policies India has raised the cost structure and lowered the efficiency of domestic industry to such an extent that the economy has become insensitive to the price and other signals which, under other conditions, would serve India's growth and distribution objectives as well as capitalize on its international comparative advantage.[19]

According to Veit, India's past foreign trade strategy has contributed to the following interrelated problems: (1) policies have, in effect, guaranteed monopoly practices, which have in turn reduced efficiency and incentives to innovate; (2) the import licensing system has operated so as to encourage expansion of capacity rather than efficient utilization of existing plant and equipment; (3) the loss of efficiency associated with the foreign trade regime is multifaceted; (4) policies do not even optimize India's foreign exchange position; and (5) there is a built-in anti-investment and antigrowth bias.

The Fund has had, and will have, limited leverage on Indian economic policy in general and on this issue in particular. The issue stands, however, as the one apt to cause the most difficulty in subsequent phases of the extended arrangement. Performance criteria require that India hold the line against further restrictions. This the government is likely to do. But, successful adjustment will require

[18] Among the many books and articles written on this aspect of India's economic strategy, see Lawrence A. Veit, *India's Second Revolution* (New York: McGraw-Hill, 1976); and Jagdish N. Bhagwati and T.N. Srinivasan, *Foreign Trade Regimes and Economic Development: India* (New York: Columbia University Press for the National Bureau for Economic Research, 1975).

[19] Veit, *ibid.*, p. 290.

more than that, and how far and how fast the government is prepared to move remains an open question. The Fund's EFF gives India a three-year cushion—to enable a high level of imports to be sustained and structural changes to be made. While much can be done to increase domestic production of some of the items that now loom large in India's import bill, growth of demand for these and other essential materials and equipment will make the import bill grow rapidly if India is to sustain a satisfactory rate of growth.[20] Most of this growth will have to be financed by rising exports, but improved export performance will, in turn, depend on both an explicit export strategy, which India previously has not had, and a range of measures to ease import restrictions, streamline cumbersome official regulations and licensing procedures, and make more efficient India's industrial structure.[21]

According to India's Letter of Intent to the Fund, export policy will be one of two principal issues discussed during the first (March 1982) review. On this point the Fund and the World Bank are allies of certain key policymakers in India; but the Letter of Intent submitted to the Fund by India contains no specific commitments on trade promotion measures, and there is much room for future confrontation on this issue. Both the availability of adequate financial assistance and moderate pacing of trade adjustment measures are, however, likely to be critical—a point made in case studies of other developing countries' adjustment efforts and, in general, in writings by Krueger and others.[22]

Outside of India, the main criticism of the country's extended program has come from the US government. Interestingly, the United States and the Indian leftist critics converge on two points—doubt about the need for so large a loan, and the preference for commercial

[20] According to World Bank projections, India's import bill in current prices will grow at an average rate of 18 percent per year through 1984/85 if the government sticks to its ambitious Sixth Plan.

[21] There are innumerable sources, both Indian and non-Indian, that might be cited on this point. Perhaps one of the most relevant is the recent Indian government report—Committee on Export Strategy for the 1980s, "Tandon Committee" (December 1980)—which argues that, because of past emphasis on self-reliance, key sectors of Indian industry have slipped behind technologically and that this is impeding the growth of Indian manufactured exports.

[22] See for example, Anne O. Krueger, *Foreign Trade Regimes and Economic Development: Liberalization Attempts and Consequences* (Cambridge, Mass.: Balinger Press, 1978).

borrowing. Whereas the left views IMF conditionality as an affront and a distortion of Indian priorities, the United States claims that the conditions are too easy. At the time of the Executive Board's vote on India's program, the US executive director criticized the "lack of specificity" regarding the policy measures to be taken and the inadequacies of the existing performance criteria as means of monitoring India's structural adjustment. Those criteria, which deal with ceilings on domestic credit, including net credit to the government, limits on official debt, and prohibitions against import and currency restrictions say nothing about India's strategy of public sector saving and investment or about its trade strategy. Nor does the agreement between India and the Fund state clearly what structural adjustments are most critical in order for India to achieve its projected current account trend and for the Board to review India's progress in making adjustments. Therefore, while it is expected that India will have no trouble in meeting the stated performance criteria, it is possible that it could satisfy those particular requirements without meeting the adjustment goals of its extended program. Stated more generally, changes in performance criteria have not kept up with changes in Fund lending policy and do not provide an adequate means of monitoring structural adjustment programs. The Fund itself has recognized the limitations of existing performance criteria and, therefore, puts emphasis on periodic reviews. But, at least in the Indian case, the agreement does not specify the areas of policy that are to be the principal subjects of review. Perhaps additional criteria are needed—ones that relate to the savings and investment goals of a structural adjustment program—if the Fund's board is to have the means to make appropriate judgments about which programs have reasonable chances of success and judgments about what constitutes reasonable progress in the course of an EFF program. What is required, however, is not quantitative targets but agreement on the means of achieving targets (i.e., policy)—and, here, what is appropriate will vary greatly country to country.

In India's case, the staff of the World Bank played a major role in assessing India's investment plans. Because of its store of expertise on and involvement in India, the Bank staff was in a position to judge India's proposed balance between new investment and better utilization of existing capacity, the soundness of India's sector priorities and plans, and the feasibility of the ambitious investment program. Given the kind of adjustment problem India faces, this contribution by the Bank was key. One has to observe, however, that there are no procedures that guarantee that such collaboration will occur in other cases. Judging from the Indian case, what is needed is a continuing working relation between regional staffs and a continuing commitment on the part of the Bank to broad-ranging country programs. Still, close collaboration is not an adequate substitute for the build-up of more expertise on the process of structural adjustment within the Fund. For no matter how good Bank-Fund collaboration, the Bank remains an "outside consultant," not a regular participant in Fund policy discussions. Ideally, if World Bank structural adjustment lending were additional, more would be done for low-income countries through the Bank than through the Fund, or there might be more parallel action that would entail both a Fund stabilization program and a longer term World Bank structural adjustment loan.

The Broader Question

Beyond the question of the effectiveness of the program, the Indian case raises the broader question of when Fund resources should be made available to countries that need medium-term balance of payments financing to enable them to make adjustments without severely cutting back on rates of growth. The United States, in abstaining on the vote on India's extended arrangement, argued that India's balance of payments position did not justify expanded access financing—or at least financing of the amount India was authorized to purchase. Approving India's EFF program, the United States held, set a wrong precedent that could threaten the Fund's liquidity position and significantly alter the character of the institution. According to the US executive director, the IMF would be moved more in the direction of a medium-term financial intermediary instead of a revolving monetary fund standing ready to provide temporary balance of payments financing on a contingent basis. There are three facets to the US argument, each of which deserves attention since each bears fundamentally on how the role of the Fund is defined.

First, the United States argued that the Fund's policy of enlarged access (which allows a country total purchases of 450 percent of quota over three successive years) applies, as stated in the agreed decision, to members "facing serious payments imbalances that are large in relation to their quotas." India, the United States said, could ease its balance of payments pressures and reduce its expected purchases from the Fund by borrowing more aggressively in the international capital markets or by pursuing a less expansionary domestic expenditure policy.

Second, the United States argued that the EFF was established, as stated in the decision, to enable the Fund to assist "an economy characterized by slow growth and an inherently weak balance of payments position which prevents pursuit of an active development policy." The Indian arrangement, which placed emphasis on an ambitious investment program, was seen by the United States to stretch that concept too far.

Third, while acknowledging that countries have been encouraged by the revised guidelines on conditionality to come early to the Fund before they are confronted with a balance of payments crisis, the United States proposed that, consistent with those guidelines, a larger proportion of the resources committed to India should have been made available on a stand-by basis with greater emphasis on the contingent nature of such resources.

The core issue that the US argument raises is whether the Fund should serve as lender of other than last resort. Despite the US contention that its own position, in defense of a last-resort role, is an effort to return the Fund to first principles, the answer to this question is not to be found in the Fund's Articles of Agreement. According to Article I, one of the purposes of the Fund is "to facilitate the expansion and balanced growth of international trade, and contribute thereby to the promotion and maintenance of high levels of employment and real income and to the development of the productive resources of all members as primary objectives of economic policy." Nowhere does it say that Fund resources should be used only if no other sources are available. The decision of when to make resources available is *a matter of policy*.

India's own point of view has been that it would rather grow less quickly than borrow what it cannot afford. Early access to expanded Fund resources gives it the possibility to adjust, grow, and avoid the political dislocations that more drastic measures, imposed under worsened conditions, would entail. This option is both in India's interest and the interest of the international economic system as a whole.

CHAPTER **21**

Turkey and the IMF: A Review of Relations, 1978–82

Osman Okyar

Turkey went through a political and economic crisis of agonizing proportions during the 1970s. Democratic processes faltered, the political authority of civilian governments weakened, and lawlessness and terrorism emerged in the cities. After 1973 left-of-center and right-of-center coalition governments succeeded one another but were unable to restore law and order, until finally the army took over power in 1980. Parallel to the growing political crisis was a deep economic crisis, which emerged in 1977. This originated from three factors: the inflationary financing of growing public sector deficits, the inefficiencies of the long-standing inward-looking development strategy, and the oil price shocks of 1973 and 1979–80.

The International Monetary Fund (IMF) became directly involved in Turkey's problems early in 1978, when the incoming left of center Ecevit coalition government decided to introduce a stabilization program and applied for a stand-by. The first section of the paper describes the two stand-bys negotiated by the Ecevit government, in 1978 and 1979, neither of which was successful in meeting the crisis. The next section of the paper examines the new stabilization policy adopted by the Demirel government which took office in November 1979, the stand-by agreement reached with the Fund in June 1980, and the subsequent complementary measures taken by the military administration in September 1980. The following section is devoted to a preliminary appraisal of the (rather successful) results of the 1980 stabilization program. The concluding section discusses whether the potentially far-reaching shift in attitudes and policies initiated in 1980 is likely to be maintained and expanded in the future.

The Stand-bys of 1978 and 1979

The economic background that led to the request for a stand-by agreement from the IMF in March 1978 by the minister of finance of the recently installed Ecevit government was very somber. In 1977, things had begun to go very badly for the Turkish economy. The rise in the wholesale price index had grown from 15.6 percent in 1976 to 24.1 percent in 1977, while in the last quarter inflation quickened to 36 percent. The situation as regards foreign exchange availability and the balance of payments had already been worsening in 1975 and 1976. In 1977, there was a dramatic turn for the worse, with a balance of payments deficit of $3,635 million, mainly due to the deterioration in the balance of trade, with strongly rising imports and falling exports. But GNP, which had continued to rise markedly in 1975 (8 percent) and 1976 (7.7 percent), rose by only around 4 percent in 1977.

The rise in GNP in 1975 and 1976 had been sustained by very large increases in the volume of short term foreign indebtedness, which had risen from the low level of $229 million in 1974, to $1,388 million in 1975 and to $3,342 million in 1976. In 1977 the amount of short-term indebtedness rose further to $6,146 million, but this figure included accumulated payment arrears to the tune of $1,580 million. This indicated the inability of the central bank to pay for the current volume of imports and raised big question marks about future economic growth.

Such was the dark economic background to the request for a stand-by agreement involving SDR 300 million for a period of two years by the incoming Ecevit government in March 1978. As stated in the Letter of Intent, the aim of the program was to bring about a sharp reduction in the current balance of payments deficit, from 7 percent of GNP in 1977 to 4 percent in 1978, through the expansion of exports that would follow the 23 percent devaluation of the Turkish currency on March 1, 1978, and through restricting the volume of imports. Parallel to the reduction in the payments deficit, the government was to control inflation by reducing the part of the public sector borrowing financed by the central bank, from 58 billion Turkish liras (TL) in 1977 to TL 38 billion, through measures involving control of budget expenditures, tax reforms, reductions in subsidies and reduced rates of growth of guaranteed prices of agricultural goods.

On April 24, 1978, the Fund accepted the request of the Turkish government to release SDR 300 million in installments over two years. It tied the right of Turkey to make purchases of SDRs to the following conditions:

- The limits established for successive periods on the ceilings of net domestic assets of the central bank and of the amounts of public sector borrowing financed by the central bank were not to be exceeded.
- The limits accepted by the Turkish government on contracting new external debts were not to be exceeded.
- No new commercial payment arrears were to be accumulated.
- A schedule would be presented by Turkey by November 1978 for the elimination of past arrears.
- The liquidity ratio of 15 percent of deposits established for commercial banks in Turkey would not be lowered.
- Turkey would not introduce new payments restrictions, multiple currency practices, or restrictions on imports and would refrain from entering into new bilateral payments agreements with Fund members.

Developments in the Turkish economy between March and September 1978 differed from the forecasts and expectations entertained in the stand-by agreement of April 1978. Although the Turkish government made an attempt in the first half of 1978 to apply stricter and better demand-management policies than previously, other unfavorable factors intervened to such an extent that the minister of finance had to write to the Fund managing director in September requesting modifications in the performance criteria and waivers for some of the rules established under the stand-by.

The principal modification concerned an increase in the ceiling for the net domestic assets of the central bank, for the period May-July 1978, from TL 224 billion to TL 229.1 billion. In addition, waivers were requested concerning the provisions disallowing new accumulations in payment arrears and new restrictions on imports. What had gone wrong?

The letter of the minister of finance, dated September 13, 1978, attributed the adverse factors to the effects of extreme shortages of imported inputs on the level of economic activity and upon public finances. The minister also referred to the problems that had arisen in Turkey's negotiations with foreign banks on rescheduling past debt.

On September 20, 1978, the Executive Board of the Fund approved the modifications requested by the Turkish government. However, the Fund's appraisal of developments in the Turkish economy and the adverse factors that had affected it in 1978 were quite different from the views put forward by the minister of finance. The Fund staff pointed out that the main reason for the poor performance of Turkish exports following the devaluation of March 1978 lay in the insufficient profitability of manufactured exports, as compared with domestic sales, rather than in the lack of needed imported inputs. The clear implication of the Fund's analysis here was that the fault lay in the rigidity of Turkish exchange rate policy, which was not corrected by the increases in export rebates introduced by the government in July. The Fund pointed out that the system of providing export subsidies on an ad hoc basis to alleviate pressures on the profitability of exports did not generate confidence on the part of exporters.

The Fund also mentioned the negative influence of the large wage settlements (between 40 percent and 80 percent) obtained by the Turkish trade unions during 1978, in spite of the government's attempts to introduce an incomes policy within a so-called social contract. These negative factors, coupled with the decline of economic activity associated with the drastic decline in imports, were responsible, in the Fund's view, for the increase in the annual rate of inflation, which jumped from 21 percent in January to 57 percent in July 1978.

Developments in the Turkish economy became even more unfavorable in the latter part of 1978 and the early months of 1979. They were marked by continued acceleration in the rate of inflation, extreme foreign exchange shortages, and the emergence of black markets and double-pricing for many goods (sugar, cigarettes, cooking oil, etc.). Petroleum shortages were also widespread and repeated. It was no surprise that the main performance criteria established in the 1978 stand-by agreement were again exceeded.

The situation took such alarming proportions at the end of 1978 that it was thought, in Turkish government quarters, that nothing short of an extraordinary rescue operation to be conducted by the Organization for Economic Cooperation and Development (OECD), on the lines of the Aid Consortium that had been set up to help Turkey in the 1960s, would rescue Turkey from the bottomless pit into which it seemed to be sinking. The leading Western countries, whose leaders met at a summit meeting in Guadaloupe in January 1979, expressed concern at the Turkish situation and readiness to contribute joint economic help of around $1 billion in 1979. Western leaders made the granting of extraordinary aid dependent, however, upon a new agreement being reached between Turkey and the IMF. It became apparent at about the same time that an agreement for rescheduling short-term credits to Turkey was also conditional on agreement being reached between Turkey and the Fund.

Although anxious to resume economic growth at the rate of 6–7 percent in 1979, the Turkish government seemed also to be aware that new measures to restrict internal demand, to control public sector borrowing from the bank and to bring the nominal value of currency more in line with its real value, would be necessary before approaching the Fund for a new stand-by to replace that of 1978, whose performance criteria had been violated. So, after passing what was proclaimed to be a restrictive consolidated budget in March 1979 and increasing somewhat the prices of petroleum and products produced by the State Economic Enterprises (SEEs), so as to yield additional annual revenues to the tune of TL 80 billion, the minister of finance had a meeting with the managing director of the Fund in Zurich in April 1979, presumably to discuss the main lines of the forthcoming stand-by agreement. This meeting had to be supplemented by another meeting, in May in Ankara, between the Turkish Prime Minister Bülent Ecevit and the director of the European Department of the Fund, and by further discussions in June in Paris, between Fund and Turkish government representatives, before the measures to be taken by the Turkish government were finalized.

The Letter of Intent dated June 30, 1979, asking for the cancellation of the two year stand-by agreement of 1978 and the approval of a one year stand-by to the amount of SDR 250 million, began by mentioning the factors that were considered to have prevented the realization of the previous program. The problem created by the excessive accumulation of foreign short-term debt under the Demirel government in 1975–77 was again mentioned. The government also blamed more recent events, such as adverse movements in the terms of trade and difficulties encountered in finding new financing abroad.

The minister of finance declared that a new stabilization program had been launched early in 1979, the aims of which were to increase self-reliance and to strengthen the economy. He pointed out that another devaluation had been put into effect on June 11, 1979, lowering the value of the Turkish currency by 43.7 percent, from TL 26.5 = $1 to TL 47.1 = $1. However, the new exchange regime involved a multiple currency system, because foreign exchange proceeds from the export of agricultural goods enjoying domestic price support and foreign exchange purchases for the imports of petroleum and chemical inputs for the manufacture of fertilizers would be valued at the rate of TL 35 = $1.

The program also involved a small rise of 5.5 percent in the deposit and lending rates of commercial banks. In the monetary field, the government fixed new ceilings on net domestic assets of the central bank and on net central bank credit to the public sector. The government made a passing reference to the major problem of internal wage increases, by mentioning that salary increases of public employees would be kept at 20 percent in 1979 and that guidelines established in the social contract of 1978 as regards wage increases in the rest of the economy would be enforced. The government declared its determination to slow down the rate of inflation without mentioning any figures, and expected that the current account deficit in the balance of payments in 1979 and 1980 would be of the same order of magnitude as in 1978, namely around $1.8 billion.

The Fund approved the new stand-by in July 1979, thus giving the green light for the application of the OECD package of aid of around $1 billion and for the agreement with foreign banks on debt rescheduling, which also involved fresh credits to the tune of $400 million. The stand-by also opened the way to various World Bank project credits and to a program credit of $150 million. The Fund staff's appraisal of the 1979 stabilization policy was positive, though reserved and cautious.

When reviewing the unsuccessful outcome of the 1978 program, the Fund's evaluation was again quite different from the government's diagnosis. The Fund thought that the failure to adjust domestic financial policies and to accept a flexible exchange rate had been the principal causes of failure. The severely restrictive stance in public sector finances that was necessary had not been realized, thus leading to the central bank's greatly exceeding the stand-by performance criteria.

As regards the new stabilization policy of 1979, and the new performance criteria and ceilings laid down by the government, the Fund's opinion was that the new ceilings could be realized only with a reduction in the annual rate of growth of the main target variable—namely reserve money—from the levels of around 60–70 percent recently observed, to 50 percent by the end of 1979, and to 32 percent by the end of the stand-by.

The Fund thought that the realization of the objectives for foreign economic relations depended upon strict observance of domestic monetary ceilings and a restructuring of the Turkish economy toward increasing production for exports. The achievement of reasonable wage settlements was another essential condition of success.

In conclusion, the Fund drew attention to the difficult political decisions necessary for success. It thought that the new program recognized the urgency of restructuring the economy in favor of export growth, and that it constituted a break with the past, deserving of Fund support.

The outcome of the 1979 stabilization program, although backed by the IMF agreement of July 1979 and the OECD package deal, was again unsuccessful, both in the internal and in the external economic fields. Internally, the government seemed unable to apply a restrictive stance in public sector finances and in the money supply, while wage settlements continued their uncontrolled upward course. Both the annual rates of growth and the absolute amounts of central bank credits to the public sector and the volume of bank notes in circulation increased very significantly in 1979. Thus, central bank credits to the public sector increased by TL 96 billion in 1979 (61 percent), while in 1978 they had increased by TL 36 billion (30 percent). The increase in bank notes in circulation in 1979 was TL 70 billion, representing a rate of increase of 61 percent over 1978 (end of period), while in 1978 the rate of increase had been 46 percent.

Consequently, in 1979 the annual rate of inflation, as reflected in the wholesale price index of the Ministry of Commerce, jumped to 81 percent from 51 percent in 1978. In the last quarter of 1979, net domestic assets of the central bank were dangerously close to the limits set in the stand-by agreement. Dangers loomed ahead as regards the observance of limits for the third tranche, November 1979 to February 1980. Without large increases in the prices of various subsidized products, the observance of limits seemed impossible.

Externally, the value of exports in 1979, $2,261 million, showed practically no change from 1978 ($2,288 million), while the value of imports increased from $4,599 million in 1978 to $5,067 million in 1979.

Growing inflation and the ensuing disruption of the economy must have played an important part in the heavy electoral defeat of the left-of-center Republican People's Party in the partial elections of October 1979, which led to the resignation of the Ecevit government and the formation of a minority government by Süleyman Demirel, leader of the right-of-center Justice Party in November 1979.

What lessons and conclusions can be drawn from the experiences of the successive and unsuccessful stabilization policies under the two stand-by agreements of 1978 and 1979? What were the attitudes of each side on the basic issues?

Obviously, a successful stabilization required a correct diagnosis of the crisis and a willingness and ability by the government to take appropriate decisions. The IMF's role and influence consisted in appraising the crisis as objectively as possible and formulating policy advice and performance criteria that were reasonable within the political and economic constraints in Turkey, but adequate to restore the situation and prepare the way for future growth.

As regards the government's approach to the problem, it appears that the political views and the ideological complexion of the left-of-center Ecevit government created almost insurmountable barriers in the way of arriving at a correct diagnosis of the situation, let alone taking decisive measures to counter it. The Ecevit government appeared convinced of the paramount virtues of government intervention in the economy, in the form of creating state economic enterprises or of intervening in the market mechanism, either directly or through subsidies. In addition, it was emotionally inclined towards a self-sufficient, even autarkic view of economic development, which restricted to a minimum the foreign role in the economy. The People's Republican Party had, in recent years, espoused undefined causes and slogans, such as total economic independence and anti-imperialism. The necessity of resorting to IMF cooperation and advice when the Party assumed power early in 1978 made the Ecevit government extremely uneasy and unhappy, since this went against its own convictions and embarrassed it in the eyes of its supporters.

It is clear that there existed a fundamental divergence of views as to the nature of Turkey's economic crisis and the measures appropriate to correct it, between the Turkish government and the IMF, right from the time the first stand-by was negotiated in March 1978. In the Turkish government's view, there was nothing structurally wrong with the Turkish economy or with the economic development policies followed in Turkey between 1960 and 1978. The causes of the crisis in foreign payments and the quickening trend in inflation that arose in the middle of 1977 were ascribed to the faulty—but quickly repairable—policies, and the events mentioned above. Correspondingly, all that was needed to restore the situation was additional foreign financing and the rescheduling of short-term foreign debts to help the balance of payments, and a period of restraint in public sector finances to control internal inflation.

The Fund's view, on the other hand, though expressed very guardedly at first (but increasingly openly as time went by and stabilization faltered), was that structural adjustments implying long-term changes in economic policies were necessary, in addition to purely monetary measures, to restore the Turkish economy. The Fund constantly referred in its reports to the necessity of correcting the long-standing bias in past policies in favor of imports and against exports, and argued for restructuring the economy toward export production. The Fund had in mind reforms to eliminate differentials in internal and external price movements, and greater reliance on the market mechanism in the commodity and monetary markets in Turkey.

The fundamental difference in the approach of the two sides can perhaps be summed up as follows: the Fund believed that, given the right policies and incentives, the Turkish economy possessed the potential for large increases in exports of goods and services that would eventually eliminate chronic deficits in the balance of payments, while the Ecevit government was deeply pessimistic about the possibilities of increasing exports and orienting the economy outward, and therefore considered increased foreign assistance as the only way out.

A typical example of the attitude of the Ecevit government toward the issues outlined above is the speech delivered by Ziya Müezzinoglu, the minister of finance of the Ecevit government, at a time when it became apparent that the second stand-by agreement was faltering, on the occasion of the annual Fund–World Bank meeting in Belgrade in October 1979. In his speech, Müezzinoglu criticized the IMF and the World Bank for applying to international problems 30-year-old formulas that had outlived their usefulness in the changed conditions of the present. He spoke about the limits imposed by oil price increases and by protectionist policies of industrial countries upon the foreign purchasing power of the non-oil developing countries. He asked the IMF and the World Bank to do more to help the non-oil developing countries to create a capacity to withstand present world economic conditions.[1]

In view of such a fundamental divergence of views, it is not surprising that the stand-by by agreements of 1978 and 1979 failed. Apart from the basic problems of restructuring the economy, the Ecevit government had also failed in internal monetary policy, partly because of its weak political position, and partly because of indecisiveness and delay. The record of the Ecevit government with respect to stabilization can be summed up as having done "too little, too late."

The 1980 Stand-by

When Süleyman Demirel formed a minority government in November 1979, he knew only too well the extent of the problems he would be facing in the fields of restoring law and order and rehabilitating the economy. After taking office, he appointed Turgut Özal—who had served under him as planning under secretary in the late 1960s and had subsequently worked in the private sector as a coordinator and economic advisor to Turkish holding companies—as planning under secretary. Demirel understood that economic recovery depended on winning back the confidence of Western economic institutions, and on taking bold and comprehensive measures to reduce the public sector deficit drastically and to impress upon the Turkish people the dimensions of the problem.

[1] Speech of the Minister of Finance at Belgrade IMF meeting, 5 October 1979 (Ankara: ANKA Agency).

Good relations with the IMF were crucial because the first step toward recovery lay in financing the minimum level of imports required for a reasonable level of activity in Turkey. However, relations with the IMF continued to be sensitive, especially with a segment of Turkish public opinion. Moreover, this was an issue that was likely to be exploited by the former prime minister after his return to opposition.

What was the least harmful and most effective way of approaching the IMF? The 1979 stand-by agreement was likely soon to run into trouble, and very large increases in subsidized prices, together with a drastic devaluation, appeared inevitable.

One possible approach would have been to proceed under the old stand-by negotiated by Ecevit and take the unpopular measures required to remain within its performance criteria. Another would have been to let the existing stand-by go quietly by default, take the drastic economic decisions required independently of the IMF, and subsequently open new negotiations with the IMF toward a new stand-by agreement. Psychologically and politically, Demirel was in favor of the second alternative. He understood that to deal with inflation, a one-blow psychological shock delivered to the bewildered and suffering public would be a sound beginning. Moreover, it would be to the government's political advantage if stabilization policy were seen to have been decided upon independently by the Turkish government. Thus, after forming his government in November 1979, Demirel played it cool and began preparing the set of measures to be subsequently known as the January 24, 1980, package. He maintained contact with the IMF through his officials, when an IMF team visited Turkey at the beginning of December 1979, on a routine trip to discuss the economic situation. Subsequently, he sent Turgut Özal to Washington to discuss with the Fund the outlines of his new stabilization package and a new stand-by agreement. Özal's mission was to relay to the IMF the message that determined and comprehensive measures were to be taken against inflation, measures that would definitely constitute a break with the past and mark the beginning of a new phase in Turkey. It seems that the IMF responded favorably to Demirel's overture, and in reply stressed the importance of the following points in a future program:

- the introduction of a flexible and realistic exchange policy
- the adjustment of interest rates to allow a positive real rate to emerge for time deposits
- the introduction of more liberal import policies to replace rigid and quantitative forms of protection and import licensing.

The IMF also indicated that price subsidies and below cost pricing by the SEEs should be terminated.

Özal responded by indicating the government's intention to carry out a large devaluation soon that would leave the exchange rate undervalued (without, however, mentioning any figures). He promised that in the future exchange rate policy would be flexible and competitive, and he explained the market-oriented approach of the new government.

After Özal's return from Washington, a very small team of experts worked in Ankara—in secret—on the preparation of the new economic measures. These were finally made public on January 24, 1980, and described to the press by Süleyman Demirel in a series of press conferences held in Ankara on January 27.

A first set of measures concerned foreign economic relations. The key measure was devaluation of the Turkish currency from $1 = TL 47 to $1 = TL 70, a devaluation of the order of 48 percent. The new rate was to apply to all sales and purchases of foreign exchange, except with regard to imports of inputs for fertilizers and agricultural chemicals, where the rate was $1 = TL 55. Further, exports of agricultural goods benefiting from government price-support programs (wheat, tobacco, cotton, dried fruits, etc.) were subject to the payment of a levy per quantity or value exported, the level of which was determined by the newly established Money and Credit Committee. The proceeds from such levies would be deposited in a fund, to be established with the central bank, and to be used to finance subsidies for agricultural inputs and for general export subsidies. The government also decreed that the stamp duty of 25 percent on the value of imports was reduced to 1 percent, to reduce the impact of devaluation on import prices. Finally, the government moved in the direction of a more flexible exchange rate policy by giving authority to the Ministry of Finance to fix the exchange rate, after consultation with the central bank, through simple communiques.

A second set of measures concerned internal prices. Huge subsidies on fertilizers were drastically curtailed, resulting in a 500 percent increase in the selling price. Süleyman Demirel, in one of his press conferences[2] explained that the total value of supplying, partly through internal production and partly through imports, 9 million tons of fertilizer to Turkish farmers was around TL 90 billion, only TL 10 billion of which were covered by sales proceeds at previous prices.

[2] See Süleyman Demirel, Istikrar Tedbirleri: Press Conferences, 27–28–29 January 1980, Prime Ministry, Ankara.

The price increase would halve the subsidy, with the remaining TL 40 billion covered through levies on agricultural exports. The other large subsidy was on petroleum products. With consumption of 18.5 million tons of petroleum products in 1980, the annual subsidy involved was estimated at some TL 160 billion at pre-January 24 prices. Drastic rises in sales prices were announced to eliminate this subsidy altogether.

Similarly, losses made by state enterprises on the basis of existing prices—in the fields of electricity, iron and steel, paper, cement, sugar, monopoly products and postal services—were also to be wiped out by price increases. On the other hand, the increases decreed in prices and fares in coal, railways, and shipping aimed only at reducing the subsidies or losses involved. This distinction in the treatment of subsidies was made on the basis of a new definition of "basic" goods, meaning goods or services, with prices fixed on social grounds by the Council of Ministers, leaving the prices of other goods produced by state economic enterprises to be determined in line with market trends. Demirel announced that the total expected value of the subsidies or losses eliminated by the price increases decreed on January 24 stood at around TL 290 billion for 1980, while the deficit that still remained to be covered amounted to TL 62 billion.

The January 24 package also abolished the Committee for Price Control within the Ministry of Industry, which had formerly been controlling the prices of manufactured products produced by private sector firms. The abolition of price controls in the private sector was aimed at giving room to market forces and removing black markets and double-pricing practices. The package also included small increases in the legal structure of interest rates chargeable on bank credits and payable on bank deposits, which brought the average interest rates on two-year credits to 22 percent and the interest on 12-month time deposits to 20 percent.

A third set of measures involved institutional changes. These involved the creation of a Money and Credit Committee under the chairmanship of the under secretary to the prime minister and composed of the planning, finance, and commerce under secretaries, the head of economic planning in the State Planning Organization (SPO), the general secretary for international cooperation in the Ministry of Finance, the governor of the central bank, and the director of revenue in the Ministry of Finance. The committee was charged with coordinating monetary and credit policies, with making recommendations in the field of agricultural support prices, and with examining developments in the balance of payments. The committee was given the authority to take decisions on certain matters outside the prerogative of the Council of Ministers.

Authority as regards foreign investment, which formerly had been divided among the ministries of Finance, Industry, and Commerce, and the SPO was unified within a single department attached to the prime minister's office. Fields open to foreign investment and the conditions attached to it were redefined openly, in a more liberal direction. The participation of foreign companies in the exploration for petroleum in Turkey was encouraged by allowing such companies to keep 35 percent of the petroleum discovered and produced.

This has been a summary description of the January 24 measures that were discussed and explained by Demirel over television and in the series of press conferences.

It was to be expected that these measures, which brought large sacrifices to the public in the shape of price increases caused by the elimination of subsidies and a drastic devaluation, and which also signified a reversal of government interventionism, would be the subject of angry comments by the left-wing press and of criticism made with regard to the supposed role of the Fund in the above package.

During the press conference, some journalists referred to the allegations put forward by Ecevit in his recent press conference to the effect that domestic and foreign interest groups were behind the January 24 package. Some journalists asked questions as regards the role of the IMF in the package. Demirel answered that his government had not acted under dictation from any side and that the January 24 package had been the government's own decision, made in the light of Turkey's conditions and requirements. Demirel added that Ecevit was under an obsession about plots hatched up by interest groups. The problem was to increase Turkey's foreign exchange earnings, and if Ecevit knew a more effective way of achieving this, he should explain it openly. As regards relations with the IMF, he simply stated that Turkey had to find new sources of foreign financing in the coming years, and that his government would approach all relevant institutions, such as the IMF, the World Bank, and the OECD.

I turn now to the talks that began in February 1980 between the Turkish representatives and international bodies such as the OECD and the IMF. These negotiations finally culminated in the signature of a new stand-by agreement in June 1980.

In February 1980, conversations took place over debt rescheduling and future concessionary finance between Turkish government representatives and the OECD. The Turks explained the new stabilization approach and expressed the hope that, under the new program, equilibrium would be achieved in the current account of the balance of payments within five years. Concessionary finance from the OECD would be required during this period. As regards official debts to OECD countries, the Turks asked for a grace period of five years, during which debt and interest repayments would stop. The OECD agreed to a three-year grace period, but added a goodwill clause stating that if relations between the IMF and Turkey proceeded satisfactorily, the grace period would be extended to five years. As regards new concessionary finance, the OECD asked for agreement to be reached between Turkey and the IMF before the release of the OECD assistance package.

In March 1980, talks were held between Turgut Özal and A. C. Woodward from the IMF. In line with its previous analysis of Turkish problems, the IMF was leaning toward a stand-by agreement of three year's duration, since in the Fund's view Turkey's problems were structural as well as monetary in character. The Fund thought that Turkey should maintain strict financial discipline over three years, during which the adjustments necessary to orient the Turkish economy outward would take place. After some hesitation, the Turks agreed to a long stand-by. So, for the first time in the history of the Fund, a three-year stand-by was accepted in principle.

During these preliminary discussions, two issues essential to the stabilization program were discussed between the Fund and Turkish representatives. The first issue was future interest policy. In Turkey bank deposits and lending rates had been determined by the government since the interventionist stance began in the early 1930s. With the annual inflation rate climbing from 25 percent in 1977 to over 80 percent in 1979, the nominal legal rates of interest had turned into high negative real interest rates, in spite of the limited legal increases that had been made. The demand for credit had to be rationed by banks through various practices, which amounted to double-pricing for credit. On the other hand, negative real rates strongly discouraged saving in the form of money and led to the diversion of savings toward real estate and gold. Clearly, the control of inflation and the establishment of more rational portfolio distribution patterns depended on action being taken in the field of interest. This issue was raised by the Fund, which thought that the small rise in legal rates allowed by the January 24 package had been quite insufficient. The Fund asked the Turkish authorities to allow for the emergence of positive real interest rates on time deposits. The Turks were not yet ready for such drastic action, which reversed the practices of 50 years: they argued that money illusion was still strong in Turkey, and that the Turkish people's Islamic tradition weakened belief in interest rates.

The Turks further argued that drastic action in this field should wait until black markets and double-pricing in commodities had been eliminated.

Another key unresolved issue had been the continued large rises in nominal wages since 1977. Between the periods 1970–72 and 1977–79, the average real wage of organized workers belonging to social insurance rose by 37 percent, while during the same time interval the average real salary of government employees fell by 26 percent.[3] This very significant shift in the distribution of income constituted an important economic factor behind the inflationary spiral, as well as a social phenomenon of great importance in a country where the bureaucracy had traditionally played the leading role.

As mentioned above, the Ecevit government had tried to introduce a social contract between employers and workers, who were to be brought together by the government to establish guidelines for wage increases. These had remained empty promises in the conditions of growing anarchy prevailing in the late 1970s, when the left-wing revolutionary trade union DISK was leading moves toward annual wage increases averaging 60–70 percent. The problems of controlling wage increases as well as putting an end to strikes and illegal work stoppages that paralyzed the economy were among the key elements of stabilization. However, the armory of weapons available to democratic governments operating within the constantly weakening parliamentary framework was quite insufficient to deal with the problem. When the IMF raised this matter in the preliminary discussions, the Turkish representatives replied that a committee attached to the prime minister's office had been formed with the function of laying down guidelines for wages. The question would be solved within the free, democratic collective bargaining framework. The Turks also argued that incomes policy was not such a critical element of stabilization, and that raising production levels toward capacity was more important for the success of the operation.

The negotiations between the Turkish government and the Fund developed satisfactorily, until the signature on June 18, 1980, of a stand-by agreement for the release of SDR 1.25 billion in installments over three years. This amount constituted the highest credit extended so far by the IMF and represented 6.5 times the Turkish quota.

[3] State Planning Organization, quoted by the World Bank Survey, Turkey, Public Sector Investment Review, Statistical Annex, December 1981, Washington.

Although the text of the Turkish government's Letter of Intent and of the three-year stand-by agreement have not been made public, it is known that the agreement contained the usual performance criteria in the form of limits assigned to the growth of net domestic assets of the central bank and of the net borrowings from the central bank by the public sector. It also contained undertakings not to introduce new multiple currency practices, to liberalize imports as soon as the foreign exchange situation permitted, and not to allow the accumulation of new payments arrears.

As regards monetary policy and the level of interest rates, the Turkish government promised to raise nominal rates of interest for medium-term time bank deposits to levels representing a positive real interest rate within two years. As regards the interest rates on credits payable by SEEs, the Turkish government accepted a rise from 1 percent to 10 percent per annum. On the suggestion of the Fund, the deposits to be made in the central bank by commercial banks, against increases in their own deposits, were maintained at 30 percent for time deposits and at 35 percent for sight deposits, and the banks' liquidity requirement was kept at 15 percent of deposits. The Fund considered these provisions necessary for continued monetary discipline. Another Fund suggestion in the monetary field had been that central bank credits should no longer be directed almost wholly to financing the public sector but should also contribute to financing the private sector, through the banks. This was agreed to by the Turks, who said this was already implied in the provisions that the central bank would henceforth finance no state enterprise except the Meat and Fish Corporation and the Office for the Products of the Soil.

In the Letter of Intent, the Turkish government indicated its intention to adopt institutional measures taken under the January 24 package, such as the creation of the Money and Credit Committee, the unification of foreign investment and of export promotion agencies under the prime minister's office, and the liberalization of petroleum exploration. Finally, the Letter of Intent contained the usual statement about the passage of a tax reform bill through parliament.

The signature of the stand-by in June 1980 was quickly followed (unexpected by the IMF) by a sweeping liberalization on July 1, 1980, of the deposit and lending rates of commercial banks. At one stroke, the government freed the determination of such rates from official control and left them to market forces. The main commercial banks soon came together to work out a gentlemen's agreement among themselves over the various deposit and lending rates, with the result that gross interest rates for time deposits shot up to around 60–70 percent, while net rates, after tax, moved to 45–50 percent per year.

Sight deposit rates increased slightly from 3–5 percent per year. Bank lending rates for ordinary commercial credit increased from around 25 percent to over 60 percent per year. The freeing of interest rates in Turkey came as a great shock to a public long accustomed to consider costs and returns with regard to borrowing and lending money as negligible. This move brought about deep changes in asset distribution behavior, the consequences of which still reverberate through the economy.

The courageous steps taken in January and July 1980 could not, however, save the life of the Demirel government, which came to an end on September 12, 1980, when the military dissolved parliament and suspended all civilian political institutions, in order to put an end to growing anarchy and terrorism. This development at first created uncertainty within the Fund as to the fate of the stabilization policy and of the stand-by agreement of June 1980. The Fund and Demirel's economic team had built up a good relationship. Would the new military administration continue the program, or would it change men and policies?

Uncertainties were dispelled with the formation of the cabinet by the Military Council, in which Turgut Özal, the principal architect of stabilization under Demirel, was appointed deputy prime minister in charge of economic affairs. This signified that the economic team that had successfully prepared and begun to implement stabilization under the stand-by agreement would be kept in charge of economic policy. In fact, it soon transpired that the military takeover, far from creating changes in economic direction, would bring about the consolidation and strengthening of the stabilization-cum-adjustment policies initiated by Demirel.

Apart from taking major decisions in the key fields of incomes policy and fiscal policy, the military government put a brake on certain dangerous developments, which had begun to surface under Demirel, as regards decisions about support levels of agricultural prices. Demirel had been keen to bring about the early dissolution of parliament and hold a new general election to gain a majority for his Justice Party. With an eye over this eventuality, Demirel had, just prior to the September 12 military takeover, accepted a substantial increase in the level of agricultural support prices for tea and hazelnuts, against the views of the team in charge of economic affairs. Politically motivated decisions in this key field ceased after September 12.

There were also actions of crucial importance in the fields of wage settlements and taxation, which complemented the January package and brought consistency to the whole program. After assuming power, the Military Council banned strikes, closed down the revolutionary trade union DISK, and suspended trade union activities and wage negotiations under collective bargaining. Under a law passed on December 27, 1980, a High Arbitration Council, under the chairmanship of a judge from the appeals court and composed of representatives of employers and workers, was set up to determine wages, in lieu of previous collective agreements. Wages were to be determined according to such criteria as prevailing economic conditions, changes in the cost of living, and the course of incomes other than wages. In effect, all wage increases during 1981 were referred to the Arbitration Council. Although no precise figures are available, it has been estimated that the average increase in nominal wages allowed during 1981 was around 25 percent, a far cry from the annual levels of 60–70 percent prevailing in earlier years, but roughly equal in percentage terms to the increase in the salaries of government officials brought about by changes in the income tax brackets introduced by the taxation laws of February 1981. Alongside wage restraint, the military also passed a decree preventing firms from discharging workers, as a social measure against unemployment.

The tax reform law enacted in February 1981 was aimed, on the one side, at considerably increasing tax revenues through various measures restricting tax exemption or threshold figures for groups such as agriculture, the professional classes, artisans, self-employed workers, etc. Absolute taxes were greatly increased, and a prepayment system was introduced for a number of taxes. On the other side, the tax reforms aimed at a more equitable distribution of the tax burden by changing the income tax brackets and rates, which had been completely distorted by the inflation of recent years. The budget expenditures for 1981–82 were prepared carefully with a view to avoiding additional increases during the budget year. Tax reforms were calculated to produce increases in tax revenues of around 80 percent, from TL 748 billion in 1980–81 to around TL 1,350 billion in 1981–82. With the addition of nontax revenues and of proceeds from special accounts, budget revenues in 1981–82 were estimated to fall short of planned budget expenditures (TL 1,630 billion) by only around TL 50 billion, representing 2.9 percent of total expenditures. This percentage is to be compared with 11.3 percent in 1980–81.

The other main developments since September 12, 1980, that were directly related to the stand-by agreement were the successive moves toward import liberalization in 1981 and 1982 and the decision in May 1981 to transfer to the central bank the authority to fix daily the value of the Turkish currency in terms of foreign currencies. Under this flexible exchange rate system, the value of the dollar, fixed at TL 70 in January 1980, gradually rose to TL 145 in February 1982.

In sum, Turkish governments have since January 24, 1980, followed strictly restrictive monetary policies, relying more and more on free market mechanisms in the internal and external economic fields, with the significant results to be described in the next section of this paper.

The above policies have been harshly and totally condemned in Turkey by radical-wing economists, who had been mostly supporting or executing the interventionist, autarkic, inward-looking policies symbolized by the third and fourth five-year development plans, and by politicians, such as former Prime Minister Bülent Ecevit. These criticisms have taken various shapes, including the accusation that the policies had been conceived by foreign international organizations (such as the IMF) and dictated without proper regard to Turkey's economic and social conditions. Turkish policy has also been labeled a blind imitation of Friedman's monetary model, or accused of taking its inspiration from South American economic and political models, with Chile or Brazil being variously mentioned as the master type. Accusations of soaking the poor in order to help the rich have been made.

The above criticisms have largely failed, I think, to carry weight and conviction with Turkish public opinion, for the following reasons:

- No real alternative policy has been put forward by the critics to rescue Turkey from its perilous state. The critics have refrained from openly suggesting a return to the policies of the late 1970s, since the disastrous results of such policies were too evident and too recent to be forgotten by the Turkish people.
- The serious deterioration in income distribution in Turkey was brought about by the inflationary policies of 1977–80 and not by the stabilization policy of January 24.
- The fact that most of the critics, and above all ex-Prime Minister Ecevit, had themselves requested in the recent past the cooperation of the IMF, involved them in a contradiction when they criticized foreign interference and dictation. This made their criticism appear biased and politically motivated.

Stabilization in 1980–81

It was impossible for substantial results to emerge within the climate of anarchy and terrorism that continued to prevail until September 12, 1980. The other reasons why economic results were slow to appear and why the rate of inflation witnessed still another big jump in the

Istanbul Chamber of Commerce wholesale index (to 90 percent in 1980) were twofold: (1) the reversal of the accelerating inflationary trend required measures such as another large devaluation and large price increases in subsidized products, which themselves were bound to produce a one-time high increase in prices; (2) key anti-inflationary measures, such as tax reforms and incomes policy, could only come into effect in 1981.

In real terms, the situation continued to be unfavorable in 1980, with GNP falling again by 1.1 percent over 1979, mainly as the direct and induced results of a fall of 5.5 percent in net industrial output, only partially offset by an increase of 1.7 percent in agricultural value added. The investment climate also deteriorated, with a fall of 10 percent in real investment, due to a sharp decrease in private investment accompanied by a slight fall in public investment.

Monetary developments were also unfavorable. The consolidated 1980–81 budget registered a record deficit of TL 139 billion, which had to be mostly financed from the central bank (TL 103 billion). The consolidated current position of the operational state enterprises improved somewhat, since their gross annual loss fell from TL 71 billion in 1979 to TL 22 billion in 1980. However, an increase in their fixed investment and a very large increase in their stocks led to a rise in required outside financing.

Total central bank credits to the economy increased from TL 382 billion in 1979 to TL 655 billion in 1980, an increase of around 70 percent. Consequently, the volume of bank notes in circulation increased by 52 percent, and total money supply by 58 percent.

Positive developments in foreign trade and in the balance of payments remained rather limited, with the exception of a surge in imports from TL 5 billion in 1979 to TL 7.7 billion in 1980, made possible by the resumption of transfer payments abroad by the central bank on the basis of the foreign credits that became available in 1980. The main factor behind the big increase in imports was the necessity of filling accumulated backlogs in the supply of imported inputs such as fuel and intermediate goods. The new measures, including devaluation, taken to encourage exports in 1980 had positive but quite limited effects. The value of total exports increased by 31 percent over 1979 and, significantly, exports of industrial products advanced by 36 percent for the first time since 1974. In invisibles there were also positive but limited developments, in items such as workers remittances and net factor service income. The main item in the capital account of the balance of payments was foreign borrowing by the public sector of $2,389 million, coupled with net drawing from the IMF of $423 million, to finance a current account deficit of $3,196 million.

The year 1981 was the first in which the full effects of the stabilization program became visible. There was, first, spectacular success in slowing down inflation. The annual rate of inflation, according to the Istanbul Chamber of Commerce index for wholesale prices, came down from 90 percent in 1980 to 35 percent in 1981. What were the main factors behind this achievement?

On the supply side, real GNP increased in 1981 by 4.4 percent, the first gain in three years. The prime factor behind the increase was the rise in value added by industry (including mining and public utilities) of 7.2 percent. This was accompanied by an increase of 4 percent in the value added of the service sector. On the other hand, net output in agriculture and in construction showed no change over 1980.

The SPO's estimates for total investment in 1981 indicate a rise of 5.5 percent. Total fixed capital investment increased by 9.3 percent, with private sector investments increasing slowly by 6 percent and public investments by 11.6 percent. There was a decrease of 12 percent in stocks, especially marked in the public sector, where stocks were very high.

Two factors, working in opposite directions, were influencing capacity utilization in industry: the fall in demand induced by monetary policy on one side, and the improvements in the supply of inputs, especially imported inputs, on the other.

The principal monetary developments behind the slow-down of inflation were:

- The reduction in the overall deficit of the public sector, which very considerably decreased the borrowing requirements of the public sector from the central bank and resulted directly in the decrease in monetary expansion.
- The freeing of interest rates in July 1980, which led to the emergence of positive real rates of interest for time deposits and to competition among banks for deposits. This changed the public's behavior as regards its asset portfolio, with a shift in favor of holding money balances, and away from holding durable goods and real assets.
- The maintenance by the central bank of high liquidity and reserve requirements against increases in deposits with commercial banks.

As a result of the shrinkage in the overall public sector deficit and the limited demands of the private sector, total credits extended by the central bank rose only by 27 percent in 1981. The volume of bank notes in circulation increased by 26 percent and the volume of money

TABLE 21.1 TURKEY: FOREIGN TRADE, 1980 AND 1981
(billion dollars)

Item	*1980*	*1981*	*Percentage change*
Imports	7.9	8.9	+13
Petroleum	3.89	3.85	−1
Exports	2.9	4.7	+62
Balance	−5.0	−4.2	−16

Source: Figures quoted by Osman Siklar, governor of the central bank, in an interview published by *Tercüman*, 3 March 1982.

supply (M1) by 22 percent. The emergence of positive interest rates for time deposits brought about a significant change in the pattern of bank deposits. While total deposits increased by around TL 542 billion (72 percent), the bulk of the increase (TL 457 billion) went into time deposits, which increased by 270 percent. In spite of high interest rates, the total demand for credit from the banking system remained strong, leading to an expansion in the volume of credits extended by the commercial banks of TL 562 billion (60 percent). Banks were faced, for the first time in their history, by strong competition in the fields of deposits with nonbank financial establishments, which collected and lent, during 1981, sums variously estimated at between TL 150 billion and TL 200 billion.

In terms of foreign economic relations, the flexible exchange rate policy applied since May 1981 has undoubtedly been the main factor behind the favorable developments in this field. It contributed to the establishment of competitive conditions for Turkish exports, especially manufactured exports, by neutralizing differential price movements in Turkey and abroad. Another important factor was the liberalization of imports, with consequent favorable effects on the supply of inputs to Turkish industry. There were also other factors, such as export incentives, including tax rebates and export credits at a preferential interest rate.

Imports continued their upward movement in 1981, while exports showed a dramatic increase, as summarized in Table 21.1. Note the absolute reduction in the import bill for crude petroleum and petroleum products. The main factor behind this fall was a reduction of 500,000 tons in Turkey's annual consumption of petroleum products, which resulted from the removal of subsidies.

Turning to exports, the main factor behind their dramatic rise in 1981 was the rise of industrial exports, which increased by 120 percent during the period January-November 1981 over the corresponding

TABLE 21.2 TURKEY: CHANGES IN SELECTED INVISIBLES, 1980–81 (million dollars)

Item	*1980*	*1981*	*Percentage change*
Workers remittances	2,100	2,500	+20
Net earnings of tourism	212	278	+30
Other invisibles[a]	245	530	+116
Interest on foreign debt[a]	−578	−960	
Balance on invisibles[a]	1,695	2,071	

a. January–November in each year.

period of 1980, while the increase in agricultural exports was 38 percent.[4] Thus, for the first time in the republic's history, the share of industrial products (47.6 percent) was almost equal to the share of agricultural products (48.1 percent). A marked change in the destination of exports was also noticeable, with the share of exports going to the OECD area declining from 65.5 percent in 1980 to 47.9 percent, while the share of exports to "other" countries (mostly Middle Eastern countries) increased from 17 percent in 1980 to 41 percent in 1981 (during the periods January to September).[5]

Although complete figures for the balance of payments in 1981 have not yet been released, it is possible to give some information from the scattered data available. These indicate that favorable movements occurred in invisibles during 1981, with the result that the current account balance of payments deficit was reduced by 40 percent over 1980, declining fron $3.29 billion to $1.97 billion in 1981. The main developments in invisibles are recorded in Table 21.2.

The improvement in the balance of payments in 1981 is also apparent from Turkish foreign debt repayments (principal and interest) of $1.7 billion in 1981, against $1.2 billion in 1980; and from the increase in gross Turkish foreign exchange reserves to over $2 billion—despite the fact that the realized international public financing flows fell much below what had been expected.

It is clear that the results of the stabilization policy initiated in January 1980 and supported by the stand-by agreement of June 1980

[4] *Quarterly Economic Report*, October–December 1981 (Ankara: Union of Chambers of Commerce anad Industry, 1982).

[5] 1981 Sonlarina Dogru Ekonomik Durum (Ankara: Union of Chambers of Commerce and Industry, 1981).

have been very significant. Although we shall have to wait until the end of 1983 before passing final judgment on the policies, it is possible to put forward an interim appraisal and evaluation of the role of the IMF.

I think it can be said that without the support of the IMF it would have been impossible to register the results achieved so far. It is theoretically conceivable that by extremely strict financial and economic discipline Turkey could have reached similar results over a much longer period of time by herself, but only at the cost of extraordinary hardships, which might have been politically impossible to inflict on the people. The key role of the IMF in stabilizing national economies and in the development process comes out clearly in the Turkish experience since 1978. The availability of outside financing—whether in the form of public credits from OECD governments and the World Bank or in the form of private bank or market loans—depended critically on an agreement of views, policies, and objectives between the Turkish government and the IMF, as symbolized by the signature and effective prosecution of the policies agreed in stand-by agreements. It is clear that recovery from the economic chaos and disruption that began with the payments crisis of 1977 depended on financing the minimum level of imports necessary for the operation of the economy.

Stabilization under the stand-by agreements of 1978 and 1979 failed principally because there was a fundamental divergence of views between the Turkish government and the IMF on the need to take actions toward outward orientation. The second cause of failure lay in the fact that stabilization policies were not pursued with enough determination and persistence to achieve results. The IMF showed flexibility in its conditionality when it agreed to waive conditions under the 1978 stand-by, and subsequently when it agreed to scrap the 1978 stand-by altogether and replace it with the new agreement of 1979.

A different atmosphere prevailed in the relations between the IMF and the Turkish government after the third stand-by of 1980. The initial drastic steps taken by the Demirel government in January 1980 proved its determination to proceed with stabilization and its dedication to the long-run objective of outward adjustment. This approach led to an agreement between the IMF and the Turkish government on monetary policy and on longer term structural adjustments. Subsequent steps, such as the freeing of interest rates, went beyond what the IMF had suggested and reinforced the climate of confidence between the two sides. The actions taken by the military government after September 12, such as incomes policy and tax reform, further reinforced relations and trust between the two sides.

The present state of relations is illustrated by the Letter of Intent of the Turkish minister of finance dated January 27, 1982, and forwarded to the managing director of the Fund. The minister of finance pointed out the results achieved in 1981 and expressed the determination of the government to pursue similar policies in 1982. He indicated that, due to difficulties that had arisen in the export of two important agricultural commodities, rises had occurred in the credits extended by the central bank to agricultural cooperatives. This had caused the stand-by limits on net domestic assets of the central bank for January–June 1982 to be exceeded. The minister of finance proposed that new limits should be established for the period in question and promised that the increase in such assets for the period June–December 1982 would be slowed down to compensate for increases during the first half of the year.[6]

Concluding Remarks

I do not want to end this paper simply on the rosy note left by the optimistic views just expressed as regards recent developments in the state of the economy and in relations between the IMF and Turkey.

There is no doubt that the shock administered to the Turkish economy by the 1980 stabilization policy and the significant long-term support given by the IMF to Turkey are contributing to establishing a new material and psychological basis upon which one can hope that new foundations, with regard to economic organization, economic policies, and individual behavior in economic affairs, will be erected. The future development of the Turkish economy depends upon far-reaching changes—in past policies, in the outlook within Turkey as regards Turkey's place and function in the international economy, and in the pattern of the people's economic behavior—toward greater rationality in economic decision making. Mostly as the result of the recent economic hardships and deprivations, and of the shocks administered by the measures taken since 1980, Turkish public opinion (with certain exceptions) seems to have realized the necessity for changes. We cannot yet predict the final outcome of these psychological and intellectual gestations, but, to my mind, the very fact that

[6] Text of the Letter of Intent, dated January 27, 1982, *Milliyet*, 17, February 1982, Istanbul.

for the first time since World War II a more sober and realistic mood is beginning to emerge is a mark of the success so far achieved by stabilization under the stand-by agreement.

However, there are question marks and clouds overhanging the present "structural" adjustments, and even monetary policy. Below I shall refer briefly to what appear to be the major problems.

First, there is the question of the hardships that the Turkish population, or at least certain segments of it, have had to put up with since the beginning of the crisis in 1977. No reliable figures are available as regards the distribution of income. The key questions concern recent changes in the real levels of low incomes, such as wages and salaries, and in their share in total income. As noted previously, the real purchasing power of salaries of government employees, which had been worsening in the late 1970s, again declined drastically in the two years of 1980 and 1981. In this period there has occurred a total nominal increase in salaries of around 40–50 percent, to be set against an increase in the cost of living of around 130 percent. Government employees number 1,170,000 within an employment total of 15,000,000. As regards changes in the purchasing power of wages, the position is not so clear. During the 1970s, real wages in general, and especially the wages of workers in the so-called organized sector (which includes 2,190,000 wage earners covered by social insurance and minimum wage legislation) had increased considerably, but the upward movement came to a halt in the late 1970s. There is less information about trends in the wages of workers not covered by social insurance, numbering around 1,775,000 in 1977.

In 1981, under the new incomes policy, there seems to have been an average rise of 25 percent in nominal wages in the organized sector. This meant a fall in real wages, since the inflation rate was around 35 percent.

The fall in real wages has begun to cause criticism of the stabilization policy in trade union circles. The policy is being accused by TÜRK-IS the largest Turkish trade union federation, of shifting the distribution of income in favor of income from capital and against income from labor. TÜRK-IS, in a report submitted to the prime minister, has quoted figures from some studies on the distribution of income in Turkey that indicate that the share of national income going to wage and salary earners fell to 33.7 percent in 1979 from 44.3 percent in 1968.[7] The federation further added that, among wage earners only 27 percent of the total work force benefit from collective

[7] *Tercüman*, 5 March 1982.

bargaining agreements and that, therefore, such agreements are far from preventing unfavorable movements in the distribution of income. Apart from the problem of the unreliability of existing studies on the distribution of income, however, it seems misleading to link together salary and wage incomes when analyzing changes in the distribution of income. These two income categories have moved differently up to the early 1980s. However, it is clear that the hardships and burdens caused by inflation in the late 1970s and by stabilization in the early 1980s are going to be increasingly discussed in Turkey, especially since the incomes policy introduced by the Military Council seems set to continue until 1984. The fact that key statistics on wages, unemployment, price indices, and the distribution of income are either missing or have been criticized on account of their unreliability is to be highly deplored, since the issue of burden-sharing is likely to remain a sensitive one for some time to come. Thus, the availability of comprehensive and reliable statistics is important not only during the period when the incomes policy is enforced but also for the time when it will presumably be lifted to make room for free collective bargaining. It is to be hoped that free collective bargaining will bring back flexibility to wages, in line with demand for labor in the various sectors of the economy, and in an atmosphere free from ideologically inspired wage demands.

Another question mark concerning flexibility in the use of labor in the economy springs from the eventual fate of the decree of the Military Council forbidding the discharge of workers by industry. This decree was introduced to protect the level of employment in industry at a critical time, after September 12, 1980. The regulation has been strictly applied, greatly embarrassing industrial firms in their effort to increase efficiency in the use of labor. However, newspaper reports mention that the application of the decree has been relaxed recently under pressure by employers. This has led to demands by the vice chairman of TÜRK-IS for strict application of the decree to maintain employment in industry. The freeze on employment in industry illustrates the gravity of the unemployment issue and the related question of expanding the depressed level of economic activity. Comprehensive indicators of the levels of employment and unemployment are not available in Turkey. The gap between the yearly overall demand and the supply of labor is estimated by the SPO to give a theoretical figure for unemployment in Turkey: this was calculated for 1981 as 3 million unemployed, representing 17 percent of the total supply of labor. One available, though only partial, indicator of unemployment is provided by statistics of the numbers of unemployed applying to the agencies of the Employment Board for jobs in urban areas. For what they may be worth, these indicate a rise in unemployment in 1980, followed by a small decline in 1981. The yearly average of such job seekers increased from 170,000 in 1979 to 255,000 in 1980 (by 50 percent), but decreased marginally to 249,000 in the first nine months of 1981.

The unemployment problem, on one side, and the low rates of profitability and of capacity utilization in industry, on the other, are leading some economists, trade unionists, and employers to criticize the severely restrictive monetary policy pursued within the stabilization policy under the stand-by agreement of 1980. They demand its relaxation with a view to increasing the level of activity and employment in the economy. The government, backed by other economists and employers, is steadfastly refusing to turn away from monetary restraint. It points out that this solution would be purely temporary and illusory, and that experiences with inflationary policies in 1978–80 proved that inflation is not the way to solve the employment problem. The Deputy Prime Minister Turgut Özal adds that he believes in the importance of reviving investment and of raising the rate of economic growth to somewhere around 6–7 percent, but that so far Turkey has lacked the real resources to finance a greater level of investment on account of the continuing constraint of the balance of payments, including the obligation to repay foreign debt. When Turkey is finally able to finance its economic development from international markets and private foreign sources, without having to rely on concessionary aid from friendly governments, it will become possible to expand investment and accelerate economic growth.

Thus, it appears that increasing pressures from various quarters will be applied on the government during 1982 for a relaxation of its restrictive stance on monetary policy, although the government is unlikely to yield on this crucial question. Indeed, the government has made public, perhaps somewhat imprudently, its determination to bring about a fall in the rate of inflation to 25 percent in 1982, while conceding that the realization of this target may be even more difficult than slowing down inflation in 1981.

Such are the issues that come to mind when long-term structural changes are considered. It is not easy at the present time to achieve a consensus on all these issues, either among Turkish public opinion or within the circle of economists and planners. This may be among the reasons for the continuing hesitation within the government in formulating definite answers to these questions.

The head of state, General Evren, in his opening address to the Second Economic Congress of Izmir in November 1981, spoke positively about Turkey's new experiences in the economic field since

1980. But few concrete ideas or proposals have emerged on the basic issues outlined above. Continuing uncertainty is hampering the full restoration of confidence, both within Turkey and among business and banking circles abroad, as to the future economic organization of Turkey and priorities in economic development.

COMMENTS, CHAPTERS 20–21

Richard S. Eckaus

The stories of the Turkish and Indian loans of the IMF, which are described so well by Okyar and Gwin, exemplify some of the most general issues of IMF lending: (1) the relation of that lending to the private international financial markets and (2) the relation of the terms of conditionality to the specific adjustment problems of the borrowing countries. These comments will attempt to relate these larger questions to the particular cases discussed. There is one conventional continuing problem of information which is also exemplified in these two stories: the lack of detailed data about the particular terms of conditionality of both the loans. Another difficulty is that, as of this writing, there has been relatively little time since the loans were made in which to judge the subsequent performance of the countries. So judgments must be made in prospect and on principle, rather than on fact.

The story about the Turkish loan told by Okyar provides only an incomplete background. What he did not mention was that, at the time of the loan, Turkey had substantial outstanding private debts on which it could not maintain payment of principal and interest. So it was in danger of "default," whatever that means for a sovereign nation. Clearly Turkey's foreign exchange reserves and earnings were so low that it was in danger of not being able to sustain levels of imports regarded as essential for public health and public order, if not maintenance of reasonable levels of economic activity. The accumulation of the private foreign debt apparently had not been accompanied by the creation of new capital facilities which would contribute to balance of payments viability but seems, for the most part, to have been short-term general "balance of payments support." Turkey had placed a lien on its foreign exchange earnings on which it could not meet the payments as they came due.

The situation of the Turkish economy, as described by Okyar, corresponds to the widely held view of an economy with low, perhaps declining, productivity. Inefficient resource use in public enterprise was supported by the general government budget and inefficient resource use in private enterprise was encouraged by a distorted domestic price system with monopolistic prices charged to consumers by both sectors. The problem of relative stagnation was not because the rate of investment was so low, but that the investment had not been nearly as productive as could have been expected.

The Turkish case seems clearly to be one in which major structural adjustments are necessary to recreate a viable economy. It is not one in which simple and conventional monetary policies could be expected to resolve the many and difficult problems of reordering the economy. The problems had been accumulating for a long time and were not resolvable quickly and with simple instruments. In fact, Turkey seems to be a case in which an extended arrangement under the Fund's enlarged access policy would have been eminently appropriate to support a long-term structural adjustment.

It is quite true that emergency action was necessary and the patient's "survival" had to be assured before a longer term treatment could be undertaken. Yet there is little evidence that, even in the emergency treatment, there has been recourse to the range of policy instruments which, while contributing to short-run improvement, would also move the economy toward a resolution of its more deep-seated problems.

It appears in fact that only the conventional monetary policies of the IMF have been applied in Turkey. There is little evidence even of the use of interest rate policy to encourage repatriation of capital and emigrant remittances and shifting of assets into the financial system. There is also little evidence of tax and exchange rate policies which would encourage investment and exports. The vaunted concern of the IMF for "supply side" economics seems in this case to be lacking from its terms of conditionality.

The Indian loan under the extended Fund facility is in many respects in striking contrast to the Turkish loan. India came to the Fund "early," that is before its balance of payments problems had reached a crisis stage and before the most pressing need was to prevent disaster of one form or another. Nonetheless the problems of the Indian economy have been described with many of the same words as those used for the Turkish economy: distorted domestic prices arising from subsidies and protection, inefficiencies resulting from indiscriminate import substitution and excessive and counterproductive controls. Like Turkey, India had achieved quite a respectable rate of investment but had been able to earn only low rates of return on it. Unlike Turkey, India had not acquired a burdensome foreign debt which it could not sustain.

The terms of the Fund conditionality on the Indian loan, while not released officially, have been leaked to the public and to a striking extent are concerned with structural adjustments and conditions intended to promote production efficiency. In fact, the range of issues covered by the terms of the Fund conditionality for the India loan are so broad and encompassing that they have engendered widespread controversy within India and charges of a "sell-out" of the Indian economy to the IMF.

The two issues with respect to the Indian loan which will be addressed in these comments may be put briefly: Should the loan have been made? And did the Fund know what it was doing when it made the loan, in the sense that it was reasonably assured that the terms agreed upon would produce the results desired?

With respect to the granting of the loan, the issue raised is not whether India was officially entitled to receive the money. There is no intent here to argue with the legalities. Rather the questions are whether the Fund is, or should be, an institution concerned with the long-term development of its members and, if the aswer is affirmative, should India have been one of the first in line for this type of assistance? Again there is no intent to argue with the legalities; the IMF charter certainly can be interpreted to justify the granting of loans for development support and the extended Fund facility was encouraged and approved by the Fund's Executive Board.

By establishing its extended Fund facility in the form in which it has, that is, as a loan program with conditionality in terms of detailed provisions for microeconomic and structural changes, the Fund is clearly moving in the direction of the mode of operation of the World Bank. Perhaps there is no harm in this. One might take the view that, "the more, the better," that is, the more funds made available for development, the more development there will be. It can also be argued that there are advantages in specialization of the two institutions. Long-term macroeconomic issues have, characteristically, been neglected by the World Bank. If the IMF conscientiously decides to become more long term in its outlook, perhaps a case can be made for its concentrating on macroeconomic and foreign trade and financial policy.

There is another aspect to the question as to whether the Fund should have made the India loan. That has to do with its relation to private international financial markets. According to Gwin, and the conventional wisdom, India could have borrowed at relatively favorable rates from private international lenders to finance its adjustment program. By comparison, when the IMF sent its rescue mission to Turkey, there were no further opportunities for Turkey to obtain private credit, being close to default on its outstanding loans. It is certainly the more typical situation that a country turning to the IMF in extremis cannot obtain private credit, even if it is not already heavily in debt. India was not in extremis, however.

There is a real question as to whether the Fund should, in a world in which private financing is available, provide subsidized finance when it is not really necessary. Moreover, if it is going to do that, what criteria should be used for the distribution of that finance? While it can be claimed that the World Bank, to some extent, tries to assist countries even to the extent of helping in making application for assistance, it cannot be said that the IMF is doing this as yet. Is the IMF, in effect, discriminating against countries which are not skilled in playing the assistance game? It would be grudging to complain about India's skills in this respect as the country is desperately poor. The possible complaint is that the IMF does not offer the same kind of help to other needy countries.

Lastly, can it be claimed that the broad-ranging terms of conditionality, described by Gwin, can be monitored by the IMF? Can it ascertain that the policies adopted by India are in the direction, sequence, and magnitude to be most effective? In effect the IMF has made a "program loan" with many conditions as to how the program should be worked out. The design of development programs is one of the most complex of economic policy undertakings. While certainly within the professional capabilities of the IMF staff, they have started with one of the most difficult cases.

Perhaps, the encompassing terms of conditionality on the India loan should not be taken too seriously. Perhaps the terms were made deliberately vague so that the IMF would not have to enforce requirements about which it lacked confidence. Perhaps the IMF intends to watch carefully only the overall outcomes and not bother too much with the details. That would be more in keeping with both its past policies and its expertise. In that case, however, it has generated a good many problems for itself in India where, as Gwin points out, it has been sharply attacked for what seems to be detailed and wide-ranging intervention in the country's economic policy.

PART IV

Conclusions and Policy Implications

CHAPTER **22**

Panel Discussion

Richard N. Cooper

I am not going to try to summarize the conference in any literal sense; that would be a hopeless task. Rather, I will make some general observations on the conference and on the issues that have been raised. Before doing that, though, I think we should congratulate John Williamson and the Institute for International Economics on the idea of the conference. International Monetary Fund (IMF) conditionality, although it is not exactly on the lips of the man in the street, has become a very contentious international issue. Drag Avramovíc has said (Chapter 23) that it is the key issue in North-South relations. It is a highly emotive issue with United Nations ambassadors and other interested but generally uninformed persons. It is enveloped by the mysteries of high finance, so it brings out the latent populism that exists just below the surface in most people. In a back-handed way, I suppose it is testimony to the importance that the IMF has come to play in the international system that the question of IMF conditionality has come forward so strongly. So I think that John Williamson should be congratulated on the idea of the conference and of pulling together the actual experiences of roughly a dozen countries under IMF programs.

Before turning to conditionality as such, I would like to make two observations of a background nature. First, recall the origins and the original purpose of the IMF. It arose out of the disastrous experience of the 1930s, which taught the architects of the postwar international system four lessons that are relevant for us. First, it is necessary to manage domestic demand, something that was not widely accepted before then. Second, it is necessary to avoid competitive depreciation of currencies, as actions which are collectively self-defeating for the system as a whole. Third, it is necessary, they thought, to avoid controls on payments for imports on the same grounds. Fourth, private credits dry up and even become perverse just when they are needed most, and therefore one cannot rely on private financial flows to deal with difficult balance of payments problems.

The IMF was created only partly as a lending institution. It was also created to oversee behavioral rules to which members committed themselves: convertibility on current account for their currencies; and fixed exchange rates, which have now been transformed into absence of manipulation of exchange rates. The lending function was designed to finance payments imbalances in this new world of policy, in which countries are presumed to be supporting full employment at home through domestic demand management even when the rest of the world was in recession, and to smooth the adjustment from a position of fundamental disequilibrium—to use the old language, to a new equilibrium following a change in the par value of the currency. So IMF lending was to finance imbalances in payments that were temporary for each of these two reasons: a country's demand policies were out of line with the rest of the world, but could be expected to correct themselves; or a country that found itself in fundamental disequilibrium, devalued, and needed some time for the devaluation to work. The purpose of the lending function was thus to ease adjustment, not to make it more difficult. Recall the point that Adolfo Diz made (Chapter 12), that the starting point of an IMF program is not the relevant point of comparison, because that is a nonsustainable point. One has to look instead at alternative paths toward equilibrium.

Now I believe that these original purposes of the Fund, making due allowance for the changes that have taken place in the last 35 years, are basically still valid, and during the course of the last two days I have not heard anything to suggest that that view is not widely shared, at least at a high-level of generalization. The operative question is whether the purposes of the Fund should be enlarged beyond those original purposes, whether it should take on new responsibilities in today's world. That is my first general observation.

The second observation is that we should not take the existence of the IMF for granted. The discussion that we have had has really done so. We have assumed that the IMF is there, will always be there, and the question is, how does it work? In raising this question, I do not mean that the IMF will actually disappear. International institutions never disappear. (The only exception I know of was the European Payments Union, which did actually go out of existence.) Old institutions never die, but they can atrophy. The IMF is in the business of lending money, and that issue concerns not just the prospective debtors, but also the prospective creditors. If the IMF is to grow with the world economy, the potential creditors have to be satisfied that their interests—and here I mean their conception of the global interest, not merely their national interests—are being served. *Ipso facto,* that will require conditions on IMF lending. It is an obvious point, but it is perhaps necessary to make it. No one at this conference has suggested that there should not be conditions. But there are many people who do in effect suggest that there should not be any conditions on IMF lending. So it is worth making the point that there are creditors as well as debtors that must be satisfied, although their identities may change over time. Already, IMF lending is being confused with foreign aid and the formal Group of 77 position as represented in forums such as the UN Conference on Trade and Development and on the floor of the UN General Assembly would push it further in that direction. In my view, that development would effectively kill the IMF in the long run, and that is in no one's interest. This position does not reflect opposition to foreign aid; rather, it is a question of the appropriate division of responsibility among institutions.

Now let me turn to the discussion. As I heard it—and it came as somewhat of a surprise to me, given the diversity of the participants—everyone here who spoke to the issue not only favors conditionality by the IMF, but favors rather tight conditionality. There was some disagreement over just what the conditions should be, but that there should be rather rigorous conditions imposed by the IMF as part of its lending programs commanded general agreement in this group.

I would go even further, although I recognize that I am on delicate ground in a room full of individualists, and guess from the tenor of the discussion that, with possibly one or two exceptions, we could choose any five people present and make a team to work up an economic adjustment program for a particular country other than our own, in particular circumstances, and we would have little difficulty in doing so. Furthermore, the program we came up with would not differ greatly from a typical IMF program. Such disagreements as would arise within that group of five people, I would guess, would not be over issues of principle, which we have addressed from time to time during this conference, but rather would reflect different judgments about the behavioral responses of the economy in question to this or that particular action. In short, arguments over a particular program would reflect differences in technical judgments rather than differences of principle. In an actual case, I suspect the differences in principle would yield to agreement that in that particular case it was overwhelmingly one of excess demand, or that it was not; that the political reality requires us to stay away from certain areas and to pay attention to others; that we would all want correction of the payments imbalance to be as costless as possible in terms of forgone output and employment, but that possibly a shock treatment might be necessary to achieve this, or clearly is not necessary to change expectations radically in order to make the program work. We would agree whether the budget deficit and the rate of credit creation are too large to be consistent with payments equilibrium and that they should be restrained, but we might disagree on how rapidly the demand for money would rise as the program takes hold—the whole question, which has been touched on several times, of how the velocity of money responds to a new policy regime, and how the authorities ought to accommodate to that—this is the kind of important but essentially technical issue on which we would probably have different judgments.

I believe further that we would agree that the objective must include restoration of payments balance in some defined period of time, and that there should be quantifiable markers along the way with respect to the instruments of policy. Those markers have to meet two criteria. First, they must be under the control of the government. There is no point in the world of practical reality to ask a government to undertake a task it cannot perform, so instruments have to be under the control of the government. Second, there have to be reasonably prompt and reasonably accurate data with respect to those instrumental variables, because if there are not, the variables do not serve their purpose. Once we lay down these two criteria, that sharply limits the number of intermediate target variables that can be used in any IMF program.

I think we would probably also agree that there are important differences among countries. That is to say, the same team looking at two countries might come up with what superficially look like quite different prescriptions, even though they operate within the same general framework. In particular, there is an important difference between countries with large and relatively free—even in the presence of exchange controls—movements of private capital, responsive to interest rate differentials, and countries where to a first approximation capital flows are largely in one direction and are largely bank credits or official credits rather than privately held capital moving in response to incentives. In this connection, remittances should be considered capital flows, and therefore this is *not* a distinction between developed and less developed countries. Thus, countries such as Egypt, Pakistan, Portugal, Turkey, Italy, and the United Kingdom all fall into the first category. Their payments positions are highly responsive to expected exchange rate developments and to real interest rates—nominal interest rates corrected for expected inflation. (Incidentally, I find it somewhat troubling how easily economists have fallen into the habit of talking about real interest rates, as though we know what they are. We do *not* know what real interest rates are. They are not observable, and while we have to use the term to distinguish them from nominal interest rates, we should always remind ourselves that we are dealing with a nonobservable. We can reckon them ex post, but we do not know what they are at any moment in time.)

In countries where capital movements (including remittances) are important and sensitive, the IMF's role is less one of financing the imbalance through a period of adjustment than of engendering confidence in the government's program and of persuading the relevant publics to move their capital into the country. For the other class of countries, in contrast, the role of the IMF as a source of interim finance will be proportionately greater even though, of course, there will be some responsive capital movements through leads and lags.

John Williamson suggested (Chapter 7), at the level of general principle, that in framing stabilization programs the IMF should take into account five broad objectives: payments balance, internal equilibrium, inflation, growth, and distribution of income. Carlos Diaz-Alejandro (Comments, Chapters 11–14) joined the issue by registering concern that the IMF get so heavily involved in the policies and objectives of individual countries, and suggested that the IMF should consider only payments equilibrium as its objective, leaving the country free, within that constraint, to determine and to pursue its other objectives.

On this spectrum, I find myself closer to Diaz than to Williamson. The IMF in effect should make a deal with the country in question: we will lend you funds if you undertake a program to restore payments balance in, say, 24 months. Rather than having to eliminate the imbalance "cold turkey," we will permit a more relaxed framework within which you can pursue your other objectives, provided you do not lose sight of the agreed aim of restoring balance in your international payments. If you ask, we might offer some side advice on your objectives, but that is not our prime concern. Furthermore, although we can work constructively with the minister of finance, we do not fully trust his cabinet colleagues, so together we will work out some criteria that will serve as markers to see whether you are making progress toward eliminating the imbalance. These, of course, must be written down, and they will look very specific and rigid, but they are really part of a process, the basis for a dialogue at quarterly intervals to see how the program for your country is proceeding. That is the deal between the IMF and the country.

If my rather bold conjecture about the workability of a team from the group here convened is correct, the practical politics of any particular case would inevitably involve the consideration of Williamson's other objectives, at least as constraints on the actions that could actually be taken to eliminate the payments imbalance; but it would be done on a pragmatic, case-by-case basis in collaboration with the financial officials of the government in question.

So far, I have just addressed the question of getting a country back to equilibrium. That does not address the important point introduced by Ray Mikesell (Chapter 3) that the IMF is not merely a lending institution, but its role also includes the pursuit of certain global objectives. The IMF is a club with club rules. Countries, after all, are not obliged to join the IMF; when they do join, they make certain undertakings about their behavior. It should be part of the IMF's role to enforce the club rules—in principle all of the time, but of course it has a little more leverage when a country comes to it for assistance than it does at other times, and therefore there should be at least a component of the global interest in each program. One of the club rules calls for current account convertibility, so the IMF should be encouraging that. Actually, the IMF has shown remarkable flexibility—one might argue too much flexibility—over the years in setting aside the club rules. It was properly way out in front of the international community when it came to the rule regarding par values: the IMF condoned various kinds of exchange rate flexibility long before the international community officially condoned it.

There is another global issue I would like to raise, one that has not formally come up in the discussion. I put it forward to stimulate discussion. Should the IMF take global economic conditions into account in framing individual country programs? At least in principle, I believe it should. If so, that has implications for IMF conditionality. It suggests that conditionality for all client states should vary over time, depending on world economic conditions. In a world slump, conditionality should ease. IMF lending technically represents expansionist monetary and fiscal policy from a global point of view. The monetary policy aspect is complicated because it depends on which currencies are actually used. When repayments exceed new lending, it is playing a contractionary role. Should its expansionary role be varied with the world business cycle, so to speak? In a period such as late 1978 or early 1979, IMF conditions would generally be stiffened compared with what they were, say, in late 1974 or 1975, or in early 1982.

Although it came up only once or twice in the entire conference, it is worth noting that an important part of IMF operations these days is the compensatory finance facility (CFF), which in a way is a built-in stabilizer. It lends virtually without conditions when a country's export earnings fall below projected levels, and of course that would typically take place during a world slump; the opposite would often be the case during a world boom. Thus, there is already some built-in fiscal-monetary stabilization at the global level, through the CFF.

There is a question in my mind about the practicality of this suggestion, on two related counts. First, the same country might find itself having gotten an IMF loan on easy terms in 1982 and going to the IMF in 1985, let us say, and finding the IMF is much stiffer. That might be hard for officials to explain. The same problem exists with the IMF bureaucracy. The IMF is, after all, a large organization, a bureaucracy. Bureaucracies function by rules. Any framework that large numbers of individuals must carry out in different parts of the world with some degree of consistency cannot involve too much subtlety. So I flag these as practical problems.

We had some discussion about the interaction between the IMF and the commercial banks. De Vries (Comments, Chapters 1–3) told us that the clientele are now largely separate. Commercial banks lend to one group of countries, and the IMF lends to another group of countries. That may be true on average, but it is not true on the margin, and, as usual in economics, it is the margin that counts, not the average. When a country runs into trouble, private funds dry up, and the country turns to the IMF for help. We have discussed some of those cases: Peru, Turkey, Jamaica, and Poland (if Poland were a member of the IMF). These are all cases in which countries were borrowing in private markets. Some would even say the private banks were too careless in their lending. In the end these countries had to turn to the IMF. The IMF program remains a certification for satisfactory economic prospects, not only with commercial banks, but, as Gerry Helleiner reminds us (see his remarks, below), with bilateral aid donors as well. For many countries, that is even more important than private banks. It was true also for Portugal and Turkey, in conjunction with special support packages that were put together for those two countries—not quite aid in the traditional sense. An IMF program has been made a precondition for official debt rescheduling, which in turn both requires and sets the pattern for private debt reschedulings. We have now seen the emergence of a pattern for dealing with countries in financial difficulty. The IMF continues to play a crucial role in all of those respects, many of which also involve the private banks, even though, as Irving Friedman emphasized (Chapter 6), the IMF program serves as information for the banks, rather than a formal go-ahead. In the end they have to make their own judgments.

Because of this pervasive role, and for other reasons, I am reluctant to see the IMF consciously and formally differentiate among its member countries. Much differentiation will take place in reality because the particular circumstances in which countries find themselves will be diverse.

I detect some frustrations from those who have been concerned with African countries, where there are desperate poverty and horrendous obstacles to development. The international community is not doing enough. There is an understandable tendency to push the IMF forward to do more in solving some of these horrendous problems. The question we have to ask is what role should the IMF appropriately play in dealing with these deep-seated problems.

My own answer is a conservative one. It is that the IMF simply cannot be all things to all men. You should not impose that burden on any institution, even a good one. It is not a source of aid funds, and I believe that if it were to come to be perceived as a source of aid funds, as I said before, it would eventually lead to a drying up of creditor support for the institution. To get heavily involved in social and developmental issues would be costly to its own integrity.

That view leads to Stanley Please's plea (Comments, Chapters 15–16) that we address the role of the World Bank. We have not discussed the World Bank much at this conference, but my own view complements what I have just said about preserving a limited role for the IMF. By the same token, however, the World Bank should be prepared to make program loans on a much larger scale than it has done hitherto. I see so-called structural adjustment loans basically as an excuse for getting back into making program loans on a consequential scale. In connection with program loans, the World Bank should feel obliged to discuss all the impediments to development with the borrowing country and even to lay down specific conditions on pricing, sectoral investments, and so forth. In other words, when the two Bretton Woods institutions were set up, a division of labor was envisaged, and it seems to me that that division of labor remains an appropriate one, with adjustments at the margin. The international community should not shrink from discussing detailed allocational issues with developing countries that turn to the international community for financial support.

However, we all have to bear in mind Drag Avramovíc's injunction (Chapter 23) that this advice should be given with a certain degree of modesty rather than with arrogance. Professional economists as a group, we must admit, do not know how to assure smooth, minimum-cost balance of payments adjustment or sustained, trouble-free development. We have some thoughts on these issues. We even think our thoughts are superior to the policies that countries sometimes follow. We should give our best professional advice on these issues, but it should be done with a certain degree of modesty. It is not impossible, moreover, to combine modesty with insistence in particular instances.

More particularly, we should note that IMF economists are fallible. They are not omniscient. They will make mistakes. Reg Green (Chapter 15) reminded us of Julius Nyrere's observation that "mistakes are mistakes." Mistakes will be made, even in a framework that is broadly correct. Like all large institutions, the IMF cannot admit its mistakes too freely because of fears that such admission would undermine its credibility. But it is perhaps a greater threat to an institution's credibility never to admit mistakes when some have obviously been made. A fine balance must be struck. Professional economists should criticize the IMF for the mistakes it makes so that mistakes can be avoided in the future. That is quite a different process from attacking the entire framework within which the IMF is operating, on the grounds that it has sometimes made mistakes.

The final point I want to make is that an IMF program is a process, not a fixed, finished product. The process starts long before the IMF program has been agreed, and it continues long after the program is agreed. The targets that are laid down are properly regarded not as rigid, come-hell-or-high-water-you've-got-to-meet-them targets, but rather as something to shoot for or to have very good reasons for not meeting. The quarterly reviews are occasions for members to go back to the IMF and either announce with pride that the targets have been met, *or* to have a good story to tell about why the targets have not been met. At least in the cases I know about, when the country does have a satisfactory reason for not meeting the targets, the IMF does not give them a lot of grief.

Again, a fine line has to be struck because often countries will in fact let their policies get out of control and *then* appeal to the IMF for relaxation of the targets. Somebody has to make the judgment whether the reasons are acceptable. Without question, that process gives rise to some tension between the IMF and a government that may well have done its best by its lights but that has not done well enough by the IMF's lights. But when a country fails to meet its credit ceilings, say, within a context of a program that otherwise is going well, we should not pronounce either that the program was a failure or that the program was wrong-headed to begin with, because the proper way to view the program is as a process and not as a set of rigid objectives.

Arnold C. Harberger

Our chairman told me last night that I was picked to represent something called the "conservative" point of view. Since that does not fit my self-image, I decided that I would try to put myself in the shoes of some sort of amalgam of former students. I pick Nicolas Ardito-Barletta, Carlos Massad, and a little bit of Ricardo Ffrench-Davis, all of whom I love and admire and what not. So I will try to represent all those people in addition to myself in this conservative exposition.

First, on conditionality. My experience and my very, very strong feelings about conditionality, stem from the case of Chile in the 1960s, and not from the International Monetary Fund (IMF) but from the US Agency for International Development (AID). We went through in Chile from 1964 to 1967 (when Carlos Massad was in the central bank, along with Ricardo Ffrench-Davis) what I consider to be one of the most beautiful stabilization efforts that has ever been done. They moved down from about 40 percent inflation to less than 20 percent inflation in three years, and they did this with continual growth at about 5 percent a year in output. It was beautifully organized, with the fiscal and the monetary aspects fully coordinated, and the technicians were all on one side. AID was giving stabilization money, but they (Carlos Massad and Sergio Molina) *wanted* us to demand what we were demanding of them so that they would have the clout to be able to sell these good ideas to a bunch of other people who wanted to do all sorts of dumb things. So it was a grand alliance of what I think of as good technicians to do good for the country, with the kind of motivation that all of us could share, and everything went well.

Now, there came a day, which I think was in 1968, when I happened to be in Chile. There was a meeting in the AID director's office at which the following conversation took place. "We need to get a new excuse to give aid to Chile. We can't go up to the Hill again on a stabilization loan. What should we use as the excuse?" One idea after another was bounced around. Somebody said sector—"oh yes, let's make it a sector loan. Now let's figure out what sector." Just like that. In that same meeting it was decided it would be the agricultural sector. The resulting agricultural sector loan was one of the biggest miseries that Chile ever had to suffer. AID put conditions on wheat prices, and things like that, that turned out to be absurd and stupid. And it was done for a purpose that had nothing to do with really trying to help Chile. It was finding a good excuse to go up to the Hill again.

Now, add to that the bilateral loan conditions on how much has to be bought in the country from which the aid money comes, in what kind of ships can it be sent, and so on. Also add all the silly paper work that has to be done. I have often felt that if I were a developing country member faced with the kinds of AID restrictions that have existed over the years, I would just tell AID to look for clients elsewhere. I would go to the private capital market and do it that way. And I think that Mexico did it like that, and I do not think Mexico really suffered for having simply resigned from the bilateral aid club. Now the multilateral agencies are much less subject to this kind of thing. But when I think of conditionality, it is the AID kind of conditionality I really do not like, and yet I have seen circumstances, as the Chile stabilization example showed, of times when AID-type conditions worked well.

Now to the business of IMF advice. I think by the way that Dick Cooper has to be congratulated for an absolutely superb statement. It is more than a summary, it is a fundamental statement, and one that touches, as far as I can see, just about all the bases. He said that the IMF as a whole, as an institution, gives good advice. I agree with that. Every now and then they make mistakes. I agree with that. I was in Indonesia this summer, and some of the people in the Indonesian government were telling me that they were getting strong signals that, if they have a fiscal deficit in rupiahs, it's just as bad if it is financed by printing money as if it's financed by converting oil proceeds. I went through the roof on that one. I wrote a whole paper trying to say that when you have oil proceeds you really *do* get to an equilibrium in which those proceeds really *do* finance the deficit. But it seems to me that, in-so-far as agency people may have been involved in spreading those signals, I'm sure that they were well-intentioned in trying to convince the Indonesians not to spend their oil money so fast. Nonetheless, the basic economics of the proposition that they were spreading was just wrong. Thus, I think one has to realize that the IMF, while on the whole tending to give good advice, sometimes makes mistakes.

Now there is another thing that has come out in the discussion that would be *extremely* well advised to say. I got the impression that Bruno (Comments, Chapters 4–6) was saying we do not have any message to give to the IMF. I think we do have a message, a very straight and concrete message: that is, *please* don't make your targets in absolute numbers. Set up your targets in a fashion that represents the best professional distillation of what I would call "contingency contracts." I think in inflationary countries wage indexation—a sort of basic underlying wage indexation—is a great thing. Why? Because neither the trade union nor the employer has any expertise in predicting the rate of inflation. Even we economists do not, but certainly they have less. So they shouldn't be arguing about that; they should pact it out. When a country is setting up a minerals concession, it does not know if the concession will be good or bad, make money or lose money. A royalty arrangement that gives an adequate percentage gives the country a lot if it wins and gives the country a little if it loses; that's a nice kind of thing. Well, the way in which IMF targeting ought to be done should be on a similarly contingent basis. And if you have to do it in the form of a couple of formulas, the people in most of the ministries of finance and central banks around the world are today sufficiently sophisticated that they can fully understand what a formula means, and that if the price level goes up the target is one thing and that if the price level goes down it's another—if the world price of coffee exports for Brazil goes up, there is one target, and that if it goes down there is another. These things can be handled, and this business of having the specific quantitative peso or cruzeiro or dollar targets for different things is simply, at this stage of our profession's development, outdated and unnecessary.

I think that Dick Cooper and others have been quite correct in saying that there is a deep role for the IMF because the commercial banks are so flighty. My favorite statement about the international commercial banking community is that it really loves to give a lot of credit to that country which always has a surplus in its government budget and a surplus in its balance of trade. That is the one they really want to lend to. And of course if that country knows well how to invest in the New York Stock Exchange, it might even win on such a loan, but it cannot do much else with a loan under those circumstances. And I think that the IMF really has been incredibly important in stepping in in the circumstances where, basically, the private banking community was just pulling the rug out from under a country. I agree, too, that the IMF should not ever let itself get sucked into the business of being a source of aid funds. It is not a development organization, and, if it starts confusing its purposes, that will only be for the worse. I also love Dick Cooper's notion of combining modesty with insistence. I think that particular turn of phrase deserves a prize. Finally, I also agree that it would be incorrect to start to attack the entire IMF framework just because some mistakes have been in the framework. My vote is a vote of thanks to Dick Cooper for a splendid summary.

Gerald K. Helleiner

I have organized my comments into two categories—those concerned with analytical issues and those concerned with the possibility of improvements in International Monetary Fund (IMF) practices. Obviously there are interrelationships between the two.

The most important analytical disagreement at this conference concerns what we mean by "internal balance." Many of us have blushed for years as we drew our internal balance schedules. With how much inflation and how much unemployment (let alone how much growth or with what income distribution) we are to be content has long been a matter for dispute. This kind of dispute surfaced in our discussions here in respect of both individual nations (e.g., Williamson, Chapter 7, versus Bacha, Chapter 14) on the relative costs of inflation and unemployment) and the global economy (e.g., Dale, Chapter 1, versus Cooper, Comments, above) on appropriate global macroeconomic approaches). I believe that the IMF, undoubtedly influenced by the similarly thinking US and British governments, is overly preoccupied with anti-inflationary objectives; with Cooper, I too see a risk of disaster if present macroeconomic policies in the United States continue. But we shall never reach technical agreement on these issues. We seem only able to reach analytical agreement on what we mean by "*external* balance"; and that fact alone constitutes a strong reason for focusing IMF conditionality primarily on external rather than internal balance. (There also seems to be agreement that external balance is an easier target than reducing the rate of inflation, a more practical reason for such a focus.)

Nor is there analytical agreement as to the elements of supply-side policies for maximizing growth or development. While liberal policies are part of IMF and World Bank wisdom, there exist examples of rapid growth achieved with an interventionist state, and the benefits and costs of protectionism are quite widely perceived as varying with the size of country, the level of development, and other factors. The cost of transition to a more liberal trade or payments regime can be calculated and compared with the possible benefits in particular country circumstances; it may be quite rational for policymakers who sincerely prefer liberal policies to hesitate before incurring the costs of taking the first steps in that general direction.

While there were severe doubts expressed about the World Bank's recent "free-market binge" (the phrase was Rudy Dornbusch's, Comments, Chapter 10) there was general agreement that "getting prices right" is an important part of supply-oriented adjustment and that we must have a better understanding of supply elasticities, particularly those of exportables. There was agreement that supply elasticities can vary greatly between sectors and over time. They are typically higher in the manufacturing sector than in agriculture, although the extent of excess capacity and the degree of marketing experience have an important bearing upon the prospect for short- to medium-term export expansion possibilities, and physical constraints such as those caused by "import strangulation" can be binding. From these variations in supply elasticities it follows that, in some kinds of economies and in particular time periods, there will be far greater difficulty achieving resource reallocation and adjustment than in others.

An interesting feature of the discussion of supply-side adjustment was the agreement that one would be unlikely to succeed in a total restructuring of tradable goods prices by undertaking it all at one stroke. Balassa (Chapter 8) and Avramovíc (Chapter 23), Sachs (Comments, Chapters 17–19) and Green (Chapter 15), all urged gradualism and, in particular, the provision of greatly increased profitability for the export sector in advance of any significant import liberalization.

Major disagreement remains as to the effect of interest rates upon savings rates. I am with those who doubt that one can show beneficial development effects from raising interest rates, whether through effects upon total savings or through improved financial intermediation, at least in the lower income membership of the IMF. Where the financial system is rudimentary (and frequently dominated on both the demand and supply side by the state), financial savings have not in the past been significantly interest responsive, and total savings rates are influenced overwhelmingly by real income. Since so few who are knowledgeable in these matters in these countries believe the IMF line, and since the IMF continues to be so insistent on major increases in interest rates, it may be useful now to explore whether such increases would be likely to do positive development *harm*. If not, it may be worth humoring "grandmother" for the sake of better relationships, while simultaneously pursuing the credit and other policies that really do matter. (I do not mean to suggest that there is a presumption that raising Tanzanian interest rates to 40 percent would be without costs.)

More important than interest rate orthodoxy in the lower-income countries is the provision of adequate credit to the "right" sectors in the adjustment process. Increased output is not necessarily best achieved via increased fixed investment. In the present desperate circumstances of many low-income countries, working capital (and foreign exchange) is what is required to permit the return to full utilization of existing capacity.

While there now seems to be a consensus that supply-side policies are an important part of any serious adjustment package (however much disagreement remains as to their precise components), the approach to income distributional questions seems to remain highly controversial. I believe there is a growing body of opinion, however, to the effect that distribution during the adjustment process is analytically important, not only in terms of a more comprehensive economic understanding but, more crucially, in terms of the politics of the process. The IMF has itself seemed to set its own "seal of approval" upon the analysis of distributional issues by its publication of the Johnson-Salop paper on the subject in its *Staff Papers.*[1] That paper, however, concludes that "it all depends," as did a lot of the discussion at this conference. What is now necessary is detailed empirical analysis of the distributional implications of alternative adjustment programs in similar countries, similar adjustment programs in different countries, and case-by-case, program-by-program assessments of the real possibilities and prospects in real places. To argue for the analytical importance of the distributional dimension of adjustment and for empirical research on the subject is *not* to say that distributional objectives should be part of IMF conditionality. The appropriate content of conditionality is an entirely separate question, although in the discussion of distributional issues it has frequently been confused with the former argument.

While "internal balance," growth prospects, and income distribution may be matters for continuing debate, the need for external balance is absolutely compelling. As David Finch (Chapter 4) put it at one point, "You cannot sit where you are. You have to do something about it." The alternative external adjustment paths may or may not involve the IMF, and John Williamson tried to force us to be specific about the contribution of the IMF to any particular adjustment process. I believe we may have spent disproportionate effort on one brand of "non-IMF" adjustment, that assisted by infusions of private capital, relative to another, that of the poorest countries which adjusted with neither private nor IMF support, perforce in a somewhat unplanned and chaotic fashion. The number of country

[1] Omotunde Johnson and Joanne Salop, "Distributional Aspects of Stabilization Programs in Developing Countries," IMF *Staff Papers* 27(1), March 1980, pp. 1–23.

cases of the latter non-IMF type far exceed that of the former, however inconsequential in global terms many of these may be. Moreover, the problems of the poorest have deteriorated still further during 1981 as their terms of trade have continued their sharp decline; these terms of trade are generally at lower levels than at any time in the past 35 years, and, despite some expansion in IMF lending to the poorest, their adjustment is more frequently than not undertaken without the IMF. Do we yet know how the adjustment burdens have been allocated, and what the implications for future growth may be?

The attempt at assessment of IMF "success," Williamson-style (Chapter 7), while more careful than many previous attempts, still leaves me somewhat uneasy. In the first place, I doubt whether we have really traveled very far in ascertaining what constitutes Williamson's "ideal set of policies" or his "potentially possible." That being so, we do not have a very firm "fix" on the adequacy of governmental performance, with or without the IMF. The discussion of country adjustment performance in this regard is reminiscent of the earlier literature on savings or tax performance. The implicit assumption underlying this approach is that performance is essentially a matter of governmental "will"—or, as some would put it, political capacity—as reflected in a social consensus or made possible by an authoritarian regime. But there are other dimensions to the capacity for adjustment additional to the sheer political ones. A country's economic structure and characteristics—its rigidity, its level of income, its access to private capital—also affect its capacity to undertake short- and medium-term adjustment. So does its technical and professional capacity in the area of macroeconomic management. As in the fiscal and savings performance literature, ought one not first to control for "capacity to adjust" before starting on an assessment of performance? Does Williamson's ideal incorporate such elements of capacity?

A second matter for disquiet is the recent empirical literature regarding the contribution of IMF programs to economic change. The most recent survey by Killick indicates that IMF programs do not seem to have statistically significant effects upon inflation, growth, the current account or basic balance.[2] Are we perhaps not making too much of the question of IMF content as opposed to the basic question of alternative means of achieving adjustment? Should we not devote a little more attention to attempting to model less orthodox adjustment paths?

[2] Tony Killick, "The Impact of IMF Stabilization Programmes in Developing Countries" (London: Overseas Development Institute, March 1982). See also his case study of Kenya, Chapter 16, this volume.

When it comes to proposals for improving the functioning of the IMF, I find myself in substantial agreement not only with what Dick Cooper has said but even with much of what Al Harberger (see his remarks, above) has suggested. But important differences among us remain.

Let me say at the outset that I favor a stronger IMF, one that is not merely a lender of last resort (least of all for the banks), and one that plays a greater role in global macroeconomic management. I would like to see an IMF that both oversees the world macroeconomic scene and provides a much larger proportion of balance of payments financing than it does at present. Reliance on the private market for monetary management involves risks, instabilities, and inequities that no nation has considered acceptable for the past 50 years or more. I also believe that a system based on special drawing rights (SDR) is likely to be much more rational and equitable than one based on gold, a variety of currencies, commercial bank lending, and official bilateral credit. But we live in irrational and inequitable times; so these are not matters that we have pursued.

Rather, we have discussed IMF (and World Bank) "grandmotherliness" toward a shrinking clientele, one that is increasingly segmented not only from that of private bank lending but also from orderly world economic progress. Increasingly, the IMF deals with the lowest income countries.

It has been striking in our discussions that exasperation with the IMF-country relationship is so thoroughly mutual. On the one hand, we hear the IMF staff complaining of "drift," "lack of seriousness," "slippage," "inability to maintain commitments" and therefore expressing reluctance to commit funds to those who patently require them the most, in the classic banker's mode. These bankers, like many grandmothers, feel misunderstood: they wring their hands over their clients' difficulties and appear genuinely to want to help. In the end, however, they see no option but to tighten conditionality. In the words of one of Edmund Lear's verses: "Tell me how you live, he said, and beat him on the head. . . ."

On the other hand, we heard the borrowers' familiar account (best expressed by Drag Avramovíc, Chapter 23), of Washington's arrogance, and messianic zeal, with periodic changes of religion, generating cynicism and eventually resorting to complex "con games" to get at the desired resources. (To be fair, the World Bank and the aid donors have changed their religion much more frequently than has the IMF.) The IMF and Bank are perceived by the developing country members as "theirs" and not "ours," and their developing country staff members frequently feel themselves alienated from their own societies. Particularly if the IMF's clientele is increasingly to be found in the developing countries, it must acquire greater credibility there, and there must be a broader consensus as to its appropriate functioning. If the IMF is not indeed to atrophy, there will have to be improvements in the ways in which the Fund interacts with its low-income members.

No one opposes the concept of conditionality in IMF lending per se. There are two major conditionality issues, however, on which there are grounds for low-income developing countries' disquiet: (1) the adequacy of low-conditionality balance of payments financing; (2) the nature of such conditionality as there is.

The IMF has provided low-conditionality credit at less than market rates of interest in limited amounts since its inception. This cheap credit has been rationed in part on the basis of formulas agreed in advance, including that introduced later which relates to export instability in the compensatory financing facility (CFF), and in part on the basis of discretionary decisions made by the IMF. Both the formulas and the discretion have been employed in pursuit of general global objectives of stability and of equity. The discretionary decisions are those associated with IMF conditionality.

There is at present very, very little low-conditionality balance of payments finance available to the poorest of the developing countries. Yet these countries have been subject to unprecedented degrees of external shock. While smoothing the flow of imports in these poorest of countries may not make much difference to global economic stability, can anyone doubt that doing so would be conducive to stability and development within these countries? Why has such financing not been made available to them? In particular, what is the rationale for shifting in 1980–81 to high-conditionality finance when in 1974–76 these countries' needs were financed to a much greater degree via low-conditionality lending? The IMF has not offered a sensible answer to these questions. The "permanence" of the most recent oil price changes *cannot* be the explanation (and this is not just because these changes do not now look so enduring). The enormous terms of trade shocks now being absorbed by the poorest primary exporters are not oil-created and can only be seen as temporary. Perhaps, instead, the IMF is now more afraid that its loans will not be repaid. But has anyone ever defaulted on an IMF loan? Is it likely that anyone would?

One must be careful to note that no one is advocating the abolition of conditional lending. As in the old arguments over program development assistance (arguments that were finally won), when no one was arguing for the abolition of project loans, what is at issue is the proportion of total finance that is available at various terms. The proportion of balance of payments financing available to the lowest income countries with minimum conditionality has fallen to pointlessly low levels, and it should rise. The provision of reasonable proportions of finance with a minimum of conditions during times of adversity such as those of the present could get IMF discussions concerning adjustment policies started with greater speed and in a better spirit. There would be less room for bitterness concerning discretionary IMF intercountry allocations and associated accusations of political favoritism, and a greater and earlier sense of joint country-IMF approaches to adjustment.

The existing model of the CFF is not a bad one for this purpose. But as Sidney Dell (Chapter 2) and others have suggested, it must be expanded to meet the dimensions of current and prospective needs. SDR allocations, not necessarily aid-linked, are another obvious possible device for increasing the low-conditionality finance available to those who cannot acquire it elsewhere.

When it comes to the conditions attached to IMF discretionary lending, there appear to be two broad schools of thought. The first advocates the expansion of conditionality to embrace broader objectives—employment, distribution, development. Balance of payments lending, in this approach, should be associated with efforts to overcome long-run problems as well as temporary ones, as the World Bank's structural adjustment lending already explicitly does. It seems that some poor countries at present experiencing severe *post-oil* balance of payments shocks are encountering difficulty receiving IMF balance of payments finance for the smoothing of these new shocks on the ground that they had not sufficiently adjusted to prior shocks. (Translation: can they repay?) The extreme distress of the moment is seen by some as an opportunity to force these previously reluctant adjusters finally to "set their house in order." Unfortunately, against the possibility of a high return from such conditional lending strategy there must be set a high risk of more chaos and suffering than ever—borne, as always, primarily by the weakest.

The second school of thought on conditionality seeks no more (and quite possibly fewer) conditions, together with greater automaticity and effectiveness in their enforcement. Many recommend only external balance targets, on which there is, as has been seen, quite broad analytical agreement, without further specification as to concomitant internal balance objectives or specific policy instruments for their attainment. While a firm believer in analyzing and prescribing for broader development strategy, I am with those who do not see a place for expanded IMF (or Bank) conditionality in these areas. To the maximum extent possible, lending and its conditions should be rule-based and relatively automatically started and stopped. It is still not clear to me how more widely ranging, development-oriented conditions—such as are already contained in the World Bank's structural adjustment lending and in the IMF's extended Fund facility—can be objectively monitored. The enforcement of these broader and vaguer conditions are bound to become a source of future frictions, the more so when, as in the Indian case, the loan is "back-end loaded."

In this connection, I fully endorse Harberger's proposal (above) for contingency clauses governing waivers and modifications in IMF performance targets. The credibility of the process of interaction between the IMF and member governments would certainly be enhanced if there were some joint character to the bearing of the risk of forecasting errors. If there can be IMF-country agreement on what is to be done, it should also be possible to reach agreement on forecasts of key export prices or the terms of trade, other capital flows (whether private or official), supply prospects, and contingency arrangements governing what both parties will do in the face of unforeseen events. Obviously such "contingency contracts" cannot be too complex. The object is to reduce the degree of arbitrariness in the waiver and modification arrangements, and to enhance the quality of the relationship between the IMF and its clients.

Finally, I should like to call attention to the relative dearth of data and skilled professionals in the macroeconomic and financial spheres in many of the countries that are emerging as those of the IMF's principal future lending operations. While the politics of adjustment is usually crucial to what a government actually does, the situation is never improved by faulty analysis, disagreement as to the quality of relevant numbers, and resulting suspicions and sensitivities. It will be necessary to improve technical capacity substantially, particularly in tropical Africa, if the IMF role there is to be understood in the years to come. In some areas, the IMF could perform a useful service simply by transmitting key data on a regular basis. Considering the amount of attention devoted in our meetings to the question of the real effective exchange rate, for instance, it is striking how rarely the country papers (Chapters 11–21) actually presented data on the subject. In part this is because such data are not at present readily available. In many countries they are not available because neither nominal nor real effective exchange rates are anywhere regularly calculated. While continuing its technical assistance and training activities, the IMF might consider the provision of such numbers (presumably using trade weights rather than a bigger multilateral exchange rate model) to *all* its members.

Sterie T. Beza

I first wish to thank Fred Bergsten, John Williamson, and the others who organized the program and ran the conference. It has been a full two-and-a-half days, packed with content. I also wish to say that I found the remarks of those who preceded me in this panel discussion to be most stimulating, and Dick Cooper's summing-up was both comprehensive and masterly.

I have been listening attentively for the last few days, trying to sift through what was being said about International Monetary Fund (IMF) conditionality. In this exercise I was trying to ascertain how this expert group saw conditionality—its role and purposes—and at the same time I was trying to check how the views expressed fit my own understanding of the workings of conditionality. I was also looking for insights into the application of conditionality.

There was no suggestion—and I did not expect it—that the Fund should not attach conditions in lending money to member countries as it seeks to assist countries in adjusting to imbalances in external payments. Adjustment is costly with or without the Fund, as was said more than once, but the presence of the Fund was generally expected to lessen these costs. There was little allusion to the Funds being too soft or too hard, and the discussion focused much more on whether the conditions were the right ones—that is, the most suitable or appropriate ones. There was not, insofar as I could detect, any feeling that conditionality should be loosened. There were suggestions that it ought to be broadened, and there were some suggestions that it might be applied in different ways. Perhaps what I found most intriguing was the thought that conditionality should be broadened, although this is probably not too surprising a suggestion from a group that obviously is interested in seeing the Fund play a more effective role.

On how conditionality might be broadened, matters were not entirely clear. Some noted that governments wanted income distribution taken into account, but after discussion it seems that the most prevalent view was that the Fund ought not to enter into this area. In general, there was support for extending conditions to supply-side aspects. However, there was some uncertainty on my part whether this was a reference to supply-side features the Fund customarily has

Note: Dr. Beza's comments are reproduced by permission of the International Monetary Fund, Washington.

covered in its programs—e.g., policies in respect of the exchange rate, interest rates, public sector prices, trade arrangements, and so forth—or whether it was a reference to other aspects of development policy. I might note that the Fund has relied heavily on the World Bank to assist it in coming to judgments on arrangements—particularly extended arrangements—in which public investment programs are critically important.

There were some suggestions for changing, in varying degrees, the approach to conditionality. Some would have the Fund de-emphasize the present performance criteria and would have it turn to agreements with the countries on policies to be monitored through reviews, at which time judgments on performance would be developed. This suggestion was, in general, associated with proposals to broaden conditionality. I wonder about this suggestion. I think it dismisses too lightly the important role of performance criteria as presently framed, including their characteristic of being subject to unambiguous reading. I would presume that those who wish the Fund to emphasize balance of payments performance would support maintenance of the existing criteria, as would those who prefer that the Fund not assume new responsibilities. For those who think the current performance criteria, with their emphasis on monetary and fiscal policies, are too onerous or irrelevant, I would note that these criteria relate to variables national authorities customarily monitor on their own, although perhaps not as precisely as is done under arrangements with the Fund.

There were some suggestions that the focus of conditionality be changed. One participant advanced the view that employment might be targeted in Fund programs. My response to this is that I do not think it is feasible to make promises about employment and unemployment in a stabilization program, and certainly not to elevate them to the status of performance criteria. The attempt to deliver on such targets could be destabilizing. There was also a suggestion that the fiscal limit should center on public consumption, and that foreign financing for public investment projects not be constrained. This suggestion is attractive in some respects, particularly since it might be seen to loosen the reins on those dynamic public sector enterprises that have good investment prospects. However, not all public investments meet the test of quality that would be implied in such treatment; furthermore, it is not unknown for top-ranking public enterprises to borrow on behalf of others. Finally, there is always the question of distinguishing effectively between public consumption and public investment.

There was one suggestion for change in the policy emphasis of programs that I would have no difficulty accepting, although it does not seem to be one that is attractive to the authorities of member countries. The suggestion was to opt for a shock approach to stabilization, accompanied by an incomes policy to minimize the effects on employment. More generally on incomes policy, it is obviously necessary, in the wake of devaluations, to avoid changes in public sector wages or minimum wages that would undo the adjustment sought through such exchange rate changes.

Some discussion took place on whether there had been a swing in conditionality in recent years. As was brought out in that discussion, in the recent past the Fund developed the capacity to increase the volume of lending and the numbers who sought assistance grew. As was also brought out, many members that had been given the benefit of the doubt as regards their adjustment programs did not deliver as had been hoped. Thus, it was inevitable that there would be more scrutiny of programs, more reliance on prior conditions as a manifestation of not being able to take for granted that there would be a follow-through on promises, and greater reliance on one-year as opposed to multiyear programs. I should note here that it is difficult to make multiyear programs more than just a series of one-year programs, given the general problems involved in projecting ahead for long periods and in framing fiscal policy much beyond the current or next budget cycle; some of the numbers in the out years of multiyear programs were just numbers. However, I think there has not been what I would term a systematic tightening of the goals of programs as expressed in the budget policy being sought, credit ceilings, and so on. There was, as I have mentioned, increased concern over making sure the programs were delivered.

In connection with the question of how conditionality has worked, I thought we had a good discussion on the difference between whether conditionality could work in principle and whether it was given a chance in practice. It was noted that if countries are not serious about adjusting, there is little that the Fund can do about it. Mention was made in this regard of instances in which governments failed to reveal any serious commitment to adjust. There also was recognition that the Fund's conditionality generally applies to members facing significant difficulties—it is not the members in strong economic positions that call upon the Fund—and it is through these cases that we see conditionality working. Therefore, instances of shortfalls in performance ought not to be viewed as surprising.

There was appropriate emphasis in this discussion, I thought, on the differences policies can make. Policies that are seen to be effective in addressing countries' problems clearly serve to improve the countries' creditworthiness. IMF conditionality has a role in this regard, although it is obvious that countries can demonstrate behavior on their own comparable to that which would have been obtained through the application of Fund conditionality, and this has been done in certain instances. I would underscore what was said in the discussion about how compliance with conditionality can help to improve the private sector's access to foreign capital.

At certain stages of the discussion, there were some questions about the relevance of the Fund and of its proper role, and in the examination of certain country cases (Chapters 11–21) it was asked whether the Fund's conditionality as applied had not been counterproductive—contributing to problems rather than to their solution. However, the response to this question was in the negative, and I will leave the matter at that. As for the speculation whether the Fund genuinely has a role—or whether its role will not indeed by very limited, as was suggested by some—these are questions best answered by others and not by an IMF insider. What I can say is that our current work load points to the continued high involvement of the Fund with countries in balance of payments difficulties.

I should like to say a few words about the suggestion that the Fund and private financial institutions will be working in different markets, that the private institutions will do most of the business, and that in effect the private institutions will apply the relevant conditionality.

I would first note in this connection that I would not normally expect the Fund to be large in financial intermediation. When conditions are "average" or reasonably smooth, there probably should not be a lot of business for the Fund. Thus, I would not judge the effectiveness of the Fund by the general volume of its operations relative to those of the private markets, although the Fund obviously has to have the capacity to put up sizable amounts of funds in dealing with countries in difficulty. I would also emphasize that I would not wish to see the Fund assume the role of leader in a lending cartel, inasmuch as I consider it important to preserve a wide diversity of views about the prospects of any individual country.

I would like to go on to say that I am not persuaded that the private financial institutions and the Fund are in fact working in different markets. Some countries that are probably now regarded as important customers of the private financial institutions were in arrangements with the Fund not long ago, and some countries have been emphasizing to the private financial markets the closeness of their relationship with the Fund, citing the discussions of their policies with the Fund, even though they are not using the Fund's resources.

As for the suggestion that private financial institutions are developing the machinery for the evaluation of country situations and moving in general to emulate conditionality, I always assume that those who lend money have to worry about the state of the borrower, and it is not surprising that efforts are being made to strengthen the machinery in question. It nevertheless remains, at least up to now, that certain features of the application of Fund conditionality are not readily duplicated by private institutions. Many private institutions have said this, and the work that the Fund is asked to do in this connection demonstrates it.

I turn next to a question about the circumstances in which conditionality is applied. It was in this area that the discussion of the last few days left me at times a little uneasy. Perhaps it was no more than a matter of language or emphasis, but I felt that the discussion of how conditionality was applied or how it might be modified assumed that the management and staff of the Fund and the national authorities met to consider the bases of financial programs with all aspects of policies open. This is not the case, of course, as I believe Mr. Diz (Chapter 12) brought out in the discussion. The variety of initial conditions faced is very large, including the history of performance under a preceding program, adjustment actions that may have been started by the authorities before approaching the Fund, the degree to which the authorities consulted the management and staff of the Fund before devising their adjustment measures, and so forth. What the Fund management and staff are charged with doing is to ensure that the programs developed give reasonable prospect of adjustment that is adequate in the light of circumstances, and that the programs are in general conformity with the policies supported by the Fund.

Before concluding my remarks, I would like to address a few issues that have arisen in the course of this panel discussion. On interest rates, those who advocate controls fail to appreciate, in my view, the flexibility that private asset holders have to change their portfolios to escape the effects of controls, and at the same time they underestimate the inefficiencies fostered by controls. On the suggestion that more financing with low conditionality is needed, I think it is crucial that countries concentrate attention on adjustment needs, and therefore the development of programs that would qualify for high-conditionality financing is more important than the financing itself. On the suggestion for inflation-indexed ceilings or targets, such devices would further remove the restraints on inflation, and thus I feel their introduction would be inappropriate. In saying this I am aware of the difficulties of projecting inflation, but at the same time most authorities are currently operating with goals to reduce inflation, and such aims are taken into account in framing programs.

CHAPTER **23**

The Role of the International Monetary Fund: The Disputes, Qualifications, and Future

Dragoslav Avramovíc

International Monetary Fund (IMF) conditionality is one of the central issues of controversy in North-South relations, and its principles and implementation are likely to be at the forefront of any serious North-South negotiations.

The Disputes

Four main reasons for the disputes are the following.

• Disagreements concerning the main source of balance of payments trouble and hence its main remedy. The borrowing country will admit that domestic inflation is a problem but will frequently insist that inflation is a result not only of excess domestic demand, but also, and sometimes primarily, of specific supply bottlenecks and external causes. The borrower will also frequently argue that excess capacity exists in the economy, that the missing element is extra supply of foreign exchange, which the country should be lent and eventually enabled to earn, and that, by depressing aggregate demand (the action normally advocated by the Fund), matters will only become worse. "Neither foreign financial experts, nor the local authorities, will ever solve the basic problems of the Argentinian economy so long as they ignore intersectoral disequilibria and insist on global, restrictive pol-

Note: Responsibility for this paper is that of the author, rather than that of the organization where he is now employed.

icies from the demand side" (Diamond 1973). Most of the country studies presented here have stressed the importance of removing specific sector bottlenecks in the adjustment process: Green (Chapter 15), Killick (Chapter 16), Marshall, Mardones, and Marshall (Chapter 13), Bacha (Chapter 14), da Silva Lopes (Chapter 19), referring to the experiences of countries as varied as Tanzania, Kenya, Argentina, Chile, Brazil, Portugal—and the same point has been argued for Peru (Shydlowsky and Wicht 1978) and Jamaica (Girvan, Bernal, and Hughes 1980). The Fund will reply that they do not deny the importance of supply, but that whatever else is done on this front will not solve the problem without free market pricing, and that, in any case, demand restraint is urgently needed if the balance of payments crisis is to be handled with despatch, as it should be. The dispute remains.

• Disagreements concerning the scope, timing, and policing of the standard Fund set of stabilization measures. The Fund is not satisfied only with assurances that its loan will be repaid over the medium term as agreed, or that the program the borrower has adopted provides a reasonable promise that such repayment would be feasible. The Fund also has other objectives, resulting in part from its Articles of Agreement and in part from the practices that have been built up during the last 30 years. The Fund now formulates its views on stabilization policy in individual countries within a formidable set of objectives and constraints. As recently stated by a senior expert on its staff, "the ultimate aim of Fund financial assistance is to restore viability of the balance of payments in a context of price stability and sustained economic growth, without resort to measures that impair the freedom of trade and payments" (Guitián 1981). Hong Kong, Singapore, and Taiwan may be able to do all five things at the same time; most developing countries cannot. Some will have to sacrifice price stability for some time to expand exports, and some will have to restrict nonessential imports. Perhaps the root cause of the difficulty is that the Fund has been trying to achieve too many things at the same time, while some of the borrowing countries have hardly been able to keep their heads above the water, caught as they are between inadequacies of domestic policies and external forces beyond their control. Under these circumstances, Fund-country relations have almost inevitably become, in a number of cases, marked by continuing haggling over what the Fund considers a desirable package and what the country feels it is able to deliver.

• The Fund adheres to a specific theory of economic policy that is at variance with the views held by a varying number of borrowing countries at any particular time. The Fund is not alone among the international organizations having a "view"; as matters have developed, most have distinct views that influence their marshaling and interpretation of facts and policy conclusions. Broadly, the Fund believes in three fundamental points: financial discipline, free trade, and market prices (Dornbusch, Comments to Chapters 7–10). Most borrowing countries will agree with the need for financial discipline, even though few will find it possible to stick with it. Most will dispute the tenet of free trade and will be able to cite Japan's growth experience with managed trade. Many will also argue the need for at least occasional market intervention on various grounds: the former Swedish prime minister said several years ago, "the invisible hand is of flesh and blood" (Palme 1982). The Fund management has been aware of the pitfalls and effects of the somewhat tenuous theoretical basis on which its policy is built:

> I have given you only the barest outline of the contents of conditionality. But I have said enough, I think, to indicate why it should have become a subject of controversy. After all, control of inflation and the effectiveness of monetary policy, or the responsiveness of savings to interest rate changes, the efficacy of exchange rate changes in inducing changes in trade flows, and the responsiveness of farmers to price incentives—these have been among lively subjects of debate among economists for decades. But what gives a particularly sharp edge to the controversy surrounding conditionality is that the manner in which these issues are resolved bears on the real income of one or another economic group. This goes to the heart of national policies in all countries. Both inflation and balance of payments difficulties reflect efforts on the part of a society, seen as a whole, to avail itself of more resources than it can currently generate. Dealing with these problems involves, especially in the short run, cutting back on real incomes and the use of resources; and fears on the part of each section of society that it may have to assume a disproportionate share of the burden of this cut-back provoke strong resistance to efforts aimed at this objective. It is not difficult to see why such matters should become highly charged political issues. (Witteveen 1978.)

The Fund staff is also aware of many of these problems—see the sophisticated review by Nowzad (1981). A recent analysis by Buira, executive director representing a group of Latin American countries, offers a comprehensive, incisive, and critical inside view of the theory and practice of conditionality and offers specific remedies (Buira 1981).

- Given the uncertainties and doubts listed above, what is surprising is the persistence and conviction with which particular policies are argued, although it must be added that this is not a monopoly of the Fund staff. The staff carries an enormous personal responsibility:

> Present dissatisfaction with Fund conditionality often arises from differences between the authorities and the staff whenever the latter—partly as a result of institutional constraints—is felt to assume a role of decisionmaker and to press for the adoption of a particular solution which may not be in accordance with the economic, social, and political priorities of the authorities. . . . The power exercised in stand-by negotiations by one or a few staff technicians, exempt from all political responsibility but taking major policy decisions, may give rise to considerable tension between the country and the Fund, particularly when the national technicians are not persuaded by the arguments of the staff and may see a broad area for the exercise of judgment in the design of a program more in accordance with national priorities. (Buira 1981.)

A growing number of developing countries are now using the advisory services of private investment banking houses on debt rescheduling, debt management, and borrowing strategy and tactics, at fees that may exceed $1 million a year: Turkey, Zaire, Jamaica, Gabon, Costa Rica, Sudan, Uganda, Zimbabwe, Peru, Bolivia, Dominican Republic, Senegal, Ghana, Indonesia, Sri Lanka, Cameroon, among others. Some of this advice, particularly concerning the establishment of contacts with potential private lenders, can perhaps be provided only by such private banking houses. However, most of the rest should be par excellence the function of international agencies. Why are the poor countries prepared to pay for the advice of Wall Street and the City in preference to the advice they should be getting free from the United Nations system? Because it is more technical, factual, and less loaded with a "view"?

The Qualifications

It is only fair to look at the other side of the coin: the actions by the Fund for the benefit of the developing countries.

Two facilities were established with very low conditionality (i.e., leading to almost automatic drawings): the oil facility and the compensatory financing facility (CFF). Regretfully, the first, entitling countries to loans to finance oil imports, was allowed to lapse. The second, CFF, entitling countries to loans to finance shortfalls in their export earnings, continues to exist and is as active as ever under present disastrous conditions in commodity markets. This facility and the buffer stock financing facility, also set up in the Fund, are the only things the international community has managed to do on a world scale so far to cope with price fluctuations of export commodities of developing countries. (The Common Fund is still in the process of signature and ratification.) The CFF is insufficient, and the buffer stock financing facility is inactive because of the way it is set up, but they are there and can be set right and expanded, thus helping to improve the entire structure.

In 1980–81 the Fund expanded its lending on an unprecedented scale in terms of amounts lent and the apparent ease with which many of the country negotiations were handled (Dale, Chapter 1). It seemed that this heralded a new beginning. Regretfully, the screws seem to have been turned back again, judging by the number of suspensions and cancellations (Gulati 1982), which the Fund attributes to non-performance or technical reasons, while other sources suggest they reflect a shift in Fund policy (Killick, Chapter 16).

There is one episode in Fund history that is little known and almost forgotten: support to Chile under the socialist government of the late Salvador Allende, when most other agencies, national and international, had stopped lending, even prior to the deterioration in Chile's economy. It is true that the IMF lending was done though the quasi-automatic CFF (see above), and therefore active decision was limited; but it is probable that a technical reason for not lending could have been found if it had been decided not to lend. The IMF's managing director then was Pierre-Paul Schweitzer, now retired, and the two key IMF officials who were involved, Fernando Vera and Jack Barnouin, are still in IMF service, although outside its main offices. The history of this support is yet to be written and set against the heavy and widespread criticism of the Fund for its close identification with right-wing political and financial interests. It may weigh little, but it is there.

There may be a curious and not yet fully understood and analyzed community of interests, and perhaps even views in some degree, between high financial officials in developing countries and the IMF management and staff. The story is that the tight fist of the IMF is being used by these officials as an argument in their internal struggles with government colleagues in the spending ministries and with political leaders in keeping the lid on budgetary and other expenditures. The importance of this point is difficult to judge by present, readily available evidence.

The Future

Five elements have been offered on different occasions to change the scope and implementation of conditionality, as follows.

• It has been proposed to establish a new IMF facility with low conditionality to finance balance of payments deficits arising from causes beyond control of developing countries (Group of 24, 1979; South-North Conference 1980). The latest in this family of proposals is a low-conditionality facility to finance import cost increases (Dell, Chapter 2).

• An alternative or a supplement to the above is a revision of the present practice of conditionality. The possible direction of movement has been indicated by Williamson in his "nonpaternalistic solution" (1977) and by Buira (1981). It is the country that formulates the adjustment program rather than the Fund; the staff of the latter serves as a technical advisor. The Fund still needs to be convinced that the prescribed path to equilibrium can in fact be satisfactorily pursued through the methods chosen, and the policy dialogue between the borrowing country and the Fund still takes place, but the choice of methods is that of the country: what gets cut, who gets the premium to expand, how it is done. It follows that some of the constraints built into the present Fund "ideal" practice (Guitián 1981) have to be given away. A senior Fund official suggested that a compromise may be possible on inflation and on exchange restrictions, provided it is made certain that payment arrears do not accumulate indefinitely and exchange rate flexibility is maintained to offset the effects of inflation on the external balance (Finch, Chapter 4). This is a promising approach. The difficulties involved in simultaneously pursuing balance of payments recovery and price stabilization were stressed by Cline (Chapter 9), Bindert (1982), and da Silva Lopes (Chapter 19).

• The present system of quantitative "performance criteria," based on credit ceilings agreed with the Fund, whose breach leads to an automatic cancellation of the Fund loan, should be replaced by a more flexible system where the emphasis is on broad policy issues instead of specific numbers (Harberger, remarks, Chapter 22; Killick, Chapter 16; Crawford, Chapter 17; Marshall, Mardones, and Marshall, Chapter 13; and da Silva Lopes, Chapter 19). The numbers have proven to be subject to large errors, leading to the need for a continuing renegotiation of ceilings, with the country placed in a position of requesting loans again and again. The very procedure of setting and policing specific limits on the countries' own credit operations, even if they have external financial effects, is an odd thing in an international cooperative endeavor.

• Lending to facilitate structural adjustments by helping expand output in critical sectors and removing the foreign exchange constraint to growth generally has almost universal support. The World Bank started such a program in 1980–81, but the aggregate amount is still relatively small (Stern, Chapter 5). The first experience with such a loan to an African country has been found encouraging (Killick, Chapter 16); criticisms have been raised with respect to a similar loan to an Asian country (*Le Monde* 1981). As more experience is acquired, it will be possible to assess better the important contribution to the adjustment process such loans can make. The danger is that they may become yet one more vehicle for conditionality, pressing the country to move faster toward free-market pricing, free trade, higher interest rates, and priority for export crops than is advisable. Some of these things may well be needed and probably are in many situations, but sight should not be lost of the primary objective that countries expect of these loans: finance for sectoral investments and for general and sectoral working capital.

- The last point has to do with the "view" as it results from the tradition and personnel makeup of the institution. The international financial agencies would benefit from an injection of management and senior staff talent with a different background, different outlook, and different style than the one that now dominates their thinking and operations. It is the "double dominance" of these institutions, by purse and by people, that ought to be modified in the direction of a cooperative and inquiring spirit. This would then represent a real change in the international order of things (Gulhati 1977).

A major question arises as to whether changes along the above lines would jeopardize the access of the institutions to funds. The risk exists, but it is controllable and probably not serious. First, the developing countries are well aware how important it is to preserve the institutions' good reputation both with the developed country governments and with the capital markets. Second, the major creditor country today and in the foreseeable future is Saudi Arabia, itself a developing country: hence, it should look favorably at changes in these institutions in the direction of greater influence by developing countries. Third, the key debtors in the developing world have shown during the last decade of economic upheaval and external shocks that they attach priority to meeting their external financial obligations. One could argue that their readiness to pay back would increase if they had a larger share of responsibility for the lending decisions than is now the case.

What if no significant changes take place and things continue as they are? The demand then for the establishment of a new institution and for a more radical reordering of matters in general will inevitably increase. A call for a United Nations Conference on International

Money and Finance was already made at the Arusha South-North Conference (1980; see also Lichtensztejn, Chapter 10).

Overshadowing all this is the rapid deterioration of the world financial scene. What role the different institutions, existing and new, will play if the world situation becomes worse is not possible to say at the present time. It will partly depend on the present institutions' diagnosis of the problem, the vision they will show in handling it, and their courage to act to prevent further deterioration. In a sense, looking back to 40 years ago, one cannot help but admire the spirit and imagination used in trying to build the financial foundations for the postwar world. The United States and the United Kingdom then—together with Canada, Australia, and a few others—could have refrained from creating international institutions and instead could have relied on their own national agencies to finance whom they wanted and on terms they wanted, without any rules and regards for other countries' interests. They did it differently: while preserving their own national interests, they went out of their way to meet the interests of others as they were known at the time. Much has changed since, and major adaptations are needed. A central question is whether it is possible to recreate the spirit in which an understanding for other people's problems and interests, particularly those who are weaker, becomes the guidance for action.

References

Buira, Ariel. 1981. "IMF Financial Programs and Conditionality." Processed. See also Ariel Buira Seira, "Recession, Inflation, and the International Monetary System." *World Development* (November/December 1981).

Diamond, Marcelo. 1973. *Doctrinas Economicas, Desarrollo e Independencia*. Buenos Aires. Cited in Shydlowsky and Wicht, p. 2–4.

Girvan, Norman, Richard Bernal, and Wesley Hughes. 1980. "The IMF and the Third World: The Case of Jamaica 1974–80." In *Development Dialogue* (Uppsala), vol. 2.

Group of Twenty-Four. 1979. "Outline for a Program of Action on International Monetary Reform." Belgrade and Washington (September).

Guitián, Manuel. 1981. "Conditionality: Access to Fund Resources." *Finance and Development.*

Gulati, I. S. 1982. *IMF Conditionality and Low Income Countries*. Trivandrum, India: Centre for Development Studies, (July).

Gulhati, Ravi. October 1977. "A Mandate on Behalf of the Poor?" *The Round Table* (London), no. 268 (October).

Le Monde. 1981. "Les Philippines sous l'emprise de la Banque Mondiale." 10, 11 October and 21 November.

Nowzad, Bahram. 1981. "The IMF and Its Critics." *Essays in International Finance* no. *146,* Princeton, NJ: Princeton University.

Palme, Olof. 1982. Statement at the Brandt Commission meeting held in Mont Pélerin, Switzerland (February).

Shydlowsky, Daniel M., and Juan M. Wicht. 1978. "The Anatomy of an Economic Failure: Peru 1968–78." Washington: Wilson International Center for Scholars. Processed.

South-North Conference on the International Monetary System and the New International Order, Arusha, Tanzania, June-July, 1980. In *Development Dialogue* (Uppsala) vol. 2 (1980).

Williamson, John. 1977. "The IMF's Conditionality Practices." London: Commonwealth Secretariat (September). Processed.

Witteveen, H. Johannes. 1978. "Financing the LDCs, the Role of Public and Private Institutions." Euromarkets Conference, London. Processed.

CHAPTER 24

The Lending Policies of the International Monetary Fund

John Williamson

The Fund's performance as a lender has been a perennial source of controversy, particularly in the borrowing countries. The Fund has been accused of adopting a doctrinaire monetarist approach and being insensitive to the individual situations of borrowing countries; imposing unreasonably onerous conditions; being ideologically biased against socialism and in favor of free markets; and even perpetuating dependency. Recently, especially since the Reagan administration took office in the United States, these familiar criticisms have been matched by contrary charges: that certain Fund-sponsored programs offer no reasonable hope of achieving lasting adjustment and therefore run the risk of devaluing the Fund's "seal of approval," and that the Fund has been guilty of overextending itself into intermediation that can perfectly well be handled by the commercial banks. The Fund has been buffeted by these conflicting criticisms: first into a major loosening of the conditionality attached to its loans in mid-1979, and subsequently, as from May or June 1981, into a new tightening. (Further details on these variations are provided below under Cyclical Variations.) This chapter draws on the body of analysis in preceding chapters as well as other relevant material to suggest answers to the main policy problems facing the Fund and to provide an evaluation of the performance of the Fund and the validity of the charges made against it.

Note: This chapter, in slightly different form, was first published as a monograph: John Williamson, *The Lending Policies of the International Monetary Fund,* POLICY ANALYSES IN INTERNATIONAL ECONOMICS (Washington: Institute for International Economics, 1982).

The five main policy questions addressed in this chapter are as follows:

• *The Role of the Fund.* What should the Fund's role be in the international financial intermediation process? Should it be more than a lender of last resort? Does the answer differ as between member countries in different situations, notably those with and without access to extensive credit from the commercial banks; and does that imply the Fund should discriminate in the way it treats different members? Is there a case for extending the low-conditionality facilities provided by the Fund?

• *Cooperation with the World Bank.* What is the basis of the present division of labor between the Fund and Bank? Is it a logical one? Is it being implemented effectively? Are there opportunities for improved collaboration?

• *The Design of Adjustment Programs.* What objectives should be sought when the Fund advises a member country on the design of an adjustment program? What policy measures should be included in an adjustment program? How rapidly should adjustment be sought?

• *Monitoring Adjustment Programs.* How should the policy measures that jointly constitute an adjustment program be divided among preconditions, performance criteria, and policy understandings (that is, actions that are not explicitly monitored)? Can and should performance criteria be made more flexible? Are there variables that could usefully be treated as performance criteria that are not at the moment?

• *Cyclical Variation.* Should the Fund vary its conditions for lending as an instrument of global anticyclical policy? Can the state of the economic cycle explain the changes in conditionality observed in 1979–82?

The concluding section of this chapter draws on the earlier discussion of specific issues, as well as on additional material, in order to evaluate the Fund's performance and the validity of the main criticisms that have been leveled against it. It closes with a brief summary of the principal policy changes suggested in earlier sections and a consideration of the implications of the analysis for the forthcoming review of the appropriate level of financial resources that should be made available to the Fund via the Eighth General Review of Quotas on which negotiations are scheduled to conclude by the end of 1983.

The Role of the Fund

The Fund was conceived as a monetary institution charged with supervising international monetary arrangements. Its lending powers were designed to support its ability to contribute to that end by helping its members respond to payments deficits without measures destructive of national or international prosperity. That was understood to mean restraining countries from deflating so far as to jeopardize full employment as well as outlawing competitive depreciation and preventing the imposition of trade restrictions for payments' purposes.

Whether those purposes would be better promoted by automatic or conditional lending was the subject of a lively debate even before Bretton Woods (Sidney Dell, 1981). The early operations of the Fund in 1947–48 involved minimal conditionality, despite pressure against automaticity by the United States. The debate continued during the prolonged curtailment of Fund lending during the years of US Marshall Plan aid, and in 1953 the US view was, in most essentials, adopted as Fund policy. Limited borrowing remained possible with little or no conditionality, but countries wishing to borrow large sums, relative to their quotas, had to submit to (high) conditionality.

Low conditionality involves merely establishment that a country has a "balance of payments need" (a deficit) coupled with a declaration, which the Fund does not ordinarily challenge, that it is taking measures to resolve its deficit.

High conditionality involves the country's design of a specific set of measures to eliminate its deficit, Fund agreement that the program will be adequate for that purpose, and the country's commitment to implement that program.

Deficits were traditionally classified into three types, each of which had associated an appropriate policy response:

Temporary deficits were due to climatic factors or cyclical variations in the terms of trade or foreign demand, and could be expected to reverse themselves without adjustment action. These should be financed rather than adjusted.

Some deficits were due to *excess demand* and should be adjusted by eliminating the excess demand. These should not be financed, although the Fund might temporarily replenish the country's liquidity until reserves flowed back.

Fundamental disequilibria were deficits that would persist over the cycle as a whole, even in the absence of excess demand. The appropriate policy was devaluation to improve competitiveness, reinforced by demand restraint if needed to prevent the emergence of excess demand, and accompanied by financing if a deficit persisted during the period of adjustment.

In each case, some financing might be called for, but it was to be temporary financing to bridge a gap until the balance of payments recovered. The Fund's resources would therefore revolve; the Fund was in the business of making temporary loans. It had a duty to make sure that those loans would indeed revolve, which required that it ensure that adjustment was taking place if the deficit was not inherently self-reversing. That was the purpose of conditionality. The Fund became—and the Fund staff clearly regards this as the essence of its mandate—an "adjustment institution."

William Dale (Chapter 1) has recalled that in the 1960s the Fund had a number of stand-by programs that were catalytic, both in strengthening the technocrats pressing for responsible policies within national governments and in sustaining the confidence necessary for countries to attract capital inflows. But not all Fund programs were welcomed even by the technocrats as in the enlightened self-interest of their countries, and indeed the Fund's stereotyped image (especially in the Third World) became that of a creditor which inflexibly insisted on rapid and sometimes brutal adjustment.

In the 1970s the Fund became much more a lender of last resort, avoided except in extremis, in consequence of the interaction between the ill-repute with which it had come to be regarded in many of the major capital importing countries and the ready availability of loans from commercial banks. Countries with access to the international capital market—which include all the industrial countries and new industrial countries (NICs), some of the socialist countries (in the decade prior to 1981), and a number of the orthodoxly managed developing countries—in normal circumstances need no longer rely on the Fund to finance a payments deficit. Only when they are imprudent to the point of undermining their creditworthiness do they turn to the Fund, whose high-conditionality credits provide not only a breathing space but, more important, a "seal of approval." The interest of these countries lies in having a Fund that can restore creditworthiness, when necessary. With this endorsement, recovery (measured in terms of reserves) can be dramatically quick, as shown by the experiences of Britain, Italy, Peru, and Portugal.

But there is also a second group of countries, which includes most of the poorer developing countries, which have no substantial access to loans from commercial banks. Because these countries have no alternative significant source of balance of payments financing, they still need the Fund for that purpose.

According to Rimmer de Vries (Comments, Chapters 1–3), the Fund clientele has shrunk to this second group of countries, in which the commercial banks seek to avoid exposure. He points out that low-income countries, which currently receive two-thirds of the Fund's total commitments, account for a mere 7 percent of the banks' exposure in non-oil developing countries. However, he has been accused of exaggerating the rigidity of the dichotomy: countries with Fund programs and significant bank borrowing in the last five years include India, Italy, Peru, Portugal, Romania, Turkey, and Yugoslavia. The amount of credit outstanding to the "potentially creditworthy" may be small at any one time, precisely because the restoration of confidence permits a prompt recovery of external borrowing, but the Fund nevertheless remains important to those countries for as long as they can conceive of circumstances where they might encounter creditworthiness problems.

While the Fund retains an important role in relation to the group of countries that borrows extensively from the commercial banks, it is most certainly a different role from the one it has with its other, generally poorer, members, which have no other available source of balance of payments finance. This raises two questions: whether the Fund should formally discriminate between members, and, if not, whether its general practices should be tailored to the needs of the "potentially creditworthy" group or the others. The Fund has always avoided dividing its members into categories and has sought to preserve the principle of uniform treatment of all members. This is attractive if it can be done without jeopardizing the interests of either group. But can it?

As already argued, the "potentially creditworthy" group needs access to the high-conditionality facilities on occasion, with a meaningful degree of conditionality to preserve the value of the IMF "seal of approval." The low-conditionality and unconditional facilities are inessential to this group, since they are in a position to resort to bank finance for the purposes to which those facilities are directed, the financing of routine fluctuations. But they would still find it expedient to tap the unconditional and low-conditionality facilities when the rules permit, since Fund credit remains relatively cheap.

In contrast, the unconditional and low-conditionality facilities remain of critical importance to the second group of countries. It is this group that Sidney Dell (1981; Chapter 2, this volume) addresses when he says that the degree of conditionality should vary depending upon the source of a deficit. The compensatory financing facility (CFF) (and the oil facilities of 1974–76), he argues, embody the principle of making available low-conditionality credit to finance a deficit that

TABLE 24.1 TERMS OF TRADE CHANGES AND DRAWINGS FROM COMPENSATORY FINANCING FACILITY BY SUB-SAHARAN AFRICA, 1978–81
(SDR million)

Year (1)	*Terms-of-trade impact on balance of payments* (2)	*Payments impact of export price changes* (3)	*Drawings on* CFF (4)	*Repayments to* CFF (5)	*Net drawings on* CFF (6)
1978	−1,300	350	151	26	125
1979	−400	2,400	216	61	155
1980	−2,500	2,400	112	160	−48
1981	−1,350	−1,100	398	193	205

Source: International Monetary Fund.

arises from circumstances *beyond a country's own control.* He asks why that principle should be restricted to the particular instance of an export shortfall, and urges its generalization to other sources of deficit.

The Fund now accepts that argument in the additional instance of increased costs for cereal imports, but a country can still get into deficit because of many other factors outside its own control—the world business cycle, protectionism in developed countries, wars between neighboring countries, or natural disasters. Dell argues for adoption of the principle of providing low-conditionality finance in all such cases so that resort to the high-conditionality facilities would essentially be restricted to cases of a deficit caused by national mismanagement.

The potential importance of this proposal can be illustrated by considering the situation in sub-Saharan Africa, an area that suffered a massive terms of trade deterioration cumulating to 20 percent over the period 1977–81 (with a further worsening still in train in mid-1982). The existing compensatory financing facility of the Fund has financed a very small part of this deterioration, especially on a net basis (Table 24.1). A major reason for CFF inactivity is that entitlement to draw on it is based on export shortfalls relative to trend, and until 1981, export prices were still rising, though much more slowly than import prices. The proposed extension of low-conditionality finance would therefore have been of significant value to the African countries in helping to tide them over this difficult period.

A well-stated version of the Fund's traditional response to this argument can be found in Bahram Nowzad's Princeton Essay (1981, p. 16):

> Despite its intuitive appeal, this proposal essentially addresses the wrong question. The necessity for adjustment policies depends not on the geographic origin of imbalance, but rather on its nature, on whether or not the imbalance is temporary and self-reversing in a reasonable period of time. If the imbalance is not transient, then whether or not its causes were within the control of the authorities (assuming that this can even be determined with sufficient accuracy) is of secondary importance. It is neither feasible nor desirable to finance a deficit over a protracted period of time or to suppress the difficulties by restriction. Unless adjustment takes place, the difficulties will reappear, perhaps in more severe form, necessitating even more stringent adjustment measures at a later date. It is true that adjustment measures must be tailored to the circumstances of the country. For a country with a good track record and a basically well-managed economy, conditionality can be somewhat relaxed if the problem is of external origin. But to propose as a general principle differential conditionality according to the source of the balance of payments difficulty is an entirely different matter.
>
> The proponents of linking adjustment efforts to the perceived source of difficulties often support their proposal by referring to the Fund's compensatory financing facility. One of the basic conditions for utilizing this facility is that an export shortfall be "largely attributable to circumstances beyond the control of the member." But the decision establishing the facility also provides that it is to apply to "payments difficulties produced by *temporary export shortfalls*" (emphasis added). In other words, there must be a clear indication that the shortfall will be self-reversing; the compensatory financing facility is not meant to deal with secular declines in exports, even if these are caused by circumstances beyond the control of the country.[1]

There is surely force in Nowzad's argument. When a country has been subjected to a permanent adverse payments shock, it has to adjust. But that does not establish the optimality of present arrangements, for two reasons.

First, and most powerfully, the CFF does not deal with many exogenous shocks that can be presumed to be temporary, as the terms of trade deterioration in 1981, shown in Table 24.1, surely must be. Problems would, of course, arise in determining which deficits were likely to be self-reversing (as in determining their exogeneity), and

[1] Quoted by permission of the International Finance Section of Princeton University, copyright © 1982.

extension of the CFF to cover other exogenous payments shocks would no doubt demand an effort toward establishing the patterns of current account deficits and surpluses that are, and should be, sought by member countries. There would be no harm in that: it is paradoxical that an "adjustment institution" should have failed over the years to delineate where adjustment ought to be leading, so as to ensure the global consistency of different countries' objectives.

Second, some critics might also contend that countries should first have the right to decide for themselves how they wish to adjust when confronted with a permanent adverse shock. After all, the Fund does not have a monopoly on knowledge of the steps necessary to secure adjustment. These individuals might argue that Nowzad's point could be adequately met by providing low-conditionality finance on a *tapering* basis when a country encounters what is judged to be a permanent adverse payments shock, so as to provide an incentive to undertake the necessary adjustment, parallel with the finance to permit the adjustment to be implemented gradually. For example, a country might be permitted automatic borrowing rights equivalent to 100 percent of an estimated permanent adverse shock in the first year, 75 percent in the second year, 50 percent in the third year, tapering down to zero after the fourth year. If a country failed to design and implement an effective adjustment program within the four-year grace period, then it would in due course exhaust its automatic borrowing rights and be forced back into accepting "grandmotherly" advice from the Fund, which its previous failures would indicate it needed.

The case for providing substantial financing to *complement* adjustment is today much stronger than it was before the oil price increases, for reasons that have been sensed but not adequately articulated by the Fund. The essential point is that the traditional three-way classification of deficits into those that are self-reversing, those due to excess demand, and those due to overvaluation was inadequate to the situation that confronted many oil-importing countries in 1974 and in 1979–80. There was little reason to consider their deficits to be self-reversing. They were clearly not in general the result of excess demand (though that was sometimes an aggravating factor). Neither did they seem to fit comfortably into the third category of deficit, "fundamental disequilibrium," inasmuch as that had been thought of as a situation in which relative price changes could switch expenditure toward domestically produced goods to whatever extent was necessary to cure a payments deficit without creating a recession.

But where domestic output of tradable goods is already as high as capacity permits and the economy lacks the elasticity for short-run substitution between tradables and nontradables in production or consumption, price signals alone are not sufficient: expenditure switching requires structural change. Price signals may be an indispensible precondition for inducing the appropriate changes, but those changes also need investment and time. And so there is a fourth type of deficit, a *structural* deficit[2] with its own implied policy response, *structural adjustment*. Since this is an inherently lengthy process, it is associated with a need for substantial financing.

The Fund's extended facility, created in 1974, was intended to address structural problems, but its terms of reference failed to focus on the reason given above for identifying certain payments deficits as structural. The official description of the problems addressed by the extended facility is: (1) serious imbalance relating to structural maladjustments in production and trade where cost and price distortions have been widespread and (2) an economy characterized by slow growth and an inherently weak balance of payments position that prevents pursuit of an active development policy.

The second part of this description is open to the objection expressed by Raymond Mikesell (Chapter 3, this volume) that it describes the problem of underdevelopment more than a situation requiring payments adjustment per se. And the first part of the description, in focusing on cost and price distortions rather than on exogenous change which undermines the previous cost-price structure and associated pattern of production and trade, distracts attention from the central distinction between a traditional fundamental disequilibrium and a structural deficit. It is time for the nature of the structural deficit to be explicitly recognized. Once that is done, it becomes clear that continued fulfillment in post-1974 circumstances of the Fund's traditional mandate as an "adjustment institution" required that it indeed accept responsibility for helping to finance structural adjustment programs.

One of the most controversial recent loans by the Fund was the extended arrangement of SDR 5 billion (a record) agreed with India in November 1981, despite criticism from the United States. The controversy did not stem primarily from doubts about the adequacy of the program agreed with India, which combined a continuation of

[2] It is of course true that the price changes needed to cure a fundamental disequilibrium may also induce structural change, but one can nevertheless usefully distinguish between a fundamental and a structural deficit depending on whether or not structural change is essential to eliminate the deficit without a permanent departure from internal balance.

prudent demand-management policies with supply-side measures to quicken export growth and promote some import substitution, especially in the energy sector. Some critics argued the Fund should have demanded more action, but others contended that India had already made major policy changes before approaching the Fund. Furthermore, India's recent payments deficit falls squarely in the category of a structural deficit, as defined above, in that a major contributing element was a sharp and presumably permanent deterioration in the terms of trade (though aggravated by temporary supply shortfalls due to civil unrest in one of the main oil-producing areas, and drought). A presumably permanent reduction in the inflow of concessional aid, especially from the International Development Association (IDA), is also in prospect. Rather, the source of controversy arose from India's decision to treat the Fund as a "lender of first resort" (Catherine Gwin, Chapter 20, this volume) instead of first exhausting its credit with the commercial banks and turning to the Fund only as its creditworthiness eroded. This is precisely what the Fund has been attempting to encourage, as William Dale (Chapter 1, this volume) has emphasized. But it is not in accord with the view of the Reagan administration on the proper relationship between the Fund and the commercial banks.

According to that view, the banks should be responsible for the normal process of intermediation, and the Fund should restrict its role to lender of last resort. Countries might still be encouraged to discuss adjustment policy with the Fund before their situation became critical, but the Fund would not be able to back up its advice with (relatively) cheap credit. At most, it might contract stand-bys to substitute for credit that was not forthcoming from the commercial banks to the extent anticipated (provided that performance criteria were satisfied). But it would not normally extend credit itself so long as private finance was available. Far from expanding low-conditionality finance, this course would complete the assault on automaticity waged by the United States in the late 1940s.

This is hardly the first time that views have clashed on where the boundary between public and private sectors should properly be drawn. To the extent that views on this issue are subject to reasoned debate, it is normal to consider whether, on the one hand, the public sector suffers from inefficiencies due to a lack of incentives, or, on the other hand, whether any "market failures" justify a preference for the public sector. Based on costs per dollar of loan, the Fund is a more efficient intermediary than the commercial banks. The more controversial question is whether an international capital market dominated by commercial bank lending can be considered susceptible to market failure.

The main reason for making such a charge is the supposed herd behavior of the banks. As long as a country's short-run prospects appear good, the banks compete with one another to lend more, which may encourage a country to postpone adjustment undesirably. However, any rumor of future difficulty can lead to an abrupt reversal of the desire to lend. Because no single bank owns more than a small proportion of a country's external debt, it is possible for any one of them to reduce its exposure, provided that it moves before most other banks do. This, so it is argued, creates a free rider problem with a vengeance. In fact, cases seem to have arisen where the banks lent to the point where adjustment was undesirably postponed and subsequently sought to reduce their exposure in a way that compounded liquidity problems. To anyone who considers the desirable demarcation between public and private sectors a pragmatic question, this suggests that no case can be made for cutting back the role of the Fund.

Whether there is a case for extending the Fund's low-conditionality facilities seems to depend on whether the risks involved in lending to poor countries are believed to be as great for the Fund as for the commercial banks. Asking the Fund to make loans it did not expect to have reimbursed would turn it into an aid agency, which is certainly not advocated here. There are, in fact, reasons for believing that the risks to the Fund would be lower, the main one being that loans beyond a certain cumulative size would be subject to conditionality. In addition, repudiation of IMF loans would be an even more hazardous act of policy than default on bank debt. Thus, for the poorer countries as well, the maintenance of effective conditionality is an important interest.

The main conclusions regarding the proper current role of the Fund's lending activities may now be summarized. The starting point is the fact that the Fund's members can be divided into two categories (albeit with a gray area in the middle): those that can tap commercial bank credit under normal circumstances and those that cannot. The former have no real need for low-conditionality credit, although they will find it expedient to use it from time to time as long as it remains available on favorable terms. They nevertheless retain an interest in the existence of the high-conditionality facilities, and, moreover, although they are often extremely reluctant to acknowledge the fact, in a meaningful degree of conditionality, so that successful negotiation of a stand-by serves to reestablish creditworthiness with private markets.

Countries in the second group have an interest in the retention and extention of the low-conditionality facilities so as to provide them with access to low-conditionality credit whenever a payments deterioration is due to circumstances beyond their own control. Implementation of that principle would require (1) either a restriction to cases where the shock is judged to be temporary or a modification providing for tapering the finance provided when a payments deterioration was judged to be permanent; (2) retention of the high-conditionality facilities with a meaningful degree of conditionality so as to minimize the risks involved in lending to countries that the private market judges not creditworthy, and perhaps also (3) an increase in the interest rates on low-conditionality credit to the point where creditworthy countries would have no financial incentive to exploit the Fund's facilities rather than borrow from the commercial banks.

The financial impact of this last measure on the poorer countries might be offset by an expansion of the interest subsidy account. Note that the Fund has already accepted the practice of discriminatory treatment of members in this specific context, so that no further violation of the principle of nondiscrimination would be called for. If the richer member countries of the Fund are not prepared to provide resources to expand the interest subsidy account, the next best solution might be to violate the principle of nondiscrimination and provide for countries to graduate from the right to use some or all of the low-conditionality facilities when they reach a certain level of per capita income.

The high-conditionality facilities, despite their unpopularity, are also important to the poorer countries. They provide consultancy services and an incentive to note the advice when local policy formation proves inadequate and in that way make it reasonable to maintain or extend the low-conditionality facilities. There may be scope for extending low conditionality or for improving high conditionality, but there is no case for just watering down high conditionality.

By implication, the Fund might reasonably be restricted to the role of lender of last resort for the countries able to tap bank credit, but preventing the Fund from being a lender of first resort to the non-creditworthy countries would deny them any borrowing other than last resort. Since India is on the frontier between the two groups, the Indian loan was understandably controversial.

These conclusions are relevant to the impending debate on the size of the increases in IMF quotas that should be agreed in 1983 (for implementation in 1985). At one extreme, a situation in which all

Fund members regularly availed themselves of low-conditionality loans to finance exogenously determined payments deficits would undoubtedly require a massive quota increase. At the other extreme, a decision to eschew financing of structural deficits and limit the Fund to a lender-of-last-resort role, even for countries that have little alternative source of balance of payments finance, might avoid the need for more than a minimal increase in quotas. Between these two extremes lies the view suggested here: that the Fund should restrict itself to the role of occasional last resort lender to the fully creditworthy countries but should seek to play a major role in financing temporary deficits—including structural deficits as defined above—for the large group of Fund members that are not major borrowers from the private international capital market. In the final section of this paper, the quantitative implications of this view are explored with regard to the desirable size of quota increases.

Cooperation with the World Bank

While the Fund is an *adjustment institution* whose short-term loans are directed to financing deficits that are either inherently temporary or intended to be temporary because of the adoption of adjustment policies, the World Bank is a *development institution* whose long-term loans are directed to the promotion of development. The Bank has traditionally pursued that responsibility by concentrating on project lending and on the microeconomic evaluation needed for project appraisal. The main significance of the Bank's operations from the standpoint of the Fund was that those project loans augmented long-term capital inflows. Since the relevant concept of payments equilibrium to the Fund is *basic balance*—a current account deficit (surplus) that matches the long-term (underlying) capital inflow (outflow)—the Bank's loans changed the implicit current account target toward which adjustment had to be directed. The Bank's and the Fund's provinces were therefore rather clearly demarcated, the Bank providing long-term project finance to promote development and the Fund providing short-term balance of payments finance to cover temporary overall deficits.

This division of labor became blurred after 1974. The oil price increase confronted most oil-importing countries, and most developing countries, with substantially larger import bills, and hence, larger payments deficits, all other factors remaining the same. As argued in the previous section, because those deficits were largely structural in character, payments adjustment demanded structural change. But supervision of a program of structural change involves Fund intrusion into questions of investment priorities, microeconomic efficiency, and the structure of incentives, all of which have traditionally been the preserve of the Bank. In the late 1970s, the Bank, for its part, concluded that, since the main constraint on more acceptable rates of development was once again the balance of payments, fulfillment of its responsibilities required it to provide a facility to support coherent programs of structural adjustment aimed at earning or saving foreign exchange. Thus, the traditional frontier between Fund and Bank was breached from both directions.

The Fund's institutional mechanism for supporting adjustment programs involving structural change is the extended facility. It is true that creation of that facility in 1974 probably owed more to the desire of some of the developed countries to respond to demands from developing countries in the Committee of Twenty for increased resource transfers, without conceding the "link" between the creation of SDRs and development assistance, than it did to prompt diagnosis of the enhanced importance of structural deficits. And, as argued in the preceding section, the terms of reference of the extended facility miss the central point about why Fund programs need to be capable of embracing structural change: that efficient payments adjustment to permanent adverse terms of trade shocks requires structural change in economies with inelastic productive structures. Fortunately, the vague specification of its terms of reference has not prevented the Fund from using the extended facility to support programs involving structural change.

The instrument that the Bank developed to deal with the borderline area between adjustment and development is *structural adjustment lending*, introduced in 1980. Some observers have regarded this as a revamped version of the program lending developed by the Bank in the early 1970s and run down in 1975 following criticism by the Ford administration and the sharply improved balance of payments position of India, the major recipient of the program money. But there is at least some difference in the emphasis now placed on the need to have a program designed to strengthen the balance of payments to justify a structural adjustment loan (SAL).

Ernest Stern (Chapter 5, this volume) has described the nature of the conditions attached to SALs. Those conditions typically involve four elements: the rationalization of prices or "restructuring of incentives," covering pricing policies, tariff reform, taxation, subsidies, and interest rates; the revision of public investment priorities; budgetary reform; and institution building. In any particular case, the Bank, in association with the borrowing country, picks out a number of key areas where it judges policy to be particularly deficient or misguided and negotiates a set of policy reforms to correct those weaknesses. In so doing, it finds itself involved in areas that have traditionally been the Fund's prerogative because, for example, import liberalization, tariff reform, and the provision of export incentives cannot be discussed sensibly without also covering exchange rate policy.

Thus, the former distinctions between the roles of the Fund and the Bank—macro versus micro, demand versus supply, adjustment versus development, financial versus real, program versus project loans, short term versus long term—have been severely eroded. According to Stern (echoed by Irving Friedman, Chapter 6, this volume) the critical distinction now relates to the respective staffs' spheres of competence rather than to the content of their respective programs. The Fund staff, usually experts in macroeconomics, demand management, and payments adjustment, consult their Bank counterparts when microeconomic supply questions like investment priorities arise, and vice versa. Both sets of expertise are regarded as valuable to the articulation of a well-conceived, medium-term adjustment program. Accordingly, in the ideal situation a country negotiates simultaneously with the Fund for an extended loan and with the Bank for a SAL. When one institution alone is negotiating, it still can and should draw on the knowledge of the other to ensure an adequate overall package. Where their responsibilities overlap, their advice must be harmonized.

Of the case studies before the conference, the one on India involved the closest cooperation between Fund and Bank. Catherine Gwin (Chapter 20, this volume) believes that the two institutions worked together well in that instance but that, despite improved cooperation in recent years, no existing procedures ensure that such cooperation will always be realized, and that in any event cooperation cannot be substituted for enlarging Fund expertise on "supply-side" policies. Tony Killick (Chapter 16, this volume), whose case study of Kenya covers the Fund's first extended loan and one of the Bank's early SALs, also takes a skeptical view of the Fund's achievements in supervising supply-side adjustment. An extended loan, in his view, amounts in practice to little more than several conventional loans running contiguously, with negotiations and policy conditions heavily concentrated on the traditional demand side and some other ad hoc supply-side measures tacked on as an afterthought (and relying heavily on Bank advice). The Bank's conditionality was no less stringent but was markedly different in character, relating to a set of agreed policy actions rather than to obligations to achieve specific numerical outcomes. He judges that the Bank's SAL achieved more good with less friction and, accordingly, urges the Fund to consider emulating the Bank.

There is therefore a clear difference of view about the way structural adjustment should be handled by the Fund (even assuming, following the discussion in the last section of this study, that the Fund should handle it at all). Gwin and Killick essentially urge the Fund to cultivate more of the staff skills and to adopt some of the program characteristics that have heretofore been a prerogative of the Bank, while Stern and Friedman urge both Bank and Fund to stick to their areas of expertise and cooperate in the borderline area where their traditional responsibilities overlap. Given that the fostering and safeguarding of prudent demand management policies is an important support for a program of structural adjustment that might fall into neglect if the Fund started to duplicate the functions of the Bank, the more promising approach would seem to be an extension and systematization of the practice of cooperation that has already developed.

What form might such an extension and systematization of cooperation take? The natural course would be for both institutions to declare joint responsibility for programs designed to adjust to a structural deficit, as defined in the previous section (a deficit caused by a presumably permanent external shock and which cannot be eliminated without structural change without a permanent departure from internal balance). Countries would be invited to apply simultaneously for an extended loan from the Fund and a SAL from the Bank and would then negotiate jointly a structural adjustment program with the two institutions. (Some countries, such as Turkey and Jamaica, have already sought simultaneous help from the two institutions.) The Fund would be responsible for negotiating the conditions needed to ensure that the country pursued a prudent demand-management policy consistent with the need for structural change. The Bank would deal with the structure of incentives, investment priorities, budgetary reform, and institutional development. It might be hoped that the Fund's negotiations with India, as described by Catherine Gwin (though no Bank program was directly involved in that instance) would provide a model for its negotiations with other countries whose demand-management policy is already set on a prudent course, in the sense that the Fund would agree to set credit ceilings and other performance criteria at levels not expected to "bite" so long as policy remains prudent.

Perhaps the main doubt about the feasibility of such a joint approach to the adjustment and financing of structural deficits arises from the differing time scales within which Fund and Bank are accustomed to operate. The Fund is used to being called on in an emergency and to negotiating a program in a matter of weeks. The Bank, in contrast, has a continuing negotiation with member countries about a series of projects and tends to negotiate SALs over the same sort of time scale of many months. Added Bank capacity to mobilize its intellectual resources for a quick diagnosis and negotiation seems necessary for joint action to be feasible. But a more extended period of negotiation than customary in Fund programs might also be possible if the Fund were ready to grant short-term interim stand-bys during negotiations.

The Design of Adjustment Programs

As a basic principle, the Fund has long conditioned access to credit from its high-conditionality facilities on the borrowing country's acceptance of an agreed adjustment program deemed adequate to restore what is variously described as a "viable" or "sustainable" balance of payments position or "external balance." What the Fund does and should press for in an adjustment program is treated in this section.

There is, however, a prior question: whether it is the Fund's business to attempt to influence the borrowing country's mix of policies at all. This question has been posed, not just by individuals who do not regard it as necessary for the Fund to seek assurances that borrowing countries will be able to repay on time, but also by individuals who accept that the Fund must satisfy itself that an adequate adjustment program is in place but who contend that the Fund should not seek to influence the content of that program. The alternative view holds that, since it is easy enough to devise policies to improve the balance of payments and the challenge is to find a set of policies that will do so without sacrificing growth, employment, and an equitable distribution of income, the Fund should be very much concerned with the mix of policies a borrowing country proposes to achieve adjustment.

Although people often take strong positions on this question, the realities of international life tend to leave little scope for choice in practice. Because the members of the Fund are sovereign states, it would be difficult to conceive of the Fund's refusing credit to a country that promised to implement a program that the Fund deemed adequate to secure a payments recovery on the ground that the program involved an unnecessary sacrifice in real income (or some other domestic objective). The Fund staff might point out such inefficiencies to the national authorities but could hardly overrule them if they refused to show interest. The Fund would satisfy its legitimate interests by extracting commitments which ensured that the country would actually implement its chosen program.

However, the Fund is rarely in the position of accepting that the program initially proposed gives reasonable assurance of a payments turnaround. On the contrary, it almost inevitably gets drawn into discussing variations and alternatives—that is, into giving *policy advice.* In this role of policy advisor, the Fund should quite evidently take into account targets other than the balance of payments, for the most certain method of improving the balance of payments—output deflation induced by monetary contraction—can also be among the most costly.

What other targets should the Fund take into account in giving policy advice? Everyone, including the Fund, agrees that these targets should include the level of output and employment ("internal balance") and the rate of growth. There is also a fair measure of agreement that the Fund should be concerned with inflation control, although many would argue that it should accept the government's judgment as to the priority to be given to fighting inflation. (Although the Fund's anti-inflation rhetoric is stronger than ever in the advice it addresses to its major members, it is an interesting fact that the priority the Fund attaches to curbing inflation in small borrowing countries has been sharply reduced since the days of Bretton Woods, presumably because, with exchange rate flexibility and a high level of world inflation, price stability is no longer a necessary condition for a sustainable balance of payments outcome.)

The most controversial issue is whether the Fund should take account of effects on income distribution in designing adjustment programs. Those who hold that it should are not necessarily saying that cutting the real income of the rural poor should always be avoided, let alone that the urban real wage should always be preserved. Rather, where possible without jeopardizing payments recovery or blunting incentives, the Fund should favor options that would benefit (or at least spare) the poor.

The starting point for Fund policy advice—or, for that matter, assessment of the adequacy of a member's adjustment proposals—is an estimate of how large an improvement in the current balance has to be targeted. That clearly depends on an assessment of the underlying capital inflow that can be expected, and productively used, once confidence is restored. The second essential analytical input is an estimate of the level of output corresponding to internal balance:

roughly speaking, this means the highest output level that a country can hope to sustain without generating pressures for the acceleration of inflation. Given estimates of the responsiveness of trade flows to changes in relative prices (the price elasticities of exports and imports), those two figures enable calculation of the real exchange rate consistent with achieving the target current balance when output is at internal balance. Since reasonable elasticity estimates are frequently unavailable, it is often necessary to resort to purchasing power parity comparisons (comparison of the real exchange rate[3] with its level in some earlier period when competitiveness appeared to be appropriate). In one way or another, the attempt is made to infer what (if any) real devaluation is necessary.

When the Fund concludes that an improvement in competitiveness is necessary, it normally urges the country in question to undertake a nominal devaluation. This raises two questions: whether a nominal devaluation can be expected to secure a real devaluation, and whether there may not be better ways of securing an improvement in competitiveness.

The efficacy of nominal devaluation as a tool for securing a real devaluation is a subject on which views have long differed. Some observers believe that nominal devaluations are inevitably nullified by inflation and are therefore quite ineffective in achieving a real devaluation. The problem with this view is that the same theory that asserts the inevitable ineffectiveness of devaluation (because of the law of one price) also implies the impossibility of overvaluation in the first place. A far more plausible view is that devaluation will usually be partially eroded through defensive wage increases and that this erosion can be substantial, or even total—especially in the absence of supporting macroeconomic policies or the presence of widespread wage indexation. It may validly be concluded that devaluation needs to be accompanied by other measures, including wage restraint, which is indeed a characteristic of many Fund programs.

Another strategy that has often been pressed by the Fund is more questionable: seeking a bigger nominal devaluation than the desired real devaluation, in the hope that enough of it will stick to produce the desired improvement in competitiveness. A better alternative is

[3] The real exchange rate is the nominal exchange rate corrected for the price level at home and abroad. If the domestic price level doubles while foreign prices stay constant, then a doubling of the nominal exchange rate (expressed as units of domestic currency per unit of foreign exchange) is needed to restore the real exchange rate to its former level.

to seek an initial devaluation estimated to produce the desired real exchange rate on the assumption that no additional inflation will occur, and subsequently to change the exchange rate if and as necessary to offset differential inflation.

This alternative has several advantages: it avoids creating unnecessary variations in the real exchange rate; it makes it more likely that the desired improvement in competitiveness will be achieved; and it eases the destabilizing monetary dynamics that are kindled by promising zero depreciation of a currency with (at least temporarily) high inflation and therefore high nominal interest rates.[4] It is fair to say that the Fund has moved toward acceptance of this strategy in recent years. More consistent and explicit rejection of the rival strategy (massive initial nominal devaluation, followed by the attempt to hold a fixed peg) could still be wished.

The second question is whether there may not be better ways of improving competitiveness than through a nominal devaluation. One such way, where it is feasible, is to reduce inflation to a rate below the international norm. Advocating this alternative, however, invites countries to submit unrealistic projections of inflation's dropping to near zero as a substitute for action.

Another policy option often advocated in this context is an intensification of import restrictions. The Fund strongly opposes this alternative, for two reasons: the Fund's Articles assign it the role of defending the general international interest in an open, liberal system, against the particular national interest that countries often think they have in the "easy option" of import restrictions; second, the Fund doubts whether restrictive policies are generally in the best interest even of the country imposing them. The reasons for this belief are discussed below in connection with the "supply-side" policies advocated by the Fund, where it is concluded that the Fund's reasons are convincing.

The preceding discussion suggests the conclusion that the Fund's policy of seeking to promote an appropriate level of competitiveness through a realistic exchange rate policy is correct. The Fund should, however, avoid urging massive initial devaluations, followed by an

[4] The high nominal interest rate coupled with zero expected depreciation leads to a capital inflow since the promised return in foreign currency terms is high. The resulting monetary expansion helps perpetuate or even accelerate inflation, which either leads to a period of overvaluation before equilibrium can be achieved or raises the possibility of another devaluation. See Dornbusch (1980, Chapter 12).

attempt to hold a fixed peg, and urge countries instead to change their peg as needed to offset differential inflation.

Orthodox theory suggests that the balance of payments depends importantly not merely on competitiveness but also on the level of demand. David Finch (Chapter 4, this volume) asserts:

> In all cases of continued payments difficulties, the authorities' attention will have to be focused on ways of reducing the level or the rate of growth of demand—which broadly means deflation—and on redirecting resources—which broadly calls for devaluation.

Hence, the second main thrust of a typical Fund program involves the design of restrictive demand management policies. This can be approached either in a generally Keynesian or a generally monetarist spirit.

The more Keynesian approach involves estimating the cutback (if any) in demand necessary to release real resources for the current account of the balance of payments, then planning what combination of increased taxes, reduced government expenditure, and monetary stringency would be needed to achieve that cutback. The mix of policies chosen to achieve the desired cutback is accepted as preeminently a national decision rather than a matter on which the Fund should press its views: indeed, the 1979 review of conditionality specified that performance criteria (which empower the Fund to ensure that commitments are respected) generally be confined to "macroeconomic variables."[5] The planned fiscal program is typically summarized by a target for credit to the public sector, expressed as a ceiling. Somewhat less convincingly, at least where capital mobility is high, a planned cutback in private demand may be translated into a figure for target or maximum credit to the private sector. Summation would then yield a figure for target or maximum domestic credit expansion (DCE).

A more monetarist approach appears to play a regular role in the Fund's financial programming. This approach starts by estimating the demand for money on the basis of the projected rate of inflation and real growth rate. The permissible level of domestic credit can be deduced as the difference between forecast money demand and a

[5] The conclusions of the 1979 review of conditionality are reproduced as Appendix 24.C. The reference is to paragraph 9. This paragraph also allows performance criteria "necessary to implement specific provisions of the Articles or policies adopted under them," a term of art for requirements that countries not intensify restrictions on trade or payments.

target reserve level. Target or maximum DCE is given by the excess of the calculated future permissible level of domestic credit over its current level. If the permissible rate of credit expansion appears incompatible with the projected rates of inflation and growth that were initially assumed, it is necessary to modify the projections and iterate until consistency is achieved. This "monetarist" approach, directed to targeting the level of reserves, does not conflict with the preceding "more Keynesian" approach, directed to targeting the current balance.

However, as James Meade's classic analysis (1951) of the prerequisites for simultaneous achievement of external and internal balance long ago taught, demand-management policy cannot simply be viewed as a tool for improving the balance of payments. If the real exchange rate is appropriate and the "Keynesian approach" has been followed, limiting the demand cutback to that necessary to release resources for the balance of payments, the economy should achieve internal as well as external balance. But one of the traditional complaints against the Fund is that it demands more deflation than needed to achieve external balance and, in the process, jeopardizes internal balance. It has also been suggested[6] that the Fund overlooks devaluation's deflationary consequences for domestic demand, for example, as price increases reduce real money balances. These effects may outweigh the expansionary effects of devaluation in switching demand toward domestically produced goods, especially in developing countries with little elasticity in the structure of production. Whether or not the Fund has been guilty of supporting "overkill" in recent years is examined later in this study.

What can surely not be doubted is that, where feasible, the most desirable of all economic strategies is the one William Cline (Chapter 9, this volume) terms "expansionary stabilization." This means a situation in which a reduction in inflation or an improvement in the balance of payments is accompanied by strong growth in output, perhaps even in domestic absorption. Historical examples of this agreeable conjunction include Britain after 1931, virtually the whole Western world in the early to mid-1950s, the Kennedy program of the early 1960s in the United States, Japan till the late 1960s, Brazil's "miracle" after 1967, and the Indonesian stabilization program of 1967–70.

Of course, expansionary stabilization is feasible only where either excess capacity is substantial to begin with or where capacity is grow-

[6] See, for example, Cooper (1971) and Krugman and Taylor (1978).

ing rapidly. Attempts to "dash for growth" in the absence of that elementary precondition have the all too predictable consequences witnessed, for example, in Britain in 1964 and 1973, and in Brazil in 1979–80. As another essential precondition, the prices of strategic macroeconomic significance (the real wage, the profit rate, the real interest rate, the real exchange rate, and, in recent years, the real oil price) must be realistically interrelated so that an increase in nominal demand calls forth more output and higher investment rather than higher prices or increased imports. Reflation accompanied by cost-raising measures rather than a concern to maintain supportive relative prices simply leads to a resurgence of inflationary pressure, as recent French experience has shown. Moreover, general confidence in the feasibility of expansionary stabilization is necessary. Without it, increased demand will feed price increases and inflationary expectations rather than stimulate growth. Confidence depends on a general perception that the government is resolutely pursuing a strategy consistent with the control of inflation: keeping the fiscal deficit within prudent limits, evincing determination to prevent excess demand from emerging, and refusing to allow monopolies in the labor or product markets to exploit their position at the expense of the rest of the economy.

These considerations have two important implications. First, it is vitally necessary for the Fund, as for its member governments, to exercise a high order of economic statesmanship in discriminating between cases in which the preconditions for expansionary stabilization exist and those in which they do not. Second, at least the starting point of the self-proclaimed dissidents from economic orthodoxy, both structuralists and Reaganomists, deserves to be embraced by all. That starting point is the proposition that economic policy should be concerned with expanding supply capacity and should not be limited to demand management.

As noted, the Fund has been paying increasing attention to "supply-side" policies. The Fund's efforts in this direction may be grouped under four headings: the form of credit controls, outward orientation, market economy, and growth planning.

Fund programs typically provide for both a ceiling on total domestic credit expansion and on credit extended to the public sector. The primary rationale for the latter is to ensure that the private sector is not crowded out, as might happen if the only ceiling were an overall limit on DCE. Continued availability of adequate credit to the private sector is necessary to sustain supply capacity in countries where productive enterprise depends heavily on bank credit for the purchase of inputs.

Fund programs almost always restrain borrowing countries from imposing additional restrictions on trade and payments, and they often go further than this and involve substantial liberalization. In part, as mentioned above, this policy represents the Fund's attempt to safeguard the systemic interest in liberal policies, but the major justification is that it promotes rational resource allocation and, thus, supply capacity. Bela Balassa (Chapter 8, this volume) summarizes much of his recent work on the relation between outward orientation and economic growth, which he interprets as showing that "outwardly oriented" development strategies have been more successful in promoting growth and adjustment than policies of import-substituting industrialization (once the "easy" first stage of import substitution is accomplished). Despite this evidence, the suspicion persists in some quarters that Balassa, and more generally the Bank and Fund, exaggerate the attractiveness of free trade as a development strategy. If it were true that Balassa advocates unqualified free trade, it would be easy to understand such reservations. In fact, neither Balassa nor the Bank nor the Fund has objected to a measure of infant-industry protection to establish or, within reason, broaden the industrial base. The new orthodoxy contends that the best way of providing protection is to tax traditional exports, rather than to protect specific import products. That view appears justified by the evidence.

In addition to its advocacy of liberal trade policies, the Fund has the reputation (in most quarters) of pressing for free market solutions more generally. For example, proposals to raise public utility prices to market levels, or to free interest rates, quite often figure in IMF programs, sometimes in provocative juxtaposition with provisions for wage restraint. The justification is, once again, that market prices that reflect scarcities lead to correct allocative decisions and thus enhance the capacity of the economy. Whether market solutions are always and everywhere the best way to promoting efficient resource allocation is, however, a contested point.

For example, Reginald Green (Chapter 15, this volume) argues strongly that it was precisely the search for microeconomic efficiency that has underlain Tanzanian policies of interventionism in an economy that cannot be expected to respond promptly to price incentives.[7]

[7] Reginald Green's questioning of the efficacy of devaluation in the Tanzanian context is, however, at least partially undermined by his argument that the market cannot be left to look after the promotion of manufactured exports because, although these would be remunerative to producers, they would be less profitable than home sales.

Others may worry about whether the Fund always gives sufficient support to national efforts to identify and correct situations of market failure: even those who support the Fund in seeking to eradicate negative real rates of interest ought to worry if laissez faire produces instead positive real interest rates so high as to threaten the continued viability of large sections of productive industry (as has happened in Argentina and Chile, though not through the Fund's urging). In short, while the Fund rightly encourages the pursuit of microefficiency and promoting market forces is often the simplest means to that end, there is not much basis for judging whether the balance is always well struck.

Extended loans are intended for use in adjustment programs involving structural change. In such cases, the Fund may look with favor on the existence of a realistic development plan, and the program may also include specific measures to improve the efficiency of public enterprises or a reordering of investment priorities. The Fund itself normally relies heavily on the Bank's advice in determining what measures of this type to include in a program. It was argued in the previous section that this practice should be systematized rather than superseded by a greater Fund effort to build up staff expertise in microeconomics.

Everyone agrees that inflation is bad, but the Fund has often been criticized for giving higher priority to anti-inflation policy than to growth. For example, the Fund opposed the switch to expansionary policies in Brazil in 1967, which initiated the "Brazilian miracle," on the ground that inflation reduction should remain the top priority. This is, however, a topic on which the terms of the debate have been profoundly modified in the last decade.

On the one hand, the Fund has reduced its priority for inflation abatement (at least for small borrowing countries), since exchange rate flexibility enables a sustainable balance of payments to be combined with continuing high inflation. The Fund has in fact moved a long way toward the position of its critics, confining its demands to what it believes necessary to sustain a viable payments performance and accepting whatever priority the borrowing country chooses to place on inflation control.

On the other hand, most economists now accept the accelerationist view of inflation,[8] irrespective of their political position; few still

[8] The accelerationist view of inflation holds that there is no long-run trade-off between unemployment and inflation. Any attempt to hold unemployment below some critical "natural rate" leads to accelerating inflation, as

consider limitation of the ability to inflate a gross assault on national well-being. As a result, from the left wing the Fund is increasingly criticized for imposing *excessive* inflation on borrowing countries, notably by requiring massive devaluations. Note that the trade-off changes when the exchange rate rather than demand management is the policy weapon: it is no longer a question of balancing higher output against higher inflation and a *weaker* balance of payments, but one of balancing higher output and a *stronger* balance of payments against higher inflation. Inflation control and payments strengthening are now *conflicting* goals.

There seems to be no reasonable basis for contesting the practice of treating as final the borrowing country's judgment on the priority to be given inflation control. At the same time, the Fund should be ready to give advice when called upon. For example, the Fund should emphasize that much more can be gained in inflation control by smoothing cyclical peaks than by deepening cyclical troughs. (Tony Killick, Chapter 16, this volume illustrates how Kenya could have benefited from such advice during the coffee boom of 1977.) The Fund should seek to restrain countries from engineering massive nominal devaluations in the hope that part of these will stick as real devaluations. Rather, it should seek to ensure that any nominal devaluation is accompanied by measures that will secure a useful measure of real devaluation. In particular cases this might involve wage restraint or the modification of indexation formulas or even price control.

The last and most controversial of the five targets toward which it has been suggested the Fund should direct its policy advice is the distribution of income. In contrast to its old view on inflation control, or its current view on output and growth, the Fund holds that distributional considerations are none of its business. It is not clear, however, that the Fund is as indifferent to distributional issues as it claims to be. A study undertaken within the Fund (Johnson and Salop, 1980) endeavored to unravel the distributional impact of four Fund programs. The Fund staff at the conference told of a specific instance where they had grasped that thorniest of nettles and urged a cut in

---

everyone adds the expected rate of inflation to his desired change in relative prices (or wages), and the latter are on average positive. Consequently, inflation exceeds the expected rate, which leads to an increase in inflationary expectations, which increases inflation. The spiral is explosive as long as policy holds unemployment below the natural rate.

arms expenditure as a part of the needed fiscal restraint. The Fund staff also argued that, in addition to the allocational effects, it is often distributionally desirable to raise food prices because this benefits rural income. These facts make it difficult to accept that the Fund is really as oblivious as it maintains to the distributional impact of its programs.

William Cline (Chapter 9, this volume) cites Malaysia's experience in 1974–75 as an example of equity-oriented stabilization. Richard Feinberg (1982) argues that designing a stabilization program typically allows some freedom to attend to distributional considerations, but he asserts that in no case has it been claimed that a Fund program actually improved the distribution of income. Hence, he argues, it would be a major step forward if the Fund were to strive consciously for a proportional distribution of the burden of adjustment. In the absence of such a systematic concern with distributional issues, there must be a danger that the typical Fund mission will find it expedient to avoid suggesting cuts that impinge on the politically powerful. With a general policy decision that distributional issues are a legitimate object of Fund concern, it would be that much easier for missions to urge, for example, elimination of subsidies on gasoline rather than on food (except perhaps on imported foods that compete with local production to the detriment of the rural poor). This much could be done without a commitment to maintain real incomes at uneconomic levels and without any implication that the Fund could override a sovereign government on distributional questions.

The design of adjustment programs involves not merely deciding on the objectives to be pursued and the measures to be adopted but also on the *speed* with which adjustment is to be effected. This is another topic on which left-wing critics have traditionally attacked the Fund. They have charged that the Fund has shown a marked preference for shock treatment rather than gradualism and has thus made adjustment far more costly than it need have been.

In discussing the proper speed of adjustment, it is again useful to distinguish between deficits due to excess demand, fundamental disequilibria, and structural deficits. There is no reason for not moving promptly to eliminate excess demand; the quicker the action, the smaller the dislocations remaining after equilibrium is restored. A fundamental disequilibrium also demands a prompt *initiation* of action, especially to bring the price changes needed to induce a redirection of expenditure toward home-produced goods. But because this redirection does not occur immediately, but rather over two or three years, it is not efficient to introduce immediately all the expenditure-reducing (deflationary) measures that may ultimately be called for. Shock treatment in this case is inefficient: it leads to a wastage of resources because the reduction in internal demand is not matched by a rise in external demand for some time.

The same is true in the case of structural deficits, where any increase in external demand cannot employ additional domestic resources until the necessary structural changes have been made. In this circumstance, it would be profoundly foolish to insist on shock treatment—an immediate end to the deficit—rather than to finance a continuing deficit until the new facilities come on stream.

While current account deficits can always be placed in one (or some combination of) the preceding categories, payments problems often involve capital flight as well as a current deficit. This may make it impracticable to adopt as leisurely a pace of adjustment as the preceding analysis might suggest to be appropriate. Once financial confidence evaporates, its restoration must become the first priority. Convincing the public that the rules of the game have changed may take shock treatment. Turkey in 1980 is a good example of successful Fund-supported shock treatment. In some other circumstances shock treatment may also be preferable to gradualism to quell inflation, for example, where the public is willing to accept an incomes policy.

Thus, shock treatment is appropriate in certain circumstances and not in others. Because it is sometimes inappropriate, the Fund must be capable of supporting gradualist adjustment progams. Until the mid-1970s, it did not have the means. Because Fund stand-bys were for a maximum of one year, its operating procedures virtually required it to oblige borrowing countries to take the whole package of measures necessary to secure adjustment within a few months (since the Fund's policy leverage erodes rapidly as undrawn commitments decline). That changed with the introduction of the extended facility (where drawings are spread over three years) in 1974, and of multiyear stand-bys in 1977. Those innovations were all to the good.

In summary, it has been argued in this section that what the Fund has a right to *insist* on when it makes a loan—the assurance that a program adequate to secure a payments turnaround will be implemented—must be distinguished from the *policy advice* that the Fund should give when negotiating a program. That policy advice should take account of a broad spectrum of objectives: not just the balance of payments, but also the level and growth of output, inflation, and more (more controversially) the distribution of income. In giving policy advice, the Fund should seek a combination of devaluation and deflation calculated to combine external and internal balance; it should be alive to opportunities for promoting expansionary stabilization; it should avoid nominal devaluations that cannot be translated in substantial measure into real devaluations, and prefer a modest initial devaluation followed by depreciation to maintain a target real exchange rate to a massive initial devaluation; it should nurture the supply side, and to that end support outwardly oriented policies and press for microeconomic efficiency; and, in the view of some observers, it should take into account the distributional impact of policy changes such as expenditure cuts and seek to spare the poor as far as possible. The Fund should consider whether shock treatment is called for in a country's specific circumstances, and it should have and use the capability to support gradual adjustment where shock treatment is not necessary. This may, for example, involve the *gradual* implementation of a program of import liberalization so that resources are not squeezed out of the import-competing sector before opportunities emerge for their absorption in an export sector.

Monitoring Adjustment Programs

The provisions of adjustment programs agreed with the Fund are divided into three categories, known as preconditions, performance criteria, and policy understandings:

Preconditions are actions taken before the program is agreed by the IMF Executive Board.

Performance criteria are undertakings given by the country which, if violated, involve suspension of further disbursements by the Fund until new understandings are reached.

Policy understandings are actions that the country agrees to take, but which do not have any explicit sanction associated with nonfulfillment.

Preconditions involve preeminently action on the exchange rate. The reason is obvious: if a significant devaluation is judged to be a desirable element of policy, it is hardly advisable to have a country commit itself to *future* action, since the commitment would undoubtedly leak and provoke speculation. (This would be most serious in countries with high capital mobility but can be troublesome even in countries with strict exchange controls.) Some domestic policies of the type needed to support a devaluation, notably tax increases, expenditure cuts, or rises in interest rates, may also be treated as preconditions. Requiring policy changes as preconditions avoids any subsequent problem of monitoring. But it does bring a problem of its own: namely, the absence of ex ante control by the Executive Board over the actions of the staff. Presumably, the right of executive directors to comment subsequently on what the staff asked for in the way of preconditions is regarded as sufficient assurance of political control in most instances. In particularly difficult cases, the staff may bring a progress report on negotiations to the Board.

Performance criteria come in two categories, qualitative and quantitative. The qualitative criteria invariably involve commitments to avoid the introduction or intensification of trade or exchange restrictions. The quantitative criteria normally involve credit ceilings of one form or another: a ceiling on domestic credit expansion (either by the central bank or the banking system); a ceiling on bank credit extended to the government or the whole public sector; and sometimes ceilings on short-term and medium-term international borrowing by the public sector. A floor under the level of net international reserves is also sometimes specified. Jorge Marshall (Chapter 13, this volume) reviews the variations in the Fund's credit ceilings since its earliest programs in southern South America in the 1950s. This detailed survey provides some insight into the factors governing the choice between alternative specifications.

Policy understandings may overlap or go beyond the content of the preconditions or performance criteria. They may, for example, involve a future exchange rate policy to maintain competitiveness, fiscal reform, investment incentives, price adjustments to promote incentives, interest rate increases to mobilize savings, incomes policy, trade or exchange liberalization, or institutional reform. Although no explicit sanctions are attached to a failure to implement a policy understanding, a country's compliance with those undertakings is discussed at the quarterly reviews that the Fund conducts with every member with drawings outstanding under the high-conditionality facilities. Because failure to take policy understandings seriously would also predispose the Fund to take an uncharitable view of any breach of the performance criteria, they are not without importance.

Nevertheless, the heart of the monitoring process involves the performance criteria. Given the combined rationale of protecting the systemic interest and promoting the borrowing country's national interest in an outward orientation that lies behind the qualitative criteria forbidding additional trade or exchange restrictions, it seems hard to fault the propriety of those criteria.

There are, however, periodic complaints that these reasonable conditions are sometimes interpreted in an unreasonably legalistic way. For example, Tony Killick (Chapter 16, this volume) details how Kenya was judged in breach of its 1979 agreement because an administrative rationalization was deemed to constitute the introduction of a multiple currency practice.

Far more difficult policy questions surround the quantitative performance criteria. A first of these is a parallel to the preliminary question considered in the previous section: namely, since the Fund's legitimate interest in a country's policies is restricted to ensuring that a payments turnaround occurs, should not the sole performance criterion be the balance of payments outcome or reserve level?

It is a fact that the Fund on occasion uses the maintenance of a minimum reserve level as a performance criterion. According to the Fund's official history (de Vries, 1976, vol. 1, p. 364), this was done where a specific need was felt to exert pressure on a country to avoid allowing its exchange rate to become overvalued. Jorge Marshall (Chapter 13, this volume) gives the impression that this case was rather routine in Latin America and interprets the Fund as regarding the exchange rate as the dominant instrument affecting the balance of payments. Nevertheless, the practice is open to criticism, inasmuch as the balance of payments is influenced by exogenous factors as well as the faithfulness with which the government honors its commitments. For example, an unexpected adverse shock to the terms of trade would simultaneously worsen the payments outcome and increase the need for finance, and it would be perverse to rule a country in breach of its undertakings in such a situation. Conversely, countries that flagrantly disregarded their undertakings might be saved by luck. An alternative approach to the selection of performance criteria is obviously needed.

The Fund has in fact set out in its official history (Horsefield, 1969, vol. 2, p. 492) three characteristics that it regards as important in the choice of performance criteria. These are objectivity; timely availability of data to assess compliance; and the significance of the variable as an indicator of overall compliance with the agreed program. The argument of the preceding paragraph is that the *outcome* of a program is not a measure of *compliance* with what was agreed. Richard Cooper (Chapter 22, this volume) formulates the point: performance criteria should relate to instruments under the fairly immediate control of the authorities—to *policy variables*.

Although exogenous developments do have some impact on the pressures to create credit, the level of credit creation is undeniably much closer to being a policy variable than is the payments outcome. That, allied with the satisfactory characteristics of credit ceilings in terms of the three criteria above, provides the basic case for using credit ceilings as performance criteria. Critics sometimes point to instability in the demand for money in opposing this approach, but there is little reason to believe that the demand for money is more unstable than the demand for anything else.

There is also a convincing case for using domestic credit expansion rather than the money supply as the basic credit variable. This is a direct consequence of the Fund's interest in the balance of payments. Suppose once again that the country suffered an unexpected adverse terms of trade shock, which led to an immediate deterioration in the balance of payments (assuming a pegged exchange rate). With a prefixed rate of monetary growth, the reserve loss would lead to additional credit creation as policy attempted to compensate for the reduction in the monetary base; this would tend to *perpetuate* the payments deficit. With a prefixed rate of DCE, in contrast, the reserve loss would lead to a reduction in the money supply, hence to pressure for a *reduction* in the deficit. The DCE target, in other words, provides a negative feedback that tends to limit the deviations from the payments target that result from unexpected exogenous developments. This does not necessarily preclude a strategy of responding to such developments by expansionary credit policies designed, for example, to safeguard employment, but it does ensure that such a response would have to be a part of a coherent plan, agreed with the Fund, and containing other measures (such as devaluation) calculated to safeguard the balance of payments. Because the Fund's primary duty is to ensure that the balance of payments does achieve the targeted outcome, this is as it should be.

The subsidiary credit targets, most usually for credit to the public sector and foreign borrowing by the public sector, are designed to support the DCE ceiling. They are typically justified by the desirability, respectively, of restraining the public sector from crowding out the credit needs of the private sector and preventing the public sector from evading the restraints aimed at it.

The main concern at the conference was not the propriety of framing performance criteria primarily in terms of credit ceilings but rather the inflexibility of those ceilings. It was argued that circumstances often could and did arise that make it appropriate to modify ceilings. Perhaps the most important circumstance thought to demand flexibility was deviation of the inflation rate from the one assumed when framing the program.

For example, it was argued that a successful stabilization program typically leads to a fall in inflationary expectations, and thereby to a rise in the demand for money. An inflexible ceiling on domestic credit prevents increases in the demand for money from being satisfied from internal sources. In an economy that can draw on the international capital market, this is not of great consequence, since such a country can import money via a capital inflow. But in countries without effective connections to the international capital market, this escape valve is absent. Increased demand for money cannot be satisfied, real interest rates rise, and recession usually results. In this way, the very success of a stabilization program can create an unnecessary recession.

To this point, the Fund responds that the review clauses can be used to introduce a modification of the credit ceiling, but the critical question is whether the Fund would always allow them to be so used. In one of the cases studied by the conference, Turkey asked for a relaxation of the credit ceiling because of a rise in the demand for money induced by the success of a stabilization program, but the Fund did not agree.

Paradoxically, it has also been argued that *faster* inflation than the rate projected when drawing up the financial program might justify additional credit creation. This argument might at first seem inconsistent with the one above, but this is not clear. Faster inflation as a result of developments regarded as exogenous, which do not undermine confidence in the government's economic management, might well have little effect in reducing the real demand for money and might therefore increase the nominal demand for money, so that enforcement of an inflexible DCE ceiling will be more restrictive than intended.

The Fund is inclined to reply that a tougher credit ceiling in real terms is just what is called for to counter a faster than expected rate of inflation. Indeed, some countries currently base their macroeconomic strategies on that thesis: namely, all those that have adopted rigid money supply targets. But there remain responsible voices challenging the wisdom of that strategy and urging more accommodative monetary policies allied with more rounded counterinflation strategies embracing incomes policies. The Fund should not compel countries to subscribe to a particular view on this controversial issue as an accidental by-product of drawing on the high-conditionality facilities.

Perhaps the strongest advice that the Institute conference sent to the Fund was that it should make greater efforts to frame performance criteria as contingent conditions rather than as inflexible ceilings. The Fund replied that the review clauses already provide sufficient flexibility. But this is far from being a wholly satisfactory substitute. Many borrowing countries regard themselves as in an adversarial relationship with the Fund and feel they need more assurance than they now have that the Fund will prove sensitive to unexpected developments. This need is accentuated in multiyear programs, which the Fund has recently been discouraging somewhat—partly on the grounds that it is difficult to fix realistic performance criteria far in the future, though quantitative criteria are seldom set beyond one year even in multiyear programs. Rather than retreat from multiyear programs, the Fund should seek to advance to the specification of contingent performance criteria.

Satisfactory contingent conditions are undoubtedly difficult to frame. It would therefore be irresponsible to leave this topic without advancing any ideas as to how such conditions might be formulated. A complete description of how a country's policies should be expected to respond to every conceivable change in the state of the world is clearly impossible. The most promising approach seems to be specifying rather fully in each Letter of Intent the assumptions on which the particular program is based; assumptions, for example, about foreign and domestic inflation rates, about world interest rates, about the terms of trade, about the physical output of principal crops, and so on. Substantial deviations of the actual values of these variables from the values assumed in constructing the program would give the country (and the Fund as well) the right to seek a revision in the performance criteria (and perhaps also in the scale of the drawings).

Ideally, those revisions would be spelled out ex ante: for example, each 10 percent fall in the internally generated inflation rate would entitle a country to an x-percent increase in its domestic credit ceiling provided that this revision did not lead to a fall in the real interest rate. But in the first instance, at least, the Executive Board would probably have to debate the form of a proposed ceiling revision as and when a deviation was reported of the actual from the assumed value of a variable. In due course, this would establish a body of case law which would give borrowing countries a basis for predicting how their performance criteria would vary as events unfolded even if explicit commitments to those variations had not been written down.

An additional way to provide a little more flexibility would be to distinguish between *ceilings* and *targets*. At present financial programs are formulated by projecting what is regarded as the optimal development of the credit variables, given the known and expected constraints, and treating those projections as ceilings (or floors). In order to give themselves leeway for unexpected contingencies, if for no other reason, borrowing countries are tempted to try to negotiate their ceilings up, which frequently results in tedious and taxing confrontations about the merits of rival projections. Some of the ill-will with which negotiations with the Fund are regarded might be eased if it were agreed that the projections would provide targets and that the sanctions associated with performance criteria would come into play only if the targets were exceeded by such a wide margin as to breach a ceiling set a specified distance from the target. As with policy understandings, any flagrant disregard of the targets could be expected to predispose the Fund toward taking a less generous attitude if the performance criteria (ceilings) were breached.

The preceding proposals for adding flexibility to the application of performance criteria are not intended to weaken the assurance that countries borrowing from the Fund will undertake effective adjustment. On the contrary, that assurance should, if possible, be strengthened, which might be done by adding at least one and possibly two additional types of variables to those treated as performance criteria.

A variable that could and should be treated as a performance criterion is the real exchange rate. As with credit criteria, the actual performance criterion might be set as a ceiling or floor at some margin away from the target. This might in fact be even more necessary than in the case of credit ceilings, because the data to construct real exchange rate indices are less promptly and readily available.[9] Although the Fund has become much more sympathetic to exchange rate flexibility, it still tends to push exchange rate adjustment into the preconditions and to rely on the review clauses to ensure that a misalignment does not arise subsequently. It is true that, in a case of a really large overvaluation when a program is first considered, a major adjustment has to be a precondition, since even countries with strict exchange controls would be ill-advised to commit themselves to a major devaluation at some future date. But the maintenance, not merely the momentary achievement, of a realistic real exchange rate must also be ensured. That need would be magnified by the adoption of two recommendations made earlier—avoidance of excessive initial devaluations and provision of flexible credit ceilings when inflation differs from the rate projected. This dilemma could be solved by using the real exchange rate as a performance criterion.

Another possible performance criterion is the overall savings rate. Jeffrey Sachs (Comments, Chapters 20–21, this volume) reports that his recent research shows that declines in the overall savings rate tend to be by far the best forward indicator of a debt crisis. It might be argued that the division of output between consumption and savings is a matter of purely national concern rather than a subject into which IMF should seek to intrude, but this is not convincing in the case of

[9] In his concluding statement to the conference (Chapter 22, this volume) Gerald Helleiner called for greater Fund assistance to its small and least developed members in providing updated information on the evolution of their real effective exchange rates. Adoption of the real exchange rate as a performance criterion might have the incidental benefit of motivating the Fund to respond to that request.

a country that has resolved to undertake a program of structural adjustment involving a high savings rate. More pertinent, statistics on the overall savings rate are unlikely to be available promptly, thus violating one of the Fund's basic requirements for performance criteria. Another problem is that the savings rate is not a policy variable, except partially via the government budget. In view of these considerations, the advisability of using the savings rate as a performance criterion is open to question.

It has been argued in this section that the heart of the IMF monitoring process lies in the performance criteria stipulated and that the Fund correctly uses credit ceilings (rather than payments outcomes) for this purpose. It was suggested that credit ceilings might usefully be supplemented by requirements for the real exchange rate and, possibly, the overall savings rate. The Fund should make a major effort to add flexibility to performance criteria, especially those relating to credit ceilings, by seeking to express them as contingent conditions rather than as fixed requirements.

Cyclical Variation

It has long been commonplace to regard a major purpose of both the IMF and the Organization for Economic Cooperation and Development (OECD) as being to secure a measure of macroeconomic coordination among the major countries. For many years it was taken for granted that this involved attempting to smooth the business cycle. Recent evidence indicates that the Fund now takes a very different attitude to anticyclical policy. For example, the 1982 issue of *World Economic Outlook* continues to exhort the major countries to restrictive demand-management policies even though the world is, by most measures, in the deepest recession for a half century. The managing director has recently urged general fiscal contraction not just for the United States in 1983, but for Britain and Japan in 1982.[10] William Dale (Chapter 1, this volume) echoes the same theme.

To justify this advice, it is argued that anti-inflation policy must be sustained to a successful conclusion. This is dubious: the efficient way to fight inflation is to smooth the top off the boom, not to deepen recession into depression. Indeed, deflationary overkill seems as likely to nurture a subsequent overrelaxation as to lead to lasting success,

[10] This was stated explicitly in response to questions following the speech reported as de Larosière (1982a).

in much the way that the conference discussion on Britain and Italy suggested had occurred in 1969–73 and 1974–76, respectively, after short-run Fund programs that were perceived as having been tougher than necessary. Of course, the Fund's current anti-inflation focus is supported by most of its major members, who have endorsed this strategy as recently as the Versailles Summit.

There is one respect in which the Fund can directly influence the world cycle—through variation in its readiness to lend to members. The compensatory financing facility has some built in stabilizing anticyclical potential because a world recession cuts commodity prices, which permits countries to draw on it. The proposal for extending low-conditionality finance, discussed above under "The Role of the Fund," would carry this much further, since a world recession is an exogenous factor which diminishes a country's receipts and thereby tends to enable it to draw.

Richard Cooper (Chapter 22, this volume) has suggested more modestly that the Fund's conditionality should vary over time, depending on world economic conditions, so that it would be somewhat weaker in a period like the present than in a period of world prosperity. The logic is that even well-managed countries can easily find themselves facing a need to borrow during a world recession, whereas this is much less likely in a boom. The proposal would have the additional advantage of making a modest contribution to a global anticyclical policy.

In the introduction it was asserted that the toughness of IMF conditionality has varied considerably over the past few years. It has been widely said that a major loosening occurred after the September 1979 annual Bank and Fund meetings in Belgrade, and that conditionality was again tightened around May or June 1981. Ironically, if these accounts are correct, the Fund had already tightened conditionality again when the Reagan administration was complaining about its looseness in the run-up to the 1981 annual meetings. But, rather than rely on hearsay evidence, it seemed more constructive to examine whether variations in the tightness of Fund conditionality might be detectable from statistical evidence.

While conditionality's many dimensions cannot all easily be reduced to a statistical basis, some facets can be measured: the frequency, size, and duration of programs and (more ambiguously) any real appreciation in a borrowing country's exchange rate since some base date. Tough conditionality is expected to be associated with a precondition of an adequate devaluation to restore competitiveness. Critics of the supposed weakening of conditionality charged that the

Fund was failing to require devaluations even when necessary to correct a preceding real appreciation.

Table 24.2 shows each high-conditionality loan approved by the Fund since 1978, the SDR equivalent, the percentage of a country's quota, the duration, and the real appreciation from the base year 1972 to the end of the month of approval. Real appreciation is calculated on the basis of consumer prices in the United States and in the borrowing country. The first measure of real appreciation is the bilateral appreciation against the dollar; the second corrects by the dollar's effective appreciation, giving a crude measure of real effective appreciation.

Table 24.2 reveals a surge in Fund lending under high-conditionality arrangements between mid-1979 and mid-1981. Before May 1979, the Fund approved an average of just over one high-conditionality program a month. In the 25 months, June 1979 to June 1981, inclusive, such approvals rose to an average of 2.5 a month before falling back to just over 1 a month in the 9 subsequent months. The surge started just before the Belgrade Annual Meetings, which some informants mentioned as the critical date, and petered out around June 1981.

Not only were more programs approved, but their value in relation to quotas also increased noticeably. For example, before 1979, 11 programs amounted to under 100 percent of quota, 8 to between 100 percent and 249 percent, and 1 to more than 250 percent of quota. Between October 1979 and December 1980 (before the upward change in quotas distorts such a comparison), 7 programs amounted to less than 100 percent of quota, 11 to between 100 percent and 249 percent, and no fewer than 11 programs to over 250 percent of quota.

It is important to consider whether the increased lending resulted from an increase in the Fund's willingness to lend, or from an increase in demand for loans by potential borrowers. Because the upsurge in lending more or less coincided with the second oil shock, a demand-side explanation appears plausible. On the other hand, the payments difficulties of the developing countries that currently form the Fund's principal clientele continued to worsen through 1981, so that the fall off in Fund lending can hardly be explained on that basis.

To the extent that the supply-side explanation is correct, some trace of tougher or weaker conditions should show up in the last three columns of Table 24.2. The division of programs by duration is shown for five subperiods in Table 24.3: the base period (before May 1979), the period of reportedly looser conditionality (October 1979 to May 1981), the period of supposedly tighter conditionality (October 1981 on), and the two ambiguous transitional periods. The swing is evident: from a rough equality between one-year and multiyear programs

TABLE 24.2 HIGH-CONDITIONALITY PROGRAMS, JANUARY 1978–MAY 1982

Date approved	*Country*	*Amount (SDR million)*	*Percent-age of quota*	*Length of program (months)*	*Percentage real appreciation (against dollar)*[a]	*(effective rate)*
February 1978	Western Samoa	1	36	12	11	2
February 1978	Spain	143	36	12	29	18
February 1978	Mauritius	8	36	12	23	13
April 1978	Zambia	250	177	24	n.a.	n.a.
April 1978	Turkey[c]	300	150	24	19	7
May 1978	Gabon	15	50	12	8	−3
June 1978	Jamaica[b,c]	200	270	36	−4	−14
June 1978	Panama	25	56	12	−4	−14
June 1978	Portugal[c]	57	33	12	4	−7
July 1978	Burma	30	41	12	23	5
July 1978	Egypt[b]	600	263	36	25	6
August 1978	Guyana	6	25	12	−2	−16
September 1978	Peru[c]	184	112	27	−28	−39
October 1978	Haiti[b]	32	139	36	16	−1
January 1979	Sri Lanka[b]	260	218	36	−63	−68
January 1979	Ghana	53	50	12	333	267
March 1979	Panama	30	67	12	−7	−20
April 1979	Congo	4	24	12	27	10
May 1979	Sudan[b]	200	227	36	41	22
May 1979	Nicaragua	34	100	19	n.a.	n.a.
June 1979	Jamaica[b,c]	260	351	24	−5	−18
June 1979	Philippines	105	50	6	26	10
June 1979	Togo	15	79	18	28	11
June 1979	Guyana[b]	63	252	36	2	−12
June 1979	Honduras[b]	48	141	24	−6	−19
July 1979	Turkey[c]	250	125	12	59	35
July 1979	Bangladesh	85	56	12	8	−8
August 1979	Peru[c]	285	174	16	−23	−35
August 1979	Western Samoa	1	25	12	−19	−31
August 1979	Zaire	69	45	18	169	128
August 1979	Kenya[c]	17	25	24	37	16
October 1979	Malawi	26	137	26	0	−14
October 1979	Mauritius	73	270	25	0	−14
November 1979	Sierra Leone	17	55	12	12	−2
November 1979	Gambia	2	18	12	38	21
November 1979	Grenada	1	22	14	n.a.	n.a.
February 1980	Bolivia	66	147	12	32	13
February 1980	Somalia	12	52	12	n.a.	n.a.
February 1980	Philippines	410	195	22	29	11
March 1980	Costa Rica	61	149	24	2	−9
March 1980	Korea	640	400	24	18	5
April 1980	Panama	66	147	19	−6	−16
May 1980	Malawi	50	263	22	13	−3

TABLE 24.2 Continued

Date approved	Country	Amount (SDR million)	Percent-age of quota	Length of program (months)	Percentage real appreciation (against dollar)[a]	(effective rate)
June 1980	Yugoslavia	339	123	18	29	8
June 1980	Gabon[b]	34	113	24	76	48
June 1980	Turkey[c]	1,250	625	36	7	−10
June 1980	Madagascar	64	190	24	28	8
July 1980	Equat. Guinea	6	55	12	n.a.	n.a.
July 1980	Guyana[b]	100	400	36	2	−13
July 1980	Mauritania	30	175	21	32	12
August 1980	Lao PDR	14	88	12	n.a.	n.a.
August 1980	Senegal[b]	185	440	36	27	10
September 1980	Mauritius	35	130	12	35	15
September 1980	Liberia	65	176	24	23	5
September 1980	Tanzania[c]	180	327	21	49	27
October 1980	Morocco[b]	147	98	36	19	2
October 1980	Kenya[c]	242	350	24	41	21
November 1980	Sudan	227	258	19	52	34
November 1980	Pakistan[b]	1,268	445	36	37	21
December 1980	Bangladesh[b]	800	351	36	−4	−14
January 1981	Yugoslavia	1,662	400	36	39	24
February 1981	Korea	576	225	12	15	7
February 1981	Panama	24	36	10	−8	−15
February 1981	Togo	48	167	24	26	17
February 1981	Dominica[b]	9	295	36	n.a.	n.a.
February 1981	Ivory Coast[b]	485	425	36	60	49
March 1981	Morocco[b]	817	363	31	2	−5
March 1981	Sierra Leone	164	352	36	1	−6
April 1981	Central African Rep.	10	43	8	18	12
April 1981	Jamaica[b,c]	236	213	36	10	4
April 1981	Madagascar	77	150	14	27	21
May 1981	Ethiopia	68	125	14	43	41
May 1981	Zambia[b]	800	378	36	12	10
May 1981	Grenada	3	76	12	n.a.	n.a.
June 1981	Solomon Islands	2	50	12	n.a.	n.a.
June 1981	Mauritania	26	101	10	26	27
June 1981	Burma	27	25	12	−16	−15
June 1981	Thailand	815	300	24	25	26
June 1981	Uganda	113	150	13	n.a.	n.a.
June 1981	Romania	1,103	300	36	−8	−7
June 1981	Costa Rica[b]	277	450	36	−45	−44
June 1981	Zaire[b]	912	400	36	37	38
July 1981	Somalia	43	125	12	224	235
July 1981	Guyana[b]	100	267	24	0	3
August 1981	Liberia	55	100	12	23	24
September 1981	Senegal	63	100	8	5	10

TABLE 24.2 Continued

Date approved	Country	Amount (SDR million)	Percentage of quota	Length of program (months)	Percentage real appreciation (against dollar)[a]	Percentage real appreciation (effective rate)
November 1981	India[b,c]	5,000	291	36	−15	−16
December 1981	Mauritius	30	74	12	3	3
January 1982	Kenya	152	147	12	8	9
February 1982	Gambia	17	125	12	11	16
February 1982	Sudan	198	150	12	n.a.	n.a.
April 1982	Morocco	281	125	12	−15	−8
April 1982	Panama	30	44	12	−10	−3

n.a. Not available due to lack of data.
Sources: IMF *Survey*, IMF *Annual Reports, International Financial Statistics.*
a. The penultimate column is the country's consumer prices in the month of the program divided by 1972 prices, deflated by the equivalent rise in US prices and the devaluation in the exchange rate over the same period, expressed as a percentage increase. (Real depreciation is presented by a negative number.)
b. Extended arrangement.
c. Covered by an Institute conference paper.

before October 1979 to a 3-to-1 preponderance of multiyear programs during the period of easier conditionality to a clear preponderance of short programs since late 1981.[11]

TABLE 24.3 ONE-YEAR VERSUS MULTIYEAR HIGH-CONDITIONALITY PROGRAMS, 1978–82

Subperiod	*Program of 12 months or less*	*Program of more than one year*
Before May 1979	7	5
June–September 1979	4	7
October 1979–May 1981	11	32
June–September 1981	6	6
October 1981 on	6	1

Source: Table 24.2.

[11] It has been claimed that the recent reduction in multiyear programs does not signify a return to requiring abrupt adjustment, since the need for gradualism is being met by a series of consecutive one-year programs. If this is true, it implies that the total number of programs being approved has dropped even more drastically than indicated by the figures cited here.

TABLE 24.4 REAL APPRECIATION SINCE 1972 AND HIGH-CONDITIONALITY PROGRAMS

	Real appreciation since 1972					
	Bilateral against dollar			Effective basis		
Subperiod	Zero or negative	1 percent to 19 percent	20 percent plus	Zero or negative	1 percent to 19 percent	20 percent plus
Prior to May 1979	6	5	7	9	7	2
June–September 1979	4	2	5	6	3	2
October 1979–May 1981	5	13	19	12	15	10
June–September 1981	4	1	5	3	2	5
October 1981 on	3	3	0	3	3	0

Source: Table 24.2.

The measures of real appreciation show, not unexpectedly, enormous variation between one program and another. Nevertheless, when the period 1978–82 is divided into the same five subperiods as in Table 24.3, a general tendency again emerges. Table 24.4 shows a marked increase during the "easier" period in the proportion of programs approved without requiring a devaluation to reduce the real appreciation since 1972, even after allowing for fluctuations in the value of the dollar. The most recent period, since October 1981, shows a reversion to a tougher approach. This evidence seems to confirm that Fund conditionality was eased in mid-1979 (though before the Belgrade Annual Meetings) and retightened in mid-1981.

With the exception of changes in the proportion of quota that may be drawn, these variations in the toughness of conditionality were never debated, let alone sanctioned, by the Executive Board of the Fund. The Board did indeed have protracted discussions that led up to agreement on new guidelines on conditionality in March 1979 (Appendix 24.C) but these seem to have been related more to codifying than modifying the Fund's past practices. Moreover, the managing director has publicly stated that the Fund has made no changes in policy, asserting instead that it has consistently applied the same basic policies against a changing background (de Larosière, 1982b).

The increase in high-conditionality lending after mid-1979 might indeed be explained on that basis, inasmuch as the 1979 oil price increase tended to cause a world recession as well as an increase in inflation. Even there, however, a question arises about the consistency of willingness to approve programs without requiring a devaluation adequate to restore competitiveness (Table 24.4) with the claim that "the content of the adjustment measures had certainly not been softened" (ibid., p. 4). Other dimensions in which the critics charged that conditionality became "too soft" were in the willingness to approve programs that did not require the elimination of negative real interest rates or a significant cut in the fiscal deficit. It was also said that the Fund proved more ready to approve programs that did not involve the expectation of a short-run output loss.

It is not so easy to see how the apparent tightening from mid-1981 can be explained as the result of consistent application of the same underlying principles in the face of changing circumstances. Since the recession had deepened by mid-1981, the tightening, based on traditional notions of anticyclical policy, was clearly perverse. The managing director (1982b) argues, however, that the evidence that the world recession was going to be more prolonged than previously assumed left the Fund no option but to require more severe adjustment action than had previously been called for. At best, that suggests that the Fund deliberately chose to override anticyclical considerations. At worst, it reinforces the doubts expressed at the beginning of this section about the Fund's stand on anticyclical policy. Since the oil deficit has proved less durable than had been foreseen in 1979–80, the greater persistence of the recession must be attributed to the perpetuation of restrictive policies, which the Fund still supports.

The variations in the ease of conditionality can, of course, be explained in other ways. The liquidity of the Fund is one possibility. In mid-1979 the Fund was embarrassed at its success in raising money for the supplementary financing facility, virtually none of which had been lent, and its liquidity was being restored by repayments by Italy and the United Kingdom and about to be further amplified by payment of the seventh quota increase. The Fund could have created a new oil facility, but that solution was rejected on the ground that the first oil facility had made it too easy to postpone adjustment. Requiring countries to borrow from the high-conditionality facilities, but easing the terms, must have seemed a reasonable compromise.

By mid-1981 the Fund had committed itself to lending the greater part of its resources. It could have borrowed more on the private market and from other sources, but the pressure of 1979, to lend money in order to justify having it, had abated.

A second factor was presumably the diplomatic situation. The easing of conditionality may have been partly an effort to parry the initiative of the Group of 77 to put IMF issues into the "Global Negotiations" under the aegis of the United Nations. When the easing became clear by early 1981, however, a number of the developed countries started to press for tighter policies.

Political factors may also have played a role. The Reagan administration took office in January 1981, markedly less supportive of a major role for the Fund than its predecessor had been. Four months later Valéry Giscard d'Estaing was defeated in the French presidential election, and some have speculated that any inclination the managing director might have had to defy the Fund's largest (and only veto-wielding) member could have been tempered by the changed outlook in his home country. In view of these developments, another change in Fund policy is not surprising. The fact remains, nevertheless, that the change was perverse from the standpoint of global anticyclical policy.

In addition to the question of the *timing* of the variations in the tightness of conditionality is the question of its form. Of course, "too easy" or "too tight" is a simplistic way of viewing a multidimensional phenomenon like the degree of conditionality. A person who accepts the line of argument developed above regarding the desirable design of adjustment programs would consider highly retrograde any failure to insist on realistic exchange rates. If the Fund does not insist on conditions that promise a reasonable prospect of adjustment, its "seal of approval" will be devalued, benefiting no one. Some commercial bankers assert that this has happened, and the current suspension of 10 of the Fund's 34 high-conditionality programs suggests that there may be reason for such a view.

Other aspects of the easing of conditionality were to be warmly applauded, however, especially the move to multiyear programs, as implied above in the section on the design of adjustment programs. The willingness to support programs that did not involve the expectation of a short-run output loss was also a major step forward, which has reportedly been jeopardized in the tightening of conditionality.[12]

It has been argued in this section that the Fund ought to vary the terms of its conditionality somewhat in the light of the world cyclical situation, although not at the cost of undermining the assurance that adjustment will ultimately be achieved. While the timing of the Fund's easing of conditionality in mid-1979 could be justified on that basis, the timing of the subsequent tightening in mid-1981 cannot be. It can be argued that tight conditionality at this time is consistent with the policy advice of giving primacy to the defeat of inflation that the Fund was then (and still is) dispensing. In that case, however, one has to

[12] News reports in the *Far Eastern Economic Review* on April 30 and May 21, 1982, assert that the Fund has been insisting on cutbacks in the Philippines' projected growth rate.

ask: on what basis the lower conditionality of 1979 to mid-1981 was justified; whether the developing countries should be expected to bear so much of the burden of curing world inflation; and whether the effort to defeat inflation by monetary restriction alone is well advised in light of the short-term costs.

As far as the merits of the tightening are concerned, some aspects are welcome—such as the insistence on borrowing countries' pursuing a realistic exchange rate policy. Other aspects are deplorable—such as the turning away from multiyear programs and the rumored insistence that countries cut real growth rates substantially for balance of payments reasons. If such rumors are in fact justified, it cannot but deepen the world recession, in contrast to the constructive role that the maintenance of demand in developing countries, aided by the oil facility, is acknowledged to have played in limiting the 1975 recession. There is a respectable case for the Fund's decision not to create a new oil facility in 1979–82, but only if the Fund's high-conditionality lending is sustained at a level that helps developing countries cope with the recession.

Evaluation and Conclusions

Richard Cooper (Chapter 22, this volume) conjectures that a random sample of any five participants would, in any specific instance not involving their own country, be able to agree among themselves on the outlines of a program, and that the agreed program would be broadly similar to that which the Fund would recommend in the circumstances involved. Cooper's conjecture was subsequently qualified further but it was not challenged outright, and—given that participation had deliberately been drawn broadly—that is surely significant. In other words, the group concluded that the Fund is neither driven by sinister motives nor professionally incompetent in overlooking preferable adjustment strategies but gets a bad press primarily because its job involves confronting countries with unpleasant realities.

This does not mean that programs are invariably successful. On the contrary, tests of the effectiveness of Fund programs by Connors (1979) and by Killick and Chapman (1982), which involve comparing variables like the balance of payments, output, and inflation before and after a program, disclose little systematic effect. In my own conference paper, I argued that such tests do not answer more tantalizing and perhaps more pertinent questions, like the difference between what would have happened without a program and what actually occurred. The previous situation may have become untenable, so that retrenchment had to occur. Indeed, that may be why a country went to the Fund. On the other hand, maybe there was a chance of expansionary stabilization that was forgone. In neither case would a historical comparison of two periods reveal the adequacy of the program. The only hope of making such judgments involves case studies of specific programs. That is why the conference involved a series of case studies.

Of the nine post-1975 case studies considered, one program (Tanzania) never got off the ground. Another (India) is still too early for final judgment (although to date the program appears successful). Five programs (Britain, Italy, Peru, Portugal, and Turkey) witnessed major payments improvements: in the first four of those cases a rapid recovery on capital account preceded the improvement in the current account. However, Britain and possibly Peru, as well as Jamaica and Kenya, involved what Reginald Green (Chapter 15, this volume) terms "stabilization without adjustment": that is, the short-run improvement in the balance of payments was secured by reducing income rather than by a switch of resources which permits a better payments performance at a given income level. In such cases the Fund simply helps to tide a country over a difficult patch, which may not be without value but cannot be counted a real success. Only in Italy, Portugal, and most conspicuously Turkey, can the Fund program plausibly be given credit for securing a measure of adjustment. India will join this group on current trends.

The other way of evaluating the performance of the Fund is to examine the various complaints against it: complaints of excessive monetarism, of overkill, of antisocialist and pro-free market bias, of perpetuating dependency, of bailing out the banks rather than helping borrowing countries—and, from other quarters, of having gone soft.

The complaint that the Fund is excessively monetarist is not convincing. It is true that Fund programs always involve a credit ceiling, but for good reasons. A credit ceiling is a convenient technical shorthand for the sum total of a government's commitments toward limiting expenditure. In general, such commitments are indeed necessary, for payments adjustment almost always calls for restricting expenditures. Moreover, credit ceilings satisfy the injunction that the Fund limit performance criteria to macroeconomic variables, and they provide a stabilizing negative feedback to the balance of payments when the outcome is tending to deviate from the projection. The recent examples of restrictive monetarist policies' being carried to the point of having a major impact on the real economy are associated with names like Martinez de Hoz, Pinochet and Margaret Thatcher, none of whom have been under the tutelage of the Fund. In some Fund programs, notably in India, the credit ceilings have been drawn sufficiently liberally as to be in no danger of "biting" provided that demand-management policy remains on a prudent course. Williamson (1980) characterized the Fund's theoretical position as "eclectic" rather than "monetarist," and there seems no reason to revise that judgment.

Edmar Bacha (Chapter 14, this volume), a longstanding critic of the Fund, discussed the decision of the Brazilian authorities not to seek a loan from the Fund during its payments crisis of the last two years. He argued that the Brazilian authorities' program to restore the confidence of the commercial banks was identical to the one the Fund would have required as a condition for a loan in the high-conditionality facilities. Going to the Fund would have reduced the interest-cost of borrowing, and, because the foreign-exchange constraint was binding, the need to deflate. Against this advantage, Brazil would have had to tie its hands for a considerable period into the future, losing its ability to relax its program of monetary restriction as and when it judges that it can safely do so.

Since Bacha advocates passive money rather than monetary discipline, and believes that Delfim Netto (Brazilian minister of planning) has similar instincts, he considers the flexibility left in Brazilian hands as a result of not going to the Fund to be a national advantage. He therefore sees the choice as one involving a trade-off between short-run gains in going to the Fund against long-term losses through the inability to relax as quickly—an interesting reversal of the Fund's traditional self-perception, in which Fund programs are regarded as taking unpleasant short-run medicine for the long-run benefit of the country involved.

But are Fund programs typically guilty of overkill, as Bacha essentially argues? Connors (1979) and Killick and Chapman (1982) failed to find any systematic or significant impact of Fund programs on the rate of real growth. Despite my own skepticism about how much such historical comparisons show, this must cast doubt on the charge that Fund involvement has a dire impact on real output. The case studies presented to the conference revealed surprisingly few instances where their authors felt the Fund had demanded actions that amounted to overkill. Britain in 1969 and Italy (by accident) by 1974 were mentioned. Perhaps Britain in 1976 also qualified, inasmuch as the necessary policy adjustments had already been made when the IMF team arrived in London, but it has to be conceded that the dent in the growth of real output was minimal.

Yet the conference considered a number of cases that were highly controversial at the time, such as Jamaica and Peru in 1977–79, Portugal in 1978, Turkey in 1978–80, and Tanzania in 1979–81. In retrospect it seems rather clear that policy in Jamaica, Peru, and Turkey was on a completely unsustainable course, and that there was no alternative to shock treatment that would mark a convincing break with the past. The Fund can be accused of a lack of political realism in both Jamaica and Peru for having started off by demanding drastic changes in policy, involving a fundamental scaling down of those countries' ambitions to accord with unpleasant realities, in return for a minimal level of Fund financial support, but that is not the same as having demanded overkill. The Turkish case also started off with governmental reluctance to make policy changes of the scale that the Fund considered necessary, but, after a government willing to adopt more market-oriented policies and to open up the economy took office in 1980, the Turkish program was a considerable success: it did involve shock treatment, but not overkill. In Portugal, there seems to be general agreement that the program succeeded, at least in the short run, although some observers claim that this was not so much because of the policy advice the Fund gave as because it was brought to see reason. On Tanzania, there is still no meeting of minds. Reginald Green clearly believes that expansionary stabilization would have been possible had the Fund been willing to provide the wherewithal to replenish inventories and work at improving what was an uneven but basically well-conceived governmental approach. The Fund, and also the World Bank, consider the Tanzanian economy grossly mismanaged and the government obtusely unwilling to face reality. The resulting perpetuation of a tragedy does not reflect credit on any of the parties.

Of all the cases considered by the conference, the clearest case of overkill—a deflationary policy pushing output below internal balance—is Brazil's deflation in 1981 to *avoid having to borrow from the Fund*. Brazil has apparently had to continue deflating farther and longer than first hoped because the restoration of its creditworthiness has been conditional on its continuing to pursue such policies. It is a striking contrast to the way reserves flowed back to countries like Britain, Italy and Portugal, and even Peru, once the corner was turned. The contrast suggests that the IMF "seal of approval" is worth something.

Thus, the charge seems unsubstantiated that the Fund has been guilty of imposing unreasonably onerous conditions on borrowing countries in recent years. Shock treatment has, on occasion, been administered, as in Peru and Turkey, but only in circumstances where it appears to have been called for. The advent of multiyear programs seems to have quieted earlier fears that shock treatment was applied where gradual adjustment would have been more appropriate. Charges of overkill have not been clearly substantiated. On the other hand, tests such as those by Connors and Killick do not by their nature ask if possibilities of expansionary stabilization were forgone. Such claims have been made, though not completely convincingly, in the case of Tanzania (Green, Chapter 15, this volume) and in the case of Peru (Schydlovsky in Cline and Weintraub, 1981).

It has also been charged that the Fund is biased against socialism. That the Fund welcomes those governments that are willing to work with market forces cannot be doubted. At the same time, the Fund clearly does not have an evangelical zeal for spreading "the magic of the market" parallel to that of, say, the Reagan administration. Its attitude, it would claim, is nonideological: it seeks to promote economic rationality, and it just happens that under a wide range of circumstances the readiest means to that end involves harnessing, instead of fighting, market forces.

What is surely true is that the Fund does not refuse to provide financial assistance to members with left-wing governments. On the contrary, at the time of the conference, some 16.5 percent of IMF credit was directed to the six communist member countries (China, Kampuchea, Laos, Romania, Vietnam, and Yugoslavia; Rimmer de Vries, Chapter 22, this volume), and Michael Manley's Jamaica was at one stage the heaviest *per capita* borrower from the Fund (Sharpley, Chapter 11, this volume). Moreover, the Fund continued to give the Allende government the benefit of the doubt in drawing from the compensatory financing facility. So, far from the Fund's discriminating against socialist governments, the question arises whether the left has not been seeking a foreign scapegoat for the policy failures that have resulted from its too frequent disdain for technical competence.

The charge that the Fund has tended to perpetuate dependency did not receive much attention at the conference. Samuel Lichtensztejn (Chapter 10, this volume) deals with the issue but could not attend the conference. In his absence this charge was rather passed by, perhaps because the general predilection of participants was one of greater sympathy for interdependence than for independence.

A final left-wing complaint against the Fund is that it is primarily concerned with bailing out banks from loans that run into trouble, rather than with helping its member countries. Once again, there can be no doubt that Fund programs in countries like Peru and Turkey have been very helpful to the banks in safeguarding the value of their loans, and the belief that the commercial banks could shelter under the Fund's umbrella has in the past helped to sustain the build up of bank lending to developing countries—sometimes excessively so.

Rimmer de Vries and Irving Friedman, two leading private bankers at the conference, agreed that this "umbrella" notion should not, and indeed could not, continue. In their view, the banks have to stand on their own feet. Presumably, this means that in future debt renegotiations maintenance of the present value of outstanding debt with a mere stretching of the maturities will not necessarily be taken for granted. Where it happens that the commercial banks rush in, tempt a country to overborrow, and do not assure themselves that the borrowing country will be in a position to repay—a situation that has been witnessed in Peru, Poland, Turkey, Zaire, and most recently in Chile—they deserve to forfeit a part of the value of their loans. This may not, however, be the right point in history to establish this principle, when an excessive cutback in lending to developing countries is the chief danger.

While the Fund has traditionally been attacked from the political left, it has recently come under fire from the right as well. On the extreme right, US Congressman Jack Kemp (R-NY) has taken to criticizing the Fund for insisting on "Keynesian" measures like devaluation and tax increases. No one at the conference expressed any sympathy for such criticisms. On the contrary, Arnold Harberger pleaded forcefully for a clear distinction between that type of self-styled "supply-side economics," unrelated to any coherent body of economic theory, and the supply-side measures like enabling markets to work and supporting investment that the Fund does promote.

The attack from the far right is important, however, not because of its intellectual force but because of its proven ability to influence policy despite the lack of any serious intellectual foundation. It may well influence the attitude of the Reagan administration. And it is, of course, the Reagan administration's unhappiness with the thrust of Fund policy that has presented a real threat to the Fund's role. That unhappiness relates to three issues:

The first issue is whether the Fund should not be restricted to the role of lender of last resort, to be called on only when other sources of finance are unavailable. Such a limitation of the Fund's role has already occurred in countries with ready access to the world capital market, and does no great harm. Indeed, since the Fund is under no circumstance going to be able to fill more than a small part of the financing needs of those countries, it makes good sense for it to withdraw from all but the residual role of restoring lost creditworthiness. But that leaves an important group of countries that need the Fund to finance payments fluctuations. It does not seem inherent in the logic of the Reagan administration's position that the Fund should be prevented from filling that role, but it seems highly likely that that would be the practical effect if the administration has its way in cutting the activities of the Fund.

A second and related issue is whether the Fund should be involved in financing structural adjustment. As argued in the discussion of the Fund's role, this is entirely proper, given the Fund's traditional responsibilities. A structural deficit—a deficit resulting from exogenous change that appears to be permanent and which can only be eliminated by depressing output below full capacity or by structural change—can be efficiently adjusted only by structural adjustment. The Fund is struggling to retain its new-found role in this area: it deserves to succeed.

The third issue is anticyclical policy. Under the traditional approach, in a recession the Fund would urge its members in strong positions to expand and help its members in weak positions to finance their deficits so as to avoid excessive contraction. The Reagan administration and many others around the world, however, are committed to the maintenance of an anti-inflationary monetary policy despite the depth of the recession that has resulted. On this issue, the Fund thus urges the industrial countries to stick to their anti-inflationary policies and the developing countries to tighten up so as to avoid deficits which cannot be financed with the weak demand and crippling terms of trade induced by the West's monetary contraction. This retreat from stabilization policy is *not* an inevitable consequence of the perfectly proper decision to try to eliminate inflation. Eliminating inflation requires a fundamentally long-term commitment to avoid excessive demand pressures, aided by sensible supply-side and, where possible, incomes policies, rather than a short-run commitment to produce whatever recession this takes (which is likely to induce irresistible counter-pressures in the longer run, in any event).

Little evidence has been found to support the main charges lodged against the Fund. The record of the programs studied by the conference is not one of unqualified success, but the main shortcoming was the failure to secure a lasting switch of resources into the balance of payments, not excessive monetarism, overkill, inappropriate shock treatment, or ideological bias against socialism, as asserted by the left. Neither were the right-wing criticisms of the Fund found convincing. Indeed, the major point on which this study has faulted the Fund is its retreat from anticyclical policy—the tightening of its conditionality in the face of severe world recession.

The preceding evaluation implies that the Fund has conducted its lending activities in a generally constructive way. This study has, however, produced criticism on several specific points and led to a number of suggestions for improvements.

Concerning cooperation with the World Bank, IMF involvement in lending to support programs designed to eliminate a structural deficit is not merely proper but, under current conditions, indispensable if the Fund is to fulfill its traditional mandate as an adjustment institution. Two actions were suggested to further the effectiveness of such programs:

The terms of reference of the extended facility should be reformulated in order to specify its role as that of aiding a country to adjust to a structural deficit, defined as a deficit caused by a presumably permanent external shock which cannot be eliminated without structural change except by a permanent departure from internal balance.

The welcome growth of cooperation with the World Bank should be extended by a joint declaration of Fund and Bank that structural adjustment programs are a joint responsibility of the two institutions. Countries would be invited to apply simultaneously for an extended loan from the Fund and a structural adjustment loan from the Bank. They would negotiate with the Bank a set of microeconomic measures designed to induce the desired structural changes, and with the Fund a set of conditions designed to ensure the maintenance of supportive macroeconomic policies.

While recognizing the principle that the Fund has no right to *insist* on any conditions other than those judged adequate to ensure that the balance of payments will indeed recover, *in giving policy advice the Fund should take account of a broad spectrum of objectives including output, growth, inflation, and income distribution (controversially) as well as the balance of payments.* To that end the Fund should encourage the country to seek a combination of devaluation and deflation calculated to combine external and internal balance, rather than allowing excess capacity to emerge or persist; it should avoid nominal devaluations that cannot be translated substantially into real devaluations, and should prefer a modest initial devaluation followed by further depreciation, as needed to maintain a target real exchange rate, to a massive initial devaluation; it should nurture the supply side; and, controversially, it should seek to shield the poor from the impact of expenditure cuts. The Fund should consider whether shock treatment is necessary in each specific case, and it should have and use the capability to support gradual adjustment where shock treatment is not necessary.

In the Fund's monitoring of its programs via performance criteria, it was argued that credit ceilings are appropriate variables to use for that purpose, despite the friction generated. However, *the Fund should make a major effort to confront the difficult task of expressing these more as contingent conditions instead of fixed requirements.* It was suggested that performance criteria might usefully be extended to cover the real exchange rate and, possibly, the overall savings rate.

Concerning cyclical variations, without threatening the assurance that adjustment will be achieved, *the Fund ought to take account of the world cyclical situation in framing its lending policies.* On this criterion, the timing of the tightening of conditionality in mid-1981 was perverse, even though some aspects of the tightening (such as the return to an insistence on a competitive exchange rate) were to be welcomed.

One possible reason for rejecting criticism of the Fund for having tightened conditionality at such an inopportune time is that it did not have the money to do otherwise. Although the Fund's immediate liquidity situation is not critical, it would become difficult if another two or three countries with large quotas applied for loans. Even then, the Fund could replenish its liquidity by borrowing, either from member governments or, if necessary, from the market. But the objection does draw attention to the fact that the role suggested for the Fund can be comfortably filled only if quotas are large enough to provide the Fund with the necessary financial resources.

Quotas therefore need to be large enough to enable the Fund to fulfill its traditional role as the major source of temporary balance of payments finance to those countries that have not achieved significant access to the international capital market, preferably by extension of low-conditionality financing where a deficit arises due to circumstances outside a country's own control. That requires it to provide resources both to finance the adjustment of structural deficits and to finance deficits caused by world recession even when these do not appear likely to reverse themselves quickly. The most difficult situation of all for the poorer countries is the one they face in 1982, where an acute and apparently lengthy world recession is superimposed on an underlying need for structural adjustment. It is therefore natural to calculate the Fund's need for financial resources from a consideration of what the principles enunciated in this study suggest the Fund ought to be doing at a time like the present.

The countries of sub-Saharan Africa have suffered a terms of trade deterioration of over 20 percent in recent years. The fact that foreign trade is typically of the order of 20 percent of GDP suggests that the type of payments shock that the Fund is in business to finance can easily reach 4 percent of GDP. Imagining a Fund program that finances a tapering proportion of an exogenously caused deficit might suggest that the Fund should have the capability of financing a deficit equal to (4 + 3 + 2 + 1) = 10 percent of one year's GDP in sum over the period of a structural adjustment program.

The countries classified as low-income by the World Bank's *World Development Report* provide a minimum estimate of the countries without access to the international capital market. Their aggregate GNP in 1979 was estimated at some $520 billion, of which $375 billion was attributable to China and India.[13] Ten percent of the $145 billion attributed to other low-income countries amounts to $14.5 billion, or some $17 billion in 1981 dollars. To that might be added $10 billion to cover the capability of lending to China and India on the scale of the 1981 India program, and another $5 billion for loans to countries not classified as low-income but which also lack extensive access to the international capital market. That gives a total potential call on the Fund for lending to low-income countries of $32 billion, in terms of 1981 magnitudes. The Fund is not likely to be subject to calls from all its low-income members simultaneously, but, because the vast majority may well be subject to similar pressures, the Fund should be given the capability of responding to calls equal to, say, 75 percent of the potential total. That would point to a need for a lending capability of some $24 billion in 1981 magnitudes, or SDR 21 billion. Even if the world succeeds reasonably well in bringing inflation under control in the 1980s, nominal GNP in the late 1980s must be expected to be at least double that of 1981, giving an estimated need for a lending capacity of SDR 42 billion to low-income members.

In addition, the Fund will continue to have programs from time to time with countries that have extensive borrowings from the international capital market, including perhaps some developed countries, but which encounter creditworthiness problems either as a result of domestic mismanagement or an unfavorable external environment. Even if the calls from this source diminish in the 1980s as compared to the 1970s, it would seem imprudent to fail to allow for loans of 100 percent of quota to the equivalent of two or three major countries simultaneously. Since the large members each have quotas of 2 or 3 percent of total quotas, the additional need for lending to the middle- and high-income members could be estimated at, say, 8 percent of total quotas.

[13] World Bank, *World Development Report 1981,* Appendix Table 1.

On the supply-of-funds side of the equation, the usual rule of thumb is that about one-half of the sum total of Fund quotas is available for lending at any one time.

The estimates made above may be fed into an equation in order to calculate the size of total quotas, Q (expressed in SDR billion), that would be needed. The left-hand side shows the demand for funds, consisting of up to SDR 42 billion for the members with little access to the international capital market and 8 percent of quotas for the remainder. The right-hand side shows the supply of funds:

$$42 + 0.08Q = 0.5Q,$$

which implies

$$Q = 100.$$

Since quotas are currently SDR 61 billion, this implies that they would have to be raised by about two-thirds at the forthcoming quota review if the Fund is to sustain the role that has been advocated for it in this study.

References

Cline, William R., and Sidney Weintraub, eds. *Economic Stabilization in Developing Countries.* Washington: Brookings Institution, 1981.

Connors, T. A. "The Apparent Effects of Recent IMF Stabilization Programs." International Finance Discussion Paper, no. 135. Washington: Board of Governors of the Federal Reserve System, 1979.

Cooper, Richard N. *Currency Devaluation in Developing Countries.* Essays in International Finance, no. 86. Princeton, NJ: Princeton University, 1971.

Dell, Sidney. *On Being Grandmotherly: The Evolution of IMF Conditionality.* Essays in International Finance, no. 144. Princeton, NJ: Princeton University, 1981.

De Larosière, J. "Restoring Fiscal Discipline: A Vital Element of a Policy for Economic Recovery." Address at the American Enterprise Institute, Washington, 1982a.

———. "The Role of the International Monetary Fund in Today's World Economy." Address at the Council on Foreign Relations, Washington, 1982b.

Development Dialogue. "The International Monetary System and the New International Order." Uppsala: Dag Hammarskjold Foundation, 1980(2).

De Vries, Margaret G. *The International Monetary Fund, 1966–71: The System Under Stress.* Washington: IMF, 1976.

Dornbusch, Rudiger. *Open Economy Macroeconomics.* New York: Basic Books, 1980.

Feinberg, Richard E. "The International Monetary Fund and Basic Human Needs." In Margaret Crahan, ed., *Human Rights and Basic Needs in the Americas.* Washington: Georgetown University Press, 1982.

Guitián, Manual. *Fund Conditionality: Evolution of Principles and Practices. International Monetary Fund.* Pamphlet Series, no. 38. Washington: IMF, 1981.

Horsefield, J. Keith, et al. *The International Monetary Fund, 1945–1965: Twenty Years of International Monetary Cooperation.* Washington: IMF, 1969.

International Monetary Fund Institute. *Financial Policy Workshops: The Case of Kenya.* Washington: IMF, 1981.

Johnson, Omotunde, and Joanne Salop. "Distributional Aspects of Stabilization in Developing Countries." International Monetary Fund *Staff Papers,* vol. 27 (March 1980).

Killick, Tony, and M. Chapman. "Much Ado About Nothing. Testing the Impact of IMF Stabilisation Programmes in Developing Countries." Processed. London: Overseas Development Institute, 1982.

Krugman, P., and L. Taylor. "Contractionary Effects of Devaluation." *Journal of International Economics,* vol. 8 (August 1978).

Meade, J. E. *The Theory of International Economic Policy: vol. 1, The Balance of Payments.* Oxford, England: Oxford University Press, 1951.

Nowzad, Bahram. *The IMF and Its Critics.* Essays in International Finance, no. 146. Princeton, NJ: Princeton University, 1981.

Payer, Cheryl. *The Debt Trap: The IMF and the Third World.* New York: Monthly Review Press, 1975.

Thorp, Rosemary, and Laurence Whitehead, eds. *Inflation and Stabilisation in Latin America.* London: MacMillan, 1979.

Williamson, John. "Economic Theory and International Monetary Fund Policies." *Carnegie-Rochester Conference Series on Public Policy,* Autumn 1980.

———. *Exchange-Rate Rules: The Theory, Performance and Prospects of the Crawling Peg.* London: MacMillan, 1981.

APPENDICES

A. The Participants at the Conference on IMF Conditionality, Airlie House, Virginia, March 24–26, 1982

Invitations to the Airlie House conference were sent to individuals with a wide range of views and backgrounds. Of the 51 who attended, 18 were academics and 9 were from the Fund (the deputy managing director, 6 staff members, and 2 executive directors). The others came from various institutes and foundations, international organizations, commercial banks, central banks, the World Bank, and consultancy. About 15 of the participants were from developing countries. A dozen or so were believed ex ante to be sympathetic to the traditional left wing criticisms of the Fund, including 2 participants at Arusha and a former minister in Michael Manley's government in Jamaica. Three other Arusha veterans were invited but were unable to attend, although one of them contributed a paper. Ex ante 5 or 6 participants were thought to hold "right of Fund" or strongly monetarist positions; once again, more were invited than were able to accept. Our final group was therefore mildly more centrist than initially planned but reasonably diverse nonetheless. The participants and their affiliations at the time of the conference were as follows:

Dragoslav Avramovíc
United Nations Conference on Trade and Development

Edmar Bacha
Pontíficia Universidade Católica do Rio de Janeiro

Bela Balassa
World Bank

C. Fred Bergsten
Institute for International Economics

Sterie T. Beza
International Monetary Fund

Rattan Bhatia
International Monetary Fund

Graham Bird
University of Surrey

Michael Bruno
Hebrew University

William R. Cline
Institute for International Economics

Richard N. Cooper
Harvard University

Malcolm Crawford
London

William B. Dale
International Monetary Fund

Sidney Dell
United Nations Center on Transnational Corporations

Bruno de Maulde
International Monetary Fund

Rimmer de Vries
Morgan Guaranty Trust Company

Carlos F. Diaz-Alejandro
Yale University

Adolfo C. Diz
Buenos Aires

Rudiger Dornbusch
Massachusetts Institute of Technology

Jacob Dreyer
US Treasury Department

Richard S. Eckaus
Massachusetts Institute of Technology

Richard Erb
International Monetary Fund

Asim Erdilek
National Science Foundation

Irving S. Friedman
First Boston Corporation

Reginald Herbold Green
Institute of Development Studies

Catherine Gwin
Carnegie Endowment for International Peace

Arnold C. Harberger
University of Chicago

Gerald K. Helleiner
University of Toronto

Tony Killick
Overseas Development Institute

Jóse Luis Mardones S.
Comisión Chileana del Cobre

Isabel Marshall L.
Comisión Chileana del Cobre

Jorge Marshall S.
University of Chile

Robert McCauley
Federal Reserve Bank of New York

Raymond F. Mikesell
University of Orgeon

Subimal Mookerjee
International Monetary Fund

Bahram Nowzad
International Monetary Fund

Osman Okyar
Hacettepe University, Ankara

Stanley Please
World Bank

Arturo Porzecanski
Morgan Guaranty Trust Company

Elisabeth Rabitsch
First Boston Corporation

Jeffrey Sachs
Harvard University

Hans O. Schmitt
International Monetary Fund

José da Silva Lopes
Caixa Geral de Depósitos, Lisbon

Luigi Spaventa
University of Rome

Ernest Stern
World Bank

Mary Sutton
Overseas Development Institute

Richard Feinberg
Overseas Development Council

C. David Finch
International Monetary Fund

Richard Fletcher
Inter-American Development Bank

Lance Taylor
Massachusetts Institute of Technology

John Williamson
Institute for International Economics

DeLisle Worrell
Central Bank of Barbados

B. The Lending Facilities of the Fund

The Fund was created as a pool of currencies and gold subscribed by its members in proportion to their quotas, which were supposed to reflect countries' importance to the international economy. Each member contributed a quarter of its quota in gold and the remainder in its national currency. In return for accepting that its currency might be drawn by another member, it acquired the right to draw other currencies (or, in principle, gold) under certain circumstances. In Fund jargon, a *drawing* involves a *purchase* of another country's currency in exchange for its own currency; a *repurchase*, a country's buying back its own currency with foreign exchange. In economic terms, these transactions involve borrowing from, and repayment to, the Fund.

For a long time a country's quota constituted the ceiling on its permissible borrowing, which was divided into five equal *tranches*. The first was called the *gold tranche* (now known as the *reserve tranche*): at this stage the country is merely withdrawing the liquidity it deposited with the Fund as part of its membership subscription. The other four tranches are known as the *credit tranches*, the first of which has, since the 1950s, been available on easier terms than the other three (the "higher credit tranches"). Since the 1950s a variety of additional facilities have been added, the cumulative effect of which has been to create the possibility of members' borrowing over five times their quota. A brief guide to the various facilities, classified by their level of conditionality, is provided below.

Unconditional Facilities

If the Fund holds a member's currency equivalent to less than 100 percent of its quota,[1] then that country has a *reserve position in the*

[1] The extent of a member's indebtedness to the Fund is measured by the Fund's holding of its currency as a percentage of its quota, as shown in the table.

Fund. That reserve position which arises both from the member's subscription of gold or foreign exchange to the Fund and from Fund lending of the member's currency constitutes a *reserve asset*, or *unconditional liquidity*, which can be drawn at any time in order to meet a balance of payments need. (However, such holdings cannot be liquidated simply to change the composition of reserves.)

In 1970 the Fund created another unconditional facility, the SDR Account. SDRs are created from time to time by a Fund decision to allocate SDR's among the participants in the Account, and are subsequently transferred between members in settlement of payments deficits. The operation of the SDR Account is not discussed in this study.

Low-Conditionality Facilities

From the mid-1950s on, low-conditionality was applied to the first credit tranche. A member requesting a drawing limited to the first credit tranche was expected to have in place a program representing reasonable efforts to overcome its balance of payments difficulties, but what constitutes *reasonable efforts* is in practice left to the borrower's discretion, since a country applying for such a drawing is given the *overwhelming benefit of the doubt* in any difference of view between the member and the Fund.

A *compensatory financing facility* was first introduced in 1963 and has subsequently been liberalized on several occasions, most recently in 1981 when it was extended to cover temporary excesses in the cost of purchasing cereals. A member with a temporary export shortfall for reasons largely beyond its control, or facing a temporary increase in the cost of cereal imports, is allowed to borrow a sum related to the estimated shortfall (or increase) relative to the five year moving average. The member has to undertake to cooperate with the Fund in an effort to find appropriate solutions for any balance of payments difficulties it may have. Drawings are limited by the size of the country's quota as well as by the size of the export shortfall or import excess. Repayment is on a fixed schedule rather than varying with ability to pay (as measured, for example, by subsequent export excesses).

The *buffer stock financing facility* provides funds to help a member contribute to an international buffer stock accepted as suitable by the Fund. A drawing member is again expected to cooperate with the Fund in finding appropriate solutions to any payments problems it may have.

During the period 1974–76, the Fund operated an *oil facility* intended to assist members in financing a part of their increased deficits attributable to the 1973 oil price increase. A member with a balance of payments *need* (deficit) was allowed to borrow a sum specified as a percentage of the increased cost of its oil imports, subject to a maximum related to its quota, provided that the Fund judged the member's policies to be adequate to secure a medium-term solution to its balance of payments problem. Although that phrase might have been interpreted to justify a high degree of conditionality, it in fact was not.

In 1977 the Fund created a *trust fund* with the profits derived from the sale of a sixth of its 1976 gold holdings. The trust fund made low-conditionality highly concessional loans to low-income members with a balance of payments need. Its resources and operation were quite distinct from those of the rest of the Fund, and technically the trust fund was simply administered by the Fund rather than a part of it.

High-Conditionality Facilities

Drawings from the higher credit tranches are subject to a high degree of conditionality. They are now virtually always provided in the form of a *stand-by agreement*; this provides a country with assurance of a *right* to draw over some future period, typically a year but sometimes nowadays stretching out to three years, should the need arise, rather than providing an immediate borrowing. Stand-bys normally provide for drawings in a series of *installments,* which are available subject to the observance of conditions known as *performance criteria.* If those conditions are violated, the country becomes ineligible to draw further sums, at least until new consultations have taken place, and led if necessary to a revised agreement with the Fund.

The *extended facility* was introduced in 1974 with the intention of providing longer term finance to support three-year programs involving structural adjustment. Programs involve drawings in installments and performance criteria. Loans from the extended facility now have a maximum term of 10 years, as against the 5-year maximum that applies to the other facilities.

In 1979 the Fund introduced a *supplementary financing facility* (initially known as the *Witteveen facility*) on the basis of funds borrowed from certain members. This was intended to enlarge the loans that could be made under the high-conditionality facilities to members that had deficits that were large in relation to their Fund quotas.

The supplementary financing facility was replaced by the *enlarged access policy* when the former exhausted its resources in 1981. The enlarged access policy serves the same purpose, allowing stand-by arrangements to be extended beyond the higher credit tranches, or extended arrangements to be enlarged beyond the regular limits, on the basis of resources borrowed by the Fund under bilateral arrangements. These resources carry a higher interest rate than the Fund's regular facilities.

When a country signifies that it is interested in borrowing from the high-conditionality facilities, an IMF staff mission is dispatched to discuss the conditions that the Fund will require for approving the loan. These can be classified into preconditions (actions the country will have to take before a drawing is approved), performance criteria (conditions that must continue to be satisfied for the duration of the program if further drawings are to be made), and policy understandings (commitments by the country that do not have specific sanctions attached to them). The performance criteria and policy understandings are set out in a *Letter of Intent,* which is in form a letter from the country's finance minister to the Fund, but is in practice negotiated between the country and the IMF staff. The Fund annexes the Letter of Intent to the stand-by arrangement that specifies the Fund's commitment to the borrower; it is that arrangement which has to be approved by the Fund's Executive Board. Incidentally, the Fund never publishes letters of intent, although its members often do, and, even when they do not, the gist of the contents customarily appears in the local press.

The Fund has on two occasions undertaken comprehensive reviews of its conditionality policies. The first of these occasions was in 1968, following the complaints of many developing countries that there was an inconsistency between the policies that the Fund had pursued toward them and the treatment that Britain received at the time of the sterling devaluation in 1967. It was resolved that from then on Fund policy would be standardized and that all drawings in the higher credit tranches would be on a stand-by basis with drawings by installments and subject to performance criteria, and this was in fact effected when Britain came back to the Fund in 1969. The next comprehensive review took place in 1978–79 and resulted in agreement on a set of guidelines reproduced as Appendix 24.C. It seems that this was more a codification of the Fund's existing practices than an occasion for making major changes, although the undertaking that performance criteria normally be confined to "macroeconomic variables" or "those necessary to implement specific provisions of the Articles" (paragraph 9) involved a limitation of the Fund's right to press for particular fiscal measures, such as the withdrawal of specific subsidies. *Macroeconomic variables* cover credit ceilings, while "implementing specific provisions of the Articles" means restraining restrictions on trade and payments.

A recent view from within the Fund of the evolution of its practices on conditionality can be found in Guitián (1981).

C. Text of Decision of IMF Executive Board, March 2, 1979, on Access to Resources from Fund And Use of Stand-by Arrangements

1. Members should be encouraged to adopt corrective measures, which could be supported by use of the Fund's general resources in accordance with the Fund's policies, at an early stage of their balance of payments difficulties or as a precaution against the emergence of such difficulties. The Article IV consultations are among the occasions on which the Fund would be able to discuss with members adjustment programs, including corrective measures, that would enable the Fund to approve a stand-by arrangement.

2. The normal period for a stand-by arrangement will be one year. If, however, a longer period is requested by a member and considered necessary by the Fund to enable the member to implement its adjustment program successfully, the stand-by arrangement may extend beyond the period of one year. This period in appropriate cases may extend up to but not beyond three years.

3. Stand-by arrangements are not international agreements and therefore language having a contractual connotation will be avoided in stand-by arrangements and letters of intent.

4. In helping members to devise adjustment programs, the Fund will pay due regard to the domestic social and political objectives, the economic priorities, and the circumstances of members, including the causes of their balance of payments problems.

5. Appropriate consultation clauses will be incorporated in all stand-by arrangements. Such clauses will include provision for consultation from time to time during the whole period in which the member has outstanding purchases in the upper credit tranches. This provision will apply whether the outstanding purchases were made under a stand-by arrangement or in other transactions in the upper credit tranches.

6. Phasing and performance clauses will be omitted in stand-by arrangements that do not go beyond the first credit tranche. They

will be included in all other stand-by arrangements but these clauses will be applicable only to purchases beyond the first credit tranche.

7. The Managing Director will recommend that the Executive Board approve a member's request for the use of the Fund's general resources in the credit tranches when it is his judgment that the program is consistent with the Fund's provisions and policies and that it will be carried out. A member may be expected to adopt some corrective measures before a stand-by arrangement is approved by the Fund, but only if necessary to enable the member to adopt and carry out a program consistent with the Fund's provisions and policies. In these cases the Managing Director will keep Executive Directors informed in an appropriate manner of the progress of discussions with the member.

8. The Managing Director will ensure adequate coordination in the application of policies relating to the use of the Fund's general resources with a view to maintaining the nondiscriminatory treatment of members.

9. The number and content of performance criteria may vary because of the diversity of problems and institutional arrangements of members. Performance criteria will be limited to those that are necessary to evaluate implementation of the program with a view to ensuring the achievement of its objectives. Performance criteria will normally be confined to (i) macroeconomic variables, and (ii) those necessary to implement specific provisions of the Articles or policies adopted under them. Performance criteria may relate to other variables only in exceptional cases when they are essential for the effectiveness of the member's program because of their macroeconomic impact.

10. In programs extending beyond one year, or in circumstances where a member is unable to establish in advance one or more performance criteria for all or part of the program period, provision will be made for a review in order to reach the necessary understandings with the member for the remaining period. In addition, in those exceptional cases in which an essential feature of a program cannot be formulated as a performance criterion at the beginning of a program year because of substantial uncertainties concerning major economic trends, provision will be made for a review by the Fund to evaluate the current macroeconomic policies of the member, and to reach new understandings if necessary. In these exceptional cases the Managing Director will inform Executive Directors in an appropriate manner of the subject matter of a review.

11. The staff will prepare an analysis and assessment of the performance under programs supported by use of the Fund's general

resources in the credit tranches in connection with Article IV consultations and as appropriate in connection with further requests for use of the Fund's resources.

12. The staff will from time to time prepare, for review by the Executive Board, studies of programs supported by stand-by arrangements in order to evaluate and compare the appropriateness of the programs, the effectiveness of the policy instruments, the observance of the programs, and the results achieved. Such reviews will enable the Executive Board to determine when it may be appropriate to have the next comprehensive review of conditionality.

GLOSSARY

BIS Bank for International Settlements

Bretton Woods conference held in July 1944 in Bretton Woods, New Hampshire, from which the International Monetary Fund and World Bank resulted.

CGBR central government borrowing rate

Committee of Twenty Committee of the Board of Governors of the International Monetary Fund on Reform of the International Monetary System and Related Issues, established July 26, 1972, and given the task of advising and reporting on all aspects of international monetary reform. A final report and an *Outline of Reform* were presented on June 14, 1974.

DCE domestic credit expansion

EAC East African Community

EC European Community. The short-form designation of adherents to the treaties forming the European Coal and Steel Community (ECSC), the European Economic Community (EEC), the European Atomic Energy Community (Euratom), and the treaties amending those treaties. Members are Belgium, France, Denmark, Federal Republic of Germany, Greece, Ireland, Italy, Luxembourg, Netherlands, and United Kingdom.

ECLA United Nations Economic Commission for Latin America

EFF extended Fund facility

EFTA European Free Trade Association

EIB European Investment Bank

EPU European Payments Union

GAB General Arrangements to Borrow

GATT General Agreement on Tariffs and Trade

Group of 24 made up of eight countries each from Africa, Asia, and Latin America, designated by the Group of 77 to consider monetary matters.

Group of 77 a group of developing countries within the United Nations Conference on Trade and Development. Originally numbering 77, the group now has over a hundred members.

IDA International Development Association, a low-interest lending arm of the World Bank

IMF International Monetary Fund

LDCs less developed countries or economies

Libor London interbank offer rate

NBER National Bureau of Economic Research

NICs newly industrializing country (economy), new industrial country, newly industrialized country

OECD Organization for Economic Cooperation and Development. Members are Australia, Austria, Belgium, Canada, Denmark, Finland, France, Federal Republic of Germany, Greece, Iceland, Ireland, Italy, Japan, Luxembourg, Netherlands, New Zealand, Norway, Portugal, Spain, Sweden, Switzerland, Turkey, United Kingdom, United States.

OPEC Organization of Petroleum Exporting Countries

PSBR public sector borrowing requirement

SDR special drawing right. A monetary reserve asset established by the International Monetary Fund in 1969. Its current value is based on a basket of the five major industrial countries' currencies.

SEE State Economic Enterprise (Turkey)

TDC total domestic credit, the flow of domestic credit which results in money creation

UNCTAD United Nations Conference on Trade and Development

World Bank International Bank for Reconstruction and Development. Conceived at Bretton Woods in 1944, established in 1945, and became a specialized agency of the United Nations in 1947. Its goals are to promote growth, trade and balance of trade equilibrium of its member countries, by "facilitating the investment of capital for productive purposes" with its own loans at conventional interest rates and guarantees for foreign investors, and by providing technical assistance.

INDEX

Authors

Countries

717067

Composed in Times Roman by FotoTypesetters, Inc., Baltimore, Md.
Printed, and bound, by R.R. Donnelly & Sons Company, Harrisonburg, Va., on
50# Bookmark blue-white 540 ppi, International Paper Company
Designed by Gerard A. Valerio, Bookmark Studio

DATE DUE

GAYLORD PRINTED IN U.S.A.

BOWLING GREEN STATE UNIVERSITY
DISCARDED
LIBRARY